Fundamentals of
Data Structures in C

Fundamentals of Data Structures in C

Ellis Horowitz
University of Southern California

Sartaj Sahni
University of Florida

Susan Anderson-Freed
Illinois Wesleyan University

COMPUTER SCIENCE PRESS

An imprint of W.H. Freeman and Company
New York

Cover Illustration by Richard Elmer

Library of Congress Cataloging-in-Publication Data

Horowitz, Ellis.
    Fundamentals of data structures in C / Ellis Horowitz, Sartaj
Sahni, Susan Anderson-Freed.
        p.   cm.
    Includes bibliographical references and index.
    ISBN 0-7167-8250-2
    1. C (Computer program language)   2. Data structures (Computer
science)   I. Sahni, Sartaj.   II. Anderson-Freed, Susan.
III. Title.
QA76.73.C15H6597   1993
005.13′3—dc20   92-2524
                                                           CIP

Printed in the United States of America

Computer Science Press

An imprint of W. H. Freeman and Company
The book publishing arm of *Scientific American*
41 Madison Avenue, New York, NY 10010
20 Beaumont Street, Oxford OX1 2NQ, England

Eighth printing, 1998

CONTENTS

PREFACE   **xi**

CHAPTER 1 BASIC CONCEPTS   **1**
1.1   Overview: System Life Cycle   1
1.2   Algorithm Specification   4
    1.2.1   Introduction   4
    1.2.2   Recursive Algorithms   10
1.3   Data Abstraction   14
1.4   Performance Analysis   18
    1.4.1   Space Complexity   19
    1.4.2   Time Complexity   21
    1.4.3   Asymptotic Notation   30
    1.4.4   Practical Complexities   37
1.5   Performance Measurement   38
1.6   References And Selected Readings   47

CHAPTER 2   ARRAYS AND STRUCTURES   **49**
2.1   The Array As An Abstract Data Type   49
2.2   Structures and Unions   53
    2.2.1   Structures   53
    2.2.2   Unions   56
    2.2.3   Internal Implementation Of Structures   57

       2.2.4   Self-Referential Structures   57
2.3   The Polynomial Abstract Data Type   59
2.4   The Sparse Matrix Abstract Data Type   66
       2.4.1   Introduction   66
       2.4.2   Transposing A Matrix   69
       2.4.3   Matrix Multiplication   73
2.5   The Representation Of Multidimensional Arrays   78
2.6   The String Abstract Data Type   80
       2.6.1   Introduction   80
       2.6.2   Pattern Matching   84
2.7   References And Selected Readings   92
2.8   Additional Exercises   92

CHAPTER 3 STACKS AND QUEUES   101
3.1   The Stack Abstract Data Type   101
3.2   The Queue Abstract Data Type   105
3.3   A Mazing Problem   112
3.4   Evaluation of Expressions   116
       3.4.1   Introduction   116
       3.4.2   Evaluatng Postfix Expressions   118
       3.4.3   Infix to Postfix   121
3.5   Multiple Stacks And Queues   128
3.6   Selected Readings And References   131
3.7   Additional Exercises   132

CHAPTER 4 LISTS   135
4.1   Pointers   135
       4.1.1   Pointer Can Be Dangerous   137
       4.1.2   Using Dynamically Allocated Storage   138
4.2   Singly Linked Lists   139
4.3   Dynamically Linked Stacks And Queues   147
4.4   Polynomials   150
       4.4.1   Representing Polynomials As Singly Linked Lists   150
       4.4.2   Adding Polynomials   152
       4.4.3   Erasing Polynomials   156
       4.4.4   Polynomials As Circularly Linked Lists   157
       4.4.5   Summary   161
4.5   Additional List Operations   163
       4.5.1   Operations For Chains   163
       4.5.2   Operations For Circularly Linked Lists   163
4.6   Equivalence Relations   166
4.7   Sparse Matrices   171
4.8   Doubly Linked Lists   179

4.9   References And Selected Readings   182
4.10 Additional Exercises   183

CHAPTER 5   TREES   186
5.1   Introduction   186
    5.1.1   Terminology   186
    5.1.2   Representation Of Trees   189
5.2   Binary Trees   191
    5.2.1   The Abstract Data Type   191
    5.2.2   Properties Of Binary Trees   193
    5.2.3   Binary Tree Representations   196
5.3   Binary Tree Traversals   200
5.4   Additional Binary Tree Operations   206
5.5   Threaded Binary Trees   211
5.6   Heaps   217
    5.6.1   The Heap Abstract Data Type   218
    5.6.2   Priority Queues   219
    5.6.3   Insertion Into A Max Heap   221
    5.6.4   Deletion From A Max Heap   223
5.7   Binary Search Trees   226
    5.7.1   Introduction   226
    5.7.2   Searching A Binary Search Tree   227
    5.7.3   Inserting Into A Binary Search Tree   228
    5.7.4   Deletion From A Binary Search Tree   230
    5.7.5   Height Of A Binary Search Tree   231
5.8   Selection Trees   232
5.9   Forests   236
    5.9.1   Transforming A Forest Into A Binary Search Tree   236
    5.9.2   Forest Traversals   237
5.10 Set Representation   238
    5.10.1   Union And Find Operations   239
    5.10.2   Equivalence Relations   247
5.11 Counting Binary Trees   247
    5.11.1   Distinct Binary Trees   247
    5.11.2   Stack Permutations   249
    5.11.3   Matrix Multiplication   251
    5.11.4   Number Of Distinct Binary Trees   253
5.12 References And Selected Readings   254
5.13 Additional Exercises   254

CHAPTER 6   GRAPHS   257
6.1   The Graph Abstract Data Type   257
    6.1.1   Introduction   257

   6.1.2 Definitions 259
   6.1.3 Graph Representations 263
  6.2 Elementary Graph Operations 272
   6.2.1 Depth First Search 272
   6.2.2 Breadth First Search 273
   6.2.3 Connected Components 276
   6.2.4 Spanning Trees 276
   6.2.4 Biconnected Components And Articulation Points 278
  6.3 Minimum Cost Spanning Trees 284
  6.4 Shortest Paths And Transitive Closure 292
   6.4.1 Single Source All Destination 292
   6.4.2 All Pairs Shortest Paths 295
   6.4.3 Transitive Closure 300
  6.5 Activity Networks 303
   6.5.1 Activity On Vertex (AOV) Networks 303
   6.5.2 Activity On Edge (AOE) Networks 309
  6.6 References And Selected Readings 316
  6.7 Additional Exercises 318

CHAPTER 7 SORTING 319
  7.1 Searching And List Verification 319
   7.1.1 Introduction 319
   7.1.2 Sequential Search 320
   7.1.3 Binary Search 321
   7.1.4 List Verification 322
  7.2 Definitions 326
  7.3 Insertion Sort 326
  7.4 Quick Sort 329
  7.5 Optimal Sorting Time 333
  7.6 Merge Sort 335
   7.6.1 Merging 335
   7.6.2 Iterative Merge Sort 340
   7.6.3 Recursive Merge Sort 340
  7.7 Heap Sort 347
  7.8 Radix Sort 350
  7.9 List And Table Sorts 357
  7.10 Summary Of Internal Sorting 366
  7.11 External Sorting 372
   7.11.1 Introduction 372
   7.11.2 k-way Merging 376
   7.11.3 Buffer Handling For Parallel Operation 378
   7.11.4 Run Generation 385
   7.11.5 Optimal Merging Of Runs 389

7.12 References And Selected Readings   393
7.13 Additional Exercises   393

CHAPTER 8 HASHING   395
8.1 The Symbol Table Abstract Data Type   395
8.2 Static Hashing   397
    8.2.1 Hash Tables   397
    8.2.2 Hashing Functions   398
    8.2.3 Overflow Handling   401
    8.2.4 Theoretical Evaluation Of Overflow Techniques   409
8.3 Dynamic Hashing   413
    8.3.1 Dynamic Hashing Using Directories   414
    8.3.2 Analysis Of Directory Dynamic Hashing   421
    8.3.3 Directoryless Dynamic Hashing   424
8.4 References And Selected Readings   428

CHAPTER 9 HEAP STRUCTURES   430
9.1 Min-Max Heaps   430
    9.1.1 Definition   430
    9.1.2 Insertion Into A Min-Max Heap   431
    9.1.3 Deletion Of Min Element   434
9.2 Deaps   439
    9.2.1 Definition   439
    9.2.2 Insertion Into A Deap   440
    9.2.3 Deletion Of Min Element   442
9.3 Leftist Trees   446
9.4 Binomial Heaps   453
    9.4.1 Cost Amortization   453
    9.4.2 Definition Of Binomial Heaps   454
    9.4.3 Insertion Into A Binomial Heap   455
    9.4.4 Combine   455
    9.4.5 Deletion Of Min Element   456
    9.4.6 Analysis   458
9.5 Fibonacci Heaps   461
    9.5.1 Definition   461
    9.5.2 Deletion From An F-heap   462
    9.5.3 Decrease Key   463
    9.5.4 Cascading Cut   463
    9.5.5 Analysis   464
    9.5.6 Application Of F-heaps   466
9.6 References And Selected Readings   469

CHAPTER 10 SEARCH STRUCTURES   470

10.1 Optimal Binary Search Trees   470
10.2 AVL Trees   470
10.3 2-3 Trees   496
    10.3.1 Definition And Properties   496
    10.3.2 Searching A 2-3 Tree   498
    10.3.3 Insertion Into A 2-3 Tree   499
    10.3.4 Deletion From A 2-3 Tree   502
10.4 2-3-4 Trees   509
    10.4.1 Definition And Properties   509
    10.4.2 Insertion Into A 2-3-4 Tree   511
    10.4.3 Deletion From A 2-3-4 Tree   515
10.5 Red-Black Trees   518
    10.5.1 Definition And Properties   518
    10.5.2 Searching A Red-Black Tree   521
    10.5.3 Top Down Insertion   521
    10.5.4 Bottom Up Insertion   524
    10.5.5 Deletion From A Red-Black Tree   525
10.6 B-Trees   528
    10.6.1 Definition Of m-way Search Trees   528
    10.6.2 Searching An m-way Search Tree   530
    10.6.3 Definition And Properties Of A B-tree   530
    10.6.4 Insertion Into A B-tree   533
    10.6.5 Deletion From A B-tree   535
    10.6.6 Variable Size Key Values   538
10.7 Splay Trees   542
10.8 Digital Search Trees   548
    10.8.1 Digital Search Tree   548
    10.8.2 Binary Tries   549
    10.8.3 Patricia   550
10.9 Tries   557
    10.9.1 Definition   557
    10.9.2 Searching A Trie   558
    10.9.3 Sampling Strategies   558
    10.9.4 Insertion Into A Trie   561
    10.9.5 Deletion From A Trie   561
10.10 Differential Files   563
10.11 References And Selected Readings   567

APPENDIX ANSI C AND K & R C   570

INDEX   579

PREFACE

Why *Fundamentals of Data Structures in C?* There are several answers. The first, and most important, is that instructors are moving to C as the language of choice. This is not surprising as C has become the main development language both on personal computers (PCs and Macs) as well as on UNIX-based workstations. Another reason is that the quality of C compilers and C programming development environments has improved to the point where it makes sense to provide instruction to beginners in a C environment. Finally, many of the concepts that need to be taught in the programming systems areas of computer science, such as virtual memory, file systems, automatic parser generators, lexical analyzers, networking, etc. are implemented in C. Thus, instructors are now teaching students C early in their academic life so that these concepts can be fully explored later on.

We have chosen to present our programs using ANSI C. ANSI C, adopted in 1983, has attempted to strengthen the C programming language by permitting a variety of features not allowed in earlier versions. Some of these features, such as typing information in the function header, improve readability as well as reliablity of programs. The alternative to ANSI C is Kernighan and Ritchie C (abbreviated as K&R C) which derives from their book *The C Programming Language*, Prentice-Hall, 1978. For those instructors who are using a K&R version of C we have provided an Appendix that discusses the changes required to get the programs working in that environment. The changes are quite simple and are easily made, so the distinctions between the two should not bother the student.

All programs and algorithms in this text have been compiled and tested. We have exercised the programs on an Intel/386 under DOS using Turbo C and Turbo C++ compilers. We have also run the programs using the C compiler on a SUN Sparcstation under SUNOS 4.1. We have directly imported the compiled programs into the body of the book, and we have avoided changing the appearance of the programs, via typesetting, so as not to inject any errors.

For those instructors who have used *Fundamentals of Data Structures in Pascal*, you will find that this book retains the in-depth discussion of the algorithms and computing time analyses. In addition we have attempted to preserve the chapter organization and the presentation style of the earlier book whenever it was desirable. But this has not kept us from making improvements, especially when dictated by the use of C rather than Pascal. For example, the discussion of strings is now found in the chapter on arrays. Also found there is a discussion of pointers, as pointer manipulation of arrays is quite common in C. Error messages are written to **stderr**. Programs that use system function calls, such as **malloc**, check that they return successfully. We use *exit(0)* and *exit(1)* for normal and abnormal program termination.

Non-C related changes include the placement of exercises immediately after the relevant section. Exercises which have a section marker, §, next to the exercise number denote difficult exercises. Exercises which are suitable for programming projects are labeled as such. In addition, we have rearranged the sections in each chapter so that the basic material appears early in the chapter and the difficult or optional material appears at the end of the chapter.

One of the major new features in this book, compared to its earlier version, is the inclusion of abstract data types. The major idea is to separate out the issue of data type specification from implementation. Languages such as Ada provide direct support for such a split, but in C there is no equivalent construct. Therefore, we have devised a straightforward notation in which we express an abstract data type. Basically, we provide a description of the objects of the type followed by the names and arguments of the functions of the type. Instructors can discuss with the students the specification of the data type before moving on to implementation issues and concerns for efficiency of the algorithms.

Over the past decade the field of data structures has not stood still, but has matured significantly. New and useful data structures have been devised and new forms of complexity measures have been introduced. In this new edition we attempt to keep up with these developments. For example, Chapter 9 is entirely devoted to heaps. Special forms are discussed including the min-max heap and the deap, both of which are forms of double ended priority queues. We also discuss a data structure that supports the combining of priority queues, leftist trees. These also have min and max forms. A Fibonacci heap is introduced as a data structure that supports all leftist tree operations. We introduce binomial trees, of which Fibonacci heaps are a special case.

A more thorough treatment of 2-3 trees now can be found in Chapter 10. In addition, we have included a section on 2-3-4 trees. The 2-3-4 tree has some advantages over the 2-3 tree, thereby supporting its presentation in this chapter. Red-black trees are a binary tree representation of a 2-3-4 tree. All of these data structures are important special cases of the B-tree. They are emphasized here because the insertion and deletion algorithms that maintain the tree's balance are substantially simpler than for AVL trees, while the O(log n) bounds are maintained.

Another issue treated more thoroughly in this edition is amortized complexity. Most of the algorithms have their best, worst, and occasionally their average computing time analyzed. Amortized complexity considers how efficiently a sequence of operations is carried out. This form of complexity measure was popularized by R. Tarjan and in many cases it is a more accurate measure of a data structure's performance than the more traditional ones.

The discussion of symbol tables and hashing is now in Chapter 8. We have updated the hashing material with a discussion of dynamic hashing. This method extends the traditional method with the ability to handle files that grow unpredictably large, without having to recompile or reset the size of a table.

USING THIS TEXT FOR A COURSE

For the instructor who intends to use this book and is teaching on a semester basis we present the following two possibilities, a medium pace and a rigorous pace. The medium pace is recommended when the course is for begining computer science majors, possibly their second or third course of the curriculum. Most people, including the authors, have taught according to the medium pace. The outline below corresponds to the curriculum recommended by the ACM, in particular course C2, (Curriculum '78, CACM 3/79, and CACM 8/85).

SEMESTER SCHEDULE - MEDIUM PACE

Week	Subject	Reading Assignment
1	Intro. to Algorithms and Data Organization	Chapter 1
2	Arrays	Chapter 2
3	Arrays (strings)	First program due
4	Stacks and Queues	Chapter 3
5	Linked Lists (singly and doubly linked)	Chapter 4
6	Linked Lists	Second program due
7	Trees (basic facts, binary trees)	Chapter 5
8	Trees (search, heap)	
9	Mid Term	
10	Graphs (basic facts, representations)	Chapter 6
11	Graphs (shortest paths, spanning trees, topological sorting)	Third program due
12	Internal Sorting (insertion, quick, and merge)	Chapter 7
13	Internal Sorting (heap, radix)	Fourth program due

14	Hashing	Chapter 8
15	Heap Structures (Selected Topics)	Chapter 9
16	Search Structures (Selected Topics)	Chapter 10

We recommend that several programming assignments be given, spaced somewhat evenly throughout the semester. The aim of the first program is primarily to get the students familiar with the computing environment. The second program should emphasize list structures, as discussed in Chapter 4. There are several suggestions for projects at the end of the exercises of Chapter 4. One topic we have chosen to skip is external sorting. This leaves time to cover one of the most important of techniques, hashing. This topic is used in several courses later on in the curriculum, so it is important to cover it this semester. The instructor will likely not have time to cover the material in the Search Structures chapter. Perhaps one or two topics can be selectively chosen.

The more rigorous pace would be appropriate when the book is used for a first year graduate course, or for an advanced undergraduate course. Our suggested outline follows.

SEMESTER SCHEDULE - RIGOROUS PACE

Week	Subject	Reading Assignment
1	Intro. to Algorithms and Data Organization	Chapter 1
2	Arrays	Chapter 2
3	Stacks and Queues	Chapter 3
		First program due
4	Linked Lists	Chapter 4
5	Trees	Chapter 5
6	Trees continued	Second program due
7	Mid Term	
8	Graphs	Chapter 6
9	Graphs continued	Third program due
10	Internal Sorting	Chapter 7
11	External Sorting	Chapter 7
12	Hashing	Chapter 8
13	Heap Structures	Chapter 9
		Fourth program due
14	Heap Structures	Chapter 9
15	Search Structures	Chapter 10
16	Search Structures	Chapter 10

The programming assignments and midterm exam are paced exactly as in the medium case. However, the lectures proceed at a faster rate. For the rigorous pace, two weeks are allotted for Chapters 9 and 10. This allows the coverage of only a few topics selected from each chapter.

Finally we present a curriculum for an advanced Data Structures course. This presupposes that the student has already encountered the basic material, in particular the material on lists, trees, and graphs. Four weeks on advanced data structures gives the instructor enough time to cover all of the relevant topics in depth.

SEMESTER SCHEDULE - ADVANCED DATA STRUCTURES COURSE

Week	Subject	Reading Assignment
1	Review of Basic Material on Algorithms	Chapters 1-2
2	Review of Basic List structures	Chapters 3-4
3	Review of Trees	Chapter 5
4	Review of Graphs	Chapter 6
5	Review of Internal Sorting	Chapter 7 First program due
6	External Sorting	Chapter 7
7	External Sorting (continued)	
8	Hashing	Chapter 8 Second program due
9	Heap Structures (min-max heaps, deaps, leftist trees)	Chapter 9
10	Mid Term	
11	Heaps Structures (Fibonacci heaps)	Chapter 9
12	Search Structures (Optimal binary search trees)	Chapter 10
13	Search Structures (AVL trees, 2-3 trees, 2-3-4 trees)	Third program due
14	Search Structures (Red-black trees, splay trees, digital trees)	
15	Search Structures (B-trees, tries)	Fourth program due
16	Search Structures	

For schools on the quarter system, the following two quarter sequence is possible. It assumes prior exposure to algorithm analysis and elementary data structures at the level obtained from an advanced programming course.

QUARTER 1

Week	Subject	Reading Assignment
1	Review of algorithms and arrays	Chapters 1-2
2	Stacks and Queues	Chapter 3
3	Linked Lists (stacks, queues, polynomials)	Chapter 4
4	Linked Lists	
5	Trees (traversal, set representation)	Chapter 5
		First program due
6	Trees (heaps, search)	
	Mid Term	
7	Graphs (traversal, components)	Chapter 6
8	Graphs (minimum spanning trees)	
9	Graphs (shortest paths)	Second program due
10	Graphs	(activity networks)

QUARTER 2

Week	Subject	Reading Assignment
1	Internal Sorting (insertion, quick, bound, O(1) space merging, merge sort)	Chapter 7
2	Sorting (heap, radix, list, table)	
3	External Sorting	Chapter 7
4	Hashing	Chapter 8
5	Mid Term	First program due
6	Heap Structures (deaps, Min-Max heaps, Leftist trees)	Chapter 9
7	Heap Structures (Fibonacci Heaps)	
8	Search Structures (AVL trees, 2-3 trees, 2-3-4 trees)	Chapter 10
9	Search Structures (Red-black trees, splay trees, digital trees)	Second program due
10	Search Structures (B-Trees, tries)	

Once again we would like to thank the people who have assisted us in preparing this edition. Thanks go to Professor Lisa Brown, Illinois Wesleyan University, and the students in her Programming III class, as well as to Dr. Dinesh Mehta, University of Florida, for their assistance in the debugging of this edition, and to Trey Short and Curtis Kelch of the Computer Services staff at Illinois Wesleyan University for providing technical assistance. Thanks also to Narain Gehani, AT&T Bell Laboratories, Tomasz Müldner, Arcadia University, and Ronald Prather, Trinity University, who reviewed early drafts of the manuscript. Special thanks go to Barbara and Art Friedman, our first publishers who nurtured the book through its early years. Thanks also to the staff at W.H. Freeman for their support and encouragement. We especially wish to thank Acquisitions Editor, Nola Hague and Associate Managing editior, Penny Hull. Their enthusiasm really helped the project along.

Ellis Horowitz
Sartaj Sahni
Susan Anderson-Freed
June 1992

CHAPTER 1

BASIC CONCEPTS

1.1 OVERVIEW: SYSTEM LIFE CYCLE

We assume that our readers have a strong background in structured programming, typically attained through the completion of an elementary programming course. Such an initial course usually emphasizes mastering a programming language's syntax (its grammar rules) and applying this language to the solution of several relatively small problems. These problems are frequently chosen so that they use a particular language construct. For example, the programming problem might require the use of arrays or **while** loops.

In this text we want to move you beyond these rudiments by providing you with the tools and techniques necessary to design and implement large-scale computer systems. We believe that a solid foundation in data abstraction, algorithm specification, and performance analysis and measurement provides the necessary methodology. In this chapter, we will discuss each of these areas in detail. We also will briefly discuss recursive programming because many of you probably have only a fleeting acquaintance with this important technique. However, before we begin we want to place these tools in a context that views programming as more than writing code. Good programmers regard large-scale computer programs as systems that contain many complex interacting parts. As systems, these programs undergo a development process called the system life cycle. We consider this cycle as consisting of requirements, analysis, design, coding, and verification phases. Although we will consider them separately, these phases are highly interrelated and follow only a very crude sequential time frame. The Selected Readings and References section lists several sources on the system life cycle and its various phases that will provide you with additional information.

(1) Requirements. All large programming projects begin with a set of specifications that define the purpose of the project. These requirements describe the information that we, the programmers, are given (input) and the results that we must produce (output). Frequently the initial specifications are defined vaguely, and we must develop rigorous input and output descriptions that include all cases.

(2) Analysis. After we have delineated carefully the system's requirements, the analysis phase begins in earnest. In this phase, we begin to break the problem down into manageable pieces. There are two approaches to analysis: bottom-up and top-down. The bottom-up approach is an older, unstructured strategy that places an early emphasis on the coding fine points. Since the programmer does not have a master plan for the project, the resulting program frequently has many loosely connected, error-ridden segments. Bottom-up analysis is akin to constructing a building from a generic blueprint. That is, we view all buildings identically; they must have walls, a roof, plumbing, and heating. The specific purpose to which the building will be put is irrelevant from this perspective. Although few of us would want to live in a home constructed using this technique, many programmers, particularly beginning ones, believe that they can create good, error-free programs without prior planning.

In contrast, the top-down approach begins with the purpose that the program will serve and uses this end product to divide the program into manageable segments. This technique generates diagrams that are used to design the system. Frequently, several alternate solutions to the programming problem are developed and compared during this phase.

(3) Design. This phase continues the work done in the analysis phase. The designer approaches the system from the perspectives of both the data objects that the program needs and the operations performed on them. The first perspective leads to the creation of abstract data types, while the second requires the specification of algorithms and a consideration of algorithm design strategies. For example, suppose that we are designing a scheduling system for a university. Typical data objects might include students, courses, and professors. Typical operations might include inserting, removing, and searching within each object or between them. That is, we might want to add a course to the list of university courses, or search for the courses taught by some professor.

Since the abstract data types and the algorithm specifications are language-independent, we postpone implementation decisions. Although we must specify the information required for each data object, we ignore coding details. For example, we might decide that the student data object should include name, social security number, major, and phone number. However, we would not yet pick a specific implementation for the list of students. As we will see in later chapters, there are several possibilities including arrays, linked lists, or trees. By deferring implementation issues as long as possible, we not only create a system that could be written in several programming languages, but we also have time to pick the most efficient implementations within our chosen language.

(4) Refinement and coding. In this phase, we choose representations for our data objects and write algorithms for each operation on them. The order in which we do this is crucial because a data object's representation can determine the efficiency of the algorithms related to it. Typically this means that we should write those algorithms that are independent of the data objects first.

Frequently at this point we realize that we could have created a much better system. Perhaps we have spoken with a friend who has worked on a similar project, or we realize that one of our alternate designs is superior. If our original design is good, it can absorb changes easily. In fact, this is a reason for avoiding an early commitment to coding details. If we must scrap our work entirely, we can take comfort in the fact that we will be able to write the new system more quickly and with fewer errors. A delightful book that discusses this "second system" phenomenon is Frederick Brooks's, *The Mythical Man-Month* cited in the Selected Readings and References section.

(5) Verification. This phase consists of developing correctness proofs for the program, testing the program with a variety of input data, and removing errors. Each of these areas has been researched extensively, and a complete discussion is beyond the scope of this text. However, we want to summarize briefly the important aspects of each area.

Correctness proofs: Programs can be proven correct using the same techniques that abound in mathematics. Unfortunately, these proofs are very time-consuming, and difficult to develop for large projects. Frequently scheduling constraints prevent the development of a complete set of proofs for a large system. However, selecting algorithms that have been proven correct can reduce the number of errors. In this text, we will provide you with an arsenal of algorithms, some of which have been proven correct using formal techniques, that you may apply to many programming problems.

Testing: We can construct our correctness proofs before and during the coding phase since our algorithms need not be written in a specific programming language. Testing, however, requires the working code and sets of test data. This data should be developed carefully so that it includes all possible scenarios. Frequently beginning programmers assume that if their program ran without producing a syntax error, it must be correct. Little thought is given to the input data, and usually only one set of data is used. Good test data should verify that every piece of code runs correctly. For example, if our program contains a **switch** statement, our test data should be chosen so that we can check each **case** within the **switch** statement.

Initial system tests focus on verifying that a program runs correctly. While this is a crucial concern, a program's running time is also important. An error-free program that runs slowly is of little value. Theoretical estimates of running time exist for many algorithms and we will derive these estimates as we introduce new algorithms. In addition, we may want to gather performance estimates for portions of our code. Constructing these timing tests is also a topic that we pursue later in this chapter.

Error removal. If done properly, the correctness proofs and system tests will indicate erroneous code. The ease with which we can remove these errors depends on the design and coding decisions made earlier. A large undocumented program written in "spaghetti" code is a programmer's nightmare. When debugging such programs, each corrected error possibly generates several new errors. On the other hand, debugging a well-documented program that is divided into autonomous units that interact through parameters is far easier. This is especially true if each unit is tested separately and then integrated into the system.

1.2   ALGORITHM SPECIFICATION

1.2.1   Introduction

The concept of an algorithm is fundamental to computer science. Algorithms exist for many common problems, and designing efficient algorithms plays a crucial role in developing large-scale computer systems. Therefore, before we proceed further we need to discuss this concept more fully. We begin with a definition.

Definition: An *algorithm* is a finite set of instructions that, if followed, accomplishes a particular task. In addition, all algorithms must satisfy the following criteria:

(1) **Input.** There are zero or more quantities that are externally supplied.

(2) **Output.** At least one quantity is produced.

(3) **Definiteness.** Each instruction is clear and unambiguous.

(4) **Finiteness.** If we trace out the instructions of an algorithm, then for all cases, the algorithm terminates after a finite number of steps.

(5) **Effectiveness.** Every instruction must be basic enough to be carried out, in principle, by a person using only pencil and paper. It is not enough that each operation be definite as in (3); it also must be feasible. □

In computational theory, one distinguishes between an algorithm and a program, the latter of which does not have to satisfy the fourth condition. For example, we can think of an operating system that continues in a *wait* loop until more jobs are entered. Such a program does not terminate unless the system crashes. Since our programs will always terminate, we will use algorithm and program interchangeably in this text.

We can describe an algorithm in many ways. We can use a natural language like English, although, if we select this option, we must make sure that the resulting instructions are definite. Graphic representations called flowcharts are another possibility, but they work well only if the algorithm is small and simple. In this text we will present most of our algorithms in C, occasionally resorting to a combination of English and C for our specifications. Two examples should help to illustrate the process of translating a problem into an algorithm.

Example 1.1 [*Selection sort*]: Suppose we must devise a program that sorts a set of $n \geq 1$ integers. A simple solution is given by the following:

From those integers that are currently unsorted, find the smallest and place it next in the sorted list.

Although this statement adequately describes the sorting problem, it is not an algorithm since it leaves several unanswered questions. For example, it does not tell us where and how the integers are initially stored, or where we should place the result. We assume that the integers are stored in an array, *list*, such that the ith integer is stored in the ith position, $list[i]$, $0 \leq i < n$. Program 1.1 is our first attempt at deriving a solution. Notice that it is written partially in C and partially in English.

```
for (i = 0; i < n; i++) {
  Examine list[i] to list[n-1] and suppose that the
  smallest integer is  at list[min];

  Interchange list[i] and list[min];
}
```

Program 1.1: Selection sort algorithm

To turn Program 1.1 into a real C program, two clearly defined subtasks remain: finding the smallest integer and interchanging it with $list[i]$. We can solve the latter problem using either a function (Program 1.2) or a macro. The function's code is easier to read than that of the macro but the macro works with any data type. Using the function, suppose a and b are declared as **int**s. To swap their values one would say:

```
swap(&a, &b);
```

passing to *swap* the addresses of a and b. The macro version of swap is:

```
#define SWAP(x,y,t) ((t) = (x), (x) = (y), (y) = (t))
```

```
void swap(int *x, int *y)
/* both parameters are pointers to ints */
{
   int temp = *x;    /* declares temp as an int and assigns
                 to it the contents of what x points to */
   *x = *y; /* stores what y points to into the location
                                where x points */
   *y = temp; /*places the contents of temp in location
                              pointed to by y */
}
```

Program 1.2: Swap function

We can solve the first subtask by assuming that the minimum is $list[i]$, checking $list[i]$ with $list[i+1]$, $list[i+2]$, $\cdots$, $list[n-1]$. Whenever we find a smaller number we make it the new minimum. When we reach $list[n-1]$ we are finished. Putting all these observations together gives us *sort* (Program 1.3). Program 1.3 contains a complete program which you may run on your computer. The program uses the *rand* function defined in *math.h* to randomly generate a list of numbers which are then passed into *sort*. This program has been successfully compiled and run on several systems including Turbo C and Turbo C++ under DOS 5.0. All programs in this book follow the rules of ANSI C, which are slightly different from those of Kernighan & Ritchie C (K&R C). Appendix A shows you the changes required to transform our ANSI C programs into K&R C. At this point, we should ask if this function works correctly.

Theorem 1.1: Function $sort(list,n)$ correctly sorts a set of $n \geq 1$ integers. The result remains in $list[0]$, $\cdots$, $list[n-1]$ such that $list[0] \leq list[1] \leq \cdots \leq list[n-1]$.

Proof: When the outer **for** loop completes its iteration for $i = q$, we have $list[q] \leq list[r]$, $q < r < n$. Further, on subsequent iterations, $i > q$ and $list[0]$ through $list[q]$ are unchanged. Hence following the last iteration of the outer **for** loop (i.e., $i = n - 2$), we have $list[0] \leq list[1] \leq \cdots \leq list[n-1]$. $\square$

Example 1.2 [*Binary search*]: Assume that we have $n \geq 1$ distinct integers that are already sorted and stored in the array *list*. That is, $list[0] \leq list[1] \leq \cdots \leq list[n-1]$. We must figure out if an integer *searchnum* is in this list. If it is we should return an index, i, such that $list[i] = searchnum$. If *searchnum* is not present, we should return -1. Since the list is sorted we may use the following method to search for the value.

Let *left* and *right*, respectively, denote the left and right ends of the list to be searched. Initially, *left* = 0 and *right* = $n-1$. Let *middle* = $(left+right)/2$ be the middle position in the list. If we compare $list[middle]$ with *searchnum*, we obtain one of three results:

```
#include <stdio.h>
#include <math.h>
#define MAX_SIZE 101
#define SWAP(x,y,t) ((t) = (x), (x)= (y), (y) = (t))
void sort(int [],int); /*selection sort */
void main(void)
{
   int i,n;
   int list[MAX_SIZE];
   printf("Enter the number of numbers to generate: ");
   scanf("%d",&n);
   if( n < 1 || n > MAX_SIZE) {
     fprintf(stderr, "Improper value of n\n");
     exit(1);
   }
   for (i = 0; i < n; i++) {/*randomly generate numbers*/
     list[i] = rand() % 1000;
     printf("%d  ",list[i]);
   }
   sort(list,n);
   printf("\n Sorted array:\n ");
   for (i = 0; i < n; i++) /* print out sorted numbers */
     printf("%d  ",list[i]);
   printf("\n");
}
void sort(int list[],int n)
{
   int i, j, min, temp;
   for (i = 0; i < n-1; i++)  {
     min = i;
     for (j = i+1; j < n; j++)
       if (list[j] < list[min])
         min = j;
     SWAP(list[i],list[min],temp);
   }
}
```

Program 1.3: Selection sort

(1)   **searchnum < list[middle]**. In this case, if *searchnum* is present, it must be in the positions between 0 and *middle* − 1. Therefore, we set *right* to *middle* − 1.

(2)   **searchnum = list[middle]**. In this case, we return *middle*.

(3)   **searchnum > list[middle]**. In this case, if *searchnum* is present, it must be in the positions between *middle* + 1 and *n* − 1. So, we set *left* to *middle* + 1.

If *searchnum* has not been found and there are still integers to check, we recalculate *middle* and continue the search. Program 1.4 implements this searching strategy. The algorithm contains two subtasks: (1) determining if there are any integers left to check, and (2) comparing *searchnum* to *list[middle]*.

```
while (there are more integers to check ) {
   middle = (left + right) / 2;
   if (searchnum < list[middle])
      right = middle - 1;
   else if (searchnum == list[middle])
         return middle;
      else left = middle + 1;
}
```

Program 1.4: Searching a sorted list

We can handle the comparisons through either a function or a macro. In either case, we must specify values to signify less than, equal, or greater than. We will use the strategy followed in C's library functions:

•   We return a negative number (−1) if the first number is less than the second.

•   We return a 0 if the two numbers are equal.

•   We return a positive number (1) if the first number is greater than the second.

Although we present both a function (Program 1.5) and a macro, we will use the macro throughout the text since it works with any data type. The macro version is:

```
#define COMPARE(x,y) (((x) < (y)) ? -1: ((x) == (y))? 0: 1)
```

We are now ready to tackle the first subtask: determining if there are any elements left to check. You will recall that our initial algorithm indicated that a comparison could cause us to move either our left or right index. Assuming we keep moving these indices, we will eventually find the element, or the indices will cross, that is, the left index will have a higher value than the right index. Since these indices delineate the search boundaries, once they cross, we have nothing left to check. Putting all this information together gives us *binsearch* (Program 1.6).

```
int compare(int x, int y)
{
/* compare x and y, return -1 for less than, 0 for equal,
1 for greater */
   if (x < y) return -1;
   else if (x == y) return 0;
        else return 1;
}
```

Program 1.5: Comparison of two integers

```
int binsearch(int list[], int searchnum, int left,
                                          int right)
{
/* search list[0] <= list[1] <=  · · ·  <= list[n-1] for
searchnum. Return its position if found. Otherwise
return -1 */
   int  middle;
   while (left <= right)  {
      middle = (left + right)/2;
      switch (COMPARE(list[middle], searchnum)) {
         case -1: left = middle + 1;
                  break;
         case 0 : return middle;
         case 1 : right = middle - 1;
      }
   }
   return -1;
}
```

Program 1.6: Searching an ordered list

The search strategy just outlined is called *binary search*. □

The previous examples have shown that algorithms are implemented as functions in C. Indeed functions are the primary vehicle used to divide a large program into manageable pieces. They make the program easier to read, and, because the functions can be tested separately, increase the probability that it will run correctly. Often we will declare a function first and provide its definition later. In this way the compiler is made aware that a name refers to a legal function that will be defined later. In C, groups of functions can be compiled separately, thereby establishing libraries containing groups of logically related algorithms.

1.2.2   Recursive Algorithms

Typically, beginning programmers view a function as something that is invoked (called) by another function. It executes its code and then returns control to the calling function. This perspective ignores the fact that functions can call themselves (*direct recursion*) or they may call other functions that invoke the calling function again (*indirect recursion*). These recursive mechanisms are not only extremely powerful, but they also frequently allow us to express an otherwise complex process in very clear terms. It is for these reasons that we introduce recursion here.

Frequently computer science students regard recursion as a mystical technique that is useful for only a few special problems such as computing factorials or Ackermann's function. This is unfortunate because any function that we can write using assignment, **if-else**, and **while** statements can be written recursively. Often this recursive function is easier to understand than its iterative counterpart.

How do we determine when we should express an algorithm recursively? One instance is when the problem itself is defined recursively. Factorials and Fibonacci numbers fit into this category as do binomial coefficients where:

$$\begin{bmatrix} n \\ m \end{bmatrix} = \frac{n!}{m!(n-m)!}$$

can be recursively computed by the formula:

$$\begin{bmatrix} n \\ m \end{bmatrix} = \begin{bmatrix} n-1 \\ m \end{bmatrix} + \begin{bmatrix} n-1 \\ m-1 \end{bmatrix}$$

We would like to use two examples to show you how to develop a recursive algorithm. In the first example, we take the binary search function that we created in Example 1.2 and transform it into a recursive function. In the second example, we recursively generate all possible permutations of a list of characters.

Example 1.3 [*Binary search*]: Program 1.6 gave the iterative version of a binary search. To transform this function into a recursive one, we must (1) establish boundary conditions that terminate the recursive calls, and (2) implement the recursive calls so that each call brings us one step closer to a solution. If we examine Program 1.6 carefully we can see that there are two ways to terminate the search: one signaling a success (*list[middle]* = *searchnum*), the other signaling a failure (the left and right indices cross). We do not need to change the code when the function terminates successfully. However, the **while** statement that is used to trigger the unsuccessful search needs to be replaced with an equivalent **if** statement whose **then** clause invokes the function recursively.

Creating recursive calls that move us closer to a solution is also simple since it requires only passing the new *left* or *right* index as a parameter in the next recursive call. Program 1.7 implements the recursive binary search. Notice that although the code has changed, the recursive function call is identical to that of the iterative function. □

```
int binsearch(int list[], int searchnum, int left,
                                          int right)
{
/* search list[0] <= list[1] <=  · · ·  <= list[n-1] for
searchnum. Return its position if found. Otherwise
return -1 */
   int middle;
   if (left <= right) {
      middle = (left + right)/2;
      switch (COMPARE(list[middle], searchnum)) {
         case -1: return
             binsearch(list, searchnum, middle + 1, right);
         case 0 : return middle;
         case 1 : return
             binsearch(list, searchnum, left, middle - 1);
      }
   }
   return -1;
}
```

Program 1.7: Recursive implementation of binary search

Example 1.4 [*Permutations*]: Given a set of $n \geq 1$ elements, print out all possible permutations of this set. For example, if the set is $\{a, b, c\}$, then the set of permutations is $\{(a, b, c), (a, c, b), (b, a, c), (b, c, a), (c, a, b), (c, b, a)\}$. It is easy to see that, given n elements, there are $n!$ permutations. We can obtain a simple algorithm for generating the permutations if we look at the set $\{a, b, c, d\}$. We can construct the set of permutations by printing:

(1) a followed by all permutations of (b, c, d)

(2) b followed by all permutations of (a, c, d)

(3) c followed by all permutations of (a, b, d)

(4) d followed by all permutations of (a, b, c)

The clue to the recursive solution is the phrase "followed by all permutations." It implies that we can solve the problem for a set with n elements if we have an algorithm that works on $n-1$ elements. These considerations lead to the development of Program 1.8. We assume that *list* is a character array. Notice that it recursively generates permutations until $i = n$. The initial function call is *perm(list, 0, n-1);*

```
void perm(char *list, int i, int n)
/* generate all the permutations of list[i] to list[n] */
{
   int j, temp;
   if (i == n) {
      for (j = 0; j <= n; j++)
         printf("%c", list[j]);
      printf("    ");
   }
   else {
   /* list[i] to list[n] has more than one permutation,
   generate these recursively */
      for (j = i; j <= n; j++) {
         SWAP(list[i],list[j],temp);
         perm(list,i+1,n);
         SWAP(list[i],list[j],temp);
      }
   }
}
```

Program 1.8: Recursive permutation generator

Try to simulate Program 1.8 on the three-element set $\{a, b, c\}$. Each recursive call of *perm* produces new local copies of the parameters *list*, *i*, and *n*. The value of *i* will differ from invocation to invocation, but *n* will not. The parameter *list* is an array pointer and its value also will not vary from call to call. □

We will encounter recursion several more times since many of the algorithms that appear in subsequent chapters are recursively defined. This is particularly true of algorithms that operate on lists (Chapter 4) and binary trees (Chapter 5).

EXERCISES

In the last several examples, we showed you how to translate a problem into a program. We have avoided the issues of data abstraction and algorithm design strategies, choosing to focus on developing a function from an English description, or transforming an iterative algorithm into a recursive one. In the exercises that follow, we want you to use the same approach. For each programming problem, try to develop an algorithm, translate it into a function, and show that it works correctly. Your correctness "proof" can employ an analysis of the algorithm or a suitable set of test runs.

1. Consider the two statements:

   (a) Is $n = 2$ the largest value of n for which there exist positive integers x, y, and z such that $x^n + y^n = z^n$ has a solution?

   (b) Store 5 divided by zero into x and go to statement 10.

   Both fail to satisfy one of the five criteria of an algorithm. Which criterion do they violate?

2. Horner's rule is a strategy for evaluating a polynomial $A(x) =$

$$a_n x^n + a_{n-1} x^{n-1} + \cdots + a_1 + a_0$$

   at point x_0 using a minimum number of multiplications. This rule is:

$$A(x_0) = (\cdots ((a_n x_0 + a_{n-1}) x_0 + \cdots + a_1) x_0 + a_0)$$

   Write a C program to evaluate a polynomial using Horner's rule.

3. Given n Boolean variables $x_1, \cdots, x_n$, we wish to print all possible combinations of truth values they can assume. For instance, if $n = 2$, there are four possibilities: <*true, true*>, <*false, true*>, <*true, false*>, and <*false, false*>. Write a C program to do this.

4. Write a C program that prints out the integer values of x, y, z in ascending order.

5. The pigeon hole principle states that if a function f has n distinct inputs but less than n distinct outputs then there are two inputs a and b such that $a \neq b$ and $f(a) = f(b)$. Write a C program to find the values a and b for which the range values are equal.

6. Given n, a positive integer, determine if n is the sum its divisors, that is, if n is the sum of all t such that $1 \leq t < n$ and t divides n.

7. The factorial function $n!$ has value 1 when $n \leq 1$ and value $n*(n-1)!$ when $n > 1$. Write both a recursive and an iterative C function to compute $n!$.

8. The Fibonacci numbers are defined as: $f_0 = 0$, $f_1 = 1$, and $f_i = f_{i-1} + f_{i-2}$ for $i > 1$. Write both a recursive and an iterative C function to compute f_i.

9. Write an iterative function to compute a binomial coefficient, then transform it into an equivalent recursive function.

10. Ackerman's function $A(m, n)$ is defined as:

$$A(m, n) = \begin{cases} n + 1 & \text{, if } m = 0 \\ A(m - 1, 1) & \text{, if } n = 0 \\ A(m - 1, A(m, n - 1)) & \text{, otherwise} \end{cases}$$

   This function is studied because it grows very quickly for small values of m and n. Write recursive and iterative versions of this function.

11. [*Towers of Hanoi*] There are three towers and 64 disks of different diameters placed on the first tower. The disks are in order of decreasing diameter as one scans up the tower. Monks were reputedly supposed to move the disk from tower 1 to tower 3 obeying the rules:

    (a)   Only one disk can be moved at any time.

    (b)   No disk can be placed on top of a disk with a smaller diameter.
    Write a recursive function that prints out the sequence of moves needed to accomplish this task.

12. If S is a set of n elements the powerset of S is the set of all possible subsets of S. For example, if $S = \{a, b, c\}$, then *powerset* $(S) = \{ \{\}, \{a\}, \{b\}, \{c\}, \{a, b\}, \{a, c\}, \{b, c\}, \{a, b, c\}\}$. Write a recursive function to compute *powerset(S)*.

1.3   DATA ABSTRACTION

The reader is no doubt familiar with the basic data types of C. These include **char**, **int**, **float**, and **double**. Some of these data types may be modified by the keywords **short**, **long**, and **unsigned**. Ultimately, the real world abstractions we wish to deal with must be represented in terms of these data types. In addition to these basic types, C helps us by providing two mechanisms for grouping data together. These are the array and the structure. *Arrays* are collections of elements of the same basic data type. They are declared implicitly, for example, *int list*[5] defines a five-element array of integers whose legitimate subscripts are in the range 0 $\cdots$ 4. *Structs* are collections of elements whose data types need not be the same. They are explicitly defined. For example,

```
struct student {
        char last_name;
        int student_id;
        char grade;
        }
```

defines a structure with three fields, two of type character and one of type integer. The structure name is *student*. Details of C structures are provided in Chapter 2.

C also provides the pointer data type. For every basic data type there is a corresponding pointer data type, such as pointer-to-an-int, pointer-to-a-real, pointer-to-a-char, and pointer-to-a-float. A pointer is denoted by placing an asterisk, *, before a variable's name. So,

```
int i, *pi;
```

declares *i* as an integer and *pi* as a pointer to an integer.

All programming languages provide at least a minimal set of predefined data types, plus the ability to construct new, or *user-defined types*. It is appropriate to ask the question, "What is a data type?"

Definition: A *data type* is a collection of *objects* and a set of *operations* that act on those objects. □

Whether your program is dealing with predefined data types or user-defined data types, these two aspects must be considered: objects and operations. For example, the data type **int** consists of the objects {0, +1, −1, +2, −2, ⋯ , INT_MAX, INT_MIN}, where INT_MAX and INT_MIN are the largest and smallest integers that can be represented on your machine. (They are defined in *limits.h*.) The operations on integers are many, and would certainly include the arithmetic operators +, −, *, /, and %. There is also testing for equality/inequality and the operation that assigns an integer to a variable. In all of these cases, there is the name of the operation, which may be a prefix operator, such as *atoi*, or an infix operator, such as +. Whether an operation is defined in the language or in a library, its name, possible arguments and results must be specified.

In addition to knowing all of the facts about the operations on a data type, we might also want to know about how the objects of the data type are represented. For example on most computers a **char** is represented as a bit string occupying 1 byte of memory, whereas an **int** might occupy 2 or possibly 4 bytes of memory. If 2 eight-bit bytes are used, then *INT_MAX* is $2^{15} - 1 = 32,767$.

Knowing the representation of the objects of a data type can be useful and dangerous. By knowing the representation we can often write algorithms that make use of it. However, if we ever want to change the representation of these objects, we also must change the routines that make use of it. It has been observed by many software designers that hiding the representation of objects of a data type from its users is a good design strategy. In that case, the user is constrained to manipulate the objects solely through the functions that are provided. The designer may still alter the representation as long as the new implementations of the operations do not change the user interface. This means that users will not have to recode their algorithms.

Definition: An *abstract data type (ADT)* is a data type that is organized in such a way that the specification of the objects and the specification of the operations on the objects is separated from the representation of the objects and the implementation of the operations. □

Some programming languages provide explicit mechanisms to support the distinction between specification and implementation. For example, Ada has a concept called a *package*, and C++ has a concept called a *class*. Both of these assist the programmer in implementing abstract data types. Although C does not have an explicit mechanism for implementing ADTs, it is still possible and desirable to design your data types using the same notion.

How does the specification of the operations of an ADT differ from the implementation of the operations? The specification consists of the names of every function, the type of its arguments, and the type of its result. There should also be a description of what the function does, but without appealing to internal representation or implementation details. This requirement is quite important, and it implies that an abstract data type is *implementation-independent*. Furthermore, it is possible to classify the functions of a data type into several categories:

(1) **Creator/constructor**: These functions create a new instance of the designated type.

(2) **Transformers**: These functions also create an instance of the designated type, generally by using one or more other instances. The difference between constructors and transformers will become more clear with some examples.

(3) **Observers/reporters**: These functions provide information about an instance of the type, but they do not change the instance.

Typically, an ADT definition will include at least one function from each of these three categories.

Throughout this text, we will emphasize the distinction between specification and implementation. In order to help us do this, we will typically begin with an ADT definition of the object that we intend to study. This will permit the reader to grasp the essential elements of the object, without having the discussion complicated by the representation of the objects or by the actual implementation of the operations. Once the ADT definition is fully explained we will move on to discussions of representation and implementation. These are quite important in the study of data structures. In order to help us accomplish this goal, we introduce a notation for expressing an ADT.

Example 1.5 [*Abstract data type* Natural_Number]: As this is the first example of an ADT, we will spend some time explaining the notation. Structure 1.1 contains the ADT definition of *Natural_Number*. The structure definition begins with the name of the structure and its abbreviation. There are two main sections in the definition: the objects and the functions. The objects are defined in terms of the integers, but we make no explicit reference to their representation. The function definitions are a bit more complicated. First, the definitions use the symbols x and y to denote two elements of the set of *Natural_Numbers*, while *TRUE* and *FALSE* are elements of the set of *Boolean* values. In addition, the definition makes use of functions that are defined on the set of integers, namely, plus, minus, equals, and less than. This is an indication that in order to define one data type, we may need to use operations from another data type. For each function, we place the result type to the left of the function name and a definition of the function to the right. The symbols "::=" should be read as "is defined as."

The first function, *Zero*, has no arguments and returns the natural number zero. This is a constructor function. The function *Successor(x)* returns the next natural number in sequence. This is an example of a transformer function. Notice that if there is no next number in sequence, that is, if the value of x is already *INT_MAX*, then we define the action of *Successor* to return *INT_MAX*. Some programmers might prefer that in such a case *Successor* return an error flag. This is also perfectly permissible. Other transformer functions are *Add* and *Subtract*. They might also return an error condition,

---

structure *Natural_Number* is
   objects: an ordered subrange of the integers starting at zero and ending at the maximum integer (*INT_MAX*) on the computer
   functions:
      for all $x, y \in$ *Nat_Number*; *TRUE, FALSE* $\in$ *Boolean*
      and where +, −, <, and == are the usual integer operations

Nat_No Zero( )	::=	0
Boolean Is_Zero(x)	::=	**if** (x) **return** *FALSE*
		else return *TRUE*
Nat_No Add(x, y)	::=	**if** $((x + y) <= INT\_MAX)$ **return** $x + y$
		else return *INT_MAX*
Boolean Equal(x, y)	::=	**if** $(x == y)$ **return** *TRUE*
		else return *FALSE*
Nat_No Successor(x)	::=	**if** $(x == INT\_MAX)$ **return** x
		else return $x + 1$
Nat_No Subtract(x, y)	::=	**if** $(x < y)$ **return** 0
		else return $x - y$

end *Natural_Number*

Structure 1.1: Abstract data type *Natural_Number*

although here we decided to return an element of the set *Natural_Number*. □

    Structure 1.1 shows you the general form that all ADT definitions will follow. However, we will not often be able to provide a definition of the functions that is so close to C functions. In fact, the nature of an ADT argues that we avoid implementation details. Therefore, we will usually use a form of structured English to explain the meaning of the functions.

EXERCISES

For each of these exercises, provide a definition of the abstract data type using the form illustrated in Structure 1.1.

1. Add the following operations to the *Natural_Number* ADT: *Predecessor, Is_Greater, Multiply, Divide*.

2. Create an ADT, *Set*. Use the standard mathematics definition and include the following operations: *Create, Insert, Remove, Is_In, Union, Intersection, Difference*.

3. Create an ADT, *Bag*. In mathematics a *bag* is similar to a *set* except that a *bag* may contain duplicate elements. The minimal operations should include: *Create, Insert, Remove,* and *Is_In*.

4. Create an ADT, *Boolean*. The minimal operations are *And, Or, Not, Xor* (Exclusive or), *Equivalent*, and *Implies*.

1.4 PERFORMANCE ANALYSIS

One of the goals of this book is to develop your skills for making evaluative judgments about programs. There are many criteria upon which we can judge a program, including:

(1) Does the program meet the original specifications of the task?

(2) Does it work correctly?

(3) Does the program contain documentation that shows how to use it and how it works?

(4) Does the program effectively use functions to create logical units?

(5) Is the program's code readable?

Although the above criteria are vitally important, particularly in the development of large systems, it is difficult to explain how to achieve them. The criteria are associated with the development of a good programming style and this takes experience and practice. We hope that the examples used throughout this text will help you improve your programming style. However, we also can judge a program on more concrete criteria, and so we add two more criteria to our list.

(6) Does the program efficiently use primary and secondary storage?

(7) Is the program's running time acceptable for the task?

These criteria focus on performance evaluation, which we can loosely divide into two distinct fields. The first field focuses on obtaining estimates of time and space that are machine independent. We call this field *performance analysis*, but its subject matter is the heart of an important branch of computer science known as *complexity theory*. The second field, which we call *performance measurement*, obtains machine-dependent running times. These times are used to identify inefficient code segments. In this section we discuss performance analysis, and in the next we discuss performance measurement. We begin our discussion with definitions of the space and time complexity of a program.

Definition: The *space complexity* of a program is the amount of memory that it needs to run to completion. The *time complexity* of a program is the amount of computer time that it needs to run to completion. □

1.4.1 Space Complexity

The space needed by a program is the sum of the following components:

(1) **Fixed space requirements:** This component refers to space requirements that do not depend on the number and size of the program's inputs and outputs. The fixed requirements include the instruction space (space needed to store the code), space for simple variables, fixed-size structured variables (such as **structs**), and constants.

(2) **Variable space requirements:** This component consists of the space needed by structured variables whose size depends on the particular instance, I, of the problem being solved. It also includes the additional space required when a function uses recursion. The variable space requirement of a program P working on an instance I is denoted $S_P(I)$. $S_P(I)$ is usually given as a function of some *characteristics* of the instance I. Commonly used characteristics include the number, size, and values of the inputs and outputs associated with I. For example, if our input is an array containing n numbers then n is an instance characteristic. If n is the only instance charcteristic we wish to use when computing $S_P(I)$, we will use $S_P(n)$ to represent $S_P(I)$.

We can express the total space requirement $S(P)$ of any program as:

$$S(P) = c + S_P(I)$$

where c is a constant representing the fixed space requirements. When analyzing the space complexity of a program we are usually concerned with only the variable space requirements. This is particularly true when we want to compare the space complexity of several programs. Let us look at a few examples.

Example 1.6: We have a function, *abc* (Program 1.9), which accepts three simple variables as input and returns a simple value as output. According to the classification given, this function has only fixed space requirements. Therefore, $S_{abc}(I) = 0$. □

```
float abc(float a, float b, float c)
{
    return a+b+b*c +(a+b-c)/(a+b)+4.00;
}
```

Program 1.9: Simple arithmetic function

Example 1.7: We want to add a list of numbers (Program 1.10). Although the output is a simple value, the input includes an array. Therefore, the variable space requirement depends on how the array is passed into the function. Programming languages like

Pascal may pass arrays by value. This means that the entire array is copied into temporary storage before the function is executed. In these languages the variable space requirement for this program is $S_{sum}(I) = S_{sum}(n) = n$, where n is the size of the array. C passes all parameters by value. When an array is passed as an argument to a function, C interprets it as passing the address of the first element of the array. C does not copy the array. Therefore, $S_{sum}(n) = 0$. $\square$

```
float sum(float list[], int n)
{
   float tempsum = 0;
   int i;
   for (i = 0; i < n; i++)
      tempsum += list[i];
   return tempsum;
}
```

Program 1.10: Iterative function for summing a list of numbers

Example 1.8: Program 1.11 also adds a list of numbers, but this time the summation is handled recursively. This means that the compiler must save the parameters, the local variables, and the return address for each recursive call.

```
float rsum(float list[], int n)
{
   if (n) return rsum(list,n-1) + list[n-1];
   return 0;
}
```

Program 1.11: Recursive function for summing a list of numbers

In this example, the space needed for one recursive call is the number of bytes required for the two parameters and the return address. We can use the *sizeof* function to find the number of bytes required by each type. On an 80386 computer, integers and pointers require 2 bytes of storage and floats need 4 bytes. Figure 1.1 shows the number of bytes required for one recursive call.

If the array has $n = MAX\_SIZE$ numbers, the total variable space needed for the recursive version is $S_{rsum}(MAX\_SIZE) = 6*MAX\_SIZE$. If $MAX\_SIZE = 1000$, the variable space needed by the recursive version is $6*1000 = 6,000$ bytes. The iterative version has no variable space requirement. As you can see, the recursive version has a far greater overhead than its iterative counterpart. $\square$

Type	Name	Number of bytes
parameter: float	*list*[]	2
parameter: integer	*n*	2
return address: (used internally)		2 (unless a far address)
TOTAL per recursive call		6

Figure 1.1: Space needed for one recursive call of Program 1.11

EXERCISES

1. Determine the space complexity of the iterative and recursive factorial functions created in Exercise 7, Section 1.2.

2. Determine the space complexity of the iterative and recursive Fibonacci number functions created in Exercise 8, Section 1.2.

3. Determine the space complexity of the iterative and recursive binomial coefficient functions created in Exercise 9, Section 1.2.

4. Determine the space complexity of the function created in Exercise 5, Section 1.2 (pigeon hole principle).

5. Determine the space complexity of the function created in Exercise 12, Section 1.2 (powerset problem).

1.4.2   Time Complexity

The time, $T(P)$, taken by a program, P, is the sum of its *compile time* and its *run* (or *execution*) *time*. The compile time is similar to the fixed space component since it does not depend on the instance characteristics. In addition, once we have verified that the program runs correctly, we may run it many times without recompilation. Consequently, we are really concerned only with the program's execution time, T_P.

Determining T_P is not an easy task because it requires a detailed knowledge of the compiler's attributes. That is, we must know how the compiler translates our source program into object code. For example, suppose we have a simple program that adds and subtracts numbers. Letting n denote the instance characteristic, we might express $T_P(n)$ as:

$$T_P(n) = c_a ADD(n) + c_s SUB(n) + c_l LDA(n) + c_{st} STA(n)$$

where c_a, c_s, c_l, c_{st} are constants that refer to the time needed to perform each operation, and *ADD*, *SUB*, *LDA*, *STA* are the number of additions, subtractions, loads, and stores that are performed when the program is run with instance characteristic n.

Obtaining such a detailed estimate of running time is rarely worth the effort. If we must know the running time, the best approach is to use the system clock to time the program. We will do this later in the chapter. Alternately, we could count the number of operations the program performs. This gives us a machine-independent estimate, but we must know how to divide the program into distinct steps.

Definition: A *program step* is a syntactically or semantically meaningful program segment whose execution time is independent of the instance characteristics. □

Note that the amount of computing represented by one program step may be different from that represented by another step. So, for example, we may count a simple assignment statement of the form $a = 2$ as one step and also count a more complex statement such as $a = 2*b+3*c/d-e+f/g/a/b/c$ as one step. The only requirement is that the time required to execute each statement that is counted as one step be independent of the instance characteristics.

We can determine the number of steps that a program or a function needs to solve a particular problem instance by creating a global variable, *count*, which has an initial value of 0 and then inserting statements that increment count by the number of program steps required by each executable statement.

Example 1.9 [*Iterative summing of a list of numbers*]: We want to obtain the step count for the sum function discussed earlier (Program 1.10). Program 1.12 shows where to place the *count* statements. Notice that we only need to worry about the executable statements, which automatically eliminates the function header, and the second variable declaration from consideration.

Since our chief concern is determining the final count, we can eliminate most of the program statements from Program 1.12 to obtain a simpler program Program 1.13 that computes the same value for *count*. This simplification makes it easier to express the count arithmetically. Examining Program 1.13, we can see that if *count*'s initial value is 0, its final value will be $2n + 3$. Thus, each invocation of *sum* executes a total of $2n + 3$ steps. □

Example 1.10 [*Recursive summing of a list of numbers*]: We want to obtain the step count for the recursive version of the summing function. Program 1.14 contains the original function (Program 1.11) with the step counts added.

To determine the step count for this function, we first need to figure out the step count for the boundary condition of $n = 0$. Looking at Program 1.14, we can see that when $n = 0$ only the **if** conditional and the second **return** statement are executed. So, the total step count for $n = 0$ is 2. For $n > 0$, the **if** conditional and the first **return** statement are executed. So each recursive call with $n > 0$ adds two to the step count. Since there are n such function calls and these are followed by one with $n = 0$, the step count for the function is $2n + 2$.

```
float sum(float list[], int n)
{
   float tempsum = 0;  count++; /* for assignment */
   int i;
   for (i = 0; i < n; i++)   {
      count++;                     /* for the for loop */
      tempsum += list[i]; count++;  /*  for assignment */
   }
   count++; /* last execution of for */
   count++; /* for return */  return tempsum;
}
```

Program 1.12: Program 1.10 with count statements

```
float sum(float list[], int n)
{
   float tempsum = 0;
   int i;
   for (i = 0; i < n; i++)
      count += 2;
   count +=3;
   return 0;
}
```

Program 1.13: Simplified version of Program 1.12

Surprisingly, the recursive function actually has a lower step count than its iterative counterpart. However, we must remember that the step count only tells us how many steps are executed, it does not tell us how much time each step takes. Thus, although the recursive function has fewer steps, it typically runs more slowly than the iterative version as its steps, on average, take more time than those of the iterative version. □

Example 1.11 [*Matrix addition*]: We want to determine the step count for a function that adds two-dimensional arrays (Program 1.15). The arrays a and b are added and the result is returned in array c. All of the arrays are of size $rows \times cols$. Program 1.16 shows the *add* function with the step counts introduced. As in the previous examples, we want to express the total count in terms of the size of the inputs, in this case *rows* and *cols*. To make the count easier to decipher, we can combine counts that appear within a single loop. This operation gives us Program 1.17.

```
float rsum(float list[], int n)
{
   count++;       /* for if conditional */
   if (n) {
      count++;   /* for return and rsum invocation */
      return rsum(list,n-1) + list[n-1];
   }
   count++;
   return list[0];
}
```

Program 1.14: Program 1.11 with count statements added

For Program 1.17, we can see that if *count* is initially 0, it will be $2rows \cdot cols + 2rows + 1$ on termination. This analysis suggests that we should interchange the matrices if the number of rows is significantly larger than the number of columns. □

By physically placing count statements within our functions we can run the functions and obtain precise counts for various instance characteristics. Another way to obtain step counts is to use a tabular method. To construct a step count table we first determine the step count for each statement. We call this the *steps/execution*, or *s/e* for short. Next we figure out the number of times that each statement is executed. We call this the *frequency*. The frequency of a nonexecutable statement is zero. Multiplying s/e by the frequency, gives us the *total steps* for each statement. Summing these totals, gives us the step count for the entire function. Although this seems like a very complicated process, in fact, it is quite easy. Let us redo our three previous examples using the tabular approach.

Example 1.12 [*Iterative function to sum a list of numbers*]: Figure 1.2 contains the step count table for Program 1.10. To construct the table, we first entered the steps/execution for each statement. Next, we figured out the frequency column. The **for** loop at line 5 complicated matters slightly. However, since the loop starts at 0 and terminates when i is equal to n, its frequency is $n + 1$. The body of the loop (line 6) only executes n times since it is not executed when $i = n$. We then obtained the total steps for each statement and the final step count. □

Example 1.13 [*Recursive function to sum a list of numbers*]: Figure 1.3 shows the step count table for Program 1.12. □

Example 1.14 [*Matrix addition*]: Figure 1.4 contains the step count table for the matrix addition function. □

```
void add(int a[][MAX_SIZE], int b[][MAX_SIZE],
                int c[][MAX_SIZE], int rows, int cols)
{
   int i, j;
   for (i = 0; i < rows; i++)
      for (j = 0; j < cols; j++)
         c[i][j] = a[i][j] + b[i][j];
}
```

Program 1.15: Matrix addition

```
void add(int a[][MAX_SIZE], int b[][MAX_SIZE],
                int c[][MAX_SIZE], int rows, int cols)
{
   int i, j;
   for (i = 0; i < rows; i++) {
      count++;  /* for i for loop */
      for (j = 0; j < cols; j++) {
         count++; /* for j for loop */
         c[i][j] = a[i][j] + b[i][j];
         count++; /*  for assignment statement */
      }
      count++; /* last time of j for loop */
   }
   count++; /* last time of i for loop */
}
```

Program 1.16: Matrix addition with count statements

EXERCISES

1. Redo Exercise 2, Section 1.2 (Horner's rule for evaluating polynomials), so that step counts are introduced into the function. Express the total count as an equation.

2. Redo Exercise 3, Section 1.2 (truth tables), so that steps counts are introduced into the function. Express the total count as an equation.

3. Redo Exercise 4, Section 1.2 so that step counts are introduced into the function. Express the total count as an equation.

```
void add(int a[][MAX_SIZE], int b[][MAX_SIZE],
              int c[][MAX_SIZE], int rows, int cols)
{
   int i, j;
   for (i = 0; i < rows; i++) {
      for (j = 0; j < cols; j++)
         count += 2;
      count += 2;
   }
   count++;
}
```

Program 1.17: Simplification of Program 1.16

Statement	s/e	Frequency	Total steps
float sum(float list[], int n)	0	0	0
{	0	0	0
float tempsum = 0;	1	1	1
int i;	0	0	0
for (i = 0; i < n; i++)	1	$n+1$	$n+1$
tempsum += list[i];	1	n	n
return tempsum;	1	1	1
}	0	0	0
Total			$2n+3$

Figure 1.2: Step count table for Program 1.10

4. (a) Rewrite Program 1.18 so that step counts are introduced into the function.

   (b) Simplify the resulting function by eliminating statements.

   (c) Determine the value of *count* when the function ends.

   (d) Write the step count table for the function.

5. Repeat Exercise 5 with Program 1.19.

6. Repeat Exercise 5 with Program 1.20

Statement	s/e	Frequency	Total steps
float rsum(float list[], int n)	0	0	0
{	0	0	0
if (n)	1	$n+1$	$n+1$
return rsum(list,n−1) + list[n−1];	1	n	n
return list[0];	1	1	1
}	0	0	0
Total			$2n+2$

Figure 1.3: Step count table for recursive summing function

Statement	s/e	Frequency	Total Steps
void add(int a[][MAX_SIZE] $\cdots$)	0	0	0
{	0	0	0
int i, j;	0	0	0
for (i=0; i<rows; i++)	1	$rows+1$	$rows+1$
for (j = 0; j < cols; j++)	1	$rows \cdot (cols+1)$	$rows \cdot cols + rows$
c[i][j] = a[i][j] + b[i][j];	1	$rows \cdot cols$	$rows \cdot cols$
}	0	0	0
Total			$2 rows \cdot cols + 2 rows + 1$

Figure 1.4: Step count table for matrix addition

7. Repeat Exercise 5 with Program 1.21

Summary

The time complexity of a program is given by the number of steps taken by the program to compute the function it was written for. The number of steps is itself a function of the instance characteristics. While any specific instance may have several characteristics (e.g., the number of inputs, the number of outputs, the magnitudes of the inputs and outputs, etc.), the number of steps is computed as a function of some subset of these. Usually, we choose those characteristics that are of importance to us. For example, we might wish to know how the computing (or run) time (i.e., time complexity) increases as the

```
void print_matrix(int matrix[][MAX_SIZE], int rows,
                                          int cols)
{
   int i, j;
   for (i = 0; i < rows; i++) {
      for (j = 0; j < cols; j++)
         printf("%d",matrix[i][j]);
      printf("\n");
   }
}
```

Program 1.18: Printing out a matrix

```
void mult(int a[][MAX_SIZE], int b[][MAX_SIZE],
                             int c[][MAX_SIZE])
{
   int i, j, k;
   for (i = 0; i < MAX_SIZE; i++)
      for (j = 0; j < MAX_SIZE; j++) {
         c[i][j] = 0;
         for (k = 0; k < MAX_SIZE; k++)
            c[i][j] += a[i][k] * b[k][j];
      }
}
```

Program 1.19: Matrix multiplication function

number of inputs increase. In this case the number of steps will be computed as a function of the number of inputs alone. For a different program, we might be interested in determining how the computing time increases as the magnitude of one of the inputs increases. In this case the number of steps will be computed as a function of the magnitude of this input alone. Thus, before the step count of a program can be determined, we need to know exactly which characteristics of the problem instance are to be used. These define the variables in the expression for the step count. In the case of *sum*, we chose to measure the time complexity as a function of the number, n, of elements being added. For function *add* the choice of characteristics was the number of rows and the number of columns in the matrices being added.

Once the relevant characteristics $(n, m, p, q, r, \ldots)$ have been selected, we can define what a step is. A step is any computation unit that is independent of the characteristics $(n, m, p, q, r, \ldots)$. Thus, 10 additions can be one step; 100 multiplications can

```
void prod(int a[][MAX_SIZE], int b[][MAX_SIZE],
     int c[][MAX_SIZE], int rowsa, int colsb, int colsa)
{
   int i, j, k;
   for (i = 0; i < rowsa; i++)
     for (j = 0; j < colsb; j++) {
        c[i][j] = 0;
        for (k = 0; k < colsa; k++)
           c[i][j] += a[i][k] * b[k][j];
     }
}
```

Program 1.20: Matrix product function

```
void transpose(int a[][MAX_SIZE])
{
   int i, j, temp;
   for (i = 0; i < MAX_SIZE-1; i++)
     for (j = i+1; j < MAX_SIZE; j++)
        SWAP(a[i][j], a[j][i], temp);
}
```

Program 1.21: Matrix transposition function

also be one step; but n additions cannot. Nor can $m/2$ additions, $p + q$ subtractions, etc., be counted as one step.

The examples we have looked at so far were sufficiently simple that the time complexities were nice functions of fairly simple characteristics like the number of elements, and the number of rows and columns. For many programs, the time complexity is not dependent solely on the number of inputs or outputs or some other easily specified characteristic. Consider the function *binsearch* (Program 1.6). This function searches an ordered list. A natural parameter with respect to which you might wish to determine the step count is the number, n, of elements in the list. That is, we would like to know how the computing time changes as we change the number of elements n. The parameter n is inadequate. For the same n, the step count varies with the position of the element *searchnum* that is being searched for. We can extricate ourselves from the difficulties resulting from situations when the chosen parameters are not adequate to determine the step count uniquely by defining three kinds of steps counts: best case, worst case and average.

The *best case step count* is the minimum number of steps that can be executed for the given paramenters. The *worst case step count* is the maximum number of steps that can be executed for the given paramenters. The *average step count* is the average number of steps executed on instances with the given parameters.

1.4.3   Asymptotic Notation (O, Ω, Θ)

Our motivation to determine step counts is to be able to compare the time complexities of two programs that compute the same function and also to predict the growth in run time as the instance characteristics change.

Determining the exact step count (either worst case or average) of a program can prove to be an exceedingly difficult task. Expending immense effort to determine the step count exactly isn't a very worthwhile endeavor as the notion of a step is itself inexact. (Both the instructions $x = y$ and $x = y + z + (x/y) + (x*y*z-x/z)$ count as one step.) Because of the inexactness of what a step stands for, the exact step count isn't very useful for comparative purposes. An exception to this is when the difference in the step counts of two programs is very large as in $3n+3$ versus $100n+10$. We might feel quite safe in predicting that the program with step count $3n+3$ will run in less time than the one with step count $100n+10$. But even in this case, it isn't necessary to know that the exact step count is $100n+10$. Something like, ''it's about $80n$, or $85n$, or $75n$,'' is adequate to arrive at the same conclusion.

For most situations, it is adequate to be able to make a statement like $c_1 n^2 \le T_P(n) \le c_2 n^2$ or $T_Q(n,m) = c_1 n + c_2 m$ where c_1 and c_2 are nonnegative constants. This is so because if we have two programs with a complexity of $c_1 n^2 + c_2 n$ and $c_3 n$, respectively, then we know that the one with complexity $c_3 n$ will be faster than the one with complexity $c_1 n^2 + c_2 n$ for sufficiently large values of n. For small values of n, either program could be faster (depending on c_1, c_2, and c_3). If $c_1 = 1, c_2 = 2$, and $c_3 = 100$ then $c_1 n^2 + c_2 n \le c_3 n$ for $n \le 98$ and $c_1 n^2 + c_2 n > c_3 n$ for $n > 98$. If $c_1 = 1, c_2 = 2$, and $c_3 = 1000$, then $c_1 n^2 + c_2 n \le c_3 n$ for $n \le 998$.

No matter what the values of c_1, c_2, and c_3, there will be an n beyond which the program with complexity $c_3 n$ will be faster than the one with complexity $c_1 n^2 + c_2 n$. This value of n will be called the *break even point*. If the break even point is 0 then the program with complexity $c_3 n$ is always faster (or at least as fast). The exact break even point cannot be determined analytically. The programs have to be run on a computer in order to determine the break even point. To know that there is a break even point it is adequate to know that one program has complexity $c_1 n^2 + c_2 n$ and the other $c_3 n$ for some constants c_1, c_2, and c_3. There is little advantage in determining the exact values of c_1, c_2, and c_3.

With the previous discussion as motivation, we introduce some terminology that will enable us to make meaningful (but inexact) statements about the time and space complexities of a program. In the remainder of this chapter, the functions f and g are nonnegative functions.

Definition: [Big ''oh''] $f(n) = O(g(n))$ (read as ''f of n is big oh of g of n'') iff (if and only if) there exist positive constants c and n_0 such that $f(n) \leq cg(n)$ for all $n, n \geq n_0$. $\square$

Example 1.15: $3n + 2 = O(n)$ as $3n + 2 \leq 4n$ for all $n \geq 2$. $3n + 3 = O(n)$ as $3n + 3 \leq 4n$ for all $n \geq 3$. $100n + 6 = O(n)$ as $100n + 6 \leq 101n$ for $n \geq 10$. $10n^2 + 4n + 2 = O(n^2)$ as $10n^2 + 4n + 2 \leq 11n^2$ for $n \geq 5$. $1000n^2 + 100n - 6 = O(n^2)$ as $1000n^2 + 100n - 6 \leq 1001n^2$ for $n \geq 100$. $6*2^n + n^2 = O(2^n)$ as $6*2^n + n^2 \leq 7*2^n$ for $n \geq 4$. $3n + 3 = O(n^2)$ as $3n + 3 \leq 3n^2$ for $n \geq 2$. $10n^2 + 4n + 2 = O(n^4)$ as $10n^2 + 4n + 2 \leq 10n^4$ for $n \geq 2$. $3n + 2 \neq O(1)$ as $3n + 2$ is not less than or equal to c for any constant c and all $n, n \geq n_0$. $10n^2 + 4n + 2 \neq O(n)$. $\square$

We write $O(1)$ to mean a computing time which is a constant. $O(n)$ is called linear, $O(n^2)$ is called quadratic, $O(n^3)$ is called cubic, and $O(2^n)$ is called exponential. If an algorithm takes time $O(\log n)$ it is faster, for sufficiently large n, than if it had taken $O(n)$. Similarly, $O(n \log n)$ is better than $O(n^2)$ but not as good as $O(n)$. These seven computing times, $O(1)$, $O(\log n)$, $O(n)$, $O(n \log n)$, $O(n^2)$, $O(n^3)$, and $O(2^n)$ are the ones we will see most often in this book.

As illustrated by the previous example, the statement $f(n) = O(g(n))$ only states that $g(n)$ is an upper bound on the value of $f(n)$ for all $n, n \geq n_0$. It doesn't say anything about how good this bound is. Notice that $n = O(n^2)$, $n = O(n^{2.5})$, $n = O(n^3)$, $n = O(2^n)$, etc. In order for the statement $f(n) = O(g(n))$ to be informative, $g(n)$ should be as small a function of n as one can come up with for which $f(n) = O(g(n))$. So, while we shall often say $3n + 3 = O(n)$, we shall almost never say $3n + 3 = O(n^2)$ even though this latter statement is correct.

From the definition of O, it should be clear that $f(n) = O(g(n))$ is not the same as $O(g(n)) = f(n)$. In fact, it is meaningless to say that $O(g(n)) = f(n)$. The use of the symbol ''='' is unfortunate as this symbol commonly denotes the ''equals'' relation. Some of the confusion that results from the use of this symbol (which is standard terminology) can be avoided by reading the symbol ''='' as ''is'' and not as ''equals.''

Theorem 1.2 obtains a very useful result concerning the order of $f(n)$ (i.e., the $g(n)$ in $f(n) = O(g(n))$) when $f(n)$ is a polynomial in n.

Theorem 1.2: If $f(n) = a_m n^m + \ldots + a_1 n + a_0$, then $f(n) = O(n^m)$.

Proof: $f(n) \leq \sum_{i=0}^{m} |a_i| n^i$

$$\leq n^m \sum_{0}^{m} |a_i| n^{i-m}$$

$$\leq n^m \sum_{0}^{m} |a_i|, \text{ for } n \geq 1$$

So, $f(n) = O(n^m)$. $\square$

Definition: [Omega] $f(n) = \Omega(g(n))$ (read as "f of n is omega of g of n") iff there exist positive constants c and n_0 such that $f(n) \geq cg(n)$ for all $n, n \geq n_0$. $\square$

Example 1.16: $3n + 2 = \Omega(n)$ as $3n + 2 \geq 3n$ for $n \geq 1$ (actually the inequality holds for $n \geq 0$ but the definition of Ω requires an $n_0 > 0$). $3n + 3 = \Omega(n)$ as $3n + 3 \geq 3n$ for $n \geq 1$. $100n + 6 = \Omega(n)$ as $100n + 6 \geq 100n$ for $n \geq 1$. $10n^2 + 4n + 2 = \Omega(n^2)$ as $10n^2 + 4n + 2 \geq n^2$ for $n \geq 1$. $6*2^n + n^2 = \Omega(2^n)$ as $6*2^n + n^2 \geq 2^n$ for $n \geq 1$. Observe also that $3n + 3 = \Omega(1)$; $10n^2 + 4n + 2 = \Omega(n)$; $10n^2 + 4n + 2 = \Omega(1)$; $6*2^n + n^2 = \Omega(n^{100})$; $6*2^n + n^2 = \Omega(n^{50.2})$; $6*2^n + n^2 = \Omega(n^2)$; $6*2^n + n^2 = \Omega(n)$; and $6*2^n + n^2 = \Omega(1)$. $\square$

As in the case of the "big oh" notation, there are several functions $g(n)$ for which $f(n) = \Omega(g(n))$. $g(n)$ is only a lower bound on $f(n)$. For the statement $f(n) = \Omega(g(n))$ to be informative, $g(n)$ should be as large a function of n as possible for which the statement $f(n) = \Omega(g(n))$ is true. So, while we shall say that $3n + 3 = \Omega(n)$ and that $6*2^n + n^2 = \Omega(2^n)$, we shall almost never say that $3n + 3 = \Omega(1)$ or that $6*2^n + n^2 = \Omega(1)$ even though both these statements are correct.

Theorem 1.3 is the analogue of Theorem 1.2 for the omega notation.

Theorem 1.3: If $f(n) = a_m n^m + \ldots + a_1 n + a_0$ and $a_m > 0$, then $f(n) = \Omega(n^m)$.

Proof: Left as an exercise. $\square$

Definition: [Theta] $f(n) = \Theta(g(n))$ (read as "f of n is theta of g of n") iff there exist positive constants c_1, c_2, and n_0 such that $c_1 g(n) \leq f(n) \leq c_2 g(n)$ for all $n, n \geq n_0$. $\square$

Example 1.17: $3n + 2 = \Theta(n)$ as $3n + 2 \geq 3n$ for all $n \geq 2$ and $3n + 2 \leq 4n$ for all $n \geq 2$, so $c_1\ 3, c_2 = 4$, and $n_0 = 2$. $3n + 3 = \Theta(n)$; $10n^2 + 4n + 2 = \Theta(n^2)$; $6*2^n + n^2 = \Theta(2^n)$; and $10*\log n + 4 = \Theta(\log n)$. $3n + 2 \neq \Theta(1)$; $3n + 3 \neq \Theta(n^2)$; $10n^2 + 4n + 2 \neq \Theta(n)$; $10n^2 + 4n + 2 \neq \Theta(1)$; $6*2^n + n^2 \neq \Theta(n^2)$; $6*2^n + n^2 \neq \Theta(n^{100})$; and $6*2^n + n^2 \neq \Theta(1)$. $\square$

The theta notation is more precise than both the "big oh" and omega notations. $f(n) = \Theta(g(n))$ iff $g(n)$ is both an upper and lower bound on $f(n)$.

Notice that the coefficients in all of the $g(n)$'s used in the preceding three examples has been 1. This is in accordance with practice. We shall almost never find ourselves saying that $3n + 3 = O(3n)$, or that $10 = O(100)$, or that $10n^2 + 4n + 2 = \Omega(4n^2)$, or that $6*2^n + n^2 = \Omega(6*2^n)$, or that $6*2^n + n^2 = \Theta(4*2^n)$, even though each of these statements is true.

Theorem 1.4: If $f(n) = a_m n^m + \ldots + a_1 n + a_0$ and $a_m > 0$, then $f(n) = \Theta(n^m)$.

Proof: Left as an exercise. $\square$

Let us reexamine the time complexity analyses of the previous section. For function *sum* (Program 1.11) we had determined that $T_{sum}(n) = 2n + 3$. So, $T_{sum}(n) = \Theta(n)$. $T_{rsum}(n) = 2n + 2 = \Theta(n)$ and $T_{add}(rows, cols) = 2rows.cols + 2rows + 1 = \Theta(rows.cols)$.

While we might all see that the O, Ω, and Θ notations have been used correctly in the preceding paragraphs, we are still left with the question: "Of what use are these notations if one has to first determine the step count exactly?" The answer to this question is that the asymptotic complexity (i.e., the complexity in terms of O, Ω, and Θ) can be determined quite easily without determining the exact step count. This is usually done by first determining the asymptotic complexity of each statement (or group of statements) in the program and then adding up these complexities.

Example 1.18 [*Complexity of matrix addition*]: Using a tabular approach, we construct the table of Figure 1.5. This is quite similar to Figure 1.4. However, instead of putting in exact step counts, we put in asymptotic ones. For nonexecutable statements, we enter a step count of 0. Constructing a table such as the one in Figure 1.5 is actually easier than constructing the one is Figure 1.4. For example, it is harder to obtain the exact step count of $rows.(cols + 1)$ for line 5 than it is to see that line 5 has an asymptotic complexity that is $\Theta(rows.cols)$. To obtain the asymptotic complexity of the function, we can add the asymptotic complexities of the individual program lines. Alternately, since the number of lines is a constant (i.e., is independent of the instance characteristics), we may simply take the maximum of the line complexities. Using either approach, we obtain $\Theta(rows.cols)$ as the asymptotic complexity. $\square$

Statement	Asymptotic complexity
void add(int a[][MAX_SIZE] $\cdots$)	0
{	0
int i, j;	0
for (i=0; i<rows; i++)	$\Theta(rows)$
for (j = 0; j < cols; j++)	$\Theta(rows.cols)$
c[i][j] = a[i][j] + b[i][j];	$\Theta(rows.cols)$
}	0
Total	$\Theta(rows.cols)$

Figure 1.5: Time complexity of matrix addition

Example 1.19 [*Binary search*]: Let us obtain the time complexity of the binary search function *binsearch* (Program 1.6). The instance characteristic we shall use is the number n of elements in the list. Each iteration of the **while** loop takes $\Theta(1)$ time. We can show that the **while** loop is iterated at most $\lceil \log_2(n+1) \rceil$ times (see the book by S. Sahni cited in the references). Since an asymptotic analysis is being performed, we don't need such an accurate count of the worst case number of iterations. Each iteration except for the last results in a decrease in the size of the segment of *list* that has to be searched by a factor of about 2. That is, the value of *right* − *left* + 1 reduces by a factor of about 2 on each iteration. So, this loop is iterated $\Theta(\log n)$ times in the worst case. As each iteration takes $\Theta(1)$ time, the overall worst case complexity of *binsearch* is $\Theta(\log n)$. Notice that the best case complexity is $\Theta(1)$ as in the best case *searchnum* is found in the first iteration of the **while** loop. □

Example 1.20 [*Permutations*]: Consider function *perm* (Program 1.8). When $i = n$, the time taken is $\Theta(n)$. When $i < n$, the **else** clause is entered. The **for** loop of this clause is entered $n - i + 1$ times. Each iteration of this loop takes $\Theta(n + T_{perm}(i + 1, n))$ time. So, $T_{perm}(i, n) = \Theta((n - i + 1)(n + T_{perm}(i + 1, n)))$ when $i < n$. Since, $T_{perm}(i + 1, n)$, is at least n when $i + 1 \leq n$, we get $T_{perm}(i, n) = \Theta((n - i + 1)T_{perm}(i + 1, n))$ for $i < n$. Solving this recurrence, we obtain $T_{perm}(1, n) = \Theta(n(n!))$, $n \geq 1$. □

Example 1.21 [*Magic square*]: As our last example of complexity analysis, we use a problem from recreational mathematics, the creation of a magic square.

A *magic square* is an $n \times n$ matrix of the integers from 1 to n^2 such that the sum of each row and column and the two major diagonals is the same. Figure 1.6 shows a magic square for the case $n = 5$. In this example, the common sum is 65.

15	8	1	24	17
16	14	7	5	23
22	20	13	6	4
3	21	19	12	10
9	2	25	18	11

Figure 1.6: Magic square for $n = 5$

Coxeter has given the following simple rule for generating a magic square when n is odd:

Put a one in the middle box of the top row. Go up and left assigning numbers in increasing order to empty boxes. If your move causes you to jump off the square (that is, you go beyond the square's boundaries), figure out where you would be if you landed on a box on the opposite side of the square. Continue with this box. If a box is occupied, go down instead of up and continue.

We created Figure 1.6 using Coxeter's rule. Program 1.22 contains the coded algorithm. Let n denote the size of the magic square (i.e., the value of the variable *size* in Program 1.22. The **if** statements that check for errors in the value of n take $\Theta(1)$ time. The two nested **for** loops have a complexity $\Theta(n^2)$. Each iteration of the next **for** loop takes $\Theta(1)$ time. This loop is iterated $\Theta(n^2)$ time. So, its complexity is $\Theta(n^2)$. The nested **for** loops that output the magic square also take $\Theta(n^2)$ time. So, the asymptotic complexity of Program 1.22 is $\Theta(n^2)$. $\square$

```c
#include <stdio.h>
#define MAX_SIZE  15 /* maximum size of square */
void main(void)
/* construct a magic square, iteratively */
{
   static int square[MAX_SIZE][MAX_SIZE];
   int i, j, row, column;   /* indices */
   int count  ;             /* counter */
   int size;                /* Square size */

   printf("Enter the size of the square: ");
   scanf("%d", &size);
   /* check for input errors */
   if (size < 1 || size > MAX_SIZE + 1) {
      fprintf(stderr, "Error!  Size is out of range\n");
      exit(1);
   }
   if (!(size % 2)) {
      fprintf(stderr, "Error!  Size is even\n");
      exit(1);
   }
   for (i = 0; i < size; i++)
      for (j = 0; j < size; j++)
         square[i][j] = 0;
   square[0][(size-1) / 2] = 1; /* middle of first row */
   /* i and j are current position */
   i = 0;
   j = (size - 1) / 2;
   for (count = 2; count <= size * size; count++) {
      row = (i-1 < 0) ? (size - 1) : (i - 1); /*up*/
      column = (j-1 < 0) ? (size - 1) : (j - 1); /*left*/
      if (square[row][column])   /*down*/
         i = (++i) % size;
      else {                     /* square is unoccupied */
         i = row;
```

```
        j = (j-1 < 0) ? (size - 1) : --j;
      }
      square[i][j] = count;
    }
    /* output the magic square */
    printf(" Magic Square of size %d : \n\n",size);
    for (i = 0; i < size; i++) {
      for (j = 0; j < size; j++)
        printf("%5d", square[i][j]);
      printf("\n");
    }
    printf("\n\n");
}
```

Program 1.22: Magic square program

When we analyze programs in the following chapters, we will normally confine ourselves to providing an upper bound on the complexity of the program. That is, we will normally use only the big oh notation. We do this because this is the current trend in practice. In many of our analyses the theta notation could have been used in place of the big oh notation as the complexity bound obtained is both an upper and a lower bound for the program.

EXERCISES

1. Show that the following statements are correct:

    (a) $5n^2 - 6n = \Theta(n^2)$

    (b) $n! = O(n^n)$

    (c) $2n^2 + n \log n = \Theta(n^2)$

    (d) $\sum_{i=0}^{n} i^2 = \Theta(n^3)$

    (e) $\sum_{i=0}^{n} i^3 = \Theta(n^4)$

    (f) $n^{2^n} + 6 \cdot 2^n = \Theta(n^{2^n})$

    (g) $n^3 + 10^6 n^2 = \Theta(n^3)$

    (h) $6n^3 / (\log n + 1) = O(n^3)$

    (i) $n^{1.001} + n \log n = \Theta(n^{1.001})$

(j) $n^k + n + n^k \log n = \Theta(n^k \log n)$ for all $k \geq 1$.

(k) $10n^3 + 15n^4 + 100n^2 2^n = O(n^2 2^n)$

2.   Show that the following statements are incorrect:

(a) $10n^2 + 9 = O(n)$

(b) $n^2 \log n = \Theta(n^2)$

(c) $n^2 / \log n = \Theta(n^2)$

(d) $n^3 2^n + 6n^2 3^n = O(n^2 2^n)$

(e) $3^n = O(2^n)$

3.   Prove Theorem 1.3.

4.   Prove Theorem 1.4.

5.   Determine the worst case complexity of Program 1.18.

6.   Determine the worst case complexity of Program 1.21.

7.   Compare the two functions n^2 and $20n + 4$ for various values of n. Determine when the second function becomes smaller than the first.

8.   Write an equivalent recursive version of the magic square program (Program 1.22).

1.4.4   Practical Complexities

We have seen that the time complexity of a program is generally some function of the instance characteristics. This function is very useful in determining how the time requirements vary as the instance characteristics change. The complexity function may also be used to compare two programs P and Q that perform the same task. Assume that program P has complexity $\Theta(n)$ and program Q is of complexity $\Theta(n^2)$. We can assert that program P is faster than program Q for "sufficiently large" n. To see the validity of this assertion, observe that the actual computing time of P is bounded from above by cn for some constant c and for all n, $n \geq n_1$, while that of Q is bounded from below by dn^2 for some constant d and all n, $n \geq n_2$. Since $cn \leq dn^2$ for $n \geq c/d$, program P is faster than program Q whenever $n \geq \max\{n_1, n_2, c/d\}$.

You should always be cautiously aware of the presence of the phrase "sufficiently large" in the assertion of the preceding discussion. When deciding which of the two programs to use, we must know whether the n we are dealing with is, in fact, "sufficiently large." If program P actually runs in $10^6 n$ milliseconds while program Q runs in n^2 milliseconds and if we always have $n \leq 10^6$, then, other factors being equal, program Q is the one to use, other factors being equal.

To get a feel for how the various functions grow with n, you are advised to study Figures 1.7 and 1.8 very closely. As you can see, the function 2^n grows very rapidly with n. In fact, if a program needs 2^n steps for execution, then when $n = 40$, the number of steps needed is approximately $1.1*10^{12}$. On a computer performing 1 billion steps per second, this would require about 18.3 minutes. If $n = 50$, the same program would run for about 13 days on this computer. When $n = 60$, about 310.56 years will be required to execute the program and when $n = 100$, about $4*10^{13}$ years will be needed. So, we may conclude that the utility of programs with exponential complexity is limited to small n (typically $n \leq 40$).

Instance characteristic n						
Time	Name	1	2	4	8	16	32
1	Constant	1	1	1	1	1	1
$\log n$	Logarithmic	0	1	2	3	4	5
n	Linear	1	2	4	8	16	32
$n \log n$	Log linear	0	2	8	24	64	160
n^2	Quadratic	1	4	16	64	256	1024
n^3	Cubic	1	8	64	512	4096	32768
2^n	Exponential	2	4	16	256	65536	4294967296
$n!$	Factorial	1	2	24	40326	20922789888000	26313×10^{33}

Figure 1.7 Function values

Programs that have a complexity that is a polynomial of high degree are also of limited utility. For example, if a program needs n^{10} steps, then using our 1 billion steps per second computer we will need 10 seconds when $n = 10$; 3,171 years when $n = 100$; and $3.17*10^{13}$ years when $n = 1000$. If the program's complexity had been n^3 steps instead, then we would need 1 second when $n = 1000$; 110.67 minutes when $n = 10,000$; and 11.57 days when $n = 100,000$.

Figure 1.9 gives the time needed by a 1 billion instructions per second computer to execute a program of complexity $f(n)$ instructions. You should note that currently only the fastest computers can execute about 1 billion instructions per second. From a practical standpoint, it is evident that for reasonably large n (say $n > 100$), only programs of small complexity (such as n, $n \log n$, n^2, n^3) are feasible. Further, this is the case even if one could build a computer capable of executing 10^{12} instructions per second. In this case, the computing times of Figure 1.9 would decrease by a factor of 1000. Now, when $n = 100$ it would take 3.17 years to execute n^{10} instructions, and $4*10^{10}$ years to execute 2^n instructions.

1.5   PERFORMANCE MEASUREMENT

Although performance analysis gives us a powerful tool for assessing an algorithm's space and time complexity, at some point we also must consider how the algorithm executes on our machine. This consideration moves us from the realm of analysis to that of

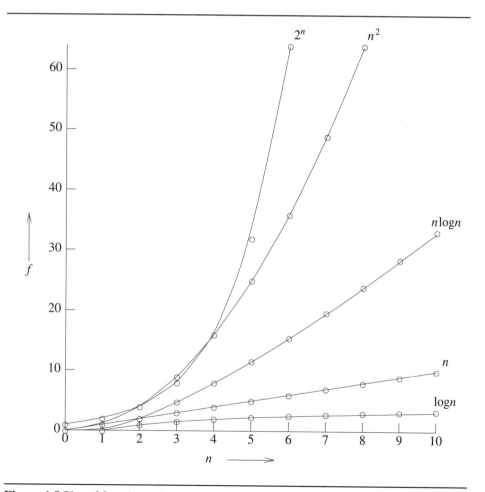

Figure 1.8 Plot of function values

measurement. We will concentrate our discussion on measuring time.

The functions we need to time events are part of C's standard library, and are accessed through the statement: *#include <time.h>*. There are actually two different methods for timing events in C. Figure 1.10 shows the major differences between these two methods.

Method 1 uses *clock* to time events. This function gives the amount of processor time that has elapsed since the program began running. To time an event we use *clock* twice, once at the start of the event and once at the end. The time is returned as a built-in type, *clock_t*. The total time required by an event is its start time subtracted from its stop time. Since this result could be any legitimate numeric type, we **type cast** it to

Time for $f(n)$ instructions on a 10^9 instr/sec computer

n	$f(n)=n$	$f(n)=\log_2 n$	$f(n)=n^2$	$f(n)=n^3$	$f(n)=n^4$	$f(n)=n^{10}$	$f(n)=2^n$
10	.01μs	.03μs	.1μs	1μs	10μs	10sec	1μs
20	.02μs	.09μs	.4μs	8μs	160μs	2.84hr	1ms
30	.03μs	.15μs	.9μs	27μs	810μs	6.83d	1sec
40	.04μs	.21μs	1.6μs	64μs	2.56ms	121.36d	18.3min
50	.05μs	.28μs	2.5μs	125μs	6.25ms	3.1yr	13d
100	.10μs	.66μs	10μs	1ms	100ms	3171yr	$4*10^{13}$ yr
1,000	1.00μs	9.96μs	1ms	1sec	16.67min	$3.17*10^{13}$ yr	$32*10^{283}$ yr
10,000	10.00μs	130.03μs	100ms	16.67min	115.7d	$3.17*10^{23}$ yr	
100,000	100.00μs	1.66ms	10sec	11.57d	3171yr	$3.17*10^{33}$ yr	
1,000,000	1.00ms	19.92ms	16.67min	31.71yr	$3.17*10^7$ yr	$3.17*10^{43}$ yr	

μs = microsecond = 10^{-6} seconds
ms = millisecond = 10^{-3} seconds
sec = seconds
min = minutes
hr = hours
d = days
yr = years

Figure 1.9 Times on a 1 billion instruction per second computer

	Method 1	Method 2
Start timing	start = clock();	start = time(NULL);
Stop timing	stop = clock();	stop = time(NULL);
Type returned	clock$_-$t	time$_-$t
Result in seconds	duration = ((double) (stop−start)) / CLK$_-$TCK;	duration = (double) difftime(stop,start);

Figure 1.10: Event timing in C

double. In addition, since this result is measured as internal processor time, we must divide it by the number of clock ticks per second to obtain the result in seconds. On our compiler the ticks per second is held in the built-in constant, *CLK$_-$TCK*. We found that this method was far more accurate on our machine. However, the second method does not require a knowledge of the ticks per second, which is why we also present it here.

Method 2 uses *time*. This function returns the time, measured in seconds, as the built-in type *time$_-$t*. Unlike *clock*, *time* has one parameter, which specifies a location to hold the time. Since we do not want to keep the time, we pass in a *NULL* value for this parameter. As was true of Method 1, we use *time* at the start and the end of the event we want to time. We then pass these two times into *difftime*, which returns the difference between two times measured in seconds. Since the type of this result is *time$_-$t*, we **type cast** it to **double** before printing it out.

The exact syntax of the timing functions varies from computer to computer and also depends on the operating system and compiler in use. For example, the constant *CLK$_-$TCK* does not exist on a SUN Sparcstation running SUNOS 4.1 Instead, the *clock( )* function returns the time in microseconds. Similarly, the function *difftime( )* is not available and one must use (stop-start) to calculate the total time taken.

We now want to look at two examples of event timing. In each case, we analyze the worst case performance.

Example 1.22 [*Worst case performance of the selection function*]: The worst case for selection sort occurs when the elements are in reverse order. That is, we want to sort into ascending order an array that is currently in descending order. To conduct our timing tests, we varied the size of the array from 0, 10, 20 , $\cdots$, 90, 100, 200 , $\cdots$, 1600. Program 1.23 contains the code we used to conduct the timing tests. (We have not included the sort function code again since it is found in Program 1.3).

To conduct the timing tests, we used a **for** loop to control the size of the array. At each iteration, a new reverse ordered array of *sizelist* [*i*] was created. We called *clock* immediately before we invoked *sort* and immediately after it returned. The results of the tests are displayed in Figures 1.11 and 1.12. The tests were conducted on an IBM

```
#include <stdio.h>
#include <time.h>
#define MAX_SIZE 1601
#define ITERATIONS 26
#define SWAP(x, y, t) ((t) = (x), (x) = (y), (y) = (t))
void main(void)
{
   int i,j,position;
   int list[MAX_SIZE];
   int sizelist[] = {0, 10, 20, 30, 40, 50, 60, 70, 80, 90,
   100, 200, 300, 400, 500, 600, 700, 800, 900, 1000, 1100,
   1200, 1300, 1400, 1500, 1600};
   clock_t start, stop;
   double duration;
   printf("    n    time\n");
   for (i = 0; i < ITERATIONS; i++) {
      for (j = 0; j < sizelist[i]; j++)
         list[j] = sizelist[i] - j;
      start = clock();
      sort(list,sizelist[i]);
      stop = clock();
      /* CLK_TCK = number of clock ticks per second */
      duration = ((double) (stop-start)) / CLK_TCK;
      printf("%6d   %f\n",sizelist[i], duration);
   }
}
```

Program 1.23: Timing program for the selection sort function

compatible PC with an 80386 cpu, an 80387 numeric coprocessor, and a turbo accelerator. We used Borland's Turbo C compiler.

What confidence can we have in the results of this experiment? The measured time for $n \leq 100$ is zero. This cannot be accurate. The sort time for all n must be larger than zero as some nonzero amount of work is being done. Furthermore, since the value of CLK_TCK is 18 on our computer, the number of clock ticks measured for $n < 500$ is less than 10. Since there is a measurement error of ± 1 tick, the measured ticks for $n < 500$ are less than 10% accurate. In the next example, we see how to obtain more accurate times.

The accuracy of our experiment is within 10% for $n > 500$. We may regard this as acceptable. The curve of Figure 1.12 resembles the n^2 curve displayed in Figure 1.8. This agrees with our analysis of selection sort. The times obtained suggest that while selection sort is good for small arrays, it is a poor sorting algorithm for large arrays. □

n	Time	n	Time
30 $\cdots$ 100	.00	900	1.86
200	.11	1000	2.31
300	.22	1100	2.80
400	.38	1200	3.35
500	.60	1300	3.90
600	.82	1400	4.54
700	1.15	1500	5.22
800	1.48	1600	5.93

Figure 1.11: Worst case performance of selection sort (in seconds)

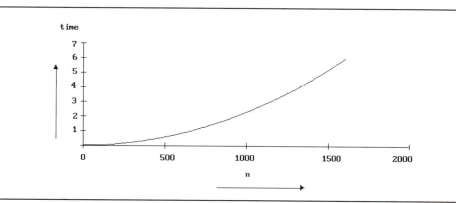

Figure 1.12: Graph of worst case performance for selection sort

Example 1.23 [*Worst case performance of sequential search*]: As pointed out in the last example, the straightforward timing scheme used to time selection sort isn't adequate when we wish to time a function that takes little time to complete. In this example, we consider a more elaborate timing mechanism. To illustrate this, we consider obtaining the worst case time of a sequential search function *seqsearch* (Program 1.24). This begins at the start of the array and compares the number it seeks, *searchnum*, with the numbers in the array until it either finds this number or it reaches the end of the array. The worst case for this search occurs if the number we seek is not in the array. In this case, all the numbers in the array are examined, and the loop is iterated $n + 1$ times.

```
int seqsearch(int list[], int searchnum, int n)
{
/*search an array, list, that has n numbers. Return i,
if list[i] = searchnum. Return -1, if searchnum is not in
the list */
    int i;
    list[n] = searchnum;
    for (i = 0; list[i] != searchnum; i++)
        ;
    return ((i < n ) ? i : -1);
}
```

Program 1.24: Sequential search function

Since searching takes less time than sorting, the timing strategy of Program 1.23 is inadequate even for small arrays. So, we needed another method to obtain accurate times. In this case, the obvious choice was to call the search function many times for each array size. Since the function runs more quickly with the smaller array sizes, we repeated the search for the smaller sizes more times than for the larger sizes. Program 1.25 shows how we constructed the timing tests. It also gives the array sizes used and the number of repetitions used for each array size. Note the need to reset element $list[sizelist[i]]$ after each invocation of *seqsearch*.

The number of repetitions is controlled by *numtimes*. We started with 30,000 repetitions for the case $n = 0$ and reduced the number of repetitions to 200 for the largest arrays. Picking an appropriate number of repetitions involved a trial and error process. The repetition factor must be large enough so that the number of elapsed ticks is at least 10 (if we want an accuracy of at least 10%). However, if we repeat too many times the total computer time required becomes excessive. Figure 1.13 shows the results of our timing tests. These were conducted on an IBM PS/2 Model 50 using Turbo C. The linear dependence of the times on the array size becomes more apparent for larger values of n. This is because the effects of the constant additive factor is more dominant for small n. □

Generating Test Data

Generating a data set that results in the worst case performance of a program isn't always easy. In some cases, it is necessary to use a computer program to generate the worst case data. In other cases, even this is very difficult. In these cases, another approach to estimating worst case performance is taken. For each set of values of the instance characteristics of interest, we generate a suitably large number of random test data. The run times for each of these test data are obtained. The maximum of these times is used

```
#include <stdio.h>
#include <time.h>
#define MAX_SIZE 1001
#define ITERATIONS 16
int seqsearch(int [], int, int);
void main(void)
{
    int i, j, position;
    int list[MAX_SIZE];
    int sizelist[] = {0, 10, 20, 30, 40, 50, 60, 70, 80, 90,
                      100, 200, 400, 600, 800, 1000};
    int numtimes[] = {30000, 12000, 6000, 5000, 4000, 4000,
                      4000, 3000, 3000, 2000, 2000,
                      1000, 500, 500, 500, 200};
    clock_t start, stop;
    double duration,total;
    for (i = 0; i < MAX_SIZE; i++)
      list[i] = i;
    for (i = 0; i < ITERATIONS; i++) {
      start = clock();
      for (j = 0; j < numtimes[i]; j++)
        position = seqsearch(list, -1, sizelist[i]);
      stop = clock();
      total = ((double)(stop-start))/CLK_TCK;
      duration = total/numtimes[i];
      printf("%5d %d  %d %f %f\n", sizelist[i], numtimes[i],
                                   (int)(stop-start), total,
      duration);
      list[sizelist[i]] = sizelist[i]; /* reset value */
    }
}
```

Program 1.25: Timing program for sequential search

as an estimate of the worst case time for this set of values of the instance characteristics.

To measure average case times, it is usually not possible to average over all possible instances of a given characteristic. While it is possible to do this for sequential and binary search, it is not possible for a sort program. If we assume that all keys are distinct, then for any given n, $n!$ different permutations need to be used to obtain the average time.

n	Iterations	Ticks	Total time (sec)	Duration
0	30000	16	0.879121	0.000029
10	12000	16	0.879121	0.000073
20	6000	14	0.769231	0.000128
30	5000	16	0.879121	0.000176
40	4000	16	0.879121	0.000220
50	4000	20	1.098901	0.000275
60	4000	23	1.263736	0.000316
70	3000	20	1.098901	0.000366
80	3000	23	1.263736	0.000421
90	2000	17	0.934066	0.000467
100	2000	18	0.989011	0.000495
200	1000	18	0.989011	0.000989
400	500	18	0.989011	0.001978
600	500	27	1.483516	0.002967
800	500	35	1.923077	0.003846
1000	300	27	1.483516	0.004945

Figure 1.13: Worst case performance of sequential search

Obtaining average case data is usually much harder than obtaining worst case data. So, we often adopt the strategy outlined above and simply obtain an estimate of the average time.

Whether we are estimating worst case or average time using random data, the number of instances that we can try is generally much smaller than the total number of such instances. Hence, it is desirable to analyze the algorithm being tested to determine classes of data that should be generated for the experiment. This is a very algorithm specific task and we shall not go into it here.

EXERCISES

For each of the exercises that follow we want to determine the worst case performance. Create timing programs that do this. For each program, pick arrays of appropriate sizes and repetition factors, if necessary. Present you results in table and graph form, and summarize your findings.

1. Repeat the experiment of Example 1.23. This time make sure that all measured times have an accuracy of at least 10%. Times are to be obtained for the same values of n as in the example. Plot the measured times as a function of n.

2. Plot the run times of Figure 1.14 as a function of n.

3. Compare the worst case performance of the iterative (Program 1.10) and recursive (Program 1.11) list summing functions.

4. Compare the worst case performance of the iterative (Program 1.6) and recursive (Program 1.7) binary search functions.

5. (a) Translate the iterative version of sequential search (Program 1.24) into an equivalent recursive function.

    (b) Analyze the worst case complexity of your function.

    (c) Measure the worst case performance of the recursive sequential search function and compare with the results we provided for the iterative version.

6. Measure the worst case performance of the matrix addition function (Program 1.15).

7. Measure the worst case performance of the matrix multiplication function (Program 1.19).

1.6 SELECTED READINGS AND REFERENCES

For a discussion of programming techniques and how to develop programs, see D. Gries, *The Science of Programming*, Springer Verlag, NY, 1981; E. Dijkstra, *A Discipline of Programming*, Prentice-Hall, Englewood Cliffs, NJ 1976; and B. W. Kernighan and P. J. Plauger, *The Elements of Programming Style*, Second Edition, McGraw Hill, NY 1978.

A good discussion of tools and procedures for developing very large software systems appears in the texts: E. Horowitz, *Practical Strategies for Developing Very Large Software Systems*, Addison-Wesley, Reading, Mass., 1975; I. Sommerville, *Software Engineering*, Third Edition, Addison-Wesley, Workingham, England, 1989; and F. Brooks, *The Mythical Man-Month*, Addison-Wesley, Reading, Mass., 1979.

For a more detailed discussion of performance analysis and measurement, see S. Sahni, *Software Development in Pascal*, Second Edition, Camelot Publishing, 1989.

For a further discussion of abstract data types see B. Liskov and J. Guttag, *Abstraction and Specification in Program Development*, MIT Press, Cambridge, Mass., 1988; J. Kingston, *Algorithms and Data Structures*, Addison-Wesley, Reading, Mass., 1990, and D. Stubbs and N. Webre, *Data Structures with Abstract Data Types and Pascal*, Brooks/Cole Publishing Co., Monterey, CA, 1985.

Writing a correct version of binary search is discussed in the papers J. Bentley, *"Programming pearls: Writing correct programs, CACM*, vol. 26, 1983, pp. 1040-1045, and R. Levisse, *"Some lessons drawn from the history of the binary search algorithm"*, *The Computer Journal*, vol. 26, 1983, pp. 154-163.

For a general discussion of permutation generation, see the paper R. Sedgewick, *"Permutation generation methods, Computer Surveys*, vol. 9, 1977, pp. 137-164.

CHAPTER **2**

ARRAYS AND STRUCTURES

2.1 THE ARRAY AS AN ABSTRACT DATA TYPE

We begin our discussion by considering an array as an ADT. This is not the usual perspective since many programmers view an array only as "a consecutive set of memory locations." This is unfortunate because it clearly shows an emphasis on implementation issues. Thus, although an array is usually implemented as a consecutive set of memory locations, this is not always the case. Intuitively an array is a set of pairs, <*index*, *value*>, such that each index that is defined has a value associated with it. In mathematical terms, we call this a *correspondence* or a *mapping*. However, when considering an ADT we are more concerned with the operations that can be performed on an array. Aside from creating a new array, most languages provide only two standard operations for arrays, one that retrieves a value, and a second that stores a value. Structure 2.1 shows a definition of the array ADT.

The *Create*(*j*, *list*) function produces a new, empty array of the appropriate size. All of the items are initially undefined. *Retrieve* accepts an *array* and an *index*. It returns the value associated with the index if the index is valid, or an error if the index is invalid. *Store* accepts an *array*, an *index*, and an *item*, and returns the original array augmented with the new <*index*, *value*> pair. The advantage of this ADT definition is that it clearly points out the fact that the array is a more general structure than "a consecutive set of memory locations."

---

structure *Array* is

    objects: A set of pairs *<index, value>* where for each value of *index* there is a value from the set *item*. *Index* is a finite ordered set of one or more dimensions, for example, {0, $\cdots$, $n-1$} for one dimension, {(0, 0), (0, 1), (0, 2), (1, 0), (1, 1), (1, 2), (2, 0), (2, 1), (2, 2)} for two dimensions, etc.

    functions:

      for all $A \in Array$, $i \in index$, $x \in item$, j, $size \in$ integer

Array Create(j, *list*)	::=	**return** an array of j dimensions where *list* is a j-tuple whose ith element is the the size of the ith dimension. *Items* are undefined.
Item Retrieve(A, i)	::=	**if** ($i \in index$) **return** the item associated with index value i in array A **else return** error
Array Store(A,i,x)	::=	**if** (i in *index*) **return** an array that is identical to array A except the new pair *<i, x>* has been inserted **else return** error.

end *Array*

Structure 2.1: Abstract Data Type *Array*

Now let's examine arrays in C. We restrict ourselves initially to one-dimensional arrays. A one-dimensional array in C is declared implicitly by appending brackets to the name of a variable. For example,

```
int list[5], *plist[5];
```

declares two arrays each containing five elements. The first array defines five integers, while the second defines five pointers to integers. In C all arrays start at index 0, so *list*[0], *list*[1], *list*[2], *list*[3], and *list*[4] are the names of the five array elements, each of which contains an integer value. Similarly, *plist*[0], *plist*[1], *plist*[2], *plist*[3], and *plist*[4] are the names of five array elements, each of which contains a pointer to an integer.

    We now consider the implementation of one-dimensional arrays. When the compiler encounters an array declaration such as the one used above to create *list*, it allocates five consecutive memory locations. Each memory location is large enough to hold a single integer. The address of the first element *list*[0], is called the *base address*. If the size of an integer on your machine is denoted by *sizeof(int)*, then we get the following memory addresses for the five elements of *list*[]:

Variable	Memory Address
list[0]	base address = α
list[1]	$\alpha + sizeof(int)$
list[2]	$\alpha + 2 \cdot sizeof(int)$
list[3]	$\alpha + 3 \cdot sizeof(int)$
list[4]	$\alpha + 4 \cdot sizeof(int)$

In fact, when we write *list*[*i*] in a C program, C interprets it as a pointer to an integer whose address is the one in the table above. Observe that there is a difference between a declaration such as

```
int *list1;
```
and
```
int list2[5];
```

The variables *list*1 and *list*2 are both pointers to an **int**, but in the second case five memory locations for holding integers have been reserved. *list*2 is a pointer to *list*2[0] and *list*2+*i* is a pointer to *list*2[*i*]. Notice that in C, we do not multiply the offset *i* with the size of the type to get to the appropriate element of the array. Thus, regardless of the type of the array *list*2, it is always the case that (*list*2 + *i*) equals &*list*2[*i*]. So, *(*list*2 + *i*) equals *list*2[*i*].

It is useful to consider the way C treats an array when it is a parameter to a function. All parameters of a C function must be declared within the function. However, the range of a one-dimensional array is defined only in the main program since new storage for an array is not allocated within a function. If the size of a one-dimensional array is needed, it must be either passed into the function as an argument or accessed as a global variable.

Consider Program 2.1. When *sum* is invoked, *input* = &*input*[0] is copied into a temporary location and associated with the formal parameter *list*. When *list*[*i*] occurs on the right-hand side of the equals sign, a dereference takes place and the value pointed at by (*list* + *i*) is returned. If *list*[*i*] appears on the left-hand side of the equals sign, then the value produced on the right-hand side is stored in the location (*list* + *i*). Thus in C, array parameters have their values altered, despite the fact that the parameter passing is done using *call-by-value*.

Example 2.1 [*One-dimensional array addressing*]: Assume that we have the following declaration:

```
int one[] = {0, 1, 2, 3, 4};
```

We would like to write a function that prints out both the address of the *i*th element of this array and the value found at this address. To do this, *print*1 (Program 2.2) uses pointer arithmetic. The function is invoked as *print*1(&*one*[0],5). As you can see

```
#define MAX_SIZE 100
float sum(float [], int);
float input[MAX_SIZE], answer;
int i;
void main(void)
{
   for (i = 0; i < MAX_SIZE; i++)
      input[i] = i;
   answer = sum(input, MAX_SIZE);
   printf("The sum is: %f\n", answer);
}
float sum(float list[], int n)
{
   int i;
   float tempsum = 0;
   for (i = 0; i < n; i++)
      tempsum += list[i];
   return tempsum;
}
```

Program 2.1: Example array program

from the **printf** statement, the address of the *i*th element is simply *ptr* + *i*. To obtain the value of the *i*th element, we use the dereferencing operator, *. Thus, *(*ptr* + *i*) indicates that we want the contents of the *ptr* + *i* position rather than the address.

```
void print1(int *ptr, int rows)
{
/* print out a one-dimensional array using a pointer */
   int i;
   printf("Address Contents\n");
   for (i = 0; i < rows; i++)
      printf("%8u%5d\n", ptr + i, *(ptr + i));
   printf("\n");
}
```

Program 2.2: One-dimensional array accessed by address

Figure 2.1 shows the results we obtained when we ran *print1*. Notice that the

Address	Contents
1228	0
1230	1
1232	2
1234	3
1236	4

Figure 2.1: One-dimensional array addressing

addresses increase by two. This is what we would expect on an Intel 386 machine. □

2.2   STRUCTURES AND UNIONS

2.2.1   Structures

Arrays are collections of data of the same type. In C there is an alternate way of group-ing data that permits the data to vary in type. This mechanism is called the **struct**, short for structure. A structure (called a record in many other programming languages) is a collection of data items, where each item is identified as to its type and name. For exam-ple,

```
struct {
        char name[10];
        int age;
        float salary;
        } person;
```

creates a variable whose name is *person* and that has three fields:

- a name that is a character array
- an integer value representing the age of the person
- a **float** value representing the salary of the individual

We may assign values to these fields as below. Notice the use of the **.** as the structure member operator. We use this operator to select a particular member of the structure.

```
strcpy(person.name,"james");
person.age = 10;
person.salary = 35000;
```

We can create our own structure data types by using the **typedef** statement as below:

```
typedef struct human_being {      or    typedef struct {
       char name[10];                           char name[10];
       int age;                                 int age;
       float salary;                            float salary;
       };                                       } human_being;
```

This says that *human_being* is the name of the type defined by the structure definition, and we may follow this definition with declarations of variables such as:

```
human_being person1, person2;
```

We might have a program segment that says:

```
 if (strcmp(person1.name, person2.name))
   printf("The two people do not have the same name\n");
 else
   printf("The two people have the same name\n");
```

It would be nice if we could write `if (person1 == person2)` and have the entire structure checked for equality, or if we could write `person1 = person2` and have that mean that the value of every field of the structure of *person 2* is assigned as the value of the corresponding field of *person 1*. ANSI C permits structure assignment, but most earlier versions of C do not. For older versions of C, we are forced to write the more detailed form:

```
strcpy(person1.name, person2.name);
person1.age = person2.age;
person1.salary = person2.salary;
```

While structures cannot be directly checked for equality or inequality, we can write a function (Program 2.3) to do this. We assume that *TRUE* and *FALSE* are defined as:

```
#define FALSE 0
#define TRUE 1
```

A typical function call might be:

```
int humans_equal(human_being person1,
                        human_being person2)
{
/* return TRUE if person1 and person2 are the same human
being otherwise return FALSE */
   if (strcmp(person1.name, person2.name))
      return FALSE;
   if (person1.age != person2.age)
      return FALSE;
   if (person1.salary != person2.salary)
      return FALSE;
   return TRUE;
}
```

Program 2.3: Function to check equality of structures

```
   if (humans_equal(person1,person2))
      printf("The two human beings are the same\n");
   else
      printf("The two human beings are not the same\n");
```

We can also embed a structure within a structure. For example, associated with our *human_being* structure we may wish to include the date of his or her birth. We can do this by writing:

```
typedef struct {
        int month;
        int day;
        int year;
        } date;

typedef struct human_being {
        char name[10];
        int age;
        float salary;
        date dob;
        };
```

A person born on February 11, 1944, would have the values for the *date* **struct** set as:

```
person1.dob.month = 2;
person1.dob.day = 11;
person1.dob.year = 1944;
```

2.2.2 Unions

Continuing with our *human_being* example, it would be nice if we could distinguish between males and females. In the case of males we might ask whether they have a beard or not. In the case of females we might wish to know the number of children they have borne. This gives rise to another feature of C called a **union**. A **union** declaration is similar to a structure, but the fields of a **union** must share their memory space. This means that only one field of the **union** is "active" at any given time. For example, to add different fields for males and females we would change our definition of *human_being* to:

```
typedef struct sex_type {
    enum tag_field {female, male} sex;
    union {
        int children;
        int beard ;
        } u;
    };
typedef struct human_being {
        char name[10];
        int age;
        float salary;
        date dob;
        sex_type sex_info;
        };
human_being person1, person2;
```

We could assign values to *person*1 and *person*2 as:

```
person1.sex_info.sex = male;
person1.sex_info.u.beard = FALSE;
```
and
```
person2.sex_info.sex = female;
person2.sex_info.u.children = 4;
```

Notice that we first place a value in the tag field. This allows us to determine which field in the **union** is active. We then place a value in the appropriate field of the **union**. For example, if the value of *sex_info.sex* was *male*, we would enter a *TRUE* or a *FALSE* in the *sex_info.u.beard* field. Similarly, if the person was a *female*, we would enter an integer value in the *sex_info.u.children* field. C does not check to make sure that we use the appropriate field. For instance, we could place a value of *female* in the *sex_info.sex* field, and then proceed to place a value of *TRUE* in the *sex_info.u.beard* field. Although we know that this is not appropriate, C does not check to make sure that we have used the correct fields of a **union**.

2.2.3   Internal Implementation of Structures

In most cases you need not be concerned with exactly how the C compiler will store the fields of a structure in memory. Generally, if you have a structure definition such as:

```
        struct {int i,j; float a, b;};
```
or
```
        struct {int i; int j; float a; float b; };
```

these values will be stored in the same way using increasing address locations in the order specified in the structure definition. However, it is important to realize that holes or padding may actually occur within a structure to permit two consecutive components to be properly aligned within memory.

The size of an object of a **struct** or **union** type is the amount of storage necessary to represent the largest component, including any padding that may be required. Structures must begin and end on the same type of memory boundary, for example, an even byte boundary or an address that is a multiple of 4, 8, or 16.

2.2.4   Self-Referential Structures

A *self-referential structure* is one in which one or more of its components is a pointer to itself. Self-referential structures usually require dynamic storage management routines (*malloc* and *free*) to explicitly obtain and release memory. Consider as an example:

```
        typedef struct list {
                char data;
                list *link ;
                } ;
```

Each instance of the structure *list* will have two components, *data* and *link*. *data* is a single character, while *link* is a pointer to a *list* structure. The value of *link* is either the address in memory of an instance of *list* or the null pointer. Consider these statements, which create three structures and assign values to their respective fields:

```
list item1, item2, item3;
item1.data = 'a';
item2.data = 'b';
item3.data = 'c';
item1.link = item2.link = item3.link = NULL;
```

Structures *item* 1, *item* 2, and *item* 3 each contain the data item *a*, *b*, and *c*, respectively, and the null pointer. We can attach these structures together by replacing the null *link* field in *item* 2 with one that points to *item* 3 and by replacing the null *link* field in *item* 1 with one that points to *item* 2.

```
item1.link = &item2;
item2.link = &item3;
```

We will see more of this linking in Chapter 4.

EXERCISES

1. Develop a structure to represent the planets in the solar system. Each planet has fields for the planet's name, its distance from the sun (in miles), and the number of moons it has. Place items in each the fields for the planets: Earth and Venus.

2. Modify the *human_being* structure so that we can include different information based on marital status. Marital status should be an enumerated type with fields: single, married, widowed, divorced. Use a **union** to include different information based on marital status as follows:

    •   *Single*. No information needed.

    •   *Married*. Include a marriage date field.

    •   *Widowed*. Include marriage date and death of spouse date fields.

    •   *Divorced*. Include divorce date and number of divorces fields.

    Assign values to the fields for some *person* of type *human_being*.

3. Develop a structure to represent each of the following geometric objects:

    •   *rectangle*

    •   *triangle*

    •   *circle*.

2.3 THE POLYNOMIAL ABSTRACT DATA TYPE

Arrays are not only data structures in their own right, we can also use them to implement other abstract data types. For instance, let us consider one of the simplest and most commonly found data structures: the *ordered*, or *linear*, *list*. We can find many examples of this data structure, including:

- Days of the week: (Sunday, Monday, Tuesday, Wednesday, Thursday, Friday, Saturday)
- Values in a deck of cards: (Ace, 2, 3, 4, 5, 6, 7, 8, 9, 10, Jack, Queen, King)
- Floors of a building: (basement, lobby, mezzanine, first, second)
- Years the United States fought in World War II: (1941, 1942, 1943, 1944, 1945)
- Years Switzerland fought in World War II: ( )

Notice that the years Switzerland fought in World War II is different because it contains no items. It is an example of an empty list, which we denote as ( ). The other lists all contain items that are written in the form ($item_0, item_1, \cdots, item_{n-1}$).

We can perform many operations on lists, including:

- Finding the length, n, of a list.
- Reading the items in a list from left to right (or right to left).
- Retrieving the ith item from a list, $0 \leq i < n$.
- Replacing the item in the ith position of a list, $0 \leq i < n$.
- Inserting a new item in the ith position of a list, $0 \leq i \leq n$. The items previously numbered $i, i+1, \cdots, n-1$ become items numbered $i+1, i+2, \cdots, n$.
- Deleting an item from the ith position of a list, $0 \leq i < n$. The items numbered $i+1, \cdots, n-1$ become items numbered $i, i+1, \cdots, n-2$.

Rather than state the formal specification of the ADT *list*, we want to explore briefly its implementation. Perhaps, the most common implementation is to represent an ordered list as an array where we associate the list element, $item_i$, with the array index i. We call this a sequential mapping because, assuming the standard implementation of an array, we are storing $item_i, item_{i+1}$ into consecutive slots i and $i+1$ of the array. Sequential mapping works well for most of the operations listed above. Thus, we can retrieve an item, replace an item, or find the length of a list, in constant time. We also can read the items in the list, from either direction, by simply changing subscripts in a controlled way. Only insertion and deletion pose problems since the sequential allocation forces us to move items so that the sequential mapping is preserved. It is precisely this overhead that leads us to consider nonsequential mappings of ordered lists in Chapter 4.

Let us jump right into a problem requiring ordered lists, which we will solve by using one-dimensional arrays. This problem has become the classical example for motivating the use of list processing techniques, which we will see in later chapters. Therefore, it makes sense to look at the problem and see why arrays offer only a partially adequate solution. The problem calls for building a set of functions that allow for the manipulation of symbolic polynomials. Viewed from a mathematical perspective, a polynomial is a sum of terms, where each term has a form ax^e, where x is the variable, a is the coefficient, and e is the exponent. Two example polynomials are:

$$A(x) = 3x^{20} + 2x^5 + 4 \text{ and } B(x) = x^4 + 10x^3 + 3x^2 + 1$$

The largest (or leading) exponent of a polynomial is called its *degree*. Coefficients that are zero are not displayed. The term with exponent equal to zero does not show the variable since x raised to a power of zero is 1. There are standard mathematical definitions for the sum and product of polynomials. Assume that we have two polynomials, $A(x) = \sum a_i x^i$ and $B(x) = \sum b_i x^i$ then:

$$A(x) + B(x) = \sum (a_i + b_i)x^i$$

$$A(x) \cdot B(x) = \sum (a_i x^i \cdot \sum (b_j x^j))$$

Similarly, we can define subtraction and division on polynomials, as well as many other operations.

We begin with an ADT definition of a polynomial. The particular operations in part are a reflection of what will be needed in our subsequent programs to manipulate polynomials. The definition is contained in Structure 2.2.

We are now ready to make some representation decisions. A very reasonable first decision requires unique exponents arranged in decreasing order. This requirement considerably simplifies many of the operations. Using our specification and this stipulation, we can write a version of *Add* that is closer to a C function (Program 2.4), but is still representation-independent.

This algorithm works by comparing terms from the two polynomials until one or both of the polynomials becomes empty. The **switch** statement performs the comparisons and adds the proper term to the new polynomial, d. If one of the polynomials becomes empty, we copy the remaining terms from the nonempty polynomial into d. With these insights, suppose we now consider the representation question more carefully.

One way to represent polynomials in C is to use **typedef** to create the type *polynomial* as below:

```
#define MAX_DEGREE 101 /*Max degree of polynomial+1*/
typedef struct {
        int degree;
```

---

structure *Polynomial* is

 objects: $p(x) = a_1 x^{e_1} + \cdots + a_n x^{e_n}$; a set of ordered pairs of $<e_i, a_i>$ where a_i in *Coefficients* and e_i in *Exponents*, e_i are integers $>= 0$

 functions:

 for all *poly, poly1, poly2* $\in$ *Polynomial*, *coef* $\in$ *Coefficients*, *expon* $\in$ *Exponents*

Polynomial Zero()	::=	**return** the polynomial, $p(x) = 0$
Boolean IsZero(*poly*)	::=	**if** (*poly*) **return** *FALSE* **else return** *TRUE*
Coefficient Coef(*poly,expon*)	::=	**if** (*expon* $\in$ *poly*) **return** its coefficient **else return** zero
Exponent Lead_Exp(*poly*)	::=	**return** the largest exponent in *poly*
Polynomial Attach(*poly, coef, expon*)	::=	**if** (*expon* $\in$ *poly*) **return** error **else return** the polynomial *poly* with the term *<coef, expon>* inserted
Polynomial Remove(*poly, expon*)	::=	**if** (*expon* $\in$ *poly*) **return** the polynomial *poly* with the term whose exponent is *expon* deleted **else return** error
Polynomial SingleMult(*poly, coef, expon*)	::=	**return** the polynomial $poly \cdot coef \cdot x^{expon}$
Polynomial Add(*poly1, poly2*)	::=	**return** the polynomial $poly1 + poly2$
Polynomial Mult(*poly1, poly2*)	::=	**return** the polynomial $poly1 \cdot poly2$

end *Polynomial*

Structure 2.2: Abstract data type *Polynomial*

```
        float coef[MAX_DEGREE];
        } polynomial;
```

Now if *a* is of type *polynomial* and *n* < *MAX_DEGREE*, the polynomial $A(x) = \sum_{i=0}^{n} a_i x^i$ would be represented as:

$$a.\text{degree} = n$$

```
/* d = a + b, where a, b, and d are polynomials */
d = Zero()
while (! IsZero(a) && ! IsZero(b)) do {
   switch COMPARE(Lead_Exp(a), Lead_Exp(b)) {
      case -1: d =
         Attach(d,Coef(b,Lead_Exp(b)),Lead_Exp(b));
         b = Remove(b,Lead_Exp(b));
         break;
      case  0: sum  =  Coef(  a,  Lead_Exp(a))  +  Coef(b,
   Lead_Exp(b));
         if (sum) {
            Attach(d,sum,Lead_Exp(a));
            a = Remove(a,Lead_Exp(a));
            b = Remove(b,Lead_Exp(b));
         }
         break;
      case 1: d =
         Attach(d,Coef(a,Lead_Exp(a)),Lead_Exp(a));
         a = Remove(a,Lead_Exp(a));
   }
}
insert any remaining terms of a or b into d
```

Program 2.4: Initial version of *padd* function

$$a.\text{coef}[i] = a_{n-i},\ 0 \le i \le n$$

In this representation, we store the coefficients in order of decreasing exponents, such that $a . coef [i]$ is the coefficient of x^{n-i} provided a term with exponent $n-i$ exists; otherwise, $a . coef [i] = 0$. Although this representation leads to very simple algorithms for most of the operations, it wastes a lot of space. For instance, if $a . degree \ll$ *MAX_DEGREE*, (the double "less than" should be read as "is much less than"), then we will not need most of the positions in $a . coef [MAX\_DEGREE]$. The same argument applies if the polynomial is sparse, that is, the number of terms with nonzero coefficient is small relative to the degree of the polynomial. To preserve space we devise an alternate representation that uses only one global array, *terms*, to store all our polynomials. The C declarations needed are:

```
MAX_TERMS 100 /*size of terms array*/
typedef struct {
        float coef;
        int expon;
```

```
      } polynomial;
  polynomial terms[MAX_TERMS];
  int avail = 0;
```

Consider the two polynomials $A(x) = 2x^{1000} + 1$ and $B(x) = x^4 + 10x^3 + 3x^2 + 1$. Figure 2.2 shows how these polynomials are stored in the array *terms*. The index of the first term of A and B is given by *starta* and *startb*, respectively, while *finisha* and *finishb* give the index of the last term of A and B. The index of the next free location in the array is given by *avail*. For our example, *starta* = 0, *finisha* = 1, *startb* = 2, *finishb* = 5, and *avail* = 6.

	starta	finisha	startb			finishb	avail
	↓	↓	↓			↓	↓
coef	2	1	1	10	3	1	
exp	1000	0	4	3	2	0	
	0	1	2	3	4	5	6

Figure 2.2: Array representation of two polynomials

This representation does not impose any limit on the number of polynomials that we can place in *terms*. The only stipulation is that the total number of nonzero terms must be no more than *MAX_TERMS*. It is worth pointing out the difference between our specification and our representation. Our specification used *poly* to refer to a polynomial, and our representation translated *poly* into a *<start, finish>* pair. Therefore, to use $A(x)$ we must pass in *starta* and *finisha*. Any polynomial A that has *n* nonzero terms has *starta* and *finisha* such that *finisha* = *starta* + *n* − 1.

Before proceeding, we should evaluate our current representation. Is it any better than the representation that uses an array of coefficients for each polynomial? It certainly solves the problem of many zero terms since $A(x) = 2x^{1000} + 1$ uses only six units of storage: one for *starta*, one for *finisha*, two for the coefficients, and two for the exponents. However, when all the terms are nonzero, the current representation requires about twice as much space as the first one. Unless we know before hand that each of our polynomials has few zero terms, our current representation is probably better.

We would now like to write a C function that adds two polynomials, A and B, represented as above to obtain D = A + B. To produce $D(x)$, *padd* (Program 2.5) adds $A(x)$ and $B(x)$ term by term. Starting at position *avail*, *attach* (Program 2.6) places the terms of D into the array, *terms*. If there is not enough space in *terms* to accommodate D, an error message is printed to the standard error device and we exit the program with an error condition.

```
void padd(int starta,int finisha,int startb, int finishb,
                                int *startd,int *finishd)
{
/* add A(x) and B(x) to obtain D(x) */
   float coefficient;
   *startd = avail;
   while (starta <= finisha && startb <= finishb)
      switch(COMPARE(terms[starta].expon,
                       terms[startb].expon)) {
         case -1: /* a expon < b expon */
                 attach(terms[startb].coef,terms[startb].expon);
                 startb++;
                 break;
         case 0: /* equal exponents */
                 coefficient = terms[starta].coef +
                               terms[startb].coef;
                 if (coefficient)
                    attach(coefficient,terms[starta].expon);
                 starta++;
                 startb++;
                 break;
         case 1: /* a expon > b expon */
                 attach(terms[starta].coef,terms[starta].expon);
                 starta++;
      }
   /* add in remaining terms of A(x) */
   for(; starta <= finisha; starta++)
      attach(terms[starta].coef,terms[starta].expon);
   /* add in remaining terms of B(x) */
   for( ; startb <= finishb; startb++)
      attach(terms[startb].coef, terms[startb].expon);
   *finishd = avail-1;
}
```

Program 2.5: Function to add two polynomials

Analysis of *padd*: Since the number of nonzero terms in A and in B are the most important factors in the time complexity, we will carry out the analysis using them. Therefore, let m and n be the number of nonzero terms in A and B, respectively. If $m > 0$ and $n > 0$, the **while** loop is entered. Each iteration of the loop requires O(1) time. At each

```
void attach(float coefficient, int exponent)
{
/* add a new term to the polynomial */
   if (avail >= MAX_TERMS) {
      fprintf(stderr,"Too many terms in the polynomial\n");
      exit(1);
   }
   terms[avail].coef = coefficient;
   terms[avail++].expon = exponent;
}
```

Program 2.6: Function to add a new term

iteration, we increment the value of *starta* or *startb* or both. Since the iteration terminates when either *starta* or *startb* exceeds *finisha* or *finishb*, respectively, the number
of iterations is bounded by $m + n - 1$. This worst case occurs when:

$$A(x) = \sum_{i=0}^{n} x^{2i} \text{ and } B(x) = \sum_{i=0}^{n} x^{2i+1}$$

The time for the remaining two loops is bounded by $O(n + m)$ because we cannot
iterate the first loop more than m times and the second more than n times. So, the asymptotic computing time of this algorithm is $O(n + m)$. □

Before proceeding let us briefly consider a few of the problems with the current
representation. We have seen that, as we create polynomials, we increment *avail* until it
equals *MAX_TERMS*. When this occurs, must we quit? Given the current representation, we must unless there are some polynomials that we no longer need. We could write
a compaction function that would remove the unnecessary polynomials and create a
large, continuous available space at one end of the array. However, this requires data
movement which takes time. In addition, we also must change the start and end indices
for each polynomial moved, that is, we change the values of *starti* and *finishi* for all
polynomials moved. In Chapter 3, we let you experiment with some "simple" compact-
ing routines.

EXERCISES

1. Write functions *readpoly* and *printpoly* that allow the user to create and print polynomials.

2. Write a function, *pmult*, that multiplies two polynomials. Figure out the computing time of your function.

3. Write a function, *peval*, that evaluates a polynomial at some value, x_0. Try to minimize the number of operations.

4. Let $A(x) = x^{2n} + x^{2n-2} + \cdots + x^2 + x^0$ and $B(x) = x^{2n+1} + x^{2n} + \cdots + x^3 + x$. For these polynomials, determine the exact number of times each statement of *padd* is executed.

5. The declarations that follow give us a third representation of the polynomial ADT. *terms*[i][0].*expon* gives the number of nonzero terms in the *i*th polynomial. These terms are stored, in descending order of exponents, in positions *terms*[i][1], *terms*[i][2], $\cdots$. Create the functions *readpoly*, *printpoly*, *padd*, and *pmult* for this representation. Is this representation better or worse than the representation used in the text? (You may add declarations as necessary.)

```
#define MAX_TERMS 101 /* maximum number of terms + 1*/
#define MAX_POLYS 15 /* maximum number of
                              polynomials*/
typedef struct {
        float coef;
        int expon;
        } polynomial;
polynomial terms[MAX_POLYS][MAX_TERMS];
```

2.4   THE SPARSE MATRIX ABSTRACT DATA TYPE

2.4.1   Introduction

We now turn our attention to a mathematical object that is used to solve many problems in the natural sciences, the matrix. As computer scientists, our interest centers not only on the specification of an appropriate ADT, but also on finding representations that let us efficiently perform the operations described in the specification.

In mathematics, a matrix contains *m* rows and *n* columns of elements as illustrated in Figure 2.3. In this figure, the elements are numbers. The first matrix has five rows and three columns; the second has six rows and six columns. In general, we write $m \times n$ (read "*m* by *n*") to designate a matrix with *m* rows and *n* columns. The total number of elements in such a matrix is *mn*. If *m* equals *n*, the matrix is square.

The standard representation of a matrix in computer science is a two-dimensional array defined as *a*[*MAX_ROWS*][*MAX_COLS*]. With this representation, we can locate quickly any element by writing *a*[i][j], where *i* is the row index and *j* is the column index. However, there are some problems with the standard representation. For

	col 0	col 1	col 2
row 0	−27	3	4
row 1	6	82	−2
row 2	109	−64	11
row 3	12	8	9
row 4	48	27	47

(a)

	col 0	col 1	col 2	col 3	col 4	col 5
row 0	15	0	0	22	0	−15
row 1	0	11	3	0	0	0
row 2	0	0	0	−6	0	0
row 3	0	0	0	0	0	0
row 4	91	0	0	0	0	0
row 5	0	0	28	0	0	0

(b)

Figure 2.3: Two matrices

instance, if you look at Figure 2.3(b), you notice that it contains many zero entries. We call this a *sparse matrix*. Although it is difficult to determine exactly whether a matrix is sparse or not, intuitively we can recognize a sparse matrix when we see one. In Figure 2.3(b), only 8 of 36 elements are nonzero and that certainly is sparse.

Since a sparse matrix wastes space, we must consider alternate forms of representation. The standard two-dimensional array implementation simply does not work when the matrices are large since most compilers impose limits on array sizes. For example, consider the space requirements necessary to store a 1000×1000 matrix. If this matrix contains mostly zero entries we have wasted a tremendous amount of space. Therefore, our representation of sparse matrices should store only nonzero elements.

Before developing a particular representation, we first must consider the operations that we want to perform on these matrices. A minimal set of operations includes matrix creation, addition, multiplication, and transpose. Structure 2.3 contains our specification of the matrix ADT.

Before implementing any of these operations, we must establish the representation of the sparse matrix. By examining Figure 2.3, we know that we can characterize uniquely any element within a matrix by using the triple < *row, col, value* >. This means that we can use an array of triples to represent a sparse matrix. Since we want our transpose operation to work efficiently, we should organize the triples so that the row indices are in ascending order. We can go one step further by also requiring that all the triples for any row be stored so that the column indices are in ascending order. In addition, to ensure that the operations terminate, we must know the number of rows and columns, and the number of nonzero elements in the matrix. Putting all this information together suggests that we implement the *Create* operation as below:

---

structure *Sparse_Matrix* is

    objects: a set of triples, <*row, column, value*>, where *row* and *column* are integers and form a unique combination, and *value* comes from the set *item*.

    functions:

        for all $a, b \in$ *Sparse_Matrix*, $x \in$ *item*, $i, j, max\_col, max\_row \in$ *index*

        Sparse_Matrix Create(*max_row, max_col*) ::=

                return a *Sparse_Matrix* that can hold up to $max\_items = max\_row \times max\_col$ and whose maximum row size is *max_row* and whose maximum column size is *max_col*.

        Sparse_Matrix Transpose(*a*) ::=

                return the matrix produced by interchanging the row and column value of every triple.

        Sparse_Matrix Add(*a, b*) ::=

                if the dimensions of *a* and *b* are the same

                return the matrix produced by adding corresponding items, namely those with identical *row* and *column* values.

                else return error

        Sparse_Matrix Multiply(*a, b*) ::=

                if number of columns in *a* equals number of rows in *b*

                return the matrix *d* produced by multiplying *a* by *b* according to the formula: $d[i][j] = \sum (a[i][k] \cdot b[k][j])$ where $d(i, j)$ is the (i, j)th element

                else return error.

Structure 2.3: Abstract data type *Sparse_Matrix*

Sparse_Matrix Create(*max_row, max_col*) ::=

```
#define MAX_TERMS 101 /* maximum number of terms +1*/
typedef struct {
        int col;
        int row;
        int value;
        } term;
term a[MAX_TERMS];
```

Since *MAX_TERMS* is greater than eight, these statements can be used to represent the second sparse matrix from Figure 2.3. Figure 2.4(a) shows how this matrix is represented in the array a. Thus, a[0].*row* contains the number of rows; a[0].*col* contains the number of columns; and a[0].*value* contains the total number of nonzero entries. Positions 1 through 8 store the triples representing the nonzero entries. The row index is in the field *row*; the column index is in the field *col*; and the value is in the field *value*. The triples are ordered by row and within rows by columns.

	row	col	value		row	col	value
a[0]	6	6	8	b[0]	6	6	8
[1]	0	0	15	[1]	0	0	15
[2]	0	3	22	[2]	0	4	91
[3]	0	5	−15	[3]	1	1	11
[4]	1	1	11	[4]	2	1	3
[5]	1	2	3	[5]	2	5	28
[6]	2	3	−6	[6]	3	0	22
[7]	4	0	91	[7]	3	2	−6
[8]	5	2	28	[8]	5	0	−15
	(a)				(b)		

Figure 2.4: Sparse matrix and its transpose stored as triples

2.4.2   Transposing a Matrix

Figure 2.4(b) shows the transpose of the sample matrix. To transpose a matrix we must interchange the rows and columns. This means that each element $a[i][j]$ in the original matrix becomes element $b[j][i]$ in the transpose matrix. Since we have organized the original matrix by rows, we might think that the following is a good algorithm for transposing a matrix:

```
for each row i
   take element <i, j, value> and store it
   as element <j, i, value> of the transpose;
```

Unfortunately, if we process the original matrix by the row indices we will not know exactly where to place element <*j, i, value*> in the transpose matrix until we have processed all the elements that precede it. For instance, in Figure 2.4, we have:

$$(0, 0,\ 15),\qquad \text{which becomes}\qquad (0, 0,\ 15)$$
$$(0, 3,\ 22),\qquad \text{which becomes}\qquad (3, 0,\ 22)$$
$$(0, 5, -15),\qquad \text{which becomes}\qquad (5, 0, -15)$$

If we place these triples consecutively in the transpose matrix, then, as we insert new triples, we must move elements to maintain the correct order. We can avoid this data movement by using the column indices to determine the placement of elements in the transpose matrix. This suggests the following algorithm:

```
for all elements in column j
   place element <i, j, value> in
   element <j, i, value>
```

The algorithm indicates that we should "find all the elements in column 0 and store them in row 0 of the transpose matrix, find all the elements in column 1 and store them in row 1, etc." Since the original matrix ordered the rows, the columns within each row of the transpose matrix will be arranged in ascending order as well. This algorithm is incorporated in *transpose* (Program 2.7). The first array, *a*, is the original array, while the second array, *b*, holds the transpose.

It is not too difficult to see that the function works correctly. The variable, *currentb*, holds the position in *b* that will contain the next transposed term. We generate the terms in *b* by rows, but since the rows in *b* correspond to the columns in *a*, we collect the nonzero terms for row *i* of *b* by collecting the nonzero terms from column *i* of *a*.

Analysis of *transpose*: Determining the computing time of this algorithm is easy since the nested **for** loops are the decisive factor. The remaining statements (two **if** statements and several assignment statements) require only constant time. We can see that the outer **for** loop is iterated *a* [0].*col* times, where *a* [0].*col* holds the number of columns in the original matrix. In addition, one iteration of the inner **for** loop requires *a* [0].*value* time, where *a* [0].*value* holds the number of elements in the original matrix. Therefore, the total time for the nested **for** loops is *columns* · *elements*. Hence, the asymptotic time complexity is O(*columns* · *elements*). □

We now have a matrix transpose algorithm with a computing time of O(*columns* · *elements*). This time is a little disturbing since we know that if we represented our matrices as two-dimensional arrays of size *rows* × *columns*, we could obtain the transpose in O(*rows* · *columns*) time. The algorithm to accomplish this has the simple form:

```
void transpose(term a[], term b[])
/* b is set to the transpose of a */
{
   int n,i,j, currentb;
   n = a[0].value;          /* total number of elements */
   b[0].row = a[0].col; /* rows in b = columns in a */
   b[0].col = a[0].row; /* columns in b = rows in a */
   b[0].value = n;
   if (n > 0 )  { /* non zero matrix */
      currentb = 1;
      for (i = 0; i < a[0].col; i++)
      /* transpose by the columns in a */
         for (j = 1; j <= n; j++)
         /* find elements from the current column */
            if (a[j].col == i) {
            /* element is in current column, add it to b */
               b[currentb].row = a[j].col;
               b[currentb].col = a[j].row;
               b[currentb].value = a[j].value;
               currentb++;
            }
   }
}
```

Program 2.7: Transpose of a sparse matrix

```
            for (j = 0; j < columns; j++)
               for (i = 0; i < rows; i++)
                  b[j][i] = a[i][j];
```

The O(*columns · elements*) time for our transpose function becomes O(*columns*^{2} · *rows*) when the number of elements is of the order *columns · rows*. Perhaps, to conserve space, we have traded away too much time. Actually, we can create a much better algorithm by using a little more storage. In fact, we can transpose a matrix represented as a sequence of triples in O(*columns + elements*) time. This algorithm, *fast_transpose* (Program 2.8), proceeds by first determining the number of elements in each column of the original matrix. This gives us the number of elements in each row of the transpose matrix. From this information, we can determine the starting position of each row in the transpose matrix. We now can move the elements in the original matrix one by one into their correct position in the transpose matrix. We assume that *MAX_COL* is defined as follows, and that the number of columns in the original matrix never exceeds it.

```
#define MAX_COL 50 /*maximum number of columns + 1*/
```

```
void fast_transpose(term a[], term b[])
{
/* the transpose of a is placed in b */
   int row_terms[MAX_COL], starting_pos[MAX_COL];
   int i,j, num_cols = a[0].col, num_terms = a[0].value;
   b[0].row = num_cols;  b[0].col = a[0].row;
   b[0].value = num_terms;
   if (num_terms > 0) { /* nonzero matrix */
      for (i = 0; i < num_cols; i++)
         row_terms[i] = 0;
      for (i = 1; i <= num_terms; i++)
         row_terms[a[i].col]++;
      starting_pos[0] = 1;
      for (i = 1; i < num_cols; i++)
         starting_pos[i] =
                  starting_pos[i-1] + row_terms[i-1];
      for (i = 1; i <= num_terms; i++) {
         j = starting_pos[a[i].col]++;
         b[j].row = a[i].col;   b[j].col = a[i].row;
         b[j].value = a[i].value;
      }
   }
}
```

Program 2.8: Fast transpose of a sparse matrix

Analysis of *fast_transpose*: We can verify that *fast_transpose* works correctly from the preceding discussion and the observation that the starting point of row i, $i > 1$ of the transpose matrix is *row_terms*[$i-1$] + *starting_pos*[$i-1$], where *row_terms*[$i-1$] is the number of elements in row $i-1$ and *starting_pos*[$i-1$] is the starting point of row $i-1$. The first two **for** loops compute the values for *row_terms*, the third **for** loop carries out the computation of *starting_pos*, and the last **for** loop places the triples into the transpose matrix. These four loops determine the computing time of *fast_transpose*. The bodies of the loops are executed *num_cols*, *num_terms*, *num_cols* − 1, and *num_terms* times, respectively. Since the statements within the loops require only constant time, the computing time for the algorithm is O(*columns* + *elements*). The time becomes O(*columns* · *rows*) when the number of elements is of the order *columns* · *rows*. This time equals that of the two-dimensional array representation, although *fast_transpose* has a larger constant factor. However, when the number of elements is sufficiently small compared to the maximum of *columns* · *rows*, *fast_transpose* is much faster. Thus, in this representation we save both time and space. This was not true of *transpose* since the number of elements is usually greater than max{*columns, rows*} and *columns · elements* is always at least *columns · rows*. In addition, the constant factor for *transpose* is bigger than that found in the two-dimensional array representation. However, *transpose* requires less space than *fast_transpose* since the latter function must allocate space for the *row_terms* and *starting_pos* arrays. We can reduce this space to one array if we put the starting positions into the space used by the row terms as we calculate each starting position. □

If we try the algorithm on the sparse matrix of Figure 2.4(a), then after the execution of the third **for** loop, the values of *row_terms* and *starting_pos* are:

	[0]	[1]	[2]	[3]	[4]	[5]
row_terms =	1	2	2	2	0	1
starting_pos =	1	2	4	6	8	8

The number of entries in row i of the transpose is contained in *row_terms*[i]. The starting position for row i of the transpose is held by *starting_pos*[i].

2.4.3 Matrix Multiplication

A second operation that arises frequently is matrix multiplication, which is defined below.

Definition: Given A and B where A is $m \times n$ and B is $n \times p$, the product matrix D has dimension $m \times p$. Its <i, j> element is :

$$d_{ij} = \sum_{k=0}^{n-1} a_{ik}\, b_{kj}$$

for $0 \le i < m$ and $0 \le j < p$. □

The product of two sparse matrices may no longer be sparse, as Figure 2.5 shows.

$$\begin{bmatrix} 1 & 0 & 0 \\ 1 & 0 & 0 \\ 1 & 0 & 0 \end{bmatrix} \begin{bmatrix} 1 & 1 & 1 \\ 0 & 0 & 0 \\ 0 & 0 & 0 \end{bmatrix} = \begin{bmatrix} 1 & 1 & 1 \\ 1 & 1 & 1 \\ 1 & 1 & 1 \end{bmatrix}$$

Figure 2.5: Multiplication of two sparse matrices

We would like to multiply two sparse matrices represented as an ordered list (Figure 2.4). We need to compute the elements of D by rows so that we can store them in their proper place without moving previously computed elements. To do this we pick a row of A and find all elements in column j of B for $j = 0, 1, \cdots, cols\_b - 1$. Normally, we would have to scan all of B to find all the elements in column j. However, we can avoid this by first computing the transpose of B. This puts all column elements in consecutive order. Once we have located the elements of row i of A and column j of B we just do a merge operation similar to that used in the polynomial addition of Section 2.2. (We explore an alternate approach in the exercises at the end of this section.)

To obtain the product matrix D, *mmult* (Program 2.9) multiplies matrices A and B using the strategy outlined above. We store the matrices A, B, and D in the arrays a, b, and d, respectively. To place a triple in d and to reset *sum* to 0, *mmult* uses *storesum* (Program 2.10). In addition, *mmult* uses several local variables that we will describe briefly. The variable *row* is the row of A that we are currently multiplying with the columns in B. The variable *row_begin* is the position in a of the first element of the current row, and the variable *column* is the column of B that we are currently multiplying with a row in A. The variable *totald* is the current number of elements in the product matrix D. The variables i and j are used to examine successively elements from a row of A and a column of B. Finally, the variable *new_b* is the sparse matrix that is the transpose of b. Notice that we have introduced an additional term into both a ($a[totala+1].row = rows\_a;$) and *new_b* ($new\_b[totalb+1].row = cols\_b;$). These dummy terms serve as sentinels that enable us to obtain an elegant algorithm.

```
void mmult(term a[], term b[], term d[])
/* multiply two sparse matrices */
{
   int i, j, column, totalb = b[0].value, totald = 0;
   int rows_a = a[0].row, cols_a = a[0].col,
   totala = a[0].value; int  cols_b = b[0].col,
   int row_begin = 1, row = a[1].row, sum = 0;
   int new_b[MAX_TERMS][3];
   if (cols_a != b[0].row) {
      fprintf(stderr,"Incompatible matrices\n");
      exit(1);
   }
   fast_transpose(b,new_b);
   /* set boundary condition */
   a[totala+1].row = rows_a;
   new_b[totalb+1].row = cols_b;
   new_b[totalb+1].col = 0;
   for (i = 1; i <= totala; ) {
      column = new_b[1].row;
      for (j = 1; j <= totalb+1;) {
```

```
    /* multiply row of a by column of b */
      if (a[i].row != row) {
        storesum(d,&totald,row,column,&sum);
        i = row_begin;
        for (; new_b[j].row == column; j++)
           ;
        column = new_b[j].row;
      }
      else if (new_b[j].row != column) {
        storesum(d, &totald, row, column, &sum);
        i = row_begin;
        column = new_b[j].row;
      }
      else switch (COMPARE(a[i].col, new_b[j].col)) {
        case -1: /* go to next term in a */
               i++;   break;
        case 0: /* add terms, go to next term in a and b*/
               sum += ( a[i++].value * new_b[j++].value);
               break;
        case 1 : /* advance to next term in b */
               j++;
      }
    }  /* end of for j <= totalb+1 */
    for (; a[i].row == row; i++)
      ;
    row_begin = i; row = a[i].row;
  } /* end of for i<=totala */
  d[0].row = rows_a;
  d[0].col = cols_b; d[0].value =  totald;
}
```

Program 2.9: Sparse matrix multiplication

Analysis of *mmult*: We leave the correctness proof of *mmult* as an exercise and consider only its complexity. Besides the space needed for *a*, *b*, *d*, and a few simple variables, we also need space to store the transpose matrix *new_b*. We also must include the additional space required by *fast_transpose*. The exercises explore a strategy for *mmult* that does not explicitly compute *new_b*.

We can see that the lines before the first **for** loop require only O(*cols_b* + *totalb*) time, which is the time needed to transpose *b*. The outer **for** loop is executed *totala* times. At each iteration either *i* or *j* or both increase by 1, or *i* and *column* are reset. The maximum total increment in *j* over the entire loop is *totalb* + 1. If *termsrow* is the total number of terms in the current row of *A*, then *i* can increase at most *termsrow* times before *i* moves to the next row of *A*. When this happens, we reset *i* to *row_begin*, and, at

```
void storesum(term d[], int *totald, int row, int column,
                                      int *sum)
{
/* if *sum != 0, then it along with its row and column
position is stored as the *totald+1 entry in d */
   if (*sum)
      if (*totald < MAX_TERMS) {
         d[++*totald].row = row;
         d[*totald].col = column;
         d[*totald].value = *sum;
         *sum = 0;
      }
      else {
         fprintf(stderr,"Numbers of terms in product
                              exceeds %d\n",MAX_TERMS);
         exit(1);
      }
}
```

Program 2.10: *storesum* function

the same time, advance *column* to the next column. Thus, this resetting takes place at most *cols_b* time, and the total maximum increment in *i* is *cols_b*termsrow*. Therefore, the maximum number of iterations of the outer **for** loop is *cols_b* + *cols_b*termsrow* + *totalb*. The time for the inner loop during the multiplication of the current row is O(*cols_b*termsrow* + *totalb*), and the time to advance to the next row is O(*termsrow*). Thus, the time for one iteration of the outer **for** loop is O(*cols_b*termsrow* + *totalb*). The overall time for this loop is:

$$O\left(\sum_{row}(cols\_b \cdot termsrow + totalb)\right) = O\left(cols\_b \cdot total\_a + rows\_a \cdot totalb\right) \quad \Box$$

Once again we can compare this time with the computing time required to multiply matrices using the standard array representation. The classic multiplication algorithm is:

```
for (i = 0; i < rows_a; i++)
   for (j = 0; j < cols_b; j++) {
      sum = 0;
      for (k = 0; k < cols_a; k++)
         sum += (a[i][k] * b[k][j]);
      d[i][j] = sum;
   }
```

This algorithm takes $O(rows\_a \cdot cols\_a \cdot cols\_b)$ time. Since $totala \leq cols\_a \cdot rows\_a$ and $totalb \leq cols\_a \cdot cols\_b$, the time for *mmult* is at most:

$$O(rows\_a \cdot cols\_a \cdot cols\_b)$$

However, its constant factor is greater than that of the classic algorithm. In the worst case, when $totala = cols\_a \cdot rows\_a$ or $totalb = cols\_a \cdot cols\_b$, *mmult* is slower by a constant factor. However, when *totala* and *totalb* are sufficiently smaller than their maximum value, that is, *A* and *B* are sparse, *mmult* outperforms the classic algorithm. The analysis of *mmult* is not trivial. It introduces some new concepts in algorithm analysis and you should make sure that you understand the analysis.

This representation of sparse matrices permits us to perform operations such as addition, transpose, and multiplication efficiently. However, there are other considerations that make this representation undesirable in certain applications. Since the number of terms in a sparse matrix is variable, we would like to represent all our sparse matrices in one array as we did for polynomials in Section 2.2. This would enable us to make efficient utilization of space. However, when this is done we run into difficulties in allocating space from the array to any individual matrix. These difficulties also occur with the polynomial representation and will become even more obvious when we study a similar representation for multiple stacks and queues in Section 3.4.

EXERCISES

1. Write C functions *read_matrix*, *print_matrix*, and *search* that read triples into a new sparse matrix, print out the terms in a sparse matrix, and search for a value in a sparse matrix. Analyze the computing time of each of these functions.

2. Rewrite *fast_transpose* so that it uses only one array rather than the two arrays required to hold *row_terms* and *starting_pos*.

3. Develop a correctness proof for the *mmult* function.

4. Analyze the time and space requirements of *fast_transpose*. What can you say about the existence of a faster algorithm?

5. Use the concept of an array of starting positions found in *fast_transpose* to rewrite *mmult* so that it multiplies sparse matrices *A* and *B* without transposing *B*. What is the computing time of your function?

6. As an alternate sparse matrix representation we keep only the nonzero terms in a one-dimensional array, *value*, in the order described in the text. In addition, we also maintain a two-dimensional array, *bits* [*rows*][*columns*], such that *bits* [*i*][*j*] = 0 if $a[i][j] = 0$ and *bits* [*i*][*j*] = 1 if $a[i][j] \neq 0$. Figure 2.6 illustrates the representation for the sparse matrix of Figure 2.4(b).

$$
\begin{bmatrix}
1 & 0 & 0 & 1 & 0 & 1 \\
0 & 1 & 1 & 0 & 0 & 0 \\
0 & 0 & 0 & 1 & 0 & 0 \\
0 & 0 & 0 & 0 & 0 & 0 \\
1 & 0 & 0 & 0 & 0 & 0 \\
0 & 0 & 1 & 0 & 0 & 0
\end{bmatrix}
\quad
\begin{bmatrix}
15 \\
22 \\
-15 \\
11 \\
3 \\
-6 \\
91 \\
28
\end{bmatrix}
$$

Figure 2.6: Alternate representation of a sparse matrix

(a) On a computer with *w* bits per word, how much storage is needed to represent a sparse matrix, *A*, with *t* nonzero terms?

(b) Write a C function to add two sparse matrices *A* and *B* represented as in Figure 2.6 to obtain $D = A + B$. How much time does your algorithm take?

(c) Discuss the merits of this representation versus the one used in the text. Consider the space and time requirements for such operations as random access, add, multiply, and transpose. Note that we can improve the random access time by keeping another array, *ra*, such that *ra* [*i*] = number of nonzero terms in rows 0 through $i - 1$.

2.5 REPRESENTATION OF MULTIDIMENSIONAL ARRAYS

The internal representation of multidimensional arrays requires more complex addressing formulas. If an array is declared $a[upper_0][upper_1] \cdots [upper_{n-1}]$, then it is easy to see that the number of elements in the array is:

$$
\prod_{i=0}^{n-1} upper_i
$$

where $\prod$ is the product of the $upper_i$'s. For instance, if we declare *a* as $a[10][10][10]$, then we require $10 \cdot 10 \cdot 10 = 1000$ units of storage to hold the array. There are two common ways to represent multidimensional arrays: *row major order* and *column major order*. We consider only row major order here, leaving column major order for the exercises.

As its name implies, row major order stores multidimensional arrays by rows. For instance, we interpret the two-dimensional array $A[upper_0][upper_1]$ as $upper_0$ rows, $row_0, row_1, \cdots, row_{upper_0-1}$, each row containing $upper_1$ elements.

If we assume that α is the address of $A[0][0]$, then the address of $A[i][0]$ is $\alpha + i \cdot upper_1$ because there are i rows, each of size $upper_1$, preceding the first element in the ith row. Notice that we haven't multiplied by the element size. This follows C convention in which the size of the elements is automatically accounted for. The address of an arbitrary element, $a[i][j]$, is $\alpha + i \cdot upper_1 + j$.

To represent a three-dimensional array, $A[upper_0][upper_1][upper_2]$, we interpret the array as $upper_0$ two-dimensional arrays of dimension $upper_1 \times upper_2$. To locate $a[i][j][k]$, we first obtain $\alpha + i \cdot upper1 \cdot upper2$ as the address of $a[i][0][0]$ because there are i two-dimensional arrays of size $upper_1 \cdot upper_2$ preceding this element. Combining this formula with the formula for addressing a two-dimensional array, we obtain:

$$\alpha + i \cdot upper_1 \cdot upper_2 + j \cdot upper_2 + k$$

as the address of $a[i][j][k]$.

Generalizing on the preceding discussion, we can obtain the addressing formula for any element $A[i_0][i_1]\ldots[i_{n-1}]$ in an n-dimensional array declared as:

$$A[upper_0][upper_1]\ldots[upper_{n-1}]$$

If α is the address for $A[0][0]\ldots[0]$ then the address of $a[i_0][0][0]\ldots[0]$ is:

$$\alpha + i_0\, upper_1\, upper_2\, \ldots\, upper\, n-1$$

The address of $a[i_0][i_1][0]\ldots[0]$ is:

$$\alpha + i_0\, upper_1\, upper_2\, \ldots\, upper_{n-1} + i_1\, upper_2\, upper_3\, \ldots\, upper_{n-1}$$

Repeating in this way the address for $A[i_0][i_1]\ldots[i_{n-1}]$ is:

$$
\begin{aligned}
&\alpha + i_0 upper_1 upper_2 \ldots upper_{n-1}\\
&+ i_1 upper_2 upper_3 \ldots upper_{n-1}\\
&+ i_2 upper_3 upper_4 \ldots upper_{n-1}\\
&\quad .\\
&\quad .\\
&\quad .\\
&+ i_{n-2} upper_{n-1}\\
&+ i_{n-1}
\end{aligned}
$$

$$= \alpha + \sum_{j=0}^{n-1} i_j a_j \text{ where: } \begin{cases} a_j = \displaystyle\prod_{k=j+1}^{n-1} upper_k \quad 0 \le j < n-1 \\[2mm] a_{n-1} = 1 \end{cases}$$

Notice that a_j may be computed from $a_{j+1}, 0 \le j < n-1$, using only one multiplication as $a_j = upper_{j+1} \cdot a_{j+1}$. Thus, a compiler will initially take the declared bounds $upper_0, \ldots, upper_{n-1}$ and use them to compute the constants $a_0 \ldots a_{n-2}$ using $n-2$ multiplications. The address of $a[i_0] \ldots a[i_{n-1}]$ can be computed using the formula, requiring $n-1$ more multiplications and n additions and n subtractions.

EXERCISES

1. Assume that we have a one-dimensional array, $a[MAX\_SIZE]$. Normally, the subscripts for this array vary from 0 to $MAX\_SIZE - 1$. However, by using pointer arithmetic we can create arrays with arbitrary bounds. Indicate how to create an array, and obtain subscripts for an array, that has bounds between -10 to 10. That is, we view the subscripts as having the values $-10, -9, -8, \cdots, 8, 9, 10$.

2. Extend the results from Exercise 1 to create a two-dimensional array where row and column subscripts each range from -10 to 10.

3. Obtain an addressing formula for the element $a[i_0][i_1] \ldots [i_{n-1}]$ in an array declared as $a[upper_0] \ldots a[upper_{n-1}]$. Assume a column major representation of the array with one word per element and α the address of $a[0][0] \ldots [0]$. In column major order, the entries are stored by columns first. For example, the array $a[3][3]$ would be stored as $a[0][0]$, $a[1][0]$, $a[2][0]$, $a[0][1]$, $a[1][1]$, $a[2][1]$, $a[0][2]$, $a[1][2]$, $a[2][2]$.

2.6   THE STRING ABSTRACT DATA TYPE

2.6.1   Introduction

Thus far, we have considered only ADTs whose component elements were numeric. For example, we created a sparse matrix ADT and represented it as an array of triples $<row, col, value>$. In this section, we turn our attention to a data type, the string, whose component elements are characters. As an ADT, we define a string to have the form, $S = s_0, \ldots, s_{n-1}$, where s_i are characters taken from the character set of the programming language. If $n = 0$, then S is an empty or null string.

There are several useful operations we could specify for strings. Some of these operations are similar to those required for other ADTs: creating a new empty string, reading a string or printing it out, appending two strings together (called *concatenation*), or copying a string. However, there are other operations that are unique to our new ADT, including comparing strings, inserting a substring into a string, removing a substring from a string, or finding a pattern in a string. We have listed the essential operations in Structure 2.4, which contains our specification of the string ADT. Actually there are many more operations on strings, as we shall see when we look at part of C's string library in Figure 2.7.

---

structure *String* is
  objects: a finite set of zero or more characters.
  functions:
    for all $s, t \in$ *String*, $i, j, m \in$ non-negative integers

String Null(m)	::=	**return** a string whose maximum length is m characters, but is initially set to *NULL* We write *NULL* as "".

Integer Compare(s, t)	::=	**if** s equals t
		 return 0
		 else if s precedes t
		    return -1
		    else return $+1$

Boolean IsNull(s)	::=	**if** (Compare(s, *NULL*)) **return** *FALSE* **else return** *TRUE*
Integer Length(s)	::=	**if** (Compare(s, *NULL*)) **return** the number of characters in s **else return** 0.
String Concat(s, t)	::=	**if** (Compare(t, *NULL*)) **return** a string whose elements are those of s followed by those of t **else return** s.
String Substr(s, i, j)	::=	**if** $((j > 0)$ && $(i + j - 1) <$ Length(s)) **return** the string containing the characters of s at positions $i, i + 1, \cdots, i + j - 1$. **else return** *NULL*.

Structure 2.4: Abstract data type *String*

In C, we represent strings as character arrays terminated with the null character \0. For instance, suppose we had the strings:

```
#define MAX_SIZE 100 /*maximum size of string */
char s[MAX_SIZE] = {"dog"};
char t[MAX_SIZE] = {"house"};
```

Figure 2.8 shows how these strings would be represented internally in memory. Notice that we have included array bounds for the two strings. Technically, we could have declared the arrays with the statements:

```
char s[] = {"dog"};
```

Function	Description
*char *strcat(char *dest, char *src)*	concatenate *dest* and *src* strings; return result in *dest*
*char *strncat(char *dest, char *src, int n)*	concatenate *dest* and *n* characters from *src*; return result in *dest*
*char *strcmp(char *str1, char *str2)*	compare two strings; return < 0 if *str1* < *str2*; 0 if *str1* = *str2*; > 0 if *str1* > *str2*
*char *strncmp(char *str1, char *str2, int n)*	compare first *n* characters return < 0 if *str1* < *str2*; 0 if *str1* = *str2*; > 1 if *str1* > *str2*
*char *strcpy(char *dest, char *src)*	copy *src* into *dest*; return *dest*
*char *strncpy(char *dest, char *src, int n)*	copy *n* characters from *src* string into *dest*; return *dest*;
*size_t strlen(char *s)*	return the length of a *s*
*char *strchr(char *s, int c)*	return pointer to the first occurrence of *c* in *s*; return *NULL* if not present
*char *strrchr(char *s, int c)*	return pointer to last occurrence of *c* in *s*; return *NULL* if not present
*char *strtok(char *s, char *delimiters)*	return a token from *s*; token is surrounded by *delimiters*
*char *strstr(char *s, char *pat)*	return pointer to start of *pat* in *s*
*size_t strspn(char *s, char *spanset)*	scan *s* for characters in *spanset*; return length of span
*size_t strcspn(char *s, char *spanset)*	scan *s* for characters not in *spanset*; return length of span
*char *strpbrk(char *s, char *spanset)*	scan *s* for characters in *spanset*; return pointer to first occurrence of a character from *spanset*

Figure 2.7: C string functions

s[0]	s[1]	s[2]	s[3]
d	o	g	\0

t[0]	t[1]	t[2]	t[3]	t[4]	t[5]
h	o	u	s	e	\0

Figure 2.8: String representation in C

```
char t[] = {"house"}
```

Using these declarations, the C compiler would have allocated just enough space to hold each word including the null character. Now suppose we want to concatenate these strings together to produce the new string, "doghouse." To do this we use the C function *strcat* (See Figure 2.7). Two strings are joined together by *strcat* (*s*, *t*), which stores the result in *s*. Although *s* has increased in length by five, we have no additional space in *s* to store the extra five characters. Our compiler handled this problem inelegantly: it simply overwrote the memory to fit in the extra five characters. Since we declared *t* immediately after *s*, this meant that part of the word "house" disappeared.

We have already seen that C provides a built-in function to perform concatenation. In addition to this function, C provides several other string functions which we access through the statement *#include <string.h>*. Figure 2.7 contains a brief summary of these functions (we have excluded string conversion functions such as *atoi*). For each function, we have provided a generic function declaration and a brief description. Rather than discussing each function separately, we next look at an example that uses several of them. For further information on string functions, including examples, look at the books by Kerninghan and Ritchie or Harbison and Steele cited in the References and Selected Readings section.

Example 2.2 [*String insertion*]: Assume that we have two strings, say *string* 1 and *string* 2, and that we want to insert *string* 2 into *string* 1 starting at the *i*th position of *string* 1. We begin with the declarations:

```
#include <string.h>
#define MAX_SIZE 100 /*size of largest string*/
char string1[MAX_SIZE], *s = string1;
char string2[MAX_SIZE],  *t = string2;
```

In addition to creating the two strings, we also have created a pointer for each string.

Now suppose that the first string contains "amobile" and the second contains "uto" (Figure 2.9). We want to insert "uto" starting at position 1 of the first string, thereby producing the word "automobile." We can accomplish this using only three function calls, as Figure 2.9 illustrates. Thus, in Figure 2.9(a), we assume that we have an empty string that is pointed to by *temp*. We use *strncpy* to copy the first *i* characters from *s* into *temp*.

Since $i = 1$, this produces the string "a." In Figure 2.9(b), we concatenate *temp* and *t* to produce the string "auto." Finally, we append the remainder of *s* to *temp*. Since *strncat* copied the first *i* characters, the remainder of the string is at address $(s + i)$. The final result is shown in Figure 2.9(c).

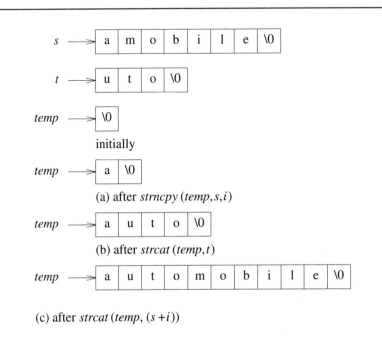

initially

(a) after *strncpy* (*temp,s,i*)

(b) after *strcat* (*temp,t*)

(c) after *strcat* (*temp*, (*s +i*))

Figure 2.9: String insertion example

Program 2.11 inserts one string into another. This particular function is not normally found in *<string.h>*. Since either of the strings could be empty, we also include statements that check for these conditions. It is worth pointing out that the call *strnins* (*s*, *t*, 0) is equivalent to *strcat* (*t*, *s*). Program 2.11 is presented as an example of manipulating strings. It should never be used in practice as it is wasteful in its use of time and space. Try to revise it so the string *temp* is not required. □

2.6.2 Pattern Matching

Now let us develop an algorithm for a more sophisticated application of strings. Assume that we have two strings, *string* and *pat*, where *pat* is a pattern to be searched for in *string*. The easiest way to determine if *pat* is in *string* is to use the built-in function *strstr*. If we have the following declarations:

```
void strnins(char *s, char *t, int i)
{
/* insert string t into string s at position i */
   char string[MAX_SIZE], *temp = string;

   if (i < 0 && i > strlen(s)) {
      fprintf(stderr,"Position is out of bounds \n");
      exit(1);
   }
   if (!strlen(s))
      strcpy(s,t);
   else if (strlen(t)) {
      strncpy(temp, s,i);
      strcat(temp,t);
      strcat(temp, (s+i));
      strcpy(s, temp);
   }
}
```

Program 2.11: String insertion function

```
      char pat[MAX_SIZE], string[MAX_SIZE], *t;
```

then we use the following statements to determine if *pat* is in *string*:

```
      if (t = strstr(string,pat))
         printf("The string from strstr is: %s\n",t);
      else
         printf("The pattern was not found with strstr\n");
```

The call (*t = strstr*(*string*,*pat*)) returns a null pointer if *pat* is not in *string*. If *pat* is in *string*, *t* holds a pointer to the start of *pat* in *string*. The entire string beginning at position *t* is printed out.

Although *strstr* seems ideally suited to pattern matching, there are two reasons why we may want to develop our own pattern matching function:

(1)   The function *strstr* is new to ANSI C. Therefore, it may not be available with the compiler we are using.

(2)   There are several different methods for implementing a pattern matching function. The easiest but least efficient method sequentially examines each character of the string until it finds the pattern or it reaches the end of the string. (We explore this approach in the Exercises.) If *pat* is not in *string*, this method has a computing

time of O($n \cdot m$) where n is the length of *pat* and m is the length of *string*. We can
do much better than this, if we create our own pattern matching function.

We can improve on an exhaustive pattern matching technique by quitting when
strlen (*pat*) is greater than the number of remaining characters in the string. Checking
the first and last characters of *pat* and *string* before we check the remaining characters is
a second improvement. These changes are incorporated in *nfind* (Program 2.12).

```
int nfind(char *string, char *pat)
{
/* match the last character of pattern first, and
then match from the beginning */
   int i,j,start = 0;
   int lasts = strlen(string)-1;
   int lastp = strlen(pat)-1;
   int endmatch = lastp;

   for (i = 0; endmatch <= lasts; endmatch++, start++) {
      if (string[endmatch] == pat[lastp])
         for (j = 0, i = start; j < lastp &&
                     string[i] == pat[j]; i++,j++)
            ;
      if (j == lastp)
         return start; /* successful */
      }
      return -1;
}
```

Program 2.12: Pattern matching by checking end indices first

Example 2.3 [*Simulation of nfind*]: Suppose *pat* = "aab" and *string* = "ababbaabaa."
Figure 2.10 shows how *nfind* compares the characters from *pat* with those of *string*. The
end of the *string* and *pat* arrays are held by *lasts* and *lastp*, respectively. First *nfind* compares *string* [*endmatch*] and *pat* [*lastp*]. If they match, *nfind* uses i and j to move
through the two strings until a mismatch occurs or until all of *pat* has been matched. The
variable *start* is used to reset i if a mismatch occurs. □

Analysis of *nfind*: If we apply *nfind* to *string* = "aa $\cdots$ a" and *pat* = "a $\cdots$ ab", then the
computing time for these strings is linear in the length of the string O(m), which is certainly far better than the sequential method. Although the improvements we made over
the sequential method speed up processing on the average, the worst case computing
time is still O($n \cdot m$). □

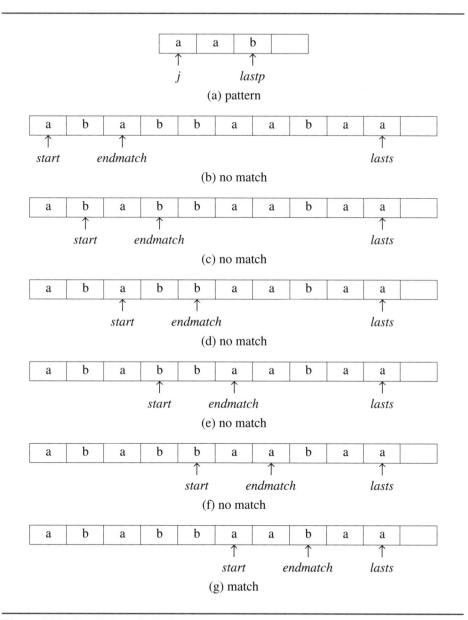

Figure 2.10: Simulation of *nfind*

Ideally, we would like an algorithm that works in O($strlen$ ($string$) + $strlen$ (pat)) time. This is optimal for this problem as in the worst case it is necessary to look at all characters in the pattern and string at least once. We want to search the string for the pattern without moving backwards in the string. That is, if a mismatch occurs we want to use our knowledge of the characters in the pattern and the position in the pattern where the mismatch occurred to determine where we should continue the search. Knuth, Morris, and Pratt have developed a pattern matching algorithm that works in this way and has linear complexity. Using their example, suppose

$$pat = `a\ b\ c\ a\ b\ c\ a\ c\ a\ b'$$

Let $s = s_0\ s_2\ \cdots\ s_{m-1}$ be the string and assume that we are currently determining whether or not there is a match beginning at s_i. If $s_i \neq a$ then, clearly, we may proceed by comparing s_{i+1} and a. Similarly if $s_i = a$ and $s_{i+1} \neq b$ then we may proceed by comparing s_{i+1} and a. If $s_i s_{i+1} = ab$ and $s_{i+2} \neq c$ then we have the situation:

$s =$	'-	a	b	?	?	?	.	.	.	.	?'
$pat =$		'a	b	c	a	b	c	a	c	a	b'

The ? implies that we do not know what the character in s is. The first ? in s represents s_{i+2} and $s_{i+2} \neq c$. At this point we know that we may continue the search for a match by comparing the first character in pat with s_{i+2}. There is no need to compare this character of pat with s_{i+1} as we already know that s_{i+1} is the same as the second character of pat, b, and so $s_{i+1} \neq a$. Let us try this again assuming a match of the first four characters in pat followed by a nonmatch, i.e., $s_{i+4} \neq b$. We now have the situation:

$s =$	'-	a	b	c	a	?	?	.	.	.	?'
$pat =$		'a	b	c	a	b	c	a	c	a	b'

We observe that the search for a match can proceed by comparing s_{i+4} and the second character in pat, b. This is the first place a partial match can occur by sliding the pattern pat towards the right. Thus, by knowing the characters in the pattern and the position in the pattern where a mismatch occurs with a character in s we can determine where in the pattern to continue the search for a match without moving backwards in s. To formalize this, we define a failure function for a pattern.

Definition: If $p = p_0 p_1\ \cdots\ p_{n-1}$ is a pattern, then its *failure function*, f, is defined as:

$$f(j) = \begin{cases} \text{largest } i < j \text{ such that } p_0 p_1\ \cdots\ p_i = p_{j-i} p_{j-i+2}\ \cdots\ p_j \text{ if such an } i \geq 0 \text{ exists} \\ -1 & \text{otherwise} \end{cases} \qquad \square$$

For the example pattern, *pat = abcabcacab*, we have:

j	0	1	2	3	4	5	6	7	8	9
pat	*a*	*b*	*c*	*a*	*b*	*c*	*a*	*c*	*a*	*b*
f	−1	−1	−1	0	1	2	3	−1	0	1

From the definition of the failure function, we arrive at the following rule for pattern matching: *If a partial match is found such that $s_{i-j} \cdots s_{i-1} = p_0 p_1 \cdots p_{j-1}$ and $s_i \neq p_j$ then matching may be resumed by comparing s_i and $p_{f(j-1)+1}$ if $j \neq 0$. If $j = 0$, then we may continue by comparing s_{i+1} and p_0.* This pattern matching rule translates into function *pmatch* (Program 2.13). The following declarations are assumed:

```
#include <stdio.h>
#include <string.h>
#define max_string_size 100
#define max_pattern_size 100
int pmatch();
void fail();
int failure[max_pattern_size];
char string[max_string_size];
char pat[max_pattern_size];
```

```
int pmatch(char *string, char *pat)
{
/* Knuth, Morris, Pratt string matching algorithm */
  int i = 0, j = 0;
  int lens = strlen(string);
  int lenp = strlen(pat);
  while ( i < lens && j < lenp ) {
    if (string[i] == pat[j]) {
      i++; j++; }
    else if (j == 0) i++;
        else j = failure[j-1]+1;
  }
  return ( (j == lenp) ? (i-lenp) : -1);
}
```

Program 2.13: Knuth, Morris, Pratt pattern matching algorithm

Note that we do not keep a pointer to the start of the pattern in the string. Instead we use the statement:

```
return ( (j == lenp) ? (i - lenp) : -1);
```

This statement checks to see whether or not we found the pattern. If we didn't find the pattern, the pattern index index j is not equal to the length of the pattern and we return -1. If we found the pattern, then the starting position is i – the length of the pattern.

Analysis of *pmatch*: The **while** loop is iterated until the end of either the string or the pattern is reached. Since i is never decreased, the lines that increase i cannot be executed more than $m = strlen(string)$ times. The resetting of j to $failure[j-1]+1$ decreases the value of j. So, this cannot be done more times than j is incremented by the statement $j++$ as otherwise, j falls off the pattern. Each time the statement $j++$ is executed, i is also incremented. So, j cannot be incremented more than m times. Consequently, no statement of Program 2.13 is executed more than m times. Hence the complexity of function *pmatch* is $O(m) = O(strlen(string))$. □

From the analysis of *pmatch*, it follows that if we can compute the failure function in $O(strlen(pat))$ time, then the entire pattern matching process will have a computing time proportional to the sum of the lengths of the string and pattern. Fortunately, there is a fast way to compute the failure function. This is based upon the following restatement of the failure function:

$$f(j) = \begin{cases} -1 & \text{if } j = 0 \\ f^m(j-1) + 1 & \text{where } m \text{ is the least integer } k \text{ for which } p_{f^k(j-1)+1} = p_j \\ -1 & \text{if there is no } k \text{ satisfying the above} \end{cases}$$

(note that $f^1(j) = f(j)$ and $f^m(j) = f(f^{m-1}(j))$).

This definition yields the function in Program 2.14 for computing the failure function of a pattern.

Analysis of *fail*: In each iteration of the **while** loop the value of i decreases (by the definition of f). The variable i is reset at the beginning of each iteration of the **for** loop. However, it is either reset to -1 (initially or when the previous iteration of the **for** loop goes through the last **else** clause) or it is reset to a value 1 greater than its terminal value on the previous iteration (i.e., when the statement $failure[j] = i+1$ is executed). Since the **for** loop is iterated only $n-1$ (n is the length of the pattern) times, the value of i has a total increment of at most $n-1$. Hence it cannot be decremented more than $n-1$ times. Consequently the **while** loop is iterated at most $n-1$ times over the whole algorithm and the computing time of *fail* is $O(n) = O(strlen(pat))$. □

```
void fail(char *pat)
{
/* compute the pattern's failure function */
  int n = strlen(pat);
  failure[0] = -1;
  for (j=1; j < n; j++) {
    i = failure[j-1];
    while ((pat[j] != pat[i+1]) && (i >= 0))
      i = failure[i];
    if (pat[j] == pat[i+1])
      failure[j] = i+1;
    else failure[j] = -1;
  }
}
```

Program 2.14: Computing the failure function

Note that when the failure function is not known in advance, the time to first compute this function and then perform a pettern match is O(*strlen* (*pat*) + *strlen* (*string*)).

EXERCISES

1. Write a function that accepts as input a *string* and determines the frequency of occurrence of each of the distinct characters in *string*. Test your function using suitable data.

2. Write a function, *strndel*, that accepts a *string* and two integers, *start* and *length*. Return a new string that is equivalent to the original string, except that *length* characters beginning at *start* have been removed.

3. Write a function, *strdel*, that accepts a *string* and a *character*. The function returns *string* with the first occurrence of *character* removed.

4. Write a function, *strpos* 1, that accepts a *string* and a *character*. The function returns an integer that represents the position of the first occurrence of *character* in *string*. If *character* is not in *string*, it returns −1. You may not use the function *strpos* which is part of the traditional <*string.h*> library, but not the ANSI C one.

5. Write a function, *strchr* 1, that does the same thing as *strpos* 1 except that it returns a pointer to *character*. If *character* is not in the list it returns *NULL*. You may not use the built-in function *strchr*.

6. Modify Program 2.11 so that it does not use a temporary string *temp*. Compare the complexity of your new function with that of the old one.

7. Write a function, *strsearch*, that uses the sequential method for pattern matching. That is, assuming we have a *string* and a *pattern*, *strsearch* examines each character in *string* until it either finds the *pattern* or it reaches the end of the *string*.

8. Show that the computing time for *nfind* is $O(n \cdot m)$ where n and m are, respectively, the lengths of the string and the pattern. Find a string and a pattern for which this is true.

9. Compute the failure function for each of the following patterns:

    (a) *a a a a b*

    (b) *a b a b a a*

    (c) *a b a a b a a b*

10. Show the equivalence of the two definitions for the failure function.

2.7 REFERENCES AND SELECTED READINGS

Several texts discuss array representation in C, including T. Plum, *Reliable Data Structures in C*, Plum Hall, Cardiff, N.J., 1985 (Chapter 3), and R. Jaesche, *Solutions in C*, Addison-Wesley, Reading, Mass., 1986 (Chapter 2). The Jaesche text includes a detailed discussion of array bounds, including altering array bounds, and pointer addressing.

Strings are discussed in B. Kernighan and K. Ritchie, *The C Programming Language, ANSI C*, Second Edition, Prentice-Hall, Englewood Cliffs, N.J., 1988, and S. Harbison and G. Steele, *C: A Reference Manual*, Third Edition, Prentice-Hall, Englewood Cliffs, N.J., 1991 (Chapter 13). A discussion of string pointers can be found in R. Traister, *Mastering C Pointers*, Academic Press, San Diego, Calif., 1990. The Knuth, Morris, Pratt pattern matching algorithm is found in *"Fast pattern matching in strings,"* *SIAM Journal on Computing*, vol. 6, no. 2, 1977.

2.8 ADDITIONAL EXERCISES

1. Given an array $a[n]$ produce the array $z[n]$ such that $z[0] = a[n-1], z[1] = a[n-2], \cdots, z[n-2] = a[1], z[n-1] = a[0]$. Use a minimal amount of storage.

2. An $m \times n$ matrix is said to have a saddle point if some entry $a[i][j]$ is the smallest value in row i and the largest value in column j. Write a C function that determines the location of a saddle point if one exists. What is the computing time of your method?

Exercises 3 through 8 explore the representation of various types of matrices that are frequently used in the solution of problems in the natural sciences.

3. A *triangular matrix* is one in which either all the elements above the main diagonal or all the elements below the main diagonal of a square matrix are zero. Figure 2.11 shows a lower and an upper triangular matrix. In a lower triangular matrix, a, with n rows, the maximum number of nonzero terms in row i is $i+1$. Thus, the total number of nonzero terms is

$$d = \sum_{i=0}^{n-1} (i+1) = n(n+1)/2.$$

Since storing a triangular matrix as a two dimensional array wastes space, we would like to find a way to store only the nonzero terms in the triangular matrix. Find an addressing formula for the elements a_{ij} so that they can be stored by rows in an array $b[n(n+1)/2-1]$, with $a[0][0]$ being stored in $b[0]$.

```
X                            X X X X X X X X X X
X X                          X                 X
X   X                          X               X
X     X                          X     non     X
X         X    zero                X   zero     X
X   non     X                        X         X
X   zero      X                  zero  X       X
X             X                          X     X
X               X                          X X X
X X X X X X X X X X                          X
```

lower triangular   upper triangular

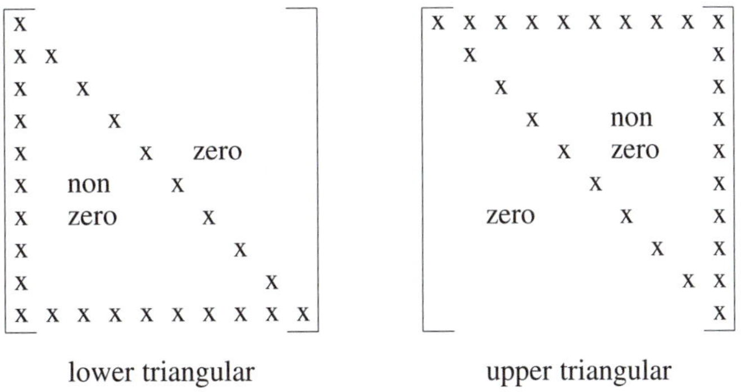

Figure 2.11: Lower and upper triangular matrices

4. Let a and b be two lower triangular matrices, each with n rows. The total number of elements in the lower triangles is $n(n+1)$. Devise a scheme to represent both triangles in an array $d[n-1][n]$. [Hint: Represent the triangle of a in the lower triangle of d and the transpose b in the upper triangle of d.] Write algorithms to determine the values of $a[i][j]$, $b[i][j]$, $0 \le i, j < n$.

5. A *tridiagonal matrix* is a square matrix in which all elements that are not on the major diagonal and the two diagonals adjacent to it are zero (Figure 2.12). The elements in the band formed by these three diagonals are represented by rows in an array, b, with $a[0][0]$ being stored in $b[0]$. Obtain an algorithm to determine the value of $a[i][j]$, $0 \le i, j < n$ from the array b.

$$\begin{bmatrix} \text{x} & \text{x} & & & & & & \\ \text{x} & \text{x} & \text{x} & & & & & \\ & \text{x} & \text{x} & \text{x} & & & & \\ & & . & \text{x} & . & & & \\ & & & . & . & . & & \text{zero} \\ & & & & . & . & . & \\ & \text{zero} & & & . & \text{x} & \text{x} & \\ & & & & & \text{x} & \text{x} & \text{x} \\ & & & & & & \text{x} & \text{x} & \text{x} \\ & & & & & & & \text{x} & \text{x} & \text{x} \end{bmatrix}$$

Figure 2.12: Tridiagonal matrix

6. A *square band matrix* $D_{n,a}$ is an $n \times n$ matrix in which all the nonzero terms lie in a band centered around the main diagonal. The band includes the main diagonal and $a - 1$ diagonals below and above the main diagonal (Figure 2.13).

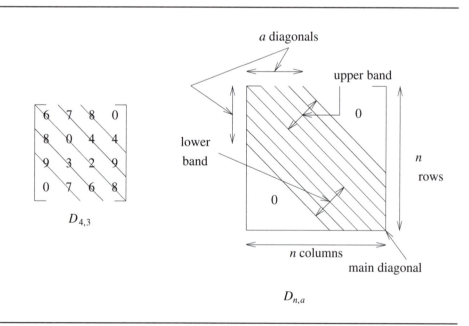

Figure 2.13: Square band matrix

(a) How many elements are there in the band $D_{n,a}$?

(b) What is the relationship between i and j for elements $d_{i,j}$ in the band $D_{n,a}$?

(c) Assume that the band of $D_{n,a}$ is stored sequentially in an array b by diagonals, starting with the lowermost diagonal. For example, the band matrix, $D_{4,3}$ of Figure 2.13 would have the following representation.

b[0]	b[1]	b[2]	b[3]	b[4]	b[5]	b[6]	b[7]	b[8]	b[9]	b[10]	b[11]	b[12]	b[13]
9	7	8	3	6	6	0	2	8	7	4	9	8	4
d_{20}	d_{31}	d_{10}	d_{21}	d_{32}	d_{00}	d_{11}	d_{22}	d_{33}	d_{01}	d_{12}	d_{23}	d_{02}	d_{13}

Obtain an addressing formula for the location of an element, $d_{i,j}$, in the lower band of $D_{n,a}$ (location(d_{10}) = 2 in the example above).

7. A *generalized band matrix* $D_{n,a,b}$ is an $n \times n$ matrix in which all the nonzero terms lie in a band made up of $a-1$ diagonals below the main diagonal, the main diagonal, and $b-1$ bands above the main diagonal (Figure 2.14).

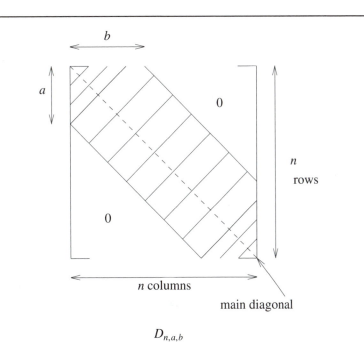

Figure 2.14: Generalized band matrix

(a)   How many elements are there in the band of $D_{n,a,b}$?

(b)   What is the relationship between i and j for the elements d_{ij} in the band of $D_{n,a,b}$?

(c)   Obtain a sequential representation of the band $D_{n,a,b}$ in the one dimensional array e. For this representation, write a C function *value* (n, a, b, i, j, e) that determines the value of element d_{ij} in the matrix $D_{n,a,b}$. The band of $D_{n,a,b}$ is represented in the array e.

8.   A complex-valued matrix X is represented by a pair of matrices $<a, b>$, where a and b contain real values. Write a function that computes the product of two complex-valued matrices $<a, b>$ and $<d, e>$, where $<a, b> * <d, e> = (a + ib)$ $* (d + ie) = (ad - be) + i (ae + bd)$. Determine the number of additions and multiplications if the matrices are all $n \times n$.

9.   § [*Programming project*] There are a number of problems, known collectively as "random walk" problems, that have been of longstanding interest to the mathematical community. All but the most simple of these are extremely difficult to solve, and, for the most part, they remain largely unsolved. One such problem may be stated as:

A (drunken) cockroach is placed on a given square in the middle of a tile floor in a rectangular room of size $n \times m$ tiles. The bug wanders (possibly in search of an aspirin) randomly from tile to tile throughout the room. Assuming that he may move from his present tile to any of the eight tiles surrounding him (unless he is against a wall) with equal probability, how long will it take him to touch every tile on the floor at least once?

Hard as this problem may be to solve by pure probability techniques, it is quite easy to solve using a computer. The technique for doing so is called "simulation." This technique is widely used in industry to predict traffic flow, inventory control, and so forth. The problem may be simulated using the following method:

An $n \times m$ array *count* is used to represent the number of times our cockroach has reached each tile on the floor. All the cells of this array are initialized to zero. The position of the bug on the floor is represented by the coordinates (*ibug*, *jbug*). The eight possible moves of the bug are represented by the tiles located at (*ibug* + *imove* [k], *jbug* + *jmove* [k]), where $0 \le k \le 7$, and

$$imove[0] = -1 \quad jmove[0] = 1$$
$$imove[1] = 0 \quad jmove[1] = 1$$
$$imove[2] = 1 \quad jmove[2] = 1$$
$$imove[3] = 1 \quad jmove[3] = 0$$
$$imove[4] = 1 \quad jmove[4] = -1$$
$$imove[5] = 0 \quad jmove[5] = -1$$
$$imove[6] = -1 \quad jmove[6] = -1$$
$$imove[7] = -1 \quad jmove[7] = 0$$

A random walk to any one of the eight neighbor squares is simulated by generating a random value for k, lying between 0 and 7. Of course, the bug cannot move outside the room, so that coordinates that lead up a wall must be ignored, and a new random combination formed. Each time a square is entered, the count for that square is incremented so that a nonzero entry shows the number of times the bug has landed on that square. When every square has been entered at least once, the experiment is complete.

Write a program to perform the specified simulation experiment. Your program MUST:

(a)   handle all values of n and m, $2 < n \leq 40$, $2 \leq m \leq 20$;

(b)   perform the experiment for (1) $n = 15$, $m = 15$, starting point (10, 10), and (2) $n = 39$, $m = 19$, starting point (1, 1);

(c)   have an iteration limit, that is, a maximum number of squares that the bug may enter during the experiment. This ensures that your program will terminate. A maximum of 50,000 is appropriate for this exercise.

For each experiment, print (1) the total number of legal moves that the cockroach makes and (2) the final count array. This will show the "density" of the walk, that is, the number of times each tile on the floor was touched during the experiment. This exercise was contributed by Olson.

10.   § [*Programming project*] Chess provides the setting for many fascinating diversions that are quite independent of the game itself. Many of these are based on the strange "L-shaped" move of the knight. A classic example is the problem of the "knight's tour," which has captured the attention of mathematicians and puzzle enthusiasts since the beginning of the eighteenth century. Briefly stated, the problem requires us to move the knight, beginning from any given square on the chessboard, successively to all 64 squares, touching each square once and only once. Usually we represent a solution by placing the numbers 0, 1, $\cdots$, 63 in the squares of the chess board to indicate the order in which the squares are reached. One of the more ingenious methods for solving the problem of the knight's tour was given by J. C. Warnsdorff in 1823. His rule stated that the knight must always move to one of the squares from which there are the fewest exits to squares not already traversed.

The goal of this programming project is to implement Warnsdorff's rule. The ensuing discussion will be easier to follow, however, if you try to construct a solution to the problem by hand, before reading any further.

The crucial decision in solving this problem concerns the data representation. Figure 2.15 shows the chess board represented as a two-dimensional array.

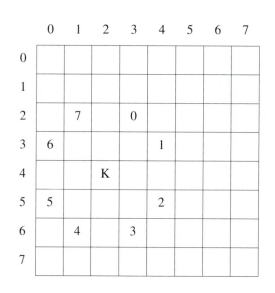

Figure 2.15: Legal moves for a knight

The eight possible moves of a knight on square (4, 2) are also shown in this figure. In general, a knight may move to one of the squares $(i - 2, j + 1)$, $(i - 1, j + 2)$, $(i + 1, j + 2)$, $(i + 2, j + 1)$, $(i + 2, j - 1)$, $(i + 1, j - 2)$, $(i - 1, j - 2)$, $(i - 2, j - 1)$. However, notice that if (i, j) is located near one of the board's edges, some of these possibilities could move the knight off the board, and, of course, this is not permitted. We can represent easily the eight possible knight moves by two arrays *ktmove* 1 and *ktmove* 2 as:

ktmove 1	ktmove 2
−2	1
−1	2
1	2
2	1
2	−1
1	−2
−1	−2
−2	−1

Then a knight at (i, j) may move to $(i + ktmove[k], j + ktmove 2[k])$, where k is some value between 0 and 7, provided that the new square lies on the chess board. Below is a description of an algorithm for solving the knight's tour problem using Warnsdorff's rule. The data representation discussed in the previous section is assumed.

(a) [*Initialize chessboard*] For $0 \leq i, \ j \leq 7$ set $board[i][j]$ to 0.

(b) [*Set starting position*] Read and print $(i, \ j)$ and then set $board[i][j]$ to 0.

(c) [*Loop*] For $1 \leq m \leq 63$, do steps (d) through (g).

(d) [*Form a set of possible next squares*] Test each of the eight squares one knight's move away from $(i, \ j)$ and form a list of the possibilities for the next square $(nexti[l], nextj[l])$. Let $npos$ be the number of possibilities. (That is, after performing this step we have $nexti[l] = i + ktmove 1[k]$ and $nextj[l] = j + ktmove 2[k]$, for certain values of k between 0 and 7. Some of the squares $(i + ktmove 1[k], j + ktmove 2[k])$ may be impossible because they lie off the chessboard or because they have been occupied previously by the knight, that is, they contain a nonzero number. In every case we will have $0 \leq npos \leq 8$.)

(e) [*Test special cases*] If $npos = 0$, the knight's tour has come to a premature end; report failure and go to step (h). If $npos = 1$, there is only one next move; set min to 1 and go to step (g).

(f) [*Find next square with minimum number of exits*] For $1 \leq l \leq npos$, set $exits[l]$ to the number of exits from square $(nexti[l], nextj[l])$. That is, for each of the values of l, examine each of the next squares $(nexti[l] + ktmove 1[k], nextj[l] + ktmove 2[k])$ to see if it is an exit from $(nexti[l], nextj[l])$, and count the number of such exits in $exits[l]$. (Recall that a square is an exit if it lies on the chessboard and has not been occupied previously by the knight.) Finally, set min to the location of the minimum value of $exits$. (If there is more than one occurrence of the minimum value, let min denote the first such occurrence. Although this does not guarantee a solution, the chances of completing the tour are very good.)

(g) [**Move knight**] Set $i = nexti[min]$, $j = nextj[min]$, and $board[i][j] = m$. Thus, (i, j) denotes the new position of the knight, and $board[i][j]$ records the move in proper sequence.

(h) [**Print**] Print out the board showing the solution to the knight's tour, and then terminate the algorithm.

Write a C program that corresponds to the algorithm. This exercise was contributed by Legenhausen and Rebman.

CHAPTER 3

STACKS AND QUEUES

3.1 THE STACK ABSTRACT DATA TYPE

In this chapter we look at two data types that are frequently found in computer science. These data types, the stack and the queue, are special cases of the more general data type, *ordered list*, that we discussed in Chapter 2. Recall that $A = a_0, a_1, \cdots, a_{n-1}$ is an ordered list of $n \geq 0$ elements. We refer to the a_i as *atoms* or *elements* that are taken from some set. The null or empty list, denoted by ( ), has $n = 0$ elements. In this section we begin by defining the ADT *Stack* and follow with its implementation. In the next section we look at the queue.

A *stack* is an ordered list in which insertions and deletions are made at one end called the *top*. Given a stack $S = (a_0, \cdots, a_{n-1})$, we say that a_0 is the bottom element, a_{n-1} is the top element, and a_i is on top of element a_{i-1}, $0 < i < n$. The restrictions on the stack imply that if we add the elements A, B, C, D, E to the stack, in that order, then E is the first element we delete from the stack. Figure 3.1 illustrates this sequence of operations. Since the last element inserted into a stack is the first element removed, a stack is also known as a *Last-In-First-Out (LIFO)* list.

Example 3.1 [*System stack*]: Before we discuss the stack ADT, we look at a special stack, called the system stack, that is used by a program at run-time to process function calls. Whenever a function is invoked, the program creates a structure, referred to as an *activation record* or a *stack frame*, and places it on top of the system stack. Initially, the

```
     |   |        |   |        | C |←top   | D |←top        | E |←top        | D |←top
     |   |        | B |←top    | B |        | C |           | D |           | C |
     | A |←top    | A |        | A |        | B |           | C |           | B |
     |   |        |   |        |   |        | A |           | B |           | A |
                                                            | A |
```

Figure 3.1: Inserting and deleting elements in a stack

activation record for the invoked function contains only a pointer to the previous stack frame and a return address. The previous stack frame pointer points to the stack frame of the invoking function, while the return address contains the location of the statement to be executed after the function terminates. Since only one function executes at any given time, the function whose stack frame is on top of the system stack is chosen. If this function invokes another function, the local variables, except those declared static, and the parameters of the invoking function are added to its stack frame. A new stack frame is then created for the invoked function and placed on top of the system stack. When this function terminates, its stack frame is removed and the processing of the invoking function, which is again on top of the stack, continues. A simple example illustrates this process. (We refer the reader who wants a more detailed discussion of stack frames to Holub's book on compiler design cited in the References and Selected Readings section.)

Assume that we have a main function that invokes function *al*. Figure 3.2(a) shows the system stack before *al* is invoked; Figure 3.2(b) shows the system stack after *al* has been invoked. Frame pointer *fp* is a pointer to the current stack frame. The system also maintains separately a stack pointer, *sp*, which we have not illustrated.

Since all functions are stored similarly in the system stack, it makes no difference if the invoking function calls itself. That is, a recursive call requires no special strategy; the run-time program simply creates a new stack frame for each recursive call. However, recursion can consume a significant portion of the memory allocated to the system stack; it could consume the entire available memory. □

Our discussion of the system stack suggests several operations that we include in the ADT specification (Structure 3.1).

The easiest way to implement this ADT is by using a one-dimensional array, say, *stack* [*MAX_STACK_SIZE*], where *MAX_STACK_SIZE* is the maximum number of entries. The first, or bottom, element of the stack is stored in *stack* [0], the second in *stack* [1], and the ith in *stack* [$i-1$]. Associated with the array is a variable, *top*, which points to the top element in the stack. Initially, *top* is set to -1 to denote an empty stack. Given this representation, we can implement the operations in Structure 3.1 as follows. Notice that we have specified that *element* is a structure that consists of only a *key* field. Ordinarily, we would not create a structure with a single field. However, we use *element* in this and subsequent chapters as a template whose fields we may add to or modify to

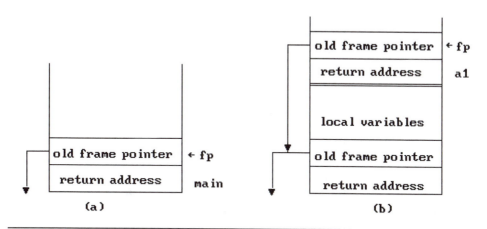

Figure 3.2: System stack after function call

meet the requirements of our application.

Stack CreateS(*max-stack-size*) ::=

```
#define MAX_STACK_SIZE 100 /*maximum stack size*/
typedef struct {
        int key;
        /* other fields */
        } element;
element stack[MAX_STACK_SIZE];
int top = -1;
```

Boolean IsEmpty(Stack) ::= `top < 0;`

Boolean IsFull(Stack) ::= `top >= MAX_STACK_SIZE-1;`

     The *IsEmpty* and *IsFull* operations are simple, and we will implement them directly in the *add* (Program 3.1) and *delete* (Program 3.2) functions. In each of these functions we have passed in the top of the stack as a parameter. The stack is kept global and "hidden" because we want to reinforce the concept that the only access to the stack is through the pointer to the top. The functions are short and require little explanation. Function *add* checks to see if the stack is full. If it is, it calls *stack-full*. Although we haven't implemented *stack-full*, minimally it should print an error message to the standard error device (*stderr*). If the stack is not full, we increment *top* and add *item* to the stack. Implementation of the delete operation parallels that of the add operation. For

---

structure *Stack* **is**

    objects: a finite ordered list with zero or more elements.

    functions:

        for all *stack* ∈ *Stack*, *item* ∈ *element*, *max_stack_size* ∈ positive integer

        Stack CreateS(*max_stack_size*) ::=

                create an empty stack whose maximum size is *max_stack_size*

        Boolean IsFull(*stack, max_stack_size*) ::=

                if (number of elements in *stack* == *max_stack_size*)

                return *TRUE*

                else return *FALSE*

        Stack Add(*stack, item*) ::=

                if (IsFull(*stack*)) *stack_full*

                else insert *item* into top of *stack* and **return**

        Boolean IsEmpty(*stack*) ::=

                if (*stack* == CreateS(*max_stack_size*))

                return *TRUE*

                else return *FALSE*

        Element Delete(*stack*) ::=

                if (IsEmpty(*stack*)) **return**

                else remove and return the *item* on the top of the stack.

Structure 3.1: Abstract data type *Stack*

deletion, the *stack_empty* function should print an error message and return an item of type *element* with a *key* field that contains an error code. Typical function calls would be *add(&top, item);* and *item = delete(&top);*. Notice that in both function calls we pass in the address of *top*. If we do not pass in the address the changes made to *top* by *add* or *delete* will not percolate back to the main program.

```
void add(int *top, element item)
{
/* add an item to the global stack */
   if (*top >= MAX_STACK_SIZE-1) {
      stack_full();
      return;
   }
   stack[++*top] = item;
}
```

Program 3.1: Add to a stack

```
element delete(int *top)
{
/* return the top element from the stack */
   if (*top == -1)
      return stack_empty(); /* returns an error key */
   return stack[(*top)--];
}
```

Program 3.2: Delete from a stack

EXERCISES

1. Implement the *stack_empty* and *stack_full* functions.

2. Using Figures 3.1 and {3.2} as examples, show the status of the system stack after each function call for the iterative and recursive functions to compute binomial coefficients (Exercise 9, Section 1.2). You do not need to show the stack frame itself for each function call. Simply add the name of the function to the stack to show its invocation and remove the name from the stack to show its termination.

3. The Fibonacci sequence is: 0, 1, 1, 2, 3, 5, 8, 13, 21, 34, $\cdots$

    It is defined as $F_0 = 0, F_1 = 1$, and $F_i = F_{i-1} + F_{i-2}, i \geq 2$

    Write a recursive function, *fibon* (n), that returns the nth fibonacci number. Show the status of the system stack for the call *fibon* (4) (see Exercise 2). What can you say about the efficiency of this function?

4. Consider the railroad switching network given in Figure 3.3. Railroad cars numbered 0, 1, $\cdots$, n−1 are at the right. Each car is brought into the stack and removed at any time. For instance, if n = 3, we could move in 0, move in 1, move in 2, and then take the cars out, producing the new order 2, 1, 0. For n = 3 and n = 4, what are the possible permutations of the cars that can be obtained? Are any permutations not possible?

3.2   THE QUEUE ABSTRACT DATA TYPE

A *queue* is an ordered list in which all insertions take place at one end and all deletions take place at the opposite end. Given a queue Q = $(a_0, a_1, \cdots , a_{n-1})$, a_0 is the front element, a_{n-1} is the rear element, and a_{i+1} is behind a_i, $0 \leq i < n-1$. The restrictions on a queue imply that if we insert A, B, C, D, in that order, then A is the first element deleted from the queue. Figure 3.4 illustrates this sequence of events. Since the first element inserted into a queue is the first element removed, queues are also known as *First-In-First-Out (FIFO)* lists. The ADT specification of the queue appears in Structure 3.2.

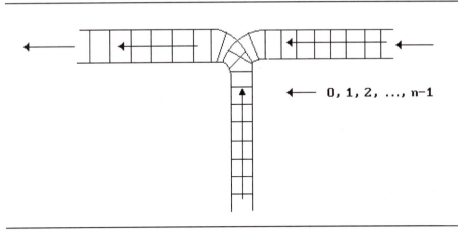

Figure 3.3: Railroad switching network

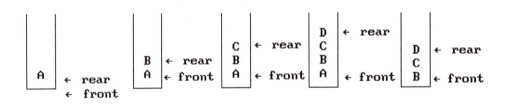

Figure 3.4: Inserting and deleting elements in a queue

The representation of a queue in sequential locations is more difficult than that of the stack. The simplest scheme employs a one-dimensional array and two variables, *front* and *rear*. Given this representation, we can define the queue operations in Structure 3.2 as:

Queue CreateQ(*max_queue_size*) ::=

```
#define MAX_QUEUE_SIZE 100 /*Maximum queue size*/
      typedef struct {
            int key;
            /* other fields */
            } element;
element queue[MAX_QUEUE_SIZE];
int rear = -1;
int front = -1;
```

Boolean IsEmptyQ(*queue*) ::= `front == rear`

---

structure *Queue* is
    objects: a finite ordered list with zero or more elements.
    functions:
        for all *queue* ∈ *Queue*, *item* ∈ *element*, *max−queue−size* ∈ positive integer
        Queue CreateQ(*max−queue−size*) ::=
                       create an empty queue whose maximum size is *max−queue−size*
        Boolean IsFullQ(*queue, max−queue−size*) ::=
                    if (number of elements in *queue* == *max−queue−size*)
                    return *TRUE*
                    else return *FALSE*
        Queue AddQ(*queue, item*) ::=
                    if (IsFullQ(*queue*)) *queue − full*
                    else insert *item* at rear of *queue* and return *queue*
        Boolean IsEmptyQ(*queue*) ::=
                    if (*queue* == CreateQ(*max−queue−size*))
                    return *TRUE*
                    else return *FALSE*
        Element DeleteQ(*queue*) ::=
                    if (IsEmptyQ(*queue*)) **return**
                    else remove and return the *item* at front of queue.

Structure 3.2: Abstract data type *Queue*

Boolean IsFullQ(*queue*) ::= `rear == MAX_QUEUE_SIZE-1`

    Since the *IsEmptyQ* and *IsFullQ* operations are quite simple, we again implement them directly in the *addq* (Program 3.3) and *deleteq* (Program 3.4) functions. Functions *addq* and *deleteq* are structurally similar to *add* and *delete* on stacks. While the stack uses the variable *top* in both *add* and *delete*, the queue increments *rear* in *addq* and *front* in *deleteq*. Typical function calls would be *addq(&rear, item);* and *item = deleteq(&front, rear);*. Notice that the call to *addq* passes in the address of *rear*. We do this so that the modification to *rear* is permanent. Similarly, in the call to *deleteq* we pass in the address of *front* so that the modification to *front* is permanent. We do not pass in the address of *rear* since *deleteq* does not modify *rear*; but it does use *rear* to check for an empty queue.

    This sequential representation of a queue has pitfalls that are best illustrated by example.

Example 3.2 [*Job scheduling*]: Queues are frequently used in computer programming, and a typical example is the creation of a job queue by an operating system. If the operating system does not use priorities, then the jobs are processed in the order they enter the system. Figure 3.5 illustrates how an operating system might process jobs if it used a sequential representation for its queue.

```
void addq(int *rear, element item)
{
/* add an item to the queue */
   if (*rear == MAX_QUEUE_SIZE-1) {
      queue_full();
      return;
   }
   queue[++*rear] = item;
}
```

Program 3.3: Add to a queue

```
element deleteq(int *front, int rear)
{
/* remove element at the front of the queue */
   if (*front == rear)
      return queue_empty(); /*return an error key */
   return queue[++*front];
}
```

Program 3.4: Delete from a queue

front	rear	Q[0]	Q[1]	Q[2]	Q[3]	Comments
−1	−1					queue is empty
−1	0	J1				Job 1 is added
−1	1	J1	J2			Job 2 is added
−1	2	J1	J2	J3		Job 3 is added
0	2		J2	J3		Job 1 is deleted
1	2			J3		Job 2 is deleted

Figure 3.5: Insertion and deletion from a sequential queue

It should be obvious that as jobs enter and leave the system, the queue gradually shifts to the right. This means that eventually the rear index equals *MAX_QUEUE_SIZE* − 1, suggesting that the queue is full. In this case, *queue_full* should move the entire queue to the left so that the first element is again at *queue*[0] and *front* is at − 1. It should also recalculate *rear* so that it is correctly positioned. Shifting an array is very time-consuming, particularly when there are many elements in it. In fact, *queue_full* has a worst case complexity of O(*MAX_QUEUE_SIZE*). □

We can obtain a more efficient queue representation if we regard the array *queue*[*MAX_QUEUE_SIZE*] as circular. In this representation, we initialize *front* and *rear* to 0 rather than −1. The *front* index always points one position counterclockwise from the first element in the queue. The *rear* index points to the current end of the queue. The queue is empty iff *front* = *rear*. Figure 3.6 shows empty and nonempty circular queues for *MAX_QUEUE_SIZE* = 6. Figure 3.7 illustrates two full queues for *MAX_QUEUE_SIZE* = 6. While these have space for one more element, the addition of such an element will result in *front* = *rear* and we won't be able to distinguish between an empty and a full queue. So, we adopt the convention that a circular queue of size *MAX_QUEUE_SIZE* will be permitted to hold at most *MAX_QUEUE_SIZE* − 1 elements.

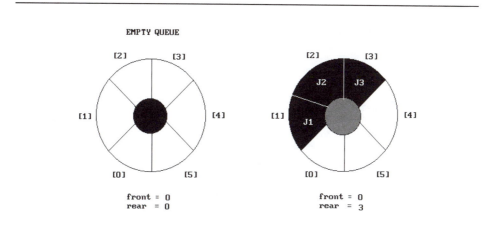

Figure 3.6: Empty and nonempty circular queues

Implementing *addq* and *deleteq* for a circular queue is slightly more difficult since we must assure that a circular rotation occurs. This is attained by using the modulus operator. The circular rotation of the rear index in *addq* (Program 3.5) occurs in the statement:

$$*rear = (*rear+1) \% \text{MAX\_QUEUE\_SIZE};$$

Notice that we rotate *rear* before we place the item in *queue*[*rear*]. Similarly, in *deleteq* (Program 3.6), we rotate *front* with the statement:

$$*front = (*front+1) \% \text{MAX\_QUEUE\_SIZE};$$

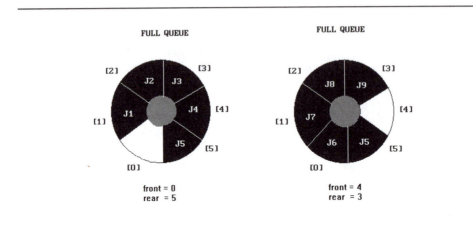

Figure 3.7: Full circular queues

and then we remove the item.

```
void addq(int front, int *rear, element item)
{
/* add an item to the queue */
   *rear = (*rear+1) % MAX_QUEUE_SIZE;
   if (front == *rear) {
      queue_full(rear); /* reset rear and print error*/
      return;
   }
   queue[*rear] = item;
}
```

Program 3.5: Add to a circular queue

Observe that the test for a full queue in *addq* and the test for an empty queue in *deleteq* are the same. In the case of *addq*, however, when *front* = *rear* is evaluated and found to be true, there is actually one space free (*queue*[*rear*]) since the first element in the queue is not at *queue*[*front*] but is one position clockwise from this point. As remarked earlier, if we insert an item here, then we will not be able to distinguish between the cases of full and empty, since the insertion would leave *front* equal to *rear*. To avoid this we signal *queue_full*, thus permitting a maximum of *MAX_QUEUE_SIZE* − 1 rather than *MAX_QUEUE_SIZE* elements in the queue at any time. We leave the implementation of *queue_full* as an exercise.

```
element deleteq(int *front, int rear)
{
   element item;
   /* remove front element from the queue and put it in
   item */
      if (*front == rear)
         return queue_empty();  /* queue_empty returns an
         error key */
      *front = (*front+1) % MAX_QUEUE_SIZE;
      return queue[*front];
}
```

Program 3.6: Delete from a circular queue

The *queue_full* and *queue_empty* functions have been used without explanation. Their implementation depends on the particular application. If the intention is to keep processing and to next delete an element, *queue_full* should restore the rear pointer to its previous value. We have suggested this strategy in our call to *queue_full*. Similarly, *queue_empty* should return an *item* with an error key that can be checked by the main program.

EXERCISES

1. Implement the *queue_full* and *queue_empty* functions for the noncircular queue.

2. Implement the *queue_full* and *queue_empty* functions for the circular queue.

3. Using the noncircular queue implementation, produce a series of adds and deletes that requires O(*MAX_QUEUE_SIZE*) for each add. (Hint: Start with a full queue.)

4. A *double-ended queue (deque)* is a linear list in which additions and deletions may be made at either end. Obtain a data representation mapping a deque into a one-dimensional array. Write functions that add and delete elements from either end of the deque.

5. We can maintain a linear list circularly in an array, *circle* [*MAX_SIZE*]. We set up *front* and *rear* indices similar to those used for a circular queue.

    (a) Obtain a formula in terms of *front*, *rear*, and *MAX_SIZE* for the number of elements in the list.

(b)   Write a function that deletes the *k*th element in the list.

(c)   Write a function that inserts an element, *item*, immediately after the *k*th element.

(d)   What is the time complexity of your functions for (b) and (c)?

3.3   A MAZING PROBLEM

Mazes have been an intriguing subject for many years. Experimental psychologists train rats to search mazes for food, and many a mystery novelist has used an English country garden maze as the setting for a murder. We also are interested in mazes since they present a nice application of stacks. In this section, we develop a program that runs a maze. Although this program takes many false paths before it finds a correct one, once found it can correctly rerun the maze without taking any false paths.

In creating this program the first issue that confronts us is the representation of the maze. The most obvious choice is a two dimensional array in which zeros represent the open paths and ones the barriers. Figure 3.8 shows a simple maze. We assume that the rat starts at the top left and is to exit at the bottom right. With the maze represented as a two-dimensional array, the location of the rat in the maze can at any time be described by the row and column position. If X marks the spot of our current location, *maze*[*row*][*col*], then Figure 3.9 shows the possible moves from this position. We use compass points to specify the eight directions of movement: north, northeast, east, southeast, south, southwest, west, and northwest, or N, NE, E, SE, S, SW, W, NW.

We must be careful here because not every position has eight neighbors. If [*row*,*col*] is on a border then less than eight, and possibly only three, neighbors exist. To avoid checking for these border conditions we can surround the maze by a border of ones. Thus an $m \times p$ maze will require an $(m+2) \times (p+2)$ array. The entrance is at position [1][1] and the exit at [*m*][*p*].

Another device that will simplify the problem is to predefine the possible directions to move in an array, *move*, as in Figure 3.10. This is obtained from Figure 3.9. We represent the eight possible directions of movement by the numbers from 0 to 7. For each direction, we indicate the vertical and horizontal offset. The C declarations needed to create this table are:

```
typedef struct {
        short int vert;
        short int horiz;
        } offsets;
offsets move[8]; /*array of moves for each direction*/
```

We assume that *move* is initialized according to the data provided in Figure 3.10. This means that if we are at position, *maze*[*row*][*col*], and we wish to find the position of the next move, *maze*[*next_row*][*next_col*], we set:

entrance →

```
0 1 0 0 0 1 1 0 0 0 1 1 1 1 1
1 0 0 0 1 1 0 1 1 1 0 0 1 1 1
0 1 1 0 0 0 0 1 1 1 1 0 0 1 1
1 1 0 1 1 1 1 0 1 1 0 1 1 0 0
1 1 0 1 0 0 1 0 1 1 1 1 1 1 1
0 0 1 1 0 1 1 1 0 1 0 0 1 0 1
0 1 1 1 1 0 0 1 1 1 1 1 1 1 1
0 0 1 1 0 1 1 0 1 1 1 1 1 0 1
1 1 0 0 0 1 1 0 1 1 0 0 0 0 0
0 0 1 1 1 1 1 0 0 0 1 1 1 1 0
0 1 0 0 1 1 1 1 1 0 1 1 1 1 0
```
→ exit

Figure 3.8: An example maze

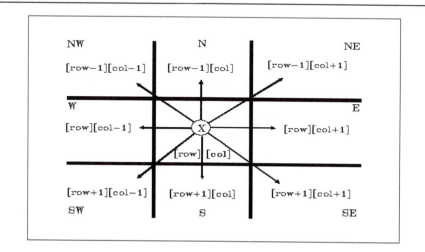

Figure 3.9: Allowable moves

Name	Dir	*move[dir].vert*	*move[dir].horiz*
N	0	−1	0
NE	1	−1	1
E	2	0	1
SE	3	1	1
S	4	1	0
SW	5	1	−1
W	6	0	−1
NW	7	−1	−1

Figure 3.10: Table of moves

```
next_row = row + move[dir].vert;
next_col = col + move[dir].horiz;
```

As we move through the maze, we may have the choice of several directions of movement. Since we do not know which choice is best, we save our current position and arbitrarily pick a possible move. By saving our current position, we can return to it and try another path if we take a hopeless path. We examine the possible moves starting from the north and moving clockwise. Since we do not want to return to a previously tried path, we maintain a second two-dimensional array, *mark*, to record the maze positions already checked. We initialize this array's entries to zero. When we visit a position, *maze[row][col]*, we change *mark[row][col]* to one. Program 3.7 is our initial attempt at a maze traversal algorithm. *EXIT_ROW* and *EXIT_COL* give the coordinates of the maze exit.

Although this algorithm describes the essential processing, we must still resolve several issues. Our first concern is with the representation of the stack. Examining Program 3.7, we see that the stack functions created in Section 3.2 will work if we redefine *element* as:

```
#define MAX_STACK_SIZE 100 /*maximum stack size*/
typedef struct {
        short int row;
        short int col;
        short int dir;
        } element;
element stack[MAX_STACK_SIZE];
```

```
initialize a stack to the maze's entrance coordinates and
direction to north;
while (stack is not empty) {
   /* move to position at top of stack */
   <row,col,dir> = delete from top of stack;
   while (there are more moves from current position) {
      <next_row, next_col> = coordinates of next move;
      dir = direction of move;
      if ((next_row == EXIT_ROW) && (next_col == EXIT_COL))
         success;
      if (maze[next_row][next_col] == 0 &&
                  mark[next_row][next_col] == 0) {
      /* legal move and haven't been there */
         mark[next_row][next_col] = 1;
         /* save current position and direction */
         add <row,col,dir> to the top of the stack;
         row = next_row;
         col = next_col;
         dir = north;
      }
   }
}
printf("No path found\n");
```

Program 3.7: Initial maze algorithm

We also need to determine a reasonable bound for the stack size. Since each position in the maze is visited no more than once, the stack need have only as many positions as there are zeroes in the maze. The maze of Figure 3.11 has only one entrance to exit path. When searching this maze for an entrance to exit path, all positions (except the exit) with value zero will be on the stack when the exit is reached. Since, an $m \times p$ maze, can have at most mp zeroes, it is sufficient for the stack to have this capacity.

Program 3.8 contains the maze search algorithm. We assume that the arrays, *maze*, *mark*, *move*, and *stack*, along with the constants *EXIT_ROW*, *EXIT_COL*, *TRUE*, and *FALSE*, and the variable, *top*, are declared as global. Notice that *path* uses a variable *found* that is initially set to zero (i.e., *FALSE*). If we find a path through the maze, we set this variable to *TRUE*, thereby allowing us to exit both **while** loops gracefully.

Analysis of *path*: The size of the maze determines the computing time of *path*. Since each position within the maze is visited no more than once, the worst case complexity of the algorithm is O(mp) where m and p are, respectively, the number of rows and columns of the maze. □

$$\begin{bmatrix} 0 & 0 & 0 & 0 & 0 & 1 \\ 1 & 1 & 1 & 1 & 1 & 0 \\ 1 & 0 & 0 & 0 & 0 & 1 \\ 0 & 1 & 1 & 1 & 1 & 1 \\ 1 & 0 & 0 & 0 & 0 & 1 \\ 1 & 1 & 1 & 1 & 1 & 0 \\ 1 & 0 & 0 & 0 & 0 & 1 \\ 0 & 1 & 1 & 1 & 1 & 1 \\ 1 & 0 & 0 & 0 & 0 & 0 \end{bmatrix}$$

Figure 3.11: Simple maze with a long path

EXERCISES

1. Describe how you could model a maze with horizontal and vertical walls by a matrix whose entries are zeroes and ones. What moves are permitted in your matrix model? Provide an example maze together with its matrix model.

2. Do the previous exercise for the case of mazes that have walls that are at 45 and 135 degrees in addition to horizontal and vertical ones.

3. What is the maximum path length from start to finish for any maze of dimensions *rows* × *columns*?

4. (a) Find a path through the maze of Figure 3.8.

   (b) Trace the action of function path on the maze of Figure 3.8. Compare this to your own attempt in (a).

5. § [***Programming project***] Using the information provided in the text, write a complete program to search a maze. Print out the entrance to exit path if successful.

3.4 EVALUATION OF EXPRESSIONS

3.4.1 Introduction

The representation and evaluation of expressions is of great interest to computer scientists. As programmers, we write complex expressions such as:

$$((rear + 1 == front) \; || \; ((rear == MAX\_QUEUE\_SIZE - 1) \; \&\& \; ! front)) \quad (3.1)$$

or complex assignment statements such as:

$$x = a/b - c + d*e - a*c \quad (3.2)$$

If we examine expression (3.1), we notice that it contains operators (==, +, −, ||, &&, !), operands (*rear*, *front*, *MAX_QUEUE_SIZE*), and parentheses. The same is true of the statement (3.2), although the operands and operators have changed, and there are

```
void path(void)
{
/* output a path through the maze if such a path exists */
   int i, row, col, next_row, next_col, dir, found = FALSE;
   element position;
   mark[1][1] = 1; top = 0;
   stack[0].row = 1;  stack[0].col = 1;  stack[0].dir = 1;
   while (top > -1 && !found) {
      position = delete(&top);
      row = position.row;  col = position.col;
      dir = position.dir;
      while (dir <  8 && !found) {
         /* move in direction dir */
         next_row = row + move[dir].vert;
         next_col = col + move[dir].horiz;
         if (next_row == EXIT_ROW && next_col == EXIT_COL)
            found = TRUE;
         else if ( !maze[next_row][next_col] &&
         ! mark[next_row][next_col]) {
            mark[next_row][next_col] = 1;
            position.row = row; position.col = col;
            position.dir = ++dir;
            add(&top, position);
            row = next_row; col = next_col; dir = 0;
         }
         else ++dir;
      }
   }
   if (found) {
      printf("The path is:\n");
      printf("row  col\n");
      for (i = 0; i <= top; i++)
         printf("%2d%5d",stack[i].row, stack[i].col);
      printf("%2d%5d\n",row,col);
      printf("%2d%5d\n",EXIT_ROW,EXIT_COL);
   }
   else printf("The maze does not have a path\n");
}
```

Program 3.8: Maze search function

no parentheses.

The first problem with understanding the meaning of these or any other expressions and statements is figuring out the order in which the operations are performed. For instance, assume that $a = 4$, $b = c = 2$, $d = e = 3$ in statement (3.2). We want to find the value of x. Is it

$$((4/2) - 2) + (3 * 3) - (4 * 2)$$
$$= 0 + 9 - 8$$
$$= 1$$

or

$$(4/(2 - 2 + 3)) * (3 - 4) * 2$$
$$= (4/3) * (-1) * 2$$
$$= -2.66666 \cdots$$

Most of us would pick the first answer because we know that division is carried out before subtraction, and multiplication before addition. If we wanted the second answer, we would have written (3.2) differently, using parentheses to change the order of evaluation:

$$x = ((a/(b - c + d)) * (e - a) * c \qquad (3.3)$$

Within any programming language, there is a precedence hierarchy that determines the order in which we evaluate operators. Figure 3.12 contains the precedence hierarchy for C. We have arranged the operators from highest precedence to lowest. Operators with the same precedence appear in the same box. For instance, the highest precedence operators are function calls, array elements, and structure or union members, while the comma operator has the lowest precedence. Operators with highest precedence are evaluated first. The associativity column indicates how we evaluate operators with the same precedence. For instance, the multiplicative operators have left-to-right associativity. This means that the expression $a*b/c\%d/e$ is equivalent to $((((a*b)/c)\%d)/e)$. In other words, we evaluate the operator that is furthest to the left first. With right associative operators of the same precedence, we evaluate the operator furthest to the right first. Parentheses are used to override precedence, and expressions are always evaluated from the innermost parenthesized expression first.

3.4.2 Evaluating Postfix Expressions

The standard way of writing expressions is known as infix notation because in it we place a binary operator in-between its two operands. We have used this notation for all of the expressions written thus far. Although infix notation is the most common way of writing expressions, it is not the one used by compilers to evaluate expressions. Instead compilers typically use a parenthesis-free notation referred to as postfix. In this notation, each operator appears after its operands. Figure 3.13 contains several infix expressions and their postfix equivalents.

Token	Operator	Precedence[1]	Associativity
() [] -> .	function call array element struct or union member	17	left-to-right
-- ++	increment, decrement[2]	16	left-to-right
-- ++ ! ~ - + & * sizeof	decrement, increment[3] logical not one's complement unary minus or plus address or indirection size (in bytes)	15	right-to-left
(type)	type cast	14	right-to-left
* / %	multiplicative	13	left-to-right
+ -	binary add or subtract	12	left-to-right
<< >>	shift	11	left-to-right
> >= < <=	relational	10	left-to-right
== !=	equality	9	left-to-right
&	bitwise and	8	left-to-right
^	bitwise exclusive or	7	left-to-right
|	bitwise or	6	left-to-right
&&	logical and	5	left-to-right
||	logical or	4	left-to-right
?:	conditional	3	right-to-left
= += -= /= *= %= <<= >>= &= ^= |=	assignment	2	right-to-left
,	comma	1	left-to-right

1. The precedence column is taken from Harbison and Steele.
2. Postfix form
3. Prefix form

Figure 3.12: Precedence hierarchy for C

Before writing a function that translates expressions from infix to postfix, we tackle the easier task of evaluating postfix expressions. This evaluation process is much simpler than the evaluation of infix expressions because there are no parentheses to consider. To evaluate an expression we make a single left-to-right scan of it. We place the operands on a stack until we find an operator. We then remove, from the stack, the correct number of operands for the operator, perform the operation, and place the result back on the stack. We continue in this fashion until we reach the end of the expression. We then remove the answer from the top of the stack. Figure 3.14 shows this processing when the input is the nine character string 6 2/3–4 2*+.

Infix	Postfix
2+3*4	2 3 4*+
$a*b$ +5	$ab*5+$
(1+2)*7	1 2+7*
$a*b/c$	$ab*c/$
$((a/(b-c+d))*(e-a)*c$	$abc-d+/ea-*c*$
$a/b-c+d*e-a*c$	$ab/c-de*+ac*-$

Figure 3.13: Infix and postfix notation

Token	Stack			Top
	[0]	[1]	[2]	
6	6			0
2	6	2		1
/	6/2			0
3	6/2	3		1
–	6/2–3			0
4	6/2–3	4		1
2	6/2–3	4	2	2
*	6/2–3	4*2		1
+	6/2–3+4*2			0

Figure 3.14: Postfix evaluation

We now consider the representation of both the stack and the expression. To simplify our task we assume that the expression contains only the binary operators +, –, *, /, and % and that the operands in the expression are single digit integers as in Figure 3.14. This permits us to represent the expression as a character array. The operands are stored on a stack of type **int** until they are needed. The stack is represented by a global array accessed only through *top*. The complete declarations are:

```
#define MAX_STACK_SIZE 100 /*maximum stack size*/
#define MAX_EXPR_SIZE 100 /*max size of expression*/
typedef enum {lparen ,rparen, plus, minus, times, divide,
                    mod, eos, operand} precedence;
int stack[MAX_STACK_SIZE]; /* global stack */
char expr[MAX_EXPR_SIZE]; /* input string */
```

The declarations include an enumerated type, *precedence*, that lists the operators by mnemonics. Although we will use it to process tokens (operators, operands, and parentheses) in this example, its real importance becomes evident when we translate infix expressions into postfix ones. Besides the usual operators, the enumerated type also includes an end-of-string (*eos*) operator.

The function *eval* (Program 3.9) contains the code to evaluate a postfix expression. Since an operand (*symbol*) is initially a character, we must convert it into a single digit integer. We use the statement, *symbol* − '0', to accomplish this task. The statement takes the ASCII value of *symbol* and subtracts the ASCII value of '0', which is 48, from it. For example, suppose *symbol* = '1'. The character, '1', has an ASCII value of 49. Therefore, the statement *symbol* − '0' produces as result the number 1.

We use an auxiliary function, *get_token* (Program 3.10), to obtain tokens from the expression string. If the token is an operand, we convert it to a number and add it to the stack. Otherwise, we remove two operands from the stack, perform the specified operation, and place the result back on the stack. When we have reached the end of expression, we remove the result from the stack.

3.4.3   Infix To Postfix

We can describe an algorithm for producing a postfix expression from an infix one as follows:

(1)   Fully parenthesize the expression.

(2)   Move all binary operators so that they replace their corresponding right parentheses.

(3)   Delete all parentheses.

For example, $a/b - c + d*e - a*c$ when fully parenthesized becomes:

$$((((a/b)-c) + (d*e))-a*c))$$

Performing steps 2 and 3 gives:

$$ab/c - de*+ac*-$$

```
int eval(void)
{
/* evaluate a postfix expression, expr, maintained as a
global variable. '\0' is the the end of the expression.
The stack and top of the stack are global variables.
get_token is used to return the tokentype and
the character symbol. Operands are assumed to be single
character digits */
   precedence token;
   char symbol;
   int op1, op2;
   int n = 0; /* counter for the expression string */
   int top = -1;
   token = get_token(&symbol, &n);
   while (token != eos) {
      if (token == operand)
         add(&top, symbol-'0'); /* stack insert */
      else {
         /* remove two operands, perform operation, and
         return result to the stack */
         op2 = delete(&top); /*stack delete */
         op1 = delete(&top);
         switch(token) {
            case plus: add(&top,op1+op2);
                       break;
            case minus: add(&top, op1-op2);
                        break;
            case times: add(&top, op1*op2);
                        break;
            case divide: add(&top,op1/op2);
                         break;
            case mod: add(&top, op1%op2);
         }
      }
      token = get_token(&symbol, &n);
   }
   return delete(&top); /* return result */
}
```

Program 3.9: Function to evaluate a postfix expression

```
precedence get_token(char *symbol, int *n)
{
/* get the next token, symbol is the character
representation, which is returned, the token is
represented by its enumerated value, which
is returned in the function name */
   *symbol = expr[(*n)++];
   switch (*symbol) {
      case '(' : return lparen;
      case ')' : return rparen;
      case '+' : return plus;
      case '-' : return minus;
      case '/' : return divide;
      case '*' : return times;
      case '%' : return mod;
      case ' ' : return eos;
      default  : return operand; /* no error checking,
                            default is operand */
   }
}
```

Program 3.10: Function to get a token from the input string

Although this algorithm works well when done by hand, it is inefficient on a computer because it requires two passes. The first pass reads the expression and parenthesizes it, while the second moves the operators. Since the order of operands is the same in infix and postfix, we can form the postfix equivalent by scanning the infix expression left-to-right. During this scan, operands are passed to the output expression as they are encountered. However, the order in which the operators are output depends on their precedence. Since we must output the higher precedence operators first, we save operators until we know their correct placement. A stack is one way of doing this, but removing operators correctly is problematic. Two examples illustrate the problem.

Example 3.3 [*Simple expression*]: Suppose we have the simple expression $a+b*c$, which yields $abc*+$ in postfix. As Figure 3.15 illustrates, the operands are output immediately, but the two operators need to be reversed. In general, operators with higher precedence must be output before those with lower precedence. Therefore, we stack operators as long as the precedence of the operator at the top of the stack is less than the precedence of the incoming operator. In this particular example, the unstacking occurs only when we reach the end of the expression. At this point, the two operators are removed. Since the operator with the higher precedence is on top of the stack, it is removed first. □

Token	Stack [0]	[1]	[2]	Top	Output
a				−1	a
+	+			0	a
b	+			0	ab
*	+	*		1	ab
c	+	*		1	abc
eos				−1	abc*+

Figure 3.15: Translation of a +b*c to postfix

Example 3.4 [*Parenthesized expression*]: Parentheses make the translation process more difficult because the equivalent postfix expression will be parenthesis-free. We use as our example the expression a*(b +c)*d, which yields abc +*d* in postfix. Figure 3.16 shows the translation process. Notice that we stack operators until we reach the right parenthesis. At this point we unstack until we reach the corresponding left parenthesis. We then delete the left parenthesis from the stack. (The right parenthesis is never put on the stack.) This leaves us with only the *d remaining in the infix expression. Since the two multiplications have equal precedences, one is output before the d, the second is placed on the stack and removed after the d is output. □

Token	Stack [0]	[1]	[2]	Top	Output
a				−1	a
*	*			0	a
(	*	(		1	a
b	*	(		1	ab
+	*	(	+	2	ab
c	*	(	+	2	abc
)	*			0	abc +
*	*			0	abc +*
d	*			0	abc +*d
eos	*			0	abc +*d*

Figure 3.16: Translation of a*(b +c)*d to postfix

The analysis of the two examples suggests a precedence-based scheme for stacking and unstacking operators. The left parenthesis complicates matters because it behaves like a low-precedence operator when it is on the stack, and a high-precedence one when it is not. It is placed in the stack whenever it is found in the expression, but it is unstacked only when its matching right parenthesis is found. Thus, we have two types of precedence, an *in-stack precedence* (*isp*) and an *incoming precedence* (*icp*). The declarations that establish these precedences and the stack are:

```
precedence stack[MAX_STACK_SIZE];
/* isp and icp arrays -- index is value of precedence
lparen, rparen, plus, minus, times, divide, mod, eos */
static int isp[] = {0,19,12,12,13,13,13,0};
static int icp[] = {20,19,12,12,13,13,13,0};
```

Notice that we are now using the stack to store the mnemonic for the token. Since the value of a variable of an enumerated type is simply the integer corresponding to the position of the value in the enumerated type, we can use the mnemonic as an index into the two arrays. For example, *isp* [*plus*] is translated into *isp* [2], which gives us an in-stack precedence of 12. The precedences are taken from Figure 3.12, but we have added precedences for the left and right parentheses and the *eos* marker. We give the right parenthesis an in-stack and incoming precedence (19) that is greater than the precedence of any operator in Figure 3.12. We give the left parenthesis an instack precedence of zero, and an incoming precedence (20) greater than that of the right parenthesis. In addition, because we want unstacking to occur when we reach the end of the string, we give the *eos* token a low precedence (0). These precedences suggest that we remove an operator from the stack only if its instack precedence is greater than or equal to the incoming precedence of the new operator.

The function *postfix* (Program 3.11) converts an infix expression into a postfix one using the process just discussed. This function invokes a function, *print_token*, to print out the character associated with the enumerated type. That is, *print_token* reverses the process used in *get_token*.

Analysis of *postfix*: Let n be the number of tokens in the expression. $\Theta(n)$ time is spent extracting tokens and outputting them. Besides this, time is spent in the two **while** loops. The total time spent here is $\Theta(n)$ as the number of tokens that get stacked and unstacked is linear in n. So, the complexity of function *postfix* is $\Theta(n)$. □

EXERCISES

1. Write the postfix form of the following expressions:

```
void postfix(void)
{
/* output the postfix of the expression. The expression
string, the stack, and top are global */
   char symbol;
   precedence token;
   int n = 0;
   int top = 0;     /* place eos on stack */
   stack[0] = eos;
   for (token = get_token(&symbol, &n); token != eos;
                       token = get_token(&symbol,&n)) {
      if (token == operand)
         printf("%c",symbol);
      else if (token == rparen) {
         /* unstack tokens until left parenthesis */
         while (stack[top] != lparen)
            print_token(delete(&top));
         delete(&top);   /* discard the left parenthesis */
      }
      else {
         /* remove and print symbols whose isp is greater
         than or equal to the current token's icp */
         while(isp[stack[top]] >= icp[token])
            print_token(delete(&top));
         add(&top, token);
      }
   }
   while ( (token=delete(&top)) != eos)
      print_token(token);
   printf("\n");
}
```

Program 3.11: Function to convert from infix to postfix

   (a) $a * b * c$

   (b) $-a + b - c + d$

   (c) $a * - b + c$

   (d) $(a + b) * d + e / (f + a * d) + c$

(e) a && b || c || ! $(e > f)$ (assuming C precedence)

(f) $!(a$ && $!((b < c) || (c > d))) || (c < e)$

2. Write the *print_token* function used in *postfix* (Program 3.11).

3. Use the precedences of Figure 3.12 together with those for '(', ')', and \0 to answer the following:

(a)   In the postfix function, what is the maximum number of elements that can be on the stack at any time if the input expression, *expr*, has *n* operators and an unlimited number of nested parentheses?

(b)   What is the answer to (a) if *expr* has *n* operators and the depth of the nesting of parentheses is at most six?

4. Rewrite the *eval* function so that it evaluates the unary operators + and −.

5. § Rewrite the *postfix* function so that it works with the following operators, besides those used in the text: &&, !!, <<, >>, <=, !=, <, >, <=, and >=. (Hint: Write the equation so that the operators, operands, and parentheses are separated with a space, for example, $a + b > c$. Then review the functions in <*string.h*>.)

6. Another expression form that is easy to evaluate and is parenthesis-free is known as prefix. In prefix notation, the operators precede their operands. Figure 3.17 shows several infix expressions and their prefix equivalents. Notice that the order of operands is the same in infix and prefix.

Infix	Prefix
$a*b/c$	$/*abc$
$a/b-c+d*e-a*c$	$-+-/abc*de*ac$
$a*(b+c)/d-g$	$-/*a+bcdg$

Figure 3.17: Infix and postfix expressions

(a)   Write the prefix form of the expressions in Exercise 1.

(b)   Write a C function that evaluates a prefix expression, *expr*. (Hint: Scan *expr* from right to left.)

(c)   Write a C function that transforms an infix expression, *expr*, into its prefix equivalent.

What is the time complexity of your functions for (b) and (c)? How much space is needed by each of these functions?

7. Write a C function that transforms a prefix expression into a postfix one. Carefully state any assumptions you make regarding the input. How much time and space does your function take?

8. Write a C function that transforms a postfix expression into a prefix one. How much time and space does your function take?

9. Write a C function that transforms a postfix expression into a fully parenthesized infix expression. A fully parenthesized expression is one in which all the subexpressions are surrounded by parentheses. For example, $a+b+c$ becomes $((a+b)+c)$. Analyze the time and space complexity of your function.

10. Write a C function that transforms a prefix expression into a fully parenthesized infix expression. Analyze the time and space complexity of your function.

11. § Repeat Exercise 5, but this time transform the infix expression into prefix.

3.5 MULTIPLE STACKS AND QUEUES

Until now we have been concerned only with the representations of a single stack or a single queue. In both cases, we have seen that it is possible to obtain efficient sequential representations. We would now like to examine the case of multiple stacks. (We leave the consideration of multiple queues as an exercise.) We again examine only sequential mappings of stacks into an array, *memory*[*MEMORY_SIZE*]. If we have only two stacks to represent, the solution is simple. We use *memory* [0] for the bottom element of the first stack, and *memory*[*MEMORY_SIZE – 1*] for the bottom element of the second stack. The first stack grows toward *memory*[*MEMORY_SIZE – 1*] and the second grows toward *memory* [0]. With this representation, we can efficiently use all the available space.

Representing more than two stacks within the same array poses problems since we no longer have an obvious point for the bottom element of each stack. Assuming that we have *n* stacks, we can divide the available memory into *n* segments. This initial division may be done in proportion to the expected sizes of the various stacks, if this is known. Otherwise, we may divide the memory into equal segments.

Assume that *stack_no* refers to the stack number of one of the *n* stacks. To establish this stack, we must create indices for both the bottom and top positions of this stack. The bottom element, *boundary*[*stack_no*], $0 \leq stack\_no < MAX\_STACKS$, always points to the position immediately to the left of the bottom element, while *top*[*stack_no*], $0 \leq stack\_no < MAX\_STACKS$ points to the top element. A stack is empty *iff* *boundary*[*stack_no*] = *top*[*stack_no*]. The relevant declarations are:

```
#define MEMORY_SIZE 100 /* size of memory */
#define MAX_STACKS 10 /* max number of stacks plus 1 */
/* global memory declaration */
element memory[MEMORY_SIZE];
int top[MAX_STACKS];
int boundary[MAX_STACKS];
int n;   /* number of stacks entered by the user */
```

To divide the array into roughly equal segments we use the following code:

```
top[0] = boundary[0] = -1;
for (i = 1; i < n;i++)
    top[i] = boundary[i] = (MEMORY_SIZE/n)*i;
boundary[n] = MEMORY_SIZE-1;
```

Figure 3.18 shows this initial configuration. In the figure, *n* is the number of stacks entered by the user, *n* < *MAX_STACKS*, and *m* = *MEMORY_SIZE*. Stack *stack_no* can grow from *boundary*[*stack_no*] + 1 to *boundary* [*stack_no* + 1] before it is full. Since we need a boundary for the last stack, we set *boundary* [*n*] to *MEMORY_SIZE*– 1. Programs 3.12 and 3.13 implement the add and delete operations for this representation.

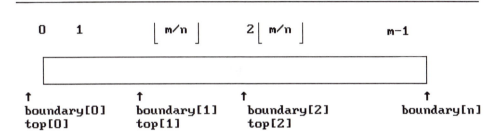

All stacks are empty and divided into roughly equal segments.

Figure 3.18: Initial configuration for *n* stacks in *memory* [*m*].

```
void add(int i, element item)
{
/* add an item to the ith stack */
   if (top[i] == boundary[i+1])
      stack_full(i);
   memory[++top[i]] = item;
}
```

Program 3.12: Add an *item* to the stack *stack_no*

The *add* (Program 3.12) and *delete* (Program 3.13) functions for multiple stacks appear to be as simple as those we used for the representation of a single stack. However, this is not really the case because the *top*[*i*] == *boundary*[*i*+1] condition in *add* implies only that a particular stack ran out of memory, not that the entire memory is full. In fact, there may be a lot of unused space between other stacks in array *memory* (see Figure 3.19). Therefore, we create an error recovery function, *stack_full*, which determines if there is any free space in memory. If there is space available, it should shift the stacks so that space is allocated to the full stack.

```
element delete(int i)
{
/* remove top element from the ith stack */
    if (top[i] == boundary[i])
        return stack_empty(i);
    return memory[top[i]--];
}
```

Program 3.13: Delete an *item* from the stack *stack_no*

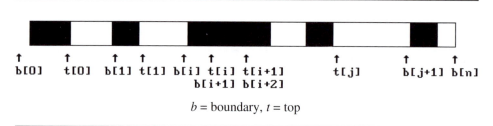

b = boundary, t = top

Figure 3.19: Configuration when stack i meets stack $i + 1$, but the memory is not full

There are several ways that we can design *stack_full* so that we can add elements to this stack until the array is full. We outline one method here. Other methods are discussed in the exercises. We can guarantee that *stack_full* adds elements as long as there is free space in array *memory* if we:

(1) Determine the least, j, *stack_no* $< j < n$, such that there is free space between stacks j and $j + 1$. That is, *top*[j] $<$ *boundary*[$j+1$]. If there is such a j, then move stacks *stack_no*+1, *stack_no*+2, $\cdots$, j one position to the right (treating *memory*[0] as leftmost and *memory*[*MEMORY_SIZE* $-$ *1*] as rightmost). This creates a space between stacks *stack_no* and *stack_no*+1.

(2) If there is no j as in (1), then look to the left of stack *stack_no*. Find the largest j such that $0 \le j <$ *stack_no* and there is space between stacks j and $j+1$. That is, *top*[j] $<$ *boundary*[$j+1$]. If there is such a j, then move stacks $j+1$, $j+2$, $\cdots$, *stack_no* one space to the left. This also creates a space between stacks *stack_no* and *stack_no*+1.

(3) If there is no j satisfying either condition (1) or condition (2), then all *MEMORY_SIZE* spaces of memory are utilized and there is no free space. In this case *stack _full* terminates with an error message.

We leave the implementation of *stack_full* as an exercise. However, it should be clear that the worst case performance of this representation for the n stacks together will be poor. In fact, in the worst case, the function has a time complexity of O(*MEMORY_SIZE*).

EXERCISES

1. We must represent two stacks in an array, *memory*[*MEMORY_SIZE*]. Write C functions that add and delete an item from stack *stack_no*, $0 \leq stack\_no \leq 1$. Your functions should be able to add elements to the stacks as long as the total number of elements in both stacks is less than *MEMORY_SIZE* − 1.

2. Obtain a data representation that maps a stack and a queue into a single array, *memory*[*MEMORY_SIZE*]. Write C functions that add and delete elements from these two data objects. What can you say about the suitability of your data representation?

3. Write a C function that implements the *stack_full* strategy discussed in the text.

4. Using the add and delete functions discussed in the text and *stack_full* from Exercise 3, produce a sequence of additions/deletions that requires O(*MEMORY_SIZE*) time for each add. Assume that you have two stacks and that your are starting from a configuration representing a full utilization of *memory*[*MEMORY_SIZE*].

5. Rewrite the *add* and *stack_full* functions so that the *add* function terminates if there are fewer than c_1 free spaces left in memory. The empirically determined constant, c_1 shows when it is futile to move items in memory. Substitute a small constant of your choice.

6. Design a data representation that sequentially maps n queues into an array *memory*[*MEMORY_SIZE*]. Represent each queue as a circular queue within memory. Write functions *addq*, *deleteq*, and *queue_full* for this representation.

3.6 REFERENCES AND SELECTED READINGS

You will find an excellent discussion of the system stack and activation records in A. Holub, *Compiler Design in C*,Prentice-Hall, Englewood Cliffs, N.J., 1990. The structure of our activation record (Figure 3.2) is based on Holub's discussion.

Several texts discuss the precedence hierarchy used in C. Among the references you might like to look at are S. Harbison and G. Steele, *C: A Reference Manual*, Third Edition, Prentice-Hall, Englewood Cliffs, N.J., 1991, and B. Kernighan and D. Ritchie, *The C Programming Language*, Second Edition, Prentice-Hall, Englewood Cliffs, N.J., 1988.

3.7 ADDITIONAL EXERCISES

1. § [*Programming project*] [Landweber] People have spent so much time playing solitaire that the gambling casinos are now capitalizing on this human weakness. A form of solitaire is described below. You must write a C program that plays this game, thus freeing hours of time for people to return to more useful endeavors.

To begin the game, 28 cards are dealt into seven piles. The leftmost pile has one card, the next pile has two cards, and so forth, up to seven cards in the rightmost pile. Only the uppermost card of each of the seven piles is turned face-up. The cards are dealt left-to-right, one card to each pile, dealing one less pile each time, and turning the first card in each round face-up. You may build descending sequences of red on black or black on red from the top face-up card of each pile. For example, you may place either the eight of diamonds or the eight of hearts on the nine of spades or the nine of clubs. All face-up cards on a pile are moved as a unit and may be placed on another pile according to the bottom face-up card. For example, the seven of clubs on the eight of hearts may be moved as a unit onto the nine of clubs or the nine of spades.

Whenever a face-down card is uncovered, it is turned face-up. If one pile is removed completely, a face-up king may be moved from a pile (together with all cards above it) or the top of the waste pile (see below) into the vacated space. There are four output piles, one for each suite, and the object of the game is to get as many cards as possible into the output piles. Each time an ace appears at the top of a pile or the top of the stack it is moved into the appropriate output pile. Cards are added to the output piles in sequence, the suit for each pile being determined by the ace on the bottom.

From the rest of the deck, called the stock, cards are turned up one by one and placed face-up on a waste pile. You may always play cards off the top of the waste pile, but only one at a time. Begin by moving a card from the stock to the top of the waste pile. If you can ever make more than one possible play, make them in the following order:

(a)   Move a card from the top of a playing pile or from the top of the waste pile to an output pile. If the waste pile becomes empty, move a card from the stock to the waste pile.

(b)   Move a card from the top of the waste pile to the leftmost playing pile to which it can be moved. If the waste pile becomes empty, move a card from the stock to the waste pile.

(c)   Find the leftmost playing pile that can be moved and place it on top of the leftmost playing pile to which it can be moved.

(d) Try (a), (b), and (c) in sequence, restarting with (a) whenever a move is made.

(e) If no move is made via (a) through (d), move a card from the stock to the waste pile and retry (a).

Only the top card of the playing piles or the waste pile may be played to an output pile. Once placed on an output pile, a card may not be withdrawn to help elsewhere. The game is over when either all the cards have been played to the output piles, or the stock pile has been exhausted and no more cards can be moved.

When played for money, the player pays the house $52 at the beginning, and wins $5 for every card played to the output piles. Write your program so that it will play several games and determine your net winnings. Use a random number generator to shuffle the deck. Output a complete record of two games in easily understandable form. Include as output the number of games played and the net winnings (+ or −).

2. § [*Programming project*] [Landweber] We want to simulate an airport landing and takeoff pattern. The airport has three runways, runway 0, runway 1, and runway 2. There are four landing holding patterns, two for each of the first two runways. Arriving planes enter one of the holding pattern queues, where the queues are to be as close in size as possible. When a plane enters a holding queue, it is assigned an integer identification number and an integer giving the number of time units the plane can remain in the queue before it must land (because of low fuel level). There is also a queue for takeoffs for each of the three runways. Planes arriving in a takeoff queue are assigned an integer identification number. The takeoff queues should be kept approximately the same size.

For each time period, no more than three planes may arrive at the landing queues and no more than three planes may enter the takeoff queues. Each runway can handle one takeoff or landing at each time slot. Runway 2 is used for takeoffs except when a plane is low on fuel. During each time period, planes in either landing queue whose air time has reached zero must be given priority over other landings and takeoffs. If only one plane is in this category, runway 2 is used. If there is more than one plane, then the other runways are also used.

Use successive even(odd) integers for identification numbers of the planes arriving at takeoff (landing) queues. At each time unit assume that arriving planes are entered into queues before takeoffs or landings occur. Try to design your algorithm so that neither landing nor takeoff queues grow excessively. However, arriving planes must be placed at the ends of queues and the queues cannot be reordered.

Your output should label clearly what occurs during each time unit. Periodically you should also output:

(a)   the contents of each queue

(b)   the average takeoff waiting time

(c)   the average landing waiting time

(d)   the number of planes that have crashed (run out of fuel and there was no open runway) since the last time period.

CHAPTER 4

LISTS

4.1 POINTERS

In the previous chapters we studied the representation of simple data structures using an array and a sequential mapping. These representations stored successive elements of the data object a fixed distance apart. Thus,

- If the ith element in a queue was at location Loc_i then the $(i + 1)$th element was at location $(Loc_i + c) \% MAX\_QUEUE\_SIZE$ for the circular representation.

- If the top element of a stack was at location, Loc_{top}, then the element beneath it was at location $Loc_{top} - c$.

These sequential representations were adequate for many operations including insertion or deletion of elements from a stack or queue. However, when we use a sequential mapping for ordered lists, operations such as insertion and deletion of arbitrary elements become expensive. For example, consider the following alphabetized list of three-letter English words ending in *at*:

$$(bat, cat, sat, vat)$$

We would like to add the word *mat* to this list. If we store this list in an array, then we must move *sat* and *vat* one position to the right before we insert *mat*. Similarly, if we want to remove the word *cat* from the list, we must move *sat* and *vat* one position to the left to maintain our sequential representation. In the general case, arbitrary insertion and deletion from arrays can be very time-consuming.

We encountered an additional difficulty with sequential representations when we used several ordered lists of varying sizes. By storing each list in a different array of maximum size, we could waste storage. However, by maintaining the lists in a single array, we might need to move data frequently. We observed this dilemma when we represented multiple stacks, queues, polynomials, and sparse matrices. These data types are examples of ordered lists. Polynomials are ordered by exponent, while matrices are ordered by rows and columns. In this chapter, we present an alternate representation for ordered lists that reduces the time needed for arbitrary insertion and deletion.

We can attain an elegant solution to the problem of data movement in sequential representations by using linked representations. Unlike a sequential representation where successive items of a list are located a fixed distance apart, in a linked representation these items may be placed anywhere in memory. In other words, in a sequential representation the order of elements is the same as in the ordered list, while in a linked representation these two sequences need not be the same. To access elements of the list in the correct order with each element, we store the address, or location, of the next element in that list. Thus, associated with each list element is a *node* which contains both a data component and a pointer to the next item in the list. The pointers are often called *links*.

C provides extensive support for pointers. In Chapter 2 we observed that an array element, *a*[*i*], is viewed as a pointer to the location containing the *i*th element of array *a*. Actually, for any type *T* in C there is a corresponding type pointer-to-*T*. The actual value of a pointer type is an address of memory. The two most important operators used with the pointer type are:

- & the address operator
- * the dereferencing (or indirection) operator

If we have the declaration:

```
int i, *pi;
```

then *i* is an integer variable and *pi* is a pointer to an integer. If we say:

```
pi = &i;
```

then &*i* returns the address of *i* and assigns it as the value of *pi*. To assign a value to *i* we can say:

```
i = 10;
```

or

```
*pi = 10;
```

In both cases the integer 10 is stored as the value of *i*. In the second case, the * in front of the pointer *pi* causes it to be dereferenced, by which we mean that instead of storing 10 into the pointer, 10 is stored into the location pointed at by the pointer *pi*.

There are other operations we can do on pointers. We may assign a pointer to a variable of type pointer. Since a pointer is just a nonnegative integer number, C allows us to perform arithmetic operations such as addition, subtraction, multiplication, and division, on pointers. We also can determine if one pointer is greater than, less than, or equal to another, and we can convert pointers explicitly to integers.

The size of a pointer can be different on different computers. In some cases the size of a pointer on a computer can vary. For example, the size of a pointer to a **char** can be longer than a pointer to a **float**. C has a special value that it treats as a null pointer. The null pointer points to no object or function. Typically the null pointer is represented by the integer 0. There is a macro called *NULL* which is defined to be this constant. The macro is defined either in *stddef.h* for ANSI C or in *stdio.h* for K&R C. The null pointer can be used in relational expressions, where it is interpreted as false. Therefore, to test for the null pointer in C we can say:

```
if (pi == NULL)
```

or more simply:

```
if (!pi)
```

4.1.1   Pointers Can Be Dangerous

In this chapter we will see that by using pointers we can attain a high degree of flexibility and efficiency. But pointers can be dangerous as well. When programming in C, it is a wise practice to set all pointers to *NULL* when they are not actually pointing to an object. This makes it less likely that you will attempt to access an area of memory that is either out of range of your program or that does not contain a pointer reference to a legitimate object. On some computers, it is possible to dereference the null pointer and the result is *NULL*, permitting execution to continue. On other computers, the result is whatever the bits are in location zero, often producing a serious error.

Another wise programming tactic is to use explicit **type casts** when converting between pointer types. For example:

```
pi = malloc(sizeof(int)); /*assign to pi a pointer to int*/
pf = (float *) pi; /*casts an int pointer to a float pointer*/
```

Another area of concern is that in many systems, pointers have the same size as type **int**. Since **int** is the default type specifier, some programmers omit the return type when defining a function. The return type defaults to **int** which can later be interpreted as a pointer. This has proven to be a dangerous practice on some computers and the programmer is urged to define explicit return types for functions.

4.1.2 Using Dynamically Allocated Storage

In your program you may wish to acquire space in which you will store information. When you write your program you may not know how much space you will need, nor do you wish to allocate some very large area that may never be required. To solve this problem C provides a mechanism, called a *heap*, for allocating storage at run-time. Whenever you need a new area of memory, you may call a function, *malloc*, and request the amount you need. If the memory is available, a pointer to the start of an area of memory of the required size is returned. At a later time when you no longer need an area of memory, you may free it by calling another function, *free*, and return the area of memory to the system. Once an area of memory is freed, it is improper to use it. Program 4.1 shows how we might allocate and deallocate storage to pointer variables.

```
int i, *pi;
float f, *pf;
pi = (int *) malloc(sizeof(int));
pf = (float *) malloc(sizeof(float));
*pi = 1024;
*pf = 3.14;
printf("an integer = %d, a float = %f\n", *pi, *pf);
free(pi);
free(pf);
```

Program 4.1: Allocation and deallocation of pointers

The call to *malloc* includes a parameter that determines the size of storage required to hold the **int** or the **float**. The result is a pointer to the first address of a storage area of the proper size. The type of the result can vary. On some systems the result of *malloc* is a **char ***, a pointer to a **char**. However, those who use ANSI C will find that the result is **void ***. The notation (*int **) and (*float **) are *type cast* expressions. They transform the resulting pointer into a pointer to the correct type. The pointer is then assigned to the proper pointer variable. The *free* function deallocates an area of memory previously allocated by *malloc*. In some versions of C, *free* expects an argument that is a **char ***, while ANSI C expects **void ***. However, the casting of the argument is generally omitted in the call to *free*.

In Program 4.1 if we insert the line:

```
pf = (float *) malloc(sizeof(float));
```

immediately after the *printf* statement, then the pointer to the storage used to hold the value 3.14 has disappeared. Now there is no way to retrieve this storage. This is an example of a *dangling reference*. Whenever all pointers to a dynamically allocated area of storage are lost, the storage is lost to the program. As we examine programs that make use of pointers and dynamic storage, we will make it a point to always return storage after we no longer need it.

4.2 SINGLY LINKED LISTS

Linked lists are drawn as an ordered sequence of nodes with links represented as arrows (Figure 4.1). The name of the pointer to the first node in the list is the name of the list. Thus, the list of Figure 4.1 is called *ptr*. Notice that we do not explicitly put in the values of the pointers, but simply draw arrows to indicate that they are there. We do this to reinforce the facts that:

(1)   the nodes do not reside in sequential locations
(2)   the locations of the nodes may change on different runs

When we write a program that works with lists, we almost never look for a specific address except when we test for the end of the list.

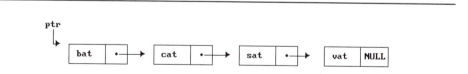

Figure 4.1: Usual way to draw a linked list

Let us now see why it is easier to make arbitrary insertions and deletions using a linked list rather than a sequential list. To insert the word *mat* between *cat* and *sat*, we must:

(1)   Get a node that is currently unused; let its address be *paddr*.
(2)   Set the data field of this node to *mat*.
(3)   Set *paddr*'s link field to point to the address found in the link field of the node containing *cat*.
(4)   Set the link field of the node containing *cat* to point to *paddr*.

Figure 4.2 shows how the list changes after we insert *mat*. The dashed line out of the node containing *cat* is the old link, while the solid line shows the new link. Notice that when we insert *mat* we do not move any elements that are already in the list. Thus, we have overcome the need to move data, but we have the additional storage needed for the link field. As we will see, this is not too severe a penalty.

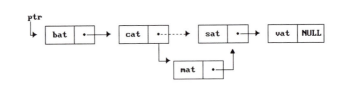

Figure 4.2: Insert *mat* after *cat*

Now suppose that we want to delete *mat* from the list. We only need to find the element that immediately precedes *mat*, which is *cat*, and set its link field to point to *mat*'s link field (Figure 4.3). We have not moved any data, and although the link field of *mat* still points to *sat*, *mat* is no longer in the list.

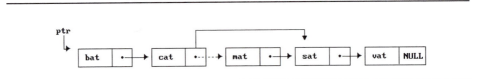

Figure 4.3: Delete *mat* from list

From this brief discussion of linked lists, we see that we need the following capabilities to make linked representations possible:

(1)   A mechanism for defining a node's structure, that is, the fields it contains. We use *self-referential structures*, discussed in Section 2.2, to do this.

(2)   A way to create new nodes when we need them. The *malloc* function handles this operation.

(3)   A way to remove nodes that we no longer need. The *free* function handles this operation.

We will present several small examples to show how to create and use linked lists in C.

Example 4.1 [*List of words ending in at*]: To create a linked list of words, we first define a node structure for the list. This structure specifies the type of each of the fields.

From our previous discussion we know that our structure must contain a character array and a pointer to the next node. The necessary declarations are:

```
typedef struct list_node *list_pointer;
typedef struct list_node {
        char data[4];
        list_pointer link;
        };
list_pointer ptr = NULL;
```

These declarations contain an example of a *self-referential structure*. Notice that we have defined the pointer (*list _ pointer*) to the **struct** before we defined the **struct** (*list _ node*). C allows us to create a pointer to a type that does not yet exist because otherwise we would face a paradox: we cannot define a pointer to a nonexistent type, but to define the new type we must include a pointer to the type.

After defining the node's structure, we create a new empty list. This is accomplished by the statement:

```
list_pointer ptr = NULL;
```

This statement indicates that we have a new list called *ptr*. Remember that *ptr* contains the address of the start of the list. Since the new list is initially empty, its starting address is zero. Therefore, we use the reserved word *NULL* to signify this condition. We also can use an *IS_EMPTY* macro to test for an empty list:

```
#define IS_EMPTY(ptr) (!(ptr))
```

To create new nodes for our list we use the *malloc* (memory allocation) function provided in *<alloc.h>*. We would apply this function as follows to obtain a new node for our list:

```
ptr = (list_pointer)malloc(sizeof(list_node));
```

From the available memory, *malloc* obtains a storage block large enough to hold *struct list_node*. We use *sizeof* to furnish *malloc* with the required block size. Since our only access to this block is through its starting address, we **type cast** the address to type pointer to *list _ node*. (The **type cast** is unnecessary in ANSI C, but we include it here for portability.) We then assign this pointer to the variable *ptr*.

We are now ready to assign values to the fields of the node. This introduces a new operator, –>. If *e* is a pointer to a structure that contains the field *name*, then *e–>name* is a shorthand way of writing the expression (**e*).*name*. The –> operator is referred to as the *structure member* operator, and its use is preferred when one has a pointer to a **struct** rather than the * and dot notation.

To place the word *bat* into our list we use the statements:

```
strcpy(ptr->data,"bat");
ptr->link = NULL;
```

These statements create the list illustrated in Figure 4.4. Notice that the node has a null link field because there is no next node in the list. □

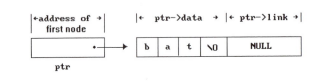

Figure 4.4: Referencing the fields of a node

Example 4.2 [*Two-node linked list*]: We want to create a linked list of integers. The node structure is defined as:

```
typedef struct list_node *list_pointer;
typedef struct list_node {
        int data;
        list_pointer link;
        };
list_pointer ptr = NULL;
```

A linked list with two nodes is created by function *create2* (Program 4.2). We set the data field of the first node to 10 and that of the second to 20. The variable *first* is a pointer to the first node; *second* is a pointer to the second node. Notice that the link field of the first node is set to point to the second node, while the link field of the second node is *NULL*. The variable *first*, which is the pointer to the start of the list, is returned by *create2*. Figure 4.5 shows the resulting list structure. □

Example 4.3 [*List insertion*]: Let *ptr* be a pointer to a linked list as in Example 4.2. Assume that we want to insert a node with a data field of 50 after some arbitrary node. Function *insert* (Program 4.3) accomplishes this task. In this function, we pass in two pointer variables. The first variable, *ptr*, is the pointer to the first node in the list. If this variable contains a null address (i.e., there are no nodes in the list), we want to change *ptr* so that it points to the node with 50 in its data field. This means that we must pass in the address of *ptr*. This is why we use the declaration *list_pointer *ptr*. Since the address of the second pointer, *node*, does not change, we do not need to pass in its address as a parameter. A typical function call would be *insert (&ptr, node)*; where *ptr* points to the start of the list and *node* points to the new node.

```
list_pointer create2()
{
/* create a linked list with two nodes */
   list_pointer first, second;
   first = (list_pointer)malloc(sizeof(list_node));
   second = (list_pointer)malloc(sizeof(list_node));
   second->link = NULL;
   second->data = 20;
   first->data = 10;
   first->link = second;
   return first;
}
```

Program 4.2: Create a two-node list

Figure 4.5: A two-node list

The function *insert* uses an **if** ··· **else** statement to distinguish between empty and nonempty lists. For an empty list, we set *temp*'s link field to *NULL* and change the value of *ptr* to the address of *temp*. For a nonempty list, we insert the *temp* node between *node* and the node pointed to by its link field. Figure 4.6 shows the list from Figure 4.5 after we insert *temp* between the first and second nodes.

Notice that we have added a new macro, *IS_FULL*, that allows us to determine if we have used all available memory. This macro is used in conjunction with *malloc*, which returns *NULL* if there is no more memory. It is defined as:

```
#define IS_FULL(ptr)  (!(ptr)) □
```

Example 4.4 [*List deletion*]: Deleting an arbitrary node from a list is slightly more complicated than insertion because deletion depends on the location of the node. Assume that we have three pointers: *ptr* points to the start of the list, *node* points to the node that we wish to delete, and *trail* points to the node that precedes it. Figures 4.7 and 4.8 show two examples. In Figure 4.7, the node to be deleted is the first node in the list. This means that we must permanently change the starting address of *ptr*. In Figure 4.8, since *node* is not the first node, we simply change the link field in *trail* to point to the link field

```
void insert(list_pointer *ptr, list_pointer node)
{
/* insert a new node with data = 50 into the list
ptr after node */
   list_pointer temp;
   temp = (list_pointer)malloc(sizeof(list_node));
   if (IS_FULL(temp)){
      fprintf(stderr, "The memory is full\n");
      exit(1);
   }
   temp->data = 50;
   if (*ptr) {
      temp->link = node->link;
      node->link = temp;
   }
   else {
      temp->link = NULL;
      *ptr = temp;
   }
}
```

Program 4.3: Simple insert into front of list

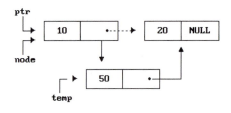

Figure 4.6: Two node list after the function call *insert(&ptr, ptr);*

in *node*.

An arbitrary node is deleted from a linked list by function *delete* (Program 4.4). In addition to changing the link fields, or the value of **ptr*, *delete* also returns the space that was allocated to the deleted node to the system memory. To accomplish this task, we use *free*. □

Example 4.5 [*Printing out a list*]: Program 4.5 prints the data fields of the nodes in a

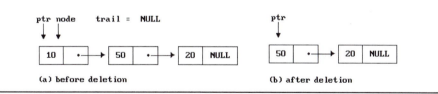

Figure 4.7: List after the function call *delete(&ptr, NULL, ptr);*

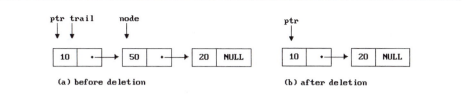

Figure 4.8: List after the function call *delete(&ptr, ptr, ptr->link);*

```
void delete(list_pointer *ptr, list_pointer trail,
                            list_pointer node)
{
/* delete node from the list, trail is the preceding node
ptr is the head of the list */
   if (trail)
      trail->link = node->link;
   else
      *ptr = (*ptr)->link;
   free(node);
}
```

Program 4.4: Deletion from a list

list. To do this we first print out the contents of *ptr*'s data field, then we replace *ptr* with the address in its *link* field. We continue printing out the *data* field and moving to the next node until we reach the end of the list. □

```
void print_list(list_pointer ptr)
{
   printf("The list contains: ");
   for (; ptr; ptr = ptr->link)
      printf("%4d",ptr->data);
   printf("\n");
}
```

Program 4.5: Printing a list

EXERCISES

1. Rewrite *delete* (Program 4.4) so that it uses only two pointers, *ptr* and *trail*.

2. Assume that we have a list of integers as in Example 4.2. Create a function that searches for an integer, *num*. If *num* is in the list, the function should return a pointer to the node that contains *num*. Otherwise it should return *NULL*.

3. Write a function that deletes a node containing a number, *num*, from a list. Use the search function (Exercise 2) to determine if *num* is in the list.

4. Write a function, *length*, that counts the number of nodes in a list.

5. Let p be a pointer to the first node in a singly linked list. Write a procedure to delete every other node beginning with node p (i.e., the first, third, fifth, etc. nodes of the list are deleted). What is the time complexity of your algorithm?

6. Let $x = (x_1, x_2, \ldots, x_n)$ and $y = (y_1, y_2, \ldots, y_m)$ be two linked lists. Assume that in each list, the nodes are in nondecreasing order of their data field values. Write an algorithm to merge the two lists together to obtain a new linked list z in which the nodes are also in this order. Following the merge, x and y do not exist as individual lists. Each node initially in x or y is now in z. No additional nodes may be used. What is the time complexity of your algorithm?

7. Let $list_1 = (x_1, x_2, \cdots, x_n)$ and $list_2 = (y_1, y_2, \cdots, y_m)$. Write a function to merge the two lists together to obtain the linked list, $list_3 = (x_1, y_1, x_2, y_2, \cdots, x_m, y_m, x_{m+1}, \cdots, x_n)$ if $m \leq n$; and $list_3 = (x_1, y_1, x_2, y_2, \cdots, x_n, y_n, x_{n+1}, \cdots, x_m)$ if $m > n$.

8. § It is possible to traverse a linked list in both directions (i.e., left to right and restricted right-to-left) by reversing the links during the left-to-right traversal. A possible configuration for the list, *ptr*, under this scheme is given in Figure 4.9. The variable *ptr* points to the node currently being examined and *left* to the node on its left. Note that all nodes to the left of *ptr* have their links reversed.

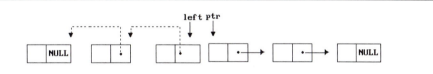

Figure 4.9: Configuration for reversing links

(a)   Write a function to move *ptr* to the right *n* nodes from a given position *(left, ptr)*.

(b)   Write a function to move *ptr* to the left *n* nodes from any given position *(left, ptr)*.

4.3   DYNAMICALLY LINKED STACKS AND QUEUES

Previously we represented stacks and queues sequentially. Such a representation proved efficient if we had only one stack or one queue. However, when several stacks and queues coexisted, there was no efficient way to represent them sequentially. Figure 4.10 shows a linked stack and a linked queue. Notice that the direction of links for both the stack and the queue facilitate easy insertion and deletion of nodes. In the case of Figure 4.10(a), we can easily add or delete a node from the top of the stack. In the case of Figure 4.10(b), we can easily add a node to the rear of the queue and add or delete a node at the front, although we normally will not add items to the front of a queue.

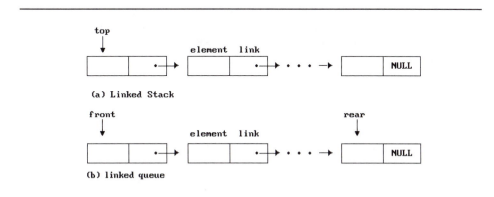

Figure 4.10: Linked stack and queue

If we wish to represent *n* stacks simultaneously, we begin with the declarations:

```
#define MAX_STACKS 10 /*maximum number of stacks*/
typedef struct {
        int key;
        /* other fields */
        } element;
typedef struct stack *stack_pointer;
typedef struct stack {
        element item;
        stack_pointer link;
        };
stack_pointer top[MAX_STACKS];
```

We assume that the initial condition for the stacks is:

$$top\,[i\,] = NULL,\ 0 \leq i < MAX\_STACKS$$

and the boundary conditions are:

$$top\,[i\,] = NULL \text{ iff the } i\text{th stack is empty}$$

and

$$IS\_FULL\,(temp\,) \text{ iff the memory is full}$$

Functions *add* (Program 4.6) and *delete* (Program 4.7) add and delete items to/from a stack. The code for each is straightforward. In both functions, we pass in the address of *top* so that *top* will point to the element that resides at the top of the stack. Function *add* creates a new node, *temp*, and places *item* in the item field and *top* in the link field. The variable *top* is then changed to point to *temp*. A typical function call would be *add* (&*top* [*stack _ no*],*item*). Function *delete* returns the item and changes *top* to point to the address contained in its link field. The removed node is then returned to system memory. A typical function call would be *item* = *delete* (&*top* [*stack _ no*]);

To represent *m* queues simultaneously, we begin with the declarations:

```
#define MAX_QUEUES 10 /* maximum number of queues */
typedef struct queue *queue_pointer;
typedef struct queue {
        element item;
        queue_pointer link;
        };
queue_pointer front[MAX_QUEUES], rear[MAX_QUEUES];
```

We assume that the initial condition for the queues is:

$$front[i] = NULL,\ 0 \leq i < MAX\_QUEUES$$

```
void add(stack_pointer *top, element item)
{
/* add an element to the top of the stack */
   stack_pointer temp =
                   (stack_pointer) malloc(sizeof (stack));
   if (IS_FULL(temp)) {
      fprintf(stderr, "The memory is full\n");
      exit(1);
   }
   temp->item = item;
   temp->link = *top;
   *top = temp;
}
```

Program 4.6: Add to a linked stack

```
element delete(stack_pointer *top) {
/* delete an element from the stack */
   stack_pointer temp = *top;
   element item;
   if (IS_EMPTY(temp)) {
      fprintf(stderr, "The stack is empty\n");
      exit(1);
   }
   item = temp->item;
   *top = temp->link;
   free(temp);
   return item;
}
```

Program 4.7: Delete from a linked stack

and the boundary conditions are:

$front[i]$ = NULL iff the ith queue is empty

and

$IS\_FULL(temp)$ iff the memory is full

Functions *addq* (Program 4.8) and *deleteq* (Program 4.9) implement the add and delete operations for multiple queues. Function *addq* is more complex than *add* because we must check for an empty queue. If the queue is empty, we change *front* to point to the new node; otherwise we change *rear*'s link field to point to the new node. In either case, we then change *rear* to point to the new node. Function *deleteq* is similar to *delete* since we are removing the node that is currently at the start of the list. Typical function calls would be *addq(&front, &rear, item)*; and *item = deleteq(&front)*;.

The solution presented above to the *n*-stack, *m*-queue problem is both computationally and conceptually simple. We no longer need to shift stacks or queues to make space. Computation can proceed as long as there is memory available. Although we need additional space for the link field, the use of linked lists makes sense because the overhead incurred by the storage of the links is overridden by (1) the ability to represent lists in a simple way, and (2) the reduced computing time required by linked representations.

EXERCISES

1. A palindrome is a word or phrase that is the same when spelled from the front or the back. For example, "reviver" and "Able was I ere I saw Elba" are both palindromes. We can determine if a word or phrase is a palindrome by using a stack. Write a C function that returns *TRUE* if a word or phrase is a palindrome and *FALSE* if it is not.

2. We can use a stack to determine if the parentheses in an expression are properly nested. Write a C function that does this.

3. Consider the hypothetical data type $X2$. $X2$ is a linear list with the restriction that while additions to the list may be made at either end, deletions can be made at one end only. Design a linked list representation for $X2$. Write addition and deletion functions for $X2$. Specify initial and boundary conditions for your representation.

4.4   POLYNOMIALS

4.4.1   Representing Polynomials As Singly Linked Lists

Let us tackle a reasonably complex problem using linked lists. This problem, the manipulation of symbolic polynomials, has become a classic example of list processing. As in Chapter 2, we wish to be able to represent any number of different polynomials as long as memory is available. In general, we want to represent the polynomial:

$$A(x) = a_{m-1}x^{e_{m-1}} + \cdots + a_0 x^{e_0}$$

where the a_i are nonzero coefficients and the e_i are nonnegative integer exponents such that $e_{m-1} > e_{m-2} > \cdots > e_1 > e_0 \geq 0$. We represent each term as a node containing

```
void addq(queue_pointer *front, queue_pointer *rear,
                         element item)
{
/* add an element to the rear of the queue */
   queue_pointer temp =
                      (queue_pointer) malloc(sizeof(queue));
   if (IS_FULL(temp)) {
      fprintf(stderr, "The memory is full\n");
      exit(1);
   }
   temp->item = item;
   temp->link = NULL;
   if (*front) (*rear)->link = temp;
   else *front = temp;
   *rear = temp;
}
```

Program 4.8: Add to the rear of a linked queue

```
element deleteq(queue_pointer *front)
{
/* delete an element from the queue */
   queue_pointer temp = *front;
   element item;
   if (IS_EMPTY(*front)) {
      fprintf(stderr, "The queue is empty\n");
      exit(1);
   }
   item = temp->item;
   *front= temp->link;
   free(temp);
   return item;
}
```

Program 4.9: Delete from the front of a linked queue

coefficient and exponent fields, as well as a pointer to the next term. Assuming that the coefficients are integers, the type declarations are:

```
typedef struct poly_node *poly_pointer;
typedef struct poly_node {
        int coef;
        int expon;
        poly_pointer link;
        };
poly_pointer a,b,d;
```

We draw *poly_node*s as:

coef	expon	link

Figure 4.11 shows how we would store the polynomials

$$a = 3x^{14} + 2x^8 + 1$$

and

$$b = 8x^{14} - 3x^{10} + 10x^6$$

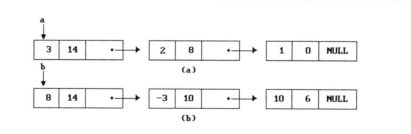

Figure 4.11: Polynomial representation

4.4.2   Adding Polynomials

To add two polynomials, we examine their terms starting at the nodes pointed to by a and b. If the exponents of the two terms are equal, we add the two coefficients and create a new term for the result. We also move the pointers to the next nodes in a and b. If the exponent of the current term in a is less than the exponent of the current term in b, then we create a duplicate term of b, attach this term to the result, called d, and advance the pointer to the next term in b. We take a similar action on a if $a->expon > b->expon$. Figure 4.12 illustrates this process for the polynomials represented in Figure 4.11.

Each time we generate a new node, we set its *coef* and *expon* fields and append it to the end of d. To avoid having to search for the last node in d each time we add a new node, we keep a pointer, *rear*, which points to the current last node in d. The complete

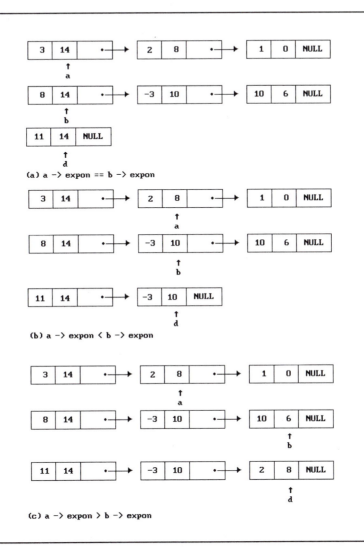

Figure 4.12: Generating the first three terms of $d = a + b$

addition algorithm is specified by *padd* (Program 4.10). To create a new node and append it to the end of d, *padd* uses *attach* (Program 4.11). To make things work out neatly, initially we give d a single node with no values, which we delete at the end of the function. Although this is somewhat inelegant, it avoids more computation.

This is our first complete example of list processing, so you should study it carefully. The basic algorithm is straightforward, using a streaming process that moves along the two polynomials, either copying terms or adding them to the result. Thus, the

```
poly_pointer padd(poly_pointer a, poly_pointer b)
{
/* return a polynomial which is the sum of a and b */
   poly_pointer front, rear, temp;
   int sum;
   rear = (poly_pointer)malloc(sizeof(poly_node));
   if (IS_FULL(rear)) {
      fprintf(stderr, "The memory is full\n");
      exit(1);
   }
   front = rear;
   while (a && b)
      switch (COMPARE(a->expon,b->expon)) {
         case -1: /* a->expon < b->expon */
               attach(b->coef,b->expon,&rear);
               b = b->link;
               break;
         case 0: /* a->expon = b->expon */
               sum = a->coef + b->coef;
               if (sum) attach(sum,a->expon,&rear);
               a = a->link;  b = b->link; break;
         case 1: /* a->expon > b->expon */
               attach(a->coef,a->expon,&rear);
               a = a->link;
      }
   /* copy rest of list a and then list b */
   for (; a; a = a->link) attach(a->coef,a->expon,&rear);
   for (; b; b = b->link) attach(b->coef,b->expon,&rear);
   rear->link = NULL;
   /* delete extra initial node */
   temp = front; front = front->link;  free(temp);
   return front;
}
```

Program 4.10: Add two polynomials

while loop has three cases depending on whether the next pair of exponents are =, < , or
>. Notice that there are five places where we create a new term, justifying our use of
function *attach*.

Analysis of *padd*: To determine the computing time of *padd*, we first determine which
operations contribute to the cost. For this algorithm, there are three cost measures:

```
void attach(float coefficient, int exponent, poly_pointer
                                  *ptr)
{
/* create a new node with coef = coefficient and expon =
exponent, attach it to the node pointed to by ptr.  ptr is
updated to point to this new node */
   poly_pointer temp;
   temp = (poly_pointer)malloc(sizeof(poly_node));
   if (IS_FULL(temp)) {
      fprintf(stderr, "The memory is full\n");
      exit(1);
   }
   temp->coef = coefficient;
   temp->expon = exponent;
   (*ptr)->link = temp;
   *ptr = temp;
}
```

Program 4.11: Attach a node to the end of a list

(1)   coefficient additions

(2)   exponent comparisons

(3)   creation of new nodes for d

If we assume that each of these operations takes a single unit of time if done once, then the number of times that we perform these operations determines the total time taken by *padd*. This number clearly depends on how many terms are present in the polynomials a and b. Assume that a and b have m and n terms, respectively:

$$A(x) = a_{m-1}x^{e_{m-1}} + \cdots + a_0 x^{e_0}$$

$$B(x) = b_{n-1}x^{f_{n-1}} + \cdots + b_0 x^{f_0}$$

where $a_i, b_i \neq 0$ and $e_{m-1} > \cdots > e_0 \geq 0$, $f_{n-1} > \cdots > f_0 \geq 0$. Then clearly the number of coefficient additions varies as:

$$0 \leq \text{number of coefficient additions} \leq \min\{m,n\}$$

The lower bound is achieved when none of the exponents are equal, while the upper is achieved when the exponents of one polynomial are a subset of the exponents of the other.

As for the exponent comparisons, we make one comparison on each iteration of the **while** loop. On each iteration, either a or b or both move to the next term. Since the total number of terms is $m + n$, the number of iterations and hence the number of exponent comparisons is bounded by $m + n$. You can easily construct a case when $m + n - 1$ comparisons will be necessary, for example, $m = n$ and

$$e_{m-1} > f_{m-1} > e_{m-2} > f_{m-2} > \cdots > e_1 > f_1 > e_0 > f_0$$

The maximum number of terms in d is $m + n$, and so no more than $m + n$ new terms are created (this excludes the additional node that is attached to the front of d and later removed).

In summary, the maximum number of executions of any statement in *padd* is bounded above by $m + n$. Therefore, the computing time is $O(m + n)$. This means that if we implement and run the algorithm on a computer, the time it takes will be $c_1 m + c_2 n + c_3$, where c_1, c_2, c_3 are constants. Since any algorithm that adds two polynomials must look at each nonzero term at least once, *padd* is optimal to within a constant factor. □

4.4.3 Erasing Polynomials

The use of linked lists is well suited to polynomial operations. We can easily imagine writing a collection of functions for input, output, addition, subtraction, and multiplication of polynomials using linked lists as the means of representation. A hypothetical user who wishes to read in polynomials $a(x)$, $b(x)$, and $d(x)$ and then compute $e(x) = a(x) * b(x) + d(x)$ would write his or her main function as:

```
poly_pointer a, b, d, e
   .
   .
   .
a = read_poly();
b = read_poly();
d = read_poly();
temp = pmult(a,b);
e = padd(temp,d);
print_poly(e);
```

If our user wishes to compute more polynomials, it would be useful to reclaim the nodes that are being used to represent *temp* (x) since we created *temp* (x) only to hold a partial result for $d(x)$. By returning the nodes of *temp* (x), we may use them to hold other polynomials. One by one, *erase* (Program 4.12) frees the nodes in *temp*.

```
void erase(poly_pointer *ptr)
{
/* erase the polynomial pointed to by ptr */
   poly_pointer temp;
   while (*ptr) {
      temp = *ptr;
      *ptr = (*ptr)->link;
      free(temp);
   }
}
```

Program 4.12: Erasing a polynomial

4.4.4 Representing Polynomials As Circularly Linked Lists

We can free all the nodes of a polynomial more efficiently if we modify our list structure so that the link field of the last node points to the first node in the list (See Figure 4.13). We call this a *circular list*. A singly linked list in which the last node has a null link is called a *chain*.

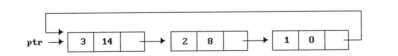

Figure 4.13: Circular representation of $ptr = 3x^{14} + 2x^8 + 1$

As we indicated earlier, we free nodes that are no longer in use so that we may reuse these nodes later. We can meet this objective, and obtain an efficient erase algorithm for circular lists, by maintaining our own list (as a chain) of nodes that have been "freed." When we need a new node, we examine this list. If the list is not empty, then we may use one of its nodes. Only when the list is empty do we need to use *malloc* to create a new node.

Let *avail* be a variable of type *poly_pointer* that points to the first node in our list of freed nodes. Henceforth, we call this list the available space list or *avail* list. Initially, we set *avail* to *NULL*. Instead of using *malloc* and *free*, we now use *get_node* (Program 4.13) and *ret_node* (Program 4.14).

```
poly_pointer get_node(void)
/* provide a node for use */
{
   poly_pointer node;
   if (avail) {
      node = avail;
      avail = avail->link;
   }
   else {
      node = (poly_pointer) malloc(sizeof(poly_node));
      if (IS_FULL(node)) {
         fprintf(stderr, "The memory is full\n");
         exit(1);
      }
   }
   return node;
}
```

Program 4.13: *get_node* function

```
void ret_node(poly_pointer ptr)
{
/* return a node to the available list */
   ptr->link = avail;
   avail = ptr;
}
```

Program 4.14: *ret_node* function

We may erase a circular list in a fixed amount of time independent of the number of nodes in the list using *cerase* (Program 4.15). Figure 4.14 shows the changes involved in erasing a circular list.

A direct changeover to the structure of Figure 4.13 creates problems when we implement the other polynomial operations since we must handle the zero polynomial as a special case. To avoid this special case, we introduce a *head node* into each polynomial, that is, each polynomial, zero or nonzero, contains one additional node. The *expon* and *coef* fields of this node are irrelevant. Thus, the zero polynomial has the representation of Figure 4.15(a), while $a(x) = 3x^{14} + 2x^8 + 1$ has the representation of Figure 4.15(b).

```
void cerase(poly_pointer *ptr)
{
/* erase the circular list ptr */
   poly_pointer temp;
   if (*ptr) {
      temp = (*ptr)->link;
      (*ptr)->link = avail;
      avail = temp;
      *ptr = NULL;
   }
}
```

Program 4.15: Erasing a circular list

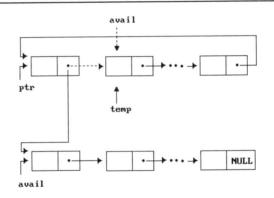

Figure 4.14: Returning a circular list to the avail list

For the circular list with head node representation, we may remove the test for (*ptr) from *cerase*. The only changes that we need to make to *padd* are:

(1)   Add two variables, *starta* = *a* and *startb* = *b*.

(2)   Prior to the **while** loop, assign *a* = *a*->*link* and *b* = *b*->*link*.

(3)   Change the **while** loop to **while** (*a* != *starta* && *b* != *startb*).

(a) Zero polynomial

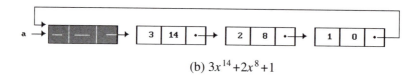

(b) $3x^{14}+2x^8+1$

Figure 4.15: Polynomial representations

(4)   Change the first **for** loop to **for** (; *a* != *starta*; *a* = *a*–>*link*).

(5)   Change the second **for** loop to **for** (; *b* != *startb*; *b* = *b*–>*link*).

(6)   Delete the lines:

> *rear*–>*link* = *NULL;*
> /* *delete extra initial node* */

(7)   Change the lines:

> *temp* = *front;*
> *front* = *front*–>*link;*
> *free*(*temp*);

to

> *rear*–>*link* = *front;*

Thus, the algorithm stays essentially the same, and we now handle zero polynomials in the same way as nonzero polynomials.

We may further simplify the addition algorithm if we set the *expon* field of the head node to −1. Now after we have examined all the nodes of *a*, *starta* = *a* and *starta*–>*expon* = −1. Since −1 ≤ *b*–>*expon*, we can copy the remaining terms of *b* by further executions of the **switch** statement. The same is true if we examine all the nodes of *b* before those of *a*. This means that we no longer need the additional code to copy the remaining terms. The final algorithm, *cpadd*, takes the simple form given in Program 4.16.

```
poly_pointer cpadd(poly_pointer a, poly_pointer b)
{
/* polynomials a and b are singly linked circular lists
with a head node. Return a polynomial which is the sum
of a and b */
   poly_pointer starta, d, lastd;
   int sum, done = FALSE;
   starta = a;              /* record start of a */
   a = a->link;             /* skip head node for a and b*/
   b = b->link;
   d = get_node();          /* get a head node for sum */
   d->expon = -1; lastd = d;
   do {
      switch (COMPARE(a->expon, b->expon)) {
         case -1: /* a->expon < b->expon */
                 attach(b->coef,b->expon,&lastd);
                 b = b->link;
                 break;
         case 0:  /* a->expon = b->expon */
                 if (starta == a)  done = TRUE;
                 else {
                     sum = a->coef + b->coef;
                     if (sum) attach(sum,a->expon,&lastd);
                     a = a->link; b = b->link;
                 }
                 break;
         case 1:  /* a->expon > b->expon */
                 attach(a->coef,a->expon,&lastd);
                 a = a->link;
      }
   } while (!done);
   lastd->link = d;
   return d;
}
```

Program 4.16: Adding circularly represented polynomials

4.4.5 Summary

Let us review what we have done so far. We have introduced the concepts of a singly linked list, a chain, and a singly linked circular list. Each node on one of these lists consists of exactly one link field and at least one other field.

In dealing with polynomials, we found it convenient to use circular lists. Another concept we introduced was an available space list. This list consisted of all nodes that had been used at least once and were not currently in use. By using the available space list and *get_node*, *ret_node*, and *cerase*, it became possible to erase circular lists in constant time, and also to reuse all nodes not currently in use. As we continue, we shall see more problems that call for variations in node structure and list representation because of the operations we wish to perform.

EXERCISES

1. Write a function, *pread*, that reads in n pairs of coefficients and exponents, ($coef_i$, $expon_i$), $0 \le i < n$ of a polynomial, x. Assume that $expon_{i+1} > expon_i$, $0 \le i < n-2$, and that $coef_i \ne 0$, $0 \le i < n$. Show that this operation can be performed in O(n) time.

2. Let a and b be pointers to two polynomials. Write a function to compute the product polynomial $d = a*b$. Your function should leave a and b unaltered and create d as a new list. Show that if n and m are the number of terms in a and b, respectively, then this multiplication can be carried out in O(nm^2) or O(n^2m) time.

3. Let a be a pointer to a polynomial. Write a function, *peval*, to evaluate the polynomial a at point x, where x is some floating point number.

4. Rewrite Exercise 1 using a circular representation for the polynomial.

5. Rewrite Exercise 2 using a circular representation for the polynomial.

6. Rewrite Exercise 3 using a circular representation for the polynomial.

7. § [***Programming project***] Design and build a linked allocation system to represent and manipulate polynomials. You should use circularly linked lists with head nodes. Each term of the polynomial will be represented as a node, using the following structure:

coef	expon	link

In order to erase polynomials efficiently, use the available space list and associated functions discussed in this section.

Write and test the following functions:

(a)   *pread*. Read in a polynomial and convert it to its circular representation. Return a pointer to the head node of this polynomial.

(b) *pwrite*. Output the polynomial using a form that clearly displays it.

(c) *padd*. Compute $d = a + b$. Do not change either a or b.

(d) *psub*. Compute $d = a - b$. Do not change either a or b.

(e) *pmult*. Compute $d = a*b$. Do not change either a or b.

(f) *eval*. Evaluate a polynomial at some point, a, where a is a floating point constant. Return the result as a floating point.

(g) *perase*. Return the polynomial represented as a circular list to the available space list.

4.5 ADDITIONAL LIST OPERATIONS

4.5.1 Operations For Chains

It is often necessary, and desirable, to build a variety of functions for manipulating singly linked lists. Some that we have seen already are *get_node* and *ret_node*, which get and return nodes to the available space list. Inverting (or reversing) a chain (Program 4.17) is another useful operation. This routine is especially interesting because we can do it "in place" if we use three pointers. We use the following declarations:

```
typedef struct list_node *list_pointer;
typedef struct list_node {
        char data;
        list_pointer link;
        };
```

Try out this function with at least three examples, an empty list and lists of one and two nodes, so that you understand how it works. For a list of *length* ≥ 1 nodes, the **while** loop is executed *length* times and so the computing time is linear or O(*length*).

Another useful function is one that concatenates two chains, *ptr*1 and *ptr*2 (Program 4.18). The complexity of this function is O(length of list *ptr*1). Since this function does not allocate additional storage for the new list, *ptr*1 also contains the concatenated list. (The exercises explore a concatenation function that does not alter *ptr*1.)

4.5.2 Operations For Circularly Linked Lists

Now let us take another look at circular lists like the one in Figure 4.16. Suppose we want to insert a new node at the front of this list. We have to change the link field of the node containing x_3. This means that we must move down the entire length of a until we find the last node. It is more convenient if the name of the circular list points to the last node rather than the first (Figure 4.16). Now we can write functions that insert a node at the front (Figure 4.17) or at the rear of a circular list in a fixed amount of time. To insert

```
list_pointer invert(list_pointer lead)
{
/* invert the list pointed to by lead */
   list_pointer middle,trail;
   middle = NULL;
   while (lead) {
      trail = middle;
      middle = lead;
      lead = lead->link;
      middle->link = trail;
   }
   return middle;
}
```

Program 4.17: Inverting a singly linked list

```
list_pointer concatenate(list_pointer ptr1,
                         list_pointer ptr2)
{
/* produce a new list that contains the list ptr1 followed
by the list ptr2. The list pointed to by ptr1 is changed
permanently */
   list_pointer temp;
   if (IS_EMPTY(ptr1)) return ptr2;
   else {
      if (!IS_EMPTY(ptr2)) {
         for (temp = ptr1; temp->link; temp = temp->link)
            ;
         temp->link = ptr2;
      }
      return ptr1;
   }
}
```

Program 4.18: Concatenating singly linked lists

node at the rear, we only need to add the additional statement **ptr = node* to the **else** clause of *insert_front* (Program 4.19).

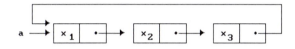

Figure 4.16: Example circular list

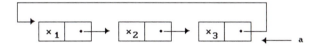

Figure 4.17: Pointing to the last node of a circular list

As a last example of a simple function for circular lists, we write a function (Program 4.20) that determines the length of such a list.

```
void insert_front(list_pointer *ptr, list_pointer node)
/* insert node at the front of the circular list ptr,
where ptr is the last node in the list */
{
   if (IS_EMPTY(*ptr)) {
   /* list is empty, change ptr to point to new entry */
      *ptr = node;
      node->link = node;
   }
   else {
   /* list is not empty, add new entry at front */
      node->link = (*ptr)->link;
      (*ptr)->link = node;
   }
}
```

Program 4.19: Inserting at the front of a list

```
int length(list_pointer ptr)
{
/* find the length of the circular list ptr */
   list_pointer temp;
   int count = 0;
   if (ptr) {
      temp = ptr;
      do {
         count++;
         temp = temp->link;
      } while (temp != ptr);
   }
   return count;
}
```

Program 4.20: Finding the length of a circular list

EXERCISES

1. Create a function that searches for an integer, *num*, in a circularly linked list. The function should return a pointer to the node that contains *num* if *num* is in the list and *NULL* otherwise.

2. Write a function that deletes a node containing a number, *num*, from a circularly linked list. Your function should first search for *num*.

3. Write a function to concatenate two circular lists together. Assume that the pointer to each such list points to the last node. Your function should return a pointer to the last node of the concatenated circular list. Following the concatenation, the input lists do not exist independently. What is the time complexity of your function?

4. Write a function to reverse the direction of pointers in a circular list.

4.6 EQUIVALENCE RELATIONS

Let us put together some of the concepts on linked and sequential representations to solve a problem that arises in the design and manufacture of very large-scale integrated (VLSI) circuits. One of the steps in the manufacture of a VLSI circuit involves exposing a silicon wafer using a series of masks. Each mask consists of several polygons. Polygons that overlap electrically are equivalent and electrical equivalence specifies a relationship among mask polygons. This relation has several properties that it shares with other equivalence relations, such as the standard mathematical equals. Suppose that we denote an arbitrary equivalence relation by the symbol $\equiv$ and that:

(1) For any polygon x, $x \equiv x$, that is, x is electrically equivalent to itself. Thus, $\equiv$ is reflexive.

(2) For any two polygons, x and y, if $x \equiv y$ then $y \equiv x$. Thus, the relation $\equiv$ is symmetric.

(3) For any three polygons, x, y, and z, if $x \equiv y$ and $y \equiv z$ then $x \equiv z$. For example, if x and y are electrically equivalent and y and z are also equivalent, then x and z are also electrically equivalent. Thus, the relation $\equiv$ is transitive.

Definition: A relation, $\equiv$, over a set, S, is said to be an *equivalence relation* over S *iff* it is symmetric, reflexive, and transitive over S. $\square$

Examples of equivalence relations are numerous. For example, the "equal to" $(=)$ relationship is an equivalence relation since

(1) $x = x$

(2) $x = y$ implies $y = x$

(3) $x = y$ and $y = z$ implies that $x = z$

We can use an equivalence relation to partition a set S into equivalence classes such that two members x and y of S are in the same equivalence class *iff* $x \equiv y$. For example, if we have twelve polygons numbered 0 through 11 and the following pairs overlap:

$$0 \equiv 4, 3 \equiv 1, 6 \equiv 10, 8 \equiv 9, 7 \equiv 4, 6 \equiv 8, 3 \equiv 5, 2 \equiv 11, 11 \equiv 0$$

then, as a result of the reflexivity, symmetry, and transitivity of the relation $\equiv$, we can partition the twelve polygons into the following equivalence classes:

$$\{0, 2, 4, 7, 11\}; \{1, 3, 5\}; \{6, 8, 9, 10\}$$

These equivalence classes are important because they define a signal net that we can use to verify the correctness of the masks.

The algorithm to determine equivalence works in two phases. In the first phase, we read in and store the equivalence pairs $<i, j>$. In the second phase we begin at 0 and find all pairs of the form $<0, j>$, where 0 and j are in the same equivalence class. By transitivity, all pairs of the form $<j, k>$ imply that k is in the same equivalence class as 0. We continue in this way until we have found, marked, and printed the entire equivalence class containing 0. Then we continue on.

Our first design attempt appears in Program 4.21. Let m and n represent the number of related pairs and the number of objects, respectively. We first must figure out which data structure we should use to hold these pairs. To determine this, we examine the operations that are required. The pair $<i, j>$ is essentially two random integers in the range 0 to $n-1$. Easy random access would dictate an array, say *pairs[n][m]*. The ith row would contain the elements, *j*, that are paired directly to *i* in the input. However, this could waste a lot of space since very few of the array elements would be used. It also might require considerable time to insert a new pair, <*i, k*>, into row *i* since we would have to scan the row for the next free location or use more storage.

```
void equivalence()
{
   initialize;
   while (there are more pairs) {
      read the next pair <i,j>;
      process this pair;
   }
   initialize the output;
   do
      output a new equivalence class;
   while (not done);
}
```

Program 4.21: First pass at equivalence algorithm

These considerations lead us to a linked list representation for each row. Our node structure requires only a data and a link field. However, since we still need random access to the *i*th row, we use a one-dimensional array, *seq* [*n*], to hold the head nodes of the *n* lists. For the second phase of the algorithm, we need a mechanism that tells us whether or not the object, *i*, has been printed. We use the array *out* [*n*] and the constants *TRUE* and *FALSE* for this purpose. Our next refinement appears in Program 4.22.

Let us simulate this algorithm, as we have developed it thus far, using the previous data set. After the **while** loop is completed the lists resemble those appearing in Figure 4.18. For each relation $i \equiv j$, we use two nodes. The variable *seq* [*i*] points to the list of nodes that contains every number that is directly equivalent to *i* by an input relation.

In phase two, we scan the *seq* array for the first *i*, $0 \le i < n$, such that *out* [*i*] = *TRUE*. Each element in the list *seq* [*i*] is printed. To process the remaining lists which, by transitivity, belong in the same class as *i*, we create a stack of their nodes. We do this by changing the link fields so that they point in the reverse direction. Program 4.23 contains the complete equivalence algorithm.

```
#include <stdio.h>
#include <alloc.h>
#define MAX_SIZE 24
#define IS_FULL(ptr) (!(ptr))
#define FALSE 0
#define TRUE 1
```

```
void equivalence()
{
   initialize seq to NULL and out to TRUE;
   while (there are more pairs) {
      read the next pair, <i,j>;
      put j on the seq[i] list;
      put i on the seq[j] list;
   }
   for (i = 0; i < n; i++)
      if (out[i]) {
         out[i] = FALSE;
         output this equivalence class;
      }
}
```

Program 4.22: A more detailed version of the equivalence algorithm

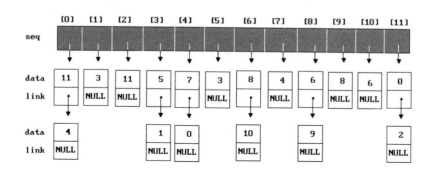

Figure 4.18: Lists after pairs are input

```
typedef struct node *node_pointer;
typedef struct node {
        int data;
        node_pointer link;
        };
void main(void)
{
   short int out[MAX_SIZE];
   node_pointer seq[MAX_SIZE];
```

```
node_pointer x,y,top;
int i,j,n;

printf("Enter the size (<= %d) ",MAX_SIZE);
scanf("%d",&n);
for (i = 0; i < n; i++) {
/* initialize seq and out */
   out[i] = TRUE;    seq[i] = NULL;
}

/* Phase 1: Input the equivalence pairs: */
printf("Enter a pair of numbers (-1 -1 to quit): ");
scanf("%d%d",&i,&j);
while (i >= 0) {
   x = (node_pointer)malloc(sizeof(node));
   if (IS_FULL(x)) {
      fprintf(stderr,"The memory is full\n");
      exit(1);
   }
   x->data = j;  x->link = seq[i];  seq[i] = x;
   x = (node_pointer)malloc(sizeof(node));
   if (IS_FULL(x)) {
      fprintf(stderr, "The memory is full\n");
      exit(1);
   }
   x->data = i;  x->link = seq[j];  seq[j] = x;
   printf("Enter a pair of numbers (-1 -1 to quit): ");
   scanf("%d%d",&i,&j);
}

/* Phase 2: output the equivalence classes */
for (i = 0; i < n; i++)
   if (out[i]) {
      printf("\nNew class: %5d",i);
      out[i] = FALSE;   /* set class to false */
      x = seq[i]; top = NULL; /* initialize stack */
      for (;;) {      /* find rest of class */
         while (x) {  /* process list */
            j = x->data;
            if (out[j]) {
               printf("%5d",j);  out[j] = FALSE;
               y = x->link; x->link = top; top = x; x = y;
            }
            else x = x->link;
```

```
        }
        if (!top) break;
        x = seq[top->data]; top = top->link; /*unstack*/
    }
  }
}
```

Program 4.23: Program to find equivalence classes

Analysis of the equivalence program: The initialization of *seq* and *out* takes $O(n)$ time. Inputting the equivalence pairs in phase 1 takes a constant amount of time per pair. Hence, the total time for this phase is $O(m +n)$ where m is the number of pairs input. In phase 2, we put each node onto the linked stack at most once. Since there are only $2m$ nodes, and we execute the **for** loop n times, the time for this phase is $O(m + n)$. Thus, the overall computing time is $O(m + n)$. Any algorithm that processes equivalence relations must look at all m equivalence pairs and at all n polygons at least once. Thus, there is no algorithm with a computing time less than $O(m+n)$. This means that the equivalence algorithm is optimal to within a constant factor. Unfortunately, the space required by the algorithm is also $O(m + n)$. In Chapter 5, we look at an alternate solution to this problem that requires only $O(n)$ space. □

4.7 SPARSE MATRICES

In Chapter 2, we saw that we could save space and computing time by retaining only the nonzero terms of sparse matrices. When the nonzero terms did not form a "nice" pattern, such as a triangle or a band, we devised a sequential scheme in which we represented each nonzero term by a node with three fields: *row, column,* and *value*. We organized these nodes sequentially. However, we found that when we performed matrix operations such as addition, subtraction, or multiplication, the number of nonzero terms varied. Matrices representing partial computations, as in the case of polynomials, were created and later destroyed to make space for further matrices. Thus, the sequential representation of sparse matrices suffered from the same inadequacies as the similar representation of polynomials. In this section, we study a linked list representation for sparse matrices. As we have seen previously, linked lists allow us to efficiently represent structures that vary in size, a benefit that also applies to sparse matrices.

In our data representation, we represent each column of a sparse matrix as a circularly linked list with a head node. We use a similar representation for each row of a sparse matrix. Each node has a tag field, which we use to distinguish between head nodes and entry nodes. Each head node has three additional fields: *down, right,* and *next* (Figure 4.19(a)). We use the *down* field to link into a column list and the *right* field to link into a row list. The *next* field links the head nodes together. The head node for row i is also the head node for column i, and the total number of head nodes is max {number of rows, number of columns}.

Each entry node has five fields in addition to the tag field: *row, col, down, right, value* (Figure 4.19(b)). We use the *down* field to link to the next nonzero term in the same column and the *right* field to link to the next nonzero term in the same row. Thus, if $a_{ij} \neq 0$, there is a node with tag field = *entry*, *value* = a_{ij}, *row* = i, and *col* = j (Figure 4.19(c)). We link this node into the circular linked lists for row i and column j. Hence, it is simultaneously linked into two different lists.

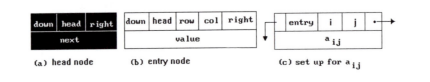

Figure 4.19: Node structure for sparse matrices

As we indicated earlier, each head node is in three lists: a list of rows, a list of columns, and a list of head nodes. The list of head nodes also has a head node that has the same structure as an entry node (Figure 4.19(b)). We use the *row* and *col* fields of this node to store the matrix dimensions.

Suppose that we have the sample sparse matrix, *a*, shown in Figure 4.20. Figure 4.21 shows the linked representation of this matrix. Although we have not shown the value of the tag fields, we can easily determine these values from the node structure. For each nonzero term of *a*, we have one entry node that is in exactly one row list and one column list. The head nodes are marked *H*0-*H*3. As the figure shows, we use the *right* field of the head node list header to link into the list of head nodes. Notice also that we may reference the entire matrix through the head node, *a*, of the list of head nodes.

$$\begin{bmatrix} 0 & 0 & 11 & 0 \\ 12 & 0 & 0 & 0 \\ 0 & -4 & 0 & 0 \\ 0 & 0 & 0 & -15 \end{bmatrix}$$

Figure 4.20: 4×4 sparse matrix *a*

If we wish to represent a *num_rows* $\times$ *num_cols* matrix with *num_terms* nonzero terms, then we need max $\{num\_rows, num\_cols\}$ + *num_terms* + 1 nodes. While each node may require several words of memory, the total storage will be less than *num_rows* $\cdot$ *num_cols* when *num_terms* is sufficiently small.

Having chosen our sparse matrix representation, we may now translate it into C declarations. Since we have two different types of nodes in our representation, we use a **union** to create the appropriate data structure. This means that our data structure is more complex than any structure we have created previously. The necessary declarations are

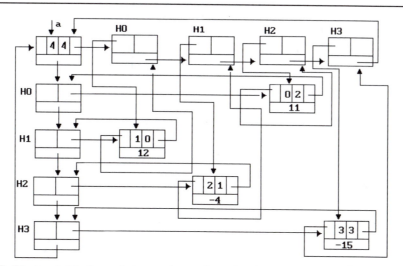

NOTE: The tag field of a node is not shown; its value for each node should be clear from the node structure.

Figure 4.21: Linked representation of the sparse matrix *a*

as follows:

```
#define MAX_SIZE 50 /*size of largest matrix*/
typedef enum {head,entry} tagfield;
typedef struct matrix_node *matrix_pointer;
typedef struct entry_node {
        int row;
        int col;
        int value;
        };
typedef struct matrix_node {
        matrix_pointer down;
        matrix_pointer right;
        tagfield tag;
        union {
            matrix_pointer next;
            entry_node entry;
            } u;
        };
matrix_pointer hdnode[MAX_SIZE];
```

The first operation we implement is that of reading in a sparse matrix and obtaining its linked representation. We assume that the first input line consists of the number of rows (*num_rows*), the number of columns (*num_cols*), and the number of nonzero terms (*num_terms*). This line is followed by *num_terms* lines of input, each of which is of the form: *row, col, value*. We assume that these lines are ordered by rows and within rows by columns. For example, Figure 4.22 shows the input for the 4×4 matrix of Figure 4.20.

	[0]	[1]	[2]
[0]	4	4	4
[1]	0	2	11
[2]	1	0	12
[3]	2	1	−4
[4]	3	3	−15

Figure 4.22: Sample input for sparse matrix

The function *mread* (Program 4.24) uses an auxiliary array, *hdnode*, which we assume is at least as large as the largest-dimensioned matrix to be input. The variable *hdnode[i]* is a pointer to the head node for column *i* and row *i*. This allows us to access efficiently columns at random, while we are setting up the input matrix. The function *mread* first sets up all the head nodes and then sets up each row list while simultaneously building the column lists. The *next* field of head node, *i*, is initially used to keep track of the last node in column *i*. The last **for** loop of the function links the head nodes together through this field.

```
matrix_pointer mread(void)
{
/* read in a matrix and set up its linked representation.
An auxiliary global array hdnode is used */
    int num_rows, num_cols,  num_terms, num_heads, i;
    int row, col, value, current_row;
    matrix_pointer temp,last,node;

    printf("Enter the number of rows, columns
                    and number of nonzero terms: ");
    scanf("%d%d%d",&num_rows, &num_cols, &num_terms);
    num_heads = (num_cols > num_rows) ? num_cols : num_rows;
    /* set up head node for the list of head nodes */
    node = new_node(); node->tag = entry;
```

```
node->u.entry.row = num_rows;
node->u.entry.col = num_cols;

if (!num_heads) node->right = node;
else { /* initialize the head nodes */
   for (i = 0; i < num_heads; i++) {
      temp = new_node;
      hdnode[i] = temp; hdnode[i]->tag = head;
      hdnode[i]->right = temp;  hdnode[i]->u.next = temp;
   }
   current_row = 0;
   last = hdnode[0]; /* last node in current row */
   for (i = 0; i < num_terms; i++) {
      printf("Enter row, column and value: ");
      scanf("%d%d%d",&row,&col,&value);
      if (row > current_row) {/* close current row */
         last->right = hdnode[current_row];
         current_row = row; last = hdnode[row];
      }
      temp = new_node();
      temp->tag = entry;  temp->u.entry.row = row;
      temp->u.entry.col = col;
      temp->u.entry.value = value;
      last->right = temp; /* link into row list */
      last = temp;
      /* link into column list */
      hdnode[col]->u.next->down = temp;
      hdnode[col]->u.next = temp;
   }
   /*close last row */
   last->right = hdnode[current_row];
   /* close all column lists */
   for (i = 0; i < num_cols; i++)
      hdnode[i]->u.next->down = hdnode[i];
   /* link all head nodes together */
   for (i = 0; i < num_heads-1; i++)
      hdnode[i]->u.next = hdnode[i+1];
   hdnode[num_heads-1]->u.next =  node;
   node->right = hdnode[0];
}
return node;
}
```

Program 4.24: Read in a sparse matrix

```
matrix_pointer new_node(void)
{
   matrix_pointer temp;
   temp = (matrix_pointer) malloc(sizeof(matrix_node));
   if (IS_FULL(temp)) {
      fprintf(stderr, "The memory is full\n");
      exit(1);
   }
   return temp;
}
```

Program 4.25: Get a new matrix node

Analysis of *mread*: Since *malloc* works in a constant amount of time, we can set up all of the head nodes in O(max {*num_rows,num_cols*}) time. We can also set up each nonzero term in a constant amount of time because we use the variable *last* to keep track of the current row, while *next* keeps track of the current column. Thus, the **for** loop that inputs and links the entry nodes requires only O(*num_terms*) time. The remainder of the function takes O(max {*num_rows,num_cols*}) time. Therefore, the total time is:

$$O(\max \{num\_rows, num\_cols\} + num\_terms)$$

$$= O(num\_rows + num\_cols + num\_terms).$$

Notice that this is asymptotically better than the input time of O(*num_rows · num_cols*) for a *num_rows* × *num_cols* matrix using a two-dimensional array. However it is slightly worse than the sequential method used in Section 2.4. □

We would now like to print out the contents of a sparse matrix in a form that resembles that found in Figure 4.22. The function *mwrite* (Program 4.26) implements this operation.

Analysis of *mwrite*: The function *mwrite* uses two **for** loops. The number of iterations of the outer **for** loop is *num_rows*. For any row, *i*, the number of iterations of the inner **for** loop is equal to the number of entries for row *i*. Therefore, the computing time of the *mwrite* function is O(*num_rows + num_terms*). □

Before closing this section we want to look at an algorithm that returns all nodes of a sparse matrix to the system memory. We return the nodes one at a time using *free*, although we could develop a faster algorithm using an available space list (see Section 4.4). The function *merase* (Program 4.27) implements the erase operation.

Analysis of *merase*: First, *merase* returns the entry nodes and the row head nodes to the

```
void mwrite(matrix-pointer node)
{
/* print out the matrix in row major form */
    int i;
    matrix-pointer temp, head = node->right;
    /* matrix dimensions */
    printf(" \n num-rows = %d, num-cols = %d \n",
                    node->u.entry.row, node->u.entry.col);
    printf(" The matrix by row, column, and value: \n\n");
    for (i = 0; i < node->u.entry.row; i++) {
    /* print out the entries in each row */
        for (temp = head->right; temp != head;
                                           temp = temp->right)
            printf("%5d%5d%5d \n",temp->u.entry.row,
                    temp->u.entry.col, temp->u.entry.value);
        head = head->u.next; /* next row */
    }
}
```

Program 4.26: Write out a sparse matrix

system memory. It uses a nested loop structure that resembles the structure found in *mwrite*. Thus, the computing time for the nested loops is O($num\_rows + num\_terms$). After these nodes are erased the remaining head nodes are erased. This requires O($num\_rows + num\_cols$) time. Hence, the computing time for *merase* is O($num\_rows + num\_cols + num\_terms$). □

EXERCISES

1. Let *a* and *b* be two sparse matrices. Write a function, *madd*, to create the matrix *d* = *a* + *b*. Your function should leave matrices *a* and *b* unchanged, and set up *d* as a new matrix. Show that if *a* and *b* are $num\_rows \times num\_cols$ matrices with num_terms_a and num_terms_b nonzero terms, then we can perform this addition in O($num\_rows + num\_cols + num\_terms_a + num\_terms_b$) time.

2. Let *a* and *b* be two sparse matrices. Write a function, *mmult*, to create the matrix *d* = *a**b. Show that if *a* is a $num\_rows_a \times num\_cols_a$ matrix with num_terms_a nonzero terms and *b* is a $num\_cols_a \times num\_cols_b$ matrix with num_terms_b nonzero terms, then we can compute *d* in O($num\_cols_b \cdot num\_terms_a + num\_rows_a \cdot num\_terms_b$) time. Can you think of a way to compute *d* in O(min $\{num\_cols_b \cdot num\_terms_a, num\_rows_a \cdot num\_terms_b\}$) time?

```
void merase(matrix_pointer *node)
{
/* erase the matrix, return the nodes to the heap */
   matrix_pointer x,y, head = (*node)->right;
   int i, num_heads;
   /* free the entry and head nodes by row */
   for (i = 0; i < (*node)->u.entry.row; i++) {
      y = head->right;
      while (y != head) {
         x = y; y = y->right; free(x);
      }
      x = head; head = head->u.next; free(x);
   }
   /* free remaining head nodes*/
   y = head;
   while (y != *node) {
      x = y; y = y->u.next; free(x);
   }
   free(*node); *node = NULL;
}
```

Program 4.27: Erase a sparse matrix

3. (a) Rewrite *merase* so that it places the erased list into an available space list rather than returning it to system memory.

   (b) Rewrite *mread* so that it first attempts to obtain a new node from the available space list rather than the system memory.

4. Write a function, *mtranspose*, to compute the matrix $b = a^T$, the transpose of the sparse matrix a. What is the computing time of your function?

5. Design a function that copies a sparse matrix. What is the computing time of your function?

6. § [*Programming project*] We want to implement a complete linked list system to perform arithmetic on sparse matrices using our linked list representation. Create a user-friendly, menu-driven system that performs the following operations. (The matrix names are used only for illustrative purposes. The functions are specified as templates to which you must add the appropriate parameters.)

   (a) *mread*. Read in a sparse matrix.

(b)   *mwrite*. Write out the contents of a sparse matrix.

(c)   *merase*. Erase a sparse matrix.

(d)   *madd*. Create the sparse matrix $d = a + b$

(e)   *mmult*. Create the sparse matrix $d = a*b$.

(f)   *mtranspose*. Create the sparse matrix $b = a^T$.

4.8   DOUBLY LINKED LISTS

Singly linked lists pose problems because we can move easily only in the direction of the links. For example, suppose that we are pointing to a specific node, say *ptr*, and we want to find the node that precedes *ptr*. We can only do this by starting at the beginning of the list and searching until we find the node whose link field points to *ptr*. Since we must know the preceding node for the deletion operation, we obviously cannot perform this operation efficiently with singly linked lists. Whenever we have a problem that requires us to move in either direction, it is useful to have doubly linked lists.

A node in a doubly linked list has at least three fields, a left link field (*llink*), a data field (*item*), and a right link field (*rlink*). The necessary declarations are:

```
typedef struct node *node_pointer;
typedef struct node {
        node_pointer llink;
        element item;
        node_pointer rlink;
        };
```

A doubly linked list may or may not be circular. A sample doubly linked circular list with three nodes is given in Figure 4.23. Besides these three nodes, we have added a head node. As was true in previous sections, a head node allows us to implement our operations more easily. The item field of the head node usually contains no information.

Now suppose that *ptr* points to any node in a doubly linked list. Then:

$$ptr = ptr->llink->rlink = ptr->rlink->llink$$

This formula reflects the essential virtue of this structure, namely, that we can go back and forth with equal ease. An empty list is not really empty since it always has a head node whose structure is illustrated in Figure 4.24.

To use these lists we must be able to insert and delete nodes. Insertion into a doubly linked list is fairly easy. Assume that we have two nodes, *node* and *newnode*, *node* may be either a head node or an interior node in a list. The function *dinsert* (Program 4.28) performs the insertion operation in constant time. Figure 4.25 shows this insertion process when *node* represents the head node of an empty list.

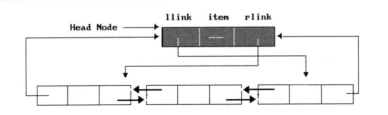

Figure 4.23: Doubly linked circular list with head node

Figure 4.24: Empty doubly linked circular list with head node

```
void dinsert(node_pointer node, node_pointer newnode)
{
/* insert newnode to the right of node */
   newnode->llink = node;
   newnode->rlink = node->rlink;
   node->rlink->llink = newnode;
   node->rlink = newnode;
}
```

Program 4.28: Insertion into a doubly linked circular list

Deletion from a doubly linked list is equally easy. The function *ddelete* (Program 4.29) deletes the node *deleted* from the list pointed to by node. To accomplish this deletion, we only need to change the link fields of the nodes that precede (*deleted−>llink−>rlink*) and follow (*deleted−>rlink−>llink*) the node we want to delete. Figure 4.26 shows the deletion in a doubly linked list with a single node.

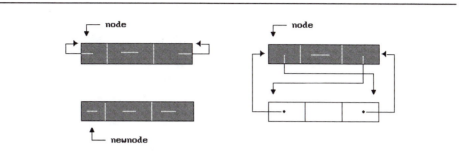

Figure 4.25: Insertion into an empty doubly linked circular list

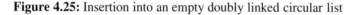

```
void ddelete(node_pointer node, node_pointer deleted)
{
/* delete from the doubly linked list */
   if (node == deleted)
      printf("Deletion of head node not permitted.\n");
   else {
      deleted->llink->rlink = deleted->rlink;
      deleted->rlink->llink = deleted->llink;
      free(deleted);
   }
}
```

Program 4.29: Deletion from a doubly linked circular list

EXERCISES

1. Assume that we have a doubly linked list, as represented in Figure 4.23, and that we want to add a new node between the second and third nodes in the list. Redraw the figure so that it shows the insertion. Label the fields of the affected nodes so that you show how each statement in the *dinsert* function is executed. For example, label *newnode–>llink*, *newnode–>rlink*, and *node–>rlink–>llink*.

2. Repeat Exercise 1, but delete the second node from the list.

3. § [***Programming project***] Assume that we have information on the employees of a computing firm as illustrated in Figure 4.27. For each employee, in addition to the employee's name, we have an occupational title, an identification number, and a location. We would like to be able to access quickly the information for any of the categories. For example, we might want to quickly retrieve the list of all

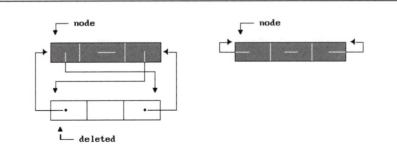

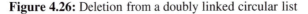

Figure 4.26: Deletion from a doubly linked circular list

employees who work in New York, or the list of all programmers. One way of doing this is to the create a data structure known as a *multilist*. This data structure contains an index table for each field, excluding the name. For instance, there is an occupation index that divides the employees into each of the occupational categories. For each category, we create a linked list. The index entry for the category contains a field that holds the identifying information for the category and a pointer to the first node in the list for that category. Figure 4.28 shows the organization for our sample data using singly linked lists. Since we want to be able to remove employees that leave the company easily, the singly linked structure appearing in Figure 4.28 is inadequate. Instead we actually want to represent the multilist as doubly linked circular lists. Write a program that creates this structure and implements the following operations:

(a)   insert a new employee record into the multilist

(b)   remove an employee record from the multilist

(c)   change the information for any field of the multilist, and relink the employee record properly

(d)   Query the multilist on any of the fields as described above.

4.9   REFERENCES AND SELECTED READINGS

For more information on pointers in C, consult R. Traister, *Mastering C Pointers*, Academic Press, San Diego, Calif., 1990.

Node	ID Number	Name	Occupation	Location
A	30	Hawkins	Programmer	Minneapolis
B	25	Smith	Analyst	New York
C	60	Jones	Programmer	New York
D	55	Austin	DataEntry	Minneapolis
E	80	Messer	Analyst	Minneapolis

Figure 4.27: Sample set of employee data

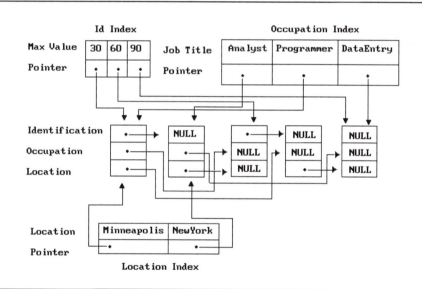

Figure 4.28: Multilist structure represented as singly linked lists

4.10 ADDITIONAL EXERCISES

1. We can obtain a simpler and more efficient representation for sparse matrices if we restrict our operations to addition, subtraction, and multiplication. In this representation, nodes have *down*, *right*, *row*, *col*, and *value* fields. We represent each nonzero term with a separate node and link these nodes together to form two circular lists. We make the first list, the row list, by linking nodes by rows and within rows by columns. This is done through the *right* field. We make the second

list, the column list, by linking nodes by columns and within columns by rows. This is done through the *down* field. These two lists share a common head node. In addition, we add a node that contains the dimensions of the matrix. Matrix *a* of Figure 4.20 is shown in Figure 4.29.

Using the same assumptions as *mread*, write a function that reads in a sparse matrix and sets up its internal representation. How much time does your function take? How much additional space is needed?

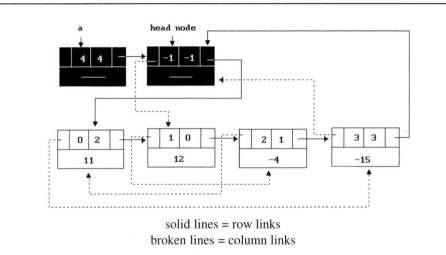

solid lines = row links
broken lines = column links

Figure 4.29: Alternate sparse matrix representation

2. For the representation of Exercise 1, write functions that:
   (a) erase a matrix
   (b) add two matrices
   (c) multiply two matrices
   (d) print out a matrix.

   For each of these operations, determine the computing time and compare these times with those obtained using the representation found in Figure 4.21.

3. Compare the sparse matrix representations found in Figure 4.29 and Figure 4.21 with respect to the following operations:
   (a) copy a matrix

(b) transpose a matrix

(c) output the entries in an arbitrary row

(d) output the entries in an arbitrary column.

4. § [***Programming project***] We want to implement a complete linked list system to perform arithmetic on sparse matrices using the linked list representation found in Figure 4.29. Create a user-friendly, menu-driven system that performs the following operations:

(a) reads in a sparse matrix

(b) writes out the contents of a sparse matrix

(c) erases a sparse matrix

(d) adds two sparse matrices

(e) subtracts two sparse matrices

(f) multiplies two sparse matrices

(g) transposes a sparse matrix.

Test your system using suitable test data.

CHAPTER 5

——————————

TREES

5.1   INTRODUCTION

5.1.1   Terminology

In this chapter we study a very important data structure, *trees*. Intuitively, the concept of a tree implies that we organize the data so that items of information are related by the branches. For example, we use a tree structure whenever we investigate genealogies. Typically, we could use either of two genealogical charts to present our data, the pedigree or the lineal chart. As Figure 5.1 shows, each chart has a characteristic treelike structure.

The pedigree chart of Figure 5.1(a) shows someone's ancestors, in this case those of Dusty. As we can see, Dusty's parents are Honey Bear and Brandy. Her maternal grandparents are Brunhilde and Terry, while her paternal grandparents are Coyote and Nugget. If we prohibit inbreeding, the pedigree chart always displays a two-way branching. Such trees, referred to as *binary trees*, have many important applications.

Although the lineal chart of Figure 5.1(b) has nothing to do with people, it is still a genealogy since it describes, in abbreviated form, the ancestry of modern European languages. Thus, this is a chart of descendants rather than ancestors. In addition, each item can have several, rather than just two, descendants. For example, Latin has as its descendants Spanish, French, and Italian. Although the lineal tree does not have the regular structure of the pedigree chart, it is a tree nonetheless.

186

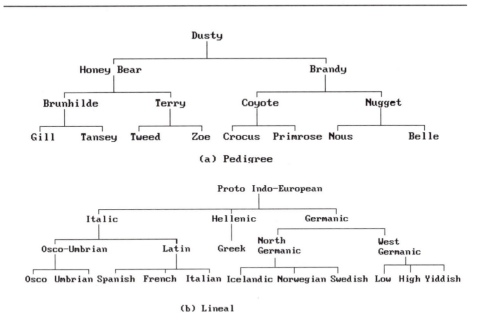

(a) Pedigree

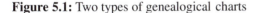

(b) Lineal

Figure 5.1: Two types of genealogical charts

Using our genealogical charts as examples, let us define formally what we mean by a tree.

Definition: A *tree* is a finite set of one or more nodes such that:

(1)   There is a specially designated node called the *root*.

(2)   The remaining nodes are partitioned into $n \geq 0$ disjoint sets $T_1, \cdots, T_n$, where each of these sets is a tree. We call $T_1, \cdots, T_n$ the subtrees of the root. □

Notice that we have an instance of a recursive definition since we define the subtrees as trees. If we return to Figure 5.1, we see that the root of tree (a) is Dusty, while that of tree (b) is Proto Indo-European. Tree (a) has two subtrees whose roots are Honey Bear and Brandy, while tree (b) has three subtrees with roots, Italic, Hellenic, and Germanic. Since $T_1, \cdots, T_n$ must be disjoint sets, we prohibit subtrees from ever connecting together, that is, we forbid crossbreeding. Our definition also indicates that every node in the tree is the root of some subtree. For instance, West Germanic is the root of a subtree of Germanic, and it has three subtrees with the following roots: Low German, High German, and Yiddish.

There are many terms that we use when referring to trees. A *node* stands for the item of information and the branches to other nodes. For example, the tree in Figure 5.2 has 13 nodes, with each item of information represented as a letter for convenience. The root of the tree is *A*. Normally we draw trees with the root at the top.

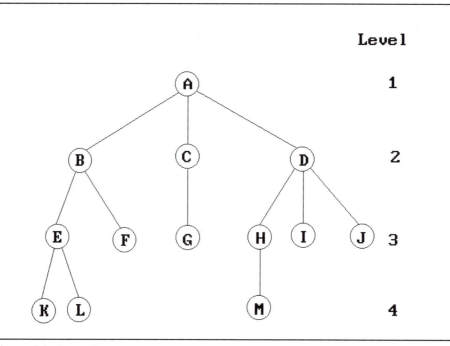

Figure 5.2: A sample tree

The *degree* of a node is the number of subtrees of the node. For example, the degree of *A* is 3, of *C* is 1, and of *F* is zero. The *degree of a tree* is the maximum degree of the nodes in the tree. For example, the tree of Figure 5.2 has degree 3. A node with degree zero is a *leaf* or *terminal* node. For instance, *K*, *L*, *F*, *G*, *M*, *I*, and *J* are all leaf nodes.

A node that has subtrees is the *parent* of the roots of the subtrees, and the roots of the subtrees are the *children* of the node. For instance, node *B* is the parent of nodes *E* and *F*, which conversely are the children of *B*. Children of the same parent are *siblings*. For instance, *H*, *I*, and *J* are siblings. We can extend this familial terminology to grandparents and grandchildren. Thus, we can say that *D* is the grandparent of *M*, and *A* is the grandparent of *E*, *F*, *G*, *H*, *I*, and *J*. The *ancestors* of a node are all the nodes along the path from the root to the node. For example, the ancestors of *M* are *A*, *D*, and *H*. Conversely, the *descendants* of a node are all the nodes that are in its subtrees. For example, *E*, *F*, *K*, and *L* are the descendants of *B*.

We define the *level* of a node by initially letting the root be at level one. For all subsequent nodes, the level is the level of the node's parent plus one. The *height* or *depth* of a tree is the maximum level of any node in the tree. Thus, the depth of the tree in Figure 5.2 is 4.

5.1.2   Representation Of Trees

List Representation

There are several ways that we can draw a tree in addition to the one presented in Figure 5.2. For example, we can write the tree of Figure 5.2 as a list in which each of the subtrees is also a list. Using this notation, the tree of Figure 5.2 is written as:

$$(A \ (B \ (E \ (K, L), F), \ C(G), \ D(\ H \ (M), I, J) \ ) \ )$$

Notice that the information in the root node comes first, followed by a list of the subtrees of that node.

We must now consider the representation of a tree in memory. If we wish to use linked lists, then a node must have a varying number of fields depending on the number of branches. Figure 5.3 shows a possible structure for a list representation. Each link field represents a child of the node.

data	*link 1*	*link 2*	$\cdots$	*link n*

Figure 5.3: Possible list representation for trees

Left Child-Right Sibling Representation

Since it is often easier to work with nodes of a fixed size, we explore such representations for trees. Both the representations we consider require exactly two link or pointer fields per node. Figure 5.4 shows the node structure used in one of these, the left child-right sibling representation.

To convert the tree of Figure 5.2 into this representation, we first note that every node has only one leftmost child and one closest right sibling. For example, in Figure 5.2, the leftmost child of A is B, and the leftmost child of D is H. Similarly, the closest right sibling of B is C, and the closest right sibling of H is I. Strictly speaking, since the order of children in a tree is not important, any of the children of a node could be its leftmost child and any of its siblings could be the closest right sibling. For the sake of definiteness, we choose the nodes based on how the tree is drawn. Figure 5.5 shows the tree of Figure 5.2 redrawn using the left child-right sibling representation.

data	
left child	right sibling

Figure 5.4: Left child-right sibling node structure

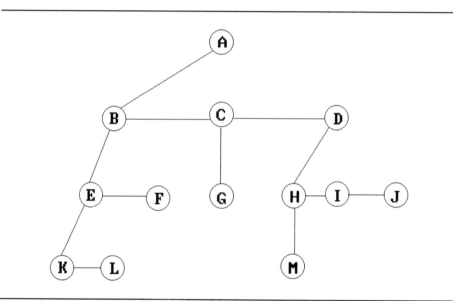

Figure 5.5: Left child-right sibling representation of a tree

Representation As A Degree Two Tree

To obtain the degree two tree representation of a tree we simply rotate the left child-right sibling tree clockwise by 45 degrees. This gives us the degree two tree displayed in Figure 5.6. We shall refer to the two children of a node as the left and right children. Notice that the right child of the root node of the tree is empty. This is always the case since the root of the tree we are transforming can never have a sibling. Figure 5.7 shows two additional examples of trees represented as left child-right sibling trees and as left child-right child (or degree two) trees. Left child-right child trees are also known as

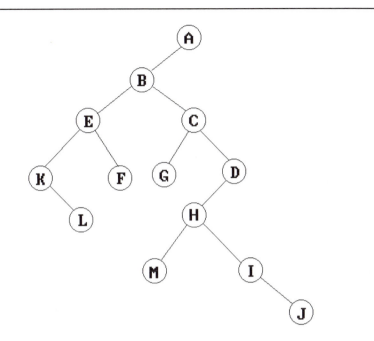

Figure 5.6: Left child-right child tree representation of a tree

binary trees.

5.2 BINARY TREES

5.2.1 The Abstract Data Type

We have seen that we can represent any tree as a binary tree. In fact, binary trees are an important type of tree structure that occurs very often. The chief characteristic of a binary tree is the stipulation that the degree of any given node must not exceed two. For binary trees, we also distinguish between the left subtree and the right subtree, while for trees the order of the subtrees is irrelevant. In addition, a binary tree may have zero nodes. Thus, a binary tree is really a different object than a tree.

Definition: A *binary tree* is a finite set of nodes that is either empty or consists of a root and two disjoint binary trees called the left subtree and the right subtree. □

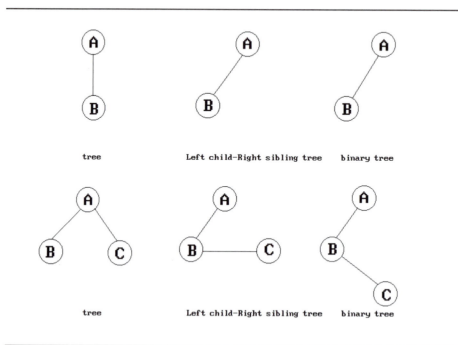

Figure 5.7: Tree representations

Structure 5.1 contains the specification for the binary tree ADT. This structure defines only a minimal set of operations on binary trees which we use as a foundation on which to build additional operations.

Let us carefully review the distinctions between a binary tree and a tree. First, there is no tree having zero nodes, but there is an empty binary tree. Second, in a binary tree we distinguish between the order of the children while in a tree we do not. Thus, the two binary trees of Figure 5.8 are different since the first binary tree has an empty right subtree, while the second has an empty left subtree. Viewed as trees, however, they are the same, despite the fact that they are drawn slightly differently.

Figure 5.9 shows two special types of binary trees. Tree (a) is a *skewed tree*. In this particular case, it is skewed to the left since each node is the left child of its parent. There is a corresponding tree that skews to the right. Tree (b) is a *complete binary tree*. Although we will formally define this tree structure shortly, for now simply notice that all the leaf nodes are on two adjacent levels. We should also point out that the same terminology we used to describe trees applies to binary trees. Thus, we can speak of the degree, level, or height of a node or a tree, and we can describe a node as a root, leaf, parent, or child.

structure *Binary_Tree* (abbreviated *BinTree*) is

   objects: a finite set of nodes either empty or consisting of a root node, left *Binary_Tree*, and right *Binary_Tree*.

   functions:

   for all *bt,bt1,bt2* ∈ *BinTree*, item ∈ *element*

BinTree Create()	::=	creates an empty binary tree
Boolean IsEmpty(*bt*)	::=	**if** (*bt* == empty binary tree) **return** *TRUE* **else return** *FALSE*
BinTree MakeBT(*bt*1, *item*, *bt*2)	::=	**return** a binary tree whose left subtree is *bt*1, whose right subtree is *bt*2, and whose root node contains the data *item*.
BinTree Lchild(*bt*)	::=	**if** (IsEmpty(*bt*)) **return** error **else return** the left subtree of *bt*.
element Data(*bt*)	::=	**if** (IsEmpty(*bt*)) **return** error **else return** the data in the root node of *bt*.
BinTree Rchild(*bt*)	::=	**if** (IsEmpty(*bt*)) **return** error **else return** the right subtree of *bt*.

Structure 5.1: Abstract data type *Binary_Tree*

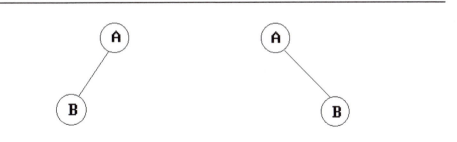

Figure 5.8: Two different binary trees

5.2.2   Properties Of Binary Trees

Before examining data representations for binary trees, let us first make some observations about such trees. In particular, we want to find out the maximum number of nodes in a binary tree of depth *k*, and we want to examine the relationship between the number of leaf nodes and the number of nodes of degree two in a binary tree. We present both

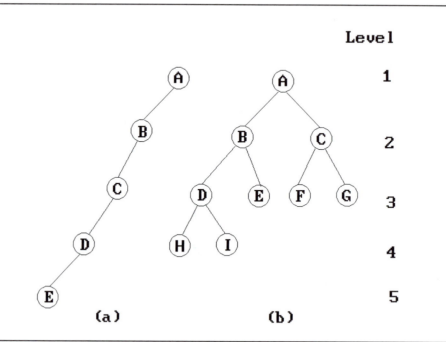

Figure 5.9: Skewed and complete binary trees

these observations as lemmas. These lemmas allow us to define full and complete binary trees.

Lemma 5.1 [*Maximum number of nodes*]:

(1)   The maximum number of nodes on level i of a binary tree is 2^{i-1}, $i \geq 1$.

(2)   The maximum number of nodes in a binary tree of depth k is $2^k - 1$, $k \geq 1$.

Proof:

(1) The proof is by induction on i.

Induction base: The root is the only node on level $i = 1$. Hence, the maximum number of nodes on level $i = 1$ is $2^{i-1} = 2^0 = 1$.

Induction hypothesis: For all j, $1 \leq j < i$, the maximum number of nodes on level j is 2^{j-1}.

Induction step: The maximum number of nodes on level $i - 1$ is 2^{i-2} by the induction hypothesis. Since each node in a binary tree has a maximum degree of 2, the maximum number of nodes on level i is two times the maximum number of nodes on level $i-1$ or 2^{i-1}.

(2) The maximum number of nodes in a binary tree of depth k is:

$$\sum_{i=1}^{k} (\text{maximum number of nodes on level } i) = \sum_{i=1}^{k} 2^{i-1} = 2^k - 1 \ \square$$

Lemma 5.2 [*Relation between number of leaf nodes and nodes of degree 2*]: For any nonempty binary tree, T, if n_0 is the number of leaf nodes and n_2 the number of nodes of degree 2, then $n_0 = n_2 + 1$.

Proof: Let n_1 be the number of nodes of degree one and n the total number of nodes. Since all nodes in T are of degree at most two, we have:

$$n = n_0 + n_1 + n_2 \tag{5.1}$$

If we count the number of branches in a binary tree, we see that every node except the root has a branch leading into it. If B is the number of branches, then $n = B+1$. All branches stem from a node of degree one or two. Thus, $B = n_1 + 2n_2$. Hence, we obtain:

$$n = 1 + n_1 + 2n_2 \tag{5.2}$$

Subtracting Eq. (5.2) from Eq. (5.1) and rearranging terms, we get:

$$n_0 = n_2 + 1 \ \square$$

In Figure 5.9(a), $n_0 = 1$ and $n_2 = 0$, while, in Figure 5.9(b), $n_0 = 5$ and $n_2 = 4$.

We are now ready to define full and complete binary trees.

Definition: A *full binary tree* of depth k is a binary tree of depth k having $2^k - 1$ nodes, $k \geq 0$. $\square$

By Lemma 5.1, $2^k - 1$ is the maximum number of nodes in a binary tree of depth k. Figure 5.10 shows a full binary tree of depth 4. An elegant sequential representation for such binary trees results from sequentially numbering the nodes, starting with the root on level 1, continuing with the nodes on level 2, and so on. Nodes on any level are numbered from left to right (see Figure 5.10). This numbering scheme gives us the definition of a complete binary tree.

Definition: A binary tree with n nodes and depth k is *complete iff* its nodes correspond to the nodes numbered from 1 to n in the full binary tree of depth k. $\square$

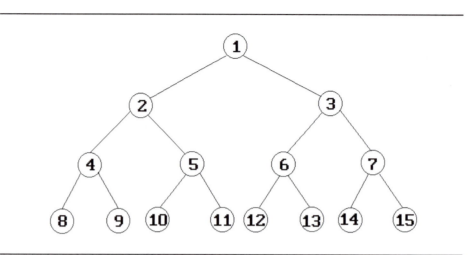

Figure 5.10: Full binary tree of depth 4 with sequential node numbers

5.2.3 Binary Tree Representations

Array Representation

The numbering scheme used in Figure 5.10 suggests our first representation of a binary tree in memory. Since the nodes are numbered from 1 to n, we can use a one-dimensional array to store the nodes. (We do not use the 0th position of the array.) Using Lemma 5.3 we can easily determine the locations of the parent, left child, and right child of any node, i, in the binary tree.

Lemma 5.3: If a complete binary tree with n nodes (depth $= \lfloor \log_2 n + 1 \rfloor$) is represented sequentially, then for any node with index i, $1 \le i \le n$, we have:

(1) *parent*(i) is at $\lfloor i / 2 \rfloor$ if $i \ne 1$ If $i = 1$, i is at the root and has no parent.
(2) *left_child*(i) is at $2i$ if $2i \le n$. If $2i > n$, then i has no left child.
(3) *right_child*(i) is at $2i + 1$ if $2i + 1 \le n$. If $2i + 1 > n$, then i has no right child.

Proof: We prove (2). (3) is an immediate consequence of (2) and the numbering of nodes on the same level from left to right. (1) follows from (2) and (3). We prove (2) by induction on i. For $i = 1$, clearly the left child is at 2 unless $2 > n$, in which case i has no left child. Now assume that for all j, $1 \leq j \leq i$, *left_child*(j) is at $2j$. Then the two nodes immediately preceding *left_child*($i+1$) are the right and left children of i. The left child is at $2i$. Hence, the left child of $i + 1$ is at $2i + 2 = 2(i + 1)$ unless $2(i + 1) > n$, in which case $i + 1$ has no left child. $\square$

We can use an array representation for all binary trees, although in most cases there will be a lot of unutilized space. For complete binary trees, this representation is ideal since it wastes no space. However, for the skewed tree in Figure 5.9(a), less than half the array is utilized. Figure 5.11 shows the array representation for both trees in Figure 5.9. Since position zero of the array isn't used, it is not shown. In the worst case, a skewed tree of depth k requires $2^k - 1$ spaces. Of these, only k spaces will be occupied.

[1]	A		[1]	A
[2]	B		[2]	B
[3]	—		[3]	C
[4]	C		[4]	D
[5]	—		[5]	E
[6]	—		[6]	F
[7]	—		[7]	G
[8]	D		[8]	H
[9]	—		[9]	I
.	.			
.	.			
.	.			
[16]	E			

Figure 5.11: Array representation of binary trees of Figure 5.9

Linked Representation

While the sequential representation is acceptable for complete binary trees, it wastes space for many other binary trees. In addition, this representation suffers from the general inadequacies of other sequential representations. Thus, insertion or deletion of nodes from the middle of a tree requires the movement of potentially many nodes to reflect the change in the level of these nodes. We can easily overcome these problems by using a linked representation. Each node has three fields, *left_child*, *data*, and *right_child*, and is defined in C as:

```
typedef struct node *tree_pointer;
typedef struct node {
        int data;
        tree_pointer left_child, right_child;
        };
```

We draw such a node using either of the representations of Figure 5.12.

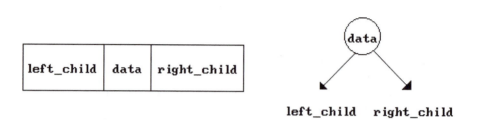

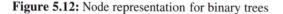

Figure 5.12: Node representation for binary trees

While this node structure makes it difficult to determine the parent of a node, it is adequate for most applications. Should we need to know the parents of random nodes, we will add a fourth field, *parent*, to the node definition. Figure 5.13 shows the representation of the trees found in Figure 5.9 using this node structure. As was true of lists, we refer to the tree by the variable that points to its root.

EXERCISES

1. For the binary tree of Figure 5.14(a), list the terminal nodes, the nonterminal nodes, and the level of each node.

2. Repeat Exercise 1 with the binary tree of Figure 5.14(b).

3. Draw the internal memory representation for the binary tree of Figure 5.14(a), using (a) list, (b) sequential, and (c) linked representations.

4. Repeat Exercise 3 with the binary tree of Figure 5.14(b).

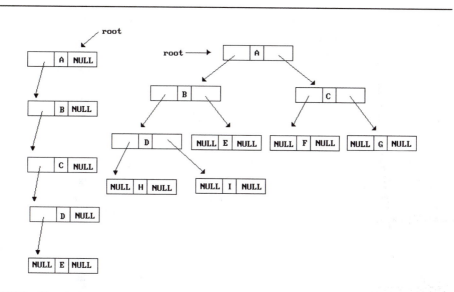

Figure 5.13: Linked representation for the binary trees of Figure 5.9

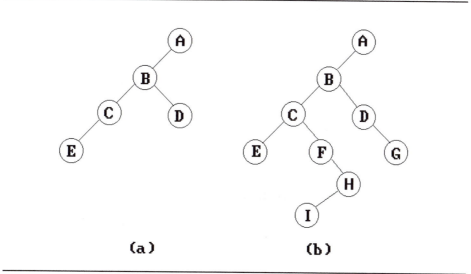

Figure 5.14: Two sample binary trees

5.3   BINARY TREE TRAVERSALS

There are many operations that we can perform on trees, but one that arises frequently is traversing a tree, that is, visiting each node in the tree exactly once. A full traversal produces a linear order for the information in a tree.

When traversing a tree we want to treat each node and its subtrees in the same way. If we let *L*, *V*, and *R* stand for moving left, visiting the node (for example, printing out the data field), and moving right, then there are six possible combinations of traversal: *LVR*, *LRV*, *VLR*, *VRL*, *RVL*, and *RLV*. If we adopt the convention that we traverse left before right, then only three traversals remain: *LVR*, *LRV*, *VLR*. We assign the names *inorder*, *postorder*, and *preorder* to these traversals because of the position of the *V* with respect to the *L* and *R*. For example, in postorder, we visit a node after we have traversed its left and right subtrees while in preorder the visiting is done before the traversal of these subtrees. There is a natural correspondence between these traversals and producing the infix, postfix, and prefix forms of an expression. To show this correspondence we will use the binary tree of Figure 5.15. This tree represents the arithmetic expression (in infix form): *A* / *B* * *C* * *D* + *E*. For the present time, we will not consider how the tree was created, but we will assume that it is available. For illustrative purposes we have included the null nodes for the tree. They are represented as shaded rectangles in Figure 5.15. We also have labeled each of the nodes, including the null nodes. We use this tree to illustrate each of the traversals.

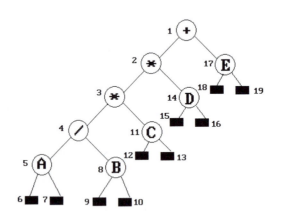

Figure 5.15: Binary tree with arithmetic expression

Inorder Traversal

Informally, an inorder traversal moves down the tree toward the left until a null node is reached. The null node's parent is then "visited," and the traversal continues with the node that is one to the right. If there is no move to the right, the traversal continues with the last unvisited node at the next higher level of the tree. We can describe this traversal in an elegant and precise way by writing it as a recursive function (Program 5.1).

```
void inorder(tree_pointer ptr)
/* inorder tree traversal */
{
   if (ptr) {
      inorder(ptr->left_child);
      printf("%d",ptr->data);
      inorder(ptr->right_child);
   }
}
```

Program 5.1: Inorder traversal of a binary tree

Figure 5.16 is a trace of *inorder* using the tree of Figure 5.15. Each step of the trace shows the call of *inorder*, the value in the root, and whether or not the **printf** function is invoked. The first three columns show the first 13 steps of the traversal. The second three columns show the remaining 14 steps. The numbers in columns 1 and 4 correspond to the node numbers displayed in Figure 5.15 and are used to show the location of the node in the tree. Since there are 19 nodes in the tree, *inorder* is invoked 19 times for the complete traversal. The data fields are output in the order:

$$A / B * C * D + E$$

which corresponds to the infix form of the expression.

Preorder Traversal

The function *preorder* (Program 5.2) contains the code for a second form of traversal. With this traversal we "visit" the node first and then follow left branches visiting all nodes encountered. This continues until we reach a null node. At this point, we back up to the closest ancestor that has a right child and continue with this child. Using a preorder traversal, the nodes of the tree in Figure 5.15 would be output as:

$$+ * * / A \, B \, C \, D \, E$$

which we recognize as the prefix form of the expression.

Call of inorder	Value in root	Action	inorder	Value in root	Action
1	+		11	C	
2	*		12	NULL	
3	*		11	C	printf
4	/		13	NULL	
5	A		2	*	printf
6	NULL		14	D	
5	A	printf	15	NULL	
7	NULL		14	D	printf
4	/	printf	16	NULL	
8	B		1	+	printf
9	NULL		17	E	
8	B	printf	18	NULL	
10	NULL		17	E	printf
3	*	printf	19	NULL	

Figure 5.16: Trace of Program 5.1

```
void preorder(tree_pointer ptr)
/* preorder tree traversal */
{
   if (ptr) {
      printf("%d",ptr->data);
      preorder(ptr->left_child);
      preorder(ptr->right_child);
   }
}
```

Program 5.2: Preorder traversal of a binary tree

Postorder Traversal

The function *postorder* (Program 5.3) contains the postorder traversal. Informally, this traversal "visits" a node's two children before it "visits" the node. This means that the node's children will be output before the node. The output produced by *postfix* for the tree of Figure 5.15 is:

$$A\ B\ /\ C * D * E +$$

which is the postfix form of our expression.

```
void postorder(tree_pointer ptr)
/* postorder tree traversal */
{
   if (ptr) {
      postorder(ptr->left_child);
      postorder(ptr->right_child);
      printf("%d",ptr->data);
   }
}
```

Program 5.3: Postorder traversal of a binary tree

Iterative Inorder Traversal

Although we have written the inorder, preorder, and postorder traversal functions recursively, we can develop equivalent iterative functions. Let us take inorder traversal as an example. To simulate the recursion, we must create our own stack. We add nodes to and remove nodes from our stack in the same manner that the recursive version manipulates the system stack. This helps us to understand fully the operation of the recursive version. Figure 5.16 implicitly shows this stacking and unstacking. A node that has no action indicates that the node is added to the stack, while a node that has a *printf* action indicates that the node is removed from the stack. Notice that the left nodes are stacked until a null node is reached, the node is then removed from the stack, and the node's right child is stacked. The traversal then continues with the left child. The traversal is complete when the stack is empty. Function *iter – inorder* (Program 5.4) stems directly from this discussion. The stack function *add* differs from that defined in Chapter 3 only in that the type of the elements in the stack is different. Similarly, the *delete* function returns a value of type *tree – pointer* rather than of type *element*. It returns *NULL* in case the stack is empty.

Analysis of *inorder2*: Let n be the number of nodes in the tree. If we consider the action of *iter – inorder*, we note that every node of the tree is placed on and removed from the stack exactly once. So, if the number of nodes in the tree is n, the time complexity is $O(n)$. The space requirement is equal to the depth of the tree which is $O(n)$. □

```
void iter-inorder(tree-pointer node)
{
    int top = -1; /* initialize stack */
    tree-pointer stack[MAX-STACK-SIZE];
    for (;;) {
        for(; node; node = node->left-child)
            add(&top, node); /* add to stack */
        node = delete(&top); /* delete from stack */
        if (!node) break; /* empty stack */
        printf("%d", node->data);
        node = node->right-child;
    }
}
```

Program 5.4: Iterative inorder traversal

Level Order Traversal

Whether written iteratively or recursively, the inorder, preorder, and postorder traversals all require a stack. We now turn to a traversal that requires a queue. This traversal, *level order*, visits the nodes using the ordering scheme suggested in Figure 5.10. Thus, we visit the root first, then the root's left child, followed by the root's right child. We continue in this manner, visiting the nodes at each new level from the leftmost node to the rightmost one.

The code for this traversal is contained in *level_order* (Program 5.5). This assumes a circular queue as in Chapter 3. Function *addq* differs from the corresponding function of Chapter 3 only in that the data type of the elements in the queue is different. Similarly, the function *deleteq* used in Program 5.5 returns a value of type *tree_pointer* rather than of type element. It returns *NULL* in case the queue is empty.

We begin by adding the root to the queue. The function operates by deleting the node at the front of the queue, printing out the node's data field, and adding the node's left and right children to the queue. Since a node's children are at the next lower level, and we add the left child before the right child, the function prints out the nodes using the ordering scheme found in Figure 5.10. The level order traversal of the tree in Figure 5.15 is:

$$+ * E * D / C A B$$

```
void level-order(tree-pointer ptr)
/* level order tree traversal */
{
   int front = rear = 0;
   tree-pointer queue[MAX-QUEUE-SIZE];
   if (!ptr) return; /* empty tree */
   addq(front, &rear, ptr);
   for (;;) {
      ptr = deleteq(&front, rear);
      if (ptr) {
         printf("%d",ptr->data);
         if(ptr->left-child)
            addq(front,&rear,ptr->left-child);
         if (ptr->right-child)
            addq(front,&rear,ptr->right-child);
      }
      else break;
   }
}
```

Program 5.5: Level order traversal of a binary tree

EXERCISES

1. Write out the inorder, preorder, postorder, and level order traversals for tree (a) of Figure 5.14.

2. Repeat Exercise 1 using tree (b) of Figure 5.14.

3. Simulate the action of *iter — inorder* using the tree of Figure 5.14(a). At each stage show the contents of the stack and what, if any, action is taken (in other words, indicate if the contents of the data field are printed).

4. Repeat the preceding exercise using the tree of Figure 5.14(b).

5. Write an iterative version of *preorder*.

6. Write an iterative version of *postorder*.

7. Write the complete C codes for the stack add and delete functions used in *iter — inorder* (Program 5.4).

8. Write the complete C codes for the queue add and delete functions used in *level — order* (Program 5.5).

9. Assume that we have a binary tree of names like the one illustrated in Figure 5.17. Prove that an inorder traversal always prints the names in alphabetical order.

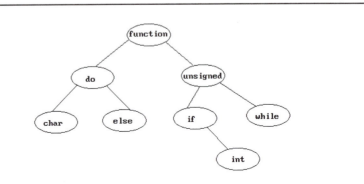

Figure 5.17: Binary tree of names

5.4   ADDITIONAL BINARY TREE OPERATIONS

Copying Binary Trees

By using the definition of a binary tree and the recursive versions of inorder, preorder, and postorder traversals, we can easily create C functions for other binary tree operations. One practical operation is copying a binary tree. The code for this operation is containted in *copy* (Program 5.6). Notice that this function is only a slightly modified version of *postorder* (Program 5.3).

Testing For Equality Of Binary Trees

Another useful operation is determining the equivalence of two binary trees. Equivalent binary trees have the same structure and the same information in the corresponding nodes. By the same structure we mean that every branch in one tree corresponds to a branch in the second tree, that is, the branching of the two trees is identical. The function *equal* (Program 5.7) uses a modification of preorder traversal to test for equality. This function returns *TRUE* if the two trees are equivalent and *FALSE* if they are not.

The Satisfiability Problem

Consider the set of formulas that we can construct by taking variables $x_1, x_2, \cdots, x_n$ and operators $\wedge$ (*and*), $\vee$ (*or*), and $\neg$ (*not*). The variables can hold only one of two

```
tree_pointer copy(tree_pointer original)
/* this function returns a tree_pointer to an exact copy
of the original tree */
{
   tree_pointer temp;
   if (original) {
      temp = (tree_pointer) malloc(sizeof(node));
      if (IS_FULL(temp)) {
         fprintf(stderr, "The memory is full\n");
         exit(1);
      }
      temp->left_child = copy(original->left_child);
      temp->right_child = copy(original->right_child);
      temp->data = original->data;
      return temp;
   }
   return NULL;
}
```

Program 5.6: Copying a binary tree

```
int equal(tree_pointer first, tree_pointer second)
{
/* function returns FALSE if the binary trees first and
second are not equal, Otherwise it returns TRUE */
   return ((!first && !second) || (first && second &&
           (first->data == second->data) &&
           equal(first->left_child,second->left_child) &&
           equal(first->right_child, second->right_child))
}
```

Program 5.7: Testing for equality of binary trees

possible values, *true* or *false*. The set of expressions that we can form using these variables and operators is defined by the following rules:

(1)   A variable is an expression.

(2)   If x and y are expressions, then $\neg\, x, x \wedge y\,, x \vee y$ are expressions.

(3)   Parentheses can be used to alter the normal order of evaluation, which is $\neg$ before $\wedge$ before $\vee$.

These rules comprise the formulas in the propositional calculus since other operations, such as implication, can be expressed using $\neg$, $\vee$, and $\wedge$.

The expression:

$$x_1 \vee (x_2 \wedge \neg\, x_3)$$

is a formula (read as "x_1 *or* x_2 *and not* x_3"). If x_1 and x_3 are *false* and x_2 is *true*, then the value of the expression is:

$$\text{\textit{false} } \vee \text{ (\textit{true} } \wedge \neg \text{ \textit{false})}$$
$$= \textit{false} \vee \textit{true}$$
$$= \textit{true}$$

The satisfiability problem for formulas of the propositional calculus asks if there is an assignment of values to the variables that causes the value of the expression to be true. This problem was originally used by Newell, Shaw, and Simon in the late 1950s to show the viability of heuristic programming (The Logic Theorist) and is still of keen interest to computer scientists.

Again let us assume that our formula is already in a binary tree. For illustrative purposes we will use the formula:

$$(x_1 \wedge \neg\, x_2) \vee (\neg\, x_1 \wedge x_3) \vee \neg\, x_3$$

Figure 5.18 shows the binary tree for this formula. The inorder traversal of this tree is:

$$x_1 \wedge \neg\, x_2 \vee \neg\, x_1 \wedge \neg\, x_3 \vee \neg\, x_3$$

which is the infix form of the expression. The most obvious algorithm to determine satisfiability is to let (x_1, x_2, x_3) take on all possible combinations of *true* and *false*, checking the formula with each combination. For n variables, there are 2^n possible combinations of *true* and *false*. For example, for $n = 3$, the eight combinations are (*false, false, false*), (*false, false, true*), (*false, true, false*), (*false, true, true*), (*true, false, false*), (*true, false, true*), (*true, true, false*), and (*true, true, true*). The algorithm takes $O(g\, 2^n)$ time, where g is the time required to substitute the *true* and *false* values for x_1, x_2, x_3 and to evaluate the expression.

To evaluate an expression we can traverse the tree in postorder, evaluating the subtrees until the entire expression is reduced to a single value. This corresponds to the postfix evaluation of an arithmetic expression that we saw earlier. Viewed from the

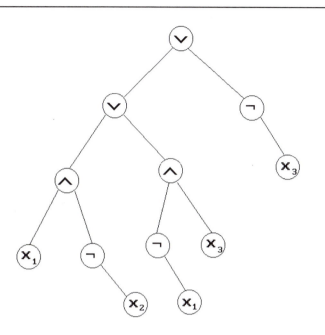

Figure 5.18: Propositional formula in a binary tree

perspective of the tree representation, for every node we reach we have already computed the values of its children. For example, when we reach the ∨ node on level 2, the values of $x_1 \wedge \neg x_2$ and $\neg x_1 \wedge x_3$ are available to us and we can apply the rule for *or*. Notice that a node containing ¬ has only a single right branch since *not* is a unary operator.

The node structure for this problem is found in Figure 5.19. The *left_child* and *right_child* fields are similar to those used previously. The field *data* holds either the value of a variable or a propositional calculus operator, while *value* holds either a value of *TRUE* or *FALSE*.

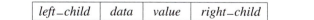

Figure 5.19: Node structure for the satisfiability problem

We define this node structure in C as:

```
typedef enum {not,and,or,true,false} logical;
typedef struct node *tree_pointer;
typedef struct node {
        tree_pointer left_child;
        logical      data;
        short int    value;
        tree_pointer right_child;
        } ;
```

We assume that for leaf nodes, *node* −> *data* contains the current value of the variable represented at this node. For example, we assume that the tree of Figure 5.18 contains either *TRUE* or *FALSE* in the data field of x_1, x_2, and x_3. We also assume that an expression tree with n variables is pointed at by *root*. With these assumptions we can write our first version of a satisfiability algorithm (Program 5.8).

```
for (all 2ⁿ possible combinations) {
   generate the next combination;
   replace the variables by their values;
   evaluate root by traversing it in postorder;
   if (root->value) {
      printf(<combination>);
      return;
   }
}
printf("No satisfiable combination\n");
```

Program 5.8: First version of satisfiability algorithm

The C function that evaluates the tree is easily obtained by modifying the original, recursive postorder traversal. The function *post_order_eval* (Program 5.9) shows the C code that implements this portion of the satisfiability algorithm.

EXERCISES

1. Write a C function that counts the number of leaf nodes in a binary tree. Determine the computing time of the function.

2. Write a C function *swap_tree* that takes a binary tree and swaps the left and right children of every node. An example is given in Figure 5.20.

```
void post_order_eval(tree_pointer node)
{
/* modified post order traversal to evaluate a
propositional calculus tree */
   if (node) {
      post_order_eval(node->left_child);
      post_order_eval(node->right_child);
      switch(node->data) {
         case not:   node->value =
               !node->right_child->value;
               break;
         case and:   node->value =
               node->right_child->value &&
               node->left_child->value;
               break;
         case or:    node->value =
               node->right_child->value ||
               node->left_child->value;
               break;
         case true:  node->value = TRUE;
               break;
         case false: node->value = FALSE;
      }
   }
}
```

Program 5.9: *post_order_eval* function

3. What is the computing time of *post_order_eval*?

4. § [***Programming project***] Devise a representation for formulas in the propositional calculus. Write a C function that inputs such a formula and creates a binary tree representation of it. Determine the computing time of your function.

5.5   THREADED BINARY TREES

If we look carefully at the linked representation of any binary tree, we notice that there are more null links than actual pointers. Specifically, there are $n + 1$ null links out of $2n$ total links. A. J. Perlis and C. Thornton have devised a clever way to make use of these null links. They replace the null links by pointers, called *threads*, to other nodes in the tree. To construct the threads we use the following rules (assume that *ptr* represents a node):

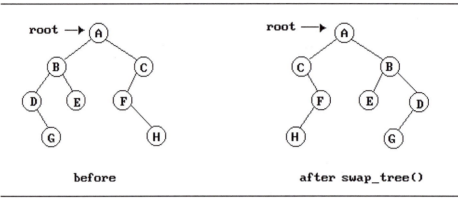

Figure 5.20 *swap_tree* example

(1)   If *ptr* −> *left_child* is null, replace *ptr* −> *left_child* with a pointer to the node that would be visited before *ptr* in an inorder traversal. That is we replace the null link with a pointer to the *inorder predecessor* of *ptr*.

(2)   If *ptr* −> *right_child* is null, replace *ptr* −> *right_child* with a pointer to the node that would be visited after *ptr* in an inorder traversal. That is we replace the null link with a pointer to the *inorder successor* of *ptr*.

Figure 5.21 shows the binary tree of Figure 5.9(b) with its threads drawn as dotted lines. This tree has nine nodes and 10 null links that we have replaced by threads. If we traverse the tree in inorder, we visit the nodes in the order *H, D, I, B, E, A, F, C, G*. To see how the threads are created we will use node *E* as an example. Since *E*'s left child is a null link, we replace it with a pointer to the node that comes before *E*, which is *B*. Similarly, since *E*'s right child is also null, we replace the null link with a pointer to the node that comes after *E* in an inorder traversal, which is *A*. We create the remaining threads in a similar fashion.

When we represent the tree in memory, we must be able to distinguish between threads and normal pointers. This is done by adding two additional fields to the node structure, *left_thread* and *right_thread*. Assume that *ptr* is an arbitrary node in a threaded tree. If *ptr* −> *left_thread* = *TRUE*, then *ptr* −> *left_child* contains a thread; otherwise it contains a pointer to the left child. Similarly, if *ptr* −> *right_thread* = *TRUE*, then *ptr* −> *right_child* contains a thread; otherwise it contains a pointer to the right child.

This node structure is given by the following C declarations:

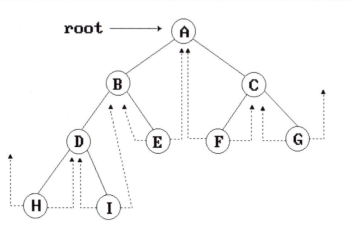

Figure 5.21: Threaded tree corresponding to Figure 5.9(b)

```
typedef struct threaded_tree *threaded_pointer;
typedef struct threaded_tree {
        short int left_thread;
        threaded_pointer left_child;
        char data;
        threaded_pointer right_child;
        short int right_thread;
        };
```

In Figure 5.21 two threads have been left dangling: one in the left child of *H*, the other in the right child of *G*. In the case of *H*, we cannot replace its null left child with a thread to the node that precedes *H* because *H* is the first node in the inorder traversal. Similarly, we cannot replace *G*'s null right child with a thread to the node that follows it since *G* is the last node in an inorder traversal. Obviously we do not want to have loose threads in our tree. Therefore, we assume that all threaded binary trees have a head node. This means that an empty threaded tree always contains one node, represented in Figure 5.22.

The complete memory representation of the tree of Figure 5.21 is shown in Figure 5.23. The variable *root* points to the head node of the tree, while *root* −> *left_child* points to the start of the first node of the actual tree. This is true for all threaded trees. Notice that we have handled the problem of the loose threads by having them point to the head node, *root*.

left_thread	left_child	data	right_child	right_thread
TRUE	•	——	•	FALSE

Figure 5.22: An empty threaded tree

Inorder Traversal of a Threaded Binary Tree

By using of threads we can simplify the algorithm for an inorder traversal. Observe that for any node, *ptr*, in a threaded binary tree, if *ptr* $\rightarrow$ *right_thread* = *TRUE*, the inorder successor of *ptr* is *ptr* $\rightarrow$ *right_child* by definition of the threads. Otherwise we obtain the inorder successor of *ptr* by following a path of left-child links from the right-child of *ptr* until we reach a node with *left_thread* = *TRUE*. The function *insucc* (Program 5.10) finds the inorder successor of any node in a threaded tree without using a stack.

To perform an inorder traversal we make repeated calls to *insucc*. The operation is implemented in *tinorder* (Program 5.11). This function assumes that the tree is pointed to by the head node's left child and that the head node's right thread is *FALSE*. The computing time for *tinorder* is still O(*n*) for a threaded binary tree with *n* nodes, although the constant factor is smaller than that of *iter − inorder*.

Inserting A Node Into A Threaded Binary Tree

We have seen how to use the threads of a threaded binary tree for an inorder traversal. We also can use the threads to simplify the algorithms for preorder and postorder traversals. Let us now consider how to make insertions into a threaded tree. We examine only the case of inserting a new node as the right child of an existing node, *parent*, leaving the insertion of a left child as an exercise.

Assume that we have a node, *parent*, that has an empty right subtree. We wish to insert *child* as the right child of *parent*. To do this we must:

(1)   change *parent* $\rightarrow$ *right_thread* to *FALSE*

(2)   set *child* $\rightarrow$ *left_thread* and *child* $\rightarrow$ *right_thread* to *TRUE*

(3)   set *child* $\rightarrow$ *left_child* to point to *parent*

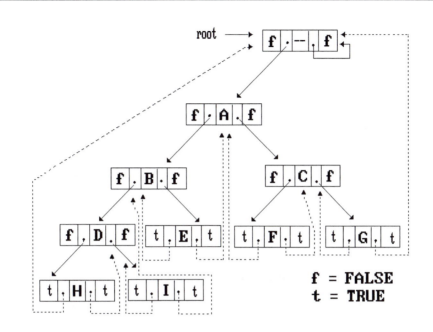

f = FALSE
t = TRUE

Figure 5.23: Memory representation of a threaded tree

```
threaded_pointer insucc(threaded_pointer tree)
{
/* find the inorder sucessor of tree in a threaded binary
tree */
   threaded_pointer temp;
   temp = tree->right_child;
   if (!tree->right_thread)
     while (!temp->left_thread)
        temp = temp->left_child;
   return temp;
}
```

Program 5.10: Finding the inorder successor of a node

```
void tinorder(threaded_pointer tree)
{
/* traverse the threaded binary tree inorder */
   threaded_pointer temp = tree;
   for (;;) {
      temp = insucc(temp);
      if (temp = tree) break;
      printf("%3c", temp->data);
   }
}
```

Program 5.11: Inorder traversal of a threaded binary tree

(4)   set *child* -> *right_child* to *parent* -> *right_child*

(5)   change *parent* -> *right_child* to point to *child*

Figure 5.24(a) is an example of this situation. In this case, we wish to insert node *D* as a right child of node *B*.

   If *parent* has a nonempty right subtree, insertion is slightly more difficult since the right subtree of parent becomes the right subtree of *child* after the insertion. When this is done, *child* becomes the inorder predecessor of the node that was previously *parent*'s inorder successor. Figure 5.24(b) illustrates this situation. In this case we wish to insert node *X* between nodes *B* and *D*. The function *insert_right* (Program 5.12) contains the C code which handles both cases.

EXERCISES

1.   Draw the binary tree of Figure 5.14(a), showing its threaded representation.

2.   Repeat Exercise 1 using the tree of Figure 5.14(b).

3.   Write a function, *insert_left*, that inserts a new node, *child*, as the left child of node *parent* in a threaded binary tree. The left child pointer of *parent* becomes the left child pointer of *child*.

4.   Write a function that traverses a threaded binary tree in postorder. What are the time and space requirements of your method?

5.   Write a function that traverses a threaded binary tree in preorder. What are the time and space requirements of your method?

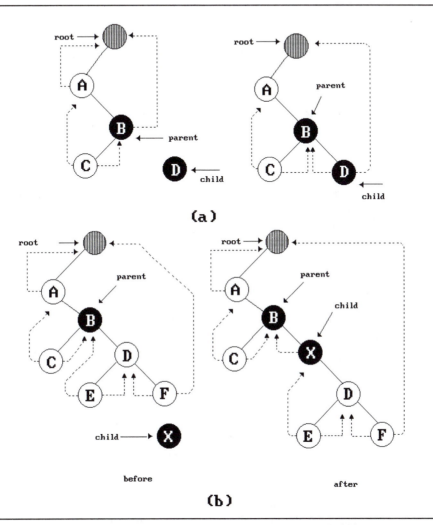

(a)

before

after

(b)

Figure 5.24: Insertion of child as a right child of parent in a threaded binary tree

5.6   HEAPS

In Section 5.2.2 we defined a complete binary tree. In this section, we present a special form of a complete binary tree that is used in many applications.

```
void insert_right(threaded_pointer parent,
                                threaded_pointer child)
{
/* insert child as the right child of parent in a threaded
binary tree */
   threaded_pointer temp;
   child->right_child = parent->right_child;
   child->right_thread = parent->right_thread;
   child->left_child = parent;
   child->left_thread = TRUE;
   parent->right_child = child;
   parent->right_thread = FALSE;
   if (!child->right_thread) {
      temp = insucc(child);
      temp->left_child = child;
   }
}
```

Program 5.12: Right insertion in a threaded binary tree

5.6.1   The Heap Abstract Data Type

Definition: A *max tree* is a tree in which the key value in each node is no smaller than the key values in its children (if any). A *max heap* is a complete binary tree that is also a max tree. □

Definition: A *min tree* is a tree in which the key value in each node is no larger than the key values in its children (if any). A *min heap* is a complete binary tree that is also a min tree. □

Figure 5.25 shows some example max heaps and Figure 5.26 shows some example min heaps. Notice that we represent a heap as an array, although we do not use position 0. This allows us to use the addressing scheme provided by Lemma 5.3. From the heap definitions it follows that the root of a min tree contains the smallest key in the tree while the root of a max tree contains the largest key in the tree.

When viewed as an ADT, a max heap is very simple. In particular the only basic operations are:

(1)   creation of an empty heap

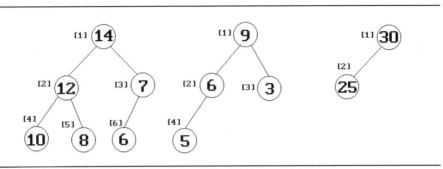

Figure 5.25: Sample max heaps

(2)   insertion of a new element into the heap

(3)   deletion of the largest element from the heap

These operations are abstractly defined in Structure 5.2. The real challenge is the design of the representation of a heap so that insertion and deletion can be carried out efficiently.

5.6.2   Priority Queues

Heaps are frequently used to implement *priority queues*. Unlike the queues we discussed in Chapter 3, a priority queue deletes the element with the highest (or the lowest) priority. At any time we can insert an element with arbitrary priority into a priority queue. If our application requires us to delete the element with the highest priority, we use a max heap. For example, suppose the job scheduler of our operating system uses a priority system in which administrators are given the highest priority and students the lowest. We would implement the priority queue that holds the jobs as a max heap. If our application requires us to delete the element with the lowest priority, we use a min heap. For example, suppose the scheduler of our operating system schedules jobs based on the anticipated amount of run time with priority given to shorter jobs. In this case, we would implement the priority queue that holds the jobs as a min heap.

Heaps are only one way to implement priority queues. Therefore, before we discuss the various heap operations, we first should examine some of the other representations. Although we will assume that each deletion removes the element with the highest value from the queue, our conclusions also apply when we remove the element with the smallest value. Figure 5.27 shows the insertion and deletion times for several representations, including a max heap.

An array is the simplest representation of a priority queue. Suppose that we have n elements in this queue. If we use an array, we can easily add to the priority queue by placing the new item at the current end of the array. Hence, insertion has a complexity

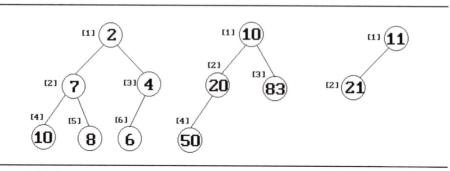

Figure 5.26: Sample min heaps

structure *MaxHeap* is

    objects: a complete binary tree of $n > 0$ elements organized so that the value in each node is at least as large as those in its children

    functions:

        for all *heap* ∈ *MaxHeap*, *item* ∈ *Element*, *n*, *max−size* ∈ integer

MaxHeap Create(*max_size*)	::=	create an empty heap that can hold a maximum of *max_size* elements.
Boolean HeapFull(*heap*, *n*)	::	**if** (*n* == *max−size*) **return** *TRUE* **else return** *FALSE*
MaxHeap Insert(*heap*, *item*, *n*)	::=	**if** (!HeapFull(*heap*, *n*)) insert *item* into *heap* and return the resulting heap **else return** error.
Boolean HeapEmpty(*heap*, *n*)	::	**if** (*n* > 0) **return** *TRUE* **else return** *FALSE*
Element Delete(*heap*, *n*)	::=	**if** (!HeapEmpty(*heap*, *n*)) **return** one instance of the largest element in the heap and remove it from the heap **else return** error.

Structure 5.2: Abstract data type *MaxHeap*

of $\Theta(1)$. To perform a deletion, we must first search for the element with the largest key and then delete this element. The search time is $\Theta(n)$ and the time to shift the array elements is $O(n)$. Switching to an unordered linked list improves our computing time only slightly. We can add to the front of the chain in $\Theta(1)$ time. However, since we still must search the list to find the element with the largest key, the time for a deletion is $\Theta(n)$. With this representation, we have eliminated only the time needed to shift elements. An ordered array permits deletion of an element in $\Theta(1)$ time, but inserting an element requires shifting some or all elements and this takes $O(n)$ time. Using a linked list

Representation	Insertion	Deletion
Unordered array	$\Theta(1)$	$\Theta(n)$
Unordered linked list	$\Theta(1)$	$\Theta(n)$
Sorted array	$O(n)$	$\Theta(1)$
Sorted linked list	$O(n)$	$\Theta(1)$
Max heap	$O(\log_2 n)$	$O(\log_2 n)$

Figure 5.27: Priority queue representations

maintained in nonincreasing order assures that the highest element is always the first element in the list. However, since we must now search the list to add an element, the time for this operation is $O(n)$. As we shall prove shortly, representing a priority queue as a heap allows us to perform both insertions and deletions in $O(\log_2 n)$ time, making it the preferred representation.

5.6.3   Insertion Into A Max Heap

To illustrate the insertion operation, we begin with the five-element max heap shown in Figure 5.28(a). When we add an element to this heap, the new six-element heap must have the structure shown in Figure 5.28(b). (We have highlighted the new node's location.) Adding the new node at any other location violates the heap definition since the result would not be a complete binary tree.

Now suppose that the new element has a key value of 1. In this case, we simply place it in the new node, that is, it becomes the left child of 2. If instead the value of the new element is a 5, we cannot insert it as the left child of 2 since this violates the heap definition. So we must move the 2 down to the new node and place the 5 at the old position of 2. Since the parent (20) of the old position of 2 is at least as large as the value being inserted (5), we do not need to change the parent. Figure 5.28(c) shows the resulting heap. Next, suppose that the new element has a value of 21 rather than 5. In this case, the 2 moves down to its left child and the 20 moves down to its right child. We then insert the 21 at the old position of 20. Figure 5.28(d) shows the resulting heap.

To implement the insertion strategy described above, we need to go from an element to its parent. If we use a linked representation, we must add a parent field to each node. However, since a heap is a complete binary tree, we also can use the array representation discussed in Section 5.2.3. Lemma 5.3 allows us to locate easily the parent of any element. The function *insert_max_heap* (Program 5.13) performs an insertion into a max heap that contains n elements. We assume that the heap is created using the following C declarations:

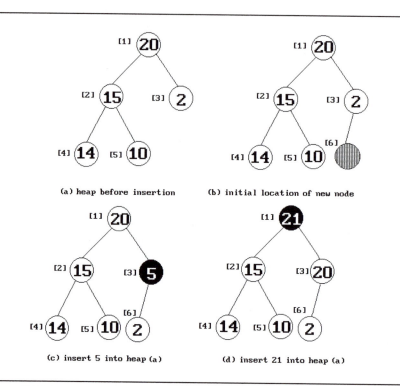

(a) heap before insertion

(b) initial location of new node

(c) insert 5 into heap (a)

(d) insert 21 into heap (a)

Figure 5.28: Insertion into a max heap

```
#define MAX_ELEMENTS 200 /* maximum heap size+1 */
#define HEAP_FULL(n) (n == MAX_ELEMENTS-1)
#define HEAP_EMPTY(n) (!n)
typedef struct {
        int key;
        /* other fields */
        } element;
element heap[MAX_ELEMENTS];
int n = 0;
```

Analysis of *insert_max_heap*: The function *insert_max_heap* first checks for a full heap. If the heap is not full, we set i to the size of the new heap $(n + 1)$. We must now determine the correct position of *item* in the heap. We use the **while** loop to accomplish this task. This follows a path from the new leaf of the max heap to the root until it either reaches the root or reaches a position i such that the value in the parent position $i/2$ is at least as large as the value to be inserted. Since a heap is a complete binary tree with n elements, it has a height of $\lceil \log_2(n + 1) \rceil$. This means that the **while** loop is iterated

```
void insert_max_heap(element item, int *n)
{
/*insert item into a max heap of current size *n */
   int i;
   if (HEAP_FULL(*n)){
      fprintf(stderr, "The heap is full. \n");
      exit(1);
   }
   i = ++(*n);
   while ((i != 1) && (item.key > heap[i/2].key)) {
      heap[i] = heap[i/2];
      i /= 2;
   }
   heap[i] = item;
}
```

Program 5.13: Insertion into a max heap

$O(\log_2 n)$ times. Hence, the complexity of the insertion function is $O(\log_2 n)$. □

5.6.4   Deletion From A Max Heap

When we delete an element from a max heap, we always take it from the root of the heap. For instance, a deletion from the heap of Figure 5.28(a) removes the element 20. Since the resulting heap has only four elements, we must restructure the tree so that it corresponds to a complete binary tree with four elements. The desired structure is illustrated in Figure 5.29(a) (the node that will be removed is highlighted). To remove the node, we place the node's element (10) in the root node (see Figure 5.29(b)). The structure is now correct, but the resulting tree violates the max heap definition. To reestablish the heap we move down the heap, comparing the parent node with its children and exchanging out-of-order elements until the heap is reestablished. Figure 5.29(c) shows the final heap. The function *delete_max_heap* (Program 5.14) implements this deletion strategy.

Analysis of *delete_max_heap*: The function *delete_max_heap* operates by moving down the heap, comparing and exchanging parent and child nodes until the heap definition is re-established. Since the height of a heap with n elements is $\lceil \log_2(n + 1) \rceil$, the **while** loop of *delete_max_heap* is iterated $O(\log_2 n)$ times. Hence, the complexity of a deletion is $O(\log_2 n)$. □

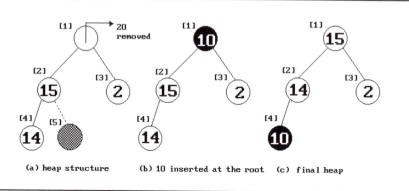

(a) heap structure   (b) 10 inserted at the root (c) final heap

Figure 5.29: Deletion from a max heap

EXERCISES

1. Two other possible representations of a priority queue would be a circular, doubly linked unordered list and a circular, doubly linked ordered list. Add these two representations to Figure 5.27. Explain your assessment of their insertion and deletion times.

2. Suppose that we have the following key values: 7, 16, 49, 82, 5, 31, 6, 2, 44.

   (a) Write out the max heap after each value is inserted into the heap.

   (b) Write out the min heap after each value is inserted into the heap.

3. Write a C function that changes the priority of an arbitrary element in a max heap. The resulting heap must satisfy the max heap definition. What is the computing time of your function?

4. Write a C function that deletes an arbitrary element from a max heap (the deleted element may be anywhere in the heap). The resulting heap must satisfy the max heap definition. What is the computing time of your function? (Hint: Change the priority of the element to one greater than that of the root, use the change priority function of Exercise 3, and then *delete_max_heap*.)

5. Write a C function that searches for an arbitrary element in a max heap. What is the computing time of your function?

6. Write insertion and deletion functions for a max heap represented as a linked binary tree. Assume that each node has a parent field as well as the usual left child, right child, and data fields.

7. § [*Programming project*] Write a user-friendly, menu-driven program that allows the user to perform the following operations on min heaps.

```
element delete_max_heap(int *n)
{
/* delete element with the highest key from the heap */
   int parent, child;
   element item, temp;
   if (HEAP_EMPTY(*n)) {
      fprintf(stderr, "The heap is empty\n");
      exit(1);
   }
   /* save value of the element with the highest key */
   item = heap[1];
   /* use last element in heap to adjust heap */
   temp = heap[(*n)--];
   parent = 1;
   child = 2;
   while (child <= *n) {
      /* find the larger child of the current parent */
      if   (child   <   *n)   &&   (heap[child].key   <
     heap[child+1].key)
         child++;
      if (temp.key >= heap[child].key) break;
      /* move to the next lower level */
      heap[parent] = heap[child];
      parent = child;
      child *= 2;
   }
   heap[parent] = temp;
   return item;
}
```

Program 5.14: Deletion from a max heap

    (a)   create a min heap

    (b)   remove the key with the lowest value

    (c)   change the priority of an arbitrary element

    (d)   insert an element into the heap.

5.7 BINARY SEARCH TREES

5.7.1 Introduction

While a heap is well suited for applications that require priority queues, it is not well suited for applications in which we must delete arbitrary elements. Deletion of an arbitrary element from an n element heap takes O(n) time. This is no better than the time needed for the deletion of an arbitrary element from an unordered list. Similarly, searching for an arbitrary element takes O(n) in a heap.

A binary search tree has a better performance than any of the data structures studied so far when the operations we wish to perform are insertion, deletion, and searching. In fact, with a binary search tree we can perform these operations by both key value (for example, delete the element with key x) and by rank (for example, delete the fifth smallest element).

Definition: A *binary search tree* is a binary tree. It may be empty. If it is not empty, it satisfies the following properties:

(1)   Every element has a key, and no two elements have the same key, that is, the keys are unique.

(2)   The keys in a nonempty left subtree must be smaller than the key in the root of the subtree.

(3)   The keys in a nonempty right subtree must be larger than the key in the root of the subtree.

(4)   The left and right subtrees are also binary search trees. □

There is some redundancy in the definition. Properties (2), (3), and (4) taken together imply that the keys must be distinct. Therefore, we can replace property (1) with the property: The root has a key. However, the definition provided above is clearer than the nonredundant version.

Some sample binary trees are shown in Figure 5.30. The tree of Figure 5.30(a) is not a binary search tree since the right subtree fails to satisfy property (4). This subtree has a root with a key value of 25 and a right child with a smaller key value (22). Figure 5.30(b) and Figure 5.30(c) are binary search trees.

Since a binary search tree is a specialized form of a binary tree, the C declarations for a binary search tree do not differ from the declarations that we previously used to create a binary tree. Similarly, all the binary tree operations discussed in Sections 5.3 and 5.4 apply directly to binary search trees. Thus, for example, we may use the inorder, preorder, and postorder traversals without modification. To these operations, we add those of insertion, deletion, and search.

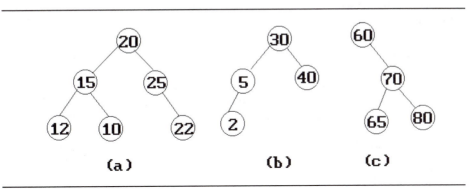

Figure 5.30: Binary trees

5.7.2 Searching A Binary Search Tree

Since the definition of a binary search tree is recursive, it is easiest to describe a recursive search method. Suppose we wish to search for an element with a *key*. We begin at the *root*. If the *root* is *NULL*, the search tree contains no elements and the search is unsuccessful. Otherwise, we compare *key* with the key value in *root*. If *key* equals *root*'s key value, then the search terminates successfully. If *key* is less than *root*'s key value, then no element in the right subtree can have a key value equal to *key*. Therefore, we search the left subtree of *root*. If *key* is larger than *root*'s key value, we search the right subtree of *root*. The function *search* (Program 5.15) recursively searches the subtrees.

```
tree_pointer search(tree_pointer root, int key)
{
/* return a pointer to the node that contains key.  If
there is no such node, return NULL. */
   if (!root) return NULL;
   if (key == root->data) return root;
   if (key < root->data)
      return search(root->left_child, key);
   return search(root->right_child,key);
}
```

Program 5.15: Recursive search of a binary search tree

We can easily replace the recursive search function with a comparable iterative one. The function *search*2 (Program 5.16) accomplishes this by replacing the recursion with a **while** loop.

```
tree_pointer search2(tree_pointer tree, int key)
{
/* return a pointer to the node that contains key.  If
there is no such node, return NULL. */
   while (tree) {
      if (key == tree->data) return tree;
      if (key < tree->data)
         tree = tree->left_child;
      else
         tree = tree->right_child;
      }
   return NULL;
}
```

Program 5.16: Iterative search of a binary search tree

Analysis of *search* and *search2*: If *h* is the height of the binary search tree, then we can perform the search using either *search* or *search*2 in $O(h)$. However, *search* has an additional stack space requirement which is $O(h)$. □

5.7.3   Inserting Into A Binary Search Tree

To insert a new element, *key*, we must first verify that the key is different from those of existing elements. To do this we search the tree. If the search is unsuccessful, then we insert the element at the point the search terminated. For instance, to insert an element with key 80 into the tree of Figure 5.30(b), we first search the tree for 80. This search terminates unsuccessfully, and the last node examined has value 40. We insert the new element as the right child of this node. The resulting search tree is shown in Figure 5.31(a). Figure 5.31(b) shows the result of inserting the key 35 into the search tree of Figure 5.31(a). This strategy is implemented by *insert_node* (Program 5.17). This uses the function *modified − search* which is a slightly modified version of function *search*2 (Program 5.16). This function searches the binary search tree **node* for the key *num*. If the tree is empty or if *num* is present, it returns *NULL*. Otherwise, it returns a pointer to the last node of the tree that was encountered during the search. The new element is to be inserted as a child of this node.

Analysis of *insert_node*: The time required to search the tree for *num* is $O(h)$ where *h* is

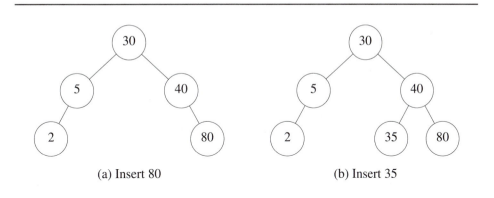

(a) Insert 80   (b) Insert 35

Figure 5.31: Inserting into a binary search tree

```
void insert_node(tree_pointer *node, int num)
/* If num is in the tree pointed at by node do nothing;
otherwise add a new node with data = num */
{
   tree_pointer ptr, temp = modified_search(*node, num);
   if (temp || !(*node)) {
      /* num is not in the tree */
      ptr = (tree_pointer)malloc(sizeof(node));
      if (IS_FULL(ptr)) {
         fprintf(stderr, "The memory is full\n");
         exit(1);
      }
      ptr->data = num;
      ptr->left_child = ptr->right_child = NULL;
      if (*node) /* insert as child of temp */
         if (num < temp->data) temp->left_child = ptr;
         else temp->right_child = ptr;
      else *node = ptr;
   }
}
```

Program 5.17: Inserting an element into a binary search tree

its height. The remainder of the algorithm takes $\Theta(1)$ time. So, the overall time needed by *insert_node* is O(h). □

5.7.4 Deletion From A Binary Search Tree

Deletion of a leaf node is easy. For example, to delete 35 from the tree of Figure 5.31(b), we set the left child field of its parent to *NULL* and free the node. This gives us the tree of Figure 5.31(a). The deletion of a nonleaf node that has only a single child is also easy. We erase the node and then place the single child in the place of the erased node. For example, if we delete 40 from the tree of Figure 5.31(a) we obtain the tree in Figure 5.32.

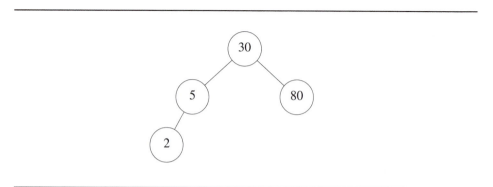

Figure 5.32: Deletion from a binary search tree

When we delete a nonleaf node with two children, we replace the node with either the largest element in its left subtree or the smallest element in its right subtree. Then we proceed by deleting this replacing element from the subtree from which it was taken. For instance, suppose that we wish to delete 60 from the tree of Figure 5.33(a). We may replace 60 with either the largest element (55) in its left subtree or the smallest element (70) in its right subtree. Suppose we opt to replace it with the largest element in the left subtree. We move the 55 into the root of the subtree. We then make the left child of the node that previously contained the 55 the right child of the node containing 50, and we free the old node containing 55. Figure 5.33(b) shows the final result. One may verify that the largest and smallest elements in a subtree are always in a node of degree zero or one. This observation simplifies the code for the deletion function. We leave the formal writing of this function as an exercise. From the examples considered, you should be able to see that a deletion can be performed in O(h) time where h is the height of the tree.

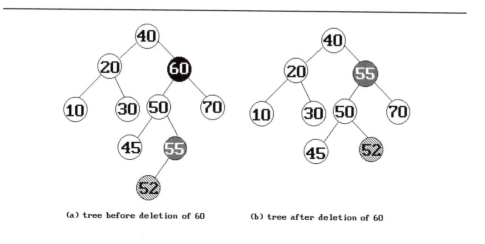

(a) tree before deletion of 60   (b) tree after deletion of 60

Figure 5.33: Deletion of a node with two children

5.7.5 Height Of A Binary Search Tree

Unless care is taken, the height of a binary search tree with n elements can become as large as n. This is the case, for instance, when we use *insert—node* to insert the keys $1, 2, 3, \cdots, n$, in that order, into an initially empty binary search tree. However, when insertion and deletions are made at random using the above functions, the height of the binary search tree is $O(\log_2 n)$, on the average.

Search trees with a worst case height of $O(\log_2 n)$ are called *balanced search trees*. Balanced search trees that permit searches, insertions, and deletions, to be performed in $O(h)$ time exist. Most notable among these are *AVL*, 2-3, and red-black trees. We discuss these in Chapter 10.

EXERCISES

1. Assume that we change the definition of a binary search tree so that equal keys are permitted and that we add a count field to the node structure.

    (a) Rewrite *insert—node* so that it increments the count field when a plural key is found. Otherwise, a new node is created.

    (b) Rewrite *delete* so that it decrements the count field when the key is found. The node is eliminated only if its count is 0.

2. Write the C code for the function *modified – search* that is used in Program 5.17.

3. Obtain a recursive version of *insert_node*. Which of the two versions is more efficient? Why?

4. Write a recursive C function to delete a key from a binary search tree. What is the time and space complexity of your function?

5. Obtain an iterative C function to delete a key from a binary search tree. The space complexity of your function should be O(1). Show that this is the case. What is the time complexity of your function?

6. Assume that a binary search tree is represented as a threaded binary search tree. Write functions to search, insert, and delete.

5.8   SELECTION TREES

Suppose we have k ordered sequences that are to be merged into a single ordered sequence. Each sequence consists of some number of records and is in nondecreasing order of a designated field called the *key*. An ordered sequence is called a *run*. Let n be the number of records in the k runs together. The merging task can be accomplished by repeatedly outputting the record with the smallest key. The smallest has to be found from k possibilities and it could be the leading record in any of the k-runs. The most direct way to merge k-runs would be to make $k - 1$ comparisons to determine the next record to output. For $k > 2$, we can achieve a reduction in the number of comparisons needed to find the next smallest element by using the idea of a selection tree. A *selection tree* is a binary tree where each node represents the smaller of its two children. Thus, the root node represents the smallest node in the tree. Figure 5.34 illustrates a selection tree for the case $k = 8$.

The construction of this selection tree may be compared to the playing of a tournament in which the winner is the record with the smaller key. Then, each nonleaf node in the tree represents the winner of a tournament and the root node represents the overall winner or the smallest key. A leaf node here represents the first record in the corresponding run. Since the records being merged are generally large, each node will contain only a pointer to the record it represents. Thus, the root node contains a pointer to the first record in run 4. The selection tree may be represented using the array representation scheme for binary trees that results from Lemma 5.3. The number above each node in Figure 5.34 represents the address of the node in this sequential representation. The record pointed to by the root has the smallest key and so may be output. Now, the next record from run 4 enters the selection tree. It has a key value of 15. To restructure the tree, the tournament has to be replayed only along the path from node 11 to the root. Thus, the winner from nodes 10 and 11 is again node 11 ($15 < 20$). The winner from nodes 4 and 5 is node 4 ($9 < 15$). The winner from 2 and 3 is node 3 ($8 < 9$). The new tree is shown in Figure 5.35. The tournament is played between sibling nodes and the result put in the parent node. Lemma 5.3 may be used to compute the address of sibling and parent nodes efficiently. After each comparison the next takes place at one

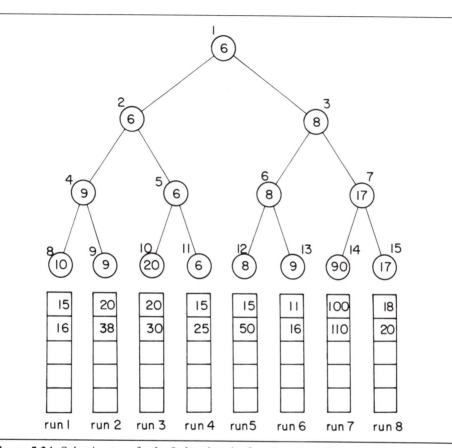

Figure 5.34: Selection tree for $k = 8$ showing the first three keys in each of the eight runs

higher level in the tree. The number of levels in the tree is $\lceil \log_2 k \rceil + 1$. So, the time to restructure the tree is $O(\log_2 k)$. The tree has to be restructured each time a record is merged into the output file. Hence, the time required to merge all n records is $O(n \log_2 k)$. The time required to set up the selection tree the first time is $O(k)$. Hence, the total time needed to merge the k runs is $O(n \log_2 k)$.

A slightly faster algorithm results if each node represents the loser of the tournament rather than the winner. After the record with smallest key is output, the selection tree of Figure 5.34 is to be restructured. Since the record with the smallest key value is in run 4, this restructuring involves inserting the next record from this run into the tree. The next record has key value 15. Tournaments are played between sibling nodes along the path from node 11 to the root. Since these sibling nodes represent the losers of tournaments played earlier, we would simplify the restructuring process by placing in each

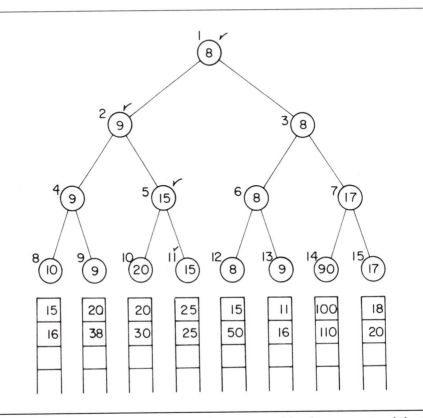

Figure 5.35: Selection tree of Figure 5.34 after one record has been output and the tree restructured (nodes that were changed are ticked)

nonleaf node a pointer to the record that loses the tournament rather than to the winner of the tournament. A tournament tree in which each nonleaf node retains a pointer to the loser is called a *tree of losers*. Figure 5.36 shows the tree of losers corresponding to the selection tree of Figure 5.34. For convenience, each node contains the key value of a record rather than a pointer to the record represented. The leaf nodes represent the first record in each run. An additional node, node 0, has been added to represent the overall winner of the tournament. Following the output of the overall winner, the tree is restructured by playing tournaments along the path from node 11 to node 1. The records with which these tournaments are to be played are readily available from the parent nodes.

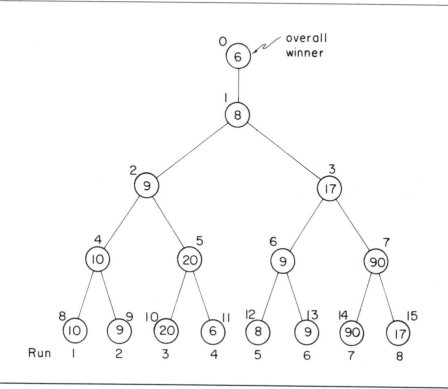

Figure 5.36: Tree of losers corresponding to Figure 5.34

EXERCISES

1. Write an algorithm to construct a tree of losers for records R_i, $1 \le i \le k$, with key values K_i, $1 \le i \le k$. Let the tree nodes be T_i, $0 \le i < k$, with T_i, $1 \le i < k$, a pointer to the loser of a tournament and T_0 a pointer to the overall winner. Show that this construction can be carried out in time $O(k)$.

2. Do the previous exercise for the case of a tree of winners.

3. Write an algorithm, using a tree of losers, to carry out a k-way merge of k runs, $k \ge 2$. Show that if there are n records in the k runs together, then the computing time is $O(n \log_2 k)$.

4. Do the previous exercise for the case when a tree of winners is used.

5. Compare the performance of your algorithms for the preceding two exercises for the case $k = 8$. Generate eight runs of data, each having 100 records in it. Use a random number generator for this (the keys obtained from the random number generator will need to be sorted before the merge can begin). Measure the time taken to merge the eight runs using the two strategies. Approximately how much faster is the tree of losers scheme?

5.9 FORESTS

Definition: A *forest* is a set of $n \geq 0$ disjoint trees. □

The concept of a forest is very close to that of a tree because if we remove the root of a tree we obtain a forest. For example, removing the root of any binary tree produces a forest of two trees. In this section, we briefly consider several forest operations, including transforming a forest into a binary tree and forest traversals. In the next section, we use forests to represent disjoint sets.

5.9.1 Transforming A Forest Into A Binary Tree

Suppose that we have a forest of three trees as illustrated in Figure 5.37. To transform this forest into a single binary tree, we first obtain the binary tree representation for each of the trees in the forest. We then link all the binary trees together through the sibling field of the root node. Applying this transformation to the forest of Figure 5.37 gives us the tree of Figure 5.38.

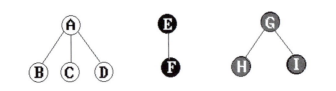

Figure 5.37: Forest with three trees

We can define this transformation formally as follows:

Definition: If $T_1, \cdots, T_n$ is a forest of trees, then the binary tree corresponding to this forest, denoted by $B(T_1, \cdots, T_n)$:

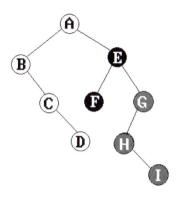

Figure 5.38: Binary tree representation of Figure 5.37

(1)   is empty, if $n = 0$

(2)   has root equal to root (T_1); has left subtree equal to $B(T_{11}, T_{12}, \cdots, T_{1m})$, where $T_{11}, T_{12}, \cdots, T_{1m}$ are the subtrees of root (T_1); and has right subtree $B(T_2, \cdots, T_n)$ □

5.9.2   Forest Traversals

Preorder, inorder, and postorder traversals of the corresponding binary tree T of a forest F have a natural correspondence with traversals of F. The preorder traversal of T is equivalent to visiting the nodes of F in tree preorder. We define this as:

(1)   If F is empty, then return.

(2)   Visit the root of the first tree of F.

(3)   Traverse the subtrees of the first tree in tree preorder.

(4)   Traverse the remaining trees of F in preorder.

Inorder traversal of T is equivalent to visiting the nodes of F in tree inorder, which is defined as:

(1)   If F is empty, then return.

(2)   Traverse the subtrees of the first tree in tree inorder.

(3)   Visit the root of the first tree.

(4)   Traverse the remaining trees in tree inorder.

There is no natural analog for the postorder traversal of the corresponding binary tree of a forest. Nevertheless, we can define the postorder traversal of a forest, F, as:

(1)   If F is empty, then return.

(2)   Traverse the subtrees of the first tree of F in tree postorder.

(3)   Traverse the remaining trees of F in tree postorder.

(4)   Visit the root of the first tree of F.

EXERCISES

1.   Define the inverse transformation of the one that creates the associated binary tree from a forest. Are these transformations unique?

2.   Prove that the preorder traversal of a forest and the preorder traversal of the associated binary tree give the same result.

3.   Prove that the inorder traversal of a forest and the inorder traversal of the associated binary tree give the same result.

4.   Prove that the postorder traversals of a forest and of its corresponding binary tree do not necessarily yield the same results.

5.10   SET REPRESENTATION

In this section, we study the use of trees in the representation of sets. For simplicity, we assume that the elements of the sets are the numbers 0, 1, 2, $\cdots$, $n-1$. In practice, these numbers might be indices into a symbol table that stores the actual names of the elements. We also assume that the sets being represented are pairwise disjoint, that is, if S_i and S_j are two sets and $i \neq j$, then there is no element that is in both S_i and S_j. For example, if we have 10 elements numbered 0 through 9, we may partition them into three disjoint sets, $S_1 = \{0, 6, 7, 8\}$, $S_2 = \{1, 4, 9\}$, and $S_3 = \{2, 3, 5\}$. Figure 5.39 shows one possible representation for these sets. Notice that for each set we have linked the nodes from the children to the parent, rather than our usual method of linking from the parent to the children. The reason for this change in linkage will become apparent when we discuss the implementation of set operations.

The minimal operations that we wish to perform on these sets are:

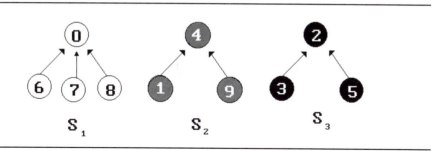

Figure 5.39: Possible forest representation of sets

(1) *Disjoint set union.* If S_i and S_j are two disjoint sets, then their union $S_i \cup S_j = \{$all elements, x, such that x is in S_i or $S_j\}$. Thus, $S_1 \cup S_2 = \{0, 6, 7, 8, 1, 4, 9\}$. Since we have assumed that all sets are disjoint, following the union of S_i and S_j we can assume that the sets S_i and S_j no longer exist independently. That is, we replace them by $S_i \cup S_j$.

(2) *Find(i).* Find the set containing the element, i. For example, 3 is in set S_3 and 8 is in set S_1.

5.10.1 Union And Find Operations

Let us consider the union operation first. Suppose that we wish to obtain the union of S_1 and S_2. Since we have linked the nodes from children to parent, we simply make one of the trees a subtree of the other. $S_1 \cup S_2$ could have either of the representations of Figure 5.40.

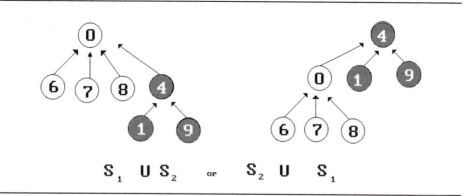

Figure 5.40: Possible representation of $S_1 \cup S_2$

To implement the set union operation, we simply set the parent field of one of the roots to the other root. We can accomplish this easily if, with each set name, we keep a pointer to the root of the tree representing that set. If, in addition, each root has a pointer to the set name, we can find which set an element is in by following the parent links to the root of its tree and then returning the pointer to the set name. Figure 5.41 shows this representation of S_1, S_2, and S_3.

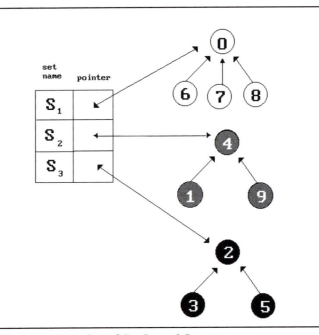

Figure 5.41: Data representation of S_1, S_2, and S_3

To simplify the discussion of the union and find algorithms, we will ignore the set names and identify the sets by the roots of the trees representing them. For example, rather than using the set name S_1 we refer to this set as 0. The transition to set names is easy. We assume that a table, *name* [ ], holds the set names. If i is an element in a tree with root j, and j has a pointer to entry k in the set name table, then the set name is just *name*[k].

Since the nodes in the trees are numbered 0 through $n - 1$ we can use the node's number as an index. This means that each node needs only one field, the index of its parent, to link to its parent. Thus, the only data structure that we need is an array, *int parent*[*MAX_ELEMENTS*], where *MAX_ELEMENTS* is the maximum number of elements. Figure 5.42 shows this representation of the sets, S_1, S_2, and S_3. Notice that root nodes have a parent of -1.

i	[0]	[1]	[2]	[3]	[4]	[5]	[6]	[7]	[8]	[9]
parent	−1	4	−1	2	−1	2	0	0	0	4

Figure 5.42: Array representation of S_1, S_2, and S_3

We can now implement $find(i)$ by simply following the indices starting at i and continuing until we reach a negative parent index. For example, $find(5)$, starts at 5, and then moves to 5's parent, 2. Since this node has a negative index we have reached the root. The operation $union(i,j)$ is equally simple. We pass in two trees with roots i and j. Assuming that we adopt the convention that the first tree becomes a subtree of the second, the statement $parent[i] = j$ accomplishes the union. Program 5.18 implements the union and find operations as just discussed.

```
int find1(int i)
{
   for(; parent[i] >= 0; i = parent[i])
      ;
   return i;
}
void union1(int i, int j)
{
   parent[i] = j;
}
```

Program 5.18: Initial attempt at union-find functions

Analysis of *union*1 and *find*1: Although *union*1 and *find*1 are easy to implement, their performance characteristics are not very good. For instance, if we start with p elements, each in a set of its own, that is, $S_i = \{i\}$, $0 \le i < p$, then the initial configuration is a forest with p nodes and $parent[i] = -1$, $0 \le i < p$. Now let us process the following sequence of union-find operations:

$$union(0, 1), find(0)$$
$$union(1, 2), find(0)$$
$$.$$
$$.$$
$$.$$
$$union(n-2, n-1), find(0)$$

This sequence produces the degenerate tree of Figure 5.43. Since the time taken for a union is constant, we can process all the $n - 1$ unions in time $O(n)$. However, for each *find*, we must follow a chain of parent links from 0 to the root. If the element is at level i, then the time required to find its root is $O(i)$. Hence, the total time needed to process the $n - 1$ finds is:

$$\sum_{i=2}^{n} i = O(n^2) \quad \square$$

Figure 5.43: Degenerate tree

By avoiding the creation of degenerate trees, we can attain far more efficient implementations of the union and find operations. We accomplish this by adopting the following *Weighting rule* for *union(i, j)*.

Definition: *Weighting rule for union(i, j)*. If the number of nodes in tree i is less than the number in tree j then make j the parent of i; otherwise make i the parent of j. $\square$

When we use this rule on the sequence of set unions described above, we obtain the trees of Figure 5.44. To implement the weighting rule, we need to know how many nodes there are in every tree. To do this easily, we maintain a count field in the root of every tree. If i is a root node, then *count[i]* equals the number of nodes in that tree. Since all nodes but the roots of trees have a nonnegative number in the parent field, we can maintain the count in the parent field of the roots as a negative number. When we incorporate the weighting rule, the union operation takes the form given in *union2* (Program 5.19). Remember that the arguments passed into *union2* must be roots of trees.

Lemma 5.4: Let T be a tree with n nodes created as a result of *union2*. No node in T has level greater than $\lfloor \log_2 n \rfloor + 1$.

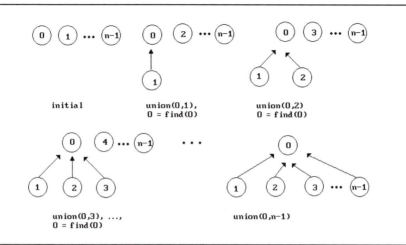

Figure 5.44: Trees obtained using the weighting rule

```
void union2(int i, int j)
{
/* union the sets with roots i and j, i != j, using
the weighting rule. parent[i] = -count[i] and
parent[j] = -count[j] */
   int temp = parent[i] + parent[j];
   if (parent[i] > parent[j]) {
      parent[i] = j; /* make j the new root */
      parent[j] = temp;
   }
   else {
      parent[j] = i; /*make i the new root */
      parent[i] = temp;
   }
}
```

Program 5.19: Union function

Proof: The lemma is clearly true for $n = 1$. Assume that it is true for all trees with i nodes, $i \leq n - 1$. We show that it is also true for $i = n$. Let T be a tree with n nodes created by *union2*. Consider the last union operation performed, *union(k, j)*. Let m be the number of nodes in tree j and $n-m$, the number of nodes in k. Without loss of generality, we may assume that $1 \leq m \leq n / 2$. Then the maximum level of any node in T is either the same as k or is one more than in j. If the former is the case, then the maximum level in T

is $\leq \lfloor \log_2(n-m) \rfloor + 1 \leq \lfloor \log_2 n \rfloor + 1$. If the latter is the case, then the maximum level is $\leq \lfloor \log_2 m \rfloor + 2 \leq \lfloor \log_2 n/2 \rfloor + 2 \leq \lfloor \log_2 n \rfloor + 1$. $\square$

Example 5.1 shows that the bound of Lemma 5.4 is achievable for some sequence of unions.

Example 5.1: Consider the behavior of *union2* on the following sequence of unions starting from the initial configuration of *parent* $[i] = -count [i] = -1, 0 \leq i < n = 2^3$:

$$union(0, 1) \quad union(2, 3) \quad union(4, 5) \quad union(6, 7)$$
$$union(0, 2) \quad union(4, 6) \quad union(0, 4)$$

When the sequence of unions is performed by columns (i.e., top to bottom within a column with column 1 first, column 2 next, and so on), the trees of Figure 5.45 are obtained. As is evident from this example, in the general case, the maximum level can be $\lfloor \log_2 m \rfloor + 1$ if the tree has m nodes. $\square$

As a result of Lemma 5.4, the time to process a find in an n element tree is $O(\log_2 n)$. If we must process an intermixed sequence of $n - 1$ union and m find operations, then the time becomes $O(n + m \log_2 n)$. Surprisingly, further improvement is possible if we add a collapsing rule to the find operation.

Definition [Collapsing rule]: If j is a node on the path from i to its root then make j a child of the root. $\square$

Program 5.20 incorporates the collapsing rule into the find operation. The new function roughly doubles the time for an individual find. However, it reduces the worst case time over a sequence of finds.

Example 5.2: Consider the tree created by *union2* on the sequence of unions of Example 5.1. Now process the following 8 finds:

$$find\,(7), find(7), \cdots, find(7)$$

Using the old version of *find*, *find(7)* requires going up three parent link fields for a total of 24 moves to process all eight finds. In the new version of *find*, the first *find(7)* requires going up three links and then resetting two links. Each of the remaining seven finds requires going up only one link field. The total cost is now only 13 moves (note that even though only two links need to be changed, function *find2* sets three including the one from node four). $\square$

The worst case behavior of the union-find algorithms while processing a sequence of unions and finds is stated in Lemma 5.5. Before stating this lemma, let us introduce a very slowly growing function, $\alpha(m, n)$, which is related to a functional inverse of Ackermann's function $A(p,q)$. We have the following definition for $\alpha(m, n)$:

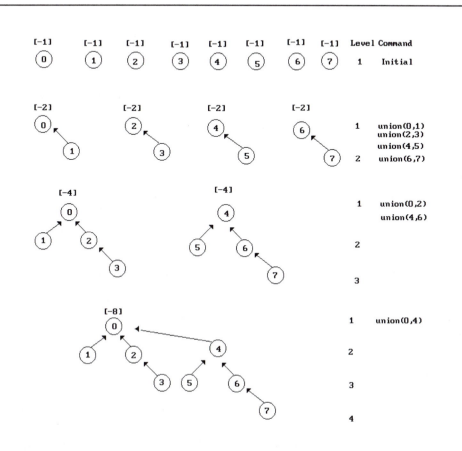

Figure 5.45: Trees achieving worst case bound

$$\alpha(m,\, n) = \min\{z \ge 1 \mid A(z,\, 4\lceil m/n \rceil) > \log_2 n\}$$

The definition of Ackermann's function used here is:

$$A(p,\, q) = \begin{cases} 2q & p = 0 \\ 0 & q = 0 \text{ and } p \ge 1 \\ 0 & p \ge 1 \text{ and } p = 1 \\ A(p-1,\, A(p,\, q-1)) & p \ge 1 \text{ and } q \ge 2 \end{cases}$$

```
int find2(int i)
{
/* find the root of the tree containing element i. Use the
collapsing rule to collapse all nodes from i to root */
    int root, trail, lead;
    for (root = i; parent[root] >= 0; root = parent[root])
        ;
    for (trail = i; trail != root; trail = lead) {
        lead = parent[trail];
        parent[trail] = root;
    }
    return root;
}
```

Program 5.20: Find function

The function $A (p, q)$ is a very rapidly growing function. You may prove that:

(1) $\quad A\,(3, 4) = 2^{2^{\cdot^{\cdot^{\cdot^2}}}}\Big\}$ 65,536 twos

(2) $\quad A\,(p,q+1) > A\,(p,q)$

(3) $\quad A\,(p+1,q) \geq A\,(p,q)$

If we assume that $m \neq 0$, then (2) and (3) together with the definition of $\alpha(m, n)$ imply that $\alpha(m, n) \leq 3$ for $\log_2 n < A(3, 4)$. But from (1), $A(3, 4)$ is a very large number indeed! In Lemma 5.5, n will be the number of unions performed. For all practical purposes we may assume $\log_2 n < A(3, 4)$ and, hence, $\alpha(m, n) \leq 3$.

Lemma 5.5 [*Tarjan*]: Let $T(m, n)$ be the maximum time required to process an intermixed sequence of $m \geq n$ finds and $n - 1$ unions. Then:

$$k_1 m\alpha(m, n) \leq T(m, n) \leq k_2 m\,\alpha(m, n)$$

for some positive constants k_1 and k_2. $\square$

Even though the function $\alpha(m, n)$ is a very slowly growing function, the complexity of the union-find is not linear in m, the number of finds. As far as the space requirements are concerned, the space needed is one for each element.

5.10.2 Equivalence Classes

Let us apply the union-find algorithms to processing the equivalence pairs of Section 4.6. We can regard the equivalence classes to be generated as sets. These sets are disjoint since no polygon can be in two equivalence classes. To begin with, all n polygons are in an equivalence class of their own; thus $parent[i] = -1$, $0 \leq i < n$. Before processing an equivalence pair, $i \equiv j$, we must first determine the sets containing i and j. If they are different, then we replace the two sets by their union. If the two sets are the same, then we do nothing since the relation $i \equiv j$ is redundant. To process each equivalence pair we need to perform two finds and at most one union. Thus, if we have n polygons and $m \geq n$ equivalence pairs, the total processing time is at most $O(m \, \alpha(2m, n))$. Although for very large n this is slightly worse than the algorithm of Section 4.6, it needs less space. In Chapter 6, we shall see another application of union-find algorithms.

Example 5.3: We use the union-find algorithms to process the set of equivalence pairs of Section 4.6. Initially, there are 12 trees, one for each variable and $parent[i] = -1$, $0 \leq i \leq 11$. The forest configuration following the processing of each equivalence pair is shown in Figure 5.46. Each tree represents an equivalence class. It is possible to determine if two elements are currently in the same equivalence class at each stage of the processing by simply making two finds. □

EXERCISES

1. Using the result of Example 5.3, draw the trees after processing the instruction *union2*(11, 9).

2. Using *union2* and *find2*, create a complete program that inputs equivalence relations and then creates and prints out the equivalence classes. Use Example 5.3 as a guide.

5.11 COUNTING BINARY TREES

As a conclusion to our chapter on trees, we consider three disparate problems that amazingly have the same solution. In particular, we wish to determine the number of distinct binary trees having n nodes, the number of distinct permutations of the numbers from 1 to n obtainable by a stack, and the number of distinct ways of multiplying $n + 1$ matrices. Let us begin with a quick look at these problems.

5.11.1 Distinct Binary Trees

We know that if $n = 0$ or $n = 1$, there is only one binary tree. If $n = 2$, then there are two distinct trees (Figure 5.47) and if $n = 3$, there are five such trees (Figure 5.48). How many distinct trees are there with n nodes? Before deriving a solution, we will examine

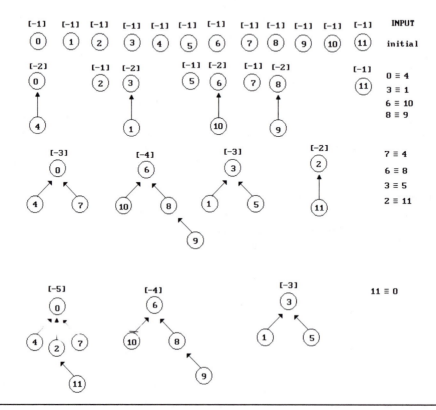

Figure 5.46: Trees for equivalence example

the two remaining problems. You might attempt to sketch out a solution of your own before reading further.

and

Figure 5.47: Distinct binary trees with $n = 2$

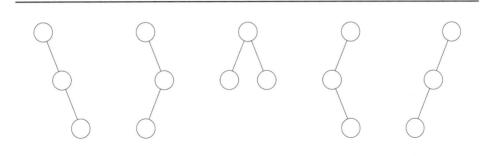

Figure 5.48: Distinct binary trees with $n = 3$

5.11.2   Stack Permutations

In Section 5.3, we introduced preorder, inorder, and postorder traversals and indicated that each traversal required a stack. Suppose we have the preorder sequence:

$$A\ B\ C\ D\ E\ F\ G\ H\ I$$

and the inorder sequence:

$$B\ C\ A\ E\ D\ G\ H\ F\ I$$

of the same binary tree. Does such a pair of sequences uniquely define a binary tree? Put another way, can this pair of sequences come from more than one binary tree?

To construct the binary tree from these sequences, we look at the first letter in the preorder sequence, A. This letter must be the root of the tree by definition of the preorder traversal (*VLR*). We also know by definition of the inorder traversal (*LVR*) that all nodes preceding A in the inorder sequence ($B\ C$) are in the left subtree, while the remaining nodes ($E\ D\ G\ H\ F\ I$) are in the right subtree. Figure 5.49(a) is our first approximation to the correct tree.

Moving right in the preorder sequence, we find B as the next root. Since no node precedes B in the inorder sequence, B has an empty left subtree, which means that C is in its right subtree. Figure 5.49(b) is the next approximation. Continuing in this way, we arrive at the binary tree of Figure 5.49(c). By formalizing this argument (see the exercises for this section), we can verify that every binary tree has a unique pair of preorder-inorder sequences.

Let the nodes of an n node binary tree be numbered from 1 to n. The inorder permutation defined by such a binary tree is the order in which its nodes are visited during an inorder traversal of the tree. A preorder permutation is similarly defined.

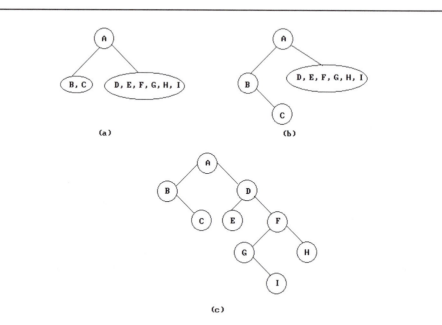

(a)   (b)

(c)

Figure 5.49: Constructing a binary tree from its inorder and preorder sequences

As an example, consider the binary tree of Figure 5.49(c) with the node numbering of Figure 5.50. Its preorder permutation is 1, 2, $\cdots$, 9, and its inorder permutation is 2, 3, 1, 5, 4, 7, 8, 6, 9.

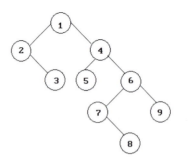

Figure 5.50: Binary tree of Figure 5.49(c) with its nodes numbered

If the nodes of the tree are numbered such that its preorder permutation is 1, 2, $\cdots, n$, then from our earlier discussion it follows that distinct binary trees define distinct inorder permutations. Thus, the number of distinct binary trees is equal to the number of distinct inorder permutations obtainable from binary trees having the preorder permutation, 1, 2, $\cdots, n$.

Using the concept of an inorder permutation, we can show that the number of distinct permutations obtainable by passing the numbers 1 to n through a stack and deleting in all possible ways is equal to the number of distinct binary trees with n nodes (see the exercises). If we start with the numbers 1, 2, 3, then the possible permutations obtainable by a stack are:

$$(1, 2, 3) \ (1, 3, 2) \ (2, 1, 3) \ (2, 3, 1) \ (3, 2, 1)$$

Obtaining (3, 1, 2) is impossible. Each of these five permutations corresponds to one of the five distinct binary trees with three nodes (Figure 5.51).

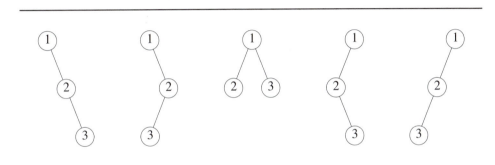

Figure 5.51: Binary trees corresponding to five permutations

5.11.3   Matrix Multiplication

Another problem that surprisingly has a connection with the previous two involves the product of n matrices. Suppose that we wish to compute the product of n matrices:

$$M_1 * M_2 * \cdots * M_n$$

Since matrix multiplication is associative, we can perform these multiplications in any order. We would like to know how many different ways we can perform these multiplications. For example, if $n = 3$, there are two possibilities:

$$(M_1 * M_2) * M_3$$
$$M_1 * (M_2 * M_3)$$

$$((M_1 * M_2) * M_3) * M_4$$
$$(M_1 * (M_2 * M_3)) * M_4$$
$$M_1 * ((M_2 * M_3) * M_4)$$
$$(M_1 * (M_2 * (M_3 * M_4)))$$
$$((M_1 * M_2) * (M_3 * M_4))$$

Let b_n be the number of different ways to compute the product of n matrices. Then $b_2 = 1$, $b_3 = 2$, and $b_4 = 5$. Let M_{ij}, $i \le j$, be the product $M_i * M_{i+1} * \cdots * M_j$. The product we wish to compute is M_{1n}. We may compute M_{1n} by computing any one of the products $M_{1i} * M_{i+1,n}$, $1 \le i \le n$. The number of distinct ways to obtain M_{1i} and $M_{i+1,n}$ are b_i and b_{n-i}, respectively. Therefore, letting $b_1 = 1$, we have:

$$b_n = \sum_{i=1}^{n-1} b_i \, b_{n-i}, n > 1$$

If we can determine the expression for b_n only in terms of n, then we have a solution to our problem.

Now instead let b_n be the number of distinct binary trees with n nodes. Again an expression for b_n in terms of n is what we want. Then we see that b_n is the sum of all the possible binary trees formed in the following way: a root and two subtrees with b_i and b_{n-i-1} nodes, for $0 \le i < n$ (Figure 5.52). This explanation says that

$$b_n = \sum_{i=0}^{n-1} b_i \, b_{n-i-1} , n \ge 1 \text{ ,and } b_0 = 1 \qquad (5.3)$$

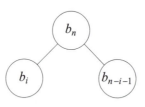

Figure 5.52: Decomposing b_n

This formula and the previous one are essentially the same. Therefore, the number of binary trees with n nodes, the number of permutations of 1 to n obtainable with a stack, and the number of ways to multiply $n + 1$ matrices are all equal.

5.11.4   Number Of Distinct Binary Trees

To obtain the number of distinct binary trees with n nodes, we must solve the recurrence of Eq. (5.5). To begin we let:

$$B(x) = \sum_{i \geq 0} b_i x^i \qquad (5.6)$$

which is the generating function for the number of binary trees. Next observe that by the recurrence relation we get the identity:

$$xB^2(x) = B(x) - 1$$

Using the formula to solve quadratics and the fact (Eq. (5.5)) that $B(0) = b_0 = 1$ we get:

$$B(x) = \frac{1 - \sqrt{1-4x}}{2x}$$

We can use the binomial theorem to expand $(1 - 4x)^{1/2}$ to obtain:

$$B(x) = \frac{1}{2x} \left[1 - \sum_{n \geq 0} \binom{1/2}{n} (-4x)^n \right]$$

$$\qquad (5.7)$$

$$= \sum_{m \geq 0} \binom{1/2}{m+1} (-1)^m \, 2^{2m+1} \, x^m$$

Comparing Eqs. (5.6) and (5.7) we see that b_n, which is the coefficient of x^n in $B(x)$, is:

$$\binom{1/2}{n+1} (-1)^n \, 2^{2n+1}$$

Some simplification yields the more compact form

$$b_n = \frac{1}{n+1} \binom{2n}{n}$$

which is approximately

$$b_n = O(4^n/n^{3/2})$$

EXERCISES

1. Prove that every binary tree is uniquely defined by its preorder and inorder sequences.

2. Do the inorder and postorder sequences of a binary tree uniquely define the binary tree? Prove your answer.

3. Do the inorder and preorder sequences of a binary tree uniquely define the binary tree? Prove your answer.

4. Do the inorder and level order sequences of a binary tree uniquely define the binary tree? Prove your answer.

5. Write an algorithm to construct the binary tree with a given preorder and inorder sequence.

6. Repeat Exercise 5 with the inorder and postorder sequences.

5.12 REFERENCES AND SELECTED READINGS

For other representations of trees, see D. Knuth, *The Art of Computer Programming: Fundamental Algorithms*, Second Edition, Addison-Wesley, Reading, Mass., 1973.

For the use of trees in generating optimal compiled code, see A. Aho, R. Sethi, and J. Ullman, *Compilers: Principles, Techniques, and Tools*, Addison-Wesley, Reading, Mass., 1986.

Tree traversal algorithms may be found in G. Lindstrom, *"Scanning list structures without stacks and tag bits,"*, *Information Processing Letters*, vol. 2, no. 2, 1973, pp 47-51, and B. Dwyer, *"Simple algorithms for traversing a tree without an auxiliary stack,"* *Information Processing Letters*, vol.2, no. 5, 1973, pp. 143-145.

For more on data structures for the set representation problems see R. Tarjan and J. Leeuwen, *"Worst case analysis of set union algorithms,"*, *Journal of the ACM*, vol. 31, no. 2, 1984, pp 245-281.

5.13 ADDITIONAL EXERCISES

1. Assume that we have a k-ary tree (a tree with degree k) of height h. Assume that all nodes are of the same size as in Figure 5.3.

    (a)   What is the maximum number of nodes in such a tree?

    (b)   How many *NULL* pointers are there?

    Prove your answers.

2. § [*Programming project*] Assume that we represent trees using the list representation and that we define the node structure as:

| tag = TRUE/FALSE | dlink/data | link |

where *tag* is a field that holds the value of *TRUE* if the node is a link node, and a value of *FALSE* if the node is a data node. Figure 5.53 show a sample tree and its representation with this node structure. This tree is written as the list:

$$(A \, (B \, (E \, (H, I \, (J, K) \,), F), C(\, G \,), D \,)$$

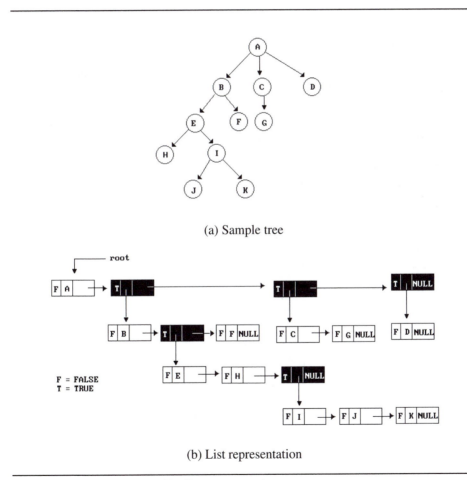

(a) Sample tree

(b) List representation

Figure 5.53: Sample tree and its list representation

Assume that we represent trees as in Figure 5.53(b). Write functions that:

    (a)   accept a list as input and create the tree corresponding to the list

    (b)   copy a tree

    (c)   test for equality between two trees

    (d)   erase a tree

    (e)   output a tree in its list notation.

3.   § [*Programming project*] In this project, we want to create a cross reference generator. We assume that we have a file of text (Lincoln's Gettysburg Address is a good candidate). We want to read in the file and print out an alphabetized list of all the words in the file, using the following format:

WORD	NUMBER OF OCCURRENCES	LINES THAT THE WORD APPEARED ON

You may assume that your cross-reference generator is not case-sensitive, that is the words *Did* and *did* are the same.

For example, running the cross-reference generator with the first two lines from the poem *Jabberwocky* by Lewis Carroll produces the following:

1 Twas brillig and the slithy toves
2 Did gyre and gimble in the wabe

Word	Count	Lines
and	2	1 2
brillig	1	1
did	1	2
gimble	1	2
gyre	1	2
in	1	2
slithy	1	1
the	2	1 2
toves	1	1
twas	1	2
wabe	1	2
Total	11	

CHAPTER 6

GRAPHS

6.1 THE GRAPH ABSTRACT DATA TYPE

6.1.1 Introduction

The first recorded evidence of the use of graphs dates back to 1736 when Leonhard Euler used them to solve the now classic Koenigsberg bridge problem. In Koenigsberg, the Pregal river flows around the island of Kneiphof. There are four land areas, labeled A through D in Figure 6.1, that have this river on their border. Seven bridges, labeled a through g, connect the land areas. The Koenigsberg bridge problem is as follows: Starting at some land area, is it possible to return to our starting location after walking across each of the bridges exactly once?

A possible walk might be:

- start from land area B
- walk across bridge a to island A
- take bridge e to area D

- take bridge g to C
- take bridge d to A
- take bridge b to B
- take bridge f to D

This walk does not cross all bridges exactly once, nor does it return to the starting land area B. We invite you to try to find a solution to the problem. You should discover quickly, as did Euler, that the people of Koenigsberg cannot walk across each bridge exactly once and return to their starting location. Euler solved the problem by using a graph (actually a multigraph) in which the land areas are vertices and the bridges are edges. His solution is not only elegant, it applies to all graphs.

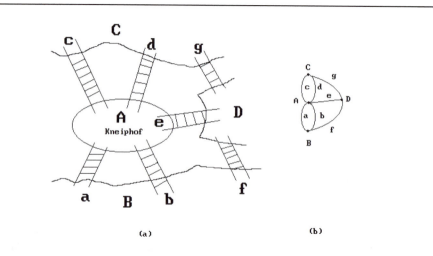

(a)

(b)

Figure 6.1: The bridges of Koenigsberg

Euler defined the degree of a vertex as the number of edges incident on it (we will explain these terms shortly). He then showed that there is a walk starting at any vertex, going through each edge exactly once, and terminating at the starting vertex *iff* the degree of each vertex is even. We now call a walk that does this an *Eulerian walk*. There is no such walk for the Koenigsberg bridge problem because all the vertices are of odd degree.

Since this first application, graphs have been used in a wide variety of applications, including analysis of electrical circuits, finding shortest routes, project planning, and the identification of chemical compounds. Indeed graphs may be the most widely used of all mathematical structures.

6.1.2   Definitions

A graph, G, consists of two sets: a finite, nonempty set of *vertices*, and a finite, possibly empty set of *edges*. $V(G)$ and $E(G)$ represent the sets of vertices and edges of G, respectively. Alternately, we may write $G = (V, E)$ to represent a graph.

An *undirected graph* is one in which the pair of vertices representing any edge is unordered. For example, the pairs (v_0, v_1) and (v_1, v_0) represent the same edge.

A *directed graph* is one in which we represent each edge as a directed pair of vertices. For example, the pair $<v_0, v_1>$ represents an edge in which v_0 is the *tail* and v_1 is the *head*. Therefore, $<v_0, v_1>$ and $<v_1, v_0>$ represent two different edges in a directed graph.

Figure 6.2 shows three sample graphs. We represent the vertices as circles numbered from 0 to $n - 1$, where n is the number of vertices currently in use. For an undirected graph, we represent the edges as lines or curves. For a directed graph, we represent the edges as arrows, drawn from the tail to the head. Graphs G_1 and G_2 are undirected, while graph G_3 is a directed graph.

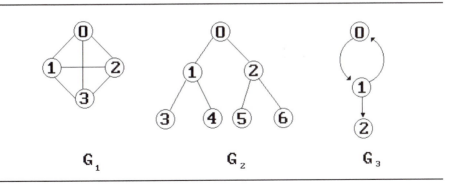

Figure 6.2: Three sample graphs

The set representation of each of these graphs is:

$V(G_1)$, = {0, 1, 2, 3} $E(G_1)$, = {(0, 1), (0, 2), (0, 3), (1, 2), (1, 3), (2, 3)}
$V(G_2)$, = {0, 1, 2, 3, 4, 5, 6} $E(G_2)$, = {(0, 1), (0, 2), (1, 3), (1, 4), (2, 5), (2, 6)}
$V(G_3)$ = {0, 1, 2} $E(G_3)$ = {<0, 1>, <1, 0>, <1, 2 >}

Notice that graph G_2 is a tree, while graphs G_1 and G_3 are not. We can define trees as a special case of graphs, but we need more terminology for that.

Since we define the edges and vertices of a graph as sets, we impose the following restrictions on graphs:

1. A graph may not have an edge from a vertex, i, back to itself. That is, the edge, (v_i, v_i) or $<v_i, v_i>$ is not legal. Such edges are known as *self loops*. If we permit self edges, we obtain graph like structures such as the one shown in Figure 6.3(a).

2. A graph may not have multiple occurrences of the same edge. If we remove this restriction, we obtain a data object referred to as a *multigraph* (see Figure 6.3(b)).

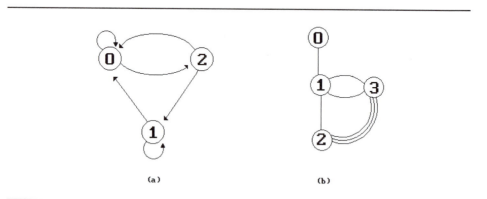

(a)   (b)

Figure 6.3: Examples of a graph with feedback loops and a multigraph

A *complete graph* is a graph that has the maximum number of edges. For an undirected graph with n vertices, the maximum number of edges is the number of distinct, unordered pairs, (v_i, v_j), $i \neq j$. This number is:

$$n(n-1)/2$$

For a directed graph on n vertices, the maximum number of edges is:

$$n(n-1)$$

Examining the graphs from Figure 6.2, we can see that G_1 is a complete graph on four vertices, while G_2 and G_3 are not complete.

If (v_0, v_1) is an edge in an undirected graph, then the vertices v_0 and v_1 are *adjacent* and the edge (v_0, v_1) is *incident on* vertices v_0 and v_1. For example, in graph G_2 vertices 3, 4, and 0 are adjacent to vertex 1; and edges (0, 2), (2, 5), and (2, 6) are incident on vertex 2. If $<v_0, v_1>$ is a directed edge, then vertex v_0 is *adjacent to* vertex v_1, while v_1 is *adjacent from* v_0. The edge $<v_0, v_1>$ is *incident on* v_0 and v_1. In G_3, the edges incident to vertex 1 are <0, 1>, <1, 0>, and <1, 2>.

A *subgraph* of G is a graph G' such that $V(G') \subseteq V(G)$ and $E(G') \subseteq E(G)$. Figure 6.4 shows some of the subgraphs of G_1 and G_3.

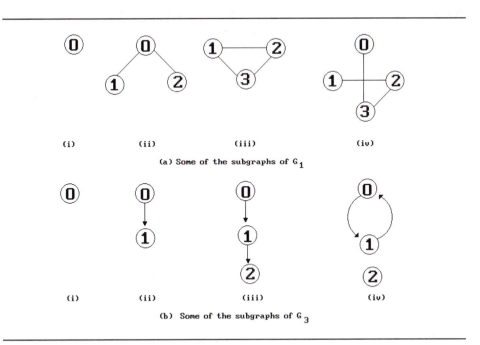

(i)   (ii)   (iii)   (iv)

(a) Some of the subgraphs of G_1

(i)   (ii)   (iii)   (iv)

(b) Some of the subgraphs of G_3

Figure 6.4: Subgraphs of G_1 and G_3

A *path* from vertex v_p to vertex v_q in a graph, G, is a sequence of vertices, v_p, v_{i_1}, v_{i_2}, $\cdots$, v_{i_n}, v_q such that (v_p, v_{i_1}), (v_{i_1}, v_{i_2}), $\cdots$, (v_{i_n}, v_q) are edges in an undirected graph. If G' is a directed graph, then the path consists of $<v_p, v_{i_1}>, <v_{i_1}, v_{i_2}>, \cdots, <v_{i_n}, v_q>$. The *length* of a path is the number of edges on it.

A *simple path* is a path in which all vertices, except possibly the first and the last, are distinct. We may write a path by simply listing the vertices. For example, the path $(0, 1), (1, 3), (3, 2)$ can be written as $0, 1, 3, 2$. In graph G_1 of Figure 6.2, paths $0, 1, 3, 2$ and $0, 1, 3, 1$ have length three. The first is a simple path, while the second is not. In graph $G_3, 0, 1, 2$ is a *simple directed path*.

A *cycle* is a simple path in which the first and the last vertices are the same. For example, $0, 1, 2, 0$ is a cycle in G_1, and $0, 1, 0$ is a cycle in G_3. For directed graphs, we usually add the prefix "directed" to the terms cycle and path.

In an undirected graph G, two vertices, v_0 and v_1, are *connected* if there is a path in G from v_0 to v_1. Since G is undirected, this means that there must also be a path from v_1 to v_0. An undirected graph is connected if, for every pair of distinct vertices v_i, v_j, there is a path from v_i to v_j in G. For example, graphs G_1 and G_2 are connected, while graph G_4 in Figure 6.5 is not.

A *connected component*, or simply a *component*, of an undirected graph is a maximal connected subgraph. For example, G_4 has two components, H_1 and H_2. A *tree* is a graph that is connected and acyclic (it has no cycles).

A directed graph is *strongly connected* if, for every pair of vertices v_i, v_j in $V(G)$, there is a directed path from v_i to v_j and also from v_j to v_i. Graph G_3 is not strongly connected since there is no path from vertex 2 to vertex 1. A *strongly connected component* is a maximal subgraph that is strongly connected. For example, G_3 has two strongly connected components, as illustrated in Figure 6.6.

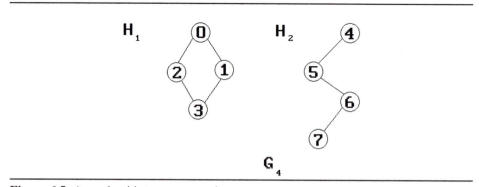

Figure 6.5: A graph with two connected components

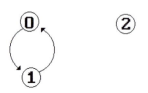

Figure 6.6: Strongly connected components of G_3

The *degree* of a vertex is the number of edges incident to that vertex. For example, the degree of vertex 0 in G_4 is 2. For a directed graph, we define the *in-degree* of a vertex v as the number of edges that have v as the head, and the *out-degree* as the number of edges that have v as the tail. For example, vertex 1 of G_3 has in-degree 1, out-degree 2, and degree 3. If d_i is the degree of a vertex i in a graph G with n vertices and e edges, then the number of edges is:

$$e = (\sum_{0}^{n-1} d_i)/2$$

In the remainder of this chapter, we shall refer to a directed graph as a *digraph*. When we use the term *graph*, we assume that it is an undirected graph. Now that we have defined all the terminology we will need, let us consider the graph as an ADT. The resulting specification is given in Structure 6.1.

---

structure *Graph* is
    objects: a nonempty set of vertices and a set of undirected edges, where each edge is a pair of vertices.
    functions:
        for all *graph* $\in$ *Graph*, *v*, v_1, and $v_2 \in$ *Vertices*

Graph Create()	::=	**return** an empty graph.
Graph InsertVertex(*graph*, *v*)	::=	**return** a graph with *v* inserted. *v* has no incident edges.
Graph InsertEdge(*graph*, v_1, v_2)	::=	**return** a graph with a new edge between v_1 and v_2.
Graph DeleteVertex(*graph*, *v*)	::=	**return** a graph in which *v* and all edges incident to it are removed.
Graph DeleteEdge(*graph*, v_1, v_2)	::=	**return** a graph in which the edge (v_1, v_2) is removed. Leave the incident nodes in the graph.
Boolean IsEmpty(*graph*)	::=	**if** (*graph* == empty graph) **return** *TRUE* **else return** *FALSE*.
List Adjacent(*graph*, *v*)	::=	**return** a list of all vertices that are adjacent to *v*.

Structure 6.1: Abstract data type *Graph*

The operations in Structure 6.1 are a basic set in that they allow us to create any arbitrary graph and do some elementary tests. In the later sections of this chapter we will see functions that traverse a graph (depth first or breadth first search) and that determine if a graph has special properties (connected, biconnected, planar).

6.1.3 Graph Representations

While several representations for graphs are possible, we shall study only the three most commonly used: adjacency matrices, adjacency lists, and adjacency multilists.

Adjacency Matrix

Let $G = (V, E)$ be a graph with *n* vertices, $n \geq 1$. The adjacency matrix of *G* is a two-dimensional $n \times n$ array, say *adj_mat*. If the edge (v_i, v_j) ($<v_i, v_j>$ for a digraph) is in

$E(G)$, *adj_mat*[i][j] = 1. If there is no such edge in $E(G)$, *adj_mat*[i][j] = 0. The adjacency matrices for graphs G_1, G_3, and G_4 are shown in Figure 6.7. The adjacency matrix for an undirected graph is symmetric since the edge (v_i, v_j) is in $E(G)$ *iff* the edge (v_j, v_i) is also in $E(G)$. In contrast, the adjacency matrix for a digraph need not be symmetric. (This is true of G_3.) For undirected graphs, we can save space by storing only the upper or lower triangle of the matrix. (We explored triangular matrices and other space-saving representations in the exercises of Chapter 2.)

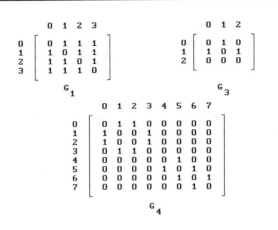

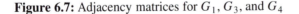

Figure 6.7: Adjacency matrices for G_1, G_3, and G_4

From the adjacency matrix, we can determine easily if there is an edge connecting any two vertices. Determining the degree of a vertex is also a simple task. For an undirected graph, the degree of any vertex, i, is its row sum:

$$\sum_{j=0}^{n-1} adj\_mat[i][j]$$

For a directed graph, the row sum is the out-degree, while the column sum is the in-degree.

Suppose we wish to answering questions such as: How many edges are there in G? or, Is G connected?. These require us to examine (potentially) all edges of the graph. Using adjacency matrices, all algorithms that answer these questions require at least $O(n^2)$ time since we must examine $n^2 - n$ entries of the matrix (the n diagonal entries equal zero and can be excluded; only half as many entries need to be examined in the case of an undirected graph as in this case the adjacency matrix is symmetric) to determine the edges of the graph. For *sparse graphs* (i.e., graphs that have a small number of edges), most of the terms in the adjacency matrix equal zero and we would like to avoid the overhead of examining $O(n^2)$ positioins in an adjacency matrix. In fact, we might expect that the former questions would be answerable in significantly less time, say $O(e + n)$ time, where e is the number of edges in G and $e \ll n^2/2$. For this, we must replace the adjacency matrix representation with an adjacency list (either sequential or linked) representation.

Adjacency Lists

In this representation, we replace the n rows of the adjacency matrix with n linked lists, one for each vertex in G. The node structure for the lists must contain at least vertex and link fields. For any given list, i, the nodes in the list contain the vertices that are adjacent from vertex i. Figure 6.8 shows the adjacency lists for G_1, G_3, and G_4. Notice that each list has a head node, and that the lists are numbered sequentially. This allows us to quickly access the adjacency list for any vertex.

The C declarations for the adjacency list representation are:

```
#define MAX_VERTICES 50 /*maximum number of vertices*/
typedef struct node *node_pointer;
typedef struct node {
        int vertex;
        struct node *link;
        };
node_pointer graph[MAX_VERTICES];
int n = 0; /* vertices currently in use */
```

In the case of an undirected graph with n vertices and e edges, this representation requires n head nodes and $2e$ list nodes. Each list node has two fields. Often, you can sequentially pack the nodes on the adjacency lists, thereby eliminating the use of pointers. In this case, an array *node* [ ] may be used. *node* [i] gives the starting point of the list for vertex i, $0 \le i < n$ and *node* [n] is set to $n + 2e + 1$. The vertices adjacent from vertex i are stored in *node* [i], $\cdots$, *node* [$i + 1$] $- 1$, $0 \le i < n$. Figure 6.9 gives such a sequential representation for the graph G_4 of Figure 6.5.

We can determine the degree of any vertex in an undirected graph by simply counting the number of nodes in its adjacency list. This also gives us the number of edges incident on the vertex. This means that if there are n vertices in the graph G, we can determine the total number of edges in G in $O(n + e)$ time. For a digraph, we can determine the out-degree of any vertex by counting the number of nodes in its adjacency list. This means that we also can determine the total number of edges in a digraph in $O(n + e)$ time. Unfortunately, finding the in-degree of a vertex in a digraph is more complex. We handle this problem and the related problem of finding all vertices adjacent to a vertex by maintaining a second set of lists. These lists are called *inverse adjacency lists*. As was true of adjacency lists, the inverse adjacency lists contain one list for each vertex. However, each list contains a node for each vertex adjacent to the vertex that the list represents. Figure 6.10 shows the inverse adjacency list for G_3.

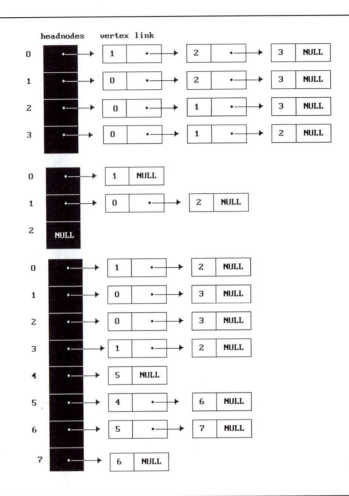

Figure 6.8: Adjacency lists for G_1, G_3, and G_4

Changing the node structure of the adjacency lists is a second approach to the problem of finding the in-degree of vertices. Figure 6.11 shows a simplified version of the node structure used in the sparse matrix representation of Section 4.7. Each node now has four fields and represents one edge. Figure 6.12 shows the representation of G_3 using the structure of Figure 6.11. We assume that the head nodes are stored sequentially.

Before discussing the third representation, we would like to quickly reconsider the lists displayed in Figure 6.8. For each graph, we arranged the nodes in each of the lists so that the vertices were in ascending order. This is not necessary, and, in fact, vertices may appear in any order. Thus, the adjacency lists of Figure 6.13 are just as valid a

[0] 9	[8] 23	[16] 2
[1] 11	[9] 1	[17] 5
[2] 13	[10] 2	[18] 4
[3] 15	[11] 0	[19] 6
[4] 17	[12] 3	[20] 5
[5] 18	[13] 0	[21] 7
[6] 20	[14] 3	[22] 6
[7] 22	[15] 1	

Figure 6.9 Sequential representation of graph G_4

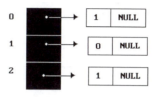

Figure 6.10: Inverse adjacency list for G_3

tail	head	column link for head	row link for tail

Figure 6.11: Alternate node structure for adjacency lists

representation of G_1 as the lists in Figure 6.8(a).

Adjacency Multilists

In the adjacency list representation of an undirected graph, we represent each edge, (v_i, v_j), by two entries. One entry is on the list for v_i, and the other is on the list for v_j. As we shall see, in some situations we need to find easily the second entry for an edge and mark it as having been examined. Maintaining the lists as *multilists*, that is, lists in which nodes are shared among several lists, facilitates this operation. For each edge there is exactly one node, but this node is on the adjacency list for each of the two

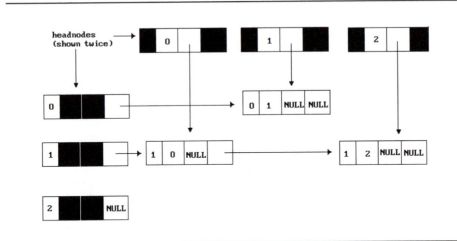

Figure 6.12: Orthogonal representation for graph G_3

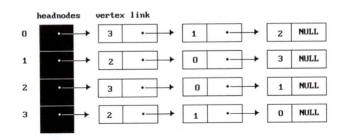

Figure 6.13: Alternate order adjacency list for G_1

vertices it is incident to. Figure 6.14 shows the new node structure.

Figure 6.14: Node structure for adjacency multilists

The C declarations to create this structure are:

```
typedef struct edge *edge_pointer;
typedef struct edge {
            short int marked;
            int vertex1;
            int vertex2;
            edge_pointer path1;
            edge_pointer path2;
            };
edge_pointer graph[MAX_VERTICES];
```

Figure 6.15 shows the adjacency multilist for G_1. In this figure the field *marked* is shown solid in each node.

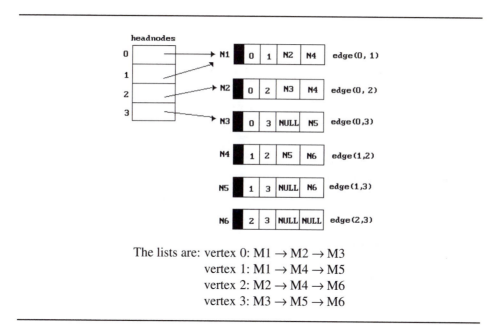

The lists are: vertex 0: M1 → M2 → M3

vertex 1: M1 → M4 → M5

vertex 2: M2 → M4 → M6

vertex 3: M3 → M5 → M6

Figure 6.15: Adjacency multilists for G_1

Weighted Edges

Thus far, we have considered only graphs that have unweighted edges. In many applications, however, the edges of a graph are assigned weights. These weights may represent the distance from one vertex to another or the cost of going from one vertex to an adjacent vertex. To handle this situation, we must modify our representations. For an adjacency matrix, we replace the 1 used to signify an edge with the weight of the edge. For adjacency lists and adjacency multilists, we must add a *weight* field to the node structure. A graph with weighted edges is called a *network*. We shall examine networks in greater detail when we consider minimum spanning trees and related topics.

EXERCISES

1. Does the multigraph of Figure 6.16 have an Eulerian walk? If so, find one.

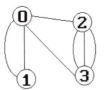

Figure 6.16: A multigraph

2. For the digraph of Figure 6.17, obtain:

    (a)   the in-degree and out-degree of each vertex

    (b)   its adjacency matrix

    (c)   its adjacency list representation

    (d)   its adjacency multilist representation

    (e)   its strongly connected components

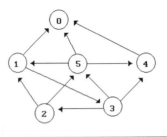

Figure 6.17: A digraph

3. Devise a suitable representation for graphs so that they can be stored on disk. Write a function that reads in such a graph and creates its adjacency matrix. Write another function that creates the adjacency lists from the disk input.

4. Draw the complete undirected graphs on one, two, three, four, and five vertices. Prove that the number of edges in an n vertex complete graph is $n(n-1)/2$.

5. Is the directed graph of Figure 6.18 strongly connected? List all the simple paths.

6. Show how the graph of Figure 6.18 would look if represented by its adjacency matrix, adjacency lists, and adjacency multilist.

Figure 6.18: A directed graph

7. For an undirected graph, G, with n vertices and e edges, show that:

$$\sum_{i=0}^{n-1} d_i = 2e$$

where d_i = degree of vertex i.

8. (a) Let G be a connected undirected graph on n vertices. Show that G must have at least $n-1$ edges, and that all connected undirected graphs with $n-1$ edges are trees.

   (b) What is the minimum number of edges in a strongly connected digraph on n vertices? What form do such digraphs have?

9. For an undirected graph, G, with n vertices, prove that the following are equivalent:

   (a) G is a tree.

   (b) G is connected, but if any edge is removed the resulting graph is not connected.

   (c) For any two distinct vertices, $u \in V(G)$ and $v \in V(G)$, there is exactly one simple path from u to v.

   (d) G contains no cycles and has $n-1$ edges

10. Write a C function to:

    (a) input the number of vertices in an undirected graph and its edges one by one.

    (b) set up the linked adjacency list representation of the graph. You may assume that no edge is input twice. Determine the time complexity of your function in terms of the number of vertices and the number of edges.

11. Write a C function that creates the inverse adjacency lists for a graph using the adjacency lists generated in Exercise 10. Create a second function that will print the adjacency lists and the inverse adjacency lists for the graph.

6.2 ELEMENTARY GRAPH OPERATIONS

When we discussed binary trees in Chapter 5, we indicated that tree traversals were among the most frequently used tree operations. Thus, we defined and implemented preorder, inorder, postorder, and level order tree traversals. An analogous situation occurs in the case of graphs. Given an undirected graph, $G = (V, E)$, and a vertex, v, in $V(G)$ we wish to visit all vertices in G that are reachable from v, that is, all vertices that are connected to v. We shall look at two ways of doing this: *depth first search* and *breadth first search*. Depth first search is similar to a preorder tree traversal, while breadth first search resembles a level order tree traversal. In our discussion of depth first search and breadth first search, we shall assume that the linked adjacency list representation for graphs is used. The excercises explore the use of other representations.

6.2.1 Depth First Search

We begin the search by visiting the start vertex, v. In this simple application, visiting consists of printing the node's vertex field. Next, we select an unvisited vertex, w, from v's adjacency list and carry out a depth first search on w. We preserve our current position in v's adjacency list by placing it on a stack. Eventually our search reaches a vertex, u, that has no unvisited vertices on its adjacency list. At this point, we remove a vertex from the stack and continue processing its adjacency list. Previously visited vertices are discarded; unvisited vertices are visited and placed on the stack. The search terminates when the stack is empty. Although this sounds like a complicated function, it is easy to implement recursively. As indicated previously, it is similar to a preorder tree traversal since we visit a vertex and then continue with the next unvisited descendant. The recursive implementation of depth first search is presented in *dfs* (Program 6.1). This function uses a global array, *visited[MAX_VERTICES]*, that is initialized to *FALSE*. When we visit a vertex, i, we change *visited[i]* to *TRUE*. The declarations are:

```
                    #define FALSE 0
                    #define TRUE 1
                    short int visited[MAX_VERTICES];
```

```
void dfs(int v)
{
/* depth first search of a graph beginning with vertex v.*/
   node_pointer w;
   visited[v] = TRUE;
   printf("%5d",v);
   for (w = graph[v]; w; w = w->link)
      if (!visited[w->vertex])
         dfs(w->vertex);
}
```

Program 6.1: Depth first search

Example 6.1: We wish to carry out a depth first search of graph G of Figure 6.19(a). Figure 6.19(b) shows the adjacency lists for this graph. If we initiate this search from vertex v_0, then the vertices of G are visited in the following order: $v_0, v_1, v_3, v_7, v_4, v_5, v_2, v_6$.

By examining Figures 6.19(a) and (b), we can verify that $dfs(v_0)$ visits all vertices connected to v_0. This means that all the vertices visited, together with all edges in G incident to these vertices, form a connected component of G. □

Analysis of *dfs*: If we represent G by its adjacency lists, then we can determine the vertices adjacent to v by following a chain of links. Since *dfs* examines each node in the adjacency lists at most once, the time to complete the search is O(e). If we represent G by its adjacency matrix, then determining all vertices adjacent to v requires O(n) time. Since we visit at most n vertices, the total time is O(n^2). □

6.2.2 Breadth First Search

Breadth first search starts at vertex v and marks it as visited. It then visits each of the vertices on v's adjacency list. When we have visited all the vertices on v's adjacency list, we visit all the unvisited vertices that are adjacent to the first vertex on v's adjacency list. To implement this scheme, as we visit each vertex we place the vertex in a queue. When we have exhausted an adjacency list, we remove a vertex from the queue and proceed by examining each of the vertices on its adjacency list. Unvisited vertices are visited and then placed on the queue; visited vertices are ignored. We have finished the search when the queue is empty.

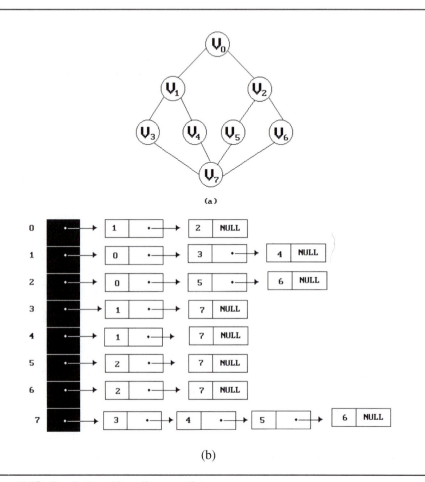

(a)

(b)

Figure 6.19: Graph *G* and its adjacency lists

To implement breadth first search, we use a dynamically linked queue as described in Chapter 4. Each queue node contains vertex and link fields. The *addq* and *deleteq* functions of Chapter 4 (Programs 4.8 and 4.9) will work correctly if we replace all references to *element* with **int**. The function *bfs* (Program 6.2) contains the C code to implement the breadth first search.

The queue definition and the function prototypes used by *bfs* are:

```
typedef struct queue *queue_pointer;
typedef struct queue {
        int vertex;
```

```
                 queue_pointer link;
                 };
        void addq(queue_pointer *, queue_pointer *, int);
        int deleteq(queue_pointer *);
```

```
void bfs(int v)
{
/* breadth first traversal of a graph, starting with node v
the global array visited is initialized to 0, the queue
operations are similar to those described in
Chapter 4. */
   node_pointer w;
   queue_pointer front,rear;
   front = rear = NULL; /* initialize queue */
   printf("%5d",v);
   visited[v] = TRUE;
   addq(&front, &rear, v);
   while (front) {
      v = deleteq(&front);
      for (w = graph[v]; w; w = w->link)
         if (!visited[w->vertex]) {
            printf("%5d", w->vertex);
            addq(&front,&rear,w->vertex);
            visited[w->vertex] = TRUE;
         }
      }
   }
}
```

Program 6.2: Breadth first search of a graph

Analysis of *bfs*: Since each vertex is placed on the queue exactly once, the **while** loop is iterated at most *n* times. For the adjacency list representation, this loop has a total cost of $d_0 + \cdots + d_{n-1} = O(e)$, where $d_i = degree\ (v_i)$. For the adjacency matrix representation, the **while** loop takes $O(n)$ time for each vertex visited. Therefore, the total time is $O(n^2)$. As was true of *dfs*, all vertices visited, together with all edges incident to them, form a connected component of *G*. □

6.2.3 Connected Components

We can use the two elementary graph searches to create additional, more interesting, graph operations. For illustrative purposes, let us look at the problem of determining whether or not an undirected graph is connected. We can implement this operation by simply calling either *dfs* (0) or *bfs* (0) and then determining if there are any unvisited vertices. For example, the call *dfs* (0) applied to graph G_4 of Figure 6.5 terminates without visiting vertices 4, 5, 6, and 7. Therefore, we can conclude that graph G_4 is not connected. The computing time for this operation is $O(n + e)$ if adjacency lists are used.

A closely related problem is that of listing the connected components of a graph. This is easily accomplished by making repeated calls to either *dfs* (v) or *bfs* (v) where v is an unvisited vertex. The function *connected* (Program 6.3) carries out this operation. Although we have used *dfs*, *bfs* may be used with no change in the time complexity.

```
void connected(void)
{
/* determine the connected components of a graph */
int i;
for (i = 0; i < n; i++)
   if(!visited[i]) {
      dfs(i);
      printf("\n");
   }
}
```

Program 6.3: Connected components

Analysis of *connected*: If G is represented by its adjacency lists, then the total time taken by *dfs* is $O(e)$. Since the **for** loop takes $O(n)$ time, the total time needed to generate all the connected components is $O(n + e)$.

If G is represented by its adjacency matrix, then the time needed to determine the connected components is $O(n^2)$. □

6.2.4 Spanning Trees

When graph G is connected, a depth first or breadth first search starting at any vertex visits all the vertices in G. The search implicitly partitions the edges in G into two sets: T (for tree edges) and N (for nontree edges). T is the set of edges used or traversed during the search and N is the set of remaining edges. We can determine the set of tree edges by adding a statement to the **if** clause of either *dfs* or *bfs* that inserts the edge (v, w) into a linked list of edges. (T represents the head of this linked list.) The edges in T form a tree that includes all vertices of G. A *spanning tree* is any tree that consists solely of edges in G and that includes all the vertices in G. Figure 6.20 shows a graph and three of its spanning trees.

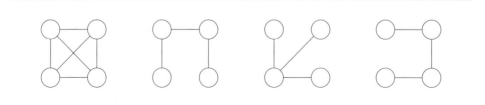

Figure 6.20: A complete graph and three of its spanning trees

As we just indicated, we may use either *dfs* or *bfs* to create a spanning tree. When *dfs* is used, the resulting spanning tree is known as a *depth first spanning tree*. When *bfs* is used, the resulting spanning tree is called a *breadth first spanning tree*. Figure 6.21 shows the spanning trees that result from a depth first and breadth first search starting at vertex v_0 in the graph of Figure 6.19.

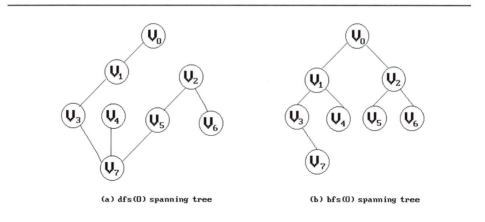

(a) dfs(0) spanning tree   (b) bfs(0) spanning tree

Figure 6.21: *dfs* and *bfs* spanning trees for graph of Figure 6.19

Now suppose we add a nontree edge, (v, w), into any spanning tree, T. The result is a cycle that consists of the edge (v, w) and all the edges on the path from w to v in T. For example, if we add the nontree edge (7, 6) to the *dfs* spanning tree of Figure 6.21(a), the resulting cycle is 7, 6, 2, 5, 7. We can use this property of spanning trees to obtain an independent set of circuit equations for an electrical network.

Example 6.2 [*Creation of circuit equations*]: To obtain the circuit equations, we must first obtain a spanning tree for the electrical network. Then we introduce the nontree edges into the spanning tree one at a time. The introduction of each such edge produces a cycle. Next we use Kirchoff's second law on this cycle to obtain a circuit equation. The cycles obtained in this way are independent (we cannot obtain any of these cycles by taking a linear combination of the remaining cycles) since each contains a nontree edge that is not contained in any other cycle. Thus, the circuit equations are also independent. In fact, we can show that the cycles obtained by introducing the nontree edges one at a time into the spanning tree form a cycle basis. This means that we can construct all other cycles in the graph by taking a linear combination of the cycles in the basis. (For further details, see the Harary text cited in the References and Selected Readings.) □

Let us examine a second property of spanning trees. A spanning tree is a *minimal subgraph*, G', of G such that $V(G') = V(G)$ and G' is connected. We define a minimal subgraph as one with the fewest number of edges. Any connected graph with n vertices must have at least $n - 1$ edges, and all connected graphs with $n - 1$ edges are trees. Therefore, we conclude that a spanning tree has $n - 1$ edges. (The exercises explore this property more fully.)

Constructing minimal subgraphs finds frequent application in the design of communication networks. Suppose that the vertices of a graph, G, represent cities and the edges represent communication links between cities. The minimum number of links needed to connect n cities is $n - 1$. Constructing the spanning trees of G gives us all feasible choices. However, we know that the cost of constructing communication links between cities is rarely the same. Therefore, in practical applications, we assign weights to the edges. These weights might represent the cost of constructing the communication link or the length of the link. Given such a weighted graph, we would like to select the spanning tree that represents either the lowest total cost or the lowest overall length. We assume that the cost of a spanning tree is the sum of the costs of the edges of that tree. Algorithms to obtain minimum cost spanning trees are studied in a later section.

6.2.5 Biconnected Components And Articulation Points

The operations that we have implemented thus far are simple extensions of depth first and breadth first search. The next operation we implement is more complex and requires the introduction of additional terminology. We begin by assuming that G is an undirected connected graph.

An *articulation point* is a vertex v of G such that the deletion of v, together with all edges incident on v, produces a graph, G', that has at least two connected components. For example, the connected graph of Figure 6.22 has four articulation points, vertices 1, 3, 5, and 7.

A *biconnected graph* is a connected graph that has no articulation points. For example, the graph of Figure 6.19 is biconnected, while the graph of Figure 6.22 obviously is not. In many graph applications, articulation points are undesirable. For instance, suppose that the graph of Figure 6.22(a) represents a communication network.

In such graphs, the vertices represent communication stations and the edges represent communication links. Now suppose that one of the stations that is an articulation point fails. The result is a loss of communication not just to and from that single station, but also between certain other pairs of stations.

A *biconnected component* of a connected undirected graph is a *maximal biconnected subgraph*, H, of G. By maximal, we mean that G contains no other subgraph that is both biconnected and properly contains H. For example, the graph of Figure 6.22(a) contains the six biconnected components shown in Figure 6.22(b). The biconnected graph of Figure 6.19, however, contains just one biconnected component: the whole graph. It is easy to verify that two biconnected components of the same graph have no more than one vertex in common. This means that no edge can be in two or more biconnected components of a graph. Hence, the biconnected components of G partition the edges of G.

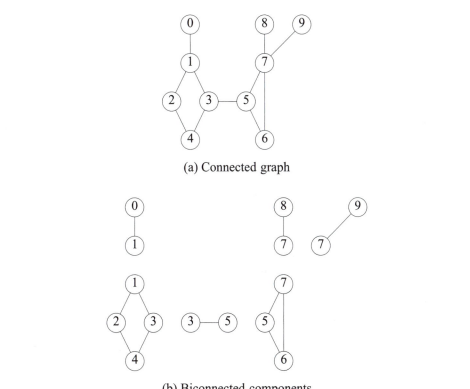

(a) Connected graph

(b) Biconnected components

Figure 6.22: A connected graph and its biconnected components

We can find the biconnected components of a connected undirected graph, G, by using any depth first spanning tree of G. For example, the function call *dfs* (3) applied to the graph of Figure 6.22(a) produces the spanning tree of Figure 6.23(a). We have redrawn the tree in Figure 6.23(b) to better reveal its tree structure. The numbers outside the vertices in either figure give the sequence in which the vertices are visited during the depth first search. We call this number the *depth first number*, or *dfn*, of the vertex. For example, *dfn* (3) = 0, *dfn* (0) = 4, and *dfn* (9) = 8. Notice that vertex 3, which is an ancestor of both vertices 0 and 9, has a lower *dfn* than either of these vertices. Generally, if u and v are two vertices, and u is an ancestor of v in the depth first spanning tree, then *dfn* (u) < *dfn* (v).

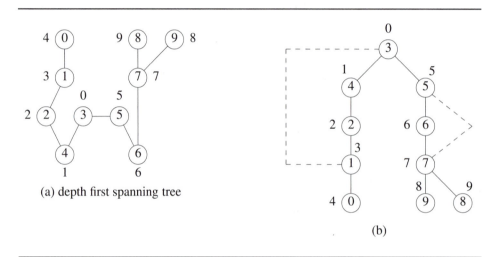

(a) depth first spanning tree

(b)

Figure 6.23: Depth first spanning tree of Figure 6.22(a)

The broken lines in Figure 6.23(b) represent nontree edges. A nontree edge (u, v) is a *back edge iff* either u is an ancestor of v or v is an ancestor of u. From the definition of depth first search, it follows that all nontree edges are back edges. This means that the root of a depth first spanning tree is an articulation point *iff* it has at least two children. In addition, any other vertex u is an articulation point *iff* it has at least one child w such that we cannot reach an ancestor of u using a path that consists of only w, descendants of w, and a single back edge. These observations lead us to define a value, *low*, for each vertex of G such that *low* (u) is the lowest depth first number that we can reach from u using a path of descendants followed by at most one back edge:

$$low (u) = \min\{dfn (u), \min\{low (w) \mid w \text{ is a child of } u\},$$
$$\min \{dfn (w) \mid (u, w) \text{ is a back edge } \} \}$$

Therefore, we can say that u is an articulation point *iff* u is either the root of the spanning tree and has two or more children, or u is not the root and u has a child w such that $low(w) \geq dfn(u)$. Figure 6.24 shows the *dfn* and low values for each vertex of the spanning tree of Figure 6.23(b). From this table we can conclude that vertex 1 is an articulation point since it has a child 0 such that $low(0) = 4 \geq dfn(1) = 3$. Vertex 7 is also an articulation point since $low(8) = 9 \geq dfn(7) = 7$, as is vertex 5 since $low(6) = 5 \geq dfn(5) = 5$. Finally, we note that the root, vertex 3, is an articulation point because it has more than one child.

Vertex	0	1	2	3	4	5	6	7	8	9
dfn	4	3	2	0	1	5	6	7	9	8
low	4	3	0	0	0	5	5	7	9	8

Figure 6.24: *dfn* and *low* values for *dfs* spanning tree with *root* = 3

We can easily modify *dfs* to compute *dfn* and *low* for each vertex of a connected undirected graph. The result is *dfnlow* (Program 6.4). We invoke the function with the call *dfnlow(x, −1)*, where x is the starting vertex for the depth first search. The function uses a *MIN2* macro that returns the smaller of its two parameters. The results are returned as two global variables, *dfn* and *low*. We also use a global variable, *num*, to increment *dfn* and *low*. The function *init* (Program 6.5) contains the code to correctly initialize *dfn*, *low*, and *num*. The global declarations are:

```
#define MIN2(x,y) ((x) < (y) ? (x) : (y))
short int dfn[MAX_VERTICES];
short int low[MAX_VERTICES];
int num;
```

We can partition the edges of the connected graph into their biconnected components by adding some code to *dfnlow*. We know that *low[w]* has been computed following the return from the function call *dfnlow(w, u)*. If $low[w] \geq dfn[u]$, then we have identified a new biconnected component. We can output all edges in a biconnected component if we use a stack to save the edges when we first encounter them. The function *bicon* (Program 6.6) contains the code. The same initialization function (Program 6.5) is used. The function call is *bicon(x, −1)*, where x is the root of the spanning tree.

Analysis of *bicon*: The function *bicon* assumes that the connected graph has at least two vertices. Technically, a graph with one vertex and no edges is biconnected, but, our implementation does not handle this special case. The complexity of *bicon* is $O(n + e)$. We leave the proof of its correctness as an exercise. □

```
void init(void)
{
   int i;
   for (i = 0; i < n; i++) {
      visited[i] = FALSE;
      dfn[i] = low[i] = -1;
   }
   num = 0;
}
```

Program 6.5: Initialization of *dfn* and *low*

```
void dfnlow(int u, int v)
{
/* compute dfn and low while performing a dfs search
beginning at vertex u, v is the parent of u (if any) */
   node_pointer ptr;
   int w;
   dfn[u] = low[u] = num++;
   for (ptr = graph[u]; ptr; ptr = ptr->link) {
      w = ptr->vertex;
      if (dfn[w] < 0) { /* w is an unvisited vertex */
         dfnlow(w,u);
         low[u] = MIN2(low[u],low[w]);
      }
      else if (w != v)
         low[u] = MIN2(low[u],dfn[w]);
   }
}
```

Program 6.4: Determining *dfn* and *low*

EXERCISES

1. Rewrite *dfs* so that it uses an adjacency matrix representation of graphs.

2. Rewrite *bfs* so that it uses an adjacency matrix representation.

3. Let *G* be a connected undirected graph. Show that no edge of *G* can be in two or more biconnected components of *G*. Can a vertex of *G* be in more than one biconnected component?

```
void bicon(int u, int v)
{
/* compute dfn and low, and output the edges of G by their
biconnected components, v is the parent (if any) of the u
(if any) in the resulting spanning tree. It is assumed that
all entries of dfn[] have been initialized to -1, num has
been initialized to 0, and the stack has been set to empty
*/
    node_pointer ptr;
    int w,x,y;
    dfn[u] = low[u] = num++;
    for (ptr = graph[u]; ptr; ptr = ptr->link) {
        w = ptr->vertex;
        if (v != w && dfn[w] < dfn[u])
            add(&top,u,w); /* add edge to stack */
            if (dfn[w] <0) { /* w has not been visited */
                bicon(w,u);
                low[u] = MIN2(low[u],low[w]);
                if (low[w] >= dfn[u]) {
                    printf("New biconnected component: ");
                    do { /* delete edge from stack */
                        delete(&top, &x, &y);
                        printf(" <%d,%d>",x,y);
                    } while (!((x == u) && (y == w)));
                    printf("\n");
                }
            }
            else if (w != v) low[u] = MIN2(low[u],dfn[w]);
    }
}
```

Program 6.6: Biconnected components of a graph

4. Let *G* be a connected graph and let *T* be any of its depth first spanning trees. Show that every edge of *G* that is not in *T* is a back edge relative to *T*.

5. Write the stack operations necessary to fully implement the *bicon* function. Use a dynamically linked representation for the stack.

6. Prove that function *bicon* correctly partitions the edges of a connected graph into the biconnected components of the graph.

7. A *bipartite graph, G = (V, E)*, is an undirected graph whose vertices can be partitioned into two disjoint sets V_1 and $V_2 = V - V_1$ with the properties:

   • no two vertices in V_1 are adjacent in G
   • no two vertices in V_2 are adjacent in G

   The graph G_4 of Figure 6.5 is bipartite. A possible partitioning of V is $V_1 = \{0, 3, 4, 6\}$ and $V_2 = \{1, 2, 5, 7\}$. Write a function to determine whether a graph is bipartite. If the graph is bipartite your function should obtain a partitioning of the vertices into two disjoint sets, V_1 and V_2, satisfying the two properties listed. Show that if G is represented by its adjacency lists, then this function has a computing time of $O(n + e)$, where $n = |V(G)|$ and $e = |E(G)|$ ($| \ |$ is the cardinality of the set, that is, the number of elements in it).

8. Show that every tree is a bipartite graph.

9. Prove that a graph is bipartite *iff* it contains no cycles of odd length.

10. Apply depth first and breadth first searches to the complete graph on four vertices. List the vertices in the order that they are visited.

11. Show how to modify *dfs* as it is used in *connected* to produce a list of all newly visited vertices.

12. Prove that when *dfs* is applied to a connected graph the edges of *T* form a tree.

13. Prove that when *bfs* is applied to a connected graph the edges of *T* form a tree.

14. An edge, (u, v), of a connected graph, G, is a *bridge iff* its deletion from G produces a graph that is no longer connected. In the graph of Figure 6.22, the edges $(0, 1)$, $(3, 5)$, $(7, 8)$, and $(7, 9)$ are bridges. Write a function that finds the bridges in a graph. Your function should have a time complexity of $O(n + e)$. (Hint: use *bicon* as a starting point.)

15. Using a complete graph with n vertices, show that the number of spanning trees is at least $2^{n-1} - 1$.

6.3 MINIMUM COST SPANNING TREES

The *cost* of a spanning tree of a weighted undirected graph is the sum of the costs (weights) of the edges in the spanning tree. A *minimum cost spanning tree* is a spanning tree of least cost. Three different algorithms can be used to obtain a minimum cost spanning tree of a connected undirected graph. All three use an algorithm design strategy called the *greedy method*. We shall refer to the three algorithms as Kruskal's, Prim's, and Sollin's algorithms, respectively.

In the greedy method, we construct an optimal solution in stages. At each stage, we make a decision that is the best decision (using some criterion) at this time. Since we cannot change this decision later, we make sure that the decision will result in a feasible solution. The greedy method can be applied to a wide variety of programming problems. Typically, the selection of an item at each stage is based on either a least cost or a highest profit criterion. A feasible solution is one which works within the constraints specified by the problem.

For spanning trees, we use a least cost criterion. Our solution must satisfy the following constraints:

(1)   we must use only edges within the graph

(2)   we must use exactly $n - 1$ edges

(3)   we may not use edges that would produce a cycle.

Kruskal's Algorithm

Kruskal's algorithm builds a minimum cost spanning tree T by adding edges to T one at a time. The algorithm selects the edges for inclusion in T in nondecreasing order of their cost. An edge is added to T if it does not form a cycle with the edges that are already in T. Since G is connected and has $n > 0$ vertices, exactly $n - 1$ edges will be selected for inclusion in T.

Example 6.3: We will construct a minimum cost spanning tree of the graph of Figure 6.25(a). Figure 6.26 shows the order in which the edges are considered for inclusion, as well as the result and the changes (if any) in the spanning tree. For example, edge (0, 5) is the first considered for inclusion. Since it obviously cannot create a cycle, it is added to the tree. The result is the tree of Figure 6.25(c). Similarly, edge (2, 3) is considered next. It is also added to the tree, and the result is shown in Figure 6.25(d). This process continues until the spanning tree has $n-1$ edges (Figure 6.25(h)). The cost of the spanning tree is 99. □

Program 6.7 presents a formal description of Kruskal's algorithm. (We leave writing the C function as an exercise.) We assume that initially E is the set of all edges in G. To implement Kruskal's algorithm, we must be able to determine an edge with minimum cost and delete that edge. We can handle both of these operations efficiently if we maintain the edges in E as a sorted sequential list. As we shall see in Chapter 7, we can sort the edges in E in O($e \log e$) time. Actually, it is not necessary to sort the edges in E as long as we are able to find the next least cost edge quickly. Obviously a min heap is ideally suited for this task since we can determine and delete the next least cost edge in O($\log e$) time. Construction of the heap itself requires O(e) time.

To check that the new edge, (v, w), does not form a cycle in T and to add such an edge to T, we may use the union-find operations discussed in Section 5.9. This means that we view each connected component in T as a set containing the vertices in that component. Initially, T is empty and each vertex of G is in a different set (see Figure 6.25(b)). Before we add an edge, (v, w), we use the find operation to determine if v and w are in the same set. If they are, the two vertices are already connected and adding the

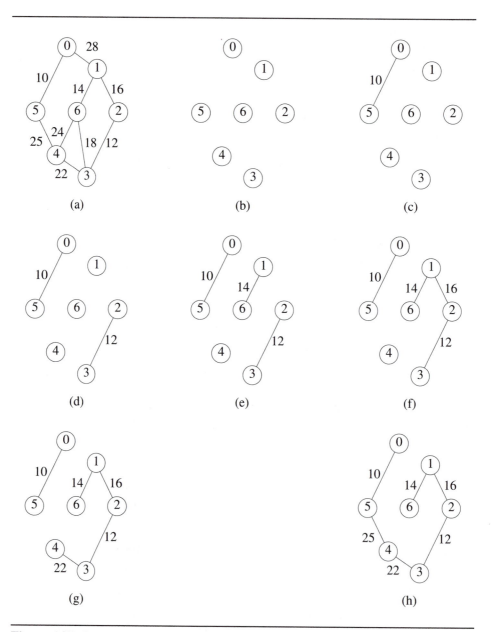

Figure 6.25: Stages in Kruskal's algorithm

Edge	Weight	Result	Figure
----	---	initial	Figure 6.25(b)
(0,5)	10	added to tree	Figure 6.25(c)
(2,3)	12	added	Figure 6.25(d)
(1,6)	14	added	Figure 6.25(e)
(1,2)	16	added	Figure 6.25(f)
(3,6)	18	discarded	
(3,4)	22	added	Figure 6.25(g)
(4,6)	24	discarded	
(4,5)	25	added	Figure 6.25(h)
(0,1)	28	not considered	

Figure 6.26: Summary of Kruskal's algorithm applied to Figure 6.25(a)

```
T = {};
while (T contains less than n-1 edges && E is not empty) {
   choose a least cost edge (v,w) from E;
   delete (v,w) from E;
   if ((v,w) does not create a cycle in T)
      add (v,w) to T;
   else
      discard (v,w);
}
if (T contains fewer than n-1 edges)
   printf("No spanning tree\n");
```

Program 6.7: Kruskal's algorithm

edge (v, w) would cause a cycle. For example, when we consider the edge $(3, 2)$, the sets would be $\{0\}, \{1, 2, 3\}, \{5\}, \{6\}$. Since vertices 3 and 2 are already in the same set, the edge $(3, 2)$ is rejected. The next edge examined is $(1, 5)$. Since vertices 1 and 5 are in different sets, the edge is accepted. This edge connects the two components $\{1, 2, 3\}$ and $\{5\}$. Therefore, we perform a union on these sets to obtain the set $\{1, 2, 3, 5\}$.

Since the union-find operations require less time than choosing and deleting an edge (lines 3 and 4), the latter operations determine the total computing time of Kruskal's algorithm. Thus, the total computing time is $O(e \log e)$. Theorem 6.1 proves that Program 6.7 produces a minimum spanning tree of G.

Theorem 6.1: Let G be an undirected connected graph. Kruskal's algorithm generates a minimum cost spanning tree.

Proof: We shall show that:

(a)   Kruskal's method produces a spanning tree whenever a spanning tree exists.

(b)   The spanning tree generated is of minimum cost.

For (a), we note that Kruskal's algorithm only discards edges that produce cycles. We know that the deletion of a single edge from a cycle in a connected graph produces a graph that is also connected. Therefore, if G is initially connected, the set of edges in T and E always form a connected graph. Consequently, if G is initially connected, the algorithm cannot terminate with $E = \{\}$ and $|T| < n - 1$.

Now let us show that the constructed spanning tree, T, is of minimum cost. Since G has a finite number of spanning trees, it must have at least one that is of minimum cost. Let U be such a tree. Both T and U have exactly $n - 1$ edges. If $T = U$, then T is of minimum cost and we have nothing to prove. So, assume that $T \neq U$. Let k, $k > 0$, be the number of edges in T that are not in U (k is also the number of edges in U that are not in T).

We shall show that T and U have the same cost by transforming U into T. This transformation is done in k steps. At each step, the number of edges in T that are not in U is reduced by exactly 1. Furthermore, the cost of U is not changed as a result of the transformation. As a result, U after k transformation steps has the same cost as the initial U and contains exactly those edges that are in T. This implies that T is of minimum cost.

For each transformation step, we add one edge, e, from T to U and remove one edge, f, from U. We select the edges e and f in the following way:

(1)   Let e be the least cost edge in T that is not in U. Such an edge must exist because $k > 0$.

(2)   When we add e to U, we create a unique cycle. Let f be any edge on this cycle that is not in T. We know that at least one of the edges on this cycle is not in T because T contains no cycles.

Given the way e and f are selected, it follows that $V = U + \{e\} - \{f\}$ is a spanning tree and that T has exactly $k - 1$ edges that are not in V. We need to show that the cost of V is the same as the cost of U. Clearly, the cost of V is the cost of U plus the cost of the edge e minus the cost of the edge f. The cost of e cannot be less than the cost of f since this would mean that the spanning tree V has a lower cost than the tree U. This is impossible. If e has a higher cost than f, then f is considered before e by Kruskal's algorithm. Since it is not in T, Kruskal's algorithm must have discarded this edge at this time. Therefore, f together with the edges in T having a cost less than or equal to the cost of f must form a cycle. By the choice of e, all these edges are also in U. Thus, U must contain a cycle. However, since U is a spanning tree it cannot contain a cycle. So the assumption that e is of higher cost than f leads to a contradiction. This means that e and f must have the same cost. Hence, V has the same cost as U. $\Box$

Prim's Algorithm

Prim's algorithm, like Kruskal's, constructs the minimum cost spanning tree one edge at a time. However, at each stage of the algorithm, the set of selected edges forms a tree. By contrast, the set of selected edges in Kruskal's algorithm forms a forest at each stage. Prim's algorithm begins with a tree, T, that contains a single vertex. This may be any of the vertices in the original graph. Next, we add a least cost edge (u, v) to T such that $T \cup \{(u, v)\}$ is also a tree. We repeat this edge addition step until T contains $n - 1$ edges. To make sure that the added edge does not form a cycle, at each step we choose the edge (u, v) such that exactly one of u or v is in T. Program 6.8 contains a formal description of Prim's algorithm. T is the set of tree edges, and TV is the set of tree vertices, that is, vertices that are currently in the tree. Figure 6.27 shows the progress of Prim's algorithm on the graph of Figure 6.25(a).

```
T = {};
TV = {0}; /* start with vertex 0 and no edges */
while (T contains fewer than n-1 edges) {
   let (u, v) be a least cost edge such that u ∈ TV and
   v ∉ TV;
   if (there is no such edge)
     break;
   add v to TV;
   add (u, v) to T;
}
if (T contains fewer than n-1 edges)
   printf("No spanning tree\n");
```

Program 6.8: Prim's algorithm

To implement Prim's algorithm, we assume that each vertex v that is not in TV has a companion vertex, *near(v)*, such that *near(v)* $\in$ TV and *cost(near(v), v)* is minimum over all such choices for *near(v)*. (We assume that *cost(v, w)* $= \infty$ if $(v, w) \notin E$). At each stage we select v so that *cost(near(v), v)* is minimum and $v \notin TV$. Using this strategy we can implement Prim's algorithm in $O(n^2)$, where n is the number of vertices in G. Asymptotically faster implementations are also possible. One of these results from the use of Fibonacci heaps which we examine in Chapter 9.

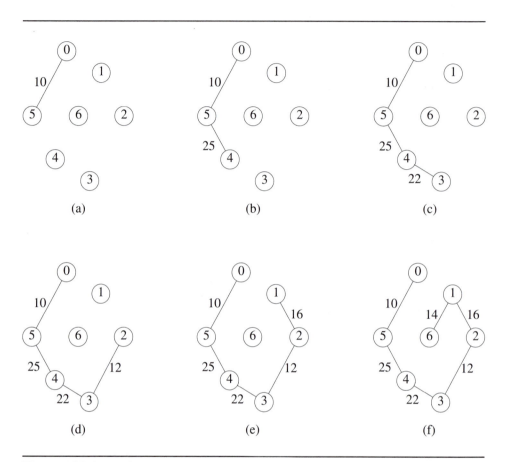

Figure 6.27: Stages in Prim's algorithm

Sollin's Algorithm

Unlike Kruskal's and Prim's algorithms, Sollin's algorithm selects several edges for inclusion in T at each stage. At the start of a stage, the selected edges, together with all n graph vertices, form a spanning forest. During a stage we select one edge for each tree in the forest. This edge is a minimum cost edge that has exactly one vertex in the tree. Since two trees in the forest could select the same edge, we need to eliminate multiple copies of edges. At the start of the first stage the set of selected edges is empty. The algorithm terminates when there is only one tree at the end of a stage or no edges remain for selection.

Figure 6.28 shows Sollin's algorithm applied to the graph of Figure 6.25(a). The initial configuration of zero selected edges is the same as that shown in Figure 6.25(b). Each tree in this forest is a a single vertex. At the next stage, we select edges for each of the vertices. The edges selected are (0, 5), (1, 6), (2, 3), (3, 2), (4, 3), (5, 0), (6, 1). After eliminating the duplicate edges, we are left with edges (0, 5), (1, 6), (2, 3), and (4, 3). We add these edges to the set of selected edges, thereby producing the forest of Figure 6.28(a). In the next stage, the tree with vertex set {0, 5} selects edge (5, 4), and the two remaining trees select edge (1, 2). After these two edges are added, the spanning tree is complete, as shown in Figure 6.28(b). We leave the development of Sollin's algorithm into a C function and its correctness proof as exercises.

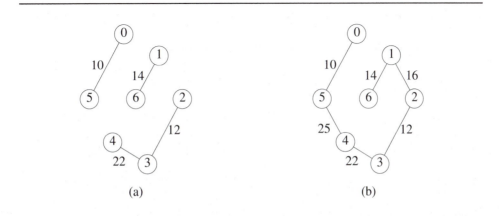

Figure 6.28: Stages in Sollin's algorithm

EXERCISES

1. Prove that Prim's algorithm finds a minimum cost spanning tree for every undirected connected graph.

2. Refine Prim's algorithm (Program 6.8) into a C function that finds a minimum cost spanning tree. The complexity of your function should be $O(n^2)$, where n is the number of vertices in the graph. Show that this is the case.

3. Prove that Sollin's algorithm finds a minimum cost spanning tree for every connected undirected graph.

4. What is the maximum number of stages in Sollin's algorithm? Give this as a function of the number of vertices, n, in the graph.

5. Write a C function that finds a minimum cost spanning tree using Sollin's algorithm. What is the complexity of your function?

6. Write a C function that finds a minimum cost spanning tree using Kruskal's algorithm. You may use the *union* and *find* functions from Chapter 5 and the *sort* function from Chapter 1 or the min heap functions from Chapter 5.

7. Show that if T is a spanning tree for an undirected graph G, then the addition of an edge e, $e \notin E(T)$ and $e \in E(G)$, to T creates a unique cycle.

6.4   SHORTEST PATHS AND TRANSITIVE CLOSURE

Suppose we have a graph that represents the highway system of a state or a country. In this graph, the vertices represent cities and the edges represent sections of the highway. Each edge has a weight representing the distance between the two cities connected by the edge. A motorist wishing to drive from city A to city B would be interested in answers to the following questions:

(1)   Is there a path from A to B?

(2)   If there is more than one path from A to B, which path is the shortest?

In this section, we explore several problems related to finding shortest paths. We define the length of a path as the sum of the weights of the edges on that path rather than the number of edges on the path. The starting vertex of the path is the source and the last vertex is the destination. Since one-way streets are possible, the graphs are directed. Unless otherwise stated, we also assume that all weights are positive.

6.4.1   Single Source All Destinations

In this problem we are given a directed graph, $G = (V, E)$, a weighting function, $w(e)$, $w(e) > 0$, for the edges of G, and a source vertex, v_0. We wish to determine a shortest path from v_0 to each of the remaining vertices of G. As an example, consider the graph of Figure 6.29(a). If v_0 is the source vertex, then the shortest path from v_0 to v_1 is v_0, v_2, v_3, v_1. The length of this path is $10 + 15 + 20 = 45$. Although there are three edges on this path, it is shorter than the path $v_0\, v_1$, which has a length of 50. Figure 6.29(b) lists the shortest paths from v_0 to v_1, v_2, v_3, and v_4 in nondecreasing order of path length. There is no path from v_0 to v_5.

We may use a greedy algorithm to generate the shortest paths in the order indicated in Figure 6.29(b). Let S denote the set of vertices, including v_0, whose shortest paths have been found. For w not in S, let *distance*[w] be the length of the shortest path starting from v_0, going through vertices only in S, and ending in w. Generating the paths in nondecreasing order of length leads to the following observations:

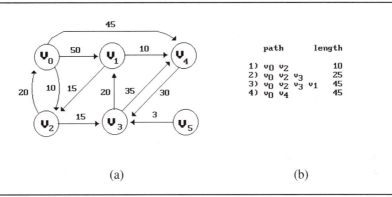

<table>
<tr><td>path</td><td></td><td></td><td>length</td></tr>
</table>

	path				length
1)	v_0	v_2			10
2)	v_0	v_2	v_3		25
3)	v_0	v_2	v_3	v_1	45
4)	v_0	v_4			45

(a)   (b)

Figure 6.29: Graph and shortest paths from v_0

(1)   If the next shortest path is to vertex u, then the path from v_0 to u goes through only those vertices that are in S. To prove this we must show that all intermediate vertices on the shortest path from v_0 to u are already in S. Assume that there is a vertex w on this path that is not in S. Then, the path from v_0 to u also contains a path from v_0 to w which has a length that is less than the length of the path from v_0 to u. Since we assume that the shortest paths are generated in nondecreasing order of path length, we must have previously generated the path from v_0 to w. This is obviously a contradiction. Therefore, there cannot be any intermediate vertex that is not in S.

(2)   Vertex u is chosen so that it has the minimum distance, $distance[u]$, among all the vertices not in S. This follows from the definition of $distance$ and observation (1). If there are several vertices not in S with the same distance, then we may select any one of them.

(3)   Once we have selected u and generated the shortest path from v_0 to u, u becomes a member of S. Adding u to S can change the distance of shortest paths starting at v_0, going through vertices only in S, and ending at a vertex, w, that is not currently in S. If the distance changes, we have found a shorter such path from v_0 to w. This path goes through u. The intermediate vertices on this path are in S and its subpath from u to w can be chosen so as to have no intermediate vertices. The length of the shorter path is $distance\,[u\,] + length\,(<u,\ w>)$.

We attribute these observations, along with the algorithm to determine the shortest paths from v_0 to all other vertices in G to Edsger Dijkstra. To implement Dijkstra's algorithm, we assume that the n vertices are numbered from 0 to $n - 1$. We maintain the set S as an array, *found*, with *found* $[i\,] = FALSE$ if vertex i is not in S and *found* $[i\,] = TRUE$ if vertex i is in S. We represent the graph by its cost adjacency matrix, with $cost[i][j]$ being the weight of edge $<i, j>$. If the edge $<i, j>$ is not in G, we set $cost[i][j]$ to some large number. The choice of this number is arbitrary, although we make two stipulations regarding its value:

(1)   The number must be larger than any of the values in the cost matrix.

(2)   The number must be chosen so that the statement *distance*[*u*] + *cost*[*u*][*w*] does not produce an overflow into the sign bit.

Restriction (2) makes *INT_MAX* (defined in *<limits.h>*) a poor choice for nonexistent edges. For *i* = *j*, we may set *cost*[*i*][*j*] to any nonnegative number without affecting the outcome. Program 6.9 contains sample declarations that create the graph of Figure 6.29(a). We may easily modify these declarations in case the graph is to be input from a file or keyboard or generated in some other manner. In these cases, the function creating the graph should keep track of the largest weight so that the weight of the nonexistent edges may be defined correctly. The function *shortest_path* (Program 6.10) contains our implementation of Dijkstra's algorithm. This function uses *choose* (Program 6.11) to return a vertex, *u*, such that *u* has the minimum distance from the start vertex, *v*.

```
#define MAX_VERTICES 6 /*maximum number of vertices */
int cost[][MAX_VERTICES] =
               {{    0,    50,    10, 1000,    45, 1000},
                {1000,     0,    15, 1000,    10, 1000},
                {  20, 1000,     0,    15, 1000, 1000},
                {1000,    20, 1000,     0,    35, 1000},
                {1000, 1000,    30, 1000,     0, 1000},
                {1000, 1000, 1000,     3, 1000,    0}};
int distance[MAX_VERTICES];
short int found[MAX_VERTICES];
int n = MAX_VERTICES;
```

Program 6.9: Declarations for the shortest path algorithm

Analysis of *shortestpath*: The time taken by the algorithm on a graph with *n* vertices is $O(n^2)$. To see this, note that the first **for** loop takes $O(n)$ time. The second **for** loop is executed *n* − 2 times. Each execution of this loop requires $O(n)$ time to select the next vertex and also to update *dist*. So the total time for this loop is $O(n^2)$. Any shortest path algorithm must examine each edge in the graph at least once since any of the edges could be in a shortest path. Hence, the minimum possible time for such an algorithm is $O(e)$. Since we represented the graph as a cost adjacency matrix, it takes $O(n^2)$ time just to determine the edges that are in *G*. Therefore, any shortest path algorithm using this representation has a time complexity of $O(n^2)$. The exercises explore several variations that speed up the algorithm, but the asymptotic time complexity remains $O(n^2)$. For the case of graphs with few edges, the use of Fibonacci heaps together with an adjacency list representation produces a more efficient implementation of the greedy algorithm for the

```
void shortestpath(int v, int cost[][MAX_VERTICES],
int distance[], int n, short int found[])
{
/* distance[i] represents the shortest path from vertex v
to i, found[i] holds a 0 if the shortest path from vertex i
has not been found and a 1 if it has, cost is the
adjacency matrix */
   int i,u,w;
   for (i = 0; i < n; i++) {
      found[i] = FALSE;
      distance[i] = cost[v][i];
   }
   found[v] = TRUE;
   distance[v] = 0;
   for (i = 0; i < n-2; i++) {
      u = choose(distance,n,found);
      found[u] = TRUE;
      for (w = 0; w < n; w++)
         if (!found[w])
            if (distance[u] + cost[u][w] < distance[w])
               distance[w] = distance[u] + cost[u][w];
   }
}
```

Program 6.10: Single source shortest paths

single-source all-destinations problem. We discuss this in Chapter 9. □

Example 6.4: Consider the eight-vertex digraph of Figure 6.30(a) and its cost adjacency matrix (Figure 6.30(b)). We would like to find the shortest paths from Boston (vertex 4) to each of the other cities on the graph. Figure 6.31 shows the vertices selected and the values of distance at each iteration of the nested **for** loops. Notice that the algorithm terminates when only seven of the eight vertices are in S. By the definition of distance, the distance of the last vertex, in this case Los Angeles, is correct since the shortest path from Boston to all other cities has been found. □

6.4.2   All Pairs Shortest Paths

In the all pairs shortest path problem we must find the shortest paths between all pairs of vertices, v_i, v_j, $i \neq j$. We could solve this problem using *shortestpath* with each of the vertices in $V(G)$ as the source. Since G has n vertices and *shortestpath* has a time

```
int choose(int distance[], int n, short int found[])
{
/* find the smallest distance not yet checked */
    int i, min, minpos;
    min = INT_MAX;
    minpos = -1;
    for (i = 0; i < n; i++)
        if (distance[i] < min && !found[i]) {
            min = distance[i];
            minpos = i;
        }
    return minpos;
}
```

Program 6.11: Choosing the least cost edge

complexity of $O(n^2)$, the total time required would be $O(n^3)$. However, we can obtain a conceptually simpler algorithm that works correctly even if some edges in G have negative weights. (We do require that G has no cycles with a negative length.) Although this algorithm still has a computing time of $O(n^3)$, it has a smaller constant factor. This new algorithm uses the dynamic programming method.

We represent the graph G by its cost adjacency matrix with $cost[i][j] = 0$, $i = j$. If the edge $<i, j>$, $i \neq j$ is not in G, we set $cost[i][j]$ to some sufficiently large number using the same restrictions discussed in the single source problem. Let $A^k[i][j]$ be the cost of the shortest path from i to j, using only those intermediate vertices with an index $\leq k$. The cost of the shortest path from i to j is $A^{n-1}[i][j]$ as no vertex in G has an index greater than $n-1$. Further, $A^{-1}[i][j] = cost[i][j]$ since the only i to j paths allowed have no intermediate vertices on them.

The basic idea in the all pairs algorithm is to begin with the matrix A^{-1} and successively generate the matrices $A^0, A^1, A^2, \cdots, A^{n-1}$. If we have already generated A^{k-1}, then we may generate A^k by realizing that for any pair of vertices i, j one of the two rules below applies.

(1) The shortest path from i to j going through no vertex with index greater than k does not go through the vertex with index k and so its cost is $A^{k-1}[i][j]$.

(2) The shortest such path does go through vertex k. Such a path consists of a path from i to k followed by one from k to j. Neither of these goes through a vertex with index greater than $k-1$. Hence, their costs are $A^{k-1}[i][k]$ and $A^{k-1}[k][j]$.

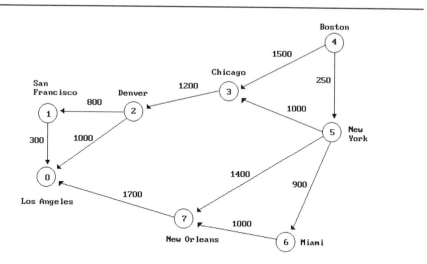

(a) Digraph of hypothetical airline routes

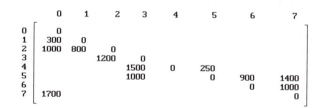

(b) Cost adjacency matrix

Figure 6.30: Digraph of airline routes

These rules yield the following formulas for $A^k[i][j]$:

$$A^k[i][j] = \min\{A^{k-1}[i][j], A^{k-1}[i][k] + A^{k-1}[k][j]\}, k \geq 0$$

and

$$A^{-1}[i][j] = cost[i][j]$$

Example 6.5: Figure 6.32 shows a digraph together with its A^{-1} matrix. For this graph $A^1[0][2] \neq \min\{A^1[0][2], A^0[0][1] + A^0[1][2]\} = 2$. Instead, $A^1[0][2] = -\infty$ because the length of the path:

$$0, 1, 0, 1, 0, 1, \cdots, 0, 1, 2$$

Iteration	S	Vertex selected	Distance LA [0]	SF [1]	DEN [2]	CHI [3]	BOST [4]	NY [5]	MIA [6]	NO [7]
Initial	--	----	$+\infty$	$+\infty$	$+\infty$	1500	0	250	$+\infty$	$+\infty$
1	{4}	5	$+\infty$	$+\infty$	$+\infty$	1250	0	250	1150	1650
2	{4,5}	6	$+\infty$	$+\infty$	$+\infty$	1250	0	250	1150	1650
3	{4,5,6}	3	$+\infty$	$+\infty$	2450	1250	0	250	1150	1650
4	{4,5,6,3}	7	3350	$+\infty$	2450	1250	0	250	1150	1650
5	{4,5,6,3,7}	2	3350	3250	2450	1250	0	250	1150	1650
6	{4,5,6,3,7,2}	1	3350	3250	2450	1250	0	250	1150	1650
	{4,5,6,3,7,2,1}									

Figure 6.31: Action of *shortestpath* on the digraph of Figure 6.30

can be made arbitrarily small. This situation occurs because we have a cycle, 0, 1, 0, that has a negative length (-1). $\square$

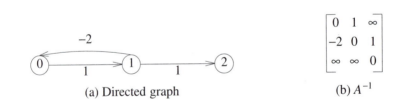

(a) Directed graph   (b) A^{-1}

Figure 6.32: Graph with negative cycle

The function *allcosts* (Program 6.12) computes $A^{n-1}[i][j]$. The computations are done in place using the array *distance*, which we define as:

```
int distance[MAX_VERTICES][MAX_VERTICES];
```

The reason this computation can be carried out in place is that $A^k[i,k] = A^{k-1}[i,k]$ and $A^k[k,j] = A^{k-1}[k,j]$ and so the in place computation does not alter the outcome.

Analysis of *allcosts*: This algorithm is especially easy to analyze because the looping is independent of the data in the distance matrix. The total time for *allcosts* is $O(n^3)$. An exercise examines the extensions needed to generate the $<i, j>$ paths with these lengths. We can speed up the algorithm by using our knowledge of the fact that the innermost **for**

```
void allcosts(int cost[][MAX_VERTICES],
              int distance[][MAX_VERTICES], int n)
{
/* determine the distances from each vertex to every other
vertex,
 cost is the adjacency matrix, distance is the matrix of
distances */
   int i,j,k;
   for (i = 0; i < n; i++)
      for (j = 0; j < n; j++)
         distance[i][j] = cost[i][j];
   for (k = 0; k < n; k++)
      for (i = 0; i < n; i++)
         for (j = 0; j < n; j++)
            if (distance[i][k] + distance[k][j] <
                                       distance[i][j])
               distance[i][j] =
               distance[i][k] + distance[k][j];
}
```

Program 6.12: All pairs, shortest paths function

loop is executed only when *distance*[i][k] and *distance*[k][j] are not equal to ∞. □

Example 6.6: Using the graph of Figure 6.33(a), we obtain the cost matrix of Figure 6.33(b). Figure 6.34 shows the initial matrix, A^{-1}, and matrices A^0, A^1, A^2. □

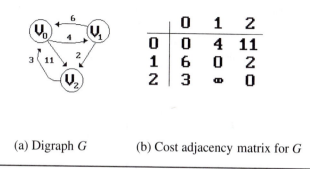

	0	1	2
0	0	4	11
1	6	0	2
2	3	∞	0

(a) Digraph G (b) Cost adjacency matrix for G

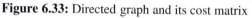

Figure 6.33: Directed graph and its cost matrix

A^{-1}	0	1	2
0	0	4	11
1	6	0	2
2	3	∞	0

A^{0}	0	1	2
0	0	4	11
1	6	0	2
2	3	7	0

A^{1}	0	1	2
0	0	4	6
1	6	0	2
2	3	7	0

A^{2}	0	1	2
0	0	4	6
1	5	0	2
2	3	7	0

Figure 6.34: Matrices A^{k} produced by *allcosts* for Figure 6.33(a)

6.4.3 Transitive Closure

We would like to end this section by studying a problem that is closely related to the all pairs, shortest path problem. Assume that we have a directed graph G with unweighted edges. We want to determine if there is a path from i to j for all values of i and j. Two cases are of interest. The first case requires positive path lengths, while the second requires only nonnegative path lengths. These cases are known as the *transitive closure* and *reflexive transitive closure* of a graph, respectively. We define them as follows:

Definition: The *transitive closure matrix*, denoted A^{+}, of a directed graph, G, is a matrix such that $A^{+}[i][j] = 1$ if there is a path of length > 0 from i to j; otherwise, $A^{+}[i][j] = 0$. $\square$

Definition: The *reflexive transitive closure matrix*, denoted A^{*}, of a directed graph, G, is a matrix such that $A^{*}[i][j] = 1$ if there is a path of length ≥ 0 from i to j; otherwise, $A^{*}[i][j] = 0$. $\square$

Figure 6.35 shows A^{+} and A^{*} for a digraph. Clearly, A^{+} and A^{*} differ only on the diagonal. Thus, $A^{+}[i][i] = 1$ *iff* there is a cycle of length > 1 containing vertex i. In contrast, $A^{*}[i][i]$ is always one since there is always a path of length 0 from i to i.

We can easily find A^+ by using *allcosts*. We first modify *cost* so that $cost[i][j] =$ 1 if $<i, j>$ is an edge in G and $cost[i][j] = +\infty$ if $<i, j>$ is not in G. When *allcosts* terminates, we obtain A^+ from *distance* by letting $A^+[i][j] = 1$ *iff distance[i][j] < +∞*. We then obtain A^* by setting all the diagonal elements in A^+ to 1. The total time is $O(n^3)$. We can simplify the algorithm by changing the **if** statement in the nested **for** loops to:

```
distance[i][j] = distance[i][j] || distance[i][k] &&
                    distance[k][j]
```

and initializing *distance* to be the adjacency matrix of the graph. With this modification, *distance* will be equivalent to A^+ when *allcosts* terminates. For an undirected graph, the (reflexive) transitive closure matrix may be computed in $O(n^2)$ time by first computing the connected components.

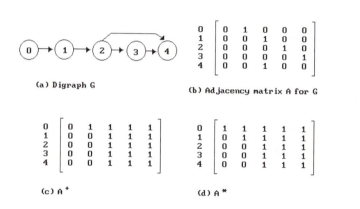

Figure 6.35: Graph G and its adjacency matrix A, A^+, A^*

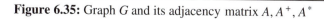

EXERCISES

1. Create a C function that allows the user to enter graphs. The graphs should be put into an adjacency matrix, *cost*[i][j], with the nonexistent edges initialized so that the cost can be used with both *shortestpath* and *allcosts*.

2. Rewrite *shortestpath* so that it generates the paths as well as the distances for each of the shortest paths.

3. Using the concepts from the shortestpath algorithm (Program 6.10), find a minimum spanning tree algorithm whose worst case time is $O(n^2)$.

4. Use *shortestpath* to obtain the lengths of the shortest paths from vertex 0 to all remaining vertices in the digraph in Figure 6.36. Generate the paths in ascending order of length.

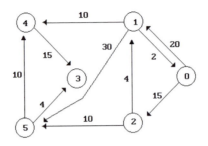

Figure 6.36: Sample digraph

5. Rewrite *shortestpath* using the following assumptions:

    (a) *G* is represented by its adjacency lists. Each node in the list has *vertex, cost,* and *link* fields, where *cost* is the length of the corresponding edge and *n* is the number of vertices in *G*.

    (b) Instead of using *S* (the set of vertices for which we have found shortest paths), use $T = V(G) - S$. Represent *T* as a linked list.

6. Using the digraph of Figure 6.37, explain why *shortestpath* does not work properly. What is the shortest path between vertices v_0 and v_6?

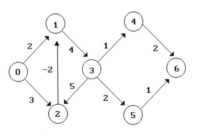

Figure 6.37: Digraph for which *shortestpath* does not work properly

7. By considering the complete graph with n vertices, show that the maximum number of simple paths between two vertices is $O((n-1)!)$.

8. Modify *allcosts* so that it prints out each of the paths as well as the length of the paths.

9. Show that $A^+ = A^* \times A$, where matrix multiplication is defined as:

$$a_{ij}^+ = \bigvee_{k=1}^{n} a_{ik}^* \wedge a_{kj}$$

where $\vee$ is the logical *or* operation and $\wedge$ is the logical *and* operation.

10. Obtain the matrices A^* and A^+ for the digraph of Figure 6.36.

11. Write a C function to compute the reflexive transitive closure of an undirected graph with n vertices in $O(n^2)$ time. Begin with the adjacency matrix of the graph and obtain its connected components.

12. Do the preceding exercise for the case of transitive closure.

6.5   ACTIVITY NETWORKS

6.5.1   Activity On Vertex (AOV) Networks

We can divide all but the simplest projects into several subprojects called *activities*. The entire project is successfully completed when each of the activities is completed. For example, a student working toward a degree in computer science has to complete several courses successfully. In this case, the project is the completed major and the activities are the individual courses. Figure 6.38(a) lists the courses needed for a computer science major at a hypothetical university. Some of these courses may be taken independently, while other courses have prerequisites. For example, a student cannot take the data structures course without first completing the beginning programming and discrete mathematics courses. Thus, prerequisites define precedence relations among courses. We may represent these relations more clearly as a directed graph in which the vertices represent courses and the directed edges represent prerequisites. This graph has an edge $<i, j>$ *iff* i is a prerequisite for course j.

Definition: An *activity on vertex*, or *AOV*, network, is a directed graph G in which the vertices represent tasks or activities and the edges represent precedence relations between tasks. □

Definition: Vertex i in an AOV network G is a *predecessor* of vertex j *iff* there is a directed path from vertex i to vertex j. Vertex i is an *immediate predecessor* of vertex j *iff* $<i, j>$ is an edge in G. If i is a predecessor of j, then j is a successor of i. If i is an immediate predecessor of j, then j is an immediate successor of i. □

Figure 6.38(b) is the AOV network corresponding to the courses of Figure 6.38(a). *C3* and *C6* are immediate predecessors of *C7*. *C9*, *C10*, *C12*, and *C13* are immediate successors of *C7*. *C14* is a successor, but not an immediate successor of *C3*. If an AOV network represents a feasible project, the precedence relations must be both transitive and irreflexive.

Definition: A relation $\cdot$ is transitive *iff* for all triples i, j, k, $i \cdot j$ and $j \cdot k \Rightarrow i \cdot k$. A relation $\cdot$ is irreflexive on a set S if $i \cdot i$ is false for all elements, i, in S. A *partial order* is a precedence relation that is both transitive and irreflexive. □

We can easily see that the precedence relation defined by the set of edges on the set of vertices in Figure 6.38(b) is transitive. Determining if the precedence relation is irreflexive is more difficult, but crucial. If the precedence relation is not irreflexive, then there is an activity which is a predecessor of itself and so must be completed before it can be started. Clearly this is impossible. When there are no inconsistencies of this type, the project is feasible.

We can show that a precedence relation is irreflexive by proving that the network contains no directed cycles. A directed graph with no cycles is a directed acyclic graph (dag). In addition to testing an AOV for feasibility, our algorithm also generates a linear ordering, $v_{i_0}, v_{i_1}, \ldots, v_{n-1}$, of the vertices (activities) in the network, referred to as the topological order.

Definition: A *topological order* is a linear ordering of the vertices of a graph such that, for any two vertices, i, j, if i is a predecessor of j in the network then i precedes j in the linear ordering. □

A topological order of the courses in Figure 6.38(b) gives a course of study that would successfully meet the degree requirements in computer science. There are several possible topological orders for the network of Figure 6.38(b), including:

C1, C2, C4, C5, C3, C6, C8, C7, C10, C13, C12, C14, C15, C11, C9

and

C4, C5, C2, C1, C6, C3, C8, C15, C7, C9, C10, C11, C12, C13, C14

An algorithm that sorts the tasks into topological order is straightforward. We begin by listing out a vertex in the network that has no predecessor. We then delete this vertex, and all edges leading out from it, from the network. We repeat these two steps until either all the vertices have been listed, or all remaining vertices have predecessors and so we cannot remove any of them. In this case, the network has a cycle and the project is infeasible. Program 6.13 contains a formal description of the topological sort.

Example 6.7: We will use Program 6.13 to find the topological order for the network of Figure 6.39. The first vertex picked is v_0 since it is the only vertex that has no predecessors. Vertex v_0 and the edges $<v_0, v_1>$, $<v_0, v_2>$, $<v_0, v_3>$ are deleted. In the resulting network (Figure 6.39(b)), v_1, v_2, and v_3 have no predecessor. Any of these can be the

Course number	Course name	Prerequisites
C1	Programming I	None
C2	Discrete Mathematics	None
C3	Data Structures	C1, C2
C4	Calculus I	None
C5	Calculus II	C4
C6	Linear Algebra	C5
C7	Analysis of Algorithms	C3, C6
C8	Assembly Language	C3
C9	Operating Systems	C7, C8
C10	Programming Languages	C7
C11	Compiler Design	C10
C12	Artificial Intelligence	C7
C13	Computational Theory	C7
C14	Parallel Algorithms	C13
C15	Numerical Analysis	C5

(a) Courses needed for a computer science degree at a hypothetical university

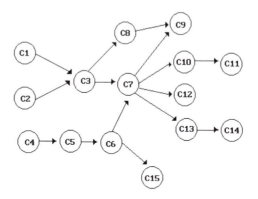

(b) AOV network representing courses as vertices and edges as prerequisites

Figure 6.38: An AOV network

next vertex in the topological order. Assume that v_3 is chosen. Deletion of v_3 and the edges $<v_3, v_5>$ and $<v_3, v_4>$ produces the network of Figure 6.39(c). Either v_1 or v_2 may be picked next. Figure 6.39(d) through Figure 6.39(g) show the progress of the algorithm. $\square$

```
for (i = 0; i < n; i++) {
   if every vertex has a predecessor {
      fprintf(stderr,"Network has a cycle.\n");
      exit(1);
   }
   pick a vertex v that has no predecessors;
   output v;
   delete v and all edges leading out of v
   from the network;
}
```

Program 6.13: Topological sort

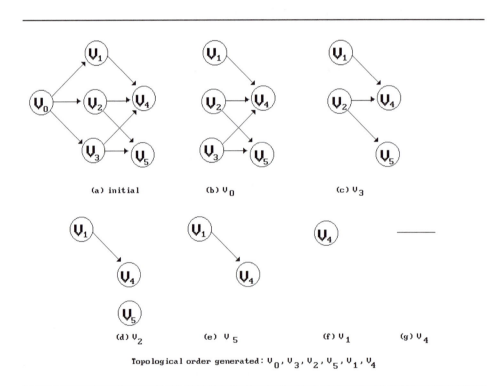

(a) initial   (b) v_0 (c) v_3

(d) v_2 (e) v_5 (f) v_1 (g) v_4

Topological order generated: $v_0, v_3, v_2, v_5, v_1, v_4$

Figure 6.39: Simulation of Program 6.13 on an AOV network

Before transforming Program 6.13 into a C function, we must specify the representation of the AOV network. As always, the choice of a representation depends on the operations that we wish to perform. In this problem, we must:

(1)   determine if a vertex has any predecessors.

(2)   delete a vertex and all of its incident edges.

We can perform the first operation efficiently if we keep a count of the number of immediate predecessors for each vertex. The second operation is easily implemented if we represent the network by its adjacency lists. Then we can carry out the deletion of all incident edges of a vertex, v, by decreasing the predecessor count of all vertices on its adjacency list. Whenever the count of a vertex drops to zero, we place the vertex on a list of vertices with a zero count. We use this list to select the next vertex. The complete C function for performing a topological sort on a network is *topsort* (Program 6.14). The function assumes that the network is represented by its adjacency lists. The head nodes of these lists now contain count and link fields.

The declarations used in *topsort* are:

```
typedef struct node *node_pointer;
typedef struct node {
        int vertex;
        node_pointer link;
        };
typedef struct {
        int count;
        node_pointer link;
        } hdnodes;
hdnodes graph[MAX_VERTICES];
```

The *count* field contains the in-degree of that vertex and *link* is a pointer to the first node on the adjacency list. Each node has two fields, *vertex* and *link*. We can easily set up the count fields at the time of input. When $<i, j>$ is input, we increment the count of vertex j. We use a stack to hold the list of vertices with zero count. We could have used a queue, but the stack is easier to implement. We link the stack through the count field of the head nodes since this field is of no use after the count reaches 0. Figure 6.40 shows the adjacency list representation of the network of Figure 6.39(a).

Analysis of *topsort*: As a result of a judicious choice of data structures, *topsort* is very efficient. The first **for** loop takes $O(n)$ time, on a network with n vertices and e edges. The second **for** loop is iterated n times. The **if** clause is executed in constant time; the **for** loop within the **else** clause takes time $O(d_i)$, where d_i is the out-degree of vertex i. Since this loop is encountered once for each vertex that is printed, the total time for this part of the algorithm is:

```
void topsort(hdnodes graph[], int n)
{
   int i,j,k,top;
   node_pointer ptr;
   /* create a stack of vertices with no predecessors */
   top = -1;
   for (i = 0; i < n; i++)
     if (!graph[i].count) {
        graph[i].count = top;
        top = i;
   }
   for (i = 0; i < n; i++)
     if (top == -1) {
        fprintf(stderr,"\nNetwork   has   a   cycle.   Sort
      terminated. \n");
        exit(1);
   }
     else {
        j = top;    /* unstack a vertex */
        top = graph[top].count;
        printf("v%d, ",j);
        for (ptr = graph[j].link; ptr; ptr = ptr->link) {
        /* decrease the count of the successor vertices
        of j */
           k = ptr->vertex;
           graph[k].count--;
           if (!graph[k].count) {
           /* add vertex k to the stack */
              graph[k].count = top;
              top = k;
        }
     }
   }
 }
}
```

Program 6.14: Topological sort

$$O((\sum_{i=0}^{n-1} d_i) + n) = O(e + n)$$

Thus, the asymptotic computing time of the algorithm is $O(e + n)$. It is linear in the size of the problem! $\square$

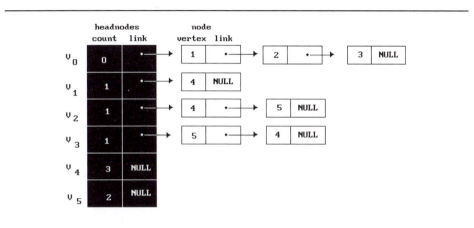

Figure 6.40: Adjacency list representation of Figure 6.39(a)

6.5.2 Activity On Edge (AOE) Networks

An *activity on edge*, or *AOE*, network is an activity network closely related to the AOV network. The directed edges in the graph represent tasks or activities to be performed on a project. The vertices represent events which signal the completion of certain activities. Hence, an event occurs only when all activities entering it have been completed. Figure 6.41(a) is an AOE network for a hypothetical project with 11 tasks or activities, $a_0, \cdots, a_{10}$. There are nine events, $v_0, \cdots, v_8$. We may interpret events, v_0 and v_8 as "start project" and "finish project," respectively. Figure 6.41(b) gives interpretations for some of the nine events. The number associated with each activity is the time required to perform the activity. Thus, activity a_0 requires 6 days, while a_{10} requires 4 days. Usually, these times are only estimates. We can perform activities a_0, a_1, and a_2 concurrently after the start of the project. However, we cannot start a_3, a_4, a_5 until events v_1, v_2, and v_3, respectively, occur. We can carry out a_6 and a_7 after the occurrence of event v_4 (after we have completed a_3 and a_4). If we must place additional constraints on the activities, we can introduce dummy activities whose time is zero. For example, if we do not want activities a_6 and a_7 to start until both events v_4 and v_5 have occurred, we add a dummy activity, a_{11}, represented by the edge $<v_5, v_4>$.

AOE networks have proved very useful for evaluating the performance of many types of projects. This evaluation includes determining not only the minimum amount of time required to complete a project, but also an assessment of the activities whose duration should be shortened to reduce the overall completion time. The most sophisticated of the techniques developed for evaluating networks include PERT (performance evaluation and review technique), CPM (critical path method), and RAMPS (resource allocation and multiproject scheduling).

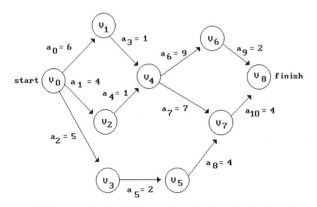

(a) AOE network. Activity graph of a hypothetical project

event	interpretation
v_0	start of project
v_1	completion of activity a_0
v_4	completion of activities a_3 and a_4
v_7	completion of activities a_7 and a_8
v_8	completion of project

(b) Interpretation of some of the events in the activity graph of (a)

Figure 6.41: An AOE network

Since we can carry out the activities in an AOE network in parallel, the minimum time required to complete the project is the length of the longest path from the start vertex to the finish vertex. (We assume that the length of a path is the sum of the times of the activities on this path.) A *critical path* is a path that has the longest length. For example, the path v_0, v_1, v_4, v_7, v_8 is a critical path in the network of Figure 6.41(a). The length of this path is 18. A network may have more than one critical path. In the network of Figure 6.41(a), the path v_0, v_1, v_4, v_6, v_8 is also a critical path.

The *earliest time* an event, v_i, can occur is the length of the longest path from the start vertex v_0 to vertex v_i. For example, the earliest time that event v_4 can occur is 7. The earliest time an event can occur determines the earliest start time for all activities represented by edges leaving that vertex. We denote this time as *early(i)* for activity a_i. For example, *early(6) = early(7) = 7*.

The *latest time, late(i)*, of activity, a_i, is defined to be the latest time the activity may start without increasing the project duration. For example, in Figure 6.41(a), *early(5) = 5* and *late(5) = 8*, *early(7) = 7* and *late(7) = 7*.

A *critical activity* is an activity for which *early(i) = late(i)*. The difference between *late(i)* and *early(i)* is a measure of how critical an activity is. It gives the time that we can delay or slow an activity without increasing the total time needed to finish the project. For example, we may add 2 two days to the time required to complete activity a_5 without affecting the project time. Clearly, all activities on a critical path are strategic and shortening the time required for noncritical activities has no effect on the project duration. A critical path analysis identifies critical activities so that we may concentrate our resources in an attempt to reduce a project's duration. Critical path methods have proved valuable in evaluating project performance and in identifying bottlenecks.

We can also perform a critical path analysis with an AOV network. The length of a path is the sum of the activity times of the vertices on that path. For each activity or vertex, we could analogously define the quantities *early(i)* and *late(i)*. Since the activity times are only estimates, we should reevaluate the project at various stages of completion as more accurate estimates of activity times become available. These changes in activity times could make previously noncritical activities critical and vice versa.

Before ending our discussion of activity networks, let us design an algorithm to compute *early(i)* and *late(i)* for all activities in an AOE network. Once we know these quantities, we can easily identify the critical activities. To determine the critical paths, we simply delete all noncritical activities from the AOE network, and generate all the paths from the start to finish vertex in the new network.

Calculation Of Earliest Times

When computing the earliest and latest activity times it is easier to first obtain the earliest event occurrence time, *earliest[j]*, and the latest event occurrence time, *latest[j]*, for all events, *j*, in the network. Then if activity a_i is represented by edge <*k*, *l*>, we can compute *early(i)* and *late(i)* from the formulas:

$$early\ (i) = earliest\ [k\ ] \tag{6.1}$$

$$late\ (i) = latest\ [l\ ] - duration\ of\ activity\ a_i \tag{6.2}$$

We compute the times *earliest[j]* and *latest[j]* in two stages: a forward stage and a backward stage. During the forward stage, we start with *earliest[0] = 0* and compute the remaining start times using the formula:

$$earliest\ [j] = \max_{i\ \in\ P(j)} \{\ earliest\ [i\ ] + duration\ of <i,\ j>\} \tag{6.3}$$

where $P(j)$ is the set of immediate predecessors of *j*. If we carry out this computation in topological order, the early times of all predecessors of *j* would have been computed prior to the computation of *earliest[j]*. We can easily obtain an algorithm that does this by inserting the following statement at the end of the **else** clause in *topsort*:

```
if (earliest[k] < earliest[j] + ptr->duration)
    earliest[k] = earliest[j] + ptr->duration;
```

We assume that *earliest[]* is initialized to zero and that *duration* is another field in the adjacency list's node structure which contains the activity duration. With this modification the evaluation of Eq. (6.3) is carried on in parallel with the generation of a topological sort. The function *earliest[j]* is updated each time the *earliest[i]* of one of its predecessors is known (that is, when *i* is ready for output).

To show how the modified topological sort algorithm works, let us try it on the network of Figure 6.41(a). Figure 6.42(a) shows the adjacency lists for the network. The order of the nodes on these lists determines the order in which the algorithm examines the vertices. Initially, the early start time for all vertices is 0, and the start vertex is the only one on the stack. When the adjacency list for this vertex is processed, the early start time of all vertices adjacent from v_0 is updated. Since vertices 1, 2, 3 are now on the stack, all their predecessors have been processed and Eq. (6.3) has been evaluated for these vertices. Next, *earliest[5]* is determined. While vertex v_5 is being processed, *earliest[7]* is updated to 11. However, this is not the final value of *earliest[7]* since we have not evaluated Eq. (6.3) for all predecessors of v_7 (for example, we have not examined v_4). This does not matter since we cannot stack v_7 until we have processed all of its predecessors. Now *earliest[4]* is updated to 5 and finally to 7. Next we obtain the values of *earliest[6]* and *earliest[7]*. Ultimately, *earliest[8]* is determined to be 18, the length of a critical path. You may readily verify that when a vertex is put onto the stack its early time has been computed correctly. The insertion of the new statement into *topsort* does not change the asymptotic computing time; it remains O($n + e$).

Calculation Of Latest Times

In the backward stage, we compute the values of *latest[i]* using a procedure analogous to that used in the forward stage. We start with *latest[n−1]* = *earliest[n−1]* and use the equation:

$$latest\,[j] = \min_{i \in S(j)} \{latest\,[i] - duration\ of<j,\ i>\} \qquad (6.4)$$

where $S(j)$ is the set of vertices adjacent from vertex j. I.e., $S(j)$ is the set of immediate successors of j. We set the initial values for *latest[i]* to *earliest[n−1]*. Eq. (6.4) states that if $<j, i>$ is an activity and the latest start time for event i is *latest[i]*, then event j must occur no later than *latest[i]* − duration of $<j, i>$. Before we can compute *latest[j]* for some event j, we must first compute the latest event for all successor events (events adjacent from j). We can obtain these times in a manner identical to the computation of the early times by using inverse adjacency lists, and inserting the following statement at the end of the **else** clause in *topsort*.

```
if (latest[k] > latest[j] - ptr->duration)
    latest[k] = latest[j] - ptr->duration;
```

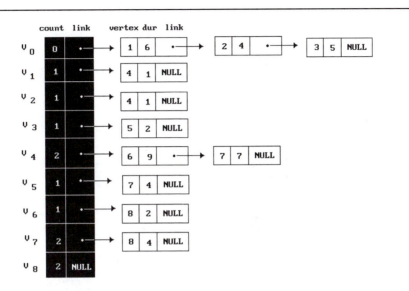

(a) Adjacency lists for Figure 6.41(a)

Earliest	[0]	[1]	[2]	[3]	[4]	[5]	[6]	[7]	[8]	Stack
initial	0	0	0	0	0	0	0	0	0	[0]
output v_0	0	6	4	5	0	0	0	0	0	[3, 2, 1]
output v_3	0	6	4	5	0	7	0	0	0	[5, 2, 1]
output v_5	0	6	4	5	0	7	0	11	0	[2, 1]
output v_2	0	6	4	5	5	7	0	11	0	[1]
output v_1	0	6	4	5	7	7	0	11	0	[4]
output v_4	0	6	4	5	7	7	16	14	0	[7, 6]
output v_7	0	6	4	5	7	7	16	14	16	[6]
output v_6	0	6	4	5	7	7	16	14	18	[8]
output v_8										

(b) Computation of *earliest*

Figure 6.42: Computing *earliest* from topological sort

Initially, the count field of a head node contains the out-degree of the vertex. Figure 6.43 describes the process of calculating latest for the network of Figure 6.41(a).

If we have already carried out the forward step and obtained a topological ordering of the vertices, we can compute the values of *latest*[i] directly using Eq. (6.4). We perform the computations in reverse topological order. Since the topological order generated in Figure 6.42(b) is v_0, v_3, v_5, v_2, v_1, v_4, v_7, v_6, v_8, we compute the values of

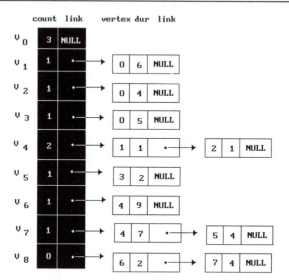

(a) Inverted adjacency lists for AOE network of Figure 6.41(a)

Latest	[0]	[1]	[2]	[3]	[4]	[5]	[6]	[7]	[8]	Stack
initial	18	18	18	18	18	18	18	18	18	[8]
output v_8	18	18	18	18	18	18	16	14	18	[7, 6]
output v_7	18	18	18	18	7	10	16	14	18	[5, 6]
output v_5	18	18	18	18	7	10	16	14	18	[3, 6]
output v_3	3	18	18	8	7	10	16	14	18	[6]
output v_6	3	18	18	8	7	10	16	14	18	[4]
output v_4	3	6	6	8	7	10	16	14	18	[2, 1]
output v_2	2	6	6	8	7	10	16	14	18	[1]
output v_1	0	6	6	8	7	10	16	14	18	[0]

(b) Computation of *latest*

Figure 6.43: Computing *latest* for AOE network of Figure 6.41(a)

latest[i] in the order 8, 6, 7, 4, 1, 2, 5, 3, 0.

    Once obtained we may use the values of *earliest* (Figure 6.42) and *latest* (Figure 6.43) to compute the *early* (i) and *late* (i) times and the degree of criticality for each task. Figure 6.44 summarizes this information. Notice that the critical activities are a_0, a_3, a_6, a_7, a_9, and a_{10}. Deleting all noncritical activities from the network gives us the graph of Figure 6.45. All paths from v_0 to v_8 in this graph are critical paths, and there are no critical paths in the original network that are not paths in the graph of Figure 6.45.

$latest[8] = earliest[8] = 18$
$latest[6] = \min\{earliest[8] - 2\} = 16$
$latest[7] = \min\{earliest[8] - 4\} = 14$
$latest[4] = \min\{earliest[6] - 9; earliest[7] - 7\} = 7$
$latest[1] = \min\{earliest[4] - 1\} = 6$
$latest[2] = \min\{earliest[4] - 1\} = 6$
$latest[5] = \min\{earliest[7] - 4\} = 10$
$latest[3] = \min\{earliest[5] - 2\} = 8$
$latest[0] = \min\{earliest[1] - 6; earliest[2] - 4; earliest[3] - 5\} = 0$

(c) Computation of *latest* from Equation (6.4) using a reverse topological order

---

Figure 6.43 (continued): Computing *latest* for AOE network of Figure 6.41(a)

As a final remark on activity networks, we note that *topsort* detects only directed cycles in the network. There may be other flaws in the network, including vertices that are not reachable from the start vertex (see Figure 6.46). When we carry out a critical path analysis on such a network, there will be several vertices with *earliest*[i] = 0. Since we assume that all activity times are greater than zero, only the start vertex can have *earliest*[i] = 0. Hence, we also can use critical path analysis to detect this kind of fault in project planning.

EXERCISES

1. Does the following set of precedence relations (<) define a partial order on the elements 0 through 4? Explain your answer.

    $$0 < 1; \ 1 < 4; \ 1 < 2; \ 2 < 3; \ 2 < 4; \ 4 < 0$$

2. (a) For the AOE network of Figure 6.47, obtain the *early* and *late* starting times for each activity. Use the forward-backward approach.

    (b) What is the earliest time the project can finish?

    (c) Which activities are critical?

    (d) Is there a single activity whose speed up would result in a reduction of the project length?

3. § [***Programming project***] Write a C program that allows the user to input an AOE network. The program should calculate and output the *early(i)* and *late(i)* times and the degree of criticality for each activity. If the project is not feasible, it should indicate this. If the project is feasible it should print out the critical activities in an appropriate format.

Activity	Early	Late	Late – Early	Critical
a_0	0	0	0	yes
a_1	0	2	2	no
a_2	0	3	3	no
a_3	6	6	0	yes
a_4	4	6	2	no
a_5	5	8	3	no
a_6	7	7	0	yes
a_7	7	7	0	yes
a_8	7	10	3	no
a_9	16	16	0	yes
a_{10}	14	14	0	yes

Figure 6.44: Early, late, and critical values

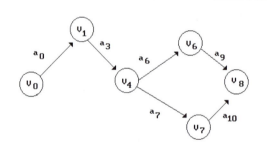

Figure 6.45: Graph with noncritical activities deleted

6.6   REFERENCES AND SELECTED READINGS

Euler's original paper on the Koenigsberg bridge problem is interesting reading. This paper has been reprinted in: *"Leonhard Euler and the Koenigsberg Bridges," Scientific American*, vol, 189, no. 1, 1953, pp. 66-70.

The biconnected component algorithm is attributed to R. Tarjan. This algorithm, together with a linear time algorithm to find the strongly connected components of a directed graph, appears in R. Tarjan, *"Depth-first search and linear graph algorithms,"* *SIAM Journal of Computing*, vol. 1 no. 2, 1972, pp. 146-149.

Prim's minimum cost spanning tree algorithm was first proposed by Jarnik in 1930 and rediscovered by Prim in 1957. Since virtually all references to this algorithm give credit to Prim, we continue to refer to it as Prim's algorithm. Similarly, the algorithm we

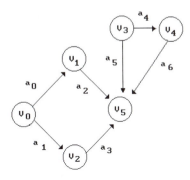

Figure 6.46: AOE network with unreachable activities

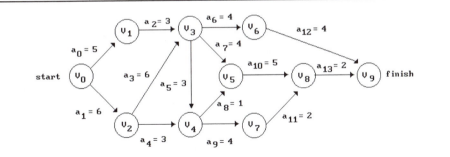

Figure 6.47: An AOE network

refer to as Sollin's algorithm was first proposed by Boruvka in 1926 and rediscovered by Sollin several years later. For an interesting history of the minimum spanning tree problem see R. Graham and P. Hell, *"On the history of the minimum spanning tree problem,"* *Annals of the History of Computing*, vol. 7, no. 1, 1985, pp. 43-57.

Additional graph algorithms may be found in A. Aho, J. Hopcroft, and J. Ullman, *The Design and Analysis of Computer Algorithms*, Addison-Wesley, Reading, Mass., 1974; N. Deo, *Graph Theory with Applications to Engineering and Computer Science*, Prentice-Hall, Englewood Cliffs, N.J., 1974; E. Lawler, *Combinatorial Optimization*, Holt, Reinhart and Winston, New York, 1976; L. Ford and D. Fulkerson,*Flows in Networks*, Princeton University Press, Princeton, N.J., 1962; T. C. Hu, *Integer Programming and Network Flows*, Addison-Wesley, Reading, Mass., 1970; S. Baase, *Computer Algorithms: Introduction to Design and Analysis*, Addison-Wesley, Reading, Mass., 1988;

and M. Paull, *Algorithm Design: A Recursion Transformation Network*, Wiley InterScience, New York, 1988.

6.7 ADDITIONAL EXERCISES

1. An *incidence matrix* is another matrix representation of a graph. In this representation, we use one row for each vertex in the graph and one column for each edge. If edge j is incident to vertex i, $incidence[i][j] = 1$; otherwise it equals 0. The incidence matrix for the graph of Figure 6.19(a) is given in Figure 6.48. We have numbered the edges of Figure 6.19(a) from left to right and top to bottom. For example, (v_0, v_1) is edge 0, (v_0, v_2) is edge 1, and so on. Rewrite *dfs* so that it works on a graph represented by its incidence matrix.

$$
\begin{array}{c@{\,}c}
 & \begin{matrix} 0 & 1 & 2 & 3 & 4 & 5 & 6 & 7 & 8 & 9 \end{matrix} \\
\begin{matrix} 0 \\ 1 \\ 2 \\ 3 \\ 4 \\ 5 \\ 6 \\ 7 \end{matrix} &
\left[\begin{matrix}
1 & 1 & 0 & 0 & 0 & 0 & 0 & 0 & 0 & 0 \\
1 & 0 & 1 & 1 & 0 & 0 & 0 & 0 & 0 & 0 \\
0 & 1 & 0 & 0 & 1 & 1 & 0 & 0 & 0 & 0 \\
0 & 0 & 1 & 0 & 0 & 0 & 1 & 0 & 0 & 0 \\
0 & 0 & 0 & 1 & 0 & 0 & 0 & 1 & 0 & 0 \\
0 & 0 & 0 & 0 & 1 & 0 & 0 & 0 & 1 & 0 \\
0 & 0 & 0 & 0 & 0 & 1 & 0 & 0 & 0 & 1 \\
0 & 0 & 0 & 0 & 0 & 0 & 1 & 1 & 1 & 1
\end{matrix} \right]
\end{array}
$$

Figure 6.48: Incidence matrix of graph of Figure 6.19(a)

2. If *ADJ* is the adjacency matrix of a graph, $G = (V, E)$ and *INC* is the incidence matrix, under what conditions does

$$ ADJ = INC \times INC^T - I $$

where INC^T is the transpose matrix of *INC*? Matrix multiplication is defined in Exercise 9, Section 6.4. I is the identity matrix.

3. The *diameter of a tree* is the maximum distance between any two vertices. Given a connected, undirected graph write a C function that finds a spanning tree of minimum diameter. Prove that your function is correct.

4. The *radius of a tree* is the maximum distance from the root to a leaf node. Given a connected, undirected graph, write a C function that finds a spanning tree of minimum radius. Prove that your function is correct.

5. § [***Programming project***] Write a C program for manipulating graphs. Your program should allow the user to input arbitrary graphs, print out graphs, and determine the connected components, articulation points, and bridges. It should also print out the spanning trees. You also should provide the capability of attaching weights to the edges.

CHAPTER 7

SORTING

7.1   SEARCHING AND LIST VERIFICATION

7.1.1   Introduction

Although the primary focus of this chapter is on sorting, we want to begin with two problems, searching and list verification, to show you why efficient sorting methods are so important. Recall that in Chapter1, we introduced two searching techniques, sequential and binary. We used simple arrays of integers to illustrate the searching techniques, but we did not examine formally the computing times of these techniques. In this chapter, we begin by searching more complicated structures.

Let us assume that we have a collection of information concerning some set of objects. If this collection fits easily within the available memory we call it a *list*; if it must be stored externally we call it a *file*. We call the information for one of the objects in the collection a *record*, and within each record we break the information into smaller units called *fields*. The structure of a record depends entirely on the application. For example, if our list was a telephone directory, we might define a *person* record consisting of name, address, and phone number fields. On the other hand, if our list was a set of numbers, we might have only a field to represent the number. Often, when searching a list of records, we wish to examine the records based on some field that serves to identify the record. This field is known as a *key*. Since we can use the same list for several different applications, the key field also depends on the particular application. For example, if we have a telephone list and we wish to locate the phone number 456-1023, the phone number field is the key. On the other hand, if we wish to figure out whether Joan Smith is listed in the directory, the name field is the key.

The efficiency of a searching strategy depends on the assumptions we make about the arrangement of records in the list. If the records are ordered by the key field, we can search the list very efficiently. On the other hand, if the records are in random order based on the key field, we must start the search at one end of the list and examine each record until we either find the desired key or we reach the other end of the list. This latter strategy is the one used by the sequential search.

7.1.2   Sequential Search

Assume that we have a *list* and a search key, *searchnum*. We wish to retrieve the record whose key field matches *searchnum*. If *list* has n records, with *list*[i].*key* referring to the key value for record i, then we can search the list by examining the key values *list*[0].*key*, $\cdots$, *list*[$n-1$].*key*, in that order, until the correct record is located, or we have examined all the records in the list. Since we examine the records in sequence, this searching technique is known as a sequential search. The function *seqsearch* (Program 7.1) contains the details. It uses the folowing declarations:

```
#define MAX_SIZE 1000 /*maximum size of list plus one*/
typedef struct {
         int key;
         /* other fields */
         } element;
element list[MAX_SIZE];
```

Analysis of *seqsearch*: Prior to the start of the search, we place *searchnum* in *list*[n].*key*. This position serves as a sentinel that signals the end of the list. By avoiding a test for the end of the list, that is, $i > n - 1$, we can simplify the loop structure. If the search is unsuccessful, $i = n$, and we return a value of -1. Therefore, an unsuccessful search requires $n + 1$ key comparisons, resulting in a worst case computing time of $O(n)$. The number of key comparisons made in a successful search depends on the position of the key in the list. If the keys are distinct and *searchnum* = *list*[i].*key*, then $i + 1$ key comparisons are made. The average number of comparisons for a successful search is:

$$\sum_{i=0}^{n-1} (i + 1)/n = (n + 1)/2 \quad \square$$

```
int seqsearch(int list[], int searchnum, int n)
{
/*search an array, list, that has n numbers. Return i, if
list[i] = searchnum.  Return -1, if searchnum is not in
the list */
    int i;
    list[n] = searchnum;
    for (i = 0; list[i] != searchnum; i++)
        ;
    return ((i < n ) ? i : -1);
}
```

Program 7.1 Sequential search

7.1.3   Binary Search

Unlike sequential search, which makes no assumptions about the order of the key fields, binary search assumes that the list is ordered on the key field such that $list[0].key \leq list[1].key \leq \cdots \leq list[n-1].key$. As we indicated in Chapter 1, this search begins by comparing *searchnum* and *list[middle].key* where $middle = (n-1)/2$. The comparison function *COMPARE* was defined in Chapter 1. There are three possible outcomes:

(1)   ***searchnum < list[middle].key:*** In this case, we discard the records between *list[middle]* and *list[n − 1]*, and continue the search with the records between *list[0]* and *list[middle−1]*.

(2)   ***searchnum = list[middle].key:*** In this case, the search terminates successfully.

(3)   ***searchnum > list[middle].key:*** In this case, we discard the records between *list[0]* and *list[middle]* and continue the search with the records between *list[middle+1]* and *list[n − 1]*.

Thus, after a comparison either the search ends successfully or the size of the unsearched portion of the list is reduced by about one half. After *j* key comparisons, the unsearched part of the list is at most $\lceil n / 2^j \rceil$, which means that this method requires $O(\log n)$ key comparisons in the worst case. The function *binsearch* (Program 7.2) implements the scheme just outlined. We pass in the number of elements, *n*, rather than the upper and lower boundaries as we did in the binary search function presented in Chapter 1. (The upper and lower boundaries are assumed to be 0 and *n − 1*, respectively.)

Analysis of *binsearch*: In *binsearch* the middle key of the current sublist is always compared with the desired key (*searchnum*). Since there are only three outcomes for each

```
int binsearch(element list[], int searchnum, int n)
{
/* search list[0], ..., list[n-1] */
   int left = 0, right = n-1, middle;
   while (left <= right) {
      middle = (left + right) / 2;
      switch (COMPARE(list[middle].key, searchnum)) {
         case -1 : left = middle + 1;
               break;
         case 0 : return middle;
         case 1 : right = middle - 1;
      }
   }
   return - 1;
}
```

Program 7.2: Binary search

comparison we can use a binary decision tree to describe the search process. For example, suppose that the input list is (4, 15, 17, 26, 30, 46, 48, 56, 58, 82, 90, 95). Figure 7.1 shows this list represented as a binary decision tree. The key values appear inside the nodes and the list indices appear outside. A path from the root to any node in the tree represents a sequence of comparisons made by *binsearch* to either find *searchnum* or determine that it is not present. From the depth of this tree, we can easily see that *binsearch* makes no more than O(log n) comparisons. □

Getting back to our example of the telephone directory, we notice that neither sequential nor binary search corresponds to the search method actually employed by humans in searching the directory. If we are looking for a name beginning with *W*, we start the search towards the end of the directory rather than at the middle. A search method based on this interpolation search would then begin by comparing key $f[i].key$ with $i = ((k - f[l].key)/(f[u].key - f[l].key)) * n$ ($f[l].key$ and $f[u].key$ are the values of the smallest and largest keys in the file). Interpolation search can be used only when the file is ordered. The behavior of such an algorithm will clearly depend on the distribution of the keys in the file.

7.1.4   List Verification

Typically, we compare lists to verify that they are identical, or to identify the discrepancies. Thus, the problem of list verification is an instance of repeatedly searching one list, using each key in the other list as the search key. Since organizations often receive duplicate material from several different sources, list verification is a problem that arises

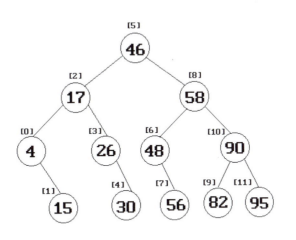

Figure 7.1: Decision tree for binary search

frequently. For example, the Internal Revenue Service (IRS) receives statements from employers indicating the salary and Social Security deductions for each of their employees. Similarly, employees must submit an income tax statement indicating their income and deductions. Naturally, the IRS would like to verify that the lists are identical with respect to the individuals entered in each list and to the information provided for each individual from the two sources. We have already shown that an ordered list increases the efficiency of the search process. Does it also speed up the process of list verification? To answer this question, we must develop list verification functions for both random and ordered lists. For each function, we assume that we have two lists, *list1* and *list2*, with keys *list1*[*i*].*key*, $0 \le i < n$, and *list2*[*j*].*key*, $0 \le j < m$. In addition, we assume that the verification process recognizes and reports three types of errors:

(1)   A record with key *list1*[*i*].*key* appears in the first list, but there is no record with the same key in the second list (*list2*).

(2)   A record with key *list2*[*j*].*key* appears in the second list, but there is no record with the same key in the first list (*list1*).

(3)   *list1*[*i*].*key* = *list2*[*j*].*key*, but the two records do not match on at least one of the other fields.

The function *verify1* (Program 7.3) assumes that the two lists are randomly arranged. We can easily prove that this function has a worst case asymptotic computing time of O(*mn*). The function *verify2* (Program 7.4) begins with the same input as does *verify1*. However, it sorts the two input lists before verifying them. Its worst case asymptotic time is O(*tsort(n)* + *tsort(m)* + *m* + *n*), where *tsort(n)* is the time needed to sort the *n* records in *list1*, and *tsort(m)* is the time needed to sort the *m* records in *list2*. As we will show in this chapter, it is possible to sort *n* records in O(*n* log *n*) time. Therefore, the worst case time for *verify2* is O(*max*[*n* log *n*, *m* log *m*]).

```
void verify1(element list1[], element list2[], int n, int m)
/* compare two unordered lists list1 and list2 */
{
   int i,j;
   int marked[MAX_SIZE];

   for (i = 0; i < m; i++)
      marked[i] = FALSE;
   for (i = 0; i < n; i++)
      if ((j = seqsearch(list2,m,list1[i].key)) < 0)
         printf("%d is not in list 2\n",list1[i].key);
      else
      /* check each of the other fields from list1[i] and
      list2[j], and print out any discrepancies */
         marked[j] = TRUE;
   for (i = 0; i < m; i++)
      if (!marked[i])
         printf("%d is not in list1\n",list2[i].key);
}
```

Program 7.3: Verifying using a sequential search

EXERCISES

1. Sequential search can be improved by transposing the *i*th record and the 0th record if the search was successful. This leads to a better performance on future searches if the same key is searched for repeatedly. Write a sequential search function that incorporates this variation.

2. Sequential search can also be improved by shifting the records between 0 and *i*−1 one position to the right, and placing the *i*th record in the 0th position. This *Move-To-Right* shifting occurs only if the search was successful. This variation allows those keys that are frequently sought to move to the front of the list. Write a function to perform this variation.

3. Assume that we have a sorted list of the 20 numbers 2, 4, ⋯ , 40. Draw the binary decision tree for the list. This tree should reflect the possible comparison sequences in a binary search. How many comparisons does it take to determine

```
void verify2(element list1[], element list2[], int n, int m)
/* Same task as verify1, but list1 and list2 are sorted */
{
   int i,j;
   sort(list1,n);
   sort(list2,m);
   i = j = 0;
   while (i < n && j < m)
      if (list1[i].key < list2[j].key) {
         printf("%d is not in list 2\n",list1[i].key);
         i++;
      }
      else if (list1[i].key == list2[j].key) {
      /* compare list1[i] and list2[j] on each of the other
      fields and report any discrepancies */
         i++;   j++;
      }
      else {
         printf("%d is not in list 1\n", list2[j].key);
         j++;
      }
   for(; i < n; i++)
      printf("%d is not in list 2\n",list1[i].key);
   for (; j < m; j++)
      printf("%d is not in list 1\n",list2[j].key);
}
```

Program 7.4: Fast verification of two lists

that 30 is in the list? How many does it take to determine that 21 is not in the list?

4. Program interpolation search and compare its performance with that of binary search. For the comparison, use sequences of numbers generated using a uniform random number generator. Sort the resulting sequence and measure the average search time for a successful search by searching for each of the numbers in the sequence. Assume that a successful search can be for any of the numbers in your sequence with equal probability. Repeat your experiment using an exponential random number generator.

7.2   DEFINITIONS

We have seen two important applications of sorting: (1) as an aid to searching, and (2) for matching entries in lists. Sorting is also used in the solution of many other more complex problems. In fact, estimates suggest that over 25 percent of all computing time is spent on sorting, with some organizations spending more than 50 percent of their computing time sorting lists. So, the problem of finding efficient sorting algorithms is immensely important. Unfortunately, no single sorting technique is the "best" for all initial orderings and sizes of the list being sorted. Therefore, we examine several techniques, indicating when one is superior to the others.

First, let us formally state the problem we are about to consider: We are given a list of records $(R_0, R_1, \cdots, R_{n-1})$, in which each record, R_i, has a key value, K_i. In addition, there is an ordering relation ($<$) on the keys such that for any two key values x and y, either $x = y$ or $x < y$ or $y < x$. This ordering relation is transitive, that is, for any three values x, y, and z, $x < y$ and $y < z$ implies $x < z$. We define the sorting problems as finding a permutation such that $K_{\sigma(i-1)} \leq K_{\sigma(i)}$, $0 < i \leq n - 1$. The desired ordering is then $(R_{\sigma(0)}, R_{\sigma(1)}, \cdots, R_{\sigma(n-1)})$.

Since a list could have several identical key values, the permutation is not unique. In some applications, we are interested in finding the unique permutation, σ_s, that has the following properties:

(1)   [*sorted*] $K_{\sigma(i-1)} \leq K_{\sigma(i)}$, for $0 < i \leq n - 1$

(2)   [*stable*] If $i < j$ and $K_i = K_j$ in the input list, then R_i precedes R_j in the sorted list.

A sorting method that generates the permutation σ_s is *stable*. Stability is only one criterion that we use to distinguish between sorting methods. In addition, we can characterize sorts based on both location and the sorting technique employed. Location refers to where the sort is carried out. Thus, an *internal sort* is one in which the list is small enough to sort entirely in main memory, while an *external sort* is used when there is too much information to fit into main memory. In the latter case, the file must be brought into the main memory in pieces until the entire file is sorted.

In Chapter 1, we developed the internal sorting method known as selection sort. In this chapter, we develop the following additional internal sorting methods: insertion sort, quick sort, heap sort, merge sort, and radix sort. The development of internal sorting methods is followed by a discussion of external sorting.

7.3   INSERTION SORT

An insertion sort is analogous to the action a card player takes when arranging a new hand: the cards arrive one at a time and each is placed in sorted order before the next one is picked up. Similarly, we pretend that the records in a list are visible to us one at a time. Thus, we insert a record R_i into a sequence of ordered records, $R_0, R_1, \cdots, R_{i-1}$,

$(K_0 \leq K_1 \leq \cdots \leq K_{i-1})$ so that the resulting sequence of size i is also ordered. We begin with the ordered sequence R_0, and then successively insert the records $R_1, R_2, \cdots,$ R_{n-1} into the sequence. Since each insertion leaves the resulting sequence ordered, we can order a list with n records by making $n-1$ insertions. This strategy is implemented by *insertion—sort* (Program 7.5). The function call is *insertion—sort(list,n);*

```
void insertion_sort(element list[], int n)
/* perform a insertion sort on the list */
{
   int i,j;
   element next;
   for (i = 1; i < n; i++) {
      next = list[i];
      for (j = i-1; j >= 0 && next.key < list[j].key; j--)
         list[j+1] = list[j];
      list[j+1] = next;
   }
}
```

Program 7.5: *insertion—sort*

Analysis of *insertion—sort*: In the worst case, the inner loop makes i comparisons before making the insertion. Hence, the computing time for inserting one record into the ordered list is $O(i)$. Since the outer loop is called for $i = 1, 2, \cdots, n-1$, the total worst case time is:

$$O(\sum_{i=0}^{n-1} i) = O(n^2) \quad \square$$

We also can estimate the computing time of an insertion sort by examining the relative disorder of the input list. To figure out the relative disorder, we measure the extent to which each record is *left out of order (LOO)*. This is defined as:

$$R_i \text{ is LOO iff } R_i < \max_{0 \leq j < i} \{R_j\}$$

Clearly, the insertion step is executed only for those records that are LOO. If k is the number of records LOO, then the computing time is $O((k + 1)n)$ and the worst case time is still $O(n^2)$. We also can show that the average time is $O(n^2)$.

Example 7.1: Assume that $n = 5$ and the input sequence is $(5, 4, 3, 2, 1)$. [Note: Only the key field is displayed.] After each insertion step, we have the following:

i	[0]	[1]	[2]	[3]	[4]
–	5	4	3	2	1
1	4	5	3	2	1
2	3	4	5	2	1
3	2	3	4	5	1
4	1	2	3	4	5

Since the list is in reverse order as each new record R_i is inserted into the ordered list $R_0, \cdots, R_{i-1}$, the entire list is shifted right by one position. Thus, this input sequence exhibits the worst case behavior of insertion sort. □

Example 7.2: Assume that $n = 5$ and the input sequence is (2, 3, 4, 5, 1). After each iteration we have:

i	[0]	[1]	[2]	[3]	[4]
–	2	3	4	5	1
1	2	3	4	5	1
2	2	3	4	5	1
3	2	3	4	5	1
4	1	2	3	4	5

In this example only R_4 is LOO, and the time for each $i = 1$, 2, and 3 is O(1); for $i = 4$ the time is O(n). □

Since the computing time of an insertion sort is O(($k + 1$)n), it is an excellent sort to use when only a few records are LOO, that is, $k \ll n$. We also can easily verify that the sort is stable. These facts, coupled with the simplicity of the method, make insertion sort a good sort for small lists, that is, $n \leq 20$ (say).

Variations

1. *Binary insertion sort:* We can reduce the number of comparisons made in an insertion sort by replacing the sequential searching technique used in *insertion_sort* with binary search. The number of record moves remains unchanged.

2. *List insertion sort:* The elements of the list are represented as a dynamically linked list rather than as an array. The number of record moves becomes zero because only the link fields require adjustment. However, we must retain the sequential search used in *insertion_sort*.

EXERCISES

1. C allows us to use a pointer to a function as a parameter in a function. Create two functions, *ascending* and *descending*. Each function takes two parameters, *x* and *y*. The ascending function returns *TRUE* if $x < y$ and *FALSE* otherwise. The descending function returns *TRUE* if $x > y$ and *FALSE* otherwise. Rewrite insertion sort to create a generic sort that can sort in either nondecreasing or nonincreasing order by passing in a pointer to one of these two functions.

2. Rewrite *insertion_sort* so that it uses binary search.

3. Rewrite *insertion_sort* so that the sorted list is returned as a linked list. The initial list is an array of records. Each record has the additional field *link* that is used to construct the sorted linked list.

4. Rewrite *insertion_sort* so that the input and output lists of records are represented as dynamically linked lists.

7.4 QUICK SORT

We now turn our attention to a sorting scheme with a very good average behavior. The quick sort scheme developed by C. A. R. Hoare has the best average behavior among all the sorting methods we shall be studying. In insertion sort the key K_i (called the pivot key) currently controlling the insertion is placed into the right spot with respect to the sorted subfile $(R_0, \ldots, R_{i-1})$. Quick sort differs from insertion sort in that the pivot key K_i controlling the process is placed at the right spot with respect to the whole file. Thus, if key K_i is placed in position $s(i)$, then $K_j \leq K_{s(i)}$ for $j < s(i)$ and $K_j \geq K_{s(i)}$ for $j > s(i)$. Hence, after this positioning has been made, the original file is partitioned into two subfiles, one consisting of records $R_0, \ldots, R_{s(i)-1}$ and the other of records $R_{s(i)+1}, \ldots, R_{n-1}$. Since in the sorted sequence all records in the first subfile may appear to the left of $s(i)$ and all in the second subfile to the right of $s(i)$, these two subfiles may be sorted independently. The function *quicksort* (Program 7.6) is our recursive version of Hoare's quick sort algorithm. The function call is *quicksort(list, 0, n-1);*

Example 7.3: The input file has 10 records with keys (26, 5, 37, 1, 61, 11, 59, 15, 48, 19). Figure 7.2 gives the status of the file at each call of *quicksort*. Square brackets are used to demarcate subfiles yet to be sorted. □

Analysis of *quicksort*: The worst case behavior of this algorithm is examined in Exercise 2 and shown to be $O(n^2)$. However, if we are lucky then each time a record is correctly positioned, the subfile to its left will be of the same size as that to its right. This would leave us with the sorting of two subfiles each of size roughly $n/2$. The time required to position a record in a file of size n is $O(n)$. If $T(n)$ is the time taken to sort a file of n records, then when the file splits roughly into two equal parts each time a record is positioned correctly we have

```
void quicksort(element list[], int left, int right)
/* sort list[left], · · · , list[right] into nondecreasing
order on the key field. list[left].key is arbitrarily
chosen as the pivot key.  It is assumed that
list[left].key ≤ list[right+1].key. */
{
   int pivot,i,j;
   element temp;
   if (left < right) {
      i = left;     j = right + 1;
      pivot = list[left].key;
      do {
      /* search for keys from the left and right sublists,
      swapping out-of-order elements until the left and
      right boundaries cross or meet */
         do
            i++;
         while (list[i].key < pivot);
         do
            j--;
         while (list[j].key > pivot);
         if (i < j)
            SWAP(list[i],list[j],temp);
      } while (i < j);
      SWAP(list[left],list[j],temp);
      quicksort(list,left,j-1);
      quicksort(list,j+1,right);
   }
}
```

Program 7.6: *quicksort* function

$$T(n) \leq cn + 2T(n/2), \text{ for some constant } c$$
$$\leq cn + 2(cn/2 + 2T(n/4))$$
$$\leq 2cn + 4T(n/4)$$

$$\cdot$$
$$\cdot$$
$$\cdot$$

$$\leq cn \log_2 n + nT(1) = O(n \log_2 n)$$

Lemma 7.1 shows that the average computing time for quick sort is $O(n \log_2 n)$. Moreover, experimental results show that as far as average computing time is concerned, it is

R_0	R_1	R_2	R_3	R_4	R_5	R_6	R_7	R_8	R_9	left	right
[26	5	37	1	61	11	59	15	48	19]	0	9
[11	5	19	1	15]	26	[59	61	48	37]	0	4
[1	5]	11	[19	15]	26	[59	61	48	37	0	1
1	5	11	[19	15]	26	[59	61	48	37]	3	4
1	5	11	15	19	26	[59	61	48	37]	6	9
1	5	11	15	19	26	[48	37]	59	[61]	6	7
1	5	11	15	19	26	37	48	59	[61]	9	9
1	5	11	15	19	26	37	48	59	61		

Figure 7.2: Simulation of *quicksort*

the best of the internal sorting methods we shall be studying.

Lemma 7.1: Let $T_{avg}(n)$ be the expected time for *quicksort* to sort a file with n records. Then there exists a constant k such that $T_{avg}(n) \leq kn\log_e n$ for $n \geq 2$.

Proof: In the call to *quicksort* $(0, n-1)$, K_0 gets placed at position j. This leaves us with the problem of sorting two subfiles of size j and $n - j - 1$, respectively. The expected time for this is $T_{avg}(j) + T_{avg}(n - j - 1)$. The remainder of the algorithm clearly takes at most cn time for some constant c. Since j may take on any of the values 0 to $n - 1$ with equal probability we have

$$T_{avg}(n) \leq cn + \frac{1}{n}\sum_{j=0}^{n-1}(T_{avg}(j) + T_{avg}(n - j - 1)) = cn + \frac{2}{n}\sum_{j=0}^{n-1}T_{avg}(j), \, n \geq 2 \quad (7.1)$$

We may assume $T_{avg}(0) \leq b$ and $T_{avg}(1) \leq b$ for some constant b. We shall now show $T_{avg}(n) \leq kn\log_e n$ for $n \geq 2$ and $k = 2(b + c)$. The proof is by induction on n.

Induction Base: For $n = 2$ we have from Eq. (7.1)

$$T_{avg}(2) \leq 2c + 2b \leq kn\log_e 2$$

Induction Hypothesis: Assume $T_{avg}(n) \leq kn\log_e n$ for $1 \leq n < m$

Induction Step: From Eq. (7.1) and the induction hypothesis we have

$$T_{avg}(m) \leq cm + \frac{4b}{m} + \frac{2}{m}\sum_{j=2}^{m-1}T_{avg}(j) \leq cm + \frac{4b}{m} + \frac{2k}{m}\sum_{j=2}^{m-1}j\log_e j \quad (7.2)$$

Since $j\log_e j$ is an increasing function of j, Eq. (7.2) yields

$$T_{avg}(m) \leq cm + \frac{4b}{m} + \frac{2k}{m}\int_2^m x\log_e x \, dx = cm + \frac{4b}{m} + \frac{2k}{m}\left[\frac{m^2\log_e m}{2} - \frac{m^2}{4}\right]$$

$$= cm + \frac{4b}{m} + km\log_e m - \frac{km}{2} \leq km\log_e m, \quad \text{for } m \geq 2 \ \square$$

Unlike insertion sort, where the only additional space needed was for one record, quick sort needs stack space to implement the recursion. In case the files split evenly as in the above analysis, the maximum recursion depth would be $\log n$ requiring a stack space of $O(\log n)$. The worst case occurs when the file is split into a left subfile of size $n-1$ and a right subfile of size 0 at each level of recursion. In this case, the depth of recursion becomes n requiring stack space of $O(n)$. The worst case stack space can be reduced by a factor of 4 by realizing that right subfiles of size less than 2 need not be stacked. An asymptotic reduction in stack space can be achieved by *sorting smaller subfiles first*. In this case the additional stack space is at most $O(\log n)$.

Variation

quicksort using a median of three: Our version of quick sort always picked the key of the first record in the current sublist as the pivot. A better choice for this pivot is the median of the first, middle, and last keys in the current sublist. Thus, *pivot = median* $\{K_{left}, K_{(left+right)/2}, K_{right}\}$. For example, median $\{10, 5, 7\} = 7$ and median $\{10, 7, 7\} = 7$.

EXERCISES

1. Produce a figure similar to Figure 7.2 for the case when the input file to be sorted is (12, 2, 16, 30, 8, 28, 4, 10, 20, 6, 18).

2. (a) Show that *quicksort* takes $O(n^2)$ time when the input file is already in sorted order.

    (b) Show that the worst case time complexity of *quicksort* is $O(n^2)$.

    (c) Why is *list* [*left*] . *key* $\leq$ *list* [*right* + 1] . *key* required in *quicksort*?

3. Write an iterative version of *quicksort* that uses the median of three rule to select the pivot record. Show that this takes $O(n \log n)$ time on an already sorted file.

4. Show that if smaller subfiles are sorted first then the recursion in *quicksort* (Program 7.6) can be simulated by a stack of depth $O(\log n)$.

5. Quick sort is unstable. Give an example of an input file in which the order of records with equal keys is not preserved.

7.5 OPTIMAL SORTING TIME

The two sorting methods discussed thus far have a worst case computing time of $O(n^2)$. At this point you might begin to wonder about the best computing time, that is, "How quickly can we hope to sort a list of n objects?" If we restrict our question to algorithms that permit only the comparison and interchange of keys, then the theorem we prove in this section shows that the best possible time is $O(n \log_2 n)$.

Our proof requires a decision tree that visually describes the sorting process. Each vertex in this tree represents a comparison between two keys, and each branch shows the result of a comparison. Thus, each path through the tree represents a sequence of computations that the sorting algorithm could produce.

Example 7.4: The decision tree for *insertion_sort* on the records R_0, R_1, and R_2 is shown in Figure 7.3. Each node is labeled by the record permutation at that node. The root label [0, 1, 2] denotes the input permutation. Inside the root, we have identified the first comparison made by *insertion_sort*. The left branch is taken if $K_0 \le K_1$, while the right branch is taken if $K_0 > K_1$. The record permutation remains the same if the left branch is taken, but changes to [1, 0, 2] if the right branch is followed. The leaf nodes are numbered I-VI and are the only points at which the algorithm may terminate. Hence only six permutations of the input sequence are obtainable from this algorithm. Since all six of these are different and $3! = 6$, it follows that this algorithm has enough leaves to constitute a valid sorting algorithm for three records. The maximum depth of this tree is 3. Figure 7.4 gives six different permutations of the keys 7, 9, 10 and the permutation needed to sort the keys. This shows that all six output permutations are possible. The decision tree of Figure 7.3 is not a full binary tree of depth 3 and so it has fewer than $2^3 = 8$ leaves. □

Theorem 7.1: Any decision tree that sorts n distinct elements has a height of at least $\log_2(n!) + 1$.

Proof: When sorting n elements there are $n!$ different possible results. Thus, any decision tree must have at least $n!$ leaves. But a decision tree is also a binary tree that can have at most 2^{k-1} leaves if its height is k. Therefore, the height must be at least $\log_2 n! + 1$. □

Corollary: Any algorithm that sorts by comparisons only must have a worst case computing time of $\Omega(n \log_2 n)$.

Proof: We must show that for every decision tree with $n!$ leaves there is a path of length $c\,n \log_2 n$, c a constant. By the theorem, there is path of length $\log_2 n!$. Now,

$$n! = n\,(n-1)(n-2),\ \cdots\,,(3)(2)(1) \ge (n/2)^{n/2}.$$

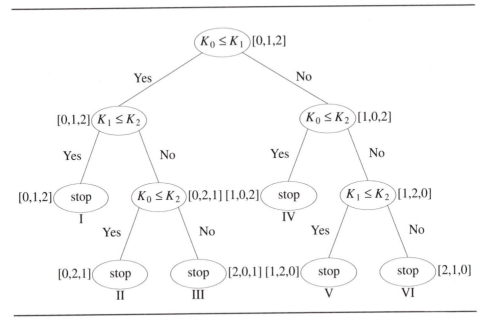

Figure 7.3: Decision tree for insertion sort

Leaf	Permutations	Sample input key values that give the permutation
I	0 1 2	(7, 9, 10)
II	0 2 1	(7, 10, 9)
III	2 0 1	(9, 10, 7)
IV	1 0 2	(9, 7, 10)
V	1 2 0	(10, 7, 9)
VI	2 1 0	(10, 9, 7)

Figure 7.4: The six permutations of 7, 9, 10

So, $\log_2 n! \geq (n/2)\log_2(n/2) = O(n\,\log_2 n)$. □

7.6 MERGE SORT

7.6.1 Merging

Before looking at the merge sort algorithm to sort n records let us see how one may merge two sorted lists to get a single sorted list. We shall examine two different algorithms for this. The first one, Program 7.7, is very simple and uses $O(n)$ additional space. It merges the sorted lists $(list[i], \cdots, list[m])$ and $(list[m+1], \cdots, list[n])$, into a single sorted list, $(sorted[i], \cdots, sorted[n])$.

```
void merge(element list[], element sorted[], int i, int m,
                                             int n)
/* merge two sorted files: list[i],...,list[m], and
list[m+1],..., list[n]. These files are sorted to
obtain a sorted list: sorted[i],..., sorted[n] */
{
   int j,k,t;
   j = m+1;        /* index for the second sublist */
   k = i;          /* index for the sorted list */

   while (i <= m && j <= n) {
      if (list[i].key <= list[j].key)
         sorted[k++] = list[i++];
      else
         sorted[k++] = list[j++];
   }
   if (i > m)
   /* sorted[k],..., sorted[n] = list[j],..., list[n] */
      for (t = j; t <= n; t++)
         sorted[k+t-j] = list[t];
      else
      /* sorted[k],..., sorted[n] = list[i],..., list[m] */
         for (t = i; t <= m; t++)
            sorted[k+t-i] = list[t];
}
```

Program 7.7: Merging two sorted lists

Analysis of *merge*: At each iteration of the **while** loop, one record is added to the sorted list, that is, k increases by 1. The total number of records added to the sorted list is $n - i +$

1. This means that we iterate the **while** loop at most $n - i + 1$ times. Therefore, the total computing time is $O(n - i + 1)$. If the records are of length M, this time is really $O(M(n - i + 1))$. When M is greater than 1, a linked list representation eliminates the additional $n - i + 1$ records required by *sorted*. However, we must now add space for $n - i + 1$ link fields. With this representation, the computing time no longer depends on M; it is simply $O(n - i + 1)$. $\square$

The second merging algorithm we shall consider is more complex than that of Program 7.7. However, it requires only $O(1)$ additional space. We assume that $i = 1$. With this assumption the total number of records in the two lists being merged is n. Our discussion will make the further simplifying assumptions that n is a perfect square and the number of records in each of the two lists to be merged is a multiple of $\sqrt{n}$. The development of the full algorithm with these assumptions removed is left as an exercise.

Suppose that $n = 36$ and that each of the two files to be merged has 18 records. The first line of Figure 7.5 gives a sample instance. Only the record keys are shown. We assume that the sorted key sequence is 0, 1, $\cdots$, a, b, $\cdots$, z. The vertical bar separates the two sorted files of size 18. Each file can be thought of as consisting of sorted blocks of size $\sqrt{n} = 6$. The first step in the $O(1)$ merge is to create a block that consists of the $\sqrt{n}$ records with the largest keys. This is done by scanning the two sorted files from the right end to the left end. From this scan we discover that the $\sqrt{n}$ largest keys are those that are boxed in line 2 of Figure 7.5.

Next, the records from the second file that are in the set of $\sqrt{n}$ records with largest keys are exchanged with the same number of records just to the left of those in the first file that are in this set. This results in the configuration of line 3 of the figure. The vertical bars partition the n records into blocks of $\sqrt{n}$ consecutive records. Notice that the $\sqrt{n}$ records with largest keys form a single block. This block is now swapped with the leftmost block and the rightmost block is sorted to get line 4. The $\sqrt{n} - 1$ blocks excluding the one with the largest keys are sorted by their rightmost records to get line 5. This completes the preprocessing needed to commence the actual merge.

The actual merge consists of several merge sub steps in each of which two segments of records are merged together. The first segment is the longest sorted sequence of records beginning at block two. Observe that this will always end at a block boundary. The second sequence consists solely of the next block. In the case of line 5, both of these sequences consist of exactly one block. A merge sub step uses three place markers which are depicted in line 5 by the symbol •. The leftmost one marks the position where the next merged record is to go. The second marker points to the next unmerged record of the first segment and the third marker points to the next unmerged record of the second segment. Initially these are, respectively, positioned at the first records of the leftmost block, segment one, and segment two. The two segments are merged by comparing the two keys pointed at by place markers two and three and exchanging the record with smaller key (in case of a tie, the record in the first segment is used) with the record pointed at by the first place marker. Following the first such exchange we get line 6. Lines 7 and 8 show the configuration following each of the next two exchanges. This merge exchanging continues until all of the first segment has been merged. In the case of our example eight more records get merged before the current

0 2 4 6 8 a c e g i j k *l* m n t w z | 1 3 5 7 9 b d f h o p q r s u v x y

0 2 4 6 8 a c e g i j k *l* m n t | w z | 1 3 5 7 9 b d f h o p q r s | u v x y |

0 2 4 6 8 a | c e g i j k | u v x y w z | 1 3 5 7 9 b | d f h o p q | r s *l* m n t

u v x y w z | c e g i j k | 0 2 4 6 8 a | 1 3 5 7 9 b | d f h o p q | *l* m n r s t

u v x y w z 0 2 4 6 8 a | 1 3 5 7 9 b | c e g i j k | d f h o p q | *l* m n r s t

0 v x y w z u 2 4 6 8 a | 1 3 5 7 9 b | c e g i j k | d f h o p q | *l* m n r s t

0 1 x y w z u 2 4 6 8 a | v 3 5 7 9 b | c e g i j k | d f h o p q | *l* m n r s t

0 1 2 y w z u x 4 6 8 a | v 3 5 7 9 b | c e g i j k | d f h o p q | *l* m n r s t

Figure 7.5: First eight lines for O(1) space merge example

merge sub step terminates. Line 1 of Figure 7.6 shows the configuration after the records with keys 3, 4, and 5 have been merged; line 2 shows the configuration following the merging of the records with keys 6, 7, and 8; and line 3 shows the status after segment one has been fully merged.

The following observations allow us to conclude that the merge of a merge sub step can always be done as described above without using extra space beyond that needed to exchange two records:

(1)   There are $\sqrt{n}$ records from the initial position of the first place marker to that of the second place marker.

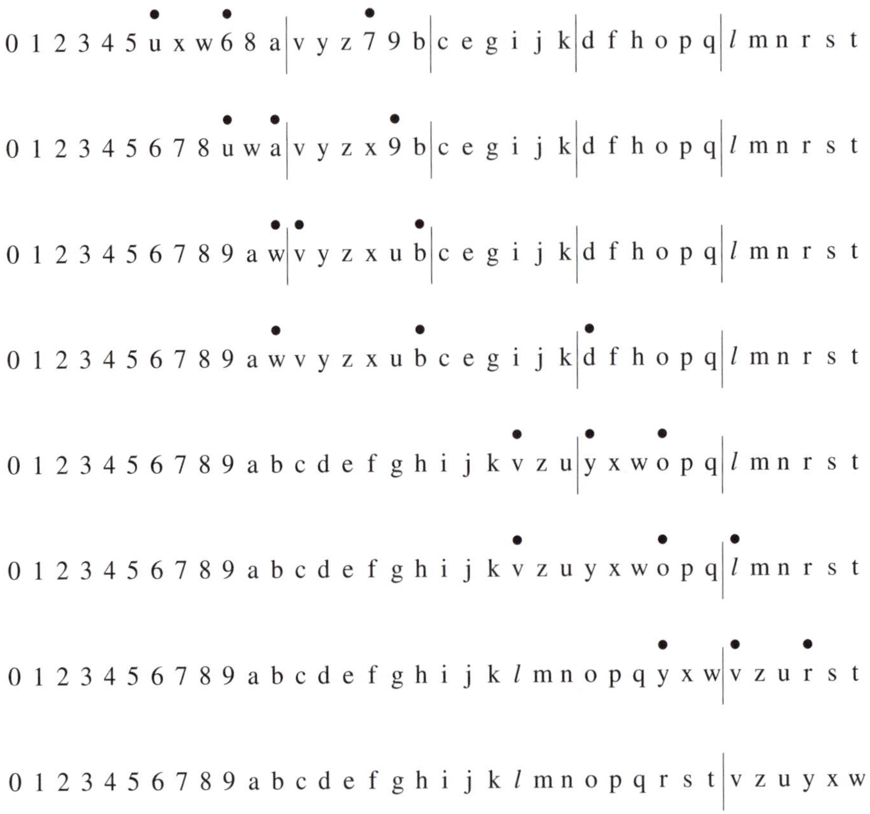

```
      •       •                 •
0 1 2 3 4 5 u x w 6 8 a|v y z 7 9 b|c e g i j k|d f h o p q‖l m n r s t

            •   •           •
0 1 2 3 4 5 6 7 8 u w a|v y z x 9 b|c e g i j k|d f h o p q‖l m n r s t

              • •                •
0 1 2 3 4 5 6 7 8 9 a w|v y z x u b|c e g i j k|d f h o p q‖l m n r s t

                •                •      •
0 1 2 3 4 5 6 7 8 9 a w v y z x u b c e g i j k|d f h o p q‖l m n r s t

                              •      •     •
0 1 2 3 4 5 6 7 8 9 a b c d e f g h i j k v z u|y x w o p q‖l m n r s t

                              •            •     •
0 1 2 3 4 5 6 7 8 9 a b c d e f g h i j k v z u y x w o p q‖l m n r s t

                                        •      •      •
0 1 2 3 4 5 6 7 8 9 a b c d e f g h i j k l m n o p q y x w|v z u r s t

0 1 2 3 4 5 6 7 8 9 a b c d e f g h i j k l m n o p q r s t|v z u y x w
```

Figure 7.6: Last eight lines for O(1) space merge example

(2)   The second segment has $\sqrt{n}$ records.

(3)   Because of the tie breaker rule and the initial ordering of blocks by their last records, the first segment will be fully merged before the second.

When a merge sub step is complete the $\sqrt{n}$ records with largest keys are contiguous and the first place marker points to the first of these records. The third place marker points to the first unmerged record in the second segment. This record begins the first segment for the next merge sub step. This segment is the longest sorted segment that begins at this record. This always ends at a block boundary. The next block forms the second segment. In the case of our example, the first segment begins at the record with key b and the second begins at the record with key d. Line 4 of Figure 7.6 shows the initial positions of the three place markers. Line 5 shows the configuration after the first segment has been fully merged.

The first segment for the next merge sub step begins at the record pointed at by the third place marker. We find a longest sorted sequence that begins here. This consists of just three records. The next block forms the second sequence. The initial positions of the three place markers for the third sort sub step is shown in line 6 of the figure. Line 7 show the status after this sub step is complete. Now the longest sorted sequence that begins at the third place marker consists of the records with keys r, s, and t. As there is no next block, the second segment is empty. The last merge sub step results in the configuration of line 8. Since the second segment is empty to begin with, the last merge sub step can be performed using just two place markers that move rightwards one position at a time. We simply exchange the records pointed at by these two place markers.

Once the merge sub steps have been performed, the block of records with largest keys is at the right end and may be sorted using an O(1) space sorting algorithm such as insertion sort. The steps involved in the O(1) space merge algorithm just described are summarized in Program 7.8.

Steps in an O(1) space merge when the total number of records, n is a perfect square */ and the number of records in each of the files to be merged is a multiple of $\sqrt{n}$ */

Step 1: Identify the $\sqrt{n}$ records with largest keys. This is done by following right to left along the two files to be merged.

Step 2: Exchange the records of the second file that were identified in Step 1 with those just to the left of those identified from the first file so that the $\sqrt{n}$ records with largest keys form a contiguous block.

Step 3: Swap the block of $\sqrt{n}$ largest records with the leftmost block (unless it is already the leftmost block). Sort the rightmost block.

Step 4: Reorder the blocks excluding the block of largest records into nondecreasing order of the last key in the blocks.

Step 5: Perform as many merge sub steps as needed to merge the $\sqrt{n} - 1$ blocks other than the block with the largest keys.

Step 6: Sort the block with the largest keys.

Program 7.8: O(1) space merge

For the complexity analysis, we see that steps 1 and 2, and the swapping of Step 3 each take $O(\sqrt{n})$ time and O(1) space. The sort of Step 3 can be done in $O(n)$ time and O(1) space using insertion sort. Step 4 can be done in $O(n)$ time and O(1) space using a selection sort (see Chapter 1). Note that selection sort sorts m records using $O(m^2)$ key comparisons and $O(m)$ record moves. When selection sort is used to implement Step 4 of Program 7.8 each block of $\sqrt{n}$ records is regarded as a single record with key equal to that of the last record in the block. So, each record move of selection sort actually moves a block of size $\sqrt{n}$. The number of key comparisons is $O(n)$ and while the number of block moves is O($\sqrt{n}$), the time needed for these is O(n). Note that if insertion sort is used in place of selection sort, the time becomes O($n^{1.5}$) as insertion sort makes O(m^2) record moves when sorting m records. So, in this application insertion sort is inferior to selection sort. The total number of merge sub steps is at most $\sqrt{n} - 1$. The end point of the first segment for each merge sub step can be found in time proportional to the number of blocks in the segment as we need merely find the first block whose last key is greater than the first key of the next block. The time for each sub step is therefore linear in the number of records merged. Hence, the total Step 5 time is O(n). The sort of Step 6 can be done in O(n) time using either a selection or an insertion sort. When the steps of Program 7.8 are implemented as above the total time is O(n) and the additional space used is O(1).

We are now ready to develop a merge sort algorithm that works on an unordered list. Both iterative and recursive implementations are possible, and we develop both versions. The iterative version uses the simple merge method found in *merge*, while the recursive version uses the linked list version of *merge* discussed above. We begin with the iterative version.

7.6.2   Iterative Merge Sort

In the iterative version, we assume that the input sequence has n sorted lists, each of length 1. We merge these lists pairwise to obtain $n / 2$ lists of size 2. (If n is odd, then one list is of size 1). We then merge the $n / 2$ lists pairwise, and so on, until a single list remains. The iterative algorithm is easier to implement if we first write a function that performs a single merge pass. The function *merge_pass* (Program 7.9) gives the details. Notice that this function invokes *merge* (Program 7.7) to merge the sorted sublists. The actual sort is found in *merge_sort* (Program 7.10). The function call is *merge_sort(list, n);*

Analysis of *merge_sort*: A merge sort consists of several passes over the input records. The first pass merges lists of size 1, the second merges lists of size 2, and the ith pass merges lists of size 2^{i-1}. Thus, the total number of passes is $\lceil \log_2 n \rceil$. As *merge* showed, we can merge two sorted lists in linear time, which means that each pass takes O(n) time. Since there are $\lceil \log_2 n \rceil$ passes, the total computing time is O($n \log n$). □

Example 7.5: The input list is (26, 5, 77, 1, 61, 11, 59, 15, 48, 19). Figure 7.7 illustrates the sublists being merged at each pass. □

7.6.3   Recursive Merge Sort

For the recursive version, we modify our record structure to accommodate a link field. The new structure is defined as:

```
void merge_pass(element list[], element sorted[], int n,
                                      int length)
{
/* perform one pass of the merge sort.  It merges adjacent
pairs of subfiles from list into sorted.  n is the
number of elements in the list. length is the length of the
subfile */
  int i,j;
  for (i = 0; i <= n - 2 * length; i += 2 * length)
    merge(list,sorted,i,i + length - 1,i + 2 * length - 1);
  if (i + length < n)
    merge(list,sorted,i,i + length - 1,n - 1);
  else
    for (j = i; j < n; j++)
      sorted[j] = list[j];
}
```

Program 7.9: *merge_pass*

```
void merge_sort(element list[], int n)
/* perform a merge sort on the file */
{
   int length = 1; /* current length being merged */
   element extra[MAX_SIZE];

   while (length < n) {
      merge_pass(list,extra,n,length);
      length *= 2;
      merge_pass(extra,list,n,length);
      length *= 2;
   }
}
```

Program 7.10: *merge_sort*

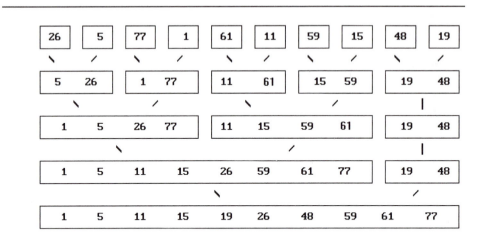

Figure 7.7: Merge tree for iterative merge sort

```
typedef struct {
        int key;
        /* other fields */
        int link;
        } element;
```

We assume that *list[i].link* and *list[i].key* refer to the *link* and *key* fields in record *i*, $0 \le i \le n - 1$. Notice that we are implementing the link field as an integer rather than a dynamic pointer. Initially *list[i].link* = −1, which means that each record is in a chain that contains only itself. The function *rmerge* (Program 7.11) implements the recursive merge sort; *rmerge* returns an integer that points to the start of the sorted list. Most of the actual merging is accomplished through *listmerge* (Program 7.12). This function takes two sorted chains, *first* and *second*, and returns an integer that points to the start of a new sorted chain that includes the first and second chains. Unlike the iterative implementation, the recursive one does not physically rearrange the list. Should this be necessary, we could use one of the schemes discussed in Section 7.9. The function call is *start = rmerge(list, 0, n−1);*

Analysis of *rmerge*: One may readily verify that this linked version of merge sort results in a stable sorting function, and that its computing time is O(*n* log *n*). □

Example 7.6: The input list is (26, 5, 77, 1, 61, 11, 59, 15, 48, 19). At each recursive call, the current list that is indexed from left to right is divided into two sublists that are indexed from *left* to ⌊ (*left* + *right*)/ 2 ⌋ and from ⌊ (*left* + *right*)/2 ⌋ + 1 to *right*,

```
int rmerge(element list[], int lower, int upper)
/* sort the list, list[lower],..., list[upper]. The link
field in each record is initially set to -1. */
{
   int middle;
   if (lower >= upper)
     return lower;
   else {
     middle = (lower + upper) / 2;
     return listmerge(list,rmerge(list,lower,middle),
                           rmerge(list,middle+1,upper));
   }
}
```

Program 7.11: Recursive merge sort

respectively. These sublists are sorted recursively and the results are later merged. Figure 7.8 shows the partitioning and merging for the sample data. You will notice that the sublists being merged are different from those produced by the iterative implementation (Figure 7.7). Figure 7.9 show the values in *start* and the *key* and *link* fields after the sort terminates. □

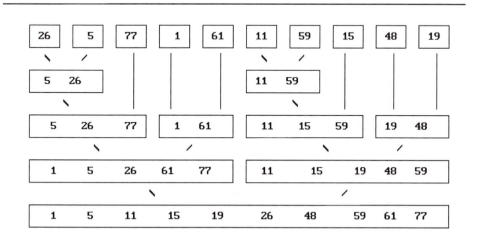

Figure 7.8: Sublist partitioning for a recursive merge sort

```
int listmerge(element list[], int first, int second)
/* merge lists pointed to by first and second */
{
    int start = n;
    while (first != -1 && second != -1)
        if (list[first].key <= list[second].key) {
        /* key in first list is lower, link this element to
        start and change start to point to first */
            list[start].link = first;
            start = first;
            first = list[first].link;
        }
        else {
        /* key second list is lower, link this element into
        the partially sorted list */
            list[start].link = second;
            start = second;
            second = list[second].link;
        }
    /* move remainder */
    if (first == -1)
        list[start].link = second;
    else
        list[start].link = first;
    return list[n].link; /* start of the new list */
}
```

Program 7.12: Merging linked lists

start = 3

i	R_0	R_1	R_2	R_3	R_4	R_5	R_6	R_7	R_8	R_9
key	26	5	77	1	61	11	59	15	48	19
link	8	5	-1	1	2	7	4	9	6	0

Figure 7.9: Simulation of *merge—sort*

Variation

Natural merge sort: We can modify *merge–sort* to take into account the prevailing order within the input list. In this implementation we make an initial pass over the data to determine the sequences of records that are in order. The merge sort then uses these initially ordered sublists for the remainder of the passes. Figure 7.10 shows the results of a natural merge sort using the input sequence found in Example 7.6.

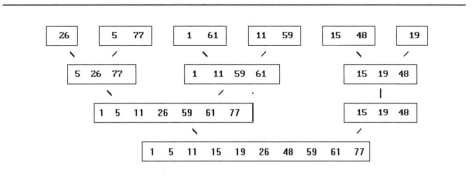

Figure 7.10: Merge sort starting with sorted sublists

EXERCISES

1. Write a function to shift the records $(x_0, \ldots, x_{n-1})$ circularly right by p, $0 \le p \le n$ positions. Your function should have time complexity $O(n)$ and space complexity $O(1)$. (Hint: Use three segment reversals.)

2. The two sorted files $(x_0, \ldots, x_m)$ and $(x_{m+1}, \ldots, x_{n-1})$ are to be merged to get the sorted file $(x_0, \ldots, x_{n-1})$. Let $s = \lfloor \sqrt{n} \rfloor$.

   (a) Assume that one of these files has fewer than s records. Write a function to merge the two sorted files in $O(n)$ time while using only $O(1)$ additional space. Show that your function actually has these complexities. (Hint: If the first list has fewer than s elements then find the position, q, in the merged file of the first element of the first file; perform a circular shift of $q-1$ as in the preceding exercise. This circular shift involves only the records of the first file and the first $q-1$ records of the second. Following the circular shift the first q records are in their final merged positions. Repeat this process for the second, third, etc., elements of the initial first file.)

(b) Assume that both files have at least s elements. Write a merge function with the same asymptotic complexity as that for (a). Show that your function actually has this complexity. (Hint: Partition the first file such that the first block has $s_1, 0 \leq s_1 < s$, records and the remainder have s records. Partition the second file so that the last block has $s_2, 0 \leq s_2 < s$ records. If $s_1 \neq 0$, then compare the first blocks of the two files to identify the s_1 records with smallest key. Perform a swap as in Step 2 of Program 7.8 so that these s_1 records are in the leftmost block of the first file. If $s_2 \neq 0$, then using a similar process we can get the s_2 records with largest keys into the rightmost block of the second file. Now, the leftmost block of size s_1 and the rightmost one of size s_2 are sorted. Following this, we may forget about them. The remaining blocks of the first and second files may be arranged in sorted order using the merge function of part (a). Next, Program 7.8 may be used to merge them.)

(c) Use the function for (a) and (b) to obtain an $O(n)$ time and $O(1)$ space function to merge two files of arbitrary size.

(d) Compare the run time of the merge function of (c) with that of Program 7.7. Use $i = 1$, $m = n/2$, and the values $n = 100, 250, 500, 1000, 2000, 5000, 10000$. For each value of n use ten randomly generated pairs of sorted files and compute the average merge time. Plot these for the two merge function. What conclusions can you draw?

(e) Modify your function for part (b) so that it does not use the function of (a) to rearrange records in the first and second files into sorted order. Rather, the last and first blocks of the first and second files, respectively, are sorted. To find the largest s records we need to look at the last two blocks of the first file and the last block of the second file. Program this function and obtain run times using the data of (d). Add these to your plot of (d).

(f) Program the $O(1)$ space merge function as described by Huang and Langston in their paper cited in the references and selected readings section. This function begins by partitioning the first file as in (b). The second file is partitioned into blocks of size except for the last block whose size s_2 is such that $s \leq s_2 < 2*s$. The largest s records are found and placed in the rightmost block of the first file. This is called the merge buffer. The rightmost block of the second file (i.e., the one with size s_2) is sorted. If $s_1 > 0$, the leftmost block of the first file is merged with the leftmost block of the second file using the last s_1 positions of the merge buffer. A swap of the leftmost s_1 records and those in the rightmost s_1 positions of the merge buffer results in moving the s_1 smallest records to their final place and also restores the merge buffer to contain the largest s records. Now we can forget about the first s_1 records and proceed to move the merge buffer to the leftmost s size block and sort the remaining blocks by their last records. One of these blocks is of size s_2. The sort of the blocks needs to be a little careful about this. Obtain the run times for this function using the data of (d). Add these results to your plot of (d). What conslusions can you draw?

3. Is *merge_sort* stable?

4. Suppose we use Program 7.8 to obtain a merge sort function. Is the resulting function a stable sort?

5. Write an algorithm to perform a natural merge sort. How much time does this algorithm take on an initially sorted list? What is the worst case computing time of the new algorithm? How much additional space is needed?

7.7 HEAP SORT

While the merge sort scheme discussed in the previous section has a computing time of $O(n \log n)$ both in the worst case and as average behavior, it requires additional storage proportional to the number of records in the file being sorted. By using the $O(1)$ space merge algorithm, the space requirements can be reduced to $O(1)$. The resulting sort algorithm is significantly slower than the original one. The sorting method, heap sort, we are about to study will require only a fixed amount of additional storage and at the same time will have as its worst case and average computing time $O(n \log n)$. While heap sort is slightly slower than merge sort using $O(n)$ additional space, it is faster than merge sort using $O(1)$ additional space.

In heap sort, we utilize the max heap structure introduced in Chapter 5. The deletion and insertion algorithms associated with max heaps directly yield an $O(n \log n)$ sorting method. The n records are first inserted into an initially empty heap. Next, the records are extracted from the heap one at a time. It is possible to create the heap of n records faster by using the function *adjust* (Program 7.13). This function takes a binary tree T whose left and right subtrees satisfy the heap property but whose root may not and adjusts T so that the entire binary tree satisfies the heap property. If the depth of the tree with root i is d, then the **while** loop is executed at most d times. Hence the computing time of *adjust* is $O(d)$.

To sort the list, we make $n - 1$ passes over the list. On each pass, we exchange the first record in the heap with the last record. Since the first record always contains the highest key, this record is now in its sorted position. We then decrement the heap size and readjust the heap. For example, on the first pass, we place the record with the highest key in the nth position; on the second pass, we place the record with the second highest key in position $n - 1$; and on the ith pass, we place the record with the ith highest key in position $n - i + 1$. The function *heapsort* (Program 7.14) implements the strategy just outlined. The function call is *heapsort(list, n);*

Analysis of *heapsort*: Suppose $2^{k-1} \le n < 2^k$ so that the tree has k levels and the number of nodes on level i is 2^{i-1}. In the first **for** loop of Program 7.14, *heapsort* calls *adjust* once for each node that has a child. Therefore, the time required for this loop is the sum, over each level, of the number of nodes on a level times the maximum distance the node

```
void adjust(element list[], int root, int n)
/* adjust the binary tree to establish the heap */
{
    int child,rootkey;
    element temp;
    temp = list[root];
    rootkey = list[root].key;
    child = 2 * root;        /* left child */
    while (child <= n) {
        if ((child < n) &&
        (list[child].key < list[child+1].key))
            child++;
        if (rootkey > list[child].key) /* compare root and
                                           max. child */
            break;
        else {
            list[child / 2] = list[child]; /* move to parent */
            child *= 2;
        }
    }
    list[child/2] = temp;
}
```

Program 7.13: Adjusting a max heap

can move. This is no more than:

$$\sum_{i=1}^{k} 2^{i-1}(k-i) = \sum_{i=1}^{k} 2^{k-i-1}\, i \le n \sum_{i=1}^{k-1} \frac{i}{2^i} < 2n = O(n)$$

In the second **for** loop, *heapsort* calls *adjust* $n-1$ times with maximum depth: $\lceil \log_2(n+1) \rceil$. Therefore, the computing time for this loop is $O(n \log n)$. So, the total computing time is $O(n \log n)$. $\square$

Example 7.7: The input list is $(26, 5, 77, 1, 61, 11, 59, 15, 48, 19)$. The initial binary tree is given in Figure 7.11. Its transformation into a max heap is given in Figure 7.12. The sorting process is illustrated in Figure 7.13. Solid circles show the records that have been placed into their sorted positions; the remaining records define the current max heap. $\square$

```
void heapsort(element list[], int n)
/* perform a heapsort on the array */
{
   int i,j;
   element temp;

   for (i = n/2; i > 0; i--)
      adjust(list,i,n);
   for (i = n-1; i > 0; i--) {
      SWAP(list[1],list[i+1],temp);
      adjust(list,1,i);
   }
}
```

Program 7.14: Heap sort

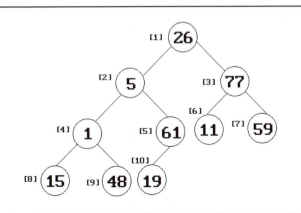

Figure 7.11: Array interpreted as a binary tree

EXERCISES

1. *heapsort* is unstable. Give an example of an input list in which the order of records with equal keys is not preserved.

2. Finish the heap sort illustrated in Figure 7.13.

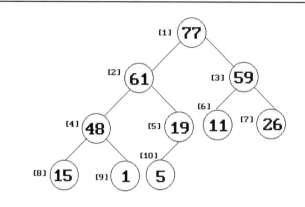

Figure 7.12: Max heap following first **for** loop of *heapsort*

7.8   RADIX SORT

Thus far we have assumed that the records to be sorted have a single key value. Let us now examine the problem of sorting records that have several keys. These keys are labeled K^0, K^1, $\cdots$, K^{r-1}, with K^0 being the most significant key and K^{r-1} the least. Let K_i^j denote key K^j of record R_i. A list of records, R_0, $\cdots$, R_{n-1}, is lexically sorted with respect to the keys K^0, K^1, ..., K^{r-1} iff $(K_i^0, K_i^1, ..., K_i^{r-1}) \leq (K_{i+1}^0, K_{i+1}^1, ..., K_{i+1}^{r-1})$, $0 \leq i < n-1$. We say that the r-tuple $(x_0, x_1, ..., x_{r-1})$ is less than or equal to the r-tuple $(y_0, ..., y_{r-1})$ *iff* either $x_i = y_i$, $0 \leq i \leq j$ and $x_{j+1} < y_{j+1}$ for some $j < r-1$ or $x_i = y_i$, $0 \leq i < r$.

For example, we can regard the problem of sorting a deck of cards as a sort on two keys, suit and face value, in which the keys have the ordering relations:

K^0 [Suit]: $\clubsuit < \diamondsuit < \heartsuit < \spadesuit$
K^1 [Face value]: $2 < 3 < 4 < \cdots < 10 < J < Q < K < A$

Thus, a sorted deck of cards has the ordering:

$$2\clubsuit, \cdots, A\clubsuit, \cdots, 2\spadesuit, \cdots, A\spadesuit$$

In the card sorting example, following the sort on suit (K^0), we would have four piles of cards, each containing all the cards in a suit. Figure 7.14 is an example of the arrangement of piles. We now independently sort the four suit piles on face value. Finally, we stack the four piles so that the spade pile is on the bottom and the club pile is on the top. We call a sort that proceeds in this fashion an MSD (Most Significant Digit)

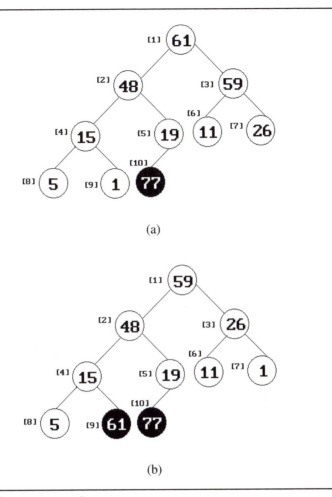

(a)

(b)

Figure 7.13: Heap sort example

sort.

    The second approach begins with the least significant key first, and is known as an LSD (Least Significant Digit) sort. Following the sort on a key, the piles are put together to obtain a single pile which is then sorted on the next least significant key. This process is continued until the pile is sorted on the most significant key. Using our card example, sorting by the least significant key first, means that we would first sort the cards by their face values. Figure 7.15 is an example of the configuration of cards after this pass. We then reform the cards into a single pile with the aces at the bottom of the pile and the twos at the top. We now resort the cards based on suit. The sorting method we employ

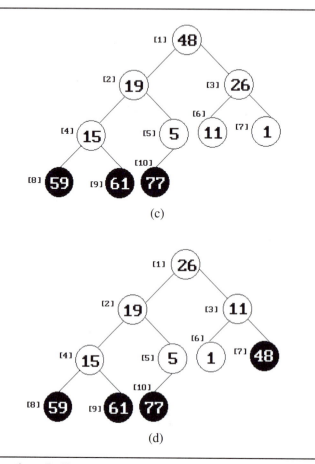

(c)

(d)

Figure 7.13 (continued): Heap sort example

in this second pass must be stable or we will undo the results of the first pass. The LSD approach is simpler than the MSD one because we do not have to sort the subpiles independently. This means that an LSD sort typically has less overhead than an MSD one.

The terms LSD or MSD indicate only the order in which the keys are sorted; they do not specify how each key is to be sorted. Generally, however, we implement either sort by creating bins to represent the different key values. For example, in an MSD card sort, we first create four "bins" to represent the different suit values. After we have placed the cards in the correct bins, we use an insertion sort to sort each of these bins. In the case of an LSD card sort, we would set up thirteen bins to represent the different face values. After we have placed the cards in the correct bins, we would reform them into a single pile, create four bins to represent the suits, and resort the cards using a stable sort.

Figure 7.14: Arrangement of cards after first pass of an MSD sort

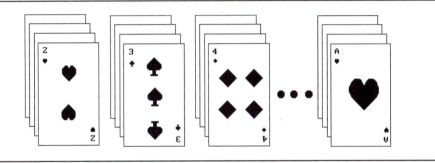

Figure 7.15: Arrangement of cards after first pass of LSD sort

If the spread in key values is O(n), a bin sort requires only O(n) time, thus, making it a very fast sorting technique.

We also can use an LSD or MSD sort when we have only one logical key, if we interpret this key as a composite of several keys. For example, an integer has several digits, and these digits are ordered so that the digit in the far right position is the least significant and the one in the far left position is the most significant. If our integers are in the range $0 \leq K \leq 999$, then we can use either an LSD or MSD sort for three keys (K^0, K^1, K^2), where K^0 is the digit in the hundredths place, K^1 the digit in the tens place, and K^2 the digit in the units place. Since all the keys lie in the range $0 \leq K^i \leq 9$, the sort for each key requires only ten bins. However, since an LSD sort does not require the maintenance of independent subpiles, it is easier to implement.

In a *radix sort*, we decompose the sort key into digits using a radix r. When $r = 10$, we get the common base 10 or decimal decomposition described above. $r = 2$ corresponds to a binary decomposition of the key. With a radix of r, r bins are needed to sort on each digit.

Let us now develop an LSD radix r sort. We assume that the records, R_0, $\cdots$, R_{n-1}, have keys that are d-tuples $(x_0, x_1, \cdots , x_{d-1})$, and that $0 \leq x_i < r$. We also assume that each record has a link field, and that the input list is stored as a dynamically linked list. We implement the bins as queues with *front[i]*, $0 \leq i < r$, pointing to the first record in bin i and *rear[i]*, $0 \leq i < r$, pointing to the last record in bin i. The function *radix—sort* (Program 7.15) implements LSD radix r sort. It assumes that the input is a linked list of records and it creates a sorted linked list. The following declarations are for the case $r = 10$, and $d = 3$.

```
#define MAX_DIGIT 3 /* numbers between 0 and 999*/
#define RADIX_SIZE 10
typedef struct list_node *list_pointer;
typedef struct list_node {
        int key[MAX_DIGIT];
        list_pointer link;
        };
```

Analysis of *radix sort*: The function *radix—sort* makes *MAX_DIGIT* passes over the data, each pass taking O(*RADIX_SIZE* + n) time. The total computing time is O(*MAX_DIGIT*(RADIX_SIZE + n)). □

The choice of the radix affects the computing time of the radix sort. A radix sort with a radix of 2 and numbers ranging from 1 to 100 billion would perform terribly, while a radix of 10 and numbers ranging from 0 $\cdots$ 999 would perform very well. Generally, we want to select carefully our radix, using the value of n and the size of the largest key to govern our final choice.

Example 7.8: The input sequence is (179, 208, 306, 93, 859, 984, 55, 9, 271, 33). The radix is 10, and since all numbers are in the range [0 $\cdots$ 999], the number of digits is 3. The list elements are labeled R_0, $\cdots$, R_9. Figure 7.16 illustrates the sort at each pass.

EXERCISES

1. Write a sort algorithm that sorts records R_0, $\cdots$, R_{n-1} lexically on keys (K_0, $\cdots$, K_{r-1}) for the case when the range of each key is much larger than n. In this case, the bin sort scheme used in *radix—sort* to sort within each key becomes inefficient (why?). What scheme would you use to sort within each key if we desired an algorithm with:

   (a)   good worst case behavior

   (b)   good average behavior

```
list_pointer radix_sort(list_pointer ptr)
/*Radix Sort using a linked list */
{
   list_pointer front[RADIX_SIZE], rear [RADIX_SIZE];
   int i, j, digit;
   for (i = MAX_DIGIT-1; i >= 0; i--) {
      for (j = 0; j < RADIX_SIZE; j++)
         front[j] = rear[j] = NULL;
      while (ptr) {
         digit = ptr->key[i];
         if (!front[digit])
            front[digit] = ptr;
         else
            rear[digit]->link = ptr;
         rear[digit] = ptr;
         ptr = ptr->link;
      }
      /* reestablish the linked list for the next pass */
      ptr = NULL;
      for (j = RADIX_SIZE-1; j >= 0; j--)
         if (front[j]) {
            rear[j]->link = ptr;  ptr = front[j];
         }
   }
   return ptr;
}
```

Program 7.15: LSD radix sort

    (c)   small values of n, say < 15?

2.   If we have n records with integer keys in the range $[0, n^2)$, then they may be sorted in $O(n \log n)$ time using heap sort or merge sort. The function *radix_sort* on a single key, that is, *MAX_DIGIT* $-1 = 1$ and radix $= n^2$ takes $O(n^2)$ time. Show how to interpret the keys as two subkeys so that radix sort takes only $O(n)$ time to sort n records. (Hint: each key, K_i, may be written as $K_i = K_i^0 n + K_i^1$ with K_i^0 and K_i^1 integers in the range $[0, n-1]$.)

3.   Generalize the method of the previous exercise to the case of integer keys in the range $[0, n^p)$ obtaining an $O(pn)$ sorting method.

$$179 \rightarrow 208 \rightarrow 306 \rightarrow 93 \rightarrow 859 \rightarrow 984 \rightarrow 55 \rightarrow 9 \rightarrow 271 \rightarrow 33$$

Initial input

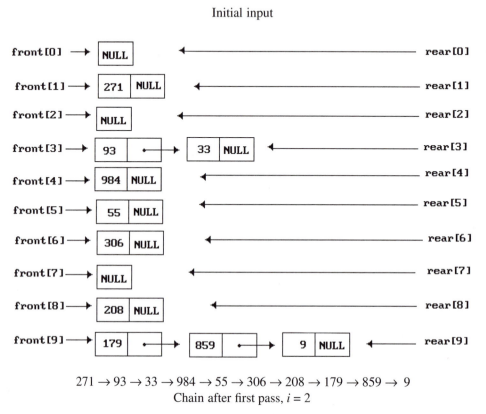

$$271 \rightarrow 93 \rightarrow 33 \rightarrow 984 \rightarrow 55 \rightarrow 306 \rightarrow 208 \rightarrow 179 \rightarrow 859 \rightarrow 9$$
Chain after first pass, $i = 2$

Figure 7.16: Simulation of *radix_sort*

4. Is *radix_sort* stable? Assume that you are sorting lists of numbers.

5. Write *convert* and *reconvert* functions that convert an array with integer keys into a linked list of the form used by *radix_sort* and reconvert the linked list back to its original form.

6. Rewrite *radix_sort* so that the radix is 2. Use the *BIT* macro to extract the bits. Try this version with keys of type *long int*. How quick is it?

7. Under what conditions would an MSD radix sort be more efficient than an LSD radix sort?

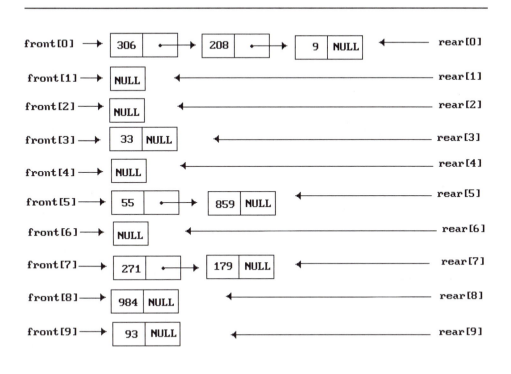

$$306 \rightarrow 208 \rightarrow 9 \rightarrow 33 \rightarrow 55 \rightarrow 859 \rightarrow 271 \rightarrow 179 \rightarrow 984 \rightarrow 93$$
Chain after second pass, $i = 1$

Figure 7.16 (continued): Simulation of *radix_sort*

7.9 LIST AND TABLE SORTS

Apart from the radix sort and the recursive merge sort, all the sorting methods we have looked at require excessive data movement since we must physically move records following some comparisons. If the records are large, this slows down the sorting process. Therefore, when sorting lists with large records we modify our sorting methods to minimize data movement. As we indicated in our discussion of the recursive merge sort, we can reduce data movement by using a linked list representation. The sort does not physically rearrange the list, but modifies the link fields to show the sorted order. In many applications this is sufficient. For example, if the sorted list is to be stored on some external media, we can send the records over using the link fields to determine the order in which the records are transmitted. However, in some applications we must physically

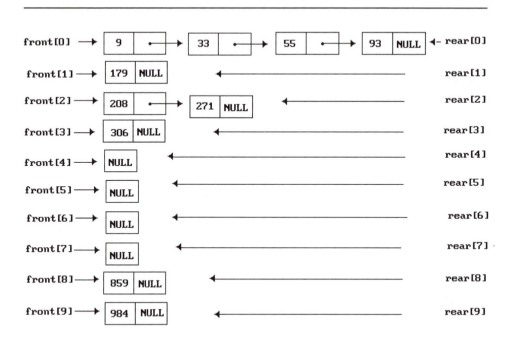

$$9 \rightarrow 33 \rightarrow 55 \rightarrow 93 \rightarrow 179 \rightarrow 208 \rightarrow 271 \rightarrow 306 \rightarrow 859 \rightarrow 984$$

Chain after third pass, $i = 0$

Figure 7.16 (continued): Simulation of *radix_sort*

rearrange the records so that they are in the required order. Even in these cases we can achieve considerable savings by first performing a linked list sort and then physically rearranging the records according to the order specified in the list. We can accomplish this rearranging in linear time using some additional space. In this section, we examine three methods for rearranging the lists into sorted order. The first two methods require a linked list representation, while the third method uses an auxiliary table that indirectly references the list's records. We begin our discussion with sorts that use a linked list representation.

Assume that the linked list has been sorted and that *start* points to the record that contains the smallest key. This record's link field points to the record with the second smallest key, and so on. (See Example 7.6, which illustrated a linked list sort using a recursive merge sort.) To physically rearrange these records into nondecreasing order, we first interchange records R_0 and R_{start}. Record R_0 now has the smallest key.

However, if *start* ≠ 0, the remaining records are no longer correctly linked. Therefore, we must find the record that contained a 0 in its link field, and change this record's link field to point to *start*. We now change *start* to point to record R_0's link field, and interchange records R_1 and R_{start}. After $n-1$ iterations the list is in ascending order.

Since the correct relinking of the list after each iteration requires a knowledge of each record's predecessor, we must use a doubly linked list. The function *list−sort*1 (Program 7.16) sorts a linked list by first converting a singly linked list into its doubly linked version. It then moves each record into its correct position. The function call is *list−sort*1(*list, n−*1, *start*). We use the following declaration:

```
typedef struct {
          int key;
          int link;
          int linkb;    /* back link */
          } element;
```

Analysis of *list−sort*1: If there are *n* records in the list, then the time required to convert the singly linked list into a doubly linked one is O(*n*). The actual sort does not begin until the second **for** loop. This loop is iterated *n−*1 times, with each iteration interchanging no more than two records. If each record is *m* words long, then the cost per interchange is 3*m*. Therefore, the total time is O(*mn*). □

Example 7.9: The input list is (26, 5, 77, 1, 61, 11, 59, 15, 48, 19). After a recursive merge sort, the list is linked as in Figure 7.17. The list with the backlinks *linkb* is found in Figure 7.18. Figure 7.19 shows the list after the first record has been placed in order, and Figure 7.20 shows the list after the next three iterations. In Figures 7.19 and 7.20, the changes in the records are highlighted. □

Although we can modify *list−sort*1 in several ways, a variation created by M. D. MacLaren is of particular interest because it does not require back links. In this algorithm (Program 7.17), after we exchange record R_{start} with R_i, we set the link field of the new R_i to *start*. This shows that we moved the original record. Since start must always be ≥ *i*, we can correctly reorder the records. The function call is *list−sort*2(*list, n−*1, *start*);

Analysis of *list−sort*2: The sequence of record moves for *list−sort*2 is identical to that of *list−sort*1. Therefore, in the worst case 3(*n* − 1) record moves are made. Since the **while** loop examines each record no more than once, the total cost of this loop is O(*n*). Thus, *list−sort*2 has a worst case time of O(*mn*). □

Although *list−sort*1 and *list−sort*2 have the same asymptotic time and make the same number of record moves, *list−sort*2 is slightly faster than *list−sort*1 since each time two records are interchanged *list−sort*1 works harder than *list−sort*2. In addition, since *list−sort*1 requires an additional link field for each record, it is also inferior to *list−sort*2 when space is considered.

```
void list_sort1(element list[], int n, int start)
/* start is a pointer to the list of n sorted elements,
linked together by the field link. linkb is assumed to be
present in each element. The elements are rearranged
so that the resulting elements list[0],..., list[n-1] are
consecutive and sorted. */
{
   int i,last,current;
   element temp;

   last = -1;
   for (current = start; current != -1;
   current = list[current].link) {
   /* establish the back links for the list */
      list[current].linkb = last;
      last = current;
   }
   for (i = 0; i < n-1; i++) {
   /* move list[start] to position i while maintaining the
   list */
      if (start != i) {
         if (list[i].link+1)
            list[list[i].link].linkb = start;
         list[list[i].linkb].link = start;
         SWAP(list[start],list[i],temp);
      }
      start = list[i].link;
   }
}
```

Program 7.16: *list_sort*1

Example 7.10: The input list is (26, 5, 77, 1, 61, 11, 59, 15, 48, 19). After the recursive merge sort we have the configuration of Figure 7.21. The configuration after each of the first two iterations of the **for** loop is shown in Figure 7.22, and Figure 7.23 shows the configurations after the next three iterations. The sort continues in this fashion until all the records are in their sorted position. □

The list sort technique is not well suited for quick sort or heap sort. For heap sort, the sequential representation of the heap is essential to the operation of the sort. We can eliminate excessive data movement in these sorts, as well as the sorts that work well with the list sort technique, by using an auxiliary table that indirectly references the records in

start = 3

i	R_0	R_1	R_2	R_3	R_4	R_5	R_6	R_7	R_8	R_9
key	26	5	77	1	61	11	59	15	48	19
link	8	5	−1	1	2	7	4	9	6	0
linkb										

Figure 7.17 Linked list following a list sort

start = 3

i	R_0	R_1	R_2	R_3	R_4	R_5	R_6	R_7	R_8	R_9
key	26	5	77	1	61	11	59	15	48	19
link	8	5	−1	1	2	7	4	9	6	0
linkb	9	3	4	−1	6	1	8	5	0	7

Figure 7.18 Doubly linked list resulting from list of Figure 7.15

start = 1

i	$\mathbf{R_0}$	R_1	R_2	$\mathbf{R_3}$	R_4	R_5	R_6	R_7	R_8	R_9
key	**1**	5	77	**26**	61	11	59	15	48	19
link	**1**	5	−1	**8**	2	7	4	9	6	**3**
linkb	**−1**	3	4	**9**	6	1	8	5	**3**	7

Figure 7.19 Configuration after first iteration of the **for** loop of function *list−sort*1

the list. The table is defined as *int table*[*MAX_SIZE*], but we refer to it as *t* in the following analysis. At the start of the sort, $t[i] = i$, $0 \le i \le n-1$. If the sorting algorithm needs to interchange R_i and R_j, then the table entries $t[i]$ and $t[j]$ are exchanged; the original list is not altered. After the sort, $R_{t[0]}$ is the record with the smallest key, $R_{t[n-1]}$ is the record with the largest key, and, in general, $R_{t[i]}$ is the record with the *i*th smallest key. Therefore, the sorted list is $R_{t[0]}, R_{t[1]}, \cdots, R_{t[n-1]}$ (see Figure 7.22). This table is sufficient for many applications that require an ordered list including a binary search. However, in some applications we must physically rearrange the records according to

$i = 2$
$start = 5$

i	R_0	R_1	R_2	R_3	R_4	R_5	R_6	R_7	R_8	R_9
key	1	5	77	26	61	11	59	15	48	19
link	1	5	−1	8	2	7	4	9	6	3
linkb	−1	3	4	9	6	1	8	5	3	7

$i = 3$
$start = 7$

i	R_0	R_1	$\mathbf{R_2}$	R_3	R_4	$\mathbf{R_5}$	R_6	R_7	R_8	R_9
key	1	5	**11**	26	61	**77**	59	15	48	19
link	1	5	**7**	8	5	**−1**	4	9	6	3
linkb	−1	3	**1**	9	6	**4**	8	5	3	7

$i = 4$
$start = 9$

i	R_0	R_1	R_2	$\mathbf{R_3}$	R_4	R_5	R_6	$\mathbf{R_7}$	R_8	R_9
key	1	5	11	**15**	61	77	59	**26**	48	19
link	1	5	7	**9**	5	−1	4	**8**	6	7
linkb	−1	3	1	**5**	6	4	8	**9**	7	7

Figure 7.20 Example for *list–sort*1

the permutation specified by t.

The algorithm to rearrange records corresponding to the permutation $t[0]$, $t[1]$, $\cdots$, $t[n-1]$ is a rather interesting application of a theorem of mathematics: Every permutation is made up of disjoint cycles. The cycle for any element i consists of i, $t[i]$, $t^2[i]$, $\cdots$, $t^k[i]$, where $t^j[i]$, $= t[t^{j-1}[i]]$, $t^0[i] = i$, and $t^k[i] = i$. Thus, the permutation t of Figure 7.24 has two cycles, the first involving R_0 and R_4 and the second involving R_3, R_2, and R_1. The function *table–sort* (Program 7.18) uses this cyclic decomposition of a permutation. First, the cycle containing R_0 is followed and all records moved to their correct positions. Next, the cycle containing R_1 is examined, unless R_1 was included in the cycle containing R_0. The cycles for R_2, R_3, $\cdots$, R_{n-2} are each examined in turn. The result is a physically sorted list.

```
void list_sort2(element list[], int n, int start)
/* list sort with only one link field */
{
   int i,next;
   element temp;
   for (i = 0; i < n-1; i++) {
      while(start < i)
         start = list[start].link;
      next = list[start].link; /* save index of next
                                       largest key */
      if (start != i) {
         SWAP(list[i],list[start],temp);
         list[i].link = start;
      }
      start = next;
   }
}
```

Program 7.17 *list_sort2*

start = 3

i	R_0	R_1	R_2	R_3	R_4	R_5	R_6	R_7	R_8	R_9
key	26	5	77	1	6	11	59	15	48	19
link	8	5	−1	1	2	7	4	9	6	0

Figure 7.21: Configuration after a recursive merge sort

Since each cycle in the sort can be classified as trivial or nontrivial, the sort uses two distinct strategies. A trivial cycle, that is, one in which $t[i] = i$ for some record R_i, is handled easily because the record with the ith smallest key is already in its correct position. Thus, no rearrangement of records is necessary. A nontrivial cycle, that is, one in which $t[i] \neq i$ for some record R_i, requires more work. First, we move R_i to a temporary position, *temp*, then we move the record at $t[i]$ to i. Next, we move the record at $t[t[i]]$ to $t[i]$. We repeat this process until we reach the end of the cycle $t^k[i]$. We then move *temp* to $t^{k-1}[i]$. The function call is *table_sort(list, n−1, table);*

Analysis of *table_sort*: If each record uses m words of storage, then the additional space

$i = 0$
$start = 1$

i	$\mathbf{R_0}$	R_1	R_2	$\mathbf{R_3}$	R_4	R_5	R_6	R_7	R_8	R_9
key	**1**	5	77	**26**	61	11	59	15	48	19
link	**3**	5	−1	**8**	2	7	4	9	6	0

$i = 1$
$start = 5$

i	R_0	R_1	R_2	R_3	R_4	R_5	R_6	R_7	R_8	R_9
key	1	5	77	26	61	11	59	15	48	19
link	3	5	−1	8	2	7	4	9	6	0

Figure 7.22: Configurations after iterations $i = 0$ and 1 of *list_sort2*

needed is m words for *temp* plus space for the index variables i, j, and k. To obtain an estimate of the computing time we observe that the **for** loop is executed $n-1$ times. If for some value of i, $t[i] \neq i$ then there is a nontrivial cycle including $k > 1$ distinct records: $R_i, R_{t[i]}, \cdots, R_{t^{k-1}[i]}$. Rearranging these records requires $k + 1$ record moves. Since no record can be in two different nontrivial cycles, these records are not moved again at any time in the algorithm. Let k_j be the number of records in a nontrivial cycle starting at R_j when $i = j$ in the algorithm. Let $k_j = 0$ for a trivial cycle. Then, the total number of record moves is:

$$\sum_{j=0, k_j \neq 0}^{n-1} (k_j + 1)$$

Since the records in nontrivial cycles must be different, $\sum k_j \leq n$. Thus, the total record moves is at its maximum when $\sum k_j = n$ and there are $\lfloor n/2 \rfloor$ cycles. When n is even, each cycle contains two records. Otherwise, one cycle contains three records and the other cycles contain two records. In either case the number of record moves is $\lfloor 3n/2 \rfloor$. Since one record move costs $O(m)$ time, the total computing time is $O(mn)$. □

Comparing *list_sort2* and *table_sort*, we see that, in the worst case, *list_sort2* makes $3(n-1)$ record moves while *table_sort* makes only $\lfloor 3n/2 \rfloor$ record moves. For larger values of m, we can attain a more efficient sort on a linked list, if we first make one pass over the list to create a table. This takes $O(n)$ time. Then we use *table_sort* to rearrange the records in the order specified by the table.

Example 7.11: Suppose that *table_sort* begins with the configuration of Figure 7.25(a).

$i = 2$

$start = 7$

i	R_0	R_1	$\mathbf{R_2}$	R_3	R_4	$\mathbf{R_5}$	R_6	R_7	R_8	R_9
key	1	5	**11**	26	61	**77**	59	15	48	19
$link$	3	5	**5**	8	2	**−1**	4	9	6	0

$i = 3$

$start = 9$

i	R_0	R_1	R_2	$\mathbf{R_3}$	R_4	R_5	R_6	$\mathbf{R_7}$	R_8	R_9
key	1	5	11	**15**	61	77	59	**26**	48	19
$link$	3	5	5	**7**	2	−1	4	**8**	6	0

$i = 4$

$start = 0$

i	R_0	R_1	R_2	R_3	$\mathbf{R_4}$	R_5	R_6	R_7	R_8	$\mathbf{R_9}$
key	1	5	11	15	**19**	77	59	26	48	**61**
$link$	3	5	5	7	**9**	−1	4	8	6	**2**

Figure 7.23: Configurations after iterations $i = 2$, 3, and 4 of *list_sort2*

There are two nontrivial cycles in the permutation specified by *table*. The first is $R_0, R_2,$ R_7, R_5, R_0. The second is R_3, R_4, R_6, R_3. During the first iteration of the **for** loop, the cycle $R_0, R_{t[0]}, R_{t^2[0]}, R_{t^3[0]}, R_0$ is followed. Record R_0 is moved to a temporary spot *temp*; $R_{t[0]}$, (R_2), is moved to position R_0; $R_{t^2[0]}$, (R_7), is moved to R_2; R_5 is moved to R_7; and finally *temp* is moved to R_5. Thus, after the first iteration we have the configuration of Figure 7.25(b).

Since $t[i] = i$, when $i = 1$ and $i = 2$ records, R_1 and R_2 are already in their correct positions. When $i = 3$, the next nontrivial cycle is discovered, and the records in this cycle (R_3, R_4, R_6, R_3) are moved to their correct positions. Following this we have the configuration of Figure 7.25(c). Since $t[i] = i$ for the remaining values of i, all the non-trivial cycles have been processed. $\square$

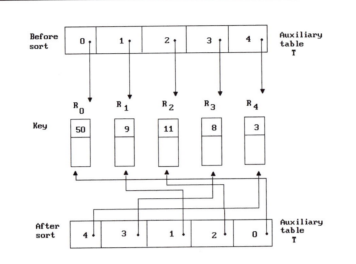

Figure 7.24: Table sort

EXERCISES

1. Trace the remaining iterations for the *list_sort1* example.

2. Trace the remaining iterations for the *list_sort2* example.

3. Rewrite selection sort (Program 1.3 from Chapter 1) so that it produces a list that we can sort using either *list_sort1* or *list_sort2*.

4. Rewrite *quicksort* so that it creates a table that contains the sorted order of the list. The records are not physically moved during the sort; instead *table*[*i*] points to the record that would have been in position *i* if records had been moved physically. Use *table_sort* to rearrange the records into the sorted order specified by *table*.

5. Repeat Exercise 4 with *insertion_sort*.

6. Do Exercise 4 for the case of selection sort.

7. Repeat Exercise 4 with *heap_sort*.

8. Repeat Exercise 4 with *merge_sort* (Program 7.10.

7.10   SUMMARY OF INTERNAL SORTING

Of the several sorting methods we have studied no one method is best. Some methods are good for small *n*, others for large *n*. An insertion sort works well when the list is already partially ordered. Because of the low overhead of this method, it is also the best sorting method for small *n*. Merge sort has the best worst case behavior, but it requires

```
void table_sort(element list[], int n, int table[])
{
/* rearrange list[0],..., list[n−1] to correspond to the
sequence list[table[0]],..., list[table[n−1]] */
    int i,current,next;
    element temp;
    for (i = 0; i < n-1; i++)
       if (table[i] != i) {
       /* nontrivial cycle starting at i */
          temp = list[i];
          current = i;
          do {
             next= table[current];
             list[current] = list[next];
             table[current] = current;
             current = next;
          } while (table[current] != i);
          list[current] = temp;
          table[current] = current;
       }
}
```

Program 7.18: *table−sort*

more storage than a heap sort, and has slightly more overhead than quick sort. Quick sort has the best average behavior, but its worst case behavior is $O(n^2)$. The behavior of radix sort depends on the size of the keys and the choice of the radix.

Figure 7.26 gives the average running times for *insertion−sort*, *quicksort*, *merge−sort*, and *heapsort*. Figure 7.27 is a plot of these times. As can be seen, for *n* up to about 20, *insertion−sort* is the fastest. For values of *n* from about 20 to 45, *quicksort* is the fastest. For larger values of *n*, *merge−sort* is the fastest. Therefore, in practice, it is worthwhile to combine *insertion−sort*, *quicksort*, and *merge−sort* so that *merge−sort* uses *quicksort* for sublists of size less than about 45 and *quicksort* uses *insertion−sort* when the sublist size is below about 20.

	R_0	R_1	R_2	R_3	R_4	R_5	R_6	R_7
key	35	14	12	42	26	50	31	18
table	2	1	7	4	6	0	3	5

(a) Initial configuration

key	12	14	18	42	26	35	31	50
table	0	1	2	4	6	5	3	7

(b) Configuration after rearrangement of first cycle

key	12	14	18	26	31	35	42	50
table	0	1	2	3	4	5	6	7

(c) Configuration after rearrangement of second cycle

Figure 7.25: Tables for Example 7.11

EXERCISES

1. The objective of this assignment is to come up with one composite sorting algorithm that is good on the worst time criterion. The candidate algorithms are:

   (a) Insertion Sort
   (b) Quick Sort
   (c) Merge Sort
   (d) Heap Sort

   To begin with, program these algorithms in C. In each case, assume that n integers are to be sorted. In the case of quick sort, use the median of 3 method. In the case of merge sort, use the iterative algorithm (as a separate exercise, you might wish to compare the run times of the iterative and recursive versions of merge sort and determine what the recursion penality is in your favorite language using your favorite compiler). Check out the correctness of the programs using some test data. Since quite detailed and working algorithms are given in the book, this part of the assignment should take little effort. In any case, no points are earned until after this step.

   To get reasonably accurate run times, you need to know the accuracy of the clock or timer you are using. Determine this by reading the appropriate manual. Let this be δ. Now, run a pilot test to determine approximate times for your four

Times in hundredths of a second

n	quick	merge	heap	insert
0	0.041	0.027	0.034	0.032
10	1.064	1.524	1.482	0.775
20	2.343	3.700	3.680	2.253
30	3.700	5.587	6.153	4.430
40	5.085	7.800	8.815	7.275
50	6.542	9.892	11.583	10.892
60	7.987	11.947	14.427	15.013
70	9.587	15.893	17.427	20.000
80	11.167	18.217	20.517	25.450
90	12.633	20.417	23.717	31.767
100	14.275	22.950	26.775	38.325
200	30.775	48.475	60.550	148.300
300	48.171	81.600	96.657	319.657
400	65.914	109.829	134.971	567.629
500	84.400	138.033	174.100	874.600
600	102.900	171.167	214.400	
700	122.400	199.240	255.760	
800	142.160	230.480	297.480	
900	160.400	260.100	340.000	
1000	181.000	289.450	382.250	

Figure 7.26: Average times for sort methods

sorting functions for $n = 5, 10, 20, 30, 40, 50$, and 100. You will notice times of 0 for many of these values of n. The other times may not be much larger than the clock accuracy.

To time an event that is smaller than or near the clock accuracy, repeat it many times and divide the overall time by the number of repetitions. You should obtain times that are accurate to within 1%.

We need worst case data for each of the 4 sort methods. The worst case data for insert sort is easy to generate. Just use the sequence $n, n-1, n-2, \cdots, 1$. Worst case data for merge sort can be obtained by working backwards. Begin with the last merge your algorithm will perform and make this work hardest. Then look at the 2nd last merge, and so on. Use this logic to obtain a program that will generate worst case data for merge sort for each of the above values of n.

Generating worst case data for heap sort is the hardest. So, here we shall use a random permutation generator (one is provided in Program 7.19). We shall

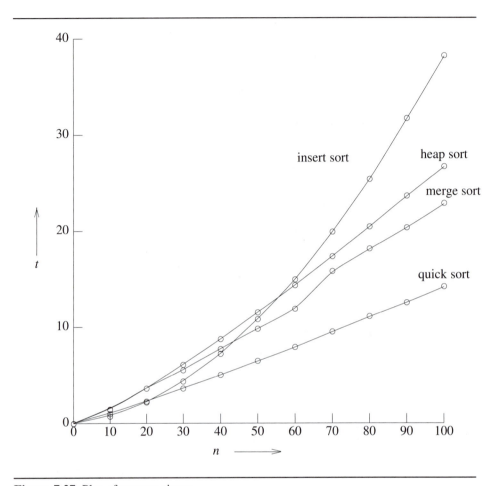

Figure 7.27: Plot of average times

generate random permutations of the desired size; clock heap sort on each of these; and use the max of these times as an approximation to the worst case time. You will be able to use more random permutations for smaller values of n than for larger. For no value of n should fewer than 10 permutations be used. Use the same technique to obtain worst case times for quick sort.

Having settled on the test data, we are ready to perform our experiment. Obtain the worst case times. From these times you will get a rough idea when one algorithm performs better than the other. Now, narrow the scope of your experiments and determine the exact value of n when one algorithm outperforms another. For some algorithms, this value may be 0. For instance, each of the other three algorithms may be faster than quick sort for all values of n.

Plot your findings on a single sheet of graph paper. Do you see the n^2 behavior of insert sort and quick sort; and the $n\log n$ behavior of the other two algorithms for suitably large n (about $n > 20$)? If not, there is something wrong with your test or your clock or with both. For each value of n determine the sort algorithm that is fastest (simply look at your graph). Write a composite algorithm with the best possible performance for all n. Clock this algorithm and plot the times on the same graph sheet you used earlier.

A word of **CAUTION**. If you are using a multi process computer, make all your final runs at about the same time. On these computers, the clocked time will vary significantly with the amount of computer work load. Comparing the run times of an insert sort run made at 2:00pm with the run times of a merge sort run made at 2:00am will not be very meaningful.

WHAT TO TURN IN
You are required to submit a report that states the clock accuracy; the number of random permutations tried for heap sort; the worst case data for merge sort and how you generated it; a table of times for the above values of n; the times for the narrowed ranges; the graph; and a table of times for the composite algorithm. In addition, your report must be accompanied by a complete listing of your program (this includes the sorting function and the main program for timing and test data generation).

```
void permute(element list[], int n)
/* random permutation */
{
   int i,j;
   element temp;

   for (i = n-1; i >= 1; i--) {
      j = rand() % (n-1) + 1;
      SWAP(list[j],list[i],temp);
   }
}
```

Program 7.19: Random permutation generator

2. Repeat the previous exercise for the case of average run times. Average case data is almost impossible to create. So, use random permutations. This time, however, don't repeat a permutation many times to overcome clock inaccuracies. Instead, use each permutation once and clock the time over all (for a fixed n).

3. We also can compare the various sorts by counting the number of comparisons and exchanges they make for different types of input data. In this experiment, we want to count the numbers of comparisons and exchanges for the following sorts and input data patterns:

Sorts	Input Data Patterns
Insertion sort	Ordered
Heap sort	Nearly ordered
Quicksort	Reverse ordered
Merge sort	Random
Radix sort	
Selection sort (see Chapter 1)	

To perform this experiment, you must:

(a) modify each of the functions provided in the text so that you can count the comparisons and exchanges.

(b) generate appropriate input data patterns.

(c) conduct your experiment on lists of size = 50, 100, 200, $\cdots$, 5000.

TURN IN:

(i) A listing of your program.

(ii) A table that shows the performance of the various sorts for the various input patterns.

(iii) A short paper summarizing the differences.

7.11 EXTERNAL SORTING

7.11.1 Introduction

In this section, we consider techniques to sort large files. The files are assumed to be so large that the whole file cannot be contained in the internal memory of a computer, making an internal sort impossible. We shall assume that the file to be sorted resides on a disk. Most of the ideas we present for a disk sort also apply for the case when the external storage media is a tape. When reading or writing from/to a disk, the following overheads apply:

(1) *Seek time:* time taken to position the read/write head to the correct track of the disk. This will depend on the number of tracks across which the head has to move.

(2) *Latency time:* time until the right sector of the track is under the read/write head.

(3) *Transmission time:* time to transmit the data to/from the disk.

We shall use the term *block* to denote the unit of data that is read from or written to the disk at one time. A block will usually contain several records.

The most popular method for sorting on external storage devices is merge sort. This method consists of essentially two distinct phases. First, segments of the input file are sorted using a good internal sort method. These sorted segments, known as *runs*, are written out onto external storage as they are generated. Second, the runs generated in phase one are merged together following the merge tree pattern of Figure 7.7, until only one run is left. Because function *merge* (Program 7.7) requires only the leading records of the two runs being merged to be present in memory at one time, it is possible to merge large runs together. It is more difficult to adapt the other internal sort methods considered in this chapter to external sorting.

We shall use an example to illustrate the basic external sort process and analyze the various contributions to the computing time. A file containing 4500 records, $A_1, \ldots, A_{4500}$, is to be sorted using a computer with an internal memory capable of sorting at most 750 records. The input file is maintained on disk and has a block length of 250 records. We have available another disk that may be used as a scratch pad. The input disk is not to be written on. One way to accomplish the sort using the approach outlined above is to:

(1) Internally sort three blocks at a time (i.e., 750 records) to obtain six runs R_1- R_6. A method such as heap sort or quick sort could be used. These six runs are written out onto the scratch disk (Figure 7.28).

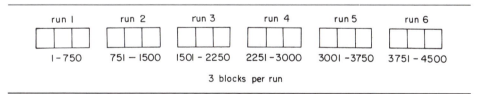

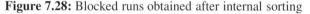

Figure 7.28: Blocked runs obtained after internal sorting

(2) Set aside three blocks of internal memory, each capable of holding 250 records. Two of these blocks will be used as input buffers and the third as an output buffer. Merge runs R_1 and R_2. This is carried out by first reading one block of each of these runs into input buffers. Blocks of runs are merged from the input buffers into the output buffer. When the output buffer gets full, it is written out onto disk. If an input buffer gets empty, it is refilled with another block from the same run. After runs R_1 and R_2 are merged, R_3 and R_4 and finally R_5 and R_6 are merged. The result of this pass is 3 runs, each containing 1500 sorted records or 6 blocks. Two of these runs are now merged using the input/output buffers set up as above to obtain a run of size 3000.

Finally, this run is merged with the remaining run of size 1500 to obtain the desired sorted file (Figure 7.29).

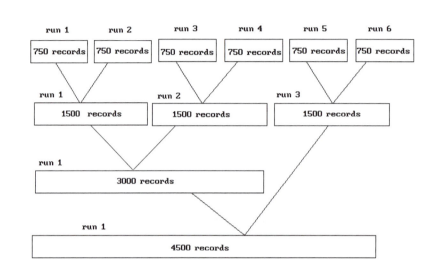

Figure 7.29: Merging the six runs

To determine the time required by the external sort, we use the following notation:

t_s = maximum seek time

t_l = maximum latency time

t_{rw} = time to read or write one block of 250 records

$t_{IO} = t_s + t_l + t_{rw}$

t_{IS} = time to internally sort 750 records

nt_m = time to merge n records from input buffers to the output buffer

We shall assume that each time a block is read from or written onto the disk, the maximum seek and latency times are experienced. While this is not true in general, it will simplify the analysis. The computing times for the various operations are given in Figure 7.30.

Note that the contribution of seek time can be reduced by writing consecutive blocks on the same track or on adjacent tracks. A close look a the final computing time indicates that it depends chiefly on the number of passes made over the data. In addition

operation	time
(1) read 18 blocks of input, $18t_{IO}$, internally sort, $6t_{IS}$, write 18 blocks, $18t_{IO}$	$36t_{IO}+6t_{IS}$
(2) merge runs 1-6 in pairs	$36t_{IO}+4500t_m$
(3) merge two runs of 1500 records each, 12 blocks	$24t_{IO}+3000t_m$
(4) merge one run of 3000 records with one run of 1500 records	$36t_{IO}+4500t_m$
total time	$132t_{IO} + 12000t_m + 6t_{IS}$

Figure 7.30 Computing times for disk sort example

to the intitial input pass made over the data for the internal sort, the merging of the runs requires 2-2/3 passes over the data (one pass to merge 6 runs of length 750 records, two thirds of a pass to merge two runs of length 1500 and one pass to merge one run of length 3000 and one of length 1500). Since one full pass covers 18 blocks, the input and output time is $2 \times (2\text{-}2/3 + 1) \times 18 \ t_{IO} = 132t_{IO}$. The leading factor of 2 appears because each record that is read is also written out again. The merge time is 2-2/3 $\times 4500t_m = 12{,}000t_m$. Because of this close relationship between the overall computing time and the number of passes made over the data, future analysis will be concerned mainly with counting the number of passes being made. Another point to note regarding the above sort is that no attempt was made to use the computer's ability to carry out input/output and CPU operation in parallel and thus overlap some of the time. In the ideal situation we would overlap almost all the input/output time with CPU processing so that the actual time would be approximately $132 \ t_{IO} \approx 12000 \ t_m + 6t_{IS}$.

If we had two disks, we could write on one while reading from the other and merging buffer loads already in memory all at the same time. In this case a proper choice of buffer lengths and buffer handling schemes would result in a time of almost $66t_{IO}$. This parallelism is an important consideration when sorting is being carried out in a non-multi-programming environment. In this situation unless input/output and CPU processing is going on in parallel, the CPU is idle during input/oputput. In a multi-programming environment, however, the need for the sorting program to carry out input/output and CPU processing in parallel may not be so critical since the CPU can be busy working on another program (if there are other programs in the system at the time), while the sort program waits for the completion of its input/output. Indeed, in many multi-programming environments it may not even be possible to achieve parallel input, output and internal computing because of the structure of the operation system.

The remainder of this section will concern itself with: (1) reduction of the number of passes being made over the data, (2) efficient utilization of program buffers so that input, output and CPU processing is overlapped as much as possible, (3) run generation, and (4) run merging.

7.11.2   *k*-way Merging

The 2-way merge algorithm *merge* is almost identical to the merge function just described (Figure 7.29). In general, if we started with *m* runs, then the merge tree corresponding to Figure 7.29 would have $\lceil \log_2 m \rceil + 1$ levels for a total of $\lceil \log_2 m \rceil$ passes over the data file. The number of passes over the data can be reduced by using a higher order merge, i.e., *k*-way merge for $k \geq 2$. In this case, we would simultaneously merge *k* runs together. Figure 7.31 illustrates a 4-way merge on 16 runs. The number of passes over the data is now 2, versus 4 passes in the case of a 2-way merge. In general, a *k*-way merge on *m* runs requires at most $\lceil \log_k m \rceil$ passes over the data (Figure 7.32). Thus, the input/output time may be reduced by using a higher order merge.

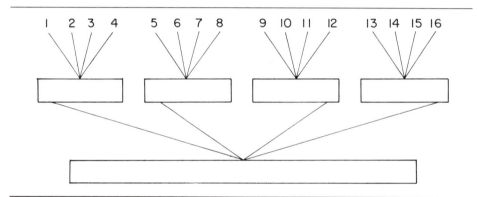

Figure 7.31: A 4-way merge on 16 runs

The use of a higher order merge, however, has some other effects on the sort. To begin with, *k*-runs of size $S_1, S_2, S_3, \ldots, S_k$ can no longer be merged internally in $O(\Sigma_1^k S_i)$ time. In a *k*-merge, as in a 2-way merge, the next record to be output is the one with the smallest key. The smallest has now to be found from *k* possibilities and it could be the leading record in any of the *k*-runs. The most direct way to merge *k*-runs would be to make $k - 1$ comparisons to determine the next record to output. The computing time for this would be $O((k - 1) \Sigma_1^k S_i)$. Since $\log_k m$ passes are being made, the total number of key comparisons being made is $n(k - 1)\log_k m = n(k - 1)\log_2 m / \log_2 k$ where *n* is the number of records in the file. Hence, $(k - 1)/\log_2 k$ is the factor by which the number of key comparisons increases. As *k* increases, the reduction in input/output time will be offset by the resulting increase in CPU time needed to perform the *k*-way merge.

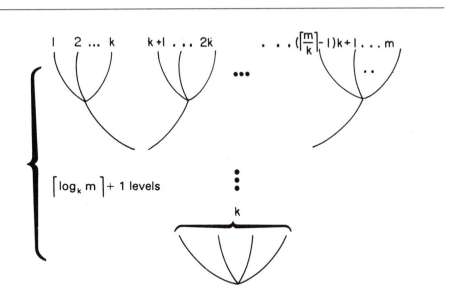

Figure 7.32: A k-way merge

For large k (say, $k \geq 6$) we can achieve a significant reduction in the number of comparisons needed to find the next smallest element by using a loser tree with k leaves (Chapter 5). In this case, the total time needed per level of the merge tree of Figure 7.32 is $O(n \log_2 k)$. Since the number of levels in this tree is $O(\log_k m)$, the asymptotic internal processing time becomes $O(n \log_2 k \log_k m) = O(n \log_2 m)$. The internal processing time is independent of k.

In going to a higher order merge, we save on the amount of input/output being carried out. There is no significant loss in internal processing speed. Even though the internal processing time is relatively insensitive to the order of the merge, the decrease in input/output time is not as much as indicated by the reduction to $\log_k m$ passes. This is so because the number of input buffers needed to carry out a k-way merge increases with k. Though $k + 1$ buffers are sufficient, we shall see in the next section that the use of $2k + 2$ buffers is more desirable. Since the internal memory available is fixed and independent of k, the buffer size must be reduced as k increases. This in turn implies a reduction in the block size on disk. With the reduced block size each pass over the data results in a greater number of blocks being written or read. This represents a potential increase in input/output time from the increased contribution of seek and latency times involved in reading a block of data. Hence, beyond a certain k value the input/output time would actually increase despite the decrease in the number of passes being made. The optimal value for k clearly depends on disk parameters and the amount of internal memory available for buffers.

7.11.3   Buffer Handling For Parallel Operation

If k runs are being merged together by a k-way merge, then we clearly need at least k input buffers and one output buffer to carry out the merge. This, however, is not enough if input, output, and internal merging are to be carried out in parallel. For instance, while the output buffer is being written out, internal merging has to be halted since there is no place to collect the merged records. This can be easily overcome through the use of two output buffers. While one is being written out, records are merged into the second. If buffer sizes are chosen correctly, then the time to output one buffer would be the same as the CPU time needed to fill the second buffer. With only k input buffers, internal merging will have to be held up whenever one of these input buffers becomes empty and another block from the corresponding run is being read in. This input delay can also be avoided if we have $2k$ input buffers. These $2k$ input buffers have to be cleverly used in order to avoid reaching a situation in which processing has to be held up because of lack of input records from any one run. Simply assigning two buffers per run does not solve the problem. To see this, consider the following example:

Example 7.12: Assume that a two way merge is being carried out using four input buffers, $in[i]$, $1 \le i \le 4$, and two output buffers, $ou[1]$ and $ou[2]$. Each buffer is capable of holding two records. The first few records of run 1 have key value 1, 3, 5, 7, 8, 9. The first few records of run 2 have key value 2, 4, 6, 15, 20, 25. Buffers $in[1]$ and $in[3]$ are assigned to run 1. The remaining two input buffers are assigned to run 2. We start the merging by reading in one buffer load from each of the two runs. At this time the buffers have the configuration of Figure 7.33(a). Now runs 1 and 2 are merged using records from $in[1]$ and $in[2]$. In parallel with this the next buffer load from run 1 is input. If we assume that buffer lengths have been chosen such that the times to input, output and generate an output buffer are all the same, then when $ou[1]$ is full we have the situation of Figure 7.33(b). Next, we simultaneously output $ou[1]$, input into $in[4]$ from run 2 and merge into $ou[2]$. When $ou[2]$ is full we are in the situation of Figure 7.33(c). Continuing in this way we reach the configuration of Figure 7.33(e). We now begin to output $ou[2]$, input from run 1 into $in[3]$ and merge into $ou[1]$. During the merge, all records from run 1 get exhausted before $ou[1]$ gets full. The generation of merged output must now be delayed until the inputting of another buffer load from run 1 is completed. □

Example 7.12 makes it clear that if $2k$ input buffers are to suffice then we cannot assign two buffers per run. Instead, the buffer must be floating in the sense that an individual buffer may be assigned to any run depending upon need. In the buffer assignment strategy we shall describe, for each run there will at any time be at least one input buffer containing records from that run. The remaining buffers will be filled on a priority basis; i.e., the run for which the k-way merging algorithm will run out of records first is the one from which the next buffer will be filled. One may easily predict which run's records will be exhausted first by simply comparing the keys of the last record read from each of

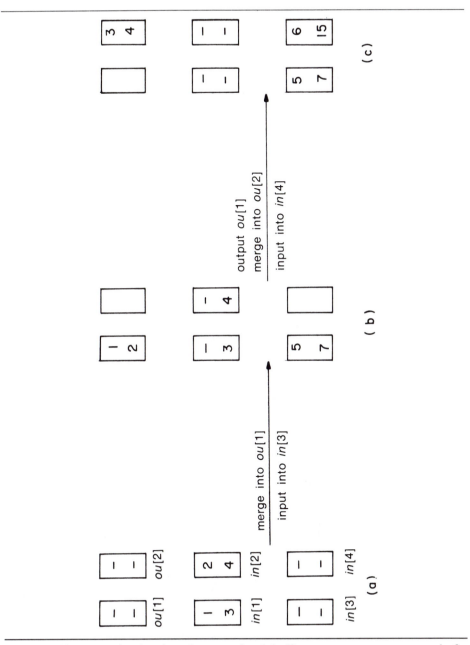

Figure 7.33: Example showing that two fixed buffers per run are not enough for continued parallel operation

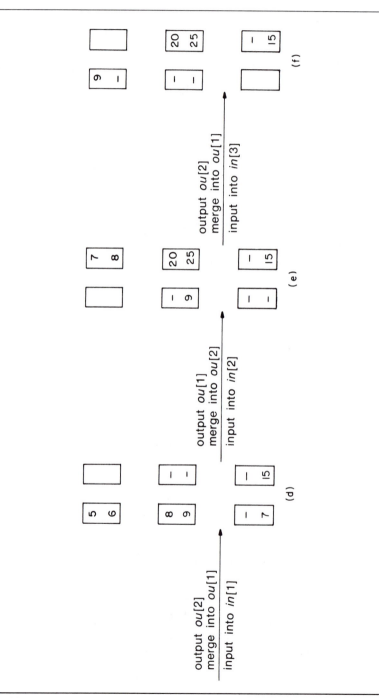

Figure 7.33 (continued): Example

the k runs. The smallest such key determines this run. We shall assume that in the case of equal keys, the merge process first merges the record from the run with least index. This means that if the key of the last record read from run i is equal to the key of the last record read from run j, and $i < j$, then the records read from i will be exhausted before those from j. So, it is possible that at any one time we might have more than two bufferloads from a given run and only one partially full buffer from another run. All bufferloads from the same run are queued together. Before formally presenting the algorithm for buffer utilization, we make the following assumptions about the parallel processing capabilities of the computer system available:

(1)   We have two disk drives and the input/output channel is such that it is possible simultaneously to read from one disk and write onto the other.

(2)   While data transmission is taking place between an input/output device and a block of memory, the CPU cannot make references to that same block of memory. Thus, it is not possible to start filling the front of an output buffer while it is being written out. If this were possible, then by coordinating the transmission and merging rate only one output buffer would be needed. By the time the first record for the new output block was determined, the first record of the previous output block would have been written out.

(3)   To simplify the discussion we assume that input and output buffers are to be the same size.

Keeping these assumptions in mind, we provide a high level description of the algorithm obtained using the strategy outlined earlier and then illustrate its working through an example. Our algorithm, Program 7.20, merges k-runs, $k \geq 2$, using a k-way merge. $2k$ input buffers and 2 output buffers are used. Each buffer is a contiguous block of memory. Input buffers are queued in k queues, one queue for each run. It is assumed that each input/output buffer is long enough to hold one block of records. Empty buffers are placed on a linked stack. The algorithm also assumes that the end of each run has a sentinel record with a very large key, say $+\infty$. It is assumed that all records other than the sentinel records have key value less than this. If block lengths, and hence buffer lengths, are chosen such that the time to merge one output buffer load equals the time to read a block, then almost all input, output, and computation will be carried out in parallel. It is also assumed that in the case of equal keys the k-way merge algorithm first outputs the record from the run with smallest index.

We make the following observations about Program 7.20.

(1)   For large k, determination of the queue that will exhaust first can be made in $\log_2 k$ comparisons by setting up a selection tree for $last[i]$, $1 \leq i \leq k$, rather than making $k - 1$ comparisons each time a buffer load is to be read in. The change in computing time will not be significant, since this queue selection represents only a very

---

/* Steps in buffering algorithm */

Step 1: Input the first block of each of the k runs setting up k linked queues each having one block of data.
Put the remaining k input blocks into a linked stack of free input blocks.
Set *ou* to 0.

Step 2: Let *lastkey* [i] be the last key input from run i. Let *nextrun* be the run for which *lastkey* is minimum. If *lastkey* [*nextrun*] $\neq +\infty$ then initiate the input of the next block from run *nextrun*.

Step 3: Use a function *kwaymerge* to merge records from the k input queues into the output buffer *ou*. Merging continues until either the output buffer gets full or a record with key $+\infty$ is merged into *ou*. If, during this merge, an input buffer becomes empty before the output buffer gets full or before a $+\infty$ is merged into *ou*, the *kwaymerge* advances to the next buffer on the same queue and returns the empty buffer to the stack of empty buffers. However, if an input buffer becomes empty at the same time as the output buffer gets full or $+\infty$ is merged into *ou*, the empty buffer is left on the queue and *kwaymerge* does not advance to the next buffer on the queue. Rather, the merge terminates.

Step 4: Wait for any ongoing disk input/output to complete.

Step 5: If an input buffer has been read, add it to the queue for the appropriate run. Determine the next run to read from by determining *nextrun* such that *lastkey* [*nextrun*] is minimum.

Step 6: If *lastkey* [*nextrun*] $\neq +\infty$, then initiate reading the next block from run *nextrun* into a free input buffer.

Step 7: Initiate the writing of output buffer *ou*. Set $ou = 1 - ou$.

Step 8: If a record with key $+\infty$ has been not been merged into the output buffer go back to step 3. Otherwise, wait for the ongoing write to complete and then terminate.

Program 7.20 Buffering

small fraction of the total time taken by the algorithm.

(2)   For large k, the function *kwaymerge* uses a tree of losers as discussed in Chapter 5.

(3)   All input/output except for the initial k blocks that are read and the last block output is done concurrently with computing. Since after k runs have been merged we would probably begin to merge another set of k runs, the input for the next set can commence during the final merge stages of the present set of runs. That is, when *lastkey* [*nextrun*] $= +\infty$ in step 6, we begin reading one by one the first blocks from each of the next set of k runs to be merged. In this case, over the entire sorting of a file, the only time that is not overlapped with the internal merging time is the time for the first k blocks of input and that for the last block of output.

(4)   The algorithm assumes that all blocks are of the same length. This may require inserting a few dummy records into the last block of each run following the sentinel record with key $+\infty$.

Example 7.13: To illustrate the working of the above algorithm, let us trace through it while it performs a three-way merge on the three runs of Figure 7.34. Each run consists of four blocks of two records each; the last key in the fourth block of each of these three runs is $+\infty$. We have six input buffers, and two output buffers. Figure 7.35 shows the status of the input buffer queues, the run from which the next block is being read and the output buffer being output at the beginning of each iteration of the loop of steps 3 through 8 of the buffering algorithm.

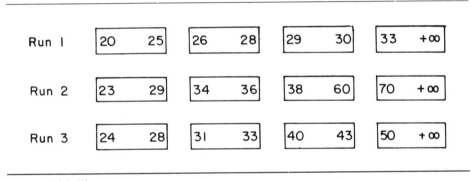

Figure 7.34: Three runs

From line 5 of Figure 7.35 it is evident that during the k-way merge the test for "output buffer full?" should be carried out before the test "input buffer empty?", as the next input buffer for that run may not have been read in yet, and so there would be no next buffer in that queue. In lines 3 and 4 all 6 input buffers are in use and the stack of free buffers is empty. □

We end our discussion of buffer handling by proving that Program 7.20 is correct. This is stated formally in Theorem 7.2.

Theorem 7.2: The following is true for Program 7.20:

(1)   In step 6, there is always a buffer available in which to begin reading the next block; and

(2)   during the k-way merge of step 3, the next block in the queue has been read in by the time it is needed.

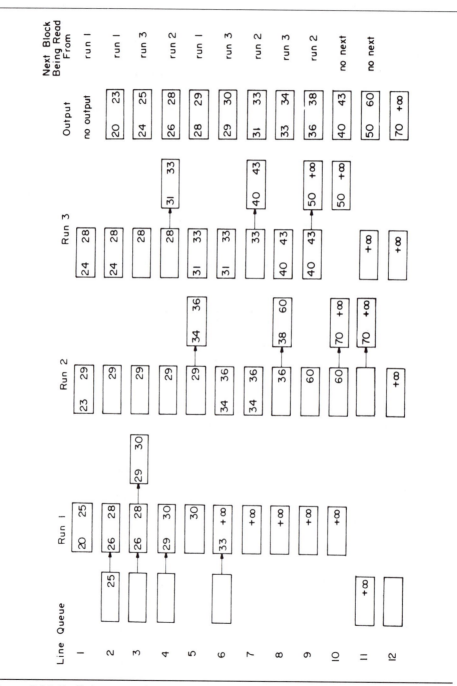

Figure 7.35: Buffering example

Proof: (1) Each time we get to step 6 of the algorithm there are at most $k+1$ buffer loads in memory, one of these being in an output buffer. For each queue there can be at most one buffer that is partially full. If no buffer is available for the next read, then the remaining k buffers must be full. This means that all the k partially full buffers are empty (as otherwise there will be more than $k+1$ buffer loads in memory). From the way the merge is set up, only one buffer can be both unavailable and empty. This may happen only if the output buffer gets full exactly when one input buffer becomes empty. But $k > 1$ contradicts this. So, there is always at least one buffer available when step 6 is being executed.

(2) Assume this is false. Let run R_i be the one whose queue becomes empty during *kwaymerge*. We may assume that the last key merged was not $+\infty$, since otherwise *kwaymerge* would terminate the merge rather then get another buffer for R_i. This means that there are more blocks of records for run R_i on the input file and *lastkey* $[i] \neq +\infty$. Consequently, up to this time whenever a block was output another was simultaneously read in. Input and output therefore proceeded at the same rate and the number of available blocks of data is always k. An additional block is being read in, but it does not get queued until step 5. Since the queue for R_i has become empty first, the selection rule for the next run to read from ensures that there is at most one block of records for each of the remaining $k-1$ runs. Furthermore, the output buffer cannot be full at this time as this condition is tested for before the input buffer empty condition. Thus there are fewer than k blocks of data in memory. This contradicts our earlier assertion that there must be exactly k such blocks of data. □

7.11.4   Run Generation

Using conventional internal sorting methods such as those of this chapter, it is possible to generate runs that are only as large as the number of records that can be held in internal memory at one time. Using a tree of losers, it is possible to do better than this. In fact, the algorithm we shall present will on the average generate runs that are twice as long as obtainable by conventional methods. This algorithm was devised by Walters, Painter, and Zalk. In addition to being capable of generating longer runs, this algorithm will allow for parallel input, output and internal processing. For almost all the internal sort methods of this chapter, this parallelism is not possible. Heap sort is an exception to this.

We describe the run generation algorithm as though input, output, and internal processing are not being overlapped. It should be obvious that these can be effectively overlapped by the use of two input and two output buffers. The run generation algorithm assumes that there is enough space in internal memory to construct a loser tree for k records, where k is the number of nodes in the tree. To construct the tree we use the following C declarations for the case $k = 16$.

```
#define k 16          /* nodes in the tree */
typedef struct {
        int key;
        int run;
        } element;
typedef struct {
        element data;
        int loser;
        } tree_node;
tree_node tree[k];
```

Each of the k record positions has a run number, *tree[i].data.run*, $0 \le i < k$. This field enables us to determine whether we can output *tree[i].data.run* as part of the run we are currently generating. Whenever we output a tournament winner, we input a new record (if there is one) and we replay the tournament. *run_generation* (Program 7.21) implements the loser tree strategy. The function uses an *open_input* function (Program 7.22) to check the input file. The variables used in *run_generation* have the following significance.

tree[i].data, $0 \le i < k$	k records in the tree
tree[i].data.key	key value of record, *tree[i].data*
tree[i].data.run	run number to which *tree[i].data* belongs
tree[i].loser	loser of the tournament played at node *i*
current_run	run number of current run
winner	position of overall tournament winner, [0]
winner_run	run number for *tree[winner].data*
max_runs	number of runs that will be generated
last_key	key value of last record output

```
void run_generation(char *in_name, char *out_name)
{
/* generate runs using a loser tree */

   int winner = 0, winner_run = 0, current_run = 0;
   int max_runs = 0, last_key = INT_MAX;
   int i, parent, loser, temp;
   FILE *in, *out;

   in = open_input(in_name);
   out = fopen(out_name,"wb");
   for (i = 1; i < k; i++) {
```

```
/*set up tree with dummy nodes */
   tree[i].data.key = 0;
   tree[i].data.run = 0;
   tree[i].loser = i;
}
tree[winner].data.run = 0;

for (;;) {
   if (winner_run != current_run) {
      if (winner_run > max_runs) {
      /* last record reached, close files and return */
         fclose(in); fclose(out);
         return;
      }
      current_run = winner_run;
   }

   if (winner_run) {
   /*suppress output if dummy records */
      fwrite(&tree[winner].data, sizeof(element),1,out);
      last_key = tree[winner].data.key;
   }
   fread(&tree[winner].data,sizeof(element),1,in);
   if(feof(in)) { /* signal to end proccessing */
      winner_run = max_runs + 1;
      tree[winner].data.run = winner_run;
   }
   else {
      if (tree[winner].data.key < last_key) {
         winner_run++;
         tree[winner].data.run = winner_run;
         max_runs = winner_run;
      }
      else
         tree[winner].data.run = current_run;
   }
   /* adjust tree */
   parent = (k + winner) / 2;
   while (parent) {
      loser = tree[parent].loser;
      if (tree[loser].data.run < winner_run ||
      (tree[loser].data.run == winner_run &&
      tree[loser].data.key < tree[winner].data.key)) {
         temp = winner;
```

```
            winner = tree[parent].loser;
            tree[parent].loser = temp;
            winner_run = tree[winner].data.run;
         }
         parent /= 2;
      }
   }
}
```

Program 7.21: Run generation using a loser tree

```
FILE *open_input(char *source_name)
{
   FILE *source;
   source = fopen(source_name, "rb");
   if (!source) {
      fprintf(stderr, "File %s cannot be opened
      for input\n",source_name);
      exit(1);
   }
   return source;
}
```

Program 7.22: *open_input* function

The **for(;;)** loop in *tree_runs* repeatedly plays the tournament, outputting records and restructuring the tree. To correctly set up the tree we create a fictitious run numbered 0. (The **for** loop prior to the **for(;;)** loop does this.) Thus, we have *tree[i].data.run* = 0 for each of the k records. Since all but one of these records must be a loser exactly once, the initialization of *tree[i].loser* = i sets up a loser tree with *tree[0].data* as the winner. Once initialized, the **for(;;)** loop can correctly set up the loser tree for run 1. The test *if(winner_run)* suppresses the output of the k fictitious records making up run 0. We use the variable *last_key* to determine whether or not we can output the new record input, *tree[winner].data*, as part of the current run. If *tree[winner].data.key < last_key* then *tree[winner].data* is smaller than the last outputted record. Therefore, we cannot output it as part of the curent run. When we readjust the tree, a record with a lower run number wins over a record with a higher run number. When the run numbers are equal, the record with the lower key value wins. This ensures that records come out of the tree in nondecreasing order of their key values. We use *max_runs* to terminate the algorithm. Thus, when we run out of input, we introduce a record with run number *max_runs* + 1. When this record is ready for output, the algorithm terminates. We may easily verify that when the input file is already sorted, only one run is generated.

Analysis of *run-generation*: On the average, the run size for *tree-runs* is almost $2k$. The time required to generate all the runs for an n record input file is $O(n \log k)$. We may speed up the algorithm slightly by explicitly initializing the loser tree using the first k records of the input file rather than k fictitious records. In this case we may remove the **if** statement that suppresses output of these records. □

7.11.5   Optimal Merging Of Runs

The runs generated by *run_generation* may not be of the same size. When runs are of different size, the run merging strategy employed so far (i.e., make complete passes over the collection of runs) does not yield minimum merge times. For example, suppose we have four runs of length 2, 4, 5, and 15, respectively. Figure 7.36 shows two possible ways to merge these runs using a series of two-way merges. The round nodes represent a two-way merge with the data in the children nodes as input. The square nodes represent the initial runs. We refer to the round nodes as *internal nodes* and the square ones as *external nodes*. Each figure is a merge tree.

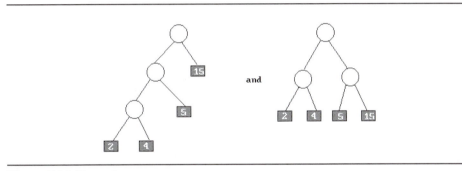

Figure 7.36: Example trees

In the first merge tree, we begin by merging the runs of size two and four to obtain a run of size six. Next, we merge this run with the run of size five to obtain a run of size 11. Finally, we merge the run with length 11 with the run of size 15 to obtain the desired sorted run of size 26. When we merge by using the first merge tree, we merge some records only once, while others may be merged up to three times. In the second merge tree, we merge each record exactly twice. This corresponds to the strategy in which we repeatedly make complete merge passes over the data.

The number of merges that involve an individual record is given by the distance of the corresponding external node from the root. For example, the records in the run of 15 records are merged only once for the first tree of Figure 7.36 and twice for the second tree of Figure 7.36. Since the time for a merge is linear in the number of records being merged, we obtain the total merge time by summing the products of the run lengths and the distance from the root of the corresponding external nodes. We call this sum the *weighted external path length*. For the two trees of Figure 7.36, the respective weighted external path lengths are:

$$2 \cdot 3 + 4 \cdot 3 + 5 \cdot 2 + 15 \cdot 1 = 43$$

and

$$2 \cdot 2 + 4 \cdot 2 + 5 \cdot 2 + 15 \cdot 2 = 52.$$

The cost of a k-way merge of n runs of length q_i, $1 \le i \le n$ is minimized by using a merge tree of degree k which has minimum weighted external path length. Although we shall explicitly consider only the case $k = 2$, we can easily generalize to the case $k > 2$ (see the exercises).

A very nice solution to the problem of finding a binary tree with minimum weighted external path length has been given by D. Huffman. We simply state his algorithm and leave the correctness proof as an exercise. The following type declarations are assumed:

```
typedef struct tree_node *tree_pointer;
typedef struct tree_node {
        tree_pointer left_child;
        int          weight;
        tree_pointer right_child;
};
tree_pointer tree;
int n;
```

The *huffman* function (Program 7.23) begins with n extended binary trees, each containing one node. These are in the array *heap* []. Each node in a tree has three fields: *weight*, *left_child*, and *right_child*. The single node in each of the initial extended binary trees has as weight of one of the q_i's. During the course of the algorithm, for any tree in *heap* with root node *tree* and depth greater than 1, *tree* $->$ *weight* is the sum of the weights of all external nodes in *tree*. The *huffman* function uses the functions *least* and *insert*; *least* finds a tree in *heap* with minimum weight and removes it from *list*; *insert* adds a new tree to *list*. These are simply the delete min and insert operations on a min heap. The function *initialize* initializes the min heap. As discussed in Section 7.7, this can be done in linear time.

We illustrate the way this algorithm works by an example. Suppose we have the weights $q_1 = 2$, $q_2 = 3$, $q_3 = 5$, $q_4 = 7$, $q_5 = 9$, and $q_6 = 13$. The sequence of trees we would get is given in Figure 7.37 (the number in a circular node represents the sum of the weights of external nodes in that subtree).

The weighted external path length of this tree is:

$$2 \cdot 4 + 3 \cdot 4 + 5 \cdot 3 + 13 \cdot 2 + 7 \cdot 2 + 9 \cdot 2 = 93$$

```
void huffman(tree_pointer heap[], int n)
{
/* heap is a list of n single node binary trees */
   tree_pointer tree;
   int i;
   /* initialize min heap */
   initialize(heap, n);
   /* create a new tree by combining the trees with the
   smallest weights until one tree remains */

   for (i = 1; i < n; i++) {
      tree = (tree_pointer)
                            malloc(sizeof(tree_node));
      if (IS_FULL(tree)) {
         fprintf(stderr, "The memory is full\n");
         exit(1);
      }
      tree ->left_child = least(heap, n-i+1);
      tree->right_child = least(heap, n-i);
      tree->weight = tree->left_child->weight +
      tree->right_child->weight;
      insert(heap,n-i-1,tree);
   }
}
```

Program 7.23: Huffman function

In comparison, the best complete binary tree has weighted path length 95.

Analysis of *huffman*: Heap initialization takes O(n) time. The main **for** loop is executed $n - 1$ times. Each call to *least* and *insert* requires only O(log n) time. Hence, the asymptotic computing time for the algorithm is O(n log n). □

EXERCISES

1. (a) n records are to be sorted on a computer with a memory capacity of S records ($S \ll n$). Assume that the entire S record capacity may be used for input/output buffers. The input is on disk and consists of m runs. Assume that each time a disk access in made the seek time is t_s and the latency time is t_l. The transmission time is t_t per record transmitted. What is the total input time for phase II of external sorting if a k-way merge is used with

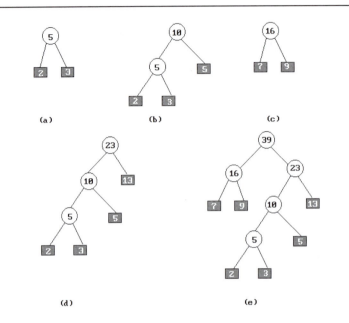

Figure 7.37: Construction of a Huffman tree

internal memory partitioned into I/O buffers so as to permit overlap of input, output and CPU processing as in algorithm *buffering*?

(b) Let the CPU time needed to merge all the runs together be t_{CPU} (we may assume it is independent of k and hence constant). Let $t_s = 80$ *ms*, $t_l = 20ms$, $n = 200,000$, $m = 64$, $t_t = 10^{-3}$ sec/record, $S = 2000$. Obtain a rough plot of the total input time, t_{input}, versus k. Will there always be a value of k for which $t_{CPU} \approx t_{input}$?

2. Modify *run_generation* so that it initializes the loser tree using the first k records rather than k fictitious records.

3. (a) Show that function *huffman* correctly generates a binary tree of minimal weighted external path length.

(b) When n runs are to be merged together using an m-way merge, Huffman's method generalizes to the following rule: First add $(1 - n) \% (m - 1)$ runs of length zero to the set of runs. Then repeatedly merge together the m shortest remaining runs until only one run is left. Show that this rule yields an optimal merge pattern for m-way merging.

7.12   REFERENCES AND SELECTED READINGS

A comprehensive discussion of sorting may be found in D. Knuth, *The Art of Computer Programming: Sorting and Searching*. vol. 3, Addison-Wesley, Reading, Massachusetts, 1973.

Two other useful sources on sorting are H. Lorin, *Sorting and Sort Systems*, Addison-Wesley, Reading, Massachusetts, 1975, and R. Rich,*Internal Sorting Methods Illustrated with PL/1 Programs*, Prentice-Hall, Englewood Cliffs, NJ, 1972.

Two references on quick sort are C. A. R. Hoare, *"Quicksort,"* The Computer Journal*, vol. 5, 1962, pp. 10-15, and R. Sedgewick, *"The analysis of quick sort programs,"* Acta Informatica*, vol. 7, 1976-1977, pp. 327-355.

Figures 7.26 and 7.27 are taken from S. Sahni, *Software Development in Pascal*, Camelot Publishing Co., 1985.

The $O(1)$ space linear time merge algorithm is from the paper B. Huang and M. Langston, *"Practical in-place merging,"* CACM*, vol. 31, no. 3, 1988, pp. 348-352.

An in-depth analysis of the computing times of several sorting techniques can be found in G. H. Gonnet, *Handbook of Algorithms and Data Structures*, Addison-Wesley, Reading, Massachusetts, 1984, and S. Baase, *Computer Algorithms: Introduction to Design and Analysis*, Addison-Wesley, Reading, Massachusetts, 1987.

7.13   ADDITIONAL EXERCISES

1. [***Count sort***] About the simplest known sorting method arises from the observation that the position of a record in a sorted list depends on the number of records with smaller keys. Associated with each record there is a count field used to determine the number of records that must precede this one in the sorted list. Write an algorithm to determine the count of each record in an unordered list. Show that if the list has *n* records, then all the counts can be determined by making at most $n(n - 1)/2$ key comparisons.

2. Write a function similar to *table_sort* to rearrange the records of a list if with each record we have a count of the number of records preceding it in the sorted list (see the preceding exercise). What is the complexity of your algorithm?

3. [***Exchange sort***] Another simple sorting technique works by exchanging adjacent elements that are out of order. The sort is frequently called a bubble sort because at each iteration the current highest element bubbles to the highest unsorted position of the array. Write a function that implements exchange sort. What is its computing time?

4. [***Exchange sort***] We can take advantage of the fact that exchange sort makes very few exchanges when the input sequence is in nearly sorted order. This requires adding an "exchange" flag to the outer loop. The flag holds *TRUE* if an exchange was made during the current iteration and *FALSE* if no exchange took place. The sort terminates when the end of the list is encountered or the flag becomes *FALSE*. Rewrite the exchange sort to take into account this variation.

5. [*Shaker sort*] This is also a variation of exchange sort in which the record with the highest key is bubbled into the last list position on the first iteration. On the second iteration, the record with the lowest key is placed in the first position. The sort alternates in this fashion until the list is sorted. Write a function that performs a shaker sort. What is its computing time?

6. Write the status of the list L = (12, 2, 16, 30, 8, 28, 4, 10, 20, 6, 18) after each phase of the following algorithms:

    (a)   *insertion_sort*

    (b)   *quicksort*

    (c)   *merge_sort*

    (d)   *heapsort*

    (e)   *radix_sort* with radix = 10

7. Assume you are working in the census department of a small town where the number of records, about 3000, is small enough to fit into the internal memory of a computer. All the people currently living in this town were born in the United States. There is one record for each person in this town. Each records contains:

    (a)   the state in which the person was born

    (b)   the person's county of birth

    (c)   the name of the person.

    How would you produce a list of all persons living in this town? The list is to be ordered by state. Within each state the persons are to be listed by their counties, the counties being arranged in alphabetical order. Justify any assumptions you may make.

CHAPTER **8**

HASHING

8.1 THE SYMBOL TABLE ABSTRACT DATA TYPE

We have all used a *dictionary*, and many of us have a word processor equipped with a limited dictionary, that is, a spelling checker. In this chapter, we consider the dictionary, as an ADT. Examples of dictionaries are found in many applications, including the spelling checker, the thesaurus, the data dictionary found in database management applications, and the symbol tables generated by loaders, assemblers, and compilers.

In computer science, we generally use the term *symbol table* rather than dictionary, when referring to the ADT. Viewed from this perspective, we define the symbol table as a *set of name-attribute pairs*. The characteristics of the name and attribute vary according to the application. For example, in a thesaurus, the name is a word, and the attribute is a list of synonyms for the word; in a symbol table for a compiler, the name is an identifier, and the attributes might include an initial value and a list of lines that use the identifier.

Generally we would want to perform the following operations on any symbol table:

> (1) determine if a particular name is in the table
> (2) retrieve the attributes of that name
> (3) modify the attributes of that name
> (4) insert a new name and its attributes

(5) delete a name and its attributes.

Structure 8.1 provides the complete specification of the symbol table ADT.

---

structure *SymbolTable(SymTab)* is
    objects: a set of name-attribute pairs, where the names are unique.
    functions:
        for all *name* ∈ *Name*, *attr* ∈ *Attribute*, *symtab* ∈ *SymbolTable*, *max−size* ∈ integer.

SymTab Create(*max−size*)	::=	create the empty symbol table whose maximum capacity is *max−size*.
Boolean IsIn(*symtab, name*)	::=	**if** (*name* is in *symtab*) **return** *TRUE* **else return** *FALSE*.
Attribute Find(*symtab, name*)	::=	**if** (*name* is in *symtab*) **return** the corresponding attribute **else return** null attribute.
SymTab Insert(*symtab, name, attr*)	::=	**if** (*name* is in *symtab*) replace its existing attribute with *attr* **else** insert the pair (*name, attr*) into *symtab*.
SymTab Delete(*symtab, name*)	::=	**if** (*name* is not in *symtab*) **return** **else** delete (*name, attr*) from *symtab*.

Structure 8.1: Abstract data type *SymbolTable*

Although Structure 8.1 lists several operations, there are only three basic operations on symbol tables: searching, inserting, and deleting. Therefore, when choosing a symbol table representation, we must make sure that we can implement these operations efficiently. For example, we could use the binary search tree introduced in Section 5.7 to represent a symbol table. If our search tree contained n identifiers, the worst case complexity for these operations would be O(n). In Chapter 10 we introduce several refinements of binary search tree that reduce the time per operation to O(log n). In this chapter we examine a technique for search, insert, and delete operations that has very good expected performance. The technique is referred to as *hashing*. Unlike search tree methods which rely on identifier comparisons to perform a search, hashing relies on a formula called the *hash function*. We divide our discussion of hashing into two parts: *static hashing* and *dynamic hashing*.

8.2 STATIC HASHING

8.2.1 Hash Tables

In *static hashing*, we store the identifiers in a fixed size table called a *hash table*. We use an arithmetic function, f, to determine the address, or location, of an identifier, x, in the table. Thus, $f(x)$ gives the hash, or home address, of x in the table. The hash table ht is stored in sequential memory locations that are partitioned into b buckets, $ht[0], \dots, ht[b-1]$. Each bucket has s slots. Usually $s = 1$, which means that each bucket holds exactly one record. We use the hash function $f(x)$ to transform the identifier x into an address in the hash table. Thus, $f(x)$ maps the set of possible identifiers onto the integers 0 through $b-1$. If we limit the length of identifiers to six characters, where the first character must be a letter and the remaining characters can be a letter or a decimal digit, then there are $T = \sum_{i=0}^{5} 26 \times 36^i > 1.6 \times 10^9$ distinct possible values for x. However, any reasonable application would never have this many identifiers. We use T, as well as b and s, to determine the *identifier* and *loading density* of a hash table. Later we will use these statistics to estimate the efficiency of hashing operations.

Definition: The *identifier density* of a hash table is the ratio n/T, where n is the number of identifiers in the table. The *loading density* or *loading factor* of a hash table is $\alpha = n/(sb)$. $\square$

Since the number of buckets b in a hash table is usually several orders of magnitude lower than the total number of possible identifiers T, the hash function f must map several different identifiers into the same bucket. Two identifiers, i_1 and i_2, are *synonyms* with respect to f if $f(i_1) = f(i_2)$. We enter distinct synonyms into the same bucket as long as the bucket has slots available. An *overflow* occurs when we hash a new identifier, i, into a full bucket. A *collision* occurs when we hash two nonidentical identifiers into the same bucket. When the bucket size is 1, collisions and overflows occur simultaneously.

Example 8.1: Consider the hash table ht with $b = 26$ buckets and $s = 2$. We have $n = 10$ distinct identifiers, each representing a C library function. This table has a loading factor, α, of $10/52 = 0.19$. The hash function must map each of the possible identifiers onto one of the numbers, 0–25. We can construct a fairly simple hash function by associating the letters, $a-z$, with the numbers, 0–25, respectively, and then defining the hash function, $f(x)$, as the first character of x. Using this scheme, the library functions **acos**, **define**, **float**, **exp**, **char**, **atan**, **ceil**, **floor**, **clock**, and **ctime** hash into buckets 0, 3, 5, 4, 2, 0, 2, 5, 2, and 2, respectively. Figure 8.1 shows the first 8 identifiers entered into the hash table.

	Slot 0	Slot 1
0	**acos**	**atan**
1		
2	**char**	**ceil**
3	**define**	
4	**exp**	
5	**float**	**floor**
6		
. . .		
25		

Figure 8.1: Hash table with 26 buckets and two slots per bucket

The identifiers **acos** and **atan** are synonyms, as are **float** and **floor**, and **ceil** and **char**. The next identifier, **clock**, hashes into the bucket ht [2]. Since this bucket is full, we have an overflow. Where in the table should we place **clock** so that we may retrieve it when necessary? We consider various solutions to the overflow problem in Sections 8.2.3. and 8.2.4 □

Assume, for a moment, that no overflows occur. Then the time required to enter, delete, or search for identifiers using hashing depends only on the time required to compute the hash function and to search one bucket. Since the bucket size is usually small, we may use a sequential search to look for an identifier within a bucket. Hence, the time required to enter, delete, or search for identifiers does not depend on the number of identifiers n in use; it is O(1).

Our choice of a hash function in Example 8.1 is not well suited for most applications since a large number of collisions and overflows is likely. For example, we have already seen that many C functions begin with the same letter; the same is true of variable names. Ideally, we would like to choose a hash function that is both easy to compute and produces few collisions. Unfortunately, since the ratio b/T is usually small, we cannot avoid collisions altogether.

8.2.2 Hashing Functions

A hash function, f, transforms an identifier, x, into a bucket address in the hash table. As mentioned above, we want a hash function that is easy to compute and that minimizes the number of collisions. Although the hash function we used in Example 8.1 was easy to compute, using only the first character in an identifier is bound to have disastrous consequences. We know that identifiers, whether they represent variable names in a program, words in a dictionary, or names in a telephone book, cluster around certain letters of the alphabet. To avoid collisions, the hash function should depend on all the characters in an identifier. It also should be unbiased. That is, if we randomly choose an identifier, x, from the identifier space (the universe of all possible identifiers), the probability that $f(x) = i$ is $1/b$ for all buckets i. This means that a random x has an equal chance of hashing into any of the b buckets. We call a hash function that satisfies this property a *uniform hash function*.

There are several types of uniform hash functions, and we shall describe four of them. We assume that the identifiers have been suitably transformed into a numerical equivalent. (Later we will describe a simple transformation.)

Mid-square

The *middle of square* hash function is frequently used in symbol table applications. We compute the function f_m by squaring the identifier and then using an appropriate number of bits from the middle of the square to obtain the bucket address. (We assume that the identifier fits into one computer word.) Since the middle bits of the square usually depend upon all the characters in an identifier, there is a high probability that different identifiers will produce different hash addresses, even when some of the characters are the same. The number of bits used to obtain the bucket address depends on the table size. If we use r bits, the range of the values is 2^r. Therefore, the size of the hash table should be a power of 2 when we use this scheme.

Division

We obtain a second simple hash function by using the modulus (%) operator. In this scheme, we divide the identifier x by some number M and use the remainder as the hash address for x. The hash function is:

$$f_D(x) = x \ \% \ M$$

This gives bucket addresses that range from 0 to $M - 1$, where M = the table size. The choice of M is critical. Recall that when we use the *middle of square* function f_m the table size should be a power of 2. In the division function, if M is a power of 2, then $f_D(x)$ depends only on the least significant bits of x. Such a choice for M results in a biased use of the hash table when several of the identifiers in use have the same suffix. If M is divisible by 2, then odd keys are mapped to odd buckets, and even keys are mapped to even buckets. Hence, an even M results in a biased use of the table when a majority of identifiers are even or when a majority are odd.

Let $X = x_1 x_2$ and $Y = x_2 x_1$ be two identifiers each consisting of the characters x_1 and x_2. If the internal binary representation of x_1 has value $C(x_1)$ and that for x_2 has value $C(x_2)$ then if each character is represented by six bits, the numeric value of X is $2^6 C(x_1) + C(x_2)$ while that for Y is $2^6 C(x_2) + C(x_1)$. If p is a prime number dividing

M then

$$(f_D(X) - f_D(Y)) \% p = (2^6 C(x_1) \% p + C(x_2) \% p$$
$$- 2^6 C(x_2) \% p - C(x_1) \% p) \% p$$

If $p = 3$, then

$$(f_D(X) - f_D(Y)) \% p = (64 \% 3 \ C(x_1) \% 3 + C(x_2) \% 3$$
$$- 64 \% 3 \ C(x_2) \% 3 - C(x_1) \% 3) \% 3$$
$$= C(x_1) \% 3 + C(x_2) \% 3 - C(x_2) \% 3 - C(x_1) \% 3$$
$$= 0 \% 3$$

i.e., permutations of the same set of characters are hashed at a distance a factor of 3 apart. So, when many identifiers are permutations of each other, a biased use of the table results. This happens because 64 % 3 = 1. The same behavior can be expected when 7 divides *M* as 64 % 7 = 1.

These difficulties can be avoided by choosing *M* as a prime number. Then, the only factors of *M* are *M* and 1. Knuth has shown that when *M* divides $r^k \pm a$ where *k* and *a* are small numbers and *r* is the radix of the character set (in the above example $r = 64$), then *X* % *M* tends to be a simple superposition of the characters in *X*. Thus, a good choice for *M* would be: *M a prime number such that M does not divide $r^k \pm a$ for small k and a*. Experience indicates that, in practice, it is sufficient to choose *M* such that it has no prime divisors less than 20.

Folding

In this method, we partition the identifier *x* into several parts. All parts, except for the last one have the same length. We then add the parts together to obtain the hash address for *x*. There are two ways of carrying out this addition. In the first method, we shift all parts except for the last one, so that the least significant bit of each part lines up with the corresponding bit of the last part. We then add the parts together to obtain $f(x)$. This method is known as *shift folding*. For example, suppose that we have divided the identifier *x* into the following parts: $x_1 = 123$, $x_2 = 203$, $x_3 = 241$, $x_4 = 112$, and $x_5 = 20$. Using shift folding, we would align x_1 through x_4 with x_5 and add. This gives us a hash address of 699.

The second method, known as *folding at the boundaries*, reverses every other partition before adding. For example, suppose the identifier *x* is divided into the same partitions as in shift folding. Using the folding at the boundaries method, we would reverse the second and fourth partitions, that is, $x_2 = 302$ and $x_4 = 211$, and add the partitions. This gives us a hash address of 897.

Digit Analysis

The last method we will examine, *digit analysis*, is used with static files. A *static file* is one in which all the identifiers are known in advance. Using this method, we first transform the identifiers into numbers using some radix, *r*. We then examine the digits of each identifier, deleting those digits that have the most skewed distributions. We continue deleting digits until the number of remaining digits is small enough to give an address in the range of the hash table. The digits used to calculate the hash address must be the same for all identifiers and must not have abnormally high peaks or valleys (the standard deviation must be small).

In Section 8.2.4, we compare the various methods used to generate a hash address. Of these methods, the one most suitable for general purpose applications is the division method with a divisor, *M*, such that *M* has no prime factors less than 20.

8.2.3   Overflow Handling

Linear Open Addressing

There are two methods for detecting collisions and overflows in a static hash table; each method using a different data structure to represent the hash table. In this section we discuss the simplest method, referred to as *linear open addressing* or *linear probing*, and in the next section we introduce *chaining*.

When we use linear open addressing, the hash table is represented as a one-dimensional array with indices that range from 0 to the desired table size − 1. The component type of the array is a **struct** that contains at least a key field. Since the keys are usually words, we use a string to denote them. The C declarations creating the hash table *ht* with one slot per bucket are:

```
#define MAX_CHAR  10 /*max number of characters in
                          an identifier*/
#define TABLE_SIZE 13 /* max table size=prime number */
typedef struct  {
        char key[MAX_CHAR];
        /* other fields */
        } element;
element hash_table[TABLE_SIZE];
```

Before inserting any elements into this table, we must initialize the table to represent the situation where all slots are empty. This allows us to detect overflows and collisions when we insert elements into the table. The obvious choice for an empty slot is the empty string since it will never be a valid key in any application. *init_table* (Program 8.1) shows the initialization function.

```
void init_table(element ht[])
{
   int i;
   for (i = 0; i < TABLE_SIZE; i++)
     ht[i].key[0] = NULL;
}
```

Program 8.1: Initialization of a hash table

To insert a new element into the hash table we convert the key field into a natural number, and then apply one of the hash functions discussed in Section 8.2.2. We can transform a key into a number if we convert each character into a number and then add these numbers together. (Apparently this is one of the most popular transformation techniques, despite the fact that it does not produce a uniform hash function.) The function *transform* (Program 8.2) uses this simplistic approach. (The exercises examine other alternatives.) To find the hash adddress of the transformed key, *hash* (Program 8.2) uses the division method.

```
int transform(char *key)
{
/* simple additive approach to create a natural number
that is within the integer range */
   int number = 0;
   while (*key)
     number += *key++;
   return number;
}

int hash(char *key)
{
/* transform key to a natural number, and return this
result modulus the table size */
   return(transform(key) % TABLE_SIZE);
}
```

Program 8.2: Creation of a hash function

We are now ready to insert elements into the hash table. If the slot at the hash address is empty, we simply place the new element into this slot. However, if the new element is hashed into a full bucket, we must find another bucket for it. The simplest solution places the new element in the closest unfilled bucket. We refer to this method of resolving overflows as *linear probing* or *linear open addressing*. Let us illustrate this technique on a 13-bucket table with one slot per bucket. As our data we will use the words **for**, **do**, **while**, **if**, **else**, and **function**. Figure 8.2 shows the hash value for each word using the simplified scheme discussed above. Inserting the first five words into the table poses no problem since they have different hash addresses. However, the last identifier, **function**, hashes to the same bucket as **if**. Using a circular rotation, the next available bucket is at *ht*[0], which is where we place **function** (Figure 8.3).

Identifier	Additive Transformation	x	Hash
for	102 + 111 + 114	327	2
do	100 + 111	211	3
while	119 + 104 + 105 + 108 + 101	537	4
if	105 + 102	207	12
else	101 + 108 + 115 + 101	425	9
function	102 + 117 + 110 + 99 + 116 + 105 + 111 + 110	870	12

Figure 8.2: Additive transformation

[0]	**function**
[1]	
[2]	**for**
[3]	**do**
[4]	**while**
[5]	
[6]	
[7]	
[8]	
[9]	**else**
[10]	
[11]	
[12]	**if**

Figure 8.3: Hash table with linear probing (13 buckets, 1 slot/bucket)

To implement the linear probing strategy, we first compute $f(x)$ for identifier x and then examine the hash table buckets $ht[(f(x) + j)\%TABLE\_SIZE]$, $0 \le j \le TABLE\_SIZE$ in this order. Four outcomes can result from the examination of a hash table bucket:

(1) The bucket contains x. In this case, x is already in the table. Depending on the application, we may either simply report a duplicate identifier, or we may update information in the other fields of the element.

(2) The bucket contains the empty string. In this case, the bucket is empty, and we may insert the new element into it.

(3) The bucket contains a nonempty string other than x. In this case we proceed to examine the next bucket.

(4) We return to the home bucket $ht [f (x)]$ $(j = TABLE - SIZE)$. In this case, the home bucket is being examined for the second time and all remaining buckets have been examined. The table is full and we report an error condition and exit.

The insertion strategy just discussed is implemented in *linear-insert* (Program 8.3).

```
void linear-insert(element item, element ht[])
{
/* insert the key into the table using the linear probing
technique, exit the function if the table is full */
   int i, hash-value;
   hash-value = hash(item.key);
   i = hash-value;
   while (strlen(ht[i].key)) {
      if (!strcmp(ht[i].key, item.key)) {
         fprintf(stderr,"Duplicate entry\n");
         exit(1);
      }
      i = (i+1) % TABLE-SIZE;
      if (i == hash-value) {
         fprintf(stderr,"The table is full\n");
         exit(1);
      }
   }
   ht[i] = item;
}
```

Program 8.3: Linear insert into a hash table

Our earlier example shows that when we use linear probing to resolve overflows, identifiers tend to cluster together. In addition, adjacent clusters tend to coalesce, thus increasing the search time. For example, suppose we enter the C built-in functions **acos**, **atoi**, **char**, **define**, **exp**, **ceil**, **cos**, **float**, **atol**, **floor**, and **ctime** into a 26-bucket hash table in that order. For illustrative purposes, we assume that the hash function uses the first character in each function name. Figure 8.4 shows the bucket number, the identifier contained in the bucket, and the number of comparisons required to insert the identifier. Notice that before we can insert **atol**, we must examine $ht[0], \ldots, ht[8]$, a total of nine comparisons. This is far worse than the worst case behavior of the search trees we will study in Chapter 10. If we retrieved each of the identifiers in ht exactly once, the average number of buckets examined would be $35/11 = 3.18$ per identifier. Analyses of the linear probing method show that the expected average number of identifier comparisons, p, required to look up an identifier is approximately $(2 - \alpha)/(2 - 2\alpha)$ where α is the loading density. In the above example, $\alpha = 11/26 = .42$ and $p = 1.36$. This indicates that the average number of probes for a loading density of .42 is 1.36. Thus, although we know that the average number of probes is small, the worst case can be large.

bucket	x	buckets searched
0	**acos**	1
1	**atoi**	2
2	**char**	1
3	**define**	1
4	**exp**	1
5	**ceil**	4
6	**cos**	5
7	**float**	3
8	**atol**	9
9	**floor**	5
10	**ctime**	9
...		
25		

Figure 8.4: Hash table with linear probing (26 buckets, 1 slot per bucket)

We have just seen that linear open addressing creates clusters of identifiers. These clusters tend to merge as we enter more identifiers into the table, thus leading to bigger clusters. We can partially curtail the growth of these clusters and hence reduce the average number of probes by using *quadratic probing*. Whereas, linear probing searches buckets $(f(x) + i)\% \, b$, $0 \le i \le b - 1$, where b is the number of buckets in the table, in quadratic probing we use a quadratic function of i as the increment. In particular, we carry out the search by examining buckets $f(x)$, $(f(x) + i^2) \% \, b$, and $(f(x) - i^2) \% \, b$ for $1 \le i \le (b - 1)/2$. When b is a prime number of the form $4j + 3$, where j is an integer, the quadratic search described above examines every bucket in the table. (We refer the reader interested in the proof to the Radke article cited in the References and Selected Readings section.) Figure 8.5 lists some primes of the form $4j + 3$.

Prime	j	Prime	j
3	0	43	10
7	1	59	14
11	2	127	31
19	4	251	62
23	5	503	125
31	7	1019	254

Figure 8.5: Some primes of the form $4j + 3$

We also can reduce the clustering that occurs with linear probing by applying a series of hash functions $f_1, f_2, \cdots, f_b$. This method is known as *rehashing*. We examine buckets $f_i(x)$, $1 \le i \le b$. A third approach for handling bucket overflow, *random probing*, is explored in the exercises.

Chaining

Linear probing and its variations perform poorly because inserting an identifier requires the comparison of identifiers with different hash values. For example, in the hash table of Figure 8.4, before we could insert **atol** we had to examine buckets $ht[0]$ to $ht[8]$, even though only the first two identifiers collided with **atol**; the remainder could not possibly be in the same bucket as **atol**. We could have eliminated most of these comparisons if we had maintained a list of synonyms for each bucket. To insert a new element we would only have to compute the hash address $f(x)$ and examine the identifiers in the list for $f(x)$. Since we would not know the sizes of the lists in advance, we should maintain them as linked chains. We now require additional space for a link field. Since we will have M lists, where M is the desired table size, we employ a head node for each chain. These head nodes only need a link field, so they are smaller than the other nodes. We maintain the head nodes in ascending order, $0, \cdots, M-1$ so that we may access the lists at random. The C declarations required to create the chained hash table are:

```
#define MAX_CHAR   10 /* maximum identifier size*/
#define TABLE_SIZE 13 /* prime number */
#define IS_FULL(ptr) (!(ptr))
```

```
typedef struct  {
        char key[MAX_CHAR];
        /* other fields */
        } element;


typedef struct list *list_pointer;
typedef struct list {
        element  item;
        list_pointer link;
        };
list_pointer hash_table[TABLE_SIZE];
```

The function *chain_insert* (Program 8.4) implements the chaining strategy. The function first computes the hash address for the identifier. It then examines the identifiers in the list for the selected bucket. If the identifier is found, we print an error message and exit. If the identifier is not in the list, we insert it at the end of the list. If the list was empty, we change the head node to point to the new entry.

Figure 8.6 shows the chained hash table corresponding to the linear table found in Figure 8.4. The number of probes needed to search for any of the identifiers is now one each for **acos**, **char**, **define**, **exp** and **float**; two each for **atoi**, **ceil**, and **float**; three each for **atol** and **cos**; and four for **ctime**. The average number of comparisons is now $21/11 = 1.91$. The expected number of identifier comparisons for a chained table is $\sim 1 + \alpha/2$, where α is the loading density n/b (b = number of headnodes). For $\alpha = 0.42$, the expected number of probes is 1.21; for $\alpha = 1$, it is about 1.5.

The results of this section and the last suggest that the performance of a hash table depends only on the method used to handle overflows, that is, chaining or linear probing. As long as a uniform hash function is used, the performance is independent of the hash function. Although this is true if we randomly select identifiers from the identifier space, it is not true in practice. In practice, our choice of identifiers is biased since we frequently use identifiers that have a common suffix or prefix or are simple permutations of other identifiers. Thus, in practice we would expect the choice of a hash function to affect hash table performance. The table of Figure 8.7 presents the results of an empirical study conducted by Lum, Yuen, and Dodd. The values in each column give the average number of bucket accesses made in searching eight different tables with 33,575, 24,050, 4909, 3072, 2241, 930, 762, and 500 identifiers each. As expected, chaining performs better than linear open addressing. Examining the performance of the various hash functions, we can see that division is generally superior. Therefore, for a general application, this is the preferred method. The divisor should be a prime number, although it is sufficient to choose a divisor that has no prime factors less than 20. Notice that the table also gives the theoretical expected number of bucket accesses based on random keys.

```
void chain_insert(element item, list_pointer ht[])
{
/* insert the key into the table using chaining */
   int hash_value  = hash(item.key);
   list_pointer ptr,trail=NULL,lead=ht[hash_value];
   for (; lead; trail = lead, lead = lead->link)
      if (!strcmp(lead->item.key,item.key)) {
         fprintf(stderr, "The key is in the table\n");
         exit(1);
      }
   }
   ptr = (list_pointer)malloc(sizeof(list));
   if (IS_FULL(ptr)) {
      fprintf(stderr, "The memory is full\n");
      exit(1);
   }
   ptr->item = item;
   ptr->link = NULL;
   if (trail)
      trail->link = ptr;
   else
      ht[hash_value] = ptr;
}
```

Program 8.4: Chain insert into a hash table

```
[0] -> acos -> atoi -> atol
[1] -> NULL
[2] -> char -> ceil -> cos -> ctime
[3] -> define
[4] -> exp
[5] -> float -> floor
[6] -> NULL
...
[25] -> NULL
```

Figure 8.6: Hash chains corresponding to Figure 8.4

$\alpha = \dfrac{n}{b}$	.50		.75		.90		.95	
Hash Function	Chain	Open	Chain	Open	Chain	Open	Chain	Open
mid square	1.26	1.73	1.40	9.75	1.45	37.14	1.47	37.53
division	1.19	4.52	1.31	7.20	1.38	22.42	1.41	25.79
shift fold	1.33	21.75	1.48	65.10	1.40	77.01	1.51	118.57
bound fold	1.39	22.97	1.57	48.70	1.55	69.63	1.51	97.56
digit analysis	1.35	4.55	1.49	30.62	1.52	89.20	1.52	125.59
theoretical	1.25	1.50	1.37	2.50	1.45	5.50	1.48	10.50

(Adapted from V. Lum, P. Yuen, and M. Dodd, *CACM*, 1971, Vol. 14, No. 4)

Figure 8.7: Average number of bucket accesses per identifier retrieved.

8.2.4 Theoretical Evaluation of Overflow Techniques

The experimental evaluation of hashing techniques indicates that they generally perform better than conventional techniques, such as binary search trees. However, the worst case performance for hashing can be very bad. In the worst case, an insertion in a hash table with n identifiers may take $O(n)$ time. In this section, we present a probabilistic analysis for the expected performance of the chaining method and state, without proof, the results of similar analyses for the other overflow handling methods. First, we formalize what we mean by expected performance.

Let $ht[\,b\,]$ be a hash table with b buckets, each bucket having one slot. Let f be a uniform hash function with range $[0, b-1]$. If we enter n identifiers $x_1, x_2, \cdots, x_n$ into the hash table, then there are b^n distinct hash sequences $f(x_1), f(x_2), \cdots, f(x_n)$. Assume that each of these is equally likely to occur. Let S_n denote the expected number of identifier comparisons needed to locate a randomly chosen x_i, $1 \le i \le n$. Then, S_n is the average number of comparisons needed to find the jth key x_j, averaged over $1 \le j \le n$, with each j equally likely and averaged over all b^n hash sequences, assuming each of these also to be equally likely. Let U_n be the expected number of identifier comparisons when a search is made for an identifier not in the hash table. This hash table contains n identifiers. The quantity U_n may be defined in a manner analogous to that used for S_n.

Theorem 8.1 Let $\alpha = n/b$ be the loading density of a hash table using a uniform hash function f. Then:

(1) for linear open addressing:

$$U_n \approx \frac{1}{2}\left[1+\frac{1}{(1-\alpha)^2}\right]$$

$$S_n \approx \frac{1}{2}\left[1+\frac{1}{1-\alpha}\right]$$

(2) for rehashing, random probing, and quadratic probing:

$$U_n \approx 1/(1-\alpha)$$

$$S_n \approx -\left[\frac{1}{\alpha}\right]\log_e(1-\alpha)$$

(3) for chaining:

$$U_n \approx \alpha$$

$$S_n \approx 1 + \alpha/2$$

Proof: Exact derivations of U_n and S_n are fairly involved and can be found in Knuth's book *The Art of Computer Programming: Sorting and Searching*. Here, we present a derivation of the approximate formulas for chaining. First, assume that we wish to insert the identifier x, where $f(x) = i$ and chain i has k nodes, excluding the headnode. If x is not on the chain, k comparisons are made. If x is j nodes away from the head node, $1 \leq j \leq k$, j comparisons are made. When the n identifiers distribute uniformly over the b possible chains, the expected number in each chain is $n/b = \alpha$. Since U_n = expected number of identifiers on a chain, $U_n = \alpha$. When we enter the ith identifier x_i into the table, the expected number of identifiers on any chain is $(i-1)/b$. Hence, the expected number of comparisons needed to insert x_i after all n identifiers have been entered is $1 + (i-1)/b$. (This assumes that new entries are added to the end of the chain.) Therefore:

$$S_n = \frac{1}{n}\sum_{i=1}^{n}\{1 + (i-1)/b\} = 1 + \frac{n-1}{2b} \approx 1 + \frac{\alpha}{2} \quad \square$$

EXERCISES

1. Why does *transform* (Program 8.2) produce a biased hash function? What transformation would you suggest?

2. Create a C function *linear_search* that returns −1 if an identifier, x, is not in the hash table, and the bucket address of x if x is in the table.

3. Write a C function that deletes identifier x from a hash table that uses hash function f and linear open addressing to resolve collisions. Show that simply setting the slot previously occupied by x to an empty string does not solve the problem. How must you modify *linear_search* so that a correct search is made in the situation when deletions are permitted? Where can a new identifier be inserted?

4. (a) Show that if quadratic searching is carried out in the sequence $(f(x) + q^2)$, $(f(x) + (q-1)^2)$, $\cdots$, $(f(x) + 1)$, $f(x)$, $(f(x) - 1)$, $\cdots$, $(f(x) - q^2)$ with $q = (b-1)/2$ then the address difference mod b between successive buckets being examined is:

$$b - 2, b - 4, b - 6, \cdots, 5, 3, 1, 1, 3, 5, \cdots, b - 6, b - 4, b - 2$$

    (b)   Write an algorithm to insert the identifier x into a hash table contain b buckets. Use quadratic hashing to resolve overflows.

5. [Morris 1968] In random probing, the search for an identifier, x, in a hash table with b buckets is carried out by examining buckets $f(x)$, $(f(x)+S(i))\ \% \ b$, $1 \le i \le b-1$, where $S(i)$ is a pseudorandom number. The random number generator must generate every number from 1 to $b - 1$ exactly once.

    (a)   Show that for a table of size 2^r, the following sequence of computations generates numbers with this property:

> Initialize R to 1 each time the search routine is called.
> On successive calls for a random number do the following:
>> $R := R * 5$
>> $R := low$ order $r + 2$ bits of R
>> $S(i) := R/4$

    (b)   Write an algorithm, incorporating the above random number generator, to insert an identifier into a hash table using random probing and the middle of square hash function f_m.

It can be shown that for this method, the expected value for the average number of comparisons needed to search for x is $-(1/\alpha)\log(1 - \alpha)$ where α is the loading factor.

6. Write an algorithm to list all the identifiers in a hash table in lexicographic order. Assume the hash function f is $f(x) =$ first character of x and linear probing is used. How much time does your algorithm take?

7. Let the binary representation of identifier x be $x_1 x_2$. Let $|x|$ denote the number of bits in x and let the first bit of x_1 be 1. Let $|x_1| = \lceil |x|/2 \rceil$ and $|x_2| = \lfloor |x|/2 \rfloor$. Consider the following hash function:

$$f(x) = \text{middle } k \text{ bits of } (x_1 \text{ XOR } x_2)$$

where XOR is the exclusive or operator. Is this a uniform hash function if identifiers are drawn at random from the space of allowable C identifiers? What can you say about the behavior of this hash function in a real symbol table usage?

8. [T. Gonzalez] Design a symbol table representation which allows you to search, insert, and delete an identifier x in $O(1)$ time. Assume that $0 \leq x < m$ and that $m + n$ units of space are available where n is the number of insertions to be made. (Hint: Use two arrays $a[n]$ and $b[m]$, where $a[i]$ will be the ith identifier inserted into the table. If x is the ith identifier inserted, then $b[x] = i$.) Write algorithms to search, insert, and delete identifiers. Note that you cannot initialize either a or b to zero as this would take $O(n + m)$ time. Note that x is an integer.

9. [T. Gonzalez] Let $S = \{x_1, x_2, \ldots, x_n\}$ and $T = \{y_1, y_2, \ldots, y_r\}$ be two sets. Assume $0 \leq x_i < m$, $1 \leq i \leq n$ and $0 \leq y_i < m$, $1 \leq i \leq r$. Using the idea of Exercise 8, write an algorithm to determine if $S \subseteq T$. Your algorithm should work in $O(r + n)$ time. Since $S = T$ iff $S \subseteq T$ and $T \subseteq S$, this implies that one can determine in linear time if two sets are equivalent. How much space is needed by your algorithm?

10. [T. Gonzalez] Using the idea of Exercise 9, write an $O(n + m)$ time algorithm to carry out the function of algorithm *verify2* of Section 7.1. How much space does your algorithm need?

11. Show that when linear open addressing is used:

$$S_n = \frac{1}{n} \sum_{i=0}^{n-1} U_i$$

Using this equation and the approximate equality:

$$U_n \approx \frac{1}{2} \left[1 + \frac{1}{(1 - \alpha)^2} \right] \quad \text{where } \alpha = \frac{n}{b}$$

show that:

$$S_n \approx \frac{1}{2} \left[1 + \frac{1}{(1 - \alpha)} \right]$$

12. [Guttag] The following set of operations defines a symbol table that handles a language with block structure. Write a specification for this data type in the style of Structure 8.1.

INIT	creates an empty table
ENTERB	indicates a new block has been entered
ADD	places an identifier and its attributes in the table
LEAVEB	deletes all identifiers that are defined in the innermost block
RETRIEVE	returns the attributes of the most recently defined identifier
ISINB	returns true if the identifier is defined in the innermost block else false

13. § [Programming project] Create a menu-driven, user-friendly program that manages the supply list of Widgets, Inc. Widgets, Inc., keeps the following information on their supplies:

- 5-digit part number (the key)

- 10-character description of part

- reorder level

- size of current inventory

You must maintain the supply list using a chained hash table. In addition, Widgets, Inc., employees must be able to perform the following operations:

(a) add a new part to the inventory

(b) delete a part from the inventory

(c) search for a part

(d) change the key field of a part

(e) change any of the remaining fields

8.3 DYNAMIC HASHING

One of the most important classes of software is the database management system or DBMS. In a DBMS the user enters a query using some language (possibly SQL) and the system translates it and retrieves the resulting data. Fast access time is essential since a DBMS is typically used to hold large sets of information. Another key characteristic of a DBMS is that the amount of information can vary a great deal over time. Various data structures have been suggested for storing the data in a DBMS. In this section, we examine an extension of hashing that permits the technique to be used by a DBMS.

Traditional hashing schemes as described in the previous sections are not ideal because we must statically allocate a portion of memory to hold the hash table. This hash table is used to point to the buckets that hold identifiers, or it may actually contain the identifiers. In either case, if we allocate a large portion of memory to hold the table, we waste space. Yet, if we allocate a minimal amount of memory, we will have to restructure the entire file when the data exceeds the capacity of the hash table. This is a very time-consuming process. *Dynamic hashing*, also referred to as *extendible hashing*, retains the fast retrieval time of conventional hashing, while extending the technique so that it can accommodate dynamically increasing and decreasing file size without penalty.

We assume that a file, F, is a collection of records, R. Each record has a key field, K, by which it is identified. Records are stored in buckets, or *pages* as they are called in dynamic hashing, whose capacity is p. The algorithms we develop must minimize page accesses since pages are usually stored on disk and their retrieval into memory dominates any operation. The measure of space utilization is the ratio of the number of records, n, divided by the total space, mp, where m is the number of pages.

8.3.1 Dynamic Hashing Using Directories

Consider an example where an identifier consists of two characters and each character is represented by 3 bits. Figure 8.8 gives a list of some of these identifiers.

Identifiers	Binary representation
a0	100 000
a1	100 001
b0	101 000
b1	101 001
c0	110 000
c1	110 001
c2	110 010
c3	110 011

Figure 8.8: Some identifiers requiring 3 bits per character

We would like to place these identifiers into a table that has four pages. Each page can hold no more than two identifiers, and the pages are indexed by the 2 bit sequence 00, 01, 10, 11, respectively. We use the two low-order bits of each identifier to determine the page address of the identifier. Figure 8.9(a) shows the placement of a0, b0, c2, a1, b1, and c3 into the table. Notice that we select the bits from least significant to most significant. Branching at the root is determined by the least significant bit. If this bit is zero, the upper branch is taken. Otherwise, the lower branch is taken. Branching at the next level is determined by the second least significant bit, and so on. a0 and b0 are in the first page since their two low-order bits are 0 and 0. The second page contains only c2. To get to this page, we first branch on the least significant bit of c2 (i.e., 0) and then on the next bit (i.e., 1). The third page contains a1 and b1. To get to this page, we first branch on the least significant bit of a1 or b1. This bit is one for both a1 and b1. Next, we branch on the next bit which is zero for both. The last page contains c3, with a bit pattern of 11. We use the term *trie* to denote a binary tree in which we locate an identifier by following its bit sequence. (We shall describe tries in greater detail in Chapter 10.) Notice that this trie has nodes that always branch in two directions corresponding to 0 or 1. Only the leaf nodes of the trie contain a pointer to a page.

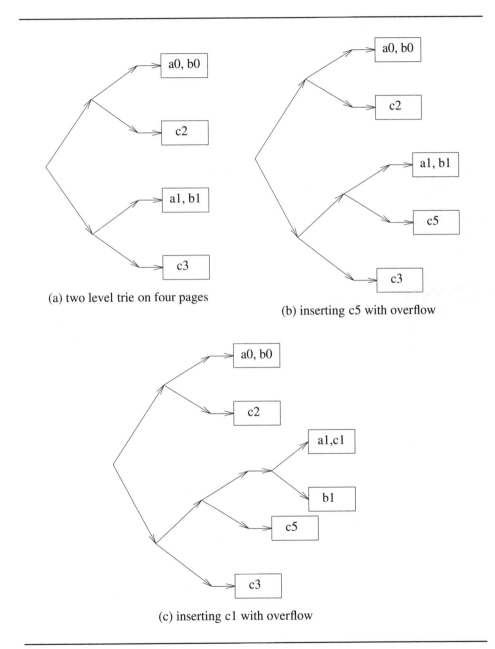

(a) two level trie on four pages

(b) inserting c5 with overflow

(c) inserting c1 with overflow

Figure 8.9: A trie to hold identifiers

Now suppose we try to insert a new identifier, say c5, into Figure 8.9(a). The two low-order bits of c5 are 1 and 0, which means that we should place it in the third page. However, since a page can hold only two identifiers, an overflow occurs. When this happens, we add a new page and increase the depth of the trie. This is shown in Figure 8.9(b). If we now insert the identifier c1, an overflow of the page containing a1 and b1 occurs. We obtain a new page and divide the identifiers among the two pages according to their four low-order bits.

From this example one can see that two major problems exist. First, the access time for a page depends on the number of bits needed to distinguish the identifiers. Second, if the identifiers have a skewed distribution, the tree is also skewed. Both these factors increase the retrieval time. Fagin et al. present a method, which they call *extendible hashing*, for solving these problems. To avoid the skewed distribution of identifiers, a hash function is used. This function takes the key and produces a random set of binary digits. To avoid the long search down the trie, the trie is mapped to a directory.

A directory is a table of page pointers. In case k bits are needed to distinguish the identifiers, the directory has 2^k entries indexed $0, \cdots, 2^k-1$. To find the page for an identifier, we use the integer with binary representation equal to the last k bits of the identifier. The page pointed at by this directory entry is searched. Figure 8.10 shows the three directories corresponding to the three tries in Figure 8.9. The first directory contains four entries indexed from 0 to 3 (the binary representation of each index is shown in Figure 8.10). Each entry contains a pointer to a page. This pointer is shown as an arrow in the figure. The letter above each pointer is a page label. The page labels were obtained by labeling the pages of Figure 8.9(a) top to bottom beginning with the label a. The page contents are shown immediately after the page pointer. To see the correspondence between the directory and the trie, notice that if the bits in the directory index are used to follow a path in the trie (beginning with the least significant bit), we will reach the page pointed at by the corresponding directory entry.

The second directory contains eight entries indexed from 0 to 7, and the third has 16 entries indexed from 0 to 15. Page a of the second directory (Figure 8.10(b)) has two directory entries (000 and 100) pointing to it. The page contents are shown only once. Page b has two pointers to it, page c has one pointer, page d has one pointer, and page e has two pointers. In Figure 8.10(c) there are six pages with the following number of pointers respectively: 4, 4, 1, 1, 2, and 4.

Using a directory to represent a trie allows the table of identifiers to grow and shrink dynamically. This, of course, assumes that the operating system can give us more pages or return pages to available storage with little or no difficulty. In addition, accessing any page requires only two steps. In the first step, we use the hash function to find the address of the directory entry, and in the second, we retrieve the page associated with the address.

Unfortunately, if the keys are not uniformly divided among the pages, the directory can grow quite large. However, most of the entries point to the same pages. To prevent this from happening, we cannot use the bit sequence of the keys themselves. Instead we translate the bits into a random sequence. This is done using a *uniform hash*

$$00 \xrightarrow{a} a0,\ b0 \qquad 000 \xrightarrow{a} a0,\ b0 \qquad 0000 \xrightarrow{a} a0,\ b0$$
$$01 \xrightarrow{c} a1,\ b1 \qquad 001 \xrightarrow{c} a1,\ b1 \qquad 0001 \xrightarrow{c} a1,\ c1$$
$$10 \xrightarrow{b} c2 \qquad 010 \xrightarrow{b} c2 \qquad 0010 \xrightarrow{b} c2$$
$$11 \xrightarrow{d} c3 \qquad 011 \xrightarrow{e} c3 \qquad 0011 \xrightarrow{f} c3$$
$$100 \xrightarrow{a} \qquad 0100 \xrightarrow{a}$$
$$101 \xrightarrow{d} c5 \qquad 0101 \xrightarrow{e} c5$$
$$110 \xrightarrow{b} \qquad 0110 \xrightarrow{b}$$
$$111 \xrightarrow{e} \qquad 0111 \xrightarrow{f}$$
$$1000 \xrightarrow{a}$$
$$1001 \xrightarrow{d} b1$$
$$1010 \xrightarrow{b}$$
$$1011 \xrightarrow{f}$$
$$1100 \xrightarrow{a}$$
$$1101 \xrightarrow{e}$$
$$1110 \xrightarrow{b}$$
$$1111 \xrightarrow{f}$$

(a) 2 bits (b) 3 bits (c) 4 bits

Figure 8.10: Tries collapsed into directories

function as discussed in the previous section. But, in contrast to the previous section, we need a *family* of hash functions, because, at any point, we may require a different number of bits to distinguish the new key. One solution is the family:

$$hash_i: key \rightarrow \{0 \ldots 2^{i-1}\},\ 1 \le i \le d$$

where $hash_i$ is simply $hash_{i-1}$ with either a zero or one appended as the new leading bit of the result. Thus, $hash\,(key, i)$ might be a function that produces a random number of i bits from the identifier *key*.

There are some important twists associated with this approach. For example, suppose a page identified by i bits overflows. We allocate a new page and rehash the identifiers into those two pages. The identifiers in both pages have their low-order i bits in common. We refer to these pages as *buddies*. When the number of identifiers in two buddy pages is no more than the capacity of a single page, then we coalesce the two pages into one.

Suppose a page that can hold only p records now contains p records and a new record is to be added. The operating system allocates a new page. All $p + 1$ keys are rehashed, using 1 more bit and divided among the two pages. If the number of bits used is greater than the depth (the number of bits or $\log_2$ of the directory size) of the directory, the whole directory doubles in size and its depth increases by 1. If all $p + 1$ records are hashed to one of the two pages the split operation has to be repeated. Fortunately, this is a fairly rare occurrence. When this happens, the depth of the directory can be reduced using a compressed trie as discussed in Chapter 10.

Program 8.5 contains a pseudo-C program that provides many of the details for implementing the directory version of dynamic hashing.

```
#include <stdio.h>
#include <alloc.h>
#include <stdlib.h>
#define WORD_SIZE  5 /* max number of directory bits */
#define PAGE_SIZE 10 /* max size of a page */
#define DIRECTORY_SIZE 32 /* max size of directory */
typedef struct page *paddr;
typedef struct page {
        int local_depth; /* page level */
        char *name[PAGE_SIZE];
        int num_idents;  /* # of identifiers in page */
        };

typedef struct {
        char *key;            /* pointer to string */
        /* other fields */
        } brecord;
int global_depth; /* trie height */
paddr directory[DIRECTORY_SIZE]; /* pointers to pages */

paddr hash(char *, short int);
paddr buddy(paddr);
short int pgsearch( char *, paddr);
int convert(paddr);
void enter(brecord, paddr);
void pgdelete(char *, paddr);
paddr find(brecord, char *);
void insert(brecord, char *);
int size(paddr);
```

```
void coalesce(paddr, paddr);
void delete(brecord, char *);

paddr hash(char *key, short int precision)
{
   /* *key is hashed using a uniform hash function, and the
   low precision bits are returned as the page address */
}

paddr buddy(paddr index)
{
   /* Take an address of a page and returns the page's
   buddy, i.e., the leading bit is complemented */
}

int size(paddr ptr)
{
   /* return the number of identifiers in the page */
}

void coalesce(paddr ptr, paddr buddy)
{
   /*  combine page ptr and its buddy into a single page */
}

short int pgsearch(char *key, paddr index)
{
   /* Search a page for a key.  If found return 1
   otherwise return 0 */
}

int convert(paddr ptr)
{
   /* Convert a pointer to a page to an equivalent
   integer */
}

void enter(brecord r, paddr ptr)
{
   /* Insert a new record into the page pointed
   at by ptr */
}

void pgdelete(char *key, paddr ptr)
```

```
{
   /*  remove the record with key, key, from the page
   pointed to by ptr */
}

short int find(char *key, paddr *ptr)
{
   /* return 0 if key is not found and 1 if it is.  Also,
   return a pointer (in ptr) to the page that was searched.
   Assume that an empty directory has one page. */

   paddr index;
   int intindex;

   index = hash(key, global_depth);
   intindex = convert(index);
   *ptr = directory[intindex];
   return pgsearch(key, ptr);
}

void insert(brecord r, char *key)
{
   paddr ptr;
   if find(key, &ptr) {
      fprintf(stderr,  "The   key   is   already   in   the
                  table.\n");
      exit(1);
   }
   if (ptr->num_idents != PAGE_SIZE) {
      enter(r,ptr);
      ptr->num_idents++;
   }
   else {
      /* Split the page into two, insert the new key, and
      update global_depth if necessary.
      If this causes global_depth to exceed WORD_SIZE
      then print an error and terminate. */
   };
}

void delete(brecord r, char *key)
{
/* find and delete the record r from the file */
   paddr ptr;
```

```
   if (!find(key, &ptr)) {
      fprintf(stderr,"Key is not in the table.\n");
      return; /* non-fatal error */
   }
   pgdelete(key,ptr);
   if (size(ptr) + size(buddy(ptr)) <= PAGE_SIZE)
      coalesce(ptr,buddy(ptr));
}

void main(void)
{
}
```

Program 8.5: Dynamic hashing

8.3.2   Analysis of Directory Dynamic Hashing

The most important feature of the directory version of extendible hashing is the guarantee that retrieving any page requires only two disk accesses. Thus, its performance is very good. However, we pay for this performance in space usage. Recall that adding identifiers that are not uniformly distributed can double the directory size. Since many of the pointers could point to the same page, we have a lot of wasted storage.

A second criterion for judging hashing schemes is the space utilization. This is defined as the ratio of the number of records stored in the table divided by the total amount of space allocated. Several researchers (Fagin, Larson, and Mendelson) have analyzed this measure for different variations of dynamic hashing. They have all reached similar conclusions, namely, that without any special strategies for handling overflows, the space utilization is approximately 69 percent. Each of their derivations is quite complex and rely on assumptions about the distributions of the identifiers. Here we will follow the derivation given by Mendelson.

Let $L(k)$ stand for the expected number of leaf nodes needed to hold k records. When the records all fit in a single page, $L(k) = 1$. The interesting case is when k exceeds the page size. In this case, the number of records in the two subtrees of the root have a symmetric binomial distribution. From this it follows that there will be j keys in the left subtree and $k - j$ in the right, each with a given probability, which is:

$$\binom{k}{j} (1/2)^k$$

This implies that the number of leaf pages in the left subtree is $L(j)$ and the number in the right subtree is $L(k - j)$. Thus, one can express $L(k)$ by the formula:

$$L(k) = \frac{1}{2^k} \sum_{j=0}^{k} \binom{k}{j} \{L(j) + L(k-j)\} = 2^{1-k} \sum_{j=0}^{k} \binom{k}{j} L(j)$$

Mendelson goes on to show that:

$$L(k) \sim \frac{k}{p \ln 2}$$

It follows that the storage utilization is the number of records k divided by the product of the page size p and the number of leaf nodes $L(k)$ or that:

$$utilization = \frac{k}{pL(k)} \sim \ln 2 \sim 0.69$$

To see that Mendelson's estimate is reasonable, suppose there is no overflow strategy other than doubling the directory size. We have a full page with p records and attempt to insert a $p + 1$'st record, which causes an overflow. With a uniform hash function we now have two pages each containing about $p/2$ identifiers, or a space utilization of 50 percent. After the process of inserting and deleting continues for a while, we would expect that a recently split page is at least half full. Thus, space utilization should be at least 50 percent, but certainly less than 100 percent.

When a page overflows, it may double the directory size. To avoid this, we introduce the concept of overflow pages. Instead of increasing the directory, an overflow causes the allocation of a new page. The pointer to this page is stored in the main page. Rather than storing new identifiers in the main page, we place them in the overflow page. As we shall see, this increases storage utilization, but at the expense of increased retrieval time.

Assume that an overflow page is the same size as a regular page and that both pages are full with p records, a total of $2p$ records. Suppose an overflow now occurs. We obtain a new page, and distribute the keys among the three pages. The utilization is $2p/3p$ or 66 percent. On the other hand, suppose that the overflow page has a capacity of $p/2$ rather than p. If we redistribute the keys as before, then a total of $3p/2$ records is divided over a capacity of $2p$. This produces a utilization of $3/4 = 75$ percent. Thus, we see that although overflow pages increase utilization, they also increase retrieval time.

Determining the ideal size for the overflow page has been investigated by Larson and others. Larson concludes that if a space utilization below 80 percent is sufficient, then the size of the overflow pages can vary widely, say, from p to $p/2$. However, higher space utilizations require a successively narrow range of overflow page sizes, because utilization begins to oscillate and access time increases significantly. To cope with this problem, we could monitor the space utilization of the file, so that when it achieves some predetermined amount, say the 80 percent ratio, the algorithm resumes splitting.

We can also analyze the size of the directory in terms of the number of records, n, that are stored in the file. Fagin estimates this as:

$$2 \lceil \log \frac{n}{p \ln 2} \rceil$$

Figure 8.11 contains a table given by Flajolet which shows the expected directory size for various numbers of records, n, and page size, p. For example, we would need a directory of size 62,500 to store one million records using a page size of 50. This is substantial, and indicates that the directory may have to be stored using auxiliary storage.

n	p 5	10	20	50	100	200
10^3	1.5K	0.3K	0.1K	0.0K	0.0K	0.0K
10^4	25.6K	4.8K	1.7K	0.5K	0.2K	0.00K
10^5	424.1K	68.2K	16.8K	4.1K	2.0K	1.0K
10^6	6.9M	1.02M	0.26M	62.5K	16.8K	8.1K
10^7	111.11M	11.64M	2.25M	0.52M	0.26M	0.13M

Figure 8.11: Directory size given n records and p page size

In the event that the hash function does not evenly distribute the identifiers across the pages, more sophisticated techniques are required. Lomet suggests that, in the directory scheme, we do not view pages as of a fixed size, but allow them to grow. Thus, any given page may be composed of several subpages. As more identifiers map to this page, its storage is expanded. This leads to different strategies for maintaining the identifiers within the page. The simplest strategy is to keep the identifiers in the order they were entered into the table. However, sequential searching is time consuming, especially as the identifier list gets long. An alternate strategy is to treat each subpage as a dynamically hashed directoryless structure. We describe its maintenance in Section 8.3.3.

Simulation

One important way to measure the performance of any new data structure is to carry out a series of experiments. Each experiment makes use of the algorithms that implement the data structure. Various distributions of identifiers are given to the algorithms and the resultant behavior is tabulated. In the case of dynamic hashing, we would want to monitor (1) access time, (2) insertion time, and (3) total space utilization. The factors influencing these attributes are (1) the number of records, (2) the page size, (3) the directory size, (4) the size of main memory for holding the directory and identifiers, and (5) the time required to process page faults.

Fagin et al. have done such a series of experiments. They found that in all cases extendible hashing performed at least as well or better than B-trees, a popular competitor. In the case of access time and insertion time, extendible hashing was clearly superior. For space utilization the two methods were about equal.

8.3.3   Directoryless Dynamic Hashing

Section 8.3.2 assumed that a directory existed that pointed to pages. One criticism of this approach is that it always requires at least one level of indirection. If we assume that we have a contiguous address space which is large enough to hold all the records, we can eliminate the directory. In effect, this leaves it to the operating system to break the address space into pages, and to manage moving them into and out of memory. This scheme is referred to as *directoryless hashing* or *linear hashing*.

Consider the trie in Figure 8.9(a) which has two levels and indexes four pages. In the new method, the 2 bit addresses are the actual addresses of these pages (actually they are an offset of some base address). Thus, the hash function delivers the actual address of a page containing the key. Moreover, every value produced by the hash function must point to an actual page. In contrast to the directory scheme where a single page might be pointed at by several directory entries, in the directoryless scheme there must exist a unique page for every possible address. Figure 8.12 shows a simple trie and its mapping to contiguous memory without a directory.

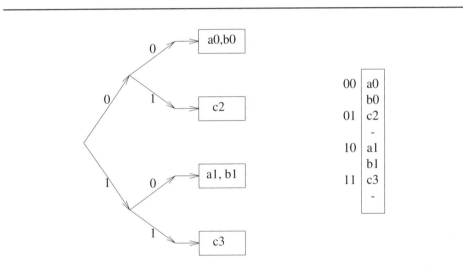

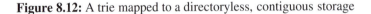

Figure 8.12: A trie mapped to a directoryless, contiguous storage

Now what happens when a page overflows? We could double the size of the address space, but this is wasteful. Instead, whenever an overflow occurs we add a new page to the end of the file, and divide the identifiers in one of the pages between its original page and the new page. This complicates the handling of the family of hash functions somewhat. However, if we had simply added one bit to the result of the hash function, the table would have to be doubled. By adding only a single page, the hash function must distinguish between pages addressed by r bits and those addressed by $r+1$. We will show how this is done in a moment.

Figure 8.13 provides an example of directoryless hashing after two insertions. Initially, there are four pages each addressed by 2 bits (Figure 8.13(a)). Two of the pages are full, and two have one identifier each. When c5 is inserted, it hashes to the page whose address is 10 (Figure 8.13(b)). Since that page is full, an overflow node is allocated to hold c5. At the same time, we add a new page at the end of the storage, rehash the identifiers in the first page, and split them between the first and new page. Unfortunately, none of the new identifiers go into the new page. The first page and the new page are now addressed by 3 bits, not 2 as shown in Figure 8.13(b). In the next step, we insert the identifier c1. Since it hashes to the same page as c5, we use another overflow node to store it. We add another new page to the end of the file and rehash the identifiers in the second page. Once again none go into the new page. (Note that this is largely a result of not using a uniform hash function.) Now the first two pages and the two new pages are all addressed using three bits. Eventually the number of pages will double, thereby completing one phase. A new phase then begins.

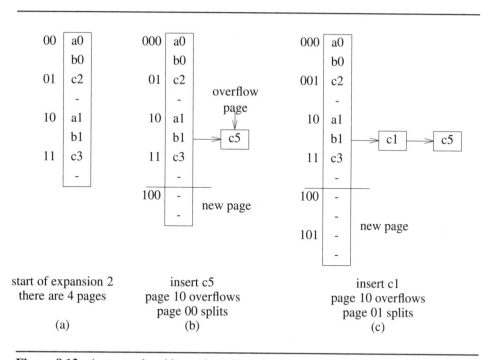

start of expansion 2 there are 4 pages	insert c5 page 10 overflows page 00 splits	insert c1 page 10 overflows page 01 splits
(a)	(b)	(c)

Figure 8.13: An example with two insertions

Consider Figure 8.14, which shows the state of file expansion during the rth phase at some time q. At the beginning of the rth phase, there are 2^r pages all addressed by r

bits. In the figure, q new pages have been added. The pages to the left of the q line have already been split. The pages between the q and r lines are waiting to be split, and the pages to the right of the r line have been added during this phase of the process. Each page in this section of the file is addressed by $r + 1$ bits. Notice that the q line indicates which page gets split next. The actual modified hash function is given in Program 8.6. All pages less than q require $r + 1$ bits. The function $hash(key, r)$ is in the range $\{0, 2^{r-1}\}$ so, if the result is less than q, we rehash using $r + 1$ bits. This gives us either the pages to the left of q or above $2^r - 1$. The directoryless method always requires overflows.

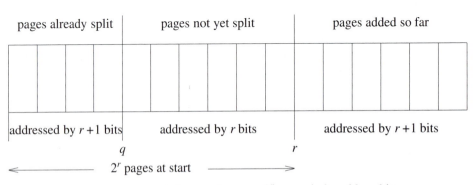

pages already split   pages not yet split   pages added so far

addressed by $r+1$ bits   addressed by r bits   addressed by $r+1$ bits

q r

2^r pages at start

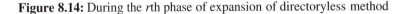

suppose we are at phase r; there are 2^r pages indexed by r bits

Figure 8.14: During the rth phase of expansion of directoryless method

One sees that many retrievals require only one access, that is, those that have identifiers that are in the page directly addressed by the hash function. However, other retrievals might require substantially more than two accesses as one moves along the overflow chain. When a new page is added and the identifiers split across the two pages, all identifiers including the overflows are rehashed.

We should also point out that the space utilization for this method is not good. As can be seen from Figure 8.13, some extra pages are empty and yet overflow pages are being used. Litwin has shown that space utilization is approximately 60 percent. He offers an alternate strategy pursued in the exercises. The term *controlled splitting* refers to splitting the *next page* only when storage utilization exceeds a predefined amount. Litwin suggests that until 80 percent utilization is reached, other pages continue to overflow.

A natural way to handle overflows is to use one of the traditional hashing schemes discussed earlier, such as open addressing. Recall that open addressing searches the file linearly from the point where the identifier hashes, either looking for the identifier or for an open spot.

```
if (hash(key,r) < q)
    page = hash(key,r+1);
else
    page = hash(key,r);
```
if needed, then follow overflow pointers;

Program 8.6: Modified hash function

From the example, one sees that the longest overflow chains occur for those pages that are near the end of the expansion phase since they are the last to be split. In contrast, those pages that are split early are generally underfull.

EXERCISES

1. The text points out that nonuniform distributions of keys result in a skewed directory and a waste of directory space. We can avoid this problem in the directory scheme if we store the directory as a forest of tries rather than a table. A new key is hashed to one of the tries and then its nodes are traversed until a leaf node is reached. The leaf node points to the page containing the desired record. Splitting is still required. The tries grow and contract with respect to the file. Write out the algorithms for maintaining a trie as a directory.

2. In extendible hashing, given a directory of size d, suppose two pointers point to the same page. How many low-order bits do all identifiers share in common? If four pointers point to the same page, how many bits do the identifiers have in common?

3. We can handle overflows in directory dynamic hashing by permitting a page to be divided into as many multiple pages as necessary to hold all identifiers that hash to that page. We assign a limit on the size of the directory. Once this limit has been reached, pages simply continue to grow. Modify the algorithms in Program 8.11 to implement this strategy.

4. Prove that in directory-based dynamic hashing a page can be pointed at by a number of pointers that is a power of 2.

5. We have not talked much about how to organize the identifiers within a page for fast retrieval. Consider an unordered list, an ordered list, and hashing and compare their merits.

6. The function *insert* is almost complete except for a few lines of pseudocode. Replace the pseudocode by actual C code that places all identifiers in page p into the *temp* area and then rehashes those identifiers back into either page p or q.

7. Program 8.5 contains a reference to a function *coalesce* that combines the identifiers in two pages into a single page. Using the types and functions already defined, write a C version of this function.

8. Take the formula given by Mendelson for the number of leaf pages required to store k records in a directory-based dynamic hashing scheme and formally derive the approximation that $L(k)$ is about equal to $k/(p \, ln \, 2)$ where p is the page size.

9. Larson has suggested using open addressing in a directoryless dynamic hashing method to handle overflows. The problem is that those pages that have yet to be split have the most overflows, but these pages are stored contiguously. Instead, Larson suggests that pages be alternately split, so next to an unsplit page is a split page. Show how the hash function must be rewritten to handle this scheme.

8.4   REFERENCES AND SELECTED READINGS

Several interesting and enlightening works on hash tables exist. Some of these are: R. Morris, "Scatter storage techniques," *CACM*, vol. 11, no. 1, 1968, pp. 38-44; V. Lum, P. Yuen, and M. Dodd, "Key to address transform techniques: A fundamental performance study on large existing formatted files," *CACM*, vol. 14, no. 4, 1971, pp. 228-239; J. Bell, "The quadratic quotient method: A hash code eliminating secondary clustering," *CACM*, vol. 13, no. 2, 1970, pp. 107-109; A. Day, "Full table quadratic searching for scatter storage," *CACM*, vol. 13, no. 8, 1970, pp. 481-482; D. Severance, "Identifier search mechanisms: A survey and generalized model," *ACM Computing Surveys*, vol. 6, no. 3, 1974, pp. 175-194; W. Mauer and T. Lewis, "Hash table methods," *ACM Computing Surveys*, vol. 7, no. 1, 1975, pp. 5-20; D. Knuth, *The Art of Computer Programmamming: Sorting and Searching*, Addison-Wesley, Reading, Massachusetts, 1973; R. Brent, "Reducing the retrieval time of scatter storage techniques," *CACM*, vol. 16, no. 2, 1973, pp. 105-109; V. Lum, "General performance analysis of key-to-address transformation methods using an abstract file concept," *CACM*, vol. 16, no. 10, 1973, pp. 603-612; and C. E. Radke, "The use of quadratic residue research, *CACM*, vol. 13, no. 2, 1970, pp. 103-105.

In the literature, Larson was the first to introduce a method he called dynamic hashing. Litwin followed. Fagin et al. called their method extendible hashing. Fagin uses a directory scheme that doubles in size on expansion. Larson used a linked tree structure as the representation of the directory with pointers to pages in the leaves. The references are: P. Larson, "Dynamic hashing," *BIT*, vol. 18, 1978, pp. 184-201; W. Litwin, "Virtual hashing: a dynamically changing hashing," *Proc. Int. conf. on very large databases*, Berlin, 1978, pp. 517-523; and R. Fagin, J. Nievergelt, N. Pippenger, and H.R. Strong, "Extendible hashing - a fast access method for dynamic files," *ACM Trans. on Database Systems*, vol. 4, no. 3, 1979, pp. 315-344.

An excellent overview of dynamic hashing techniques and variations can be found in R.J. Enbody and H.C. Du, "Dynamic Hashing Schemes," *ACM Computing Surveys*, vol. 20, no 2, 1988, pp. 85-113.

Some other papers on dynamic hashing are: P. Flajolet, "On the performance evaluation of extendible hashing and trie searching," *Acta Informatica*, 20, 1983, pp. 345-369; D.B. Lomet, "Bounded index exponential hashing," *ACM Trans. on Database Systems*, vol. 8, no. 1, 1983, pp. 136-165; H. Mendelson, "Analysis of extendible hashing," *IEEE Trans. on Software Engineering*, vol. 8, no. 6, 1982, pp. 611-619; and K. Ramamohanarao and J.W. Lloyd, "Dynamic hashing schemes," *The Computer Journal*, vol. 25, no. 4, 1982, pp. 478-485.

Scholl introduces two methods to improve storage utilization by deferring the splitting of pages and handling overflows internally. This gives a tradeoff between storage utilization and access time. See M. Scholl, "New file organizations based on dynamic hashing," *ACM Trans. of Database Systems*, vol. 6, no. 1, 1981, pp. 194-211.

CHAPTER 9

HEAP STRUCTURES

9.1 MIN-MAX HEAPS

9.1.1 Definition

A *double-ended priority queue* is a data structure that supports the following operations:

(1) Insert an element with arbitrary key.

(2) Delete an element with the largest key.

(3) Delete an element with the smallest key.

When only insertion and one of the two deletion operations is supported, we may use a min heap or a max heap (see Chapter 5). A min-max heap supports all of the operations just described.

Definition: A *min-max heap* is a complete binary tree such that if it is not empty, each element has a field called *key*. Alternating levels of this tree are min levels and max levels, respectively. The root is on a min level. Let x be any node in a min-max heap. If x is on a min level then the element in x has the minimum key from among all elements in the subtree with root x. We call this node a *min* node. Similarly, if x is on a max level then the element in x has the maximum key from among all elements in the subtree with root *x*. We call this node a *max* node. □

Figure 9.1 shows an example 12 element min-max heap. The value in each node is the key of the element in that node. Notice that we are using the array representation discussed in Section 5.2.

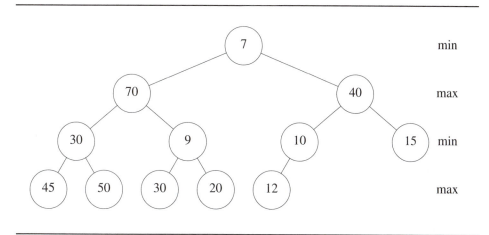

The figure shows, from top to bottom, labels on the right: min, max, min, max.

Figure 9.1: A 12 element min-max-heap

9.1.2   Insertion Into A Min-Max Heap

Suppose we wish to insert the element with key 5 into this min-max heap. Following the insertion, we will have a 13 element min-max-heap. This has the shape shown in Figure 9.2. As in the case of heaps, the insertion algorithm for min-max-heaps follows the path from the new node *j* to the root. Comparing the new key 5 with the key 10 that is in the parent of *j*, we see that since the node with key 10 is on a min level and 5 < 10, 5 is guaranteed to be smaller than all keys in nodes that are both on max levels and on the path from *j* to the root. Hence, the min-max-heap property is to be verified only with respect to min nodes on the path from *j* to the root. First, the element with key 10 is moved to node *j*. Then the element with key 7 is moved to the former position of 10. Finally, the new element with key 5 is inserted into the root. The min-max-heap following the insertion is shown in Figure 9.3(a).

Next, suppose we wish to insert an element with key 80 into the min-max-heap of Figure 9.1. The resulting min-max-heap has 13 elements and has the shape shown in Figure 9.2. Since 80 > 10 and 10 is on a min level, we are assured that 80 is larger than all keys in nodes that are both on min levels and on the path from *j* to the root. Hence, the min-max-heap property is to be verified only with respect to max nodes on the path from *j* to the root. There is only one such node in the min-max-heap of Figure 9.1. This

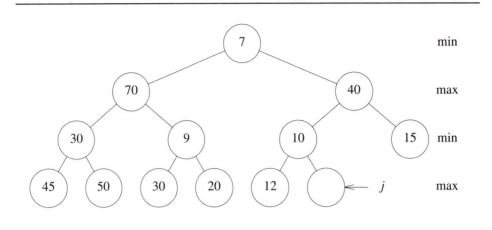

Figure 9.2: Min-max-heap of Figure 9.1 with new node *j*

node has key 40. The element with key 40 is moved to *j* and the new element inserted into the node formerly occupied by this element. The resulting min-max-heap is shown in Figure 9.3(b).

The preceding insertion examples lead to the insertion function *min_max_insert* (Program 9.1). The C declarations necessary to create the min-max heap are:

```
#define MAX_SIZE    100 /* maximum size of heap plus 1
*/
#define FALSE 0
#define TRUE 1
#define SWAP(x,y,t) ((t) = (x), (x) = (y), (y) = (t))
typedef struct {
        int key;
        /* other fields */
        } element;
element heap[MAX_SIZE];
```

Notice that we store a min-max heap in a one-dimensional array using the standard array representation of a complete binary tree (see Section 5.3). The function *min_max_insert* uses *verify_max*, *verify_min*, and *level* functions. The function *level* determines whether a node is on a min or a max level of a min-max heap; it returns *FALSE* for a min level and *TRUE* for a max level. The function *verify_max* (Program 9.2) begins at a max node *i* and follows the path of max nodes from *i* to the root of the min-max heap. It searches for the correct node in which to insert *item*. This node has the property that all max nodes above it and on the path to the root have key values at least as large as *item.key*. In addition, all max nodes below it and on the path from *i* to

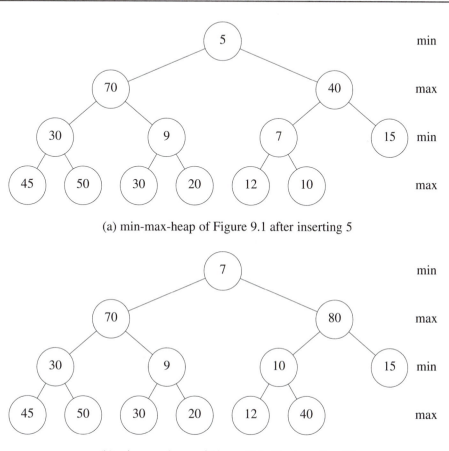

(a) min-max-heap of Figure 9.1 after inserting 5

(b) min-max-heap of Figure 9.1 after inserting 80

Figure 9.3: Insertion into a min-max-heap

the root have key values smaller than *item.key*. During the search, max nodes with keys smaller than *item.key* are moved one max level down.

The functions *verify_min* and *verify_max* are similar except that *verify_min* begins at a min node i and follows the path of min nodes from i to the root. To preserve the min-max heap property, *item* is inserted into one of these min nodes. We leave the formal development of *verify_min* and *level* as an exercise.

Analysis of *min_max_insert*: We may easily establish the correctness of *min_max_insert*. In addition, since a min-max heap with n elements has $O(\log n)$ levels, the complexity of the *min_max_insert* function is $O(\log n)$. □

```
void min_max_insert(element heap[], int *n, element item)
{
/* insert item into the min-max heap */
   int parent;
   (*n) ++;
   if (*n == MAX_SIZE) {
     fprintf(stderr,"The heap is full\n");
     exit(1);
   }
   parent = (*n)/2;
   if (!parent)
   /* heap is empty, insert item into first position */
     heap[1] = item;
   else switch(level(parent)) {
       case FALSE: /* min level */
               if (item.key < heap[parent].key) {
                  heap[*n] = heap[parent];
                  verify_min(heap,parent,item);
               }
               else
                  verify_max(heap,*n,item);
               break;
       case TRUE: /* max level */
               if (item.key > heap[parent].key) {
                  heap[*n] = heap[parent];
                  verify_max(heap,parent,item);
               }
               else
                  verify_min(heap,*n,item);
   }
}
```

Program 9.1: Procedure to insert into a min-max heap

9.1.3   Deletion Of Min Element

Let us now take a look at deletion from a min-max-heap. If we wish to delete the element with smallest key, then this element is in the root. In the case of the min-max-heap of Figure 9.1, we are to delete the element with key 7. Following the deletion, we will be left with a min-max-heap that has 11 elements. Its shape is shown in Figure 9.4. The node with key 12 is deleted from the heap and the element with key 12 is reinserted into

```
void verify_max(element heap[], int i, element item)
{
/* follow the nodes from the max node i to the root and
insert item into its proper place */
   int grandparent = i/4;
   while (grandparent)
      if (item.key > heap[grandparent].key) {
         heap[i] = heap[grandparent];
         i = grandparent;
         grandparent /= 4;
      }
      else
         break;
   heap[i] = item;
}
```

Program 9.2: *verify_max:* function

the heap. As in the case of deletion from a min or max-heap, the reinsertion is done by
examining the nodes of Figure 9.4 from the root down towards the leaves.

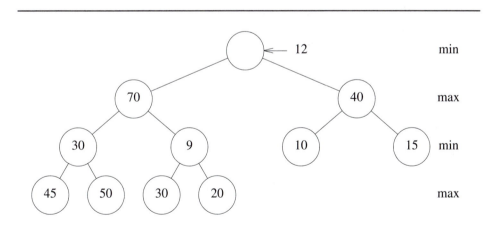

Figure 9.4: Shape of Figure 9.1 following a delete min

In a general situation, we are to reinsert an element *item* into a min-max-heap,
heap, whose root is empty. We consider the two cases:

(1)   *The root has no children.* In this case *item* is to be inserted into the root.

(2)   *The root has at least one child.* Now, the smallest key in the min-max-heap is in one of the children or grandchildren of the root. We determine which of these nodes has the smallest key. Let this be node k. The following possibilities need to be considered:

(a)   *item. key* $\leq heap\,[k]. key.$ *item* may be inserted into the root as there is no element in *heap* with key smaller than *item. key.*

(b)   *item. key* $> heap\,[k]. key$ and k is a child of the root. Since k is a max node, it has no descendants with key larger than *heap*[k]. *key*. Hence, node k has no descendants with key larger than *item. key*. So, the element *heap* [k] may be moved to the root and *item* inserted into node k.

(c)   *item. key* $> heap\,[k]. key$ and k is a grandchild of the root. In this case too, *heap* [k] may be moved to the root. Let *parent* be the parent of k. If *item. key* $> heap$ [*parent*]. *key*, then *heap* [*parent*] and *item* are to be interchanged. This ensures that the max node *parent* contains the largest key in the sub-heap with root *parent*. At this point, we are faced with the problem of inserting *item* into the sub-heap with root k. The root of this sub-min-max heap is presently empty. This is quite similar to our initial situation where we were to insert *item* into the min-max-heap *heap* with root 1 and node 1 is initially empty. Therefore, we repeat the above process.

In our example, *x. key* = 12 and the smallest key in the children and grandchildren of the root node is 9. Let k denote the node that contains this key and let p be its parent. Since, 9 < 12 and k is a grandchild of the root, we are in case 2 (c). The element with key 9 (i.e., $h\,[k\,]$) is moved to the root. Since *x. key* = 12 < 70 = $h\,[p\,].\, key$, we do not interchange x and $h\,[p\,]$. The current configuration is shown in Figure 9.5. We must now reinsert x into the sub-min-max-heap with root k. The smallest key from among the children and grandchildren of node k is 20. Since 12 < 20, we are in case 2 (a) and the element x is inserted into $h\,[k\,]$.

The function *delete_min* (Program 9.3) implements the deletion of the node with the minimum key from a min-max heap. This function uses a *min_child_grandchild(i)* function to determine the child or grandchild of the node i that has the smallest key. If both a child and a grandchild of i have the smallest key, *min_child_grandchild* should return the address of the child since this prevents further iterations of the **for** loop of *delete_min*. Notice that although *delete_min* does not explicitly check for the case when $n = 1$, this is handled correctly and an empty min-max heap results from the deletion.

Analysis of *delete_min*: In each iteration of the **for** loop of *delete_min* a constant amount of work is done. Also, in each iteration (except possibly the last), i moves down two levels. Since a min-max heap is a complete binary tree, *heap* has O(log n) levels. Hence, the complexity of *delete_min* is O(log n). □

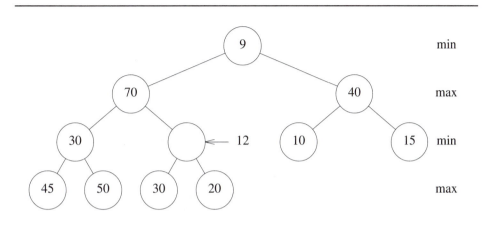

Figure 9.5: Figure 9.4 following the move of the element with key 9

The function to delete the element with the maximum key is similar to *delete _min*. We leave its development as an exercise.

EXERCISES

1. Write the *verify _min* function defined in connection with insertion into a min-max heap.

2. Write the *level* (i) function that determines whether node i of a min-max heap is on a min or a max level.

3. Write the *min _child _grandchild(i, n)* function that returns the child or grandchild of node i of a min-max heap that has the smallest key. You may assume that i has at least one child. n is the current size of the min-max heap.

4. Write a *delete _max* function to delete the element with the maximum key in a min-max heap. Your function should run in O(log n) time for a min-max heap with n elements.

5. Write a function that initializes a min-max heap with n elements. Use a series of *adjusts* as described in the initialization of a min (or max) heap (see Section 5.6). Show that your function takes O(n) time rather than the O(n log n) time that would be taken if initialization is done by performing n insertions into an initially empty heap.

```
element delete_min(element heap[], int *n)
{
/* delete the minimum element from the min-max heap */
   int i, last, k, parent;
   element temp, x;

   if (!(*n)) {
      fprintf(stderr, "The heap is empty\n");
      heap[0].key = INT_MAX; /* error key in heap[0] */
      return heap[0];
   }
   heap[0] = heap[1]; /* save the element */
   x = heap[(*n)--];
   /* find place to insert x */
   for (i = 1, last = (*n) /2; i <= last;) {
      k = min_child_grandchild(i, *n);
      if (x.key <= heap[k].key) break;
      /* case 2(b) or 2(c) */
      heap[i] = heap[k];
      if (k <= 2*i+1) {    /* 2(b) */
         i = k;
         break;
      }
      /* case 2(c), k is a grandchild of i */
      parent = k/2;
      if (x.key > heap[parent].key)
         SWAP(heap[parent], x, temp);
      i = k;
   } /* for */
   heap[i] = x;
   return heap[0];
}
```

Program 9.3: Function to delete the element with minimum key

9.2   DEAPS

9.2.1   Definition

A *deap* is a double-ended heap that supports the double-ended priority queue operations of insert, delete min, and delete max. As in the case of the min-max heap, these operations take logarithmic time on a deap. However, the deap is faster by a constant factor and the algorithms are simpler.

Definition: A *deap* is a complete binary tree that is either empty or satisfies the following properties:

(1)   The root contains no element.

(2)   The left subtree is a min-heap.

(3)   The right subtree is a max-heap.

(4)   If the right subtree is not empty, then let i be any node in the left subtree. Let j be the corresponding node in the right subtree. If such a j does not exist, then let j be the node in the right subtree that corresponds to the parent of i. The key in node i is less than or equal to the key in node j. □

An example of an 11-element deap is shown in Figure 9.6. The root of the min-heap contains 5, while that of the max-heap contains 45. The min-heap node with key 10 corresponds to the max-heap node with key 25, while the min-heap node with key 15 corresponds to the max-heap node with key 20. For the node containing 9, the node j defined in property (4) of the deap definition is the max-heap node that contains 40.

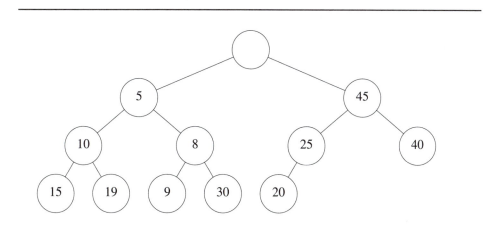

Figure 9.6: An 11 element deap

From the definition of a deap, it is evident that in an n element deap, $n > 1$, the min element is in the root of the min-heap while the max element is in the root of the max-heap. If $n = 1$, then the min and max elements are the same and are in the root of the min-heap. Since a deap is a complete binary tree, it may stored as an implicit data structure in a one dimensional array much the same way as min-, max-, and min-max-heaps are stored. In the case of a deap, position 1 of the array is not utilized (we may simply begin the array indexing at 2 rather than at 1). Let n denote the last occupied position in this array. Then the number of elements in the deap is $n - 1$. If i is a node in the min-heap, then its corresponding node in the max-heap is $i + 2^{\lfloor \log_2 i \rfloor - 1}$. Hence the j defined in property (4) of the definition is given by:

$$j = i + 2^{\lfloor \log_2 i \rfloor - 1};$$
$$\text{if } (j > n) \ j \ /= 2;$$

Notice that if property (4) of the deap definition is satisfied by all leaf nodes i of the min-heap, then it is satisfied by all remaining nodes of the min-heap too.

The double-ended priority queue operations are particularly easy to implement on a deap. The complexity of each operation is bounded by the height of the deap which is logarithmic in the number of elements in the deap.

9.2.2 Insertion Into A Deap

Suppose we wish to insert an element with key 4 into the deap of Figure 9.6. Following this insertion, the deap will have 12 elements in it and will thus have the shape shown in Figure 9.7. j points to the new node in the deap.

The insertion process begins by comparing the key 4 to the key in j's corresponding node, i, in the min-heap. This node contains a 19. To satisfy property (4), we move the 19 to node j. Now, if we use the min-heap insertion algorithm to insert 4 into position i, we get the deap of Figure 9.8.

If instead of inserting a 4, we were to insert a 30 into the deap of Figure 9.6, then the resulting deap has the same shape as in Figure 9.7. Comparing 30 with the key 19 in the corresponding node i, we see that property (4) may be satisfied by using the max-heap insertion algorithm to insert 30 into position j. This results in the deap of Figure 9.9.

The case when the new node, j, is a node of the min-heap is symmetric to the case just discussed. The function *deap_insert* (Program 9.4) implements the insert operation. The data type, *deap*, is defined as:

```
element deap [MAX_SIZE]
```

The position of the last element in the deap is n and $n = 1$ denotes an empty deap.

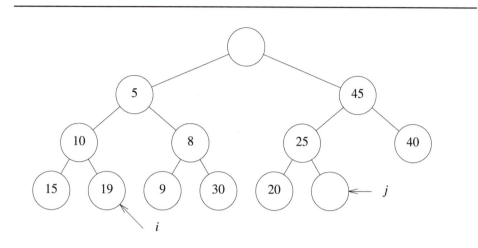

Figure 9.7: Shape of a 12 element deap

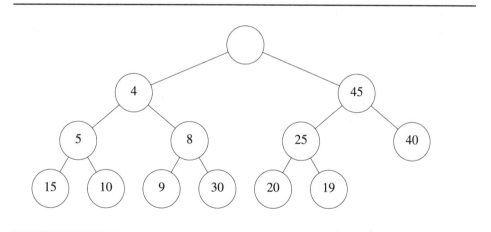

Figure 9.8: Deap of Figure 9.6 following the insertion of 4

The function *deap_insert* uses the following functions whose implementation we leave as exercises:

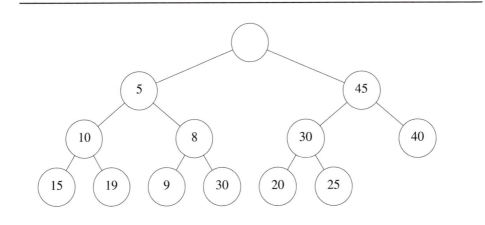

Figure 9.9: Deap of Figure 9.6 following the insertion of 30

(1)   *max_heap(n)*. This function returns *TRUE iff n* is a position in the max-heap of the deap.

(2)   *min_partner(n)*. This function computes the min-heap node that corresponds to the max-heap position *n*. This is given by $n - 2^{\lfloor \log_2 n \rfloor - 1}$

(3)   *max_partner(n)*. This function computes the max-heap node that corresponds to the parent of the min-heap position *n*. This is given by $(n + 2^{\lfloor \log_2 n \rfloor - 1}) / 2$.

(4)   *min_insert* and *max_insert*. These functions insert an element into a specified position of a min- and max-heap, respectively. This is done by following the path from this position toward the root of the respective heap. Elements are moved down as necessary until the correct place to insert the new element is found. This process differs from that used in Chapter 5 to insert into a min- or max-heap only in that the root is now at position 2 or 3 rather than at 1.

Analysis of *deap_insert*: The correctness of this function is easily established. Its complexity is O(log*n*) as the height of the deap is O(log*n*). □

9.2.3   Deletion Of Min Element

Now consider the delete min operation. A description of the deletion process is given in Program 9.5. The strategy is to first transform the deletion of the element from the root of the min-heap to the deletion of an element from a leaf position in the min-heap. This is done by following a root to leaf path in the min-heap ensuring that the min-heap properties are satisfied on the preceding levels of the heap. This process has the effect of shifting the empty position initially at the min-heap root to a leaf node *p*. This leaf node

```
void deap_insert(element deap[], int *n, element x)
{
/* insert x into the deap */
   int i;
   (*n) ++;
   if (*n == MAX_SIZE) {
      fprintf(stderr, "The heap is full\n");
      exit(1);
   }
   if (*n == 2)
      deap[2] = x; /* insert into empty deap */
   else switch(max_heap(*n)) {
      case FALSE:  /* *n is a position on min side */
              i = max_partner(*n);
              if (x.key > deap[i].key)  {
                 deap[*n] = deap[i];
                 max_insert(deap,i,x);
              }
              else
                 min_insert(deap,*n,x);
              break;
      case TRUE: /* *n is a position on max side */
              i = min_partner(*n);
              if (x.key < deap[i].key) {
                 deap[*n] = deap[i];
                 min_insert(deap,i,x);
              }
              else
                 max_insert(deap,*n,x);
   }
}
```

Program 9.4: Function to insert an item into a deap

is then filled by the element, t, initially in the last position of the deap. The insertion of t into position p of the min-heap is done as in *deap_insert* except that the specification of *max_partner*(i) is changed to:

$$j = i + 2^{\lfloor \log_2 i \rfloor - 1};$$
$$\text{if } (j > n)\, j \mathrel{/}= 2;$$

and the insertion does not increase the size of the deap. Function *modified_deap_insert* does this insertion. We leave the writing of this function as an exercise.

```
element deap_delete_min(element deap[], int *n)
{
/* delete the minimum element from the heap */
   int i,j;
   element temp;
   if (*n <  2) {
      fprintf(stderr, "The deap is empty\n");
      /* return an error code to user */
      deap[0].key = INT_MAX;
      return deap[0];
   }
   deap[0] = deap[2];  /* save min element */
   temp = deap[(*n)--];
   for (i = 2; i*2 <= *n; deap[i] = deap[j], i = j) {
   /* find node with smaller key */
   j = i*2;
   if (j+1 <= *n) {
      if (deap[j].key > deap[j+1].key)
         j++;
   }
 }
modified_deap_insert(deap,i,temp);
return deap[0];
 }
```

Program 9.5: Delete min function

For example, suppose that we wish to remove the minimum element from the deap of Figure 9.6. To do this, we first place the last element (the one with key 20) in the deap into a temporary element, *temp*, since the deletion removes this node from the heap structure. Next, we fill the vacancy created in the min-heap root (node 2) by the removal of the minimum element. To fill this vacancy we move along the path from the root to a leaf node. Prior to each move, we place the smaller of the elements in the current node's children into the current node. We then move to the node previously occupied by the moved element. In this example, we first move 8 into node 2. Then we move 9 into the node formerly occupied by 8. Now, we have an empty leaf and proceed to insert 20 into this. We compare 20 with the key 40 in its max partner. Since 20 < 40, no exchange is needed and we proceed to insert the 20 into the min-heap beginning at the empty position. This operation results in the deap of Figure 9.10.

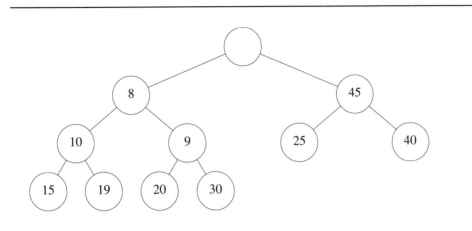

Figure 9.10: Deap of Figure 9.6 following a delete min

Analysis of *deap_delete_min*: We may easily verify that *deap_delete_min* works correctly regardless of whether the last position in the deap is in the min- or max-heap. The complexity is O(log$n$) as the height of a deap is O(log$n$). □

The *deap_delete_max* operation is performed in a similar manner.

EXERCISES

1. Complete the *deap_insert* function (Program 9.4) by writing all the functions that it uses. Test the insertion function by running it on a computer. Generate your own test data.

2. Complete the *deap_delete_min* function (Program 9.5) by writing all the functions that it uses. Test the correctness of your function by running it on a computer using test data of your choice.

3. Write a function to initialize a deap with n elements. Your function must run in O(n) time. Show that it actually has this running time. (Hint: Use a series of adjusts as discussed in Section 5.6.)

4. Write the functions to perform all double-ended priority queue operations for a min-max heap and for a deap.

   (a) Use suitable test data to test the correctness of your functions.

(b)   Create a random list of *n* elements and a random sequence of insert, delete min, and delete max operations of length *m*. Create the latter sequence so that the probability of an insert is approximately .5 and the probability for each type of delete is approximately .25. Initialize a min-max heap and a deap to contain the *n* elements in the first random list. Now, measure the time to perform the *m* operations using the min-max heap as well as the deap. Divide this time by *m* to get the average time per operation. Do this for $n = 100, 500, 1000, 2000, \cdots, 5000$. Let *m* be 5000. Tabulate your computing times.

(c)   Based on your experiments, what can you say about the relative merits of the two double-ended priority queue schemes?

5.   Obtain an exact count of the worst case number of key comparisons that can be made during each of the double-ended priority queue operations when a min-max heap is used. Do this also for the case when a deap is used. What can you say about the expected worst case performance of these two methods? Can you think of a way to reduce the worst case number of comparisons using a binary search (this will not affect the number of element moves though)?

9.3   LEFTIST TREES

In the preceding section we extended the definition of a priority queue by requiring that both delete max and delete min operations be permissible. In this section, we consider a different extension. Suppose that in addition to the normal priority queue operations, we are also required to support the operation of *combine*. This requires us to combine two priority queues into a single priority queue. One application for this is when the server for one priority queue shuts down. At this time, it is necessary to combine its priority queue with that of a functioning server.

Let *n* be the total number of elements in the two priority queues that are to be combined. If heaps are used to represent priority queues, then the combine operation takes $O(n)$ time. Using a leftist tree, the combine operation as well as the normal priority queue operations take logarithmic time.

In order to define a leftist tree, we need to introduce the concept of an extended binary tree. An *extended binary* tree is a binary tree in which all empty binary subtrees have been replaced by a square node. Figure 9.11 shows two example binary trees. Their corresponding extended binary trees are shown in Figure 9.12. The square nodes in an extended binary tree are called *external nodes*. The original (circular) nodes of the binary tree are called *internal nodes*.

Let *x* be a node in an extended binary tree. Let *left – child* (*x*) and *right – child* (*x*), respectively, denote the left and right children of the internal node *x*. Define *shortest* (*x*) to be the length of a shortest path from *x* to an external node. It is easy to see that *shortest* (*x*) satisfies the following recurrence:

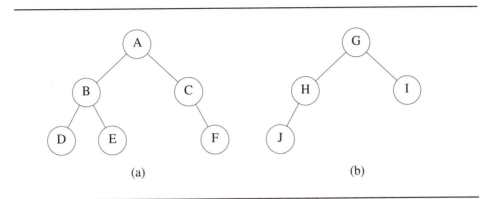

Figure 9.11: Two binary trees

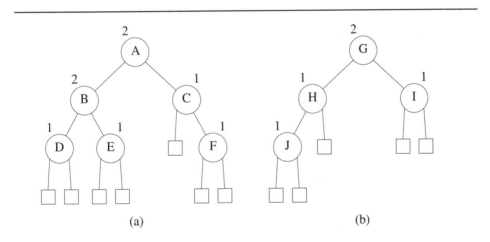

Figure 9.12: Extended binary trees corresponding to Figure 9.11

$$shortest(x) = \begin{cases} 0 & \text{if } x \text{ is an external node} \\ 1 + \min\{shortest(left-child(x)), shortest(right-child(x))\} & \text{otherwise} \end{cases}$$

The number outside each internal node x of Figure 9.12 is the value of $shortest(x)$.

Definition: A *leftist tree* is a binary tree such that if it is not empty, then

$$shortest(left-child(x)) \geq shortest(right-child(x))$$

for every internal node x. □

The binary tree of Figure 9.11(a) which corresponds to the extended binary tree of Figure 9.12(a) is not a leftist tree as $shortest(left\_child(C)) = 0$ while $shortest(right\_child(C)) = 1$. The binary tree of Figure 9.11(b) is a leftist tree.

Lemma 9.1: Let x be the root of a leftist tree that has n (internal) nodes.

(a) $n \geq 2^{shortest(x)} - 1$

(b)   The rightmost root to external node path is the shortest root to external node path. Its length is $shortest(x)$.

Proof: (a) From the definition of $shortest(x)$ it follows that there are no external nodes on the first $shortest(x)$ levels of the leftist tree. Hence, the leftist tree has at least

$$\sum_{i=1}^{shortest(x)} 2^{i-1} = 2^{shortest(x)} - 1$$

internal nodes.

(b) This follows directly from the definition of a leftist tree. □

We represent leftist trees with nodes that have the fields $left\_child$, $right\_child$, $shortest$, and $data$. We assume that $data$ is a **struct** with at least a key field. We should note that we introduced the concept of an external node to arrive at clean definitions. The external nodes are never physically present in the representation of a leftist tree. Rather the appropriate child field of the parent of an external node is set to *NULL*. The C declarations are:

```
typedef struct {
        int key;
        /* other fields */
        } element;
typedef struct leftist *leftist_tree;
        struct leftist {
                leftist_tree left_child;
                element data;
                leftist_tree right_child;
                int shortest;
                } ;
```

Definition: A *min-leftist tree* (*max leftist tree*) is a leftist tree in which the key value in each node is no larger (smaller) than the key values in its children (if any). In other words, a min (max) leftist tree is a leftist tree that is also a min (max) tree. □

Figure 9.13 depicts two min-leftist trees. The number inside a node x is the key of the element in x and the number outside x is *shortest*(x). The operations insert, delete min (delete max), and combine can be performed in logarithmic time using a min (max) leftist tree. We shall continue our discussion using min leftist trees.

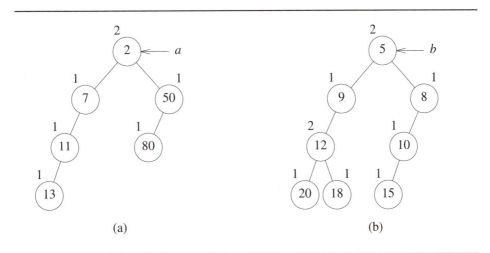

(a)   (b)

Figure 9.13: Example min leftist trees

We can implement both insert and delete min operations by using the combine operation. To insert an element, x, into a min-leftist tree, a, we first create a min-leftist tree, b, that contains the single element x. Then we combine the min-leftist trees a and b. To delete the min element from a nonempty min-leftist tree, a, we combine the min-leftist trees $a \rightarrow left\_child$ and $a \rightarrow right\_child$ and delete node a.

The combine operation is itself simple. Suppose that we wish to combine the min-leftist trees a and b. First, we obtain a new binary tree containing all elements in a and b by following the rightmost paths in a and/or b. This binary tree has the property that the key in each node is no larger than the keys in its children (if any). Next, we interchange the left and right subtrees of nodes as necessary to convert this binary tree into a leftist tree. The insert and delete min operations can both be performed by using the combine operation. To insert an element x into a min leftist tree a, we first create a min leftist tree b that contains the single element x. Then we combine the min leftist trees a and b. To delete the min element from a non empty min leftist tree a, we combine the min leftist trees $a \rightarrow left\_child$ and $a \rightarrow right\_child$ and delete the node a.

As an example, consider combining the min leftist trees a and b of Figure 9.13. To obtain a binary tree that contains all the elements in a and b and that satisfies the required relationship between parent and child keys, we first compare the root keys 2 and

5. Since $2 < 5$, the new binary tree should have 2 in its root. We shall leave the left subtree of a unchanged and combine the right subtree of a and the entire binary tree b. The resulting binary tree will become the new right subtree of a. When combining the right subtree of a and the binary tree b, we notice that $5 < 50$. So, 5 should be in the root of the combined tree. Now, we proceed to combine the subtrees with root 8 and 50. Since $8 < 50$ and 8 has no right subtree, we can make the subtree with root 50 the right subtree of 8. This gives us the binary tree of Figure 9.14(a). Hence, the result of combining the right subtree of a and the tree b is the tree of Figure 9.14(b). When this is made the right subtree of a, we get the binary tree of Figure 9.14(c). To convert this into a leftist tree, we begin at the last modified root (i.e., 8) and trace back to the overall root ensuring that *shortest* ($left - child$ ( )) $\geq$ *shortest* ($right - child$ ( )). This inequality holds at 8 but not at 5 and 2. Simply interchanging the left and right subtrees at these nodes causes the inequality to hold. The result is the leftist tree of Figure 9.14(d).

The function *min_combine* (Program 9.6) contains the code to combine two leftist trees. This function uses the recursive function *min_union* (Program 9.7) to actually combine two nonempty leftist trees. The function *min_union* intertwines the two steps:

(1) Create a binary tree that contains all elements while ensuring that the root of each subtree has the smallest key in that subtree.

(2) Ensure that each node has a left subtree whose *shortest* value is greater than or equal to that of its right subtree.

Analysis of *min_combine*: Since *min_union* moves down the rightmost paths in the two leftist trees being combined and since the lengths of these paths is at most logarithmic in the number of elements in each tree, the combining of two leftist trees with a total of n elements is done in time $O(\log n)$. □

EXERCISES

1. Let t be an arbitrary binary tree represented using the node structure for a leftist tree.

    (a) Write a function to initialize the *shortest* field of each node in t.

    (b) Write a function to convert t into a leftist tree.

    (c) Determine the complexity of each of the these functions.

2. Write a function to initialize a min-leftist tree with n elements. Assume that nodes have the same structure as that used in the text. Your function must run in $O(n)$ time. Show that this is the case. Can you think of a way to do this initialization in $O(n)$ time, and such that the resulting min-leftist tree is also a complete binary tree?

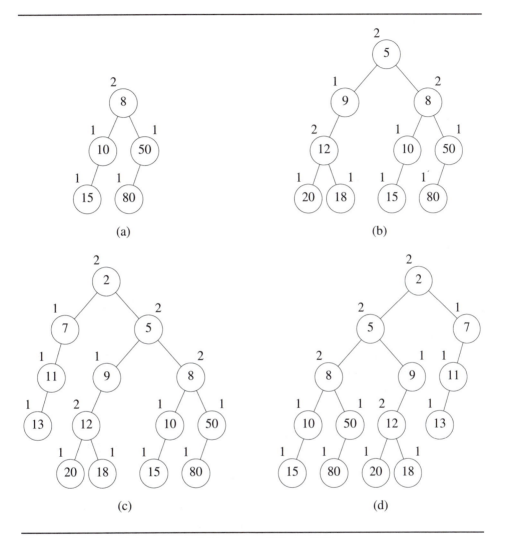

Figure 9.14: Combining the min leftist trees of Figure 9.13

3. Write a function to delete the element in node x of the min-leftist tree a. Assume that each node has the fields *left_child*, *right_child*, *parent*, *shortest*, and *data*. The *parent* field of a node points to its parent in the leftist tree. Show we can perform this deletion in O(log n), where n is the number of elements in a.

4. [Lazy deletion] Another way to handle the deletion of arbitrary elements from a min-leftist tree is to use a field, *deleted*, in place of the parent field of the previous exercise. When we delete an element, we set its *deleted* field to *TRUE*. However,

```
void min_combine(leftist_tree *a, leftist_tree *b)
{
/* combine the two min leftist trees *a and *b.  The
resulting min leftist tree is returned in *a, and *b
is set to NULL */
   if (!*a)
      *a = *b;
   else if (*b)
      min_union(a,b);
   *b = NULL;
}
```

Program 9.6: : Combining two leftist trees

we do not physically delete the node. When we perform a *delete_min* operation, we first search for the minimum element not deleted by carrying out a limited preorder search. This preorder search traverses only the upper part of the tree as needed to identify the min element. All deleted elements encountered are physically deleted and their subtrees combined to obtain the new min-leftist tree.

(a)   Write a function to delete the element in node *x* of the min-leftist tree *a*.

(b)   Write another function to delete the min element from a min-leftist tree from which several elements have been deleted using the former function.

(c)   Determine the complexity of this latter function as a function of the number of deleted elements encountered and the number of elements in the entire tree.

5.   [Skewed heaps] A *skewed heap* is a min-tree that supports the min-leftist tree operations insert, delete min, and combine in amortized time (see the next section for a definition of amortized time) $O(\log n)$ per operation. As in the case of min-leftist trees, inserts and deletes are performed using the combine operation which is carried out by following the rightmost paths in the two heaps being combined. However, unlike min-leftist trees, we interchange the left and right subtrees of all nodes (except the last) on the rightmost path in the resulting heap.

(a)   Write insert, delete min, and combine functions for skewed heaps.

(b)   Compare the running times of these with those for the same operations on a min-leftist tree. Use random sequences of insert, delete min, and combine operations.

```
void min_union(leftist_tree *a, leftist_tree *b)
{
/* recursively combine two nonempty min leftist trees */
   leftist_tree temp;
   /* set a to be the tree with smaller root */
   if ((*a)->data.key > (*b)->data.key)
      SWAP(*a,*b,temp);
   /* create binary tree such that the smallest key in each
   subtree is in the root */
   if (!(*a)->right_child)
      (*a)->right_child = *b;
   else
      min_union(&(*a)->right_child, b);
   /*leftist tree property */
   if (!(*a)->left_child) {
      (*a)->left_child = (*a)->right_child;
      (*a)->right_child = NULL ;
   }
   else if ((*a)->left_child->shortest <
   (*a)->right_child->shortest)
      SWAP((*a)->left_child,(*a)->right_child, temp);
   (*a)->shortest = (!(*a)->right_child) ? 1 :
   (*a)->right_child->shortest + 1;
}
```

Program 9.7: Combining two min-leftist trees

9.4 BINOMIAL HEAPS

9.4.1 Cost Amortization

A binomial heap is a data structure that supports the same functions (i.e., insert, delete min or max, and combine) as supported by leftist trees. Unlike leftist trees where an individual operation can be performed in $O(\log n)$ time, certain individual operations performed on a binomial heap may take $O(n)$ time. However, if we amortize part of the cost of expensive operations over the inexpensive ones, then the amortized complexity of an individual operation is either $O(1)$ or $O(\log n)$ depending on the type of the operation.

Let us examine the concept of cost (we shall use the terms *cost* and *complexity* interchangeably) amortization more closely. Suppose that a sequence I1, I2, D1, I3, I4, I5, I6, D2, I7 of insert and delete min operations is performed. Assume that the *actual cost* of each of the seven inserts is one. By this, we mean that each insert takes one unit of time. Further, suppose that the delete min operations D1 and D2 have an actual cost of eight and ten, respectively. The total cost of the sequence of operations is therefore 25.

In an amortization scheme we charge some of the actual cost of an operation to other operations. This reduces the charged cost of some operations and increases that of others. The *amortized cost* of an operation is the total cost charged to it. The cost transferring (amortization) scheme is required to be such that the sum of the amortized costs of the operations is greater than or equal to the sum of their actual costs. If we charge one unit of the cost of a delete min to each of the inserts since the last delete min (if any), then two units of the cost of D1 get transferred to I1 and I2 (the charged cost of each increases by one) and four units of the cost of D2 get transferred to I3 - I6. The amortized cost of each of I1 - I6 becomes two, that of I7 is equal to its actual cost (i.e., one), and that of each of D1 and D2 becomes 6. The sum of the amortized costs is 25 which is the same as the sum of the actual costs.

Now suppose we can prove that no matter what sequence of insert and delete min operations is performed, we can charge costs in such a way that the amortized cost of each insert is no more than two and that of each delete min is no more than six. This will enable us to make the claim that the actual cost of any insert / delete min sequence is no more that $2*i+6*d$ where i and d are, respectively, the number of insert and delete min operations in the sequence. Suppose that the actual cost of a delete min is no more than ten, while that of an insert is one. Using actual costs, we can conclude that the sequence cost is no more than $i + 10 * d$. Combining these two bounds, we obtain $\min\{2 * i + 6 * d, i + 10 * d\}$ as a bound on the sequence cost. Hence, using the notion of cost amortization it is possible to obtain tighter bounds on the complexity of a sequence of operations. We shall use the notion of cost amortization to show that while individual delete operations on an binomial heap may be expensive, the cost of any sequence of binomial heap operations is actually quite small.

9.4.2 Definition Of Binomial Heaps

As in the case of heaps and leftist trees, there are two varieties of binomial heaps: min and max. A *min-binomial heap* is a collection of min-trees while a *max-binomial heap* is a collection of max-trees. We shall explicitly consider min-binomial heaps only. These will be referred to as *B-heaps*. Figure 9.15 shows an example B-heap that is comprised of three min-trees.

Using B-heaps, we can perform an insert and a combine in O(1) actual and amortized time and a delete min in O(log$n$) amortized time. B-heaps are represented using nodes that have the fields: *degree*, *child*, *left_link*, *right_link*, and *data*. The *degree* of a node is the number of children it has; the *child* field is used to point to any one of its children (if any); the *left_link* and *right_link* fields are used to maintain doubly linked circular lists of siblings. All the children of a node form a doubly linked circular list and the node points to one of these children. Additionally, the roots of the min-trees that comprise a B-heap are linked to form a doubly linked circular list. The B-heap is then

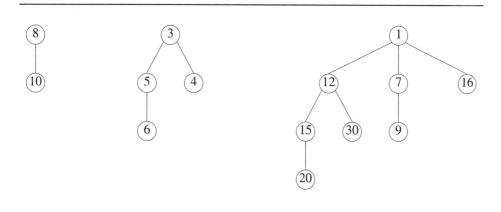

Figure 9.15: A B-heap with three min-trees

pointed at by a single pointer to the min-tree root with smallest key. In an exercise, we examine the possibility of replacing all doubly linked circular lists by singly linked circular lists.

Figure 9.16 shows the representation for the example of Figure 9.15. *child* fields are shown by broken arrows and *parent* fields by solid arrows. To enhance the readability of this figure, we have used bidirectional arrows to join together nodes that are in the same doubly linked circular list. When such a list contains only one node, no such arrows are drawn. Each of the key sets: {10}, {6}, {5,4}, {20}, {15, 30}, {9}, {12, 7, 16}, and {8, 1, 3} denotes the keys in one of the doubly linked circular lists of Figure 9.16 . *a* is the pointer to the B-heap. Note that an empty B-heap has a *NULL* pointer.

9.4.3 Insertion Into A Binomial Heap

We insert an element, *x*, into an B-heap, *a*, by first putting *x* into a new node and then placing this node into the doubly linked circular list pointed at by *a*. We reset *a* to this new node only if *a* is *NULL* or *x*'s key is smaller than the key in the node pointed at by *a*. It is evident that we can perform these insertion steps in O(1) time.

9.4.4 Combine

To combine two nonempty B-heaps *a* and *b*, we combine the top doubly linked circular lists of *a* and *b* into a single doubly linked circular list. The new B-heap pointer is either *a* or *b* depending on which has the smaller key. This can be determined with a single comparison. Since two doubly linked circular lists can be combined into a single one in O(1) time, a combine takes only O(1) time.

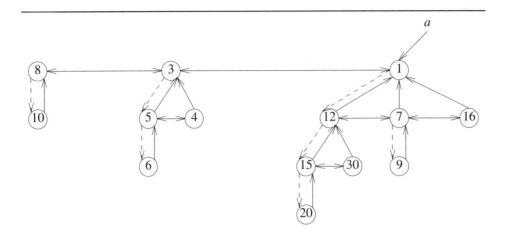

Figure 9.16: B-heap of Figure 9.15 showing parent pointers and sibling lists

9.4.5 Deletion Of Min Element

Now, let's take a look at the delete min operation. Let *a* be the pointer of the B-heap from which the min element is to be deleted. If *a* is *NULL*, then the B-heap is empty and a deletion cannot be performed. Assume that *a* is not *NULL*. *a* points to the node that contains the min element. This node is deleted from its doubly linked circular list. The new B-heap consists of the remaining min-trees and the sub min-trees of the deleted root. Figure 9.17 shows the situation for the example of Figure 9.15.

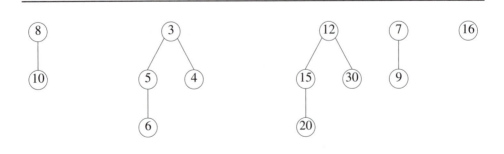

Figure 9.17: The B-heap of Figure 9.15 following the deletion of the min element

Before forming the doubly linked circular list of min-tree roots, we repeatedly join together pairs of min-trees that have the same degree (the degree of a nonempty min-tree is the degree of its root). *This min-tree joining is done by making the min-tree whose root has larger key a subtree of the other (ties are broken arbitrarily).* When two min-trees are joined, the degree of the resulting min-tree is one larger than the original degree of each min-tree and the number of min-trees decreases by one. For our example, we may first join either the min-trees with roots 8 and 7 or those with roots 3 and 12. If the first pair is joined, the min-tree with root 8 is made a subtree of the min-tree with root 7. We now have the min-tree collection of Figure 9.18. There are three min-trees of degree two in this collection. If the pair with roots 7 and 3 is picked for joining, the resulting min-tree collection is that of Figure 9.19. Since the min-trees in this collection have different degrees, the min-tree joining process terminates.

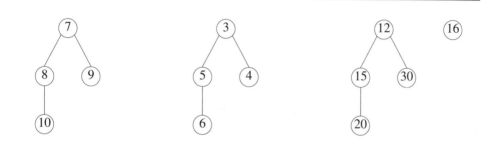

Figure 9.18: The B-heap of Figure 9.17 following the joining of the two degree one min-trees

After we have finished joining min-trees, we link the roots of the min-trees to form a doubly linked circular list. We also reset the B-heap pointer so as to point to the min-tree root with smallest key. The steps involved in a delete min operation are summarized in Program 9.8.

Steps 1 and 2 take O(1) time. Step 3 may be implemented by using an array *tree* indexed from 0 to the maximum possible degree, *MAX_DEGREE*, of a min-tree. Initially all entries in this array are *NULL*. Let s be the number of min-trees in a and y. The lists a and y created in step 2 are scanned. For each min-tree p in the lists a and y created in step 2, the code of Program 9.9 is executed. The function *join_min_trees* makes the input tree with larger root a sub tree of the other tree. The resulting tree is returned in the first parameter. In the end, the array *tree* contains pointers to the min-trees that are to be linked together in step 4. Since each time a pair of min-trees is joined the total number of min-trees decreases by one, the number of joins is at most $s-1$. Hence, the complexity of step 3 is O(*MAX_DEGREE* + s). Step 4 is accomplished by scanning *tree* and linking together the min-trees found. During this scan, the min-tree with minimum key may also be determined. The complexity of step 4 is O(*MAX_DEGREE*).

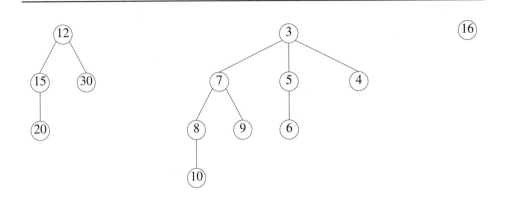

Figure 9.19: The B-heap of Figure 9.18 following the joining of two degree two min-trees

{Delete the min element from a B-heap *a*, this element is returned in *x*}

Step 1: [Handle empty B-heap] if (*a = NULL*) *deletion – error* else perform steps 2 - 4;

Step 2: [Deletion from nonempty B-heap] *x = a–>data*; *y = a–>child*; Delete *a* from its doubly linked circular list; Now, *a* points to any remaining node in the resulting list; If there is no such node, then *a = NULL*;

Step 3: [Min-tree joining] Consider the min-trees in the lists *a* and *y*; Join together pairs of min-trees of the same degree until all remaining min-trees have different degree;

Step 4: [Form min-tree root list] Link the roots of the remaining min-trees (if any) together to form a doubly linked circular list; Set *a* to point to the root (if any) with minimum key;

Program 9.8: Steps in a delete min

9.4.6 Analysis

Definition: The *binomial tree, B_k, of degree k* is a tree such that if $k = 0$, then the tree has exactly one node and if $k > 0$, then it consists of a root whose degree is k and whose sub-trees are $B_0, B_1, \cdots, B_{k-1}$. □

```
for (degree = p->degree; tree[degree]; degree++) {
  join_min_trees(p,tree[degree]);
  tree[degree] = NULL;
}
tree[degree] = p;
```

Program 9.9: Code to handle min-tree p encountered during a scan of lists a and y

The min-trees of Figure 9.15 are B_1, B_2, and B_3, respectively. One may verify that B_k has exactly 2^k nodes. Further, if we start with a collection of empty B-heaps and perform only the operations insert, combine, and delete min, then the min-trees in each B-heap are binomial trees. These observations enable us to prove that when only inserts, combines, and delete mins are performed, we can amortize costs such that the amortized cost of each insert and combine is O(1) and of each delete min is O(log$n$).

Lemma 9.2: Let a be a B-heap with n elements that results from a sequence of insert, combine, and delete min operations performed on initially empty B-heaps. Each min-tree in a has degree $\leq \log_2 n$. Consequently, $MAX\_DEGREE \leq \lfloor \log_2 n \rfloor$ and the actual cost of a delete min is O(log$n$ + s).

Proof: Since each of the min-trees in a is a binomial tree with at most n nodes, none can have degree greater than $\lfloor \log_2 n \rfloor$. $\square$

Theorem 9.1: If a sequence of n insert, combine, and delete min operations is performed on initially empty B-heaps, then we can amortize costs such that the amortized time complexity of each insert and combine is O(1) and that of each delete min is O(log$n$).

Proof: For each B-heap define the quantities *#insert* and *last_size* in the following way. When an initially empty B-heap is created or when a delete min is performed on an B-heap, its *#insert* value is set to zero. Each time an insert is done on a B-heap, its *#insert* value is increased by one. When two B-heaps are combined, the *#insert* value of the resulting B-heap is the sum of the *#insert* values of the B-heaps combined. Hence *#insert* counts the number of inserts performed on a B-heap or its constituent B-heaps since the last delete min performed in each. When an initially empty B-heap is created its *last_size* value is zero. When a delete min is performed on a B-heap its *last_size* is set to the number of min-trees it contains following this delete min. When two B-heaps are combined the *last_size* value for the resulting B-heap is the sum of the *last_size* values in the two B-heaps that were combined. One may verify that the number of min-trees in a B-heap is always equal to *#insert* + *last_size*.

Consider any individual delete min in the operation sequence. Assume this is from the B-heap a. Observe that the total number of elements in all the B-heaps is at most n as only inserts add elements and at most n inserts can be present in a sequence of n operations. Let $u = a{-}>degree \leq \log_2 n$.

From Lemma 9.2, the actual cost of this delete min is $O(\log n + s)$. The $\log n$ term is due to MAX_DEGREE and represents the time needed to initialize the array $tree$ and the step 4 time. The s term represents the time to scan the lists a and y and to perform the at most $s-1$ min-tree joins. We see that $s = \#insert + last\_size + u - 1$. If we charge $\#insert$ units of cost to the insert operations that contribute to the count $\#insert$ and $last\_size$ units to the delete mins that contribute to the count $last\_size$ (each such delete min gets charged a number of cost units equal to the number of min-trees it left behind), then only $u-1$ of the s cost units remain. Since $u \leq \log_2 n$ and since the number of min-trees in a B-heap immediately following a delete min is $\leq \log_2 n$, the amortized cost of a delete min becomes $O(\log_2 n)$.

Since the above charging scheme adds at most one unit to the cost of any insert, the amortized cost of an insert becomes $O(1)$. The amortization scheme used does not charge anything extra to a combine. So the actual and amortized cost of a combine are also $O(1)$. $\square$

From the preceding theorem and the definition of cost amortization, it follows that the actual cost of any sequence of i inserts, c combines, and dm delete mins is $O(i + c + dm \log i)$.

EXERCISES

1. Let S be an initially empty stack. We wish to perform two kinds of operations on S: $add(x)$ and $delete\_until(x)$. These are defined as follows:

   (a) $add(x)$ ... add the element x to the top of the stack S. This operation takes $O(1)$ time per invocation.

   (b) $delete\_until(x)$ ... delete elements from the top of the stack upto and including the first x encountered. If p elements are deleted, the time taken is $O(p)$.

   Consider any sequence of n stack operations (adds and $delete\_until$s). Show how to amortize the cost of the add and $delete\_until$ operations so that the amortized cost of each is $O(1)$. From this, conclude that the time needed to perform any such sequence of operations is $O(n)$.

2. Let x be an unsorted array of n elements. The function $search(x,n,i,y)$ searches x for y by examining $x[i], x[i+1], ...,$ in that order, for the least j such that $x[j] = y$. In case no such j is found, j is set to $n+1$. On termination, $search$ sets i to j. Assume that the time required to examine a single element of x is $O(1)$.

(a) What is the worst case complexity of *search*?

(b) Suppose that a sequence of m searches is performed beginning with $i = 0$. Use a cost amortization scheme that assigns costs to both elements and search operations. Show that it is always possible to amortize costs so that the amortized cost of each element is $O(1)$ and that of each search is also $O(1)$. From this, conclude that the cost of the sequence of m searches is $O(m + n)$.

3. Prove that the binomial tree B_k has 2^k nodes, $k \geq 0$.

4. Can all the functions on a B-heap be performed in the same time using singly linked circular lists rather than doubly linked circular lists? Note that we can delete from an arbitrary node x of a singly linked circular list by copy over the data from the next node and then deleting the next node rather than the node x.

5. Compare the performance of leftist trees and B-heaps under the assumption that the only permissible operations are insert and delete min. For this, do the following:

(a) Create a random list of n elements and a random sequence of insert and delete min operations of length m. The number of delete mins and inserts should be approximately equal. Initialize a min-leftist tree and a B-heap to contain the n elements in the first random list. Now, measure the time to perform the m operations using the min-leftist tree as well as the B-heap. Divide this time by m to get the average time per operation. Do this for $n = 100, 500, 1000, 2000, \cdots, 5000$. Let m be 5000. Tabulate your computing times.

(b) Based on your experiments, make some statements about the relative merits of the two data structures?

9.5 FIBONACCI HEAPS

9.5.1 Definition

A Fibonacci heap is a data structure that supports the three binomial heap operations: insert, delete min or max, and combine as well as the operations:

(1) *delete*, delete the element in a specified node

(2) *decrease key*, decrease the key of a specified node by a given positive amount.

The first of these can be done in $O(1)$ amortized time and the second in $O(\log n)$ amortized time. The binomial heap operations can be performed in the same asymptotic times using a Fibonacci heap as using a binomial heap.

There are two varieties of Fibonacci heaps: min and max. A *min-Fibonacci heap* is a collection of min-trees while a *max-Fibonacci heap* is a collection of max-trees. We shall explicitly consider min-Fibonacci heaps only. These will be referred to as *F-heaps*. B-heaps are a special case of F-heaps. Thus, all the example B-heaps of the preceding section are also examples of F-heaps. As a consequence, we shall, in this section, refer to these examples as example F-heaps. To represent an F-heap, the B-heap representation is augmented by adding two fields: *parent* and *child − cut* to each node. The *parent* field is used to point to the node's parent (if any). The significance of the *child − cut* field will be described later. The basic operations: insert, delete min, and combine are performed exactly as for the case of B-heaps. Let us examine the remaining two operations.

9.5.2   Deletion From An F-heap

To delete an arbitrary node b from the F-heap a, we do the following:

(1)   If $a = b$, then do a delete min; otherwise do steps 2, 3, and 4 below.

(2)   Delete b from the doubly linked list it is in.

(3)   Combine the doubly linked list of b's children with the doubly linked list of a's min-tree roots to get a single doubly linked list. Trees of equal degree are not joined together as in a delete min.

(4)   Dispose of node b.

For example, if we delete the node containing 12 from the F-heap of Figure 9.15, we get the F-heap of Figure 9.20. The actual cost of an arbitrary delete is O(1) unless the min element is being deleted. In this case the deletion time is the time for a delete min operation.

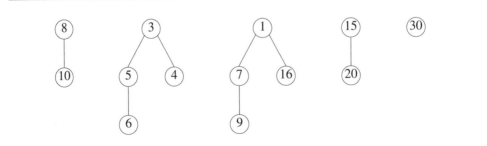

Figure 9.20: F-heap of Figure 9.15 following the deletion of 12

9.5.3   Decrease Key

To decrease the key in node b we do the following:

(1)   Reduce the key in b.

(2)   If b is not a min-tree root and its key is smaller than that in its parent, then delete b from its doubly linked list and insert it into the doubly linked list of min-tree roots.

(3)   Change a to point to b in case the key in b is smaller than that in a.

Suppose we decrease the key 15 in the F-heap of Figure 9.15 by 4. The resulting F-heap is shown in Figure 9.21. The cost of performing a decrease key is $O(1)$.

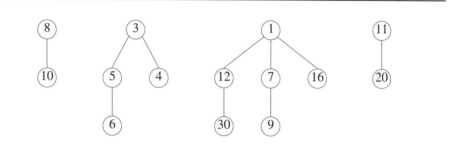

Figure 9.21: F-heap of Figure 9.15 following the reduction of 15 by 4

9.5.4   Cascading Cut

With the addition of the delete and decrease key operations, the min-trees in an F-heap need not be binomial trees. In fact, it is possible to have degree k min-trees with as few as $k+1$ nodes. As a result, the analysis of Theorem 9.1 is no longer valid. The analysis of Theorem 9.1 requires that each min-tree of degree k have an exponential (in k) number of nodes. When decrease key and delete operations are performed as described above, this is no longer true. To ensure that each min-tree of degree k has at least c^k nodes for some c, $c > 1$, each delete and decrease key operation must be followed by a *cascading cut* step. For this, we add the boolean field *child_cut* to each node. The value of this field is useful only for nodes that are not a min-tree root. In this case, the *child_cut* field of node x has the value *TRUE* iff one of the children of x was cut off (i.e., removed) after the most recent time x was made the child of its current parent. This means that each time two min-trees are joined in a delete min operation, the *child_cut* field of the root with larger key should be set to *FALSE*. Further, whenever a delete or decrease key operation deletes a node q that is not a min-tree root from its doubly linked list (step 2 of delete and decrease key), then the cascading cut step is invoked. During this, we examine the nodes on the path from the parent p of the deleted node q up to the nearest ancestor of the deleted node with $child\_cut = FALSE$. In case there is no such ancestor, then the path goes from p to the root of the min-tree containing p. All non root nodes on this path with $child\_cut$ field $TRUE$ are deleted from their respective doubly linked lists and added to the doubly linked list of min-tree root nodes of the F-heap. If the path has a node with $child\_cut$ field $FALSE$, this field is changed to $TRUE$.

Figure 9.22 gives an example of a cascading cut. Figure 9.22(a) is the min-tree containing 14 before a decrease key operation that reduces this key by 4. The $child\_cut$ fields are shown only for the nodes on the path from the parent of 14 to its nearest ancestor with $child\_cut = FALSE$. A $TRUE$ value is indicated by T. During the decrease key operation, the min-tree with root 14 is deleted from the min-tree of Figure 9.22(a) and becomes a min-tree of the F-heap. Its root now has key 10. This is the first min-tree of Figure 9.22(b). During the cascading cut, the min-trees with roots 12, 10, 8, and 6 are cut off from the min tree with root 2. Thus the single min-tree of Figure 9.22(a) becomes six min-trees of the resulting F-heap. The $child\_cut$ value of 4 becomes $TRUE$. All other $child\_cut$ values are unchanged.

9.5.5   Analysis

Lemma 9.3: Let a be an F-heap with n elements that results from a sequence of insert, combine, delete min, delete, and decrease key operations performed on initially empty F-heaps.

(a)   Let b be any node in any of the min-trees of a. The degree of b is at most $\log_\phi m$, where $\phi = (1+\sqrt{5})/2$ and m is the number of elements in the subtree with root b.

(b) $MAX\_DEGREE \leq \lfloor \log_\phi n \rfloor$ and the actual cost of a delete min is $O(\log n + s)$.

Proof: We shall prove (a) by induction on the degree of b. Let N_i be the minimum number of elements in the subtree with root b when b has degree i. We see that $N_0 = 1$ and $N_1 = 2$. So, the inequality of (a) holds for degrees 0 and 1. For $i > 1$, let $c_1, \cdots, c_i$ be the i children of b. Assume that c_j was made a child of b before c_{j+1}, $j < i$. Hence, when c_k, $k \leq i$ was made a child of b, the degree of b was at least $k-1$. The only F-heap operation that makes one node a child of another is delete min. Here, during a join min-tree step, one min-tree is made a sub tree of another min-tree of equal degree. Hence, at the time of joining, the degree of c_k must have been equal to that of b. Subsequent to joining, its degree can decrease as a result of a delete or decrease key operation. However, following such a join, the degree of c_k can decrease by at most one as an attempt to cut off a second child of c_k results in a cascading cut at c_k. Such a cut causes c_k to become the root of a min-tree of the F-heap. Hence, the degree, d_k, of c_k is at least $\max\{0, k-2\}$. So, the number of elements in c_k is at least N_{d_k}. This implies that

$$N_i = N_0 + \sum_{k=0}^{i-2} N_k + 1 = \sum_{k=0}^{i-2} N_k + 2$$

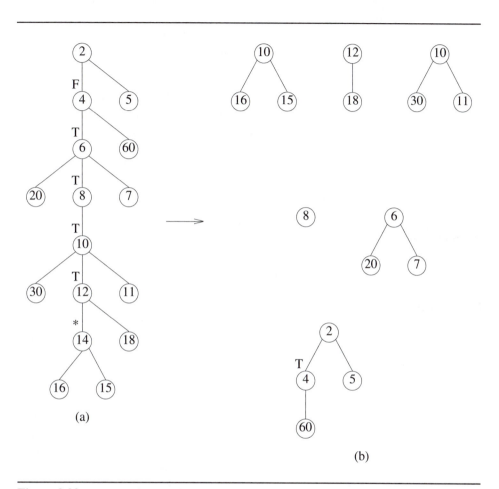

Figure 9.22: A cascading cut following a decrease of key 14 by 4

One may show (see the exercises) that the Fibonacci numbers satisfy the equality

$$F_h = \sum_{k=0}^{h-2} F_k + 1, h > 1, F_0 = 0, \text{ and } F_1 = 1$$

From this we may obtain the equality $N_i = F_{i+2}$, $i \geq 0$. Further, since $F_{i+2} \geq \phi^i$, $N_i \geq \phi^i$. Hence, $i \leq \log_\phi m$.

(b) is a direct consequence of (a). □

Theorem 9.2: If a sequence of n insert, combine, delete min, delete, and decrease key operations is performed on an initially empty F-heap, then we can amortize costs such that the amortized time complexity of each insert, combine, and decrease key operation is O(1) and that of each delete min and delete is O(log$n$). The total time complexity of the entire sequence is the sum of the amortized complexities of the individual operations in the sequence.

Proof: The proof is similar to that of Theorem 9.1. The definition of *#insert* is unchanged. However, that of *last_size* is augmented by requiring that following each delete and decrease key *last_size* be changed by the net change in the number of min-trees in the F-heap (in the example of Figure 9.22 *last_size* is increased by 5). With this modification, we see that at the time of a delete min operation s = *#insert* + *last_size* + $u - 1$. *#insert* units of cost may me charged, one each, to the *#insert* insert operations that contribute to this count and *last_size* units may be charged to the delete min, delete, and decrease key operations that contribute to this count. This results in an additional charge of at most $\log_\phi n$ to each contributing delete min and delete operation and of one to each contributing decrease key operation. As a result, the amortized cost of a delete min is O(log$n$).

Since the total number of cascading cuts is limited by the total number of deletes and decrease key operations (as these are the only operations that can set *child_cut* to *TRUE*), the cost of these cuts may be amortized over the delete and decrease key operations by adding one to their amortized costs. The amortized cost of deleting an element other than the min element becomes O(log$n$) as its actual cost is O(1) (excluding the cost of the cascading cut sequence that may be performed); at most one unit is charged to it from the amortization of all the cascading cuts; and at most $\log_\phi n$ units are charged to it from a delete min.

The amortized cost of a decrease key operation is O(1) as its actual cost is O(1) (excluding the cost of the ensuing cascading cut); at most one unit is charged to it from the amortization of all cascading cuts; and at most one unit is charged from a delete min.

The amortized cost of an insert is O(1) as its actual cost is one and at most one cost unit is charged to it from a delete min. Since the amortization scheme transfers no charge to a combine, its actual and amortized costs are the same. This cost is O(1). $\square$

From the preceding theorem, it follows that the complexity of any sequence of F-heap operations is O($i + c + dk + (dm + d)$log$i$) where i, c, dk, dm, and d are, respectively, the number of insert, combine, decrease key, delete min, and delete operations in the sequence.

9.5.6 Application Of F-heaps

We conclude this section on F-heaps by considering their application to the single source all destinations algorithm of Chapter 6. Let S be the set of vertices to which a shortest path has been found and let *distance* (i) be the length of a shortest path from the source vertex to vertex i, $i \in S$, that goes through only vertices in S. On each iteration of the shortest path algorithm, we need to determine an i, $i \in \bar{S}$, such that $distance\,(i)$ is minimum and add this i to S. This corresponds to a delete min operation on $\bar{S}$. Further, the $distance$ values of the remaining vertices in $\bar{S}$ may decrease. This corresponds to a decrease key operation on each of the affected vertices. The total number of decrease key operations is bounded by the number of edges in the graph and the number of delete min operations is $n-2$. $\bar{S}$ begins with $n-1$ vertices. If we implement $\bar{S}$ as an F-heap using $distance$ as the key, then $n-1$ inserts are needed to initialize the F-heap. Additionally, $n-2$ delete min operations and at most e decrease key operations are needed. The total time for all these operations is the sum of the amortized costs for each. This is $O(n \log n + e)$. The remainder of the algorithm takes $O(n)$ time. Hence if an F-heap is used to represent $\bar{S}$, the complexity of the shortest path algorithm becomes $O(n \log n + e)$. This is an asymptotic improvement over the implementation discussed in Chapter 6 if the graph does not have $\Omega(n^2)$ edges. If this single source algorithm is used n times, once with each of the n vertices in the graph as the source, then we can find a shortest path between every pair of vertices in $O(n^2 \log n + ne)$ time. Once again, this represents an asymptotic improvement over the $O(n^3)$ dynamic programming algorithm of Chapter 6 for graphs that do not have $\Omega(n^2)$ edges. It is interesting to note that $O(n \log n + e)$ is the best possible implementation of the single source algorithm of Chapter 6 as the algorithm must examine each edge and may be used to sort n numbers (which requires $O(n \log n)$ time).

EXERCISES

1. Prove that if we start with empty F-heaps and perform only the operations insert, combine, and delete min, then all min-trees in the F-heaps are binomial trees.

2. Can all the functions on an F-heap be performed in the same time using singly linked circular lists rather than doubly linked circular lists? Note that we can delete from an arbitrary node x of a singly linked circular list by copy over the data from the next node and then deleting the next node rather than the node x.

3. Show that if we start with empty F-heaps and do not perform cascading cuts, then it is possible for a sequence of F-heap operations to result in degree k min-trees that have only $k+1$ nodes, $k \geq 1$.

4. Suppose we change the rule for a cascading cut so that such a cut is performed only when a node loses a third child rather than when it loses a second child. For this, the $child\_cut$ field is changed so that it can have the values 0, 1, and 2. When a node acquires a new parent, its $child\_cut$ field is set to 1. Each time a node has a child cut off (during a delete or decrease key operation), its $child\_cut$ field is increased by one (unless this field is already two). In case the $child\_cut$ field is already two, a cascading cut is performed.

(a) Obtain a recurrence equation for N_i, the minimum number of nodes in a min-tree with degree i. Assume that we start with an empty F-heap and that all operations (except cascading cut) are performed as described in the text. Cascading cuts are performed as described above.

(b) Solve the recurrence of part (a) to obtain a lower bound on N_i.

(c) Does the modified rule for cascading cuts ensure that the minimum number of nodes in any min-tree of degree i is exponential in i?

(d) For the new cascading cut rule, can you establish the same amortized complexities as for the original rule? Prove the correctness of your answer.

(e) Answer parts (c) and (d) under the assumtion that cascading cuts are performed only after k children of a node have been cut off. Here, k is a fixed constant ($k = 2$ for the rule used in the text and $k = 3$ for the rule used earlier in this exercise).

(f) How do you expect the performance of F-heaps to change as larger values of k (see part (e)) are used?

5. Write C functions to do the following:

(a) Create an empty F-heap

(b) Insert element x into an F-heap

(c) Perform a delete min from an F-heap. The deleted element is to be returned to the invoking function.

(d) Delete the element in node b of an F-heap a. The deleted element is to be returned to the invoking function.

(e) Decrease the key in the node b of an F-heap a by some positive amount c.

Note that all operations must leave behind properly structured F-heaps. Your functions for (d) and (e) must perform cascading cuts. Test the correctness of your procedures by running them on a computer using suitable test data.

6. For the Fibonacci numbers F_k and the numbers N_i of Lemma 9.3, prove the following:

(a) $F_h = \sum_{k=0}^{h-2} F_k + 1, h > 1$

(b) Use (a) to show that $N_i = F_{i+2}, i \geq 0$.

(c) Use the equality $F_k = \dfrac{1}{\sqrt{5}}(\dfrac{1+\sqrt{5}}{2})^k - \dfrac{1}{\sqrt{5}}(\dfrac{1-\sqrt{5}}{2})^k, k \geq 0$ to show that $F_{k+2} \geq \phi^k, k \geq 0$, where $\phi = (1+\sqrt{5})/2$.

7. Implement the single source shortest path algorithm of Chapter 6 using the data structures recommended there as well as using F-heaps. However, use adjacency lists rather than an adjacency matrix. Generate 10 connected undirected graphs with different edge densities (say 10%, 20%, $\cdots$, 100% of maximum) for each of

the cases $n = 100, 200, \cdots, 500$. Assign random costs to the edges (use a uniform random number generator in the range [1, 1000]). Measure the run times of the two implementations of the shortest path algorithms. Plot the average times for each n.

9.6 REFERENCES AND SELECTED READINGS

Min-max-heaps were developed in: ''Min-max-heaps and generalized priority queues,'' by M. Atkinson, J. Sack, N. Santoro, and T. Strothotte, *Communications of the ACM*, pp. 996-1000, 29, 10, Oct. 1986. This paper also contains extensions of min-max-heaps.

The deap data structure was invented by Svante Carlsson. The reference is: ''The deap - A double-ended heap to implement double-ended priority queues,'' *Information Processing Letters*, 26, pp. 33-36, 1987.

Leftist trees were invented by C. Crane: *Linear lists and priority queues as balanced binary trees*, Technical report CS-72-259, Computer Science Dept., Stanford University, CA, 1972.

Further discussion of leftist trees may be found in: *Data structures and network algorithms*, by R. Tarjan, SIAM, Philadelphia, PA, 1983.

The exercise on lazy deletion is from: ''Finding minimum spanning trees,'' by D. Cheriton and R. Tarjan, *SIAM Jr on Computing*, 5, 1976, pp. 724-742.

B-heaps and F-heaps were invented by M. Fredman and R. Tarjan. Their work is reported in the paper: ''Fibonacci heaps and their uses in improved network optimization algorithms,'' *JACM*, 34, 3, July 1987, pp. 596-615. This paper also describes several variants of the basic F-heap as discussed here as well as the application of F-heaps to the assignment problem and to the problem of finding a minimum cost spanning tree. Their result is that using F-heaps, minimum cost spanning trees can be found in $O(e\beta(e,n))$ time where $\beta(e,n) \le \log^* n$ when $e \ge n$. $\log^* n = \min\{i \mid \log^{(i)} n \le 1\}$, $\log^{(0)} n = n$, and $\log^{(i)} n = \log(\log^{(i-1)} n)$. The complexity of finding minimum cost spanning trees has been further reduced to $O(e\log\beta(e,n))$. The reference for this is: ''Efficient algorithms for finding minimum spanning trees in undirected and directed graphs,'' by H. Gabow, Z. Galil, T. Spencer, and R. Tarjan, *Combinatorica*, 6, 2, 1986, pp. 109-122.

CHAPTER 10

SEARCH STRUCTURES

10.1   OPTIMAL BINARY SEARCH TREES

We introduced binary search trees in Chapter 5, and in this section we look at the construction of these search trees for a static set of identifiers. That is, we make no additions to or deletions from the tree; we only perform searches.

We begin by examining the correspondence between a binary search tree and the binary search function we studied in Chapter 7. In Chapter 7 we showed that we could construct a binary search tree that corresponds to a binary search on a sorted list (see Figure 7.1). For example, a binary search on the list (**do, if, while**) is equivalent to using the function *search* 2 (Program 5.17) on the binary search tree of Figure 10.1. Although this is a full binary tree, it may not be an optimal binary search tree for this list if the identifiers are searched for with different frequency. That is, the probability that we will search for one of the identifiers is higher than the probability that we will search for the other identifiers.

To find an optimal binary search tree for a given static list, we must first decide on a cost measure for search trees. Assume that we wish to search for an identifier at level k of a binary search tree using the *search* 2 function. We know that *search* 2 makes k iterations of the **while** loop. Generally, the number of iterations of this loop equals the level number of the identifier we seek. Since the **while** loop determines the computing time of the search, it is reasonable to use the level number of a node as its cost.

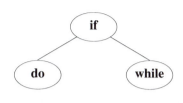

Figure 10.1: Binary search tree corresponding to a binary search on the list (**do, if, while**)

Consider the two search trees of Figure 10.2. The second tree requires at most three comparisons to decide whether the identifier we seek is in the tree. The first binary tree may require four comparisons, since any identifier that alphabetically comes after **for** but precedes **void** tests four nodes. Thus, the second binary tree has a better worst case search time than the first tree. Searching for an identifier in the first tree requires one comparison for **for**, two comparisons each for **do** and **while**, three comparisons for **void**, and four comparisons for **if**. If we search for each with equal probability, the average number of comparisons for a successful search is 2.4. The average number of comparisons for the second tree is only 2.2. Thus, the second tree also has better average behavior.

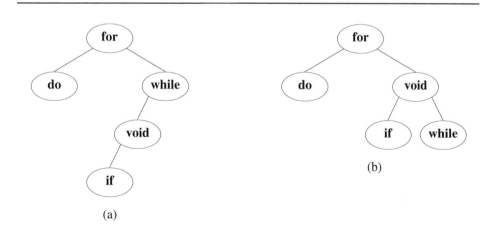

Figure 10.2: Two possible binary search trees

In evaluating binary search trees, it is useful to add a special *square* node at every place there is a null link. Doing this to the trees of Figure 10.2 yields the trees of Figure 10.3. Remember that every binary tree with *n* nodes has *n* + 1 null links and hence has *n* + 1 square nodes. We call these nodes *external* nodes because they are not part of the original tree. The remaining nodes are *internal* nodes. Each time we search for an identifier that is not in a binary search tree, the search terminates at an external node. Since all such searches represent unsuccessful searches, we also refer to external nodes as *failure* nodes. A binary tree with external nodes added is an *extended binary tree*. Figure 10.3 shows the extended binary trees corresponding to the search trees of Figure 10.2.

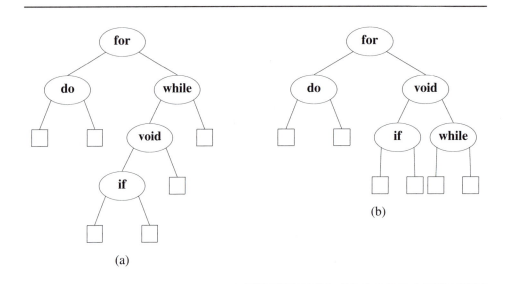

(a)

(b)

Figure 10.3: Extended binary trees corresponding to search trees of Figure 10.2

We define the *external path length* of a binary tree as the sum over all external nodes of the lengths of the paths from the root to those nodes. Analogously, the *internal path length* is the sum over all internal nodes of the lengths of the paths from the root to those nodes. For example, the internal path length, I, of the tree of Figure 10.3(a) is:

$$I = 0 + 1 + 1 + 2 + 3 = 7$$

Its external path length, E, is:

$$E = 2 + 2 + 4 + 4 + 3 + 2 = 17$$

Exercise 1 shows that the internal and external path lengths of a binary tree with n internal nodes are related by the formula $E = I + 2n$. Hence, binary trees with the maximum E also have maximum I. What are the maximum and minimum possible values for I over all binary trees with n internal nodes? Clearly, the worst case occurs when the tree is skewed, that is, the tree has a depth of n. In this case,

$$I = \sum_{i=0}^{n-1} i = n(n-1)/2$$

To obtain trees with minimal I, we must have as many internal nodes as close to the root as possible. We can have at most 2 nodes at distance 1, 4 at distance 2, 8 at distance 3, and so on. In general, the smallest value for I is:

$$0 + 2*1 + 4*2 + 8*3 + \ldots +$$

One tree with minimal internal path length is the complete binary tree defined in Section 5.2. If we number the nodes in a complete binary tree as in Section 5.2, then we see that the distance of node i from the root is $\lfloor \log_2 i \rfloor$. Hence, the smallest value for I is:

$$\sum_{i=1}^{n} \lfloor \log_2 i \rfloor = O(n\log_2 n)$$

Let us now return to our original problem of representing a static list of identifiers as a binary search tree. If the binary search tree contains the identifiers $a_1, a_2, \ldots, a_n$ with $a_1 < a_2 < \cdots < a_n$ and the probability of searching for each a_i is p_i, then the total cost of any binary search tree is:

$$\sum_{i=1}^{n} p_i \cdot \text{level}(a_i)$$

when only successful searches are made. Since unsuccessful searches, that is, searches for identifiers not in the table, are also made, we should include the cost of these searches in our cost measure. Unsuccessful searches terminate with *NULL* returned in function *search2*. Every node with a null subtree defines a point at which such a termination can take place. If we replace every null subtree by a failure node, we may partition the identifiers that are not in the binary search tree into $n + 1$ classes E_i, $0 \leq i \leq n$. E_0 contains all identifiers x such that $x < a_1$. E_i contains all identifiers x such that $a_i < x < a_{i+1}$, $1 \leq i < n$, and E_n contains all identifiers x, $x > a_n$. It is easy to see that for all identifiers in a particular class, E_i, the search terminates at the same failure node; it terminates at different failure nodes for identifiers in different classes. We may number the failure nodes from 0 to n with i being the failure node for class E_i, $0 \leq i \leq n$. If q_i is the probability that the identifier we are searching for is in E_i, then the cost of the failure nodes is:

$$\sum_{i=0}^{n} q_i \cdot (\text{level(failure node } i) - 1)$$

Therefore, the total cost of a binary search tree is:

$$\sum_{i=1}^{n} p_i \cdot \text{level}(a_i) + \sum_{i=0}^{n} q_i \cdot (\text{level (failure node } i)-1) \tag{10.1}$$

An *optimal binary search tree* for the identifier set $a_1, \cdots, a_n$ is one that minimizes Eq.(10.1) over all possible binary search trees for this identifier set. Since all searches must terminate either successfully or unsuccessfully, we have:

$$\sum_{i=1}^{n} p_i + \sum_{i=0}^{n} q_i = 1$$

Example 10.1: Figure 10.4 shows the possible binary search trees for the identifier set $(a_1, a_2, a_3) = (\textbf{do, if, while})$. If we search for the identifiers with equal probabilities, $p_i = a_j = 1/7$ for all i and j, we have:

> cost (tree a) = 15/7; cost (tree b) = 13/7
> cost (tree c) = 15/7; cost (tree d) = 15/7
> cost (tree e) = 15/7

As expected, tree b is optimal. However, with $p_1 = .5$, $p_2 = .1$, $p_3 = .05$, $q_0 = .15$, $q_1 = .1, q_2 = .05$, and $q_3 = .05$, we have:

> cost (tree a) = 2.65; cost (tree b) = 1.9
> cost (tree c) = 1.5; cost (tree d) = 2.05
> cost (tree e) = 1.6

Tree c is optimal with this assignment of p's and q's. $\square$

How do we determine the optimal tree from all the possible binary search trees for a given set of identifiers? We could proceed as in Example 10.1 and explicitly generate all possible binary search trees. Thus, we would compute the cost of each such tree and determine the optimal tree. We can determine the cost of each of the binary search trees in $O(n)$ time for an n node tree. If $N(n)$ is the total number of distinct binary search trees with n identifiers, the complexity of the algorithm is $O(n\, N(n))$. From Section 5.10 we know that $N(n) = O(4^n/n^{3/2})$, which makes this brute force algorithm impractical for

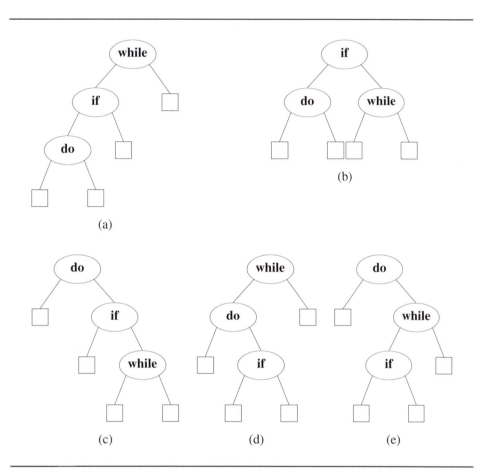

Figure 10.4: Binary search trees with three identifiers

large values of n. However, we can find a fairly efficient algorithm by making some observations about the properties of optimal binary search trees.

Let $a_1 < a_2 < \ldots < a_n$ be the n identifiers represented in a binary search tree. Let T_{ij} denote an optimal binary search tree for $a_{i+1}, \cdots, a_j, i < j$. T_{ii} is an empty tree for $0 \leq i \leq n$ and T_{ij} is not defined for $i > j$. Let c_{ij} denote the cost of the search tree T_{ij}. By definition c_{ii} is 0. Let r_{ij} denote the root of T_{ij} and let

$$w_{ij} = q_i + \sum_{k=i+1}^{j} (q_k + p_k)$$

denote the weight of T_{ij}. By definition, $r_{ii} = 0$ and $w_{ii} = q_i, 0 \leq i \leq n$. T_{0n} is an optimal binary search tree for $a_1, \cdots, a_n$. Its cost is c_{on}, its weight is w_{on}, and its root is r_{on}.

If T_{ij} is an optimal binary search tree for $a_{i+1}, \cdots, a_j$ and $r_{ij} = k$, then k satisfies the inequality $i < k \leq j$. T_{ij} has two subtrees L and R. L is the left subtree and contains the identifiers $a_{i+1}, \cdots, a_{k-1}$ and R is the right subtree and contains the identifiers $a_{k+1}, \cdots, a_j$ (Figure 10.5). The cost c_{ij} of T_{ij} is

$$c_{ij} = p_k + \text{cost } (L) + \text{cost } (R) + \text{weight } (L) + \text{weight } (R) \qquad (10.2)$$

where weight $(L) = $ weight $(T_{i,k-1}) = w_{i,k-1}$, and weight $(R) = $ weight $(T_{kj}) = w_{kj}$.

$$L \qquad\qquad R$$

Figure 10.5: An optimal binary search tree T_{ij}

From Eq. (10.2) it is clear that c_{ij} is minimal only if $\text{cost}(L) = c_{i,k-1}$ and $\text{cost}(R) = c_{kj}$. Otherwise we could replace either L or R with a subtree of lower cost and thus obtain a binary search tree for $a_{i+1}, \ldots, a_j$ with a lower cost than c_{ij}. This violates the assumption that T_{ij} is optimal. Hence, Eq. (10.2) becomes:

$$c_{ij} = p_k + c_{i,k-1} + c_{kj} + w_{i,k-1} + w_{kj}$$

$$= w_{ij} + c_{i,k-1} + c_{kj} \qquad (10.3)$$

Since T_{ij} is optimal, it follows from Eq. (10.3) that $r_{ij} = k$ is such that

$$w_{ij} + c_{i,k-1} + c_{kj} = \min_{i < l \leq j}\{w_{ij} + c_{i,l-1} + c_{lj}\}$$

or

$$c_{i,k-1} + c_{kj} = \min_{i < l \leq j}\{c_{i,l-1} + c_{lj}\} \qquad (10.4)$$

Equation (10.4) shows us how to obtain T_{on} and c_{on}, starting from the knowledge that $T_{ii} = \phi$ and $c_{ii} = 0$.

Example 10.2: Let $n = 4$ and $(a_1, a_2, a_3, a_4) = $ (**do, for, void, while**). Let $(p_1, p_2, p_3, p_4) = (3, 3, 1, 1)$ and $(q_0, q_1, q_2, q_3, q_4) = (2, 3, 1, 1, 1)$. (We have multiplied the original p's and q's by 16 for convenience.) Initially, $w_{i,i} = q_i$, $c_{ii} = 0$, and $r_{ii} = 0$, $0 \le i \le 4$. Using Eqs. (10.3) and (10.4) we get:

$$
\begin{aligned}
w_{01} &= p_1 + w_{00} + w_{11} = p_1 + q_1 + w_{00} = 8 \\
c_{01} &= w_{01} + \min\{c_{00} + c_{11}\} = 8 \\
r_{01} &= 1 \\
w_{12} &= p_2 + w_{11} + w_{22} = p_2 + q_2 + w_{11} = 7 \\
c_{12} &= w_{12} + \min\{c_{11} + c_{22}\} = 7 \\
r_{12} &= 2 \\
w_{23} &= p_3 + w_{22} + w_{33} = p_3 + q_3 + w_{22} = 3 \\
c_{23} &= w_{23} + \min\{c_{22} + c_{33}\} = 3 \\
r_{23} &= 3 \\
w_{34} &= p_4 + w_{33} + w_{44} = p_4 + q_4 + w_{33} = 3 \\
c_{34} &= w_{34} + \min\{c_{33} + c_{44}\} = 3 \\
r_{34} &= 4
\end{aligned}
$$

Knowing $w_{i,i+1}$ and $c_{i,i+1}$, $0 \le i < 4$ we can again use Eqs. (10.3) and (10.4) to compute $w_{i,i+2}$, $c_{i,i+2}$, $r_{i,i+2}$, $0 \le i < 3$. We repeat this process until we obtain w_{04}, c_{04}, and r_{04}. The table of Figure 10.6 shows the results of this computation. From the table, we see that $c_{04} = 32$ is the minimal cost of a binary search tree for a_1 to a_4. The root of tree T_{04} is a_2. Hence, the left subtree is T_{01} and the right subtree T_{24}. T_{01} has root a_1 and subtrees T_{00} and T_{11}. T_{24} has root a_3; its left subtree is therefore T_{22} and right subtree T_{34}. Thus, with the data in the table it is possible to reconstruct T_{04} (Figure 10.7). $\square$

Example 10.2 illustrates how we use Eq.(10.4) to determine the c's and r's, and how to reconstruct T_{on} knowing the r's. Let us examine the complexity of the function that evaluates the c's and r's. The evaluation function described in Example 10.2 requires us to compute c_{ij} for $(j - i) = 1, 2, \cdots, n$ in that order. When $j - i = m$ there are $n - m + 1$ c_{ij}'s to compute. To compute each of these c_{ij}'s we must find the minimum of m quantities (see Equation (10.4)). Hence, we can compute each such c_{ij} in $O(m)$ time. Therefore, the total time for all c_{ij}'s with $j - i = m$ is $O(nm - m^2)$. The total time to evaluate all the c_{ij}'s and r_{ij}'s is:

$$
\sum_{m=1}^{n} (nm - m^2) = O(n^3)
$$

Actually we can do better than this by using a result attributed to D. E. Knuth. He states that we can find the optimal l in Eq.(10.4) by limiting the search to the range $r_{i,j-1} \le l \le r_{i+1,j}$. In this case, the computing time becomes $O(n^2)$ (Exercise 3). The function *obst* (Program 10.1) uses this result to obtain the values of w_{ij}, r_{ij}, and c_{ij}, $0 \le i \le j \le n$ in $O(n^2)$ time. We may construct the actual tree, T_{0n}, from the values of r_{ij} in

$W_{00} = 2$ $C_{00} = 0$ $R_{00} = 0$	$W_{11} = 3$ $C_{11} = 0$ $R_{11} = 0$	$W_{22} = 1$ $C_{22} = 0$ $R_{22} = 0$	$W_{33} = 1$ $C_{33} = 0$ $R_{33} = 0$	$W_{44} = 1$ $C_{44} = 0$ $R_{44} = 0$
$W_{01} = 8$ $C_{01} = 8$ $R_{01} = 1$	$W_{12} = 7$ $C_{12} = 7$ $R_{12} = 2$	$W_{23} = 3$ $C_{23} = 3$ $R_{23} = 3$	$W_{34} = 3$ $C_{34} = 3$ $R_{34} = 4$	
$W_{02} = 12$ $C_{02} = 19$ $R_{02} = 1$	$W_{13} = 9$ $C_{13} = 12$ $R_{13} = 2$	$W_{24} = 5$ $C_{24} = 8$ $R_{24} = 3$		
$W_{03} = 14$ $C_{03} = 25$ $R_{03} = 2$	$W_{14} = 11$ $C_{14} = 19$ $R_{14} = 2$			
$W_{04} = 16$ $C_{04} = 32$ $R_{04} = 2$				

Computation is carried out row-wise from row 0 to row 4

Figure 10.6: Computation of c_{04} and r_{04}.

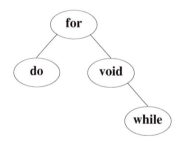

Figure 10.7: Optimal search tree for Example 10.2

$O(n)$ time. We leave this as an exercise. The data types used by *obst* are:

```
#define MAX_SIZE 200 /*max # of ids plus 1*/
#define MAX_CHAR  30 /*max characters/id*/
/* set of identifiers */
char words[MAX_SIZE][MAX_CHAR], *ptr = words[0];
int  q[MAX_SIZE];
int  p[MAX_SIZE];
int  cost[MAX_SIZE][MAX_SIZE];
```

```
int   root[MAX_SIZE][MAX_SIZE];
int   weight[MAX_SIZE][MAX_SIZE];
int n;   /* number of identifiers */
```

```
void obst(int p[], int q[], int cost[][MAX_SIZE],
     int root[][MAX_SIZE], int weight[][MAX_SIZE], int n)
{
/* given n distinct identifiers a[1] ... a[n] and
probabilities p[1] ... p[n], and q[0] ... q[n] compute
the cost c[i][j]  of the optimal binary search tree for
a[i]  ... a[j], 1 ≤ i ≤ j ≤ n. Also compute the weight
and root of the tree */
   int i,j,k,m,min,minpos;
   /* initialize 0 and 1 node trees */
   for (i = 0; i < n; i++) {
     weight[i][i] = q[i];
     root[i][i] = 0;
     cost[i][i] = 0;
     cost[i][i+1] = weight[i][i+1] =
                    q[i] + q[i+1] + p[i+1];
     root[i][i+1] = i+1;
   }
   weight[n][n] = q[n];
   root[n][n] = 0;
   cost[n][n] = 0;
   /* compute remaining diagonals */
   for (m = 2; m <= n; m++)
     for (i = 0; i <= n-m; i++) {
        j = i + m;
        weight[i][j] = weight[i][j-1] + p[j] + q[j];
        k = knuth_min(cost,root,i,j);
        /* knuth_min returns a value, k, in the range
        root[i][j-1] to root[i+1][j], that minimizes
        cost[i][k-1] + cost[k][j] */
        cost[i][j] = weight[i][j] + cost[i][k-1]
                                  + cost[k][j];
        root[i][j] = k;
     }
}
```

Program 10.1: Function to find an optimal binary search tree

EXERCISES

1. (a) Prove by induction that if T is a binary tree with n internal nodes, I its internal path length, and E its external path length, then $E = I + 2n$, $n \geq 0$.

    (b) Using the result of (a), show that the average number of comparisons s in a successful search is related to the average number of comparisons, u, in an unsuccessful search by the formula:

    $$s = (1 + 1/n)u - 1, \; n \geq 1$$

2. Using function *obst*, compute w_{ij}, r_{ij}, and c_{ij}, $0 \leq i < j \leq 4$ for the identifier set (a_1, a_2, a_3, a_4) = (**else, malloc, printf, scanf**) with $p_1 = 1/20$, $p_2 = 1/5$, $p_3 = 1/10$, $p_4 = 1/20$, $q_0 = 1/5$, $q_1 = 1/10$, $q_2 = 1/5$, $q_3 = 1/20$, $q_4 = 1/20$. Using the r_{ij}'s, construct the optimal binary search tree.

3. (a) Complete function *obst* by providing the code for the *knuth_min* function.

    (b) Show that the computing time of *obst* is $O(n^2)$.

    (c) Write an algorithm to construct the optimal binary search tree T_{on} given the roots r_{ij}, $0 \leq i < j \leq n$. Show that this can be done in $O(n)$ time.

4. Since often only the approximate values of the p's and q's are known, it is just as meaningful to find a binary search tree that is nearly optimal; that is, its cost, Eq. (10.1), is almost minimal for the given p's and q's. This exercise explores an $O(n \log n)$ algorithm that creates nearly optimal binary search trees. The search tree heuristic we will study is:

    Choose the root a_k such that $|w_{0,k-1} - w_{k,n}|$ is as small as possible. Repeat this function to find the left and right subtrees of a_k.

    (a) Using this heuristic obtain the resulting binary search tree for the list of Exercise 2. What is its cost?

    (b) Write a C algorithm implementing the above heuristic. Your algorithm should have time complexity $O(n \log n)$.

    An analysis of the performance of this heuristic may be found in the paper by Melhorn.

10.2   AVL TREES

We also may maintain dynamic tables as binary search trees. In Chapter 5, we discussed how to insert elements into and delete them from binary search trees. Figure 10.8 shows the binary search tree obtained by entering the months *January* to *December*, in that order, into an initially empty binary search tree. We used *add_node* (Program 5.18).

The maximum number of comparisons needed to search for any identifier in the tree of Figure 10.8 is six (for *November*). The average number of comparisons is (1 for *January* + 2 each for *February* and *March* + 3 each for *April, June,* and *May* + $\cdots$ + 6 for *November*) = $42/12 = 3.5$. If we enter the months into the tree in the order *July,*

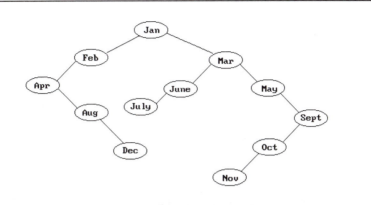

Figure 10.8: Binary search tree obtained for the months of the year

February, May, August, January, March, October, April, December, June, November, and *September,* we obtain the tree of Figure 10.9. This tree is well balanced and does not have any paths to leaf nodes that are much longer than others. In contrast, the tree of Figure 10.8 has six nodes on the path from the root to *November,* but only three nodes on the path from the root to *April.* The tree of Figure 10.9 has other advantages. The maximum number of comparisons needed to search for any identifier is now four, and the average number of comparisons is $37/12 \approx 3.1$. In addition, all the intermediate trees created during the construction of the tree of Figure 10.9 are also well balanced. Suppose that we now enter the months into an initially empty tree in alphabetical order. The tree degenerates into the chain shown in Figure 10.10. The maximum search time is now 12 identifier comparisons and the average is 6.5. Thus, in the worst case, binary search trees correspond to sequential searching in an ordered list. However, when we enter the identifiers in a random order, the tree tends to be balanced as in Figure 10.9. If all permutations are equally probable, then we can prove that the average search and insertion time is $O(\log n)$ for an n node binary search tree.

From our earlier study of binary trees, we know that we can minimize the average and maximum search time if we maintain the binary search tree as a complete binary tree at all times. Unfortunately, since we have a dynamic environment, we will search for identifiers as we are building the tree. This makes it is difficult to maintain a complete binary tree without a significant increase in the time required to add new elements. The increased time arises because, in some cases, we may have to restructure the entire tree to accommodate a new entry. However, we can maintain a balanced tree that ensures that the average and worst case search time for a tree with n nodes is $O(\log n)$. In this section, we study one method of growing balanced binary trees. These balanced trees have satisfactory search and insertion times. Other balanced tree structures are studied in subsequent sections.

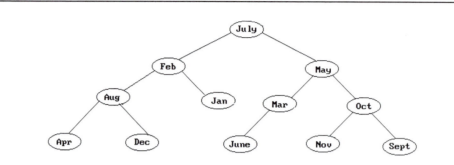

Figure 10.9:A balanced tree for the months of the year

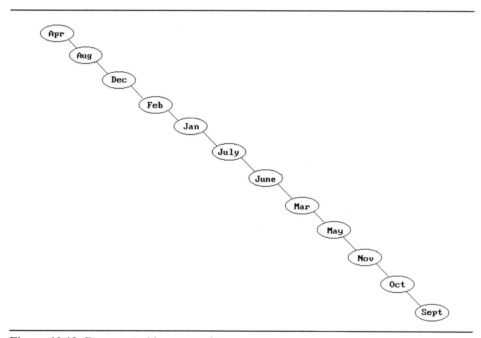

Figure 10.10: Degenerate binary search tree

In 1962, Adelson-Velskii and Landis introduced a binary tree structure that is balanced with respect to the heights of subtrees. Since the trees are balanced, we can perform dynamic retrievals in $O(\log n)$ time for a tree with n nodes. We also can enter an element into the tree, or delete an element from it, in $O(\log n)$ time. The resulting tree remains height balanced. We refer to the trees introduced by Adelson-Velskii and Landis as *AVL trees*. As with binary trees, we may define AVL trees recursively.

Definition: An empty binary tree is height balanced. If T is a nonempty binary tree with T_L and T_R as its left and right subtrees, then T is *height balanced iff*

(1) T_L and T_R are height balanced

and

(2) $|h_L - h_R| \le 1$ where h_L and h_R are the heights of T_L and T_R, respectively. □

The definition of a height balanced binary tree requires that every subtree also be height balanced. The binary tree of Figure 10.8 is not height balanced since *April*'s left subtree has a height of 0 and its right subtree has a height of 2. The tree of Figure 10.9 is height balanced, while the tree of Figure 10.10 is not. To illustrate the processes involved in maintaining a height balanced binary search tree, let us construct such a tree for the months of the year. This time we will insert the months into the tree in the order *March, May, November, August, April, January, December, July, February, June, October,* and *September*. Figure 10.11 shows the tree as it grows, and the restructuring involved in keeping it balanced. The numbers by each node represent the difference in heights between the left and right subtrees of that node. We refer to this as the balance factor of the node.

Definition: The *balance factor*, *BF* (*T*), of a node, *T*, in a binary tree is defined as $h_L - h_R$, where h_L and h_R are, respectively, the heights of the left and right subtrees of *T*. For any node *T* in an AVL tree *BF* (*T*) = $-1, 0$, or 1. □

Inserting *March* and *May* results in the binary search trees (a) and (b) of Figure 10.11. When we add *November* to the tree, the height of *March*'s right subtree becomes 2, while that of the left subtree is 0. The tree is now unbalanced. To rebalance the tree, we perform a rotation. This rotation involves the two gray nodes. Since the tree is unbalanced to the right, we rotate it to the left. Thus, we make *March* the left child of *May*, and *May* the root of the tree. The introduction of *August* leaves the tree balanced. However, the next insertion, *April*, causes the tree to become unbalanced again. Since the tree is now unbalanced to the left, we rotate the two gray nodes to the right. Thus, we make *March* the right child of August, and we make *August* the root of the subtree (Figure 10.11(e)). Notice that we performed both of the previous rotations when the closest ancestor of the new node that had a balance factor of ±2. The insertion of *January* also produces an unbalanced tree. However, this time the rotation is more complex since the imbalance is not in one direction. In this case, we must rotate the three shaded nodes along with their subtrees. We make *March* the new root. *August*, together with its left subtree, becomes the left subtree of *March*. The left subtree of *March* becomes the right subtree of *August*. *May* and its right subtree, which have identifiers greater than *March*, become the right subtree of *March*. If *March* had a nonempty right subtree, this would have become the left subtree of *May* since all identifiers would have been less than *May*.

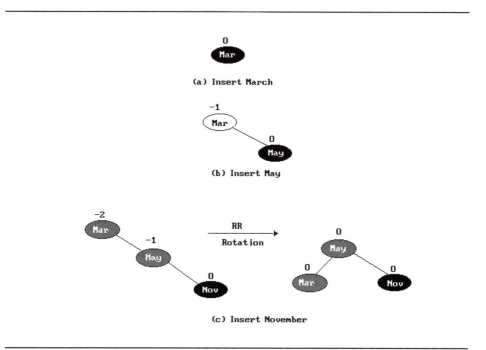

(a) Insert March

(b) Insert May

RR
Rotation

(c) Insert November

Figure 10.11: Insertion into an AVL tree

Inserting *December* and *July* necessitates no rebalancing. However, when we insert *February*, the tree again becomes unbalanced. The rebalancing process is similar to the one we used after we inserted *January*. It again involves the three gray nodes. The imbalance occurs at *August*. In this case, we make *December* the new root of that subtree. *August*, with its left subtree, becomes the left subtree of *December*. *January*, and its right subtree, becomes the right subtree of *December*. We make *February* the left subtree of *January*. If *December* had a left subtree, it would have become the right subtree of *August*. The insertion of *June* requires the same rebalancing as in Figure 10.11(f). Inserting *October* also requires rebalancing. In this case, the rotation is identical to the one we used after we placed *November* in the tree. Inserting *September* leaves the tree balanced.

In the preceding example we saw that the addition of a node to a balanced binary search tree could unbalance it. We carried out the rebalancing using four different kinds of rotations: *LL*, *RR*, *LR*, and *RL* (Figure 10.11 (e), (c), (f), and (i), respectively). *LL* and *RR* are symmetric as are *LR* and *RL*. These rotations are characterized by the nearest ancestor, *A*, of the inserted node, *Y*, whose balance factor becomes ±2. We characterize the rotation types as follows:

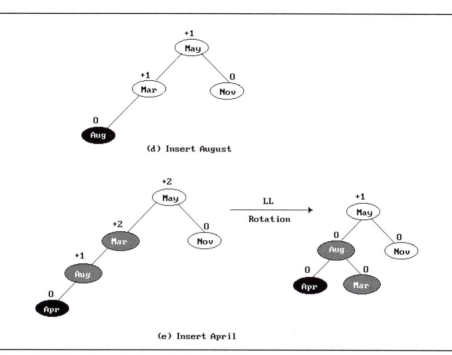

Figure 10.11 (continued): Insertion into an AVL tree

LL: new node Y is inserted in the left subtree of the left subtree of A

LR: Y is inserted in the right subtree of the left subtree of A

RR: Y is inserted in the right subtree of the right subtree of A

RL: Y is inserted in the left subtree of the right subtree of A

Figure 10.12 shows the *LL*, *LR*, and *RR* rotations in terms of abstract binary trees. The *RL* rotations are similar to the *LR* ones. The root node in each of the trees of the figure represents the nearest ancestor whose balance factor has become ±2 as a result of the insertion. A moment's reflection shows that if a height balanced binary tree becomes unbalanced as a result of an insertion, then these are the only four cases possible for rebalancing (if a moment's reflection doesn't convince you, then try Exercise 1). In both the example of Figure 10.11 and the rotations of Figure 10.12, the height of the subtrees which are not involved in the rotation remain unchanged. This means that once we have rebalanced the subtree in question, we do not need to examine the remaining portions of the tree. The only nodes whose balance factors can change are those in the subtree that is rotated.

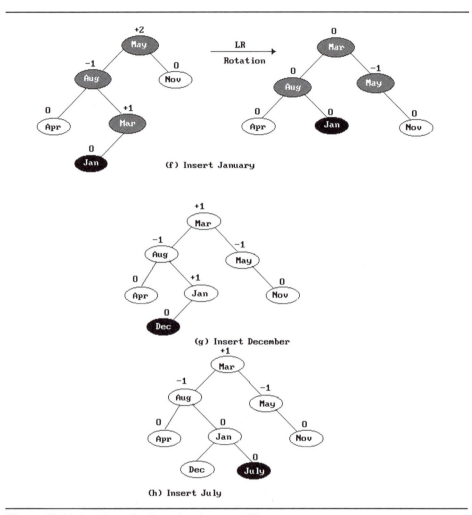

(f) Insert January

(g) Insert December

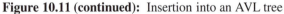

(h) Insert July

Figure 10.11 (continued): Insertion into an AVL tree

To perform a rotation, we must first locate the nearest ancestor, A, of the newly inserted node whose balance factor becomes ± 2. A node's balance factor cannot change to ± 2 unless its balance factor was ± 1 prior to insertion. Therefore, the insertion function may use this information to determine when a node's balance factor increases to ± 2. To complete an *LL* or *RR* rotation, we also must know the parent of A since after the rotation one of the parent's pointers is changed to point to the new root of the subtree. Figure 10.12 shows the changes in the nodes and their balance factors.

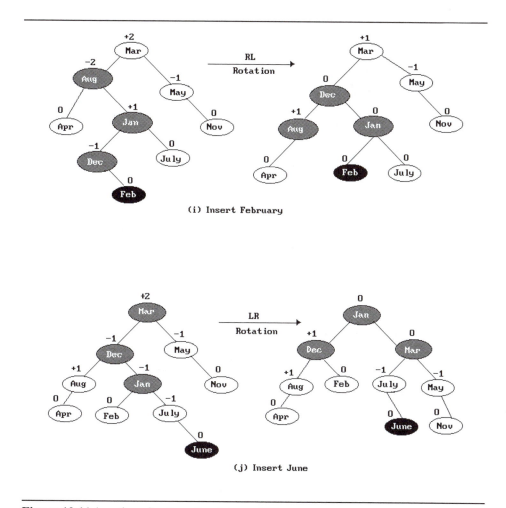

(i) Insert February

(j) Insert June

Figure 10.11 (continued): Insertion into an AVL tree

What happens when the insertion of a node does not result in an unbalanced tree (Figure 10.11 (a), (b), (d), (g), (h), and (l))? While no restructuring of the tree is needed, the balance factors of several nodes change. Let A be the nearest ancestor of the new node with balance factor ±1 before insertion. If as a result of the insertion the tree does not become unbalanced even though some path length increased by 1, the new balance factor of A must be 0. In case there is no ancestor A with balance factor ±1 (as in Figure 10.11 (a), (b), (d), (g), and (l)), let A be the root. The balance factors of nodes from A to the parent of the new node will change to ±1 (see Figure 10.11 (h), $A = January$). Notice that in both cases the function for determining A is the same as when rebalancing is needed. The remaining details of the insertion-rebalancing process are spelled out in

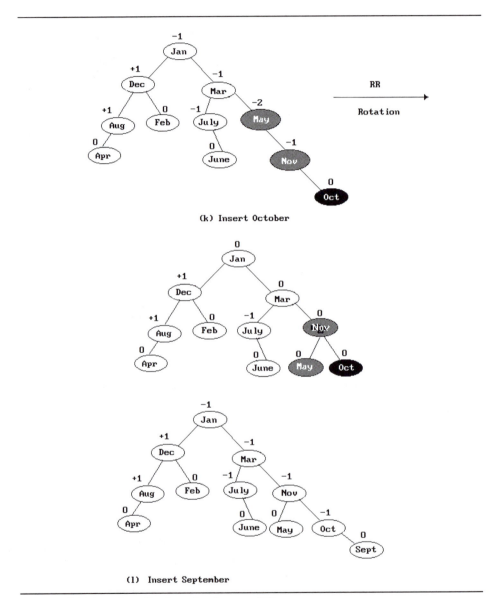

(k) Insert October

(l) Insert September

Figure 10.11 (continued): Insertion into an AVL tree

avl–insert (Program 10.2). The function *left–rotation* (Program 10.3) gives the code for
the *LL* and *LR* rotations. The code for the *RR* and *RL* rotations is symmetric and we
leave it as an exercise. The type definitions in use are:

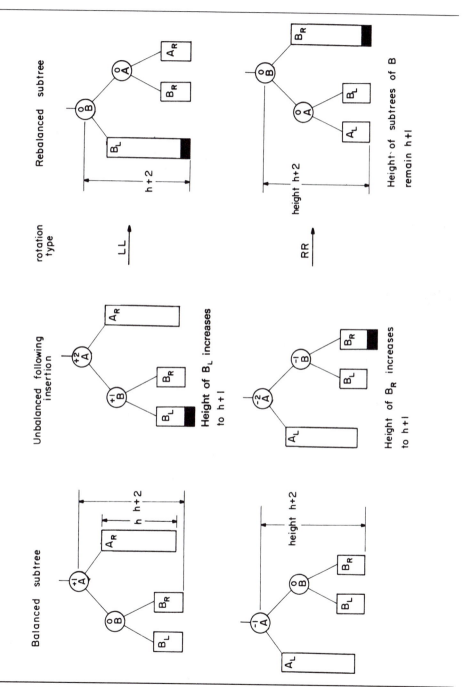

Figure 10.12: Rebalancing rotations

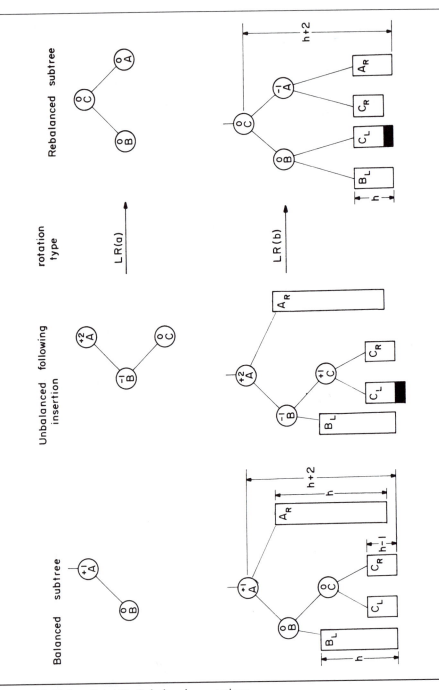

Figure 10.12 (continued): Rebalancing rotations

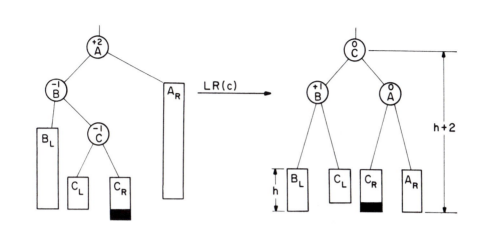

Figure 10.12 (continued): Rebalancing rotations

```
#define IS_FULL(ptr) (!(ptr))
#define FALSE = 0
#define TRUE = 1
typedef struct {
        int key;
        } element;
typedef struct tree_node *tree_pointer;
        struct tree_node {
                tree_pointer left_child;
                element      data;
                short int    bf;
                tree_pointer right_child;
                };
int unbalanced = FALSE;
tree_pointer root = NULL;
```

The pointer to the tree *root* is set to *NULL* before to the first call of *avl_insert*. We also set *unbalanced* to *FALSE* **before each call** to *avl_insert*. The function call is *avl_insert(&root, x, &unbalanced)*.

```
void avl_insert(tree_pointer *parent, element x,
                                    int *unbalanced)
{
   if (!*parent) {
   /* insert element into null tree */
      *unbalanced = TRUE;
      *parent = (tree_pointer)
                          malloc(sizeof(tree_node));
      if (IS_FULL(*parent)) {
         fprintf(stderr, "The memory is full\n");
         exit(1);
      }
      (*parent)->left_child =
                  (*parent)->right_child = NULL;
      (*parent)->bf = 0;
      (*parent)->data = x;
   }
   else if (x.key < (*parent)->data.key) {
      avl_insert(&(*parent)->left_child, x, unbalanced);
      if (*unbalanced)
      /* left branch has grown higher */
         switch ((*parent)->bf) {
            case -1: (*parent)->bf = 0;
                     *unbalanced = FALSE;
                     break;
            case  0: (*parent)->bf = 1;
                     break;
            case  1: left_rotation(parent,unbalanced);
         }
   }
   else if (x.key > (*parent)->data.key) {
      avl_insert(&(*parent)->right_child, x, unbalanced);
      if (*unbalanced)
         /* right branch has grown higher */
         switch((*parent)->bf) {
            case 1 : (*parent)->bf = 0;
                     *unbalanced = FALSE;
                     break;
            case 0 : (*parent)->bf = -1;
                     break;
            case -1: right_rotation(parent, unbalanced);
         }
   }
```

```
    else {
      *unbalanced = FALSE;
      printf("The key is already in the tree");
    }
  }
}
```

Program 10.2: Insertion into an AVL tree

To really understand the insertion algorithm, you should apply it to the example of Figure 10.11. Once you are convinced that it keeps the tree balanced, then the next question is how much time does it take to make an insertion? An analysis of the algorithm reveals that if h is the height of the tree before insertion, then the time to insert a new identifier is O(h). This is the same as for unbalanced binary search trees, although the overhead is significantly greater now. In the case of binary search trees, however, if there were n nodes in the tree, then h could be n (Figure 10.10) and the worst case insertion time would be O(n). In the case of AVL trees, since h is at most O(log n), the worst case insertion time is O(log n). To see this, let N_h be the minimum number of nodes in a height balanced tree of height h. In the worst case, the height of one of the subtrees is $h - 1$ and the height of the other is $h - 2$. Both these subtrees are also height balanced. Hence, $N_h = N_{h-1} + N_{h-2} + 1$ and $N_0 = 0$, $N_1 = 1$ and $N_2 = 2$. Notice the similarity between this recursive definition for N_h and the definition of the Fibonacci numbers $F_n = F_{n-1} + F_{n-2}$, $F_0 = 0$, and $F_1 = 1$. In fact, we can show (Exercise 2) that $N_h = F_{h+2} - 1$ for $h \geq 0$. From Fibonacci number theory we know that $F_h \approx \phi^h / \sqrt{5}$ where $\phi = (1 + \sqrt{5})/2$. Hence, $N_h \approx \phi^{n+2} / \sqrt{5} - 1$. This means that if there are n nodes in the tree, then its height, h, is at most $\log_\phi (\sqrt{5}(n + 1)) - 2$. Therefore, the worst case insertion time for a height balanced tree with n nodes is O(log n).

The exercises show that it is possible to find and delete a node with identifier x and to find and delete the kth node from a height balanced tree in O(log n) time. The paper by Karlton et al. gives the results of an empirical study of deletion in height balanced trees. Their study indicates that the probability that a random insertion will require no rebalancing is .5349; the probability that it will require a single rotation (*LL* or *RR*) is .2324; and the probability that it will require a double rotation (*LR* or *RL*) is .2324. Figure 10.13 compares the worst case times of certain operations on sorted sequential lists, sorted linked lists, and AVL trees.

EXERCISES

1. (a) Complete Figure 10.12 by drawing the tree configurations for the rotations *RL* (a), (b), and (c).

```
void left-rotation(tree-pointer *parent, int *unbalanced)
{
   tree-pointer grand-child, child;
   child = (*parent)->left-child;
   if (child->bf == 1) {
      /* LL rotation */
      (*parent)->left-child = child->right-child;
      child->right-child = *parent;
      (*parent)->bf = 0;
      (*parent) = child;
   }
   else {
   /* LR rotation */
      grand-child = child->right-child;
      child->right-child = grand-child->left-child;
      grand-child->left-child = child;
      (*parent)->left-child = grand-child->right-child;
      grand-child->right-child = *parent;
      switch(grand-child->bf) {
         case  1 : (*parent)->bf = -1;
                 child->bf = 0;
                 break;
         case 0:   (*parent)->bf = child->bf = 0;
                 break;
         case -1:   (*parent)->bf = 0;
                 child->bf = 1;
      }
      *parent = grand-child;
   }
   (*parent)->bf = 0;
   *unbalanced = FALSE;
}
```

Program 10.3: Left rotation function

(b) Convince yourself that the completed Figure 10.12 takes care of all the possible situations that may arise when a height balanced binary tree becomes unbalanced as a result of an insertion. Alternately, come up with an example that is not covered by any of the cases in this figure.

Operation	Sequential list	Linked list	AVL tree
Search for x	$O(\log n)$	$O(n)$	$O(\log n)$
Search for kth item	$O(1)$	$O(k)$	$O(\log n)$
Delete x	$O(n)$	$O(1)^1$	$O(\log n)$
Delete kth item	$O(n-k)$	$O(k)$	$O(\log n)$
Insert x	$O(n)$	$O(1)^2$	$O(\log n)$
Output in order	$O(n)$	$O(n)$	$O(n)$

1. Doubly linked list and position of x known.
2. If position for insertion is known.

Figure 10.13: Comparison of various structures

2. Prove by induction that the minimum number of nodes in an AVL tree of height h is $N_h = F_{h+2} - 1$, $h \geq 0$.

3. Complete *avl–insert* by writing the *right–rotation* function.

4. Obtain the height balanced trees corresponding to those of Figure 10.11 using algorithm *avl–insert*, starting with an empty tree, on the following sequence of insertions:

December, January, April, March, July, August,
October, February, September November, May, June

Label the rotations according to type.

5. Assume that each node in an AVL tree t has the field *lsize*. For any node, a, $a\rightarrow lsize$ is the number of nodes in its left subtree plus one. Write an algorithm *avl–find(t, k)* to locate the kth smallest identifier in the subtree t. Show that this can be done in $O(\log n)$ time if there are n nodes in t.

6. Rewrite algorithm *avl–insert* with the added assumption that each node has a *lsize* field as in Exercise 5. Show that the insertion time remains $O(\log n)$.

7. Write an algorithm to list the nodes of an AVL tree T in ascending order of the *key* fields. Show that this can be done in $O(n)$ time if T has n nodes.

8. It is known that any algorithm that merges together two sorted lists of size n and m, respectively, must make at least $n + m - 1$ comparisons in the worst. What implications does this result have on the time complexity of any comparison based algorithm that combines together two AVL trees that have n and m elements, respectively?

9. In Chapter 7, we showed that every comparison based algorithm to sort n elements must make $O(n \log n)$ comparisons in the worst case. What implications does this result have on the complexity of initializing an AVL tree with n elements?

10. Write an algorithm to delete the node with identifier x from an AVL tree t. The resulting tree should be restructured if necessary. Show that the time required for this is $O(\log n)$ when there are n nodes in t.

11. Do Exercise 5 for the case when each node has a *lsize* field and the kth smallest identifier is to be deleted.

12. Write an algorithm to merge the nodes of the two AVL trees, T_1 and T_2, together to obtain a new AVL tree. What is the computing time of your algorithm?

13. Write an algorithm to split an AVL tree, T, into two AVL trees T_1 and T_2 such that all identifiers in T_1 are $\leq x$ and all those in T_2 are $> x$.

14. Complete Figure 10.13 by adding a column for hashing.

15. § For a fixed k, $k \geq 1$, we define a height balanced tree $HB(k)$ as follows:

    Definition: An empty binary tree is an $HB(k)$ tree. If T is a nonempty binary tree with T_L and T_R as its left and right subtrees, then T is $HB(k)$ *iff*:

    (1) T_L and T_R are $HB(k)$

    (2) $|h_L - h_R| \leq k$, where h_L and h_R are the heights of T_L and T_R, respectively.   □

    (a)   Obtain the rebalancing transformations for $HB(2)$ trees.

    (b)   Write an insertion function for $HB(2)$ trees.

10.3   TWO-THREE TREES (2-3 TREES)

10.3.1   Definition And Properties

By considering search trees of degree greater than 2, we can arrive at tree structures for which the insertion and deletion algorithms are simpler than that for AVL trees. Yet, these algorithms have $O(\log n)$ complexity. The tree structure we consider is called a 2-3 tree. This name reflects the fact that each internal node in a 2-3 tree has degree two or three. A degree two node is called a 2-*node* while a degree three node is called a 3-*node*.

Definition: A 2-3 tree is a search tree that is either empty or satisfies the following properties:

(1)   Each internal node is either a 2-node or a 3-node. A 2-node has one element while a 3-node has two elements.

(2)   Let *left_child* and *middle_child* denote the children of a 2-node. Let *data_l* be the element in this node and let *data_l.key* be its key. All elements in the 2-3 subtree with root *left_child* have key less than *data_l.key*, while all elements in the 2-3 subtree with root *middle_child* have key greater than *data_l.key*.

(3)   Let *left_child*, *middle_child*, and *right_child* denote the children of a 3-node. Let *data_l* and *data_r* be the two elements in this node. Then, *data_l.key* < *data_r.key*; all keys in the 2-3 subtree with root *left_child* are less than *data_l.key*; all keys in the 2-3 subtree with root *middle_child* are less than *data_r.key* and greater than *data_l.key*; and all keys in the 2-3 subtree with root *right_child* are greater than *data_r.key*.

(4)   All external nodes are at the same level. □

An example 2-3 tree is given in Figure 10.14. As in the case of leftist trees, external nodes are introduced only to make it easier to define and talk about 2-3 trees. External nodes are not physically represented inside a computer. Rather, the corresponding child field of the parent of each external node is set to *NULL*.

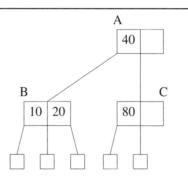

Figure 10.14: An example 2-3 tree

The number of elements in a 2-3 tree with height h (i.e., the external nodes are at level $h+1$) is between $2^h - 1$ and $3^h - 1$. To see this, note that the first bound applies when each internal node is a 2-node while the second bound applies when each internal node is a 3-node. These two cases represent the two extremes. A 2-3 tree with some 2-nodes and some 3-nodes will have a number of elements somewhere between these two bounds. Hence, the height of a 2-3 tree with n elements is between $\lceil \log_3(n+1) \rceil$ and $\lceil \log_2(n+1) \rceil$.

We may represent a 2-3 tree using nodes of the type *two_three* defined as:

```
typedef struct two_three *two_three_ptr;
        struct two_three {
```

```
element data_l, data_r;
two_three_ptr left_child, middle_child,
right_child ;
};
```

We assume that no valid element has key *INT_MAX* (defined in *<limits.h>*), and adopt the convention that a 2-node has *data_r.key* = *INT_MAX*. Its single element is kept in *data_l*, and *left_child* and *middle_child* point to its two children. Its *right_child* field is set to *NULL*.

10.3.2   Searching A 2-3 Tree

We can easily extend the search algorithm for binary search trees to obtain the search function *search* 23 (Program 10.4), which searches a 2-3 tree, *t*, for a node that contains an element with key *x*. We assume that the keys are integers. The search function uses a *compare* function that compares a key, *x*, with the keys in a given node *p*. It returns the value 1, 2, 3, or 4, respectively, depending on whether *x* is less than the first key, between the first and second keys, greater than the second key, or equal to one of the keys in *p*. The number of iterations of the **while** loop is bounded by the height of the 2-3 tree, *t*. Hence, if *t* has *n* nodes, the complexity of *search* 23 is $O(\log n)$.

```
two_three_ptr search23(two_three_ptr t, element x)
{
/* search the 2-3 tree t for an element that matches x.key.
If such an element is found, a pointer to its node is
returned, otherwise a null pointer is returned */
   while (t)
     switch(compare(x,t)) {
        case 1: t = t->left_child;
                break;
        case 2: t = t->middle_child;
                break;
        case 3: t = t->right_child;
                break;
        case 4: return t;
     }
   return NULL;
}
```

Program 10.4: Function to search a 2-3 tree

10.3.3   Insertion Into A 2-3 Tree

Insertion into a 2-3 tree is fairly simple. Consider inserting an element with key 70 into the 2-3 tree of Figure 10.14. First we search for this key. If the key is already in the tree then the insertion fails as all keys in a 2-3 tree are distinct. Since 70 is not in our example 2-3 tree, it may be inserted. For this, we need to know the leaf node encountered during the search for 70. Note that whenever we search for a key that is not in the 2-3 tree, the search encounters a unique leaf node. The leaf node encountered during the search for 70 is the node C with key 80. Since this node has only one element, the new element may be inserted here. The resulting 2-3 tree is shown in Figure 10.15(a).

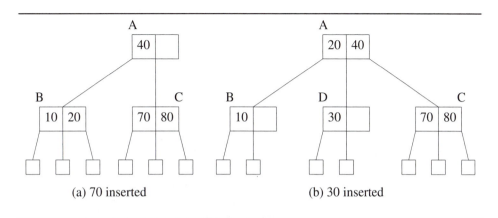

(a) 70 inserted   (b) 30 inserted

Figure 10.15: Insertion into the 2-3 tree of Figure 10.14

Next, consider inserting an element x with key 30. This time the search encounters the leaf node B. Since B is a 3-node, it is necessary to create a new node D. D will contain the element that has the largest key from amongst the two elements currently in B and x. The element with the smallest key will be in B and the element with the median key together with a pointer to D will be inserted into the parent A of B. The resulting 2-3 tree is shown in Figure 10.15(b).

As a final example, consider the insertion of an element x with key 60 into the 2-3 tree of Figure 10.15(b). The leaf node encountered during the search for 60 is node C. Since C is a 3-node, a new node E is created. This contains the element with largest key (80). Node C contains the element with smallest key (60). The element with the median key (70) together with a pointer to the new node E are to be inserted into the parent A of C. Again, since A is a 3-node, a new node F containing the element with largest key amongst {20, 40, 70} is created. As before, A contains the element with the smallest key. B and D remain the left and middle children of A, respectively and C and E become these children of F. If A had a parent, then the element with the median key 40 and a pointer to the new node F would be inserted into this parent node. Since A does not have a parent, we create a new root G for the 2-3 tree. This contains the element with key 40 together with a left child pointer to A and a middle child pointer to F. The new 2-3 tree is as shown in Figure 10.16.

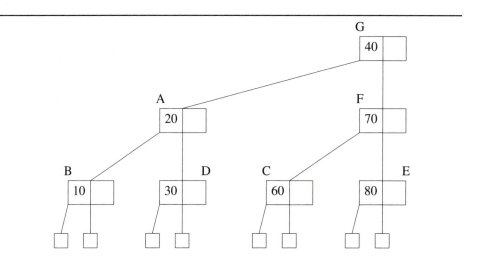

Figure 10.16: Insertion of 60 into the 2-3 tree of Figure 10.15(b)

Each time we attempt to add an element into a 3-node, p, we create a new node, q. We refer to this as a node *split*. We say that p is split into p, q, and the median element. Putting the ideas in the preceding discussion together, we get the insertion function of *insert* 23 (Program 10.5).

This function makes use of several functions whose development we leave as an exercise. We specify the task performed by each as follows:

(1)   *new_root*. We invoke this function when the root of the 2-3 tree is to change. The inputs to this function are the left child of the new root, its single element, and its middle child. A pointer to the new root is returned in the first parameter.

(2)   *find_node*. This function is a modified version of *search* 23. It searches a nonempty 2-3 tree, t, for the presence of an element with key $y.key$. If this key is present in t, then we set return *NULL*. Otherwise, we return the leaf node, p, encountered in the search. Additionally, *find_node* creates a global stack so that we can find the ancestors from the leaf p to the root t. The stack keeps a list of nodes from the closest ancestor to the most distant one. We need such a list since following a node split we must access the parent of the node that was split.

(3)   *put_in*. We use this function to insert an element, y, into a node, p, that has exactly one element in it. We place the subtree q immediately to the right of y. Thus, if y becomes *data_l*, then q becomes *middle_child* and the previous values of *data_l* and *middle_child* move to *data_r* and *right_child*. If y becomes *data_r*, then q becomes *right_child*.

```
void insert23(two_three_ptr *t, element y)
{
/* insert the element y into the 2-3 tree */
   two_three_ptr q, p, temp;

   if (!(*t))  /* tree is empty */
      new_root(t, y, NULL);
   else {
   /* insert into a non-empty tree */
      p = find_node(*t,y);
      if (!p) {
         fprintf(stderr, "The key is currently in the
                          tree\n");
         exit(1);
      }
      q = NULL;
      for(;;)
         if (p->data_r.key == INT_MAX) { /*2-node */
            put_in(&p,y,q);
            break;
         }
         else {    /* 3-node */
            split(p,&y,&q);
            if (p == *t) { /* split the root */
               new_root(t,y,q);
               break;
            }
            else
               /*remove a node from stack */
               p = delete();
         }
      }
   }
}
```

Program 10.5: Insertion into a 2-3 tree

(4) *split*. This function takes a node, *p*, that has two elements in it and creates a new
     node, *q*. The new node contains the record with largest key from among the ele-
     ments initially in *p* and the element *y*. The element with smallest key is the only
     element left in *p*. The three original children pointers of *p* and the pointer *q*
     occupy the four children fields that need to be defined in *p* and the new node. On
     return, *y* is the element with median key and *q* points to the newly formed node.

(5)   *delete*. This function removes a node from the global stack. The pointer to the top of the stack is also a global variable.

In *insert* 23, *y* denotes the element to be inserted into the 2-3 tree and *q* denotes the node that was newly created at the last iteration of the **for** loop. As for the complexity analysis, we see that the total time taken is proportional to the height of the 2-3 tree. Hence, insertion into a 2-3 tree with *n* elements takes O(log *n*) time.

10.3.4   Deletion From A 2-3 Tree

Deletion from a 2-3 tree is conceptually no harder than insertion. In case we are deleting an element that is not in a leaf node, then we transform this into a deletion from a leaf node by replacing the deleted element by a suitable element that is in a leaf. For example, if we are to delete the element with key 50 that is in the root of Figure 10.17(a), then this element may be replaced by either the element with key 20 or the element with key 60. Both are in leaf nodes. In a general situation, we may use either the element with largest key in the subtree on the left or the element with smallest key in the subtree on the right of the element being deleted.

Henceforth, we consider only the case of deletion from a leaf node. Let us begin with the tree of Figure 10.17(a). To delete the element with key 70, we need merely set $data\_r.key = INT\_MAX$ in node C. The result is shown in Figure 10.17(b). To delete the element with key 90 from the 2-3 tree of Figure 10.17(b), we need to shift $data\_r$ to $data\_l$ and set $data\_r.key = INT\_MAX$ in node D. This results in the 2-3 tree of Figure 10.17(c).

Next consider the deletion of the element with key 60. This leaves node C empty. Since the left sibling, B, of C is a 3-node, we can move the element with key 20 into the $data\_l$ position of the parent node, A, and move the element with key 50 from the parent to node C. After setting $data\_r.key = INT\_MAX$ in B, the 2-3 tree takes the form shown in Figure 10.17(d). This data movement operation is called a *rotation*. When the element with key 95 is deleted, node D becomes empty. The rotation performed when the 60 was deleted isn't possible now as the left sibling C is a 2-node. This time, we move the 80 into the left sibling C and delete the node D. We shall refer to this operation as a *combine*. In a combine one node is deleted, while no nodes are deleted in a rotation. The deletion of 95 results in the 2-3 tree of Figure 10.17(e). Deleting the element with key 50 from this tree results in the 2-3 tree of Figure 10.17(f). Now consider deleting the element with key 10 from this tree. Node B becomes empty. At this time, we examine B's right sibling C to see if it is a 2-node or a 3-node. If it is a 3-node, we can perform a rotation similar to that done during the deletion of 60. If it is a 2-node, then a combine is performed. Since C is a 2-node, we proceed in a manner similar to the deletion of 95. This time, the elements with keys 20 and 80 are moved into B and the node C deleted. This, however, causes the parent node A to have no elements. If the parent had not been a root, we would examine its left or right sibling as we did when nodes C (deletion of 60) and D (deletion of 95) became empty. Since A is the root, it is simply deleted and B

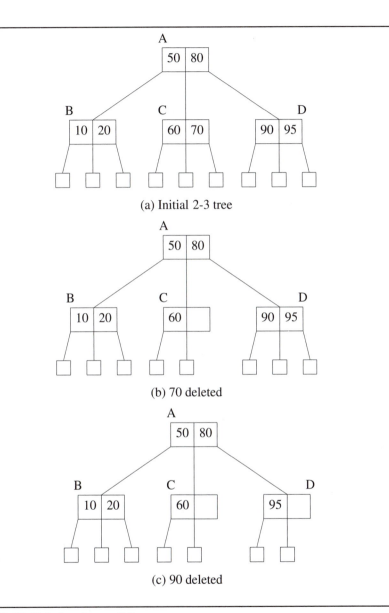

(a) Initial 2-3 tree

(b) 70 deleted

(c) 90 deleted

Figure 10.17: Deletion from a 2-3 tree

becomes the new root (Figure 10.17(g)).

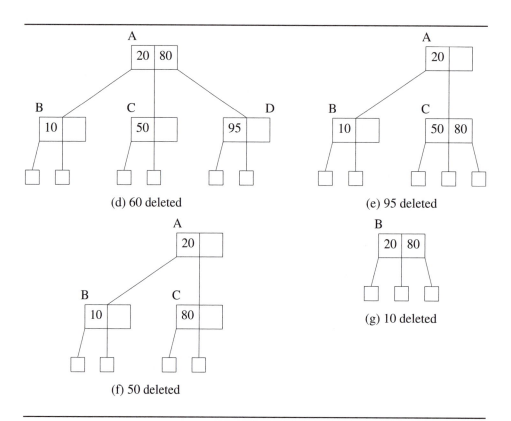

(d) 60 deleted

(e) 95 deleted

(f) 50 deleted

(g) 10 deleted

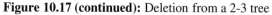

Figure 10.17 (continued): Deletion from a 2-3 tree

Program 10.6 summarizes the steps involved in deletion from a leaf node p of a 2-3 tree t.

There are three cases for a rotation depending on whether p is the left, middle, or right child of its parent r. If p is the left child of r, then let q be the right sibling of p. Otherwise, let q be the left sibling of p. Note that regardless of whether r is a 2-node or a 3-node, q is well defined. The three rotation cases are shown pictorially in Figure 10.18. A ''?'' denotes a don't care situation. a, b, c, and d denote the children (i.e., roots of sub-trees) of nodes.

Figure 10.19 shows the two cases for a combine when p is the left child of r. We leave it as an exercise to obtain the figures for the cases when p is a middle child and when p is a right child.

The refinement of step 1 of Program 10.6 into C code is shown in Program 10.7. Programs 10.8 and 10.9 show the code for the rotate and combine operations when p is the left child of r. We leave the development of the complete deletion function as an exercise.

Step 1: Modify p as necessary to reflect its status after the desired element has been deleted.

Step 2: **while** (p has zero elements && p is not the root) {
    let r be the parent of p;
    let q be the left or right sibling of p (as appropriate);
    if (q is a 3-node)
        rotate;
    else
        combine;
    $p = r$;
    }

Step 3: If p has zero elements, then p must be the root. The left child of p becomes the new root and p is deleted.

Program 10.6: Steps in deleting from a leaf node, p, of a 2-3 tree

Analysis of deletion: It should be obvious that an individual rotation or combine operation takes O(1) time. If a rotation is performed, the deletion is complete. If a combine is performed, p moves up one level in the 2-3 tree. Hence, the number of combines that we can perform during a deletion cannot exceed the height of the 2-3 tree. Consequently, deletion from a 2-3 tree with n elements takes O(log n) time. $\square$

EXERCISES

1. Write the *compare* function used in Program 10.4.

2. (a) Develop the functions *find_node*, *new_root*, *put_in*, and *split* used by function *insert* 23 (Program 10.5). Use these functions to test the correctness of *insert* 23.

    (b) Next, use random insertions and measure the height of the resulting 2-3 trees with $n = 100$, 1000, and 10,000 elements.

3. Complete Figure 10.19 by providing the figures for the cases p is a middle child and p is a right child.

4. Develop a complete C function to delete the element with key x from the 2-3 tree t. Test this function using at least five different 2-3 trees of your choice. For each of these perform at least six successive deletions.

5. It is known that any algorithm that merges together two sorted lists of size n and m, respectively, must make at least $n + m - 1$ comparisons in the worst. What implications does this result have on the time complexity of any comparison based algorithm that combines together two 2-3 trees that have n and m elements,

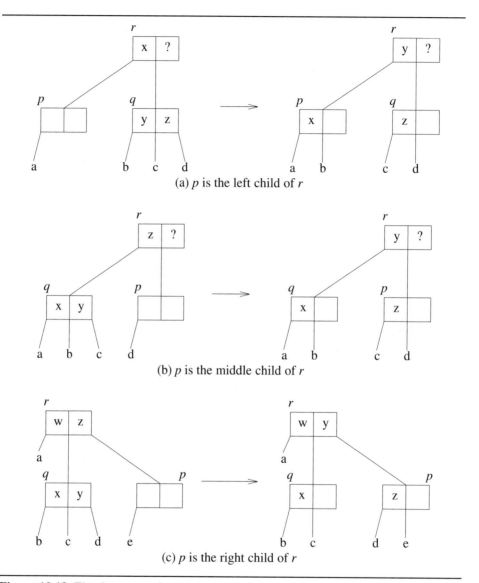

Figure 10.18: The three cases for rotation in a 2-3 tree

respectively?

6.   In Chapter 7, we showed that every comparison based algorithm to sort n elements must make $O(n \log n)$ comparisons in the worst case. What implications does this result have on the complexity of initializing a 2-3 tree with n elements?

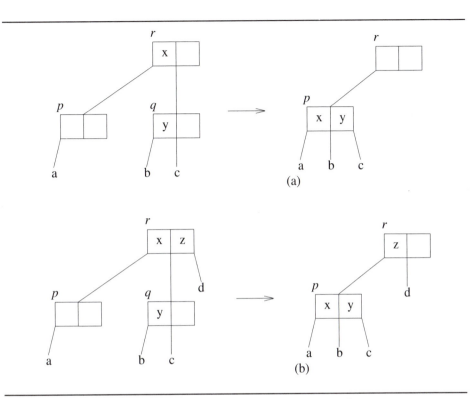

(a)

(b)

Figure 10.19: Combining in a 2-3 tree when p is a the left child of r

7. Consider a variation of a 2-3 tree in which elements are kept only in leaf nodes. Each leaf has exactly one element. The remaining nodes are 2-nodes or 3-nodes. Each such node keeps only the values $large - a$ = largest key in any leaf in its left subtree and $large - b$ = largest key in any leaf in its middle subtree. As before, all external nodes are at the same level.

    (a) Define two node structures such that one is suitable to represent a leaf node and the other to represent a nonleaf node.

    (b) Write a procedure to search such a 2-3 tree represented in this way.

    (c) Write a procedure to insert an element x into this tree.

    (d) Write a deletion procedure for such a 2-3 tree.

    (e) Show that each of the above operations can be performed in O(log$n$) time where n is the number of elements (i.e., leaf nodes) in the tree.

8. Let T and U be two 2-3 trees in which keys are kept in the leaves only (see preceding exercise). Let V be a similar tree that contains all key values in T and U. Write an algorithm to construct V from T and U. What is the complexity of your

```
/*delete x from the leaf p */
if (x.key == p->data_l.key)
   if (p->data_r.key !=  INT_MAX) {
      /* p is a 3-node */
      p->data_l = p->data_r;
      p->data_r.key = INT_MAX;
   }
   else
      /* p is a 2-node */
      p->data_l.key = INT_MAX;
else
   /* delete second element */
   p->data_r.key = INT_MAX;
```

Program 10.7: Refinement of step 1 of Program 10.6

```
/* rotation when p is left child of r */
p->data_l = r->data_l;
r->data_l = q->data_l;
q->data_l = q->data_r;
q->data_r.key = INT_MAX;
p->middle_child  = q->left_child;
q->left_child = q->middle_child;
q->middle_child = q->right_child;
```

Program 10.8: Rotation when p is the left child of r

algorithm?

9. Write insertion and deletion algorithms for 2-3 trees assuming that an additional
    field f is associated with each key value. $f = 1$ iff the corresponding key value has
    not been deleted. Deletions should be accomplished by simply setting the
    corresponding $f = 0$ and insertions should make use of deleted space whenever
    possible without restructuring the tree.

10. Write algorithms to search and delete keys from a 2-3 tree by position; that is,
    search (k) finds the kth smallest key and *delete* (k) deletes the kth smallest key in
    the tree. (Hint: In order to do this efficiently additional information must be kept
    in each node. With each pair (K_i, A_i) keep $N_i = \sum_{j=0}^{i-1}$ (number of key values in the
    subtree $A_j + 1$).) What are the worst case computing times of your algorithms?

```
/* p is the left child of r */
p->data_l = r->data_l;
p->data_r = q->data_l;
p->middle_child = q->left_child;
p->right_child = q->middle_child;
if (r->data_r.key == INT_MAX)
   /* r was a two node */
   r->data_l.key = INT_MAX;
else {
   r->data_l = r->data_r;
   r->data_r.key = INT_MAX;
   r->middle_child = r->right_child;
}
```

Program 10.9: Combine when *p* is the left child of r

11. Modify the 2-3 insertion algorithm so that we first check to see if either the nearest left sibling or the nearest right sibling of *p* has fewer than 2 keys. If so, no node is split. Instead, a rotation is performed moving either the smallest or largest key in *p* to its parent. The corresponding key in the parent together with a subtree is moved to the sibling of *p* which has space for another key value.

10.4 TWO-THREE-FOUR TREES (2-3-4 TREES)

10.4.1 Definition And Properties

A 2-3-4 tree extends a 2-3 tree so that 4-nodes are also permitted (4-nodes may have up to four children).

Definition: A *2-3-4 tree* is a search tree that is either empty or satisfies the following properties:

(1) Each internal node is a 2-, 3-, or 4-node. A 2-node has one element, a 3-node has two elements, and a 4-node has three elements.

(2) Let *left_child* and *left_mid_child* denote the children of a 2-node. Let *data_l* be the element in this node and let *data_l.key* be its key. All elements in the 2-3-4 subtree with root *left_child* have key less than *data_l.key*, while all elements in the 2-3-4 subtree with root *left_mid_child* have key greater than *data_l.key*.

(3)   Let *left_child*, *left_mid_child*, and *right_mid_child* denote the children of a 3-node. Let *data_l* and *data_m* be the two elements in this node. Then, *data_l.key* < *data_m.key*; all keys in the 2-3-4 subtree with root *left_child* are less than *data_l.key*; all keys in the 2-3-4 subtree with root *left_mid_child* are less than *data_m.key* and greater than *data_l.key*; and all keys in the 2-3-4 subtree with root *right_mid_child* are greater than *data_m.key*.

(4)   Let *left_child*, *left_mid_child*, *right_mid_child* and *right_child* denote the children of a 4-node. Let *data_l*, *data_m* and *data_r* be the three elements in this node. Then, *data_l.key* < *data_m.key* < *data_r.key*; all keys in the 2-3-4 subtree with root *left_child* are less than *data_l.key*; all keys in the 2-3-4 subtree with root *left_mid_child* are less than *data_m.key* and greater than *data_l.key*; all keys in the 2-3-4 subtree with root *right_mid_child* are greater than *data_m.key* but less than *data_r.key*; and all keys in the 2-3-4 subtree with root *right_child* are greater than *data_r.key*.

(5)   All external nodes are at the same level. □

We may represent a 2-3-4 tree using nodes of the type *two* 34*pointer* defined as:

```
typedef struct two34 *two34pointer;
typedef struct two34  {
        element data_l;
        element data_m;
        element data_r;
        two34pointer left_child;
        two34pointer left_mid_child;
        two34pointer right_mid_child;
        two34pointer right_child;
        } ;
```

As in the case of 2-3 trees, we assume that no valid element has *key* = *INT_MAX*. We adopt the convention that a 2-node has *data_m.key* = *INT_MAX*. The single element is kept in *data_l* and *left_child* and *left_mid_child* point to its two children. A 3-node has *data_r.key* = *INT_MAX* and the *left_child*, *left_mid_child*, and *right_mid_child* fields point to its three subtrees. An example 2-3-4 tree using these conventions and nodes of type *two* 34 is shown in Figure 10.20.

If a 2-3-4 tree of height *h* has only 2-nodes, then it contains $2^h - 1$ elements. If it contains only 4-nodes, then the number of elements is $4^h - 1$. A height *h* 2-3-4 tree with a mixture of 2-, 3-, and 4-nodes has between $2^h - 1$ and $4^h - 1$ elements. In other words, the height of a 2-3-4 tree with *n* elements is between $\lceil \log_4(n+1) \rceil$ and $\lceil \log_2(n+1) \rceil$.

An advantage 2-3-4 trees have over 2-3 trees is that we may insert an element into, or delete an element from, a 2-3-4 tree by a single root to leaf pass. The same operations on a 2-3 tree require a forward root to leaf pass followed by a backward leaf to root pass. As a result, the corresponding 2-3-4 tree algorithms are simpler. More interestingly, we

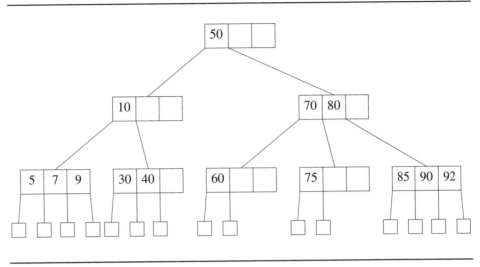

Figure 10.20: An example 2-3-4 tree

can efficiently represent a 2-3-4 tree as a binary tree called a red-black tree. As we shall see in the next section, red-black trees utilize space more efficiently than either 2-3 or 2-3-4 trees. In this section, however, we shall see how we can insert elements into, and delete them from, a 2-3-4 tree by making a single top-down root to leaf pass over the tree.

10.4.2   Insertion Into A 2-3-4 Tree

If the leaf node into which the element is to be inserted is a 4-node, then this node splits and a backward leaf to root pass is initiated. This backward pass terminates when either a 2- or 3-node is encountered or when the root is split. To avoid the backward leaf to root pass, we split 4-nodes on the way down the tree. As a result, the leaf node into which the insertion is to be made is guaranteed to be a 2- or 3-node. The element to be inserted may be added to this node without any further node splitting.

There are essentially three different situations to consider for a 4-node:

(1)   it is the root of the 2-3-4 tree

(2)   its parent is a 2-node

(3)   its parent is a 3-node

The splitting transformations for cases (1) and (2) are shown in Figure 10.21 and Figure 10.22, respectively. For case (3), Figure 10.23 shows the transformation when the 4-node is the left child of the 3-node and Figure 10.24 shows it for the case when the 4-node is the left middle child. The remaining case when the 4-node is the right middle child of the 3-node is symmetric to the case when it is the left child and is left as an exercise. It is easy to see that if the transformations of Figure 10.21, Figure 10.22, and Figure 10.23 are used to split 4-nodes on the way down the 2-3-4 tree, then whenever a non root 4-node is encountered, its parent cannot be a 4-node. Notice that the transformation for a root 4-node increases the height of the 2-3-4 tree by one, while the remaining transformations do not affect its height.

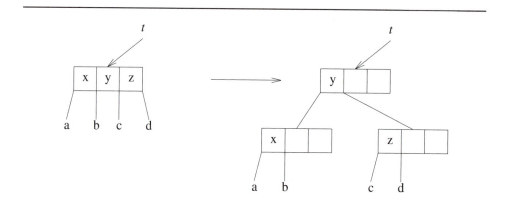

Figure 10.21: Transformation when the 4-node is the root

The function to insert element y into the 2-3-4 tree t represented with nodes of type *two34* takes the form given in Program 10.10. The functions used by *insert234* are specified as follows:

(1) *new_root*. This function creates a single node 2-3-4 tree, t, with only the element y in it.

(2) *four_node*. This function returns *TRUE iff* the given node is a 4-node, and *FALSE* otherwise.

(3) *split_root*. This function uses the transformation of Figure 10.21 to split a root that is a 4-node.

(4) *node_type*. This function returns the value *two_node* if the given node is a 2-node and the value *three_node* otherwise. We use the following declaration to define the *node_type*:

```
typedef enum {two_node,three_node} node_result;
```

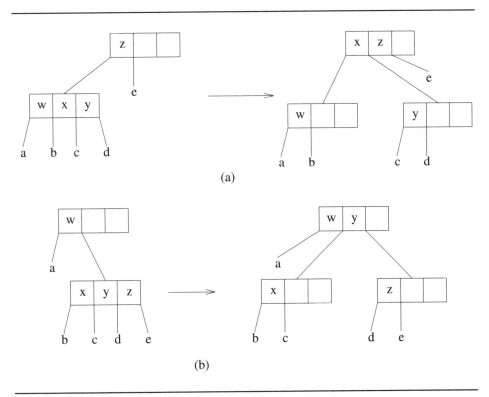

Figure 10.22: Transformation when the 4-node is the child of a 2-node

(5) *split–child–of2*. This function uses the transformations of Figure 10.22 to split a 4-node that is a child of a 2-node.

(6) *split–child–of3*. This function uses the transformations of Figures 10.23 and 10.24 to split a 4-node that is a child of a 3-node.

(7) *compare*. The function compares *y.key* with the keys in *p*. The possible outputs from this function and the corresponding conditions are:

    (a)   `equal.`   *y.key* equals the key of one of the elements in *p*

    (b)   `leaf.`   *p* is a leaf node

    (c)   `lchild.` $y.key < p \rightarrow data\_l.key$

    (d)   `lmchild.` $p \rightarrow data\_l.key < y.key < p \rightarrow data\_m.key$

    (e)   `rmchild.` $p \rightarrow data\_m.key < y.key < p \rightarrow data\_r.key$

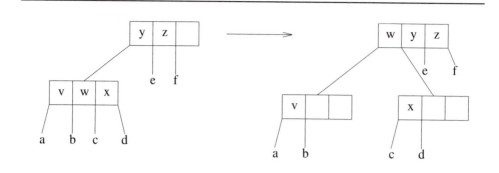

Figure 10.23: Transformation when the 4-node is the left child of a 3-node

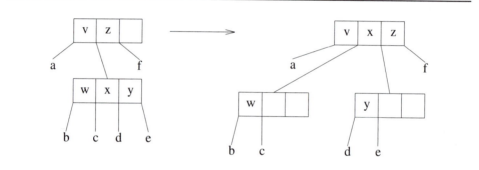

Figure 10.24: Transformation when the 4-node is the left middle child of a 3-node

(f)   `rchild.`   *y.key > p−>data−r.key*

If *y* and *p* satisfy more than one of the above conditions, then we use the first condition encountered. The following declaration creates the enumerated type used by *compare* to return the result:

```
typedef enum {equal,leaf,lchild,lmchild,rmchild,rchild}
                                            compare_result;
```

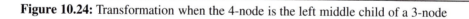

(8)   *put_in*. This function adds the new element to a leaf node. This leaf node is either a 2-node or a 3-node.

We may easily show that the complexity of *insert* 234 is O(log *n*), where *n* is the number of elements in *root*.

10.4.3   Deletion From A 2-3-4 Tree

As in the case of 2-3 trees, the deletion of an arbitrary element may be reduced to that of a deletion of an element that is in a leaf node. If the element to be deleted is in a leaf that is a 3-node or a 4-node, then its deletion leaves behind a 2-node or a 3-node. In this case, no restructuring work is required. Hence, to avoid a backward leaf to root restructuring path (as performed in the case of 2-3 trees) it is necessary to ensure that at the time of deletion, the element to be deleted is in a 3-node or a 4-node. This is accomplished by restructuring the 2-3-4 tree during the downward root to leaf pass.

The restructuring strategy requires that whenever the search moves to a node on the next level, this node must be a 3-node or a 4-node. Suppose the search is presently at node *p* and will move next to node *q*. Note that *q* is a child of *p* and is determined by the relationship between the key of the element to be deleted and the keys of the elements in *p*. The following cases are to be considered:

(1)   *p* is a leaf. In this case, the element to be deleted is either in *p* or not in the tree. If the element to be deleted is not in *p*, then the deletion is unsuccessful. Assume this is not the case. By the nature of the restructuring process, *p* can be a 2-node only if it is also the root. The deletion results in an empty tree.

(2)   *q* is not a 2-node. In this case, the search moves to *q* and no restructuring is needed.

(3)   *q* is a 2-node and its nearest sibling *r* is also a 2-node (if *q* is the left child of *p*, then its nearest sibling is the left middle child of *p*; otherwise, the nearest sibling is its left sibling). Now, if *p* is a 2-node, it must be the root and we perform the transformation of Figure 10.21 in reverse. That is, *p*, *q*, and *r* are combined to form a 4-node and the height of the tree decreases by 1. If *p* is a 3-node or a 4-node, then we perform, in reverse, the 4-node splitting transformation for the corresponding case (Figures 10.22 through 10.24).

(4)   *q* is a 2-node and its nearest sibling *r* is a 3-node. In this case, we perform the transformation of Figure 10.25. This figure only shows the transformations for the case when *q* is the left child of a 3-node *p*. The cases when *q* is the left middle child, right middle child, or right child and when *p* is a 2-node (in this case *p* is the root) or a 4-node are similar.

```
void insert234(two34pointer *t, element y)
{
/* insert y into the 2-3-4 tree t */
   two34pointer p, r;
   if (!*t)
      new_root(t, y);
   else {
      if (four_node(*t))
         split_root(t);
      p = *t;    r = NULL;
      for (;;) {
         if (four_node(p)) {
            if (node_type(r) == two_node)
               split_child_of2(&p,&r);
            else
               split_child_of3(&p,&r);
            p = r;
         }
         r = p;
         switch (compare(y,p)) {
            case equal:    fprintf(stderr,"The key is in the
                           tree\n");
                           exit(1);
            case leaf:     put_in(y, &p);
                           return;
            case lchild:   p = p->left_child;
                           break;
            case lmchild:  p = p->left_mid_child;
                           break;
            case rmchild:  p = p->right_mid_child;
                           break;
            case rchild:   p = p->right_child;
         }
      }
   }
}
```

Program 10.10: Insertion into a 2-3-4 tree

(5) q is a 2-node and its nearest sibling r is a 4-node. This is similar to the case when r is a 3-node.

The above transformations guarantee that a backward restructuring pass is not needed following the deletion from a leaf node. We leave the development of the deletion procedure as an exercise.

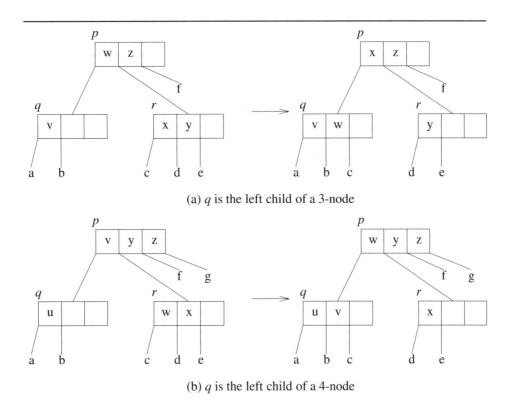

(a) q is the left child of a 3-node

(b) q is the left child of a 4-node

Figure 10.25: Deletion transformation when the nearest sibling is a 3-node

EXERCISES

1. Complete Figure 10.23 by drawing the splitting transformations for the case when the 4-node is the right middle child of a 3-node.

2. Complete function *insert* 234 (Program 10.10) by writing the code for all the functions used. Test your function using randomly generated keys.

3. Use the deletion transformations described in the text to obtain a function to delete an element, *y*, from a 2-3-4 tree represented using nodes of type *two34*. Show that the complexity of you algorithm is O(log *n*), where *n* is the number of elements initially in the tree.

10.5 RED-BLACK TREES

10.5.1 Definition And Properties

A *red-black* tree is a binary tree representation of a 2-3-4 tree. The child pointers of a node in a red-black tree are of two types: *red* and *black*. If the child pointer was present in the original 2-3-4 tree, it is a black pointer. Otherwise, it is a red pointer. The node structure *red−black* is defined as:

```
typedef enum {red,black} color;
typedef struct red_black *red_black_ptr;
typedef struct red_black {
        element data;
        red_black_ptr left_child;
        red_black_ptr right_child;
        color left_color;
        color right_color;
        }
```

An alternate node structure in which each node has a single color field may also be used. The value of this field is the color of the pointer from the node's parent. Thus a red node has a red pointer from its parent while a black node has a black pointer from its parent. The root node, is by definition, a black node. We examine this structure in the exercises. The former structure is better suited for top down insertion and deletion while the latter is better suited for algorithms that make a bottom to top restructuring pass. When drawing a red-black tree, we shall use a solid line to represent a black pointer and a broken one to represent a red pointer. We transform a 2-3-4 tree using nodes of type *two* 34 into red-black trees as follows:

(1) We represent a 2-node, *p*, by a *red−black* node, *q*, with both its color fields black and *data = data−l*; *q −>left−child = p−>left−child*, and *q−>right−child = p−>left−mid−child*.

(2) A 3-node *p* is represented by two *red−black* nodes connected by a red pointer. There are two ways in which this may be done (see Figure 10.26, color fields are not shown).

(3) A 4-node is represented by three *red−black* nodes one of which is connected to the remaining two by red pointers (see Figure 10.27).

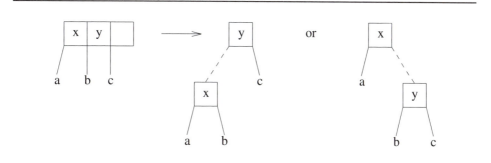

Figure 10.26: Transforming a 3-node into two *red – black* nodes

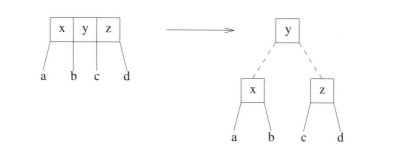

Figure 10.27: Transforming a 4-node into three *red – black* nodes

The red-black tree representation of the 2-3-4 tree of Figure 10.20 is given in Figure 10.28. External nodes and color fields are not shown. One may verify that a red-black tree satisfies the following properties:

(P1) It is a binary search tree.

(P2) Every root to external node path has the same number of black links (this follows from the fact that all external nodes of the original 2-3-4 tree are on the same level and black pointers represent original pointers).

(P3) No root to external node path has two or more consecutive red pointers (this follows from the nature of the transformations of Figure 10.26 and Figure 10.27).

An alternate definition of red-black trees is possible. In this, we associate a rank with each node x in the tree. This value is not explicitly stored in each node. Rather, if the rank of the root (also called rank of the tree) is known, then the rank of every other

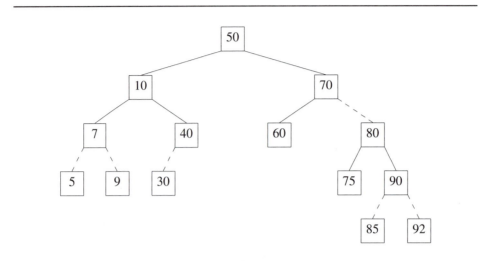

Figure 10.28: Red-black representation of 2-3-4 tree of Figure 10.20

node can be computed by traversing the binary tree and using the color information of the nodes/pointers. A binary tree is a red-black tree iff it satisifies the following properties:

(Q1) It is a binary search tree.

(Q2) The rank of each external node is 0.

(Q3) Every internal node that is the parent of an external node has rank 1.

(Q4) For every node x that has a parent $p(x)$, $rank(x) \leq rank(p(x)) \leq rank(x) + 1$.

(Q5) For every node x that has a grandparent $gp(x)$, $rank(x) < rank(gp(x))$.

Intuitively, each node x of a 2-3-4 tree T is represented by a collection of nodes in its corresponding red-black tree. All nodes in this collection have a rank equal to $height(T) - level(x) + 1$. So, each time there is a rank change in a path from the root of the red-black tree, there is a level change in the corresponding 2-3-4 tree. Black pointers go from a node of a certain rank to one whose rank is one less while red pointers connect two nodes of the same rank. The following lemma is an immediate consequence of the properties of a 2-3-4 tree.

Lemma 10.1: Every red-black tree RB with n (internal) nodes satisifies the following:

(1) $height\,(RB) \le 2\lceil \log_2(n+1) \rceil$

(2) $height\,(RB) \le 2rank\,(RB)$

(3) $rank\,(RB) \le \lceil \log_2(n+1) \rceil$ □

10.5.2   Searching A Red-Black Tree

Since every red-black tree is a binary search tree, it can be searched using exactly the same algorithm as used to search an ordinary binary search tree. The pointer colors are not used during this search.

10.5.3   Top Down Insertion

An insertion can be carried out in one of two ways: top down and bottom up. In a top down insertion a single root to leaf pass is made over the red-black tree. A bottom up insertion makes both a root to leaf and a leaf to root pass. To make a top down insertion, we use the 4-node splitting transformations described in Figures 10.21 through 10.24. In terms of red-black trees, these take the form given in Figures 10.29 through 10.32. The case when a 4-node is the right middle child of a 3-node is symmetric to the case when it is the left child (Figure 10.31).

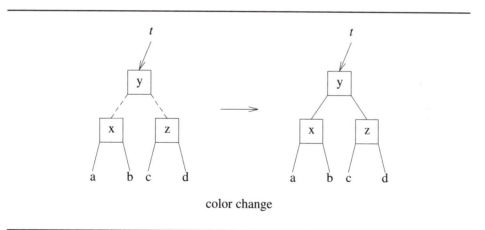

color change

Figure 10.29: Transformation for a root 4-node

We can detect a 4-node by simply looking for nodes q for which both color fields are red. Such nodes together with their two children form a 4-node. When such a q is detected, the transformations of Figures 10.29 through 10.32 are accomplished as below:

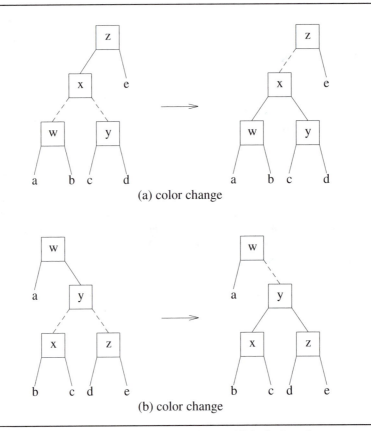

(a) color change

(b) color change

Figure 10.30: Transformation for a 4-node that is the child of a 2-node

(1)   Change both the colors of q to black.

(2)   If q is the left (right) child of its parent, then change the left (right) color of its parent to red.

(3)   If we now have two consecutive red pointers, then one is from the grandparent, gp, of q to the parent, p of q and the other from p to q. Let the direction of the first of these be X and that of the second be Y. We shall use L (R) to denote a left (right) direction. XY = LL, LR, and RL in the case of Figures 10.31(a), 10.32(a), and 10.32(b), respectively. For the case symmetric to Figure 10.31(a) that arises when the 4-node is a right middle child of a 3-node, XY = RR. A rotation similar to that performed in AVL trees is needed. We describe the rotation for the case XY = LL. Now, node p takes the place previously occupied by pp; the right child of p becomes the left child of pp and pp becomes the right child of p.

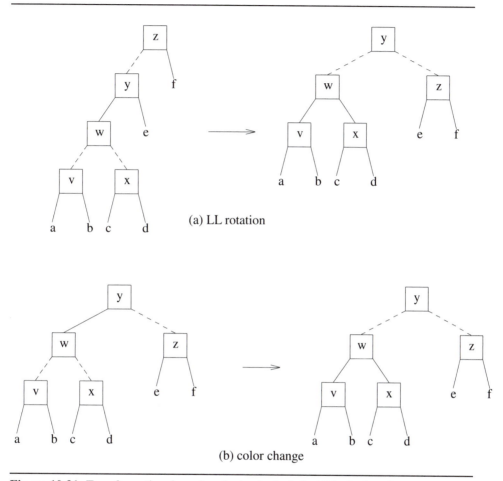

(a) LL rotation

(b) color change

Figure 10.31: Transformation for a 4-node that is the left child of a 3-node

It is interesting to note that when the 4-node to be split is a root or the child of a 2-node or that of a "nicely" oriented 3-node (as in Figure 10.31(b), color changes suffice. Pointers need to be changed only when the 4-node is the child of a 3-node that is not "nicely" oriented (as in Figures 10.31(a) and 10.32). We leave the development of the formal insertion procedure as an exercise.

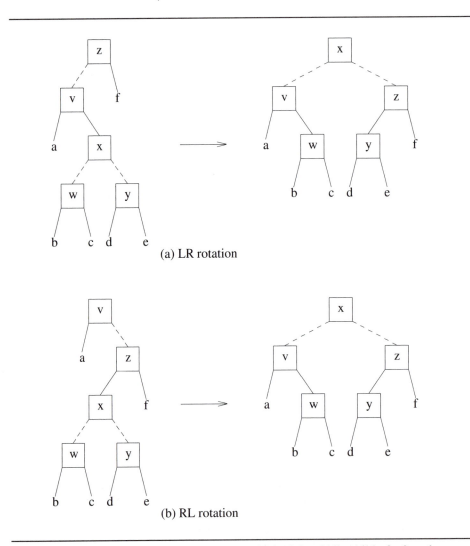

(a) LR rotation

(b) RL rotation

Figure 10.32: Transformation for a 4-node that is the left middle child of a 3-node

10.5.4   Bottom Up Insertion

In a bottom up insertion, we search the red-black tree for the key to be inserted. This search is unsuccessful. No transformations are made during this downward pass. The element to be inserted is added as the appropriate child of the node last encountered. A red pointer is used to join the new node to its parent. Following this, all root to external node paths have the same number of black pointers. However, it is possible for one such path to have two consecutive red pointers. This violates the red-black property P3 that no root to external node path has two consecutive red pointers. Let these two pointers be $<p, q>$ and $<q, r>$. The first is from node p to node q and the second from node q to node r. Let s be the sibling (if any) of node q. $s = NULL$, if q has no sibling. The violation is classified as an XYZ violation where X = L if $<p, q>$ is a left pointer and X = R otherwise; Y = L if $<q, r>$ is a left pointer and Y = R otherwise; and Z = r (for red) if $s \neq NULL$ and $<p, s>$ is a red pointer and Z = b (for black) otherwise.

The color change transformation of Figure 10.33 handles the violation cases LLr and LRr. Similar transforms handle the cases RRr and RLr. In these figures the subtrees a, b, c, d, and e may be empty and the pointer from the parent of y nonexistent (in case y is the root). These color changes potentially propagate the violation up the tree and may need to be reapplied several times. Note that the color change does not affect the number of black pointers on a root to external node path. Figure 10.34 shows the rotations needed for the cases LLb and LRb. The cases RRb and RLb are symmetric. The rotations of this figure do not propagate the violation. Hence, at most one rotation can be performed. Once again, we observe that the above rotations do not affect the number of black pointers on any root to external node path.

In comparing the top down and the bottom up insertion methods, we note that in the top down method O(log$n$) rotations can be performed while only one rotation is possible in the bottom up method. Both methods may perform O(log$n$) color changes. However, the top down method can be used in pipeline mode to perform several insertions in sequence. The bottom up method cannot be so used.

10.5.5 Deletion Fron A Red-Black Tree

For top down deletion from a leaf, we note that if the leaf from which the deletion is to occur is the root, then the result is an empty red-black tree. If the leaf is connected to its parent by a red pointer, then it is part of a 3-node or a 4-node and the leaf may be deleted from the tree. If the pointer from the parent to the leaf is a black pointer, then the leaf is a 2-node. Deletion from a 2-node requires a backward restructuring pass. To avoid this, we ensure that the deletion leaf has a red pointer from its parent. This is accomplished by using the insertion transformations in the reverse direction together with red-black transformations corresponding to the 2-3-4 deletion transformations (3) and (4) (q is a 2-node whose nearest sibling is a 3- or 4-node), and a 3-node transformation that switches from one 3-node representation to the other as necessary to ensure that the search for the element to be deleted moves down a red pointer.

Since most of the insertion and deletion transformations can be accomplished by color changes and require no pointer changes or data shifts, these operations actually take less time using red-black trees than when a 2-3-4 tree is represented using nodes of type *two* 34.

The development of the bottom up deletion transformations is left as an exercise.

526 Search Structures

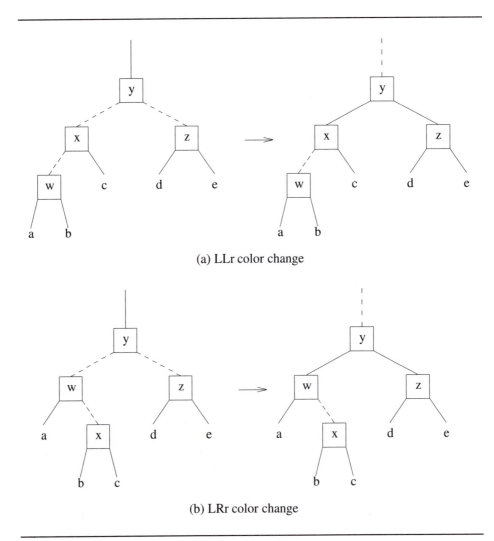

(a) LLr color change

(b) LRr color change

Figure 10.33: LLr and LRr color changes for bottom up insertion

EXERCISES

1. (a) Show that every binary tree obtained by transforming a 2-3-4 tree as described in the text satisfies properties Q1-Q5.

   (b) Show that every binary tree that satisfies properties Q1-Q5 represents a 2-3-4 tree and can be obtained from this 2-3-4 tree using the transformations of the text.

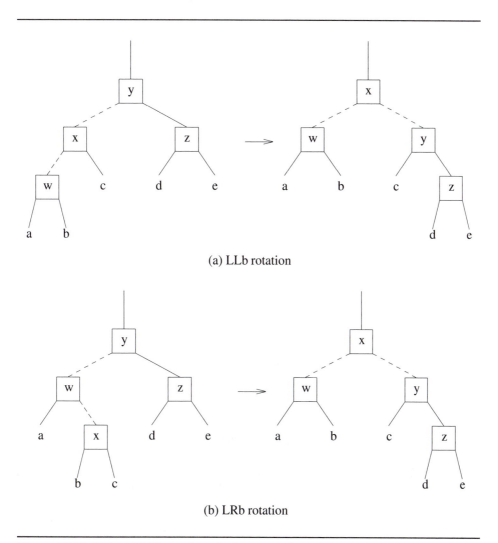

(a) LLb rotation

(b) LRb rotation

Figure 10.34: LLb and LRb rotations for bottom up insertion

2. Write a function to convert a 2-3-4 tree into its red-black representation. What is the time complexity of your function?

3. Write a function to convert a red-black tree into its 2-3-4 representation. What is the time complexity of your function?

4. Let T be a red-black tree with rank r. Write a procedure to compute the rank of each node in the tree. The time complexity of your procedure should be linear in the number of nodes in the tree. Show that this is the case.

5. Compare the worst case height of a red-black tree with n nodes and that of an AVL tree with the same number of nodes.

6. Rewrite function *insert* 234 (Program 10.10) so that it inserts an element into a 2-3-4 tree represented as a red-black tree.

7. Obtain the symmetric transforms for Figure 10.33 and Figure 10.34.

8. § Obtain a function to delete an element y from a 2-3-4 tree represented as a red-black tree. Use the top down method. Test the correctness of this procedure by running it on a computer. Generate your own test data.

9. § Do the preceding exercise using the bottom up method.

10. § The number of color fields in a node of a red-black tree may be reduced to one. In this case the color of a node represents the color of the pointer (if any) from the node's parent to that node. Write the corresponding insert and delete procedures using the top down approach. How would this change in the node structure affect the efficiency of the insert and delete procedures?

11. § Do the previous exercise for the bottom up approach.

10.6 B-TREES

10.6.1 Definition Of m-way Search Trees

The balanced search trees that we have studied so far (AVL trees, 2-3 trees, 2-3-4 trees, and red-black trees) allow us to search, insert, and delete entries from a table in $O(\log n)$ time, where n is the number of entries in the table. These structures are well suited to applications in which the table is small enough to be accommodated in internal memory. However, when the table is too large for this, these structures do not have good performance. This is because we must now retrieve the nodes of the search tree structure from a disk (say). These nodes are retrieved one at a time as needed. So, for example, when searching a 2-3 tree for an element with key x, we would retrieve only those nodes that are on the search path from the root to the node that contains the desired element. As a result, the number of disk accesses for a search is $O(h)$ where h is the height of the 2-3 tree. When $n = 1000$, h could be as high as 10. So, searching a 2-3 tree that is stored on a disk and which has 1000 elements would require up to 10 disk accesses. Since the time required for a disk access is significantly more than that for an an internal memory access, we seek structures that would reduce the number of disk acceses.

We shall use the term *index* to refer to a symbol table that resides on a disk. The symbol table may be assumed to be too large to be accommodated in the internal memory of the target computer. To obtain better performance, we shall use search trees whose degree is quite large.

Definiton: An *m-way search tree*, is either empty or satisfies the following properties;

(1)   The root has at most m subtrees and has the structure:

$$n, A_0, (K_1, A_1), (K_2, A_2), \ldots, (K_n, A_n)$$

where the A_i, $0 \leq i \leq n < m$ are pointers to subtrees and the K_i, $1 \leq i \leq n < m$ are key values.

(2) $K_i < K_{i+1}$, $1 \leq i < n$.

(3)   All key values in the subtree A_i are less than K_{i+1} and greater than K_i, $0 < i < n$.

(4)   All key values in the subtree A_n are greater than K_n and those in A_0 are less than K_1.

(5)   The subtrees A_i, $0 \leq i \leq n$ are also m-way search trees. □

We may verify that AVL trees are 2-way search trees, 2-3 trees are 3-way search trees, and 2-3-4 trees are 4-way search trees. Of course, there are 2-way search trees that are not AVL trees, 3-way search trees that are not 2-3 trees, and 4-way search trees that are not 2-3-4 trees. A 3-way search tree that is not a 2-3 tree is shown in Figure 10.35.

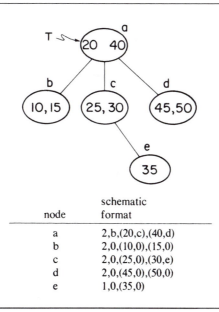

node	schematic format
a	2,b,(20,c),(40,d)
b	2,0,(10,0),(15,0)
c	2,0,(25,0),(30,e)
d	2,0,(45,0),(50,0)
e	1,0,(35,0)

Figure 10.35: Example of a 3-way search tree that is not a 2-3 tree

10.6.2 Searching An *m*-way Search Tree

Suppose we wish to search the *m*-way search tree T for the key value x. Assume that T resides on a disk. We begin by retrieving the root node from the disk. Assume that this node has the structure given in the definition of an *m*-way search tree. For convenience, assume that $K_0 = -\infty$ and $K_{n+1} = +\infty$. By searching the keys of the root, we determine i such that $K_i \leq x < K_{i+1}$. If $x = K_i$, then the search is complete. If $x \neq K_i$, then from the definition of an *m*-way search tree, it follows that if x is in the tree, it must be in subtree A_i. So, we retrieve the root of this subtree from the disk and proceed to search it. This process continues until we either find x or we have determined that x is not in the tree (the search leads us to an empty subtree). When the number of keys in the node being searched is small, a sequential search (as in the case of 2-3 and 2-3-4 trees) is used. When this number is large, a binary search may be used.

In a tree of degree m and height h the maximum number of nodes is $\sum_{0 \leq i \leq h-1} m^i = (m^h - 1)/(m - 1)$. Since each node has at most $m - 1$ keys, the maximum number of keys in an *m*-way tree index of height h is $m^h - 1$. For a binary tree with $h = 3$ this figure is 7. For a 200-way tree with $h = 3$ we have $m^h - 1 = 8 * 10^6 - 1$.

Clearly, the potentials of high order search trees are much greater than those of low order search trees. To achieve a performance close to that of the best *m*-way search trees for a given number of keys n, the search tree must be balanced. The particular variety of balanced *m*-way search trees we shall consider here is known as a B-tree. In defining a B-tree, it is convenient to reintroduce the concept of failure nodes. Recall that a failure node represents a node which can be reached during a search only if the value x being searched for is not in the tree.

10.6.3 Definition And Properties Of A B-tree

Definition: A B-tree of order m is an *m*-way search tree that is either empty or satisfies the following properties:

(1) The root node has at least 2 children.

(2) All nodes other than the root node and failure nodes have at least $\lceil m/2 \rceil$ children.

(3) All failure nodes are at the same level. □

Observe that a 2-3 tree is a B-tree of order 3 and a 2-3-4 tree is a B-tree of order 4. Also, notice that all B-trees of order 2 are full binary trees. Hence, B-trees of order 2 exist only when the number of key values is $2^k - 1$ for some k. It is not too difficult to see that for any given number of keys and any $m, m > 2$, there is a B-tree of order m that contains this many keys.

Number Of Key Values In A B-Tree

A B-tree of order m in which all failure nodes are at level $l+1$ has at most $m^l - 1$ keys. What is the minumum number, N, of keys in such a B-tree? From the definition of a B-tree we know that if $l > 1$, the root node has at least two children. Hence, there are at least two nodes at level 2. Each of these nodes must have at least $\lceil m/2 \rceil$ children. Thus, there are at least $2\lceil m/2 \rceil$ nodes at level 3. At level 4 there must be at least $2\lceil m/2 \rceil^2$ nodes, and continuing this argument, we see that there are at least $2\lceil m/2 \rceil^{l-2}$ nodes at level l when $l > 1$. All of these nodes are nonfailure nodes. If the key values in the tree are $K_1, K_2, \cdots, K_N$ and $K_i < K_{i+1}$, $1 \le i < N$, then the number of failure nodes is $N + 1$. This is so because failures occur for $K_i < x < K_{i+1}$, $0 \le i \le N$ where $K_0 = -\infty$ and $K_{N+1} = +\infty$. This results in $N + 1$ different nodes that one could reach while searching for a key value x that is not in the B-tree. Therefore, we have,

$$
\begin{aligned}
N + 1 &= \text{number of failure nodes} \\
&= \text{number of nodes at level } l + 1 \\
&\ge 2\lceil m/2 \rceil^{l-1}
\end{aligned}
$$

and so, $N \ge 2\lceil m/2 \rceil^{l-1} - 1$, $l \ge 1$.

This in turn implies that if there are N key values in a B-tree of order m, then all nonfailure nodes are at levels less than or equal to l, $l \le \log_{\lceil m/2 \rceil}\{(N + 1)/2\} + 1$. The maximum number of accesses that have to be made for a search is l. Using a B-tree of order $m = 200$, an index with $N \le 2 \times 10^6 - 2$ will have $l \le \log_{100}\{(N + 1)/2\} + 1$. Since l is integer, we obtain $l \le 3$. For $n \le 2 \times 10^8 - 2$ we get $l \le 4$. Thus, the use of a high order B-tree results in a tree index that can be searched making a very small number of disk accesses even when the number of entries is very large.

Choice Of m

B-trees of high order are desirable since they result in a reduction in the number of disk accesses needed to search an index. If the index has N entries, then a B-tree of order $m = N + 1$ would have only one level. This choice of m clearly is not reasonable, since by assumption the index is too large to fit in internal memory. Consequently, the single node representing the index cannot be read into memory and processed. In arriving at a reasonable choice for m, we must keep in mind that we are really interested in minimizing the total amount of time needed to search the B-tree for a value x. This time has two components, one, the time for reading in the node from the disk and, two, the time needed to search this node for x. Let us assume that each node of a B-tree of order m is of a fixed size and is large enough to accommodate n, A_0 and $m-1$ triples (K_i, A_i, B_i), $1 \le j < m$. Notice that while in the definition of an m-way search tree we had tuples (K_i, A_i), in practice, these will really be triples (K_i, A_i, B_i) where B_i gives the address, on disk, of the record with key K_i (as before, A_i points to a subtree of the B-tree). If the K_i are at most α characters long and the A_i and B_i each β characters long, then the size of a node is approximately $m(\alpha + 2\beta)$ characters. The time, t_i, required to read in a node is therefore:

$$
\begin{aligned}
t_i &= t_s + t_l + m(\alpha + 2\beta)\, t_c \\
&= a + bm
\end{aligned}
$$

where

$$
a = t_s + t_l = \text{ seek time + latency time}
$$
$$
b = (\alpha + 2\beta)t_c \text{ and } t_c = \text{transmission time per character}
$$

If binary search is used to search each node of the B-tree, then the internal processing time per node is $c \log_2 m + d$ for some constants c and d. The total processing time per node is thus,

$$
\tau = a + bm + c \log_2 m + d
$$

For an index with N entries, the number of levels, l, is bounded by:

$$
l \leq \log_{\lceil m/2 \rceil} \{(N+1)/2\} + 1
$$

$$
\leq f \frac{\log_2 \{(N+1)/2\}}{\log_2 m} \text{ for some constant } f
$$

The maximum search time is therefore:

$$
\text{maximum search time} = g \left\{ \frac{a+d}{\log_2 m} + \frac{bm}{\log_2 m} + c \right\} \text{ seconds}
$$

where $g = f * \log_2 \{(N+1)/2\}$.

We therefore desire a value of m that minimizes the maximum search time. If the disk drive available has a $t_s = 1/100$ sec and $t_l = 1/40$ sec, then $a = 0.035$ sec. Since d will typically be a few microseconds, we may ignore it in comparison with a. Hence, $a + d \approx a = 0.035$ sec. If each key value is at most six characters long and that each A_i and B_i is three characters long, $\alpha = 6$ and $\beta = 3$. If the transmission rate t_c is 5×10^{-6} sec/charac (corresponding to a track capacity of 5000 characters), then $b = (\alpha + 2\beta)t_c = 6 \times 10^{-5}$ sec. The formula for the maximum search time now becomes:

$$g \left\{ \frac{35}{\log_2 m} + \frac{0.06m}{\log_2 m} + 1000c \right\} \text{ milliseconds}$$

This function is tabulated in Figure 10.36 and plotted in Figure 10.37. It is evident that there is a wide range of values of m for which nearly optimal performance is achieved. This corresponds to the almost flat region $m \in [50,400]$. In case the lowest value of m in this region results in a node size greater than the allowable capacity of an input buffer, the value of m will be determined by the buffer size.

m	Search time (sec)
2	35.12
4	17.62
8	11.83
16	8.99
32	7.38
64	6.47
128	6.10
256	6.30
512	7.30
1024	9.64
2048	14.35
4096	23.40
8192	40.50

Figure 10.36: Values of $(35 + .06m)/\log_2 m$

10.6.4   Insertion Into A B-tree

The algorithm to insert a new key into a B-tree is a generalization of the two pass insertion algorithm for 2-3 trees. While, for $m > 3$, we could also generalize the top-down insertion algorithm described for 2-3-4 trees, this is not desirable as this algorithm splits many nodes and each time we change a node, it has to be written to disk. This increases the number of disk accesses.

The insertion algorithm for B-trees of order m first performs a search to determine the leaf node, p, into which the new key is to be inserted. If the insertion of the new key into p results in p having m keys, the node p is split. Otherwise, the new p is written to the disk and the insertion is complete. To split the node, assume that following the insertion of the new key, p has the format:

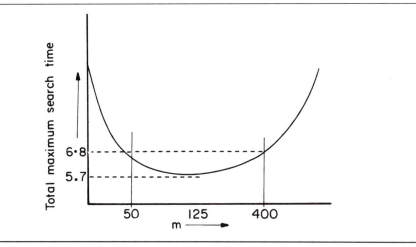

Figure 10.37: Plot of $(35+.06m)/\log_2 m$

$$m, A_0, (K_1, A_1), \ldots, (K_m, A_m), \quad \text{and} \quad K_i < K_{i+1}, \; 1 \le i < m$$

The node is split into two nodes p and q with the following formats:

$$\text{node } p: \lceil m/2 \rceil - 1, A_0, (K_1 A_1), \ldots, (K_{\lceil m/2 \rceil - 1}, A_{\lceil m/2 \rceil - 1})$$

$$\text{node } q: m - \lceil m/2 \rceil, A_{\lceil m/2 \rceil}, (K_{\lceil m/2 \rceil + 1}, A_{\lceil m/2 \rceil + 1}), \ldots, (K_m, A_m)$$

The remaining key $K_{\lceil m/2 \rceil}$ and a pointer to the new node q form a tuple $(K_{\lceil m/2 \rceil}, q)$. This is to be inserted into the parent of p. Before attempting this, the nodes p and q are written to disk.

As in the case of 2-3 trees, inserting into the parent may require us to split the parent and this splitting process can propagate all the way up to the root. When the root splits, a new root with a single key is created and the height of the B-tree increases by one. Since this insertion process is almost identical to that used for 2-3 trees, we do not provide any further details.

Analysis of B-tree insertion: If h is the height of the B-tree, then h disk accesses are made during the top-down search. In the worst case, all h of the accessed nodes may split during the bottom-up splitting pass. When a node other than the root splits, we need to write out two nodes. When the root splits, three nodes are written out. If we assume that the h nodes read in during the top-down pass can be saved in memory so that they are not to be fetched from disk during the bottom-up pass, then the number of disk accesses for an insertion is at most h (downward pass) + $2(h - 1)$ (nonroot splits) + 3 (root split) = $3h + 1$.

The average number of disk accesses is, however, approximately $h + 1$ for large m. To see this, suppose we start with an empty B-tree and insert N values into it. The total number of nodes split is at most $p - 2$ where p is the number of nonfailure nodes in the final B-tree with N entries. This upper bound of $p - 2$ follows from the observation that each time a node splits, at least one additional node is created. When the root splits, two additional nodes are created. The first node created results from no splitting, and if a B-tree has more than one node then the root must have split at least once. Figure 10.38 shows that $p - 2$ is the best possible upper bound on the number of nodes split in the creation of a p node B-tree when $p > 2$ (note that there is no B-tree with $p = 2$). A B-tree of order m with p nodes has at least

$$1 + (\lceil m/2 \rceil - 1)(p - 1)$$

keys as the root has at least one key and remaining nodes have at least $\lceil m/2 \rceil - 1$ keys each. The average number of splits, s, may now be determined as below:

$$
\begin{aligned}
s &= \text{(total number of splits)}/N \\
&\leq (p - 2)/\{1 + (\lceil m/2 \rceil - 1)(p - 1)\} \\
&< 1/(\lceil m/2 \rceil - 1)
\end{aligned}
$$

For $m = 200$ this means that the average number of node splits is less than 1/99 per key inserted. The average number of disk accesses is therefore only $l + 2s + 1 < l + 101/99 \approx l + 1$.

10.6.5 Deletion From A B-tree

The deletion algorithm for B-trees is also a generalization of the deletion algorithm for 2-3 trees. First, we search for the key x that is to be deleted. In case x is found in a node, z, that is not a leaf, then the position occupied by x in z is filled by a key from a leaf node of the B-tree. Suppose that x is the ith key in z (i.e., $x = K_i$). Then x may be replaced by either the smallest key in the subtree A_i or the largest in the subtree A_{i-1}. Both of these keys are in leaf nodes. In this way the deletion of x from a nonleaf node is transformed into a deletion from a leaf.

There are four cases when deleting from a leaf node p. In the first, p is also the root. If the root is left with at least one key, the changed root is written to disk and we are done. Otherwise, the B-tree is empty following the deletion. In the remaining cases, p is not the root. In the second case, following the deletion, p, has at least $\lceil m/2 \rceil - 1$ keys. The modified leaf is written to disk and we are done.

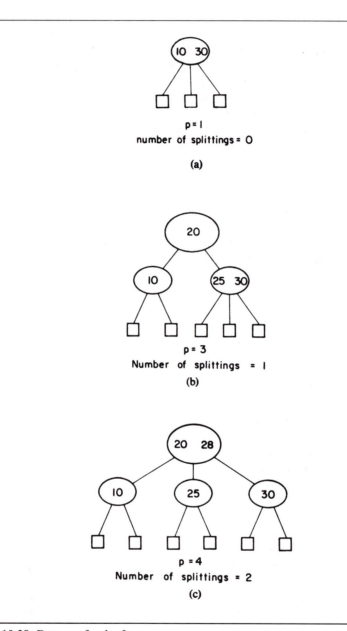

Figure 10.38: B-trees of order 3

In the third case, p has $\lceil m/2 \rceil - 2$ keys and its nearest sibling, q, has at least $\lceil m/2 \rceil$. To determine this, we examine only one of the at most two nearest siblings that p may have. p is deficient as it has one less than the minimum number of keys required. q has more keys than the minimum required. As in the case of a 2-3 tree, a rotation is performed. In this rotation, the number of keys in q decreases by one while the number in p increases by one. As a result, neither p nor q are deficient following the rotation. The rotation leaves behind a valid B-tree. Let r be the parent of p and q. If q is the nearest right sibling of p, then let i be such that K_i is the ith key in r, all keys in p are less than K_i, and all those in q are greater than K_i. For the rotation, K_i is replaced by the first (i.e., smallest) key in q, K_i becomes the rightmost key in p, and the leftmost subtree of q becomes the rightmost subtree of p. The changed nodes p, q, and r are written to disk and the deletion is complete. The case when q is the nearest left sibling of p is similar.

In the fourth case for deletion, p has $\lceil m/2 \rceil - 2$ keys while q has $\lceil m/2 \rceil - 1$. So, p is deficient and q has the minimum number of keys permissible for a nonroot node. Now, nodes p and q and the key K_i are combined to form a single node. The combined node has $(\lceil m/2 \rceil - 2) + (\lceil m/2 \rceil - 1) + 1 = 2\lceil m/2 \rceil - 2 \le m - 1$ keys which will at most fill the node. The combined node is written to disk. The combining operation reduces the number of keys in the parent node r by one. If the parent does not become deficient (i.e., it has at least one key in case it is the root and at least $\lceil m/2 \rceil - 1$ keys if it is not the root), the changed parent is written to disk and we are done. Otherwise, if the deficient parent is the root, it is discarded as it has no keys. If the deficient parent is not the root, it has exactly $\lceil m/2 \rceil - 2$ keys. To remove this deficiency, we first attempt a rotation with one of r's nearest siblings. If this isn't possible, a combine is done. This process of combining can continue up the B-tree only until the children of the root are combined.

Analysis of B-tree deletion: For a B-tree of height h, h disk accesses are made to find the node from which the key is to be deleted and to transform the deletion to that from a leaf. In the worst case, a combine takes place at each of the last $h - 2$ nodes on the root to leaf path and a rotation takes place at the second node on this path. The $h - 2$ combines require this many disk accesses to retrieve a nearest sibling for each node and another $h - 2$ to write out the combined nodes. The rotation requires one access to read a nearest sibling and three to write out the three nodes that get changed. The total number of disk accesses is $3h - 1$.

The deletion time can be reduced at the expense of disk space and a slight increase in node size by including a delete bit, F_i, for each key value K_i in a node. Then we can set $F_i = 1$ if K_i has not been deleted and $F_i = 0$ if it has. No physical deletion takes place. In this case a delete requires a maximum of $h + 1$ accesses (h to locate the node containing x and 1 to write out this node with the appropriate delete bit set to 0). With this strategy, the number of nodes in the tree never decreases. However, the space used by deleted entries can be reused during further insertions (see exercises). As a result, this strategy would have little effect on search and insert times (the number of levels increases very slowly when m is large). Insert times may even decrease slightly due to the ability to reuse deleted entry space. Such reuses would not require us to split any nodes. □

Some variations of B-trees are examined in the exercises.

10.6.6   Variable Size Key Values

With a node format of the form n, A_0, (K_1, A_1), $\cdots$, (K_n, A_n), the first problem created by the use of variable size key values, K_i, is that a binary search can no longer be carried out since, given the location of the first tuple (K_1, A_1) and n, we cannot easily determine K_n or even the location of $K_{(1+n)/2}$. When the range of key value size is small, it is best to allocate enough space for the largest size key value. When the range in sizes is large, storage may be wasted and another node format may become better, i.e., the format $n, A_0, \alpha_1, \alpha_2, \cdots, \alpha_n, (K_1, A_1), \cdots, (K_n, A_n)$ where α_i is the address of K_i in internal memory, i.e., $K_i =$ memory (α_i). In this case, a binary search of the node can still be made. The use of variable size nodes is not recommended since this would require a more complex storage management system. More importantly, the use of variable size nodes would result in degraded performance during insertion, as an insertion into a node would require us to request a larger node to accommodate the new value being inserted. Consequently, nodes of a fixed size should be used. The size should be such as to allow for at least $m - 1$ key values of the largest size. During insertions, however, we can relax the requirement that each node have $\leq m - 1$ key values. Instead, a node will be allowed to hold as many values as can fit into it and will contain at least $\lceil m/2 \rceil - 1$ values. The resulting performance will be at least as good as that of a B-tree of order m. Another possibility is to use some kind of key sampling scheme to reduce the key value size so as not to exceed some predetermined size, d. Some possibilities are prefix and suffix truncation, removing vowels, etc. Whatever the scheme used, some provision will have to be made for handling synonyms (i.e., distinct key values that have the same sampled value).

EXERCISES

1. Show that all B-trees of order 2 are full binary trees.

2. (a)   Insert the keys 62, 5, 85, 75, one at a time, into the order 5 B-tree of Figure 10.39. Show the new tree after each key is added. Do the insertion using the insertion process described in the text.

    (b)   Assuming that the tree is kept on a disk and one node may be fetched at a time, how many disk acceses are needed to make this insertion? State any assumptions you make.

    (c)   Delete the keys 45, 40, 10, 25 from the order 5 B-tree of Figure 10.39. Show the tree after each key is deleted. The deletions are to be performed using the deletion process described in the text.

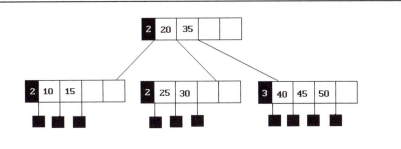

Figure 10.39: B-tree of order 5

    (d)   How many disk accesses are made for each of the deletions?

3.   Write a C function to search an m-way search tree that is stored on a disk. You may assume a function that reads a record from a specified disk address.

4.   Write a C function to insert a key x into a B-tree of order m that is stored on a disk. You may assume functions to read and write records from and to a specified disk address. Use the strategy described in the text.

5.   Write a C function to delete a key x from a B-tree of order m that is stored on a disk. You may assume functions to read and write records from and to a specified disk address. Use the strategy described in the text.

6.   Write insertion and deletion algorithms for B-trees assuming that an additional field f is associated with each key. $f = 1$ iff the coresponding key value has not been deleted. Deletions should be accomplished by simply setting the corresponding $f = 0$ and insertions should make use of deleted space whenever possible without restructuring the tree.

7.   § Write algorithms to search and delete keys from a B-tree by position; i.e., *search* (k) finds the kth smallest key and *delete* (k) deletes the kth smallest key in the tree. (Hint: In order to do this efficiently additional information must be kept in each node. With each pair (K_i, A_i) keep $N_i = \Sigma_{j=0}^{i-1}$ (number of key values in the subtree $A_j + 1$).) What are the worst case computing times of your algorithms?

8.   Modify the B-tree insertion algorithm so that we first check to see if either the nearest left sibling or the nearest right sibling of p has fewer than $m - 1$ key values. If so, then no additional nodes are created. Instead, a rotation is performed moving either the smallest or largest key in p to its parent. The corresponding key in the parent together with a subtree is moved to the sibling of p which has space for another key value.

9.   [Bayer and McCreight] The idea of the preceding exercise can be extended to obtain improved B-tree performance. In case the nearest sibling, Q, of P already has $m - 1$ key values, then we can spilt both P and Q to obtain three nodes P, Q,

and R with each node containing $\lfloor(2m-2)/3\rfloor, \lfloor(2m-1)/3\rfloor$ and $\lfloor 2m/3 \rfloor$ key values. Figure 10.40 below describes this splitting procedure when Q is P's nearest right sibling.

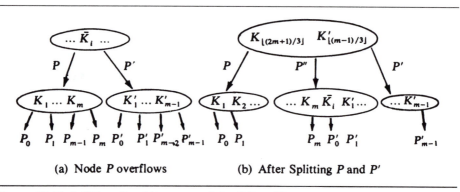

(a) Node P overflows   (b) After Splitting P and P'

Figure 10.40: Splitting P and its nearest right sibling P'

Write a B-tree insertion algorithm so that node splittings occur only as described above.

10. A B*-tree, t, of order m is a search tree that is either empty or satisfies the following properties:

(a) The root node has at least 2 and at most $2\lfloor(2m-2)/3\rfloor + 1$ children.

(b) The remaining nonfailure nodes have at most m and at least $\lceil(2m-1)/3\rceil$ children each.

(c) All failure nodes are on the same level.

For a B*-tree of order m and containing N key values, show that if $x = \lceil(2m-1)/3\rceil$ then

(a) The height, h, of the B*-tree satisfies:

$$h \leq 1 + \log_x\{(N+1)/2\}$$

(b) the number of nodes p in the B*-tree satisifies:

$$p \leq 1 + (N-1)/(x-1)$$

What is the average number of splits per insert if a B*-tree is built up starting from an empty B*-tree?

11. § Using the splitting technique of Exercise 9 write an algorithm to insert a new key x into a B*-tree, t, of order m. How many disk accesses are made in the worst case and on the average? Assume that t was initially of depth l and that t is maintained on a disk. Each access retrieves or writes one node.

12. § Write an algorithm to delete the identifier x from the B*-tree, t, of order m. What is the maximum number of accesses needed to delete x from a B*-tree of depth l? Make the same assumptions as in Exercise 11.

13. The basic idea of a B-tree may be modified differently to obtain a B'-tree. A B'-tree of order m is similar to a B-tree of order m except that in a B'-tree all identifiers are placed in leaf nodes. If P is a nonleaf node in a B'-tree and is of degree j, then the node format for P is: $j, L(1), L(2), \cdots, L(j-1)$ where $L(i), 1 \le i < j$, is the value of the largest key in the ith subtree of P. Figure 10.41 shows a B'-tree of order 5. Notice that in a B'-tree, the key values in the leaf nodes will be increasing left to right. Only the leaf nodes contain such information as the address of records having that key value. If there are n key values in the tree then there are n leaf nodes. Write an algorithm to search for x in a B'-tree t of order m. Show that the time for this is O($\log n$).

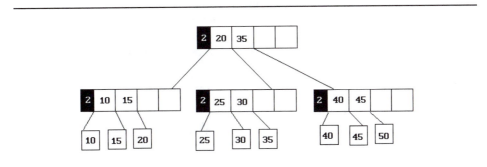

Figure 10.41: Example B'-tree

14. § For a B'-tree of order m write a function to insert x. How many disk accesses are needed?

15. Write an algorithm to delete x from a B'-tree, t, of order m. Since all key values are in leaf nodes, this always corresponds to a deletion from a leaf. How many disk accesses are needed.

16. Let T and U be two B'-trees of order m. Let V be a B'-tree of order m containing all key values in T and U. Write a C function to construct V from T and U. What is the complexity of your algorithm?

17. Obtain search, insert, and delete algorithms for B'-trees of order m. If the tree resides on disk, how many disk accesses are needed in the worst case for each of the three operations? Assume the tree has n leaf nodes.

18. § [Programming Project] Evaluate the relative performance of B-trees, B*-trees, and B'-trees when the required operations are search for x, insert x, and delete x.

10.7 SPLAY TREES

AVL, 2-3, 2-3-4, and red-black trees allow one to perform the search tree operations: insert, delete, and search in $O(\log n)$ worst case time per operation. In the case of priority queues we saw that if we are interested in amortized complexity rather than worst case complexity, simpler structures can be used. This is true even for search trees. Using a splay tree the search tree operations can be performed in $O(\log n)$ amortized time per operation.

A *splay tree* is a binary search tree in which each search, insert, and delete is performed in the same way as in an ordinary binary search tree (Chapter 5). However, each of these operations is followed by a *splay*. A splay consists of a sequence of rotations. For simplicity, we assume that each of the three operations is always successful. A failure can be modeled as a different successful operation. For example, an unsuccesful search may be modeled as a search for the element in the last node encountered in the unsuccessful search and an unsuccessful insert may be modeled as a successful search. With this assumption, the starting node for a splay is obtained as follows:

(1)   search. The splay starts at the node containing the searched for element.

(2)   insert. The start node for the splay is the newly inserted node.

(3)   delete. The parent of the physically deleted node is used as the start node for the splay. If this node is the root, then the splay start node is *NULL*.

Splay rotations are performed along the path from the start node to the root of the binary search tree. These rotations are similar to those performed for AVL trees and red-black trees. Let q be the node at which the splay is being performed. Initially, q is the splay start node. The following steps define a splay:

(1)   If q is either *NULL* or the root, then the splay terminates.

(2)   If q has a parent p but no grandparent, then the rotation of Figure 10.42 is performed and the splay terminates.

(3)   If q has a parent p, and a grandparent gp, then the rotation is classified as LL (p is the left child of gp and q is the left child of p), LR (p is the left child of gp and q is the right child of p), RR, or RL. The RR and RL rotations are shown in Figure 10.43. LL and LR rotations are symmetric to these. The splay is repeated at the new location of q.

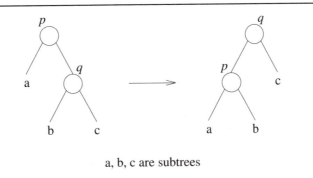

a, b, c are subtrees

Figure 10.42: Rotation when q is a right child and has no grandparent

Notice that all rotations move q up the tree and that following a splay q becomes the new root of the search tree. Figure 10.44 shows an example binary search tree before, during, and after a splay at node *.

In the case of Fibonnaci heaps, we obtained the amortized complexity of an operation by using an explicit cross charging scheme. The analysis for splay trees will use a *potential* technique. Let P_0 be the initial potential of the search tree and let P_i be its potential following the ith operation in a sequence of n operations. The amortized time for the ith operation is defined to be:

$$\text{(actual time for the } i\text{th operation)} + P_i - P_{i-1}$$

That is, the amortized time is the actual time plus the change in the potential. Rearranging terms, we see that the actual time for the ith operation is

$$\text{(amortized time for the } i\text{th operation)} + P_{i-1} - P_i$$

Hence, the actual time needed to perform the n operations in the sequence is

$$\sum_i \text{(amortized time for the } i\text{th operation)} + P_0 - P_n$$

Since each operation is followed by a splay whose actual complexity is of the same order as that of the whole operation, it is sufficient to consider only the time spent performing splays. Each splay consists of several rotations. We shall assign to each rotation a fixed cost of one unit. The choice of a potential function is rather arbitrary. The objective is to use one that results in as small a bound on the time complexity as is possible. The potential function we shall use is obtained in the following way. Let the size, $s(i)$, of the subtree with root i be the total number of nodes in it. The rank, $r(i)$, of node i is equal to $\log_2 s(i)$. The potential of the tree is $\sum_i r(i)$. The potential of an empty

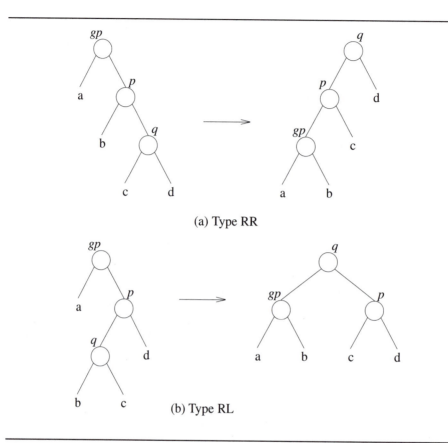

(a) Type RR

(b) Type RL

Figure 10.43: RR and RL rotations

tree is defined to be zero. Suppose that in the tree of Figure 10.44(a), the subtrees a, b, $\cdots$, j are all empty. Then, $(s(1), \cdots, s(9)) = (9, 6, 3, 2, 1, 4, 5, 7, 8)$; $r(4) = 1$, $r(5) = 0$, and $r(9) = 3$. In the following lemma we use r and r' to, respectively, denote the rank of a node before and after a rotation.

Lemma 10.2: Consider a binary search that has n elements / nodes. The amortized cost of a splay operation that begins at node q is at most $3(\log_2 n - r(q)) + 1$.

Proof: Consider the three steps in the definition of a splay.

(1)   In this step, q is either *NULL* or is the root. This step does not alter the potential of the tree. So its amortized and actual costs are the same. This cost is 1.

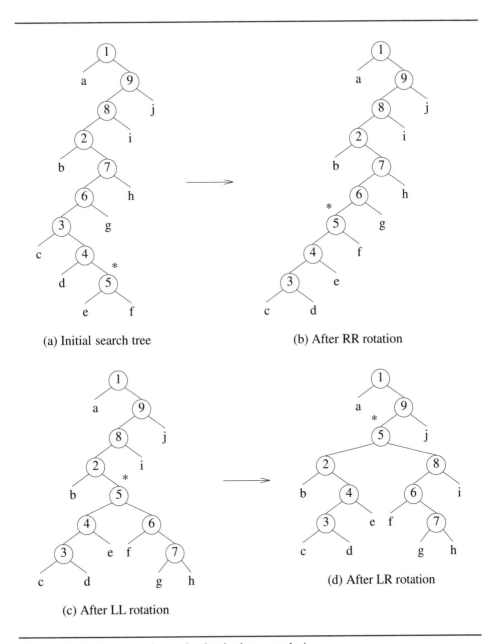

(a) Initial search tree

(b) After RR rotation

(c) After LL rotation

(d) After LR rotation

Figure 10.44: Rotations in a splay beginning at node *

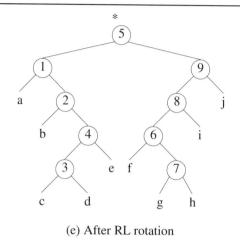

(e) After RL rotation

Figure 10.44 (continued): Rotations in a splay beginning at node *

(2)   In this step, the rotation of Figure 10.42 (or the symmetric rotation for the case q is the left child of p) is performed. Since only the ranks of p and q are affected, the potential change is $r'(p)+r'(q)-r(p)-r(q)$. Further, since $r'(p) < r(p)$ the potential change is less than $r'(q)-r(q)$. The amortized cost of this step (actual cost plus potential change) is, therefore, no more than $1+r'(q)-r(q)$.

(3)   In this step only the ranks of q, p, and gp change. So, the potential change is $r'(q) + r'(p) + r'(gp) - r(q) - r(p) - r(gp)$. Consider an RR rotation. From Figure 10.43(a), we see that $r(gp) = r'(q)$, $r'(q) > r'(p)$, and $r(p) > r(q)$. Using these in the equation for potential change, we see that the potential change cannot exceed $r'(q) + r'(gp) - 2r(q)$. This is at most $3(r'(q)-r(q))-2$. To prove this, we need to show that $2r'(q) - r'(gp) - r(q) \geq 2$. Let s and s', respectively, denote the size function before and after the rotation. So, $2r'(q) - r'(gp) - r(q) = 2\log_2 s'(q) - \log_2 s'(gp) - \log_2 s(q) = -(\log_2 A + \log_2 B)$, where $A = s'(gp)/s'(q)$ and $B = s(q)/s'(q)$. From Figure 10.43, we see that $A + B < 1$. So, $\log_2 A + \log_2 B \leq -2$. Hence, the amortized cost of an RR rotation is at most $1+3(r'(q)-r(q))-2 = 3(r'(q)-r(q))-1$. This bound may similarly be obtained for LL, LR, and RL rotations.

The lemma now follows by observing that steps 1 and 2 are mutually exclusive and can occur at most once. Step 3 occurs zero or more times. Summing up over the amortized cost of a single occurrence of steps 1 or 2 and all occurrences of step 3 we obtain the bound of the lemma. □

Theorem 10.1: The total time needed for a sequence of n search, insert, and delete operations performed on an initially empty splay tree is $O(n \log i)$ where $i, i > 0$, is the number of inserts in the sequence.

Proof: From our definition of the amortized cost of a splay operation, it follows that the time for the sequence of operations is the sum of the amortized costs of the splays and the potential change, $P_0 - P_n$. From Lemma 10.2, it follows that the sum of the amortized costs is $O(n \log i)$. The initial potential, P_0, is 0 and the final potential P_n is ≥ 0. So, the total time is $O(n \log i)$. $\square$

EXERCISES

1. Obtain figures corresponding to Figure 10.42 and Figure 10.43 for the symmetric splay rotations.

2. What is the maximum height of a splay tree that is created as the result of n insertions made into an initially empty splay tree? Give an example of a sequence of inserts that results in a splay tree of this height.

3. Complete the proof of Lemma 10.2 by providing the proof for the case of an RL rotation. Note that the proofs for LL and LR rotations are similar to those for RR and RL rotations, respectively, as the rotations are symmetric.

4. [Sleator and Tarjan] Suppose we modify the definition of $s(i)$ used in connection with the complexity analysis of splay trees. Let each node i have a positive weight $p(i)$. Let $s(i)$ be the sum of the weights of all nodes in the subtree with root i. The rank of a i is $\log_2 s(i)$.

   (a) Let t be a splay tree. Show that the amortized cost of a splay that begins at node q is at most $3(r(t) - r(q)) + 1$ where r is the rank just before the splay.

   (b) Let S be a sequence of n inserts and m searches. Assume that each of the n inserts adds a new element to the splay tree and that all searches are successful. Let $p(i), p(i) > 0$, be the number of times element i is searched for. The $p(i)$'s satisfy the equality

   $$\sum_{i=1}^{n} p(i) = m$$

   Show that the total time spent on the m searches is

   $$O(m + \sum_{i=1}^{n} p(i) \log(m / p(i)))$$

   Note that since $\Omega(m + \sum_{i=1}^{n} p(i) \log(m / p(i)))$ is an information theoretic bound on the search time in a static search tree (the optimal binary search tree of this Section 10.1 is an example of such a tree), splay trees are optimal to within a constant factor for the representation of a static set of elements.

10.8 DIGITAL SEARCH TREES

10.8.1 Digital Search Tree

A *digital search tree* is a binary tree in which each node contains one element. The element to node assignment is determined by the binary representation of the element keys. Suppose that we number the bits in the binary representation of a key left to right beginning at one. Then bit one of 1000 is 1, while bits two, three, and four are 0. All keys in the left subtree of a node at level i have bit i equal to zero while those in the right subtree of nodes at this level have bit $i = 1$. Figure 10.45 shows an example digital search tree. This contains the keys 1000, 0010, 1001, 0001, 1100, and 0000.

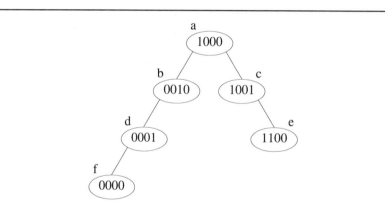

Figure 10.45: Example digital search tree

A search in a digital search tree is performed in the following way. Suppose we are to search for the key $k = 0011$ in the tree of Figure 10.45. k is first compared with the key in the root. Since k is different from the key in the root and since bit one of k is 0, we move to the left child, b, of the root. Now, since k is different from the key in node b and bit two of k is 0, we move to the left child, d, of b. As k is different from the key in node d and since bit three of k is one, we move to the right child of d. Node d has no right child to move to. From this we conclude that $k = 0011$ is not in the search tree. If we wish to insert k into the tree, then it is to be added as the right child of d. When this is done, we get the digital search tree of Figure 10.46.

The digital search tree procedures to search, insert, and delete are quite similar to the corresponding procedures for binary search trees. The essential difference is that the subtree to move to is determined by a bit in the search key rather than by the result of the

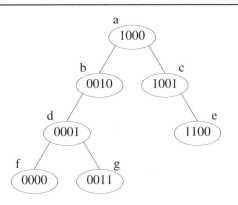

Figure 10.46: Digital search tree of Figure 10.45 following insertion of 0011

comparison of the search key and the key in the current node. We leave the formal development of these procedures as an exercise.

Each of the above search tree operations can be performed in O(h) time where h is the height of the digital search tree. If each key in a digital search tree has *KeySize* bits, then the height of the digital search tree is at most *KeySize* + 1.

10.8.2   Binary Tries

When we have very long keys, the cost of a key comparison is high. We can reduce the number of key comparisons to one by using a related structure called *Patricia* (*P*ractical *a*lgorithm *t*o *r*etrieve *i*nformation *c*oded *in* *a*lphanumeric). We shall develop this structure in three steps. First, we introduce a structure called a binary trie. Then we transform binary tries into compressed binary tries. Finally, from compressed binary tries we obtain Patricia. Since binary tries and compressed binary tries are introduced only as a means of arriving at Patricia, we do not dwell much on how to manipulate these structures. A more general version of binary tries (called a trie) is considered in the next section.

A *binary trie* is a binary tree that has two kinds of nodes *branch nodes* and *element nodes*. A branch node has the two fields *left*_*child* and *right*_*child*. It has no *data* field. An element node has the single field *data*. We use branch nodes to build a binary tree search structure similar to that of a digital search tree. This search structure leads to element nodes.

Figure 10.47 shows a six-element binary trie. To search for an element with key k, we use a branching pattern determined by the bits of k. The *i*th bit of k is used at level *i*. If it is zero, the search moves to the left subtree. Otherwise, it moves to the right subtree. To search for 0010 we first follow the left child, then again the left child, and finally the right child.

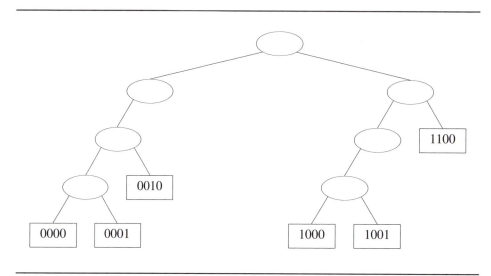

Figure 10.47: Example binary trie

Observe that a successful search in a binary trie always ends at an element node. Once this element node is reached, the key in this node is compared with the key we are searching for. This is the only key comparison that takes place. An unsuccessful search may terminate at either an element node or at a *NULL* pointer.

The binary trie of Figure 10.47 contains branch nodes whose degree is one. By adding another field *bit _ number* to each branch node, we can eliminate all degree one branch nodes from the trie. The *bit _ number* field of a branch node gives the bit number of the key that is to be used at this node. Figure 10.48 gives the binary trie that results from the elimination of degree one branch nodes from the binary trie of Figure 10.47. The number outside a node is its *bit _ number*. A binary trie that has been modified in this way to contain no branch nodes of degree one is called a *compressed binary trie*.

10.8.3   Patricia

Compressed binary tries may be represented using nodes of a single type. The new nodes, called *augmented branch nodes* are the original branch nodes augmented by the field *data*. The resulting structure is called *Patricia* and is obtained from a compressed binary trie in the following way:

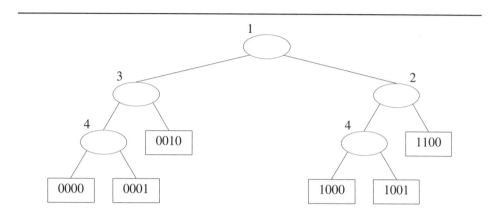

Figure 10.48: Binary trie of Figure 10.47 with degree one nodes eliminated

(1)   Replace each branch node by an augmented branch node.

(2)   Eliminate the element nodes.

(3)   Store the data previously in the element nodes in the data fields of the augmented branch nodes. Since every non empty compressed binary trie has one fewer branch node than it has element nodes, it is necessary to add one augmented branch node. This node is called the *head node*. The remaining structure is the left subtree of the head node. The head node has *bit – number* equal to zero. Its right child field is not used. The assignment of data to augmented branch nodes is done in such a way that the *bit – number* in the augmented branch node is less than or equal to that in the parent of the element node that contained this data.

(4)   Replace the original pointers to element nodes by pointers to the respective augmented branch nodes.

When the above transformations are performed on the compressed trie of Figure 10.48, we get the structure of Figure 10.49. Let *t* be an instance of Patricia. *t* is *NULL* iff the instance is empty. An instance, *t*, with one element is represented by a head node whose left child field points to itself (Figure 10.50(a)).

We can distinguish between pointers that were originally to branch nodes and those that were to element nodes by noting that, in Patricia, the former pointers are directed to nodes with a greater *bit – number* value, while pointers of the latter type are directed to nodes whose *bit – number* value is either equal to or less that that in the node where the pointer originates.

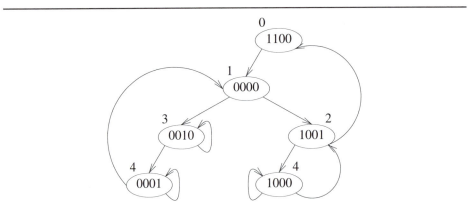

Figure 10.49: An example of Patricia

Search

To search for an element with key k we begin at the head node and follow a path determined by the bits in k. When an element pointer is followed, the key in the reached node is compared with k. This is the only key comparison made. No comparisons are made on the way down. Suppose we wish to search for $k = 0000$ in the Patricia instance of Figure 10.49. We begin at the head node and follow the left child pointer to the node with 0000. The bit number field of this node is 1. Since bit one of k is 0, we follow the left child pointer to the node with 0010. Now bit three of k is used. Since this is 0, the search moves to the node with 0001. The bit number field of this node is 4. The fourth bit of k is zero, so we follow the left child field. This gets us to a node with bit number field less than that of the node we moved from. Hence, an element pointer was used. Comparing the key in this node with k we find a match and the search is successful.

Next, suppose that we are to search for $k = 1011$. We begin at the head node. The search successively moves to the nodes with 0000, 1001, 1000, 1001. k is compared with 1001. Since k is not equal to 1001, we conclude that there is no element with this key. The function to search Patricia tree t is given in Program 10.11. This function returns, a pointer to the last node encountered in the search. If the key in this node is k, the search is successful. Otherwise, t contains no element with key k. The function $bit(i, j)$ returns the jth bit (the leftmost bit is bit one) of i. The C declarations used to define a Patricia tree are:

```
typedef struct patricia_tree *patricia;
     struct patricia_tree {
        int bit_number;
        element data;
```

```
            patricia left_child, right_child;
            };
    patricia root;
```

```
patricia search(patricia t, unsigned k)
{
/* search the Patricia tree t; return the last node y
encountered; if k = y->data.key, the key is in
the tree */
   patricia p, y;
   if (!t) return NULL; /* empty tree */
   y = t->left_child;
   p = t;
   while (y->bit_number > p->bit_number) {
      p = y;
      y = (bit(k, y->bit_number)) ?
      y->right_child : y->left_child;
   }
   return y;
}
```

Program 10.11: Searching Patricia

Insertion

Let us now examine how we can insert new elements. Suppose we begin with an empty instance and wish to insert an element with key 1000. The result is an instance that has only a head node (Figure 10.50(a)). Next, consider inserting an element with key $k = 0010$. First, we search for this key using function *search* (Program 10.11). The search terminates at the head node. Since 0010 is not equal to the key $q = 1000$ in this node, we know that 0010 isn't currently in the Patricia instance and so the element may be inserted. For this, the keys k and q are compared to determine the first (i.e., leftmost) bit at which they differ. This is bit one. A new node containing the element with key k is added as the left child of the head node. Since bit one of k is zero, the left child field of this new node points to itself and its right child field points to the head node. The bit number field is set to 1. The resulting Patricia instance is shown in Figure 10.50(b).

Suppose that the next element to be inserted has $k = 1001$. The search for this key ends at the node with $q = 1000$. The first bit where k and q differ is bit $j = 4$. Now we search the instance of Figure 10.50(b) using only the first $j-1 = 3$ bits of k. The last move is from the node with 0010 to that with 1000. Since this is a right child move, a

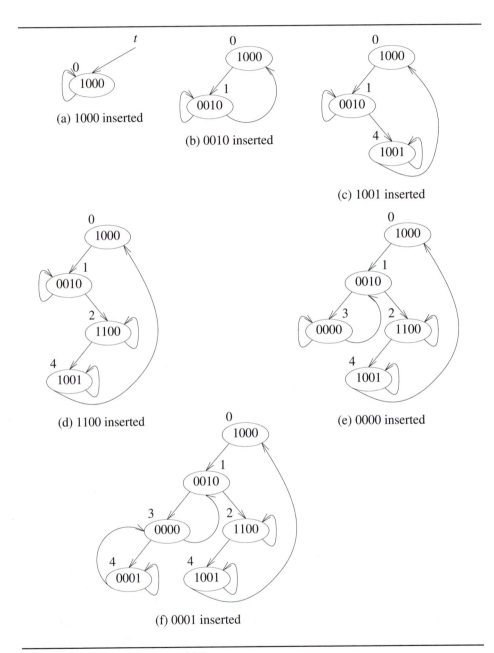

(a) 1000 inserted

(b) 0010 inserted

(c) 1001 inserted

(d) 1100 inserted

(e) 0000 inserted

(f) 0001 inserted

Figure 10.50: Insertion into Patricia

new node containing the element with key k is to be inserted as the right child of 0010. The bit number field of this node is set to $j = 4$. As bit four of k is 1, the right child field of the new node points to itself and its left child field points to the node with q. Figure 10.50(c) shows the resulting structure.

To insert $k = 1100$ into Figure 10.50(c), we first search for this key. Once again, $q = 1000$. The first bit where k and q differ is $j = 2$. The search using only the first $j-1$ bits ends at the node with 1001. The last move is a right child move from 0010. A new node containing the element with key k and bit number field $j = 2$ is added as the right child of 0010. Since bit j of k is one, the right child field of the new node points to itself. Its left child field points to the node with 1001 (this was previously the right child of 0010). The new Patricia instance is shown in Figure 10.50(d). Figure 10.50(e) shows the result of inserting an element with key 0000, and Figure 10.50(f) shows the Patrcia instance following the insertion of 0001.

The preceding discussion leads to the insertion finction *insert* of Program 10.12. Its complexity is seen to be O(h) where h is the height of t. h can be as large as min$\{key\_size + 1, n\}$ where key_size is the number of bits in a key and n is the number of elements. When the keys are uniformly distributed the height is O(log$n$). We leave the development of the deletion procedure as an exercise.

```
void insert(patricia *t, element x)
{
/* insert x into the Patricia tree *t */
   patricia s, p, y, z;
   int i;
   if (!(*t)) {/* empty tree */
      *t = (patricia)malloc(sizeof(patricia_tree));
      if (IS_FULL(*t)) {
         fprintf(stderr, "The memory is full\n");
         exit(1);
      }
      (*t)->bit_number = 0;
      (*t)->data = x;
      (*t)->left_child = *t;
   }
   y = search(*t,x.key);
   if (x.key == y->data.key) {
      fprintf(stderr, "The key is in the tree. Insertion
                       fails.\n");
      exit(1);
   }
   /* find the first bit where x.key and y->data.key differ
   */
   for (i = 1; bit(x.key,i) == bit(y->data.key,i); i++);
```

```
        ;
        /* search tree using the first i-1 bits */
        s = (*t)->left_child;
        p = *t;
        while (s->bit_number > p->bit_number &&
                            s->bit_number < i) {
           p = s;
           s = (bit(x.key,s->bit_number)) ?
                        s->right_child : s->left_child;
        }
        /* add x as a child of p */
        z = (patricia)malloc(sizeof(patricia_tree));
        if (IS_FULL(z)) {
           fprintf(stderr, "The memory is full\n");
           exit(1);
        }
        z->data = x;
        z->bit_number = i;
        z->left_child = (bit(x.key,i)) ? s: z;
        z->right_child = (bit(x.key,i)) ? z : s;
        if (s == p->left_child)
           p->left_child = z;
        else
           p->right_child = z;
}
```

Program 10.12: Insertion function for Patricia

EXERCISES

1. § Write the digital search tree functions for the search, insert, and delete operations. Assume that each key has *key – size* bits and that the function *bit* (*k, i*) returns the *i*th (from the left) bit of the key *k*. Show that each of your functions has complexity O(*h*) where *h* is the height of the digital search tree.

2. § Write the binary trie functions for the search, insert, and delete operations. Assume that each key has *key – size* bits and that the function *bit* (*k, i*) returns the *i*th (from the left) bit of the key *k*. Show that each of your functions has complexity O(*h*) where *h* is the height of the binary trie.

3. § Write the compressed binary trie functions for the search, insert, and delete operations. Assume that each key has *key – size* bits and that the function *bit* (*k, i*) returns the *i*th (from the left) bit of the key *k*. Show that each of your functions has complexity O(*h*), where *h* is the height of the compressed binary trie.

4. Write a function to delete the element with key k from the Patricia tree t. The complexity of your algorithm should be O(h), where h is the height of t. Show that this is the case.

10.9 TRIES

10.9.1 Definition

A trie is an index structure that is particularly useful when the keys vary in length. It is a generalization of the binary trie we introduced in the preceding section.

A *trie* is a tree of degree $m \geq 2$ in which the branching at any level is determined not by the entire key value but by only a portion of it. As an example, consider the trie of Figure 10.51 This trie contains two types of nodes. The first type we call a *branch node* because it contains pointers only. Since we assume that all characters in a key are one of the 26 letters of the alphabet, a branch node contains 27 link fields. We use the extra link field to hold a blank character. For example, suppose we have two keys, *an* and *ant*. If we are to correctly place *an* in the trie we must insert an imaginary blank after the *n*.

At the first level of a trie, we partition the keys into disjoint classes depending on their first character. Thus, $t->u.letters[i]$ points to a subtrie containing all key values beginning with the ith letter. On the jth level the branching is determined by the jth character. When a subtrie contains only one key value, we replace it with an *element node*. This node contains the key and any other information, such as the address of the record with this key value, etc. In Figure 10.51, we represent branch nodes as clear rectangles and element nodes as solid rectangles. We use the following C declarations to create a trie:

```
#define MAX_LETTERS 27
#define MAX_CHAR    30 /*maximum length of key*/
typedef enum {data, pointer} node_type;
typedef struct trie_node *trie_pointer;
     struct trie_node {
        node_type tag;
        union {
           char *key; /*data */
           trie_pointer letters[MAX_LETTERS];
        } u;
     } ;
  trie_pointer root;
```

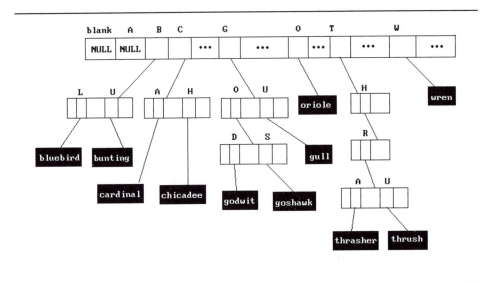

Figure 10.51: Trie created using characters of key value left to right, one at a time

10.9.2   Searching A Trie

To search a trie for a key, *x*, we must break *x* into its constituent characters and follow the branches determined by these characters. The function *search* (Program 10.13) assumes that $p{-}{>}u$. *key* is the key represented in node *p* if *p* is an element node and that a blank has been appended to the search key before invocation. The function invocation is *search* $(t,key,$ 1). *search* uses the function $get\_index\,(key,i)$ which performs the *i*th level sampling of the key. In the case of left to right single character sampling, this function extracts the *i*th character of the key and converts it to an integer index that tells us which pointer field of the branch node to use.

Analysis of *search*: The *search* function is straightforward and we may readily verify that the worst case search time is O(*l*), where *l* is the number of levels in the trie (including both branch and element nodes). □

10.9.3   Sampling Strategies

In the case of an index, all nodes reside on disk and so at most *l* accesses are made during a search. Given a set of keys to be represented in an index, the number of levels in the trie depends on the key sampling technique used to determine the branching at each level. We can define this by a sampling function *sample* (*x*, *i*), which appropriately samples *x* for branching at the *i*th level. The example trie of Figure 10.52 and the *search*

```
trie_pointer search(trie_pointer t, char *key, int i)
{
/* search the trie t */
   if (!t) return NULL; /* not found */
   if (t->tag == data)
      return ((strcmp(t->u.key,key)) ? NULL : t);
   return search(t->u.letters[get_index(key,i)], key, i+1);
}
```

Program 10.13: Searching a trie

function use sampling technique (1):

(1) *sample* $(x, i) = i$th character of x

Some other possible choices for this function are ($x = x_0x_1 \ldots x_{n-1}$):

(2) *sample* $(x, i) = x_{n-i}$

(3) *sample* $(x, i) = x_{r(x,i)}$ for $r(x, i)$ a randomization function

(4) *sample* $(x, i) = \begin{cases} x_{i/2} \text{ if } i \text{ is even} \\ x_{n-(i+1)/2} \text{ if } i \text{ is odd} \end{cases}$

For each of these functions, we may easily construct key value sets for which that particular function is best, that is, it results in a trie with the fewest number of levels. The trie of Figure 10.51 has five levels. Using the function (2) on the same key values yields the trie of Figure 10.52, which has only three levels. An optimal sampling function for this data set will yield a trie that has only two levels (Figure 10.53). Choosing the optimal sampling function for any particular set of values is very difficult. In a dynamic situation, with insertion and deletion, we wish to optimize average performance. In the absence of any further information on key values, probably the best choice would be (3).

Although all our examples of sampling have involved single character sampling we need not restrict ourselves to this. We may interpret the key values as digits using any radix we desire. Using a radix of 27^2 produces a two-character sampling. Other radixes give different samplings.

We can keep the maximum number of levels in a trie low if we design the element nodes so that they hold more than one key value. If the maximum number of levels allowed is l, then we enter all key values that are synonyms up to level $l-1$ into the same element node. If we choose the sampling function correctly, there will be only a few synonyms in each element node. Therefore, the element node will be small and can be processed in internal memory. Figure 10.54 shows the use of this strategy on the trie of Figure 10.51 with $l = 3$. In further discussion we shall, for simplicity, assume that the sampling function in use is (1) and that we place no restriction on the number of levels in the trie.

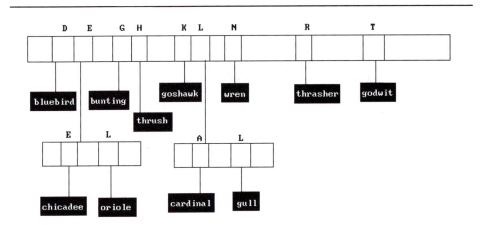

Sampling one character at a time, right to left

Figure 10.52: Trie constructed for the data of Figure 10.51

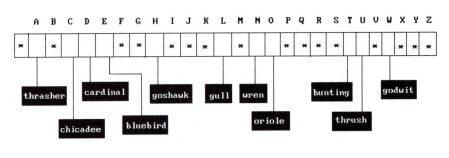

* = NULL node

Sampling on the first level done by using the fourth character of the key values

Figure 10.53: An optimal trie for the data of Figure 10.51

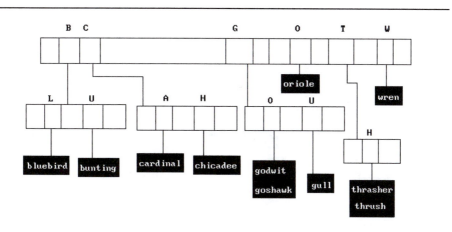

Keys have been sampled from left to right, one character at a time

Figure 10.54: Trie obtained for the data of Figure 10.51 when the number of levels is limited to 2

10.9.4 Insertion Into A Trie

Insertion into a trie is straightforward. We shall indicate the process by means of two examples and leave the writing of the algorithm as an exercise. Let us consider the trie of Figure 10.51 and insert into it the two entries: *bobwhite* and *bluejay*. First, we have $x = bobwhite$ and we attempt to search for *bobwhite*. This leads us to node σ, where we discover that $\sigma{-}{>}u \, . \, letters[15] = NULL$. (The letter O resides in the 15th index.) Hence, x is not in the trie and we may insert it here. Next, $x = bluejay$ and a search of the trie leads us to the element node which contains *bluebird*. We sample *bluebird* and *bluejay* until the two keys differ. This occurs when we compare the fifth letters of the two keys. Figure 10.55 shows the trie after both insertions.

10.9.5 Deletion From A Trie

Once again, we will not present the deletion algorithm formally, but will look at two examples to illustrate some of the ideas involved in deleting entries from a trie. From the trie of Figure 10.55 let us first delete *bobwhite*. To do this we just set $\sigma{-}{>}u \, . \, letters[15] = NULL$. We do not need to make any other changes. Next, let us delete *bluejay*. This deletion leaves us with only one key in the subtrie, δ_3. This means that we may delete node δ_3 and move node ρ up one level. The same can be done for nodes δ_1 and δ_2. Finally, we reach node σ. The subtrie with root σ has more than one key value.

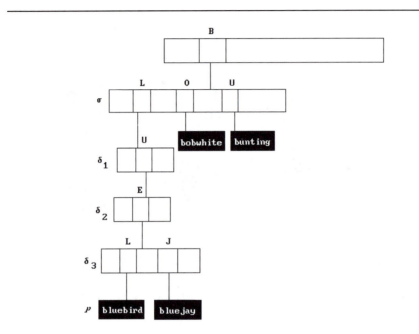

Figure 10.55: Section of the trie of Figure 10.51 after inserting *bobwhite* and *blue jay*

Therefore, we cannot move ρ up any more levels and we set $\sigma{-}{>}u \,.\, letters[12] = \rho$. To facilitate deletions from tries, it is useful to add a *count* field in each branch node. This field contains the number of children that a node has.

As in the case of binary tries, we can define compressed tries in which each branch node has at least two children. In this case, each brach node is augmeneted to have an additional field *skip* which indicates the number of levels of branching that have been eliminated (alternately, we can have a field *sample* which indicates the smapling level to use).

EXERCISES

1. (a) Draw the trie obtained for the following data:

> *Amiot, Avenger, Avro, Heinkel, HellDiver, Macchi,*
> *Marauder, Mustang, SpitFire, Sykhoi*

Sample the keys left to right one character at a time.

(b)   Using single character sampling, obtain a trie, for the above data, with the fewest number of levels.

2.   Write a C function to insert a key into a trie. What is the complexity of your function?

3.   § Do Exercise 2 with the added assumption that the trie is to have no more than six levels. Synonyms are to be packed into the same element node.

4.   § Write a function that deletes x from a trie using the assumptions of Exercişe 2. Assume that each branch node has a count field equal to the number of element nodes in the subtrie for which it is the root.

5.   § Do Exercise 4 for the trie of Exercise 3.

6.   § In the trie of Figure 10.55 the nodes δ_1 and δ_2 each have only one child. Branch nodes with only one child may be eliminated from tries by maintaining a *skip* field with each node. The value of this field equals the number of characters to be skipped before obtaining the next character to be sampled. Thus, we can have *skip* $[\delta_3] = 2$ and delete the nodes δ_1 and δ_2. Write algorithms to search, insert and delete from tries in which each branch node has a skip field.

10.10   DIFFERENTIAL FILES

Consider an application where we are maintaining an indexed file. For simplicity, assume that there is only one index and hence just a single key. Further assume that this is a dense index (that is, one which has an entry for each record in the file) and that updates to the file (inserts, deletes, and changes to an existing record) are permitted. We must keep a back-up copy of the index and file so that we can recover from an accidental loss or failure of the working copy. This loss or failure may occur for a variety of reasons including corruption of the working copy due to a malfunction of the hardware or software. We refer to the working copies of the index and file as the *master index* and *master file*, respectively.

Since updates to the file and index are permitted, the back-up copies will generally differ from the working copies at the time of failure. For failure recovery, we must have both the back-up copies and a log of all updates made since the back up copies were created. We call this log the *transaction log*. To recover from the failure, we process the back-up copies and the transaction log to reproduce an index and file that correspond to the working copies at the time of failure. This means that the recovery time is a function of the sizes of the back-up index and file and the size of the transaction log. We can reduce the recovery time by making frequent back-ups. This results in a smaller transaction log. However, making sufficiently frequent back-ups of the master index and file is not practical when the index and file are very large or the update rate is very high.

When only the file, but not the index, is very large, we can reduce the recovery time by keeping updated records in a separate file called the *differential file*. Although the master file is unchanged, we do change the master index to reflect the position of the most current version of the record with a given key. We assume that differential file records and master file records have different addresses. This means that the address obtained from a search of the master index tells us whether the most current version of the record we are seeking is in the master file or the differential file. Program 10.14(b) shows the necessary steps to follow when accessing a record with a given key. Program 10.14(a) shows the steps taken when we do not use a differential file.

Step 1: Search master index for record address.

Step 2: Access record from this master file address.

Step 3: If this is an update, then update master index, master file, and transaction log.

(a) No differential file

Step 1: Search master index for record address.

Step 2: Access record from either the master or differential file depending on the address obtained in Step 1.

Step 3: If this is an update, then update master index, differential file, and transaction log.

(b) Differential file in use

Step 1: Search differential index for record address. If the search is unsuccessful, then search the master index.

Step 2: Access record from either the master or differential file depending on the address obtained in Step 1.

Step 3: If this is an update, then update differential index, differential file, and transaction log.

(c) Differential index and file in use

Step 1: Query the Bloom filter.
If the answer is ''maybe'', then search differential index for record address.
If the Bloom filter answer is ''no'' or if the differential index search is unsuccessful, then search the master index.

Step 2: Access record from either the master or differential file depending on the address obtained in Step 1.

Step 3: If this is an update, then update Bloom filter, differential index, differential file, and transaction log.

(d) Differential index and file and Bloom filter in use

Program 10.14: Access steps

Notice that when we use a differential file, the back-up file is an exact replica of the master file. Hence, we need to back-up only the master index and differential file frequently. Since they are relatively small this is feasible. To recover from a failure of the master index or differential file, we must process the transactions in the transaction log using the back-up copies of the master file, master index, and differential file. The transaction log is usually relatively small since back-ups are done more frequently. To recover from a failure of the master file, we need merely make a new copy of its back-up. When the differential file becomes too large, we create a new version of the master file by merging together the old master file and the differential file. This also results in a new index and an empty differential file. It is interesting to note that the use of a differential file does not affect the number of disk accesses needed to perform a file operation (see Program 10.14).

Suppose that both the index and the file are very large. In this case the differential file scheme discussed above does not work as well since it is not feasible to back-up the master index as frequently as necessary to keep the transaction log sufficiently small. We can get around this difficulty by using a differential index as well as a differential file. The master index and file remain unchanged as updates are made. The differential file contains all newly inserted records and the current version of all changed records. The differential index is an index to the differential file. It also has null address entries for deleted records. Program 10.14(c) shows the steps needed to perform a file operation when both a differential index and file are used. Notice that compared to Program 10.14(a), Program 10.14(c) frequently requires additional disk accesses since we will often first query the differential index and then the master index. (Observe that the differential file is much smaller than the master file, so most requests are satisfied from the master file.)

When we use both a differential index and file, we must back them up with high frequency. This is possible since they are relatively small. To recover from a loss of the differential index or file, we need to process the transactions in the transaction log using the available back-up copies. To recover from a loss of the master index or master file, we only need to make a copy of the appropriate back-up. When the differential index and/or file becomes too large, we reorganize the master index and/or file so that the differential index and/or file becomes empty.

We can considerably reduce the performance degradation that results from the use of a differential index by using a Bloom filter. A *Bloom filter* is a device that resides in internal memory and accepts queries of the type *Is key in the differential index?* If we can answer queries of this type accurately, then we will never need to search both the differential and master indexes for a record address. Clearly, the only way to answer queries of this type accurately is to keep a list of all keys in the differential index. This is not possible for differential indexes of reasonable size.

A Bloom filter does not answer queries of the above type accurately. Instead of returning an answer of *yes* and *no*, it returns one of *maybe* and *no*. When the answer is *no*, then we are assured that the search key is not in the differential index. In this case, we search only the master index and the number of disk accesses is the same as when a differential index is not used. If the answer is *maybe*, we search the differential index.

The master index is searched only if we do not find the key in the differential index. Program 10.14(d) shows the steps to follow when a Bloom filter is used in conjunction with a differential index.

A *filter error* occurs whenever the answer to the Bloom filter query is *maybe* and the key is not in the differential index. Both the differential and master indexes are searched only when a filter error occurs. To obtain a performance close to that obtained when a differential index is not used, we must ensure that the probability of a filter error is close to zero.

Let us take a closer look at a Bloom filter. Typically, it consists of m bits of memory and h uniform and independent hash functions $f_0, \cdots, f_{h-1}$. Initially, all m filter bits are zero and the differential index and file are empty. When we add a key, k, to the differential index, we set bits $f_0(k), \cdots, f_{h-1}(k)$ of the filter to 1. When we make a query of the type *Is k in the differential index?*, we examine bits $f_0(k), \cdots, f_{h-1}(k)$. The query answer is *maybe* if all these bits are 1. Otherwise, the answer is *no*. We may verify that whenever the answer is *no*, the key cannot be in the differential index, and that when the answer is *maybe*, the key may or may not be in the differential index.

We compute the probability of a filter error in the following way. Assume that there are initially n records and u updates are made. Assume that none of these updates is an insert or a delete. Hence, the number of records remains unchanged. Further, assume that the record keys are uniformly distributed over the key (or identifier) space and that the probability that an update request is for record i is $1/n$, $1 \leq i \leq n$. From these assumptions, it follows that the probability that a particular update does not modify record i is $1 - 1/n$. So, the probability that none of the u updates modifies record i is $(1 - 1/n)^u$. Hence, the expected number of unmodified records is $n(1 - 1/n)^u$ and the probability that the $(u+1)$'st update is for an unmodified record is $(1 - 1/n)^u$.

Next, consider bit i of the Bloom filter and the hash function f_j, $0 \leq j \leq h-1$. Let k be the key corresponding to one of the u updates. Since f_j is a uniform hash function, the probability that $f_j(k) \neq i$ is $1 - 1/m$. Since the h hash functions are independent, the probability that $f_j(k) \neq i$ for all h hash functions is $(1 - 1/m)^h$. If this is the only update, the probability that bit i of the filter is zero is $(1 - 1/m)^h$. From the assumption on update requests, it follows that the probability that bit i is zero following the u updates is $(1 - 1/m)^{uh}$. From this, we can conclude that if the $(u+1)$'st update is for an unmodified record, the probability of a filter error is $(1 - (1 - 1/m)^{uh})^h$. The probability $P(u)$ that the $(u+1)$'st update results in a filter error is this quantity times the probability that the $(u+1)$'st update is for an unmodified record. Hence:

$$P(u) = (1 - 1/n)^u (1 - (1 - 1/m)^{uh})^h$$

Using the approximation:

$$(1 - 1/x)^q \sim e^{-q/x}$$

for large x, we obtain:

$$P(u) \sim e^{-u/n}(1 - e^{-uh/m})^h$$

when n and m are large.

Suppose we wish to design a Bloom filter that minimizes the probability of a filter error. This probability is highest just before the master index is reorganized and the differential index becomes empty. Let u denote the number of updates done up to this time. In most applications, m is determined by the amount of memory available and n is fixed. So the only variable in design is h. Differentiating $P(u)$ with respect to h and setting the result to zero yields:

$$h = (\log_e 2)m/u \sim 0.693m/u$$

We may verify that this h yields a minimum for $P(u)$. Actually since h has to be an integer, the number of hash functions to use is either $\lceil 0.693m/u \rceil$ or $\lfloor 0.693m/u \rfloor$ depending on which results in a smaller $P(u)$.

EXERCISES

1. By differentiating $P(u)$ with respect to h, show that $P(u)$ is minimized when $h = (\log_e 2)m/u$.

2. Suppose that you are to design a Bloom filter with minimum $P(u)$ and that $n = 100,000$, $m = 5000$, and $u = 1000$.

   (a) Using any of the results obtained in the text, compute the number h of hash functions to use. Show your computations.

   (b) What is the probability $P(u)$ of a filter error when h has this value?

10.11   REFERENCES AND SELECTED READINGS

The O(n^2) optimum binary search tree algorithm is from: ''Optimum Binary Search Trees,'' by D. Knuth, *Acta Informatica*, 1, 1, 1971, pp. 14-25.

For a discussion of heuristics that obtain in O(n log$n$) time nearly optimal binary search trees see: ''Nearly Optimal Binary Search Trees,'' by K. Melhorn, *Acta Informatica*, 5, 1975, pp. 287-295; and ''Binary Search Trees and File Organization,'' by J. Nievergelt, *ACM Computing Surveys*, Vol.6, No. 3, Sept. 1974, pp. 195-207.

The original paper on AVL trees by G. M. Adelson-Velskii and E. M. Landis appears in *Dokl. Acad. Nauk.*, SSR (Soviet Math), 3, 1962, pp. 1259-1263. Additional algorithms to manipulate AVL trees may be found in: ''Linear lists and priority queues as balanced binary trees,'' by C. Crane, STAN-CS-72-259, Computer Science Department, Stanford University, February 1972, and *The Art of Computer Programming: Sorting and Searching* by D. Knuth, Addison-Wesley, Reading, Massachusetts, 1973 (Section 6.2.3).

Results of an empirical study of height balanced trees appear in: ''Performance of Height-Balanced Trees,'' by P. L. Karlton, S. H. Fuller, R. E. Scroggs and E. B. Koehler, *CACM*, 19, 1, Jan. 1976, pp. 23-28.

2-3 trees and 2-3-4 trees are a special case of B-trees. A good reference is: *The art of computer programming: Sorting and searching*, vol. 3, by D. Knuth, Addison-Wesley, Reading, Massachussetts, 1973. The variations of 2-3 trees referred to in the exercises are from: *The design and analysis of computer algorithms*, by A. Aho, J. Hopcroft, and J. Ullman, Addison-Wesley, Reading, MA, 1974, and *Data structures and algorithms*, by A. Aho, J. Hopcroft, and J. Ullman, Addison-Wesley, Reading, MA, 1983.

Red-black trees were invented by R. Bayer. The reference is: ''Symmetric binary B-trees: data structure and maintenence,'' *Acta. Infor.*, Vol 1, No 4, 1972, pp. 290-306.

Our treatment of red-black trees is due to Guibas and Sedgewick. The top-down single pass insertion and deletion algorithms for 2-3-4 trees are also due to them. The reference is: ''A dichromatic framework for balanced trees,'' by L. Guibas and R. Sedgewick, *Proceedings 19th IEEE symposium on foundations of computer science*, pp. 8-21, 1978.

Bottom up insertion and deletion algorithms for red-black trees were proposed by R. Tarjan in the paper: ''Updating a balanced search tree in O(1) rotations,'' *Info. Process. Letters*, 16, 5, 1983, pp. 253-257.

The paper: ''Planar point location using persistent search trees,'' by N. Sarnak and R. Tarjan, *CACM*, 27, 7, 1986, pp. 669-679, develops a persistent variety of red-black trees. A persistent data structure is one which all previous versions plus the current version of the data structure can be accessed efficiently. The above paper also applies persistent red-black trees to the planar point location problem.

Splay trees were invented by D. Sleator and R. Tarjan. Their paper: ''Self-adjusting binary search trees,'' *JACM*, 32, 3, July 1985, pp. 652-686, provides several other analyses of splay trees as well as variants of the basic splaying technique discussed in the text. There are several other data structures that provide good amortized performance for priority queue and search tree operations. The exercises examine some of these. The references for these additional structures are: ''Self-adjusting heaps,'' by D. Sleator and R. Tarjan, *SIAM Jr. on Computing*, 15, 1, Feb 1986, pp. 52-69, and ''Biased search trees,'' by S. Bent, D. Sleator, and R. Tarjan, *SIAM Jr. on Computing*, 14, 3, Aug 1985, pp. 545-568.

Digital search trees were first proposed by E. Coffman and J. Eve in *CACM*, 13, 1970, pp. 427-432.

The structure Patricia is due to D. Morrison. Digital search trees, tries, and Patricia are analyzed in the book: *The Art of Computer Programming: Sorting and Searching* by D. Knuth, Addison-Wesley, Reading, Massachusetts, 1973 (Section 6.3).

The linear time suffix tree construction algorithm is due to E. McCreight. It is described in: ''A space-economical suffix tree construction algorithm,'' by E. McCreight, *JACM*, 23, 2, April 1978, pp. 262-272.

Our development of differential files parallels that of Severence and Lohman in the paper: ''Differential files: Their application to the maintenance of large databases,'' by D. Severence and G. Lohman, *ACM Trans. on Database Systems*, 1, 3, 1976, pp 256-267.

This paper also provides several advantages of using differential files. The assumptions of uniformity made in the filter error analysis are unrealistic as, in practice, future accesses are more likely to be for records previously accessed. Several authors have attempted to take this into account. Two references are: ''A practical guide to the design of differential file architectures,'' by H. Aghili and D. Severance, *ACM Trans. on Database Systems*, 7, 2, 1982, pp 540-565, and ''A regression approach to performance analysis for the differential file architecture,'' by T. Hill and A. Srinivasan, *Proceedings Third IEEE International Conference On Data Engineering*, 1987, pp 157-164.

ANSI C AND K&R C

In this appendix we examine many of the differences between the American National Standard X3.159-1989 version of C (ANSI C) and the more traditional versions of C as represented by Kernighan and Ritchie in their book *"The C Programming Language"*, Prentice Hall, 1978, (K&R C).

In this book we follow the standards of ANSI C. We do so for two reasons. Most important is the fact that ANSI C provides mechanisms for improving readability and reliability of programs. The second reason is that with increased frequency ANSI C is being supported by all computer manufacturers. Nevertheless many C compilers still exist that do not support ANSI C. One notable example is SUN Sparcstations which run a version of Berkeley UNIX. All of the programs in this book were transformed to K&R C and successfully run on a SUN Sparcstation.

ANSI C Is Bigger Than K&R C

There are many small changes and additions in ANSI C. For example you are likely aware that a source line can be continued onto the next line by ending the first line with backslash (\). ANSI C introduces a "trigraph", a three character sequence, such that the trigraph ??/ can be used to denote continuation on the next line.

ANSI C introduces the ideas of multibyte and wide character sets. There purpose is to accommodate international alphabets, many of which require more than one byte for their representation. A wide character can be declared as *wchar t*, which is defined in *stddef.h*. A multibyte character is the external representation of a wide character. It appears as a normal C character string.

ANSI C has added two new type qualifiers: **const** and **volatile**. The word **const** refers to objects that cannot be assigned to. For example,

```
const int i = 47; /* i cannot be changed */
int * const cptr; /* cptr is a pointer that cannot
                                      be changed */
const int *ptrc; /* pointer to constant data can be
                    assigned to but not
                    the object it points to */
...
i = 10;    /* this is illegal */
i++;       /* this is illegal */
```

The word **volatile** is used whenever the object it refers to can be modified sufficiently often that we want the compiler to avoid performing optimizations on it.

One of the major extensions of ANSI C is the function prototype. In K&R C one begins a function definition by providing the name of the function and a list of names to stand for the parameters. Facts about the parameters occur later. In ANSI C parameters and their types appear together in the function heading. A function prototype is similar to a function heading except that only the types of the parameters appear. Function prototypes are typically placed near the **#define** and **#include** directives in a C program and allow the C compiler to perform type-checking on function calls. For example:

```
small(x,y)           /* K&R C function heading */
small(int, int)      /* ANSI C function prototype */
small(int x, int y)  /* ANSI C function heading */
```

Even for functions with no arguments, e.g. f(), ANSI C provides the form **void f(void)** as a prototype. In traditional C when a function is encountered the following steps are taken:

(i)   the arguments are converted using standard defaults;

(ii)   no type checking is done, nor is checking for agreement in the number of arguments;

(iii) any function can take a variable number of arguments.

When a function prototype is used, the steps are:

(i)   arguments are converted to the declared types of the formal parameters, just as if assignments occurred;

(ii)   the number and type of arguments are checked against the prototype and an error is raised if there is a discrepancy

(iii)   functions that do require a variable number of arguments must have been specified earlier.

ANSI C introduces the initialization of variables in the language. The initial values are enclosed within curly braces. Some compilers will initialize static storage to zero, but this is not part of the language definition and cannot be depended upon. For example,

```
int numbers [] [MAX_NUMBERS] = {{1, 2, 3}, {4, 5, 6},
                                {7, 8, 9}}
```

initialiazes a two-dimensional array, *numbers*, such that *numbers*[0][0] = 1, *numbers*[0][1] = 2, *numbers*[0][2] = 3, *numbers*[1][0] = 4, ...

Void
Scalar types
     pointer
     arithmetic types
        integral
            integers
            enumerations
            character
        floating point
     Function types
     Union types
     Aggregate types
        array
        structure

Figure A.1: The types of C

It is useful to see how the types of ANSI C are organized, and this is shown in Figure A.1. It is required that type **int** is not smaller than **short**, and **long** is not smaller than **int**. Many implementations represent a character in 8 bits, **short** in 16 bits, **long** in 32 bits and **int** in 16 or 32 bits. ANSI C requires that at least these widths be used.

ANSI C requires that each compiler implementation document ranges of integers in the header file *limits.h* The values in this file include: **CHAR_BIT**, **INT_MIN**, **INT_MAX**, **CHAR_MIN**, **CHAR_MAX**, and others.

C's real numbers come in two forms, **float** and **double**. In K&R C it was assumed that all **float**s were converted to **double**s before being operated upon. This is not true in ANSI C. C has addressed the issue of pointers and conversions from **int**s to pointers, by introducing the special null pointer called **void**. There is a macro, *NULL*, which is defined as the constant that represents a null pointer, either 0, 0L or (**void** *) 0.

Multidimensional arrays are declared as an array of arrays. They are stored in row major order. If *arr* is a 3 x 2 array, e.g. *int arr*[3][2], then the expression *arr*[2][1] is the same as the pointer expression *(*(*arr*+2)+1). To see why, *arr* is a pointer to *arr*[0][0]. *(*arr*+2) is a pointer to *arr*[2][0] and therefore the final expression points to *arr*[2][1].

Dangerous Practices

Some programmers assume that the alphabetic characters are consecutively represented, so that 'Z'-'A'+ 1 should equal 26. This is true for ASCII, but not for EBCDIC. ANSI C specifies that /* begins a comment and */ ends a comment. It does not permit nested comments, though many C implementations do. If there is a need to comment out a large segment of C code, that may contain comments, one should use the C preprocessor commands

```
#if 0
...
#endif
```

In traditional C the compound operators, such as **+=** or **-=**, are treated as two tokens and can contain white space between them. ANSI C treats them as a single token. Traditional C specified that identifiers would only be distinguished based upon their first eight characters. Thus identifiers *looknice* and *looknice2* would be regarded as the same. ANSI C permits at least 31 characters to determine the uniqueness of an identifier, thereby encouraging the use of informative names. However, external identifiers in C must be handled by debuggers and linkers. These tools are often more restrictive, and thus longer names are still discouraged.

In a C program, a line that begins with a **#** is interpreted as a directive to the C preprocessor. The **#** is generally followed by a command, which may be followed by arguments. ANSI C permits whitespace to precede and follow the use of **#**, but many traditional C compilers expect to see **#** in column 1 with the command immediately following. ANSI C allows the keyword register to be used with any type of variable or parameter. However, non-ANSI C compilers often restrict the use of register to scalar types. Other differences may exist such as the widening of small objects declared with register.

C permits the type specifier of a variable or a function definition to be left out. In such a case the default is int. In ANSI C this is considered poor programming practice. ANSI C has introduced the special type **void** to indicate that the return value is ignored. C permits unrestricted jumps into the middle of compound statements. This is in sharp contrast to Ada, Modula-2, and Pascal which do not. This practice should be avoided.

It is impossible to cover all of the differences between K&R C and ANSI C in one appendix. For the interested reader we suggest the book by Harbison and Steele, *"C A Reference Manual"*, for a complete exposition of the differences.

Conversion Of Programs In This Text To K&R C

It is easy to convert the programs in this book from ANSI C to your own local version. Here we present a complete example that was done so the program could run on a SUN Sparcstation. In Program A.1 you see a sample program that was taken from Chapter 9 of this book. It is a "complete" program, in that it is designed to execute. It demonstrates the maintenance of a hash table. To the right of certain statements we have placed the equivalent K&R C statements, for comparison. To the left of each statement we have placed a line number to help you locate the source of the compiler errors produced when we ran the program on a SUN Sparcstation.

```
1 /* file name: Hash1.c */
2 #include <stdio.h>
3 #include <string.h>
4 #include <stdlib.h>
5 #define MAX_CHAR 10
6 #define TABLE_SIZE 13
7
8 typedef struct {
9        char key[MAX_CHAR];
10 } element;
11                              /* K&R C correct form */
12 element hash_table[TABLE_SIZE];
13 int transform(char *);            /*int transform(); */
14 int hash(char *);                 /*int hash(); */
15 void init_table(element []);      /*void init_table(); */
16 void linear_insert(element, element []);   /*void linear_insert();*/
17 int linear_search(element, element []); /*int linear_search(); */
18 void print_table(element []);     /*void print_table(); */
19
20 void main(void)                   /*void main() */
21 {
22   char key[MAX_CHAR];
23   element info;
24   int position;
25   init_table(hash_table);
26   printf("Enter a key <zzz> to quit: ");
27   scanf("%s", &key);              /* scanf("%s", key) */
28   while (strcmp(key,"zzz")) {
```

```
29    strcpy(info.key, key);
30    linear_insert(info,hash_table);
31    print_table(hash_table);
32    printf("Enter a key <zzz> to quit: ");
33    scanf("%s",&key);                    /* scanf("%s", key) */
34  }
35  printf("Enter a key to search <zzz> to quit: ");
36  scanf("%s",&key);              /* scanf("%s", key) */
37  while (strcmp(key,"zzz")) {
38    strcpy(info.key, key);
39    if ((position = linear_search(info,hash_table) ) < 0)
40    printf("The Key is not in the table \n");
41    else
42    printf("The key was found in the %d position 0,position);
43     printf("Enter a key to search <zzz> to quit: ");
44     scanf("%s",&key);                    /* scanf("%s", key) */
45   }
46 }
47
48 int transform(char *key)              /* int transform(key) */
49 {                                     /* char *key; */
50 /* simple additive approach to create a natural number, that is
51    within the integer range */
52    int number = 0;
53    int i;
54    int length = strlen(key);
55    for  (i = 0; i  < length; i++)
56      number += key[i];
57    return number;
58 }
59
60 int hash(char *key)              /* int hash(key) */
61 {                                /* char *key; */
62 /* transform key to a natural number, and return this result modulus
63 the table size */
64    return(transform(key) % TABLE_SIZE);
65 }
66
67 void linear_insert(element item,element ht[])/*void linear_insert(item,ht)*/
68 {                                    /*element item, ht[]; */
69 /* insert the key into the table using the linear probing technique,
70 exit the function if the table is full */
71
72    int i, hash_value;
```

```
73
74   hash_value = hash(item.key);
75   i = hash_value;
76   printf("Hash value is: %d0,i);
77   while (strlen(ht[i].key)) {
78     i = (i+1) % TABLE_SIZE;
79     if (i == hash_value) {
80       fprintf(stderr,"The Table is full \n");
81       exit(1);
82     }
83   }
84   ht[i] = item;
85 }
86
87 int linear_search(element item, element ht[])/*int linear_search(item, ht)*/
88 {                                  /*element item, ht[]; */
89 /* search for the key contained in item, return -1 if the key is not
90 in the table, and the position (j),  if it is.  */
91
92   int j, hash_value;
93
94   hash_value = hash(item.key);
95   j = hash_value;
96   for (;;) {
97     if (!strlen(ht[j].key))
98       return -1;
99     if (!strcmp(ht[j].key,item.key))
100      return j;
101    j = (j+1) % TABLE_SIZE;
102    if (j == hash_value)
103      return -1;
104   }
105 }
106 }
107
108 void init_table(element ht[])          /* void init_table(ht) */
109 {                                      /* element ht[]; */
110 int i;
111 for (i = 0; i < TABLE_SIZE; i++)
112   ht[i].key = NULL;
113 }
```

```
114
115 void print_table(element ht[])        /* void print_table(ht) */
116 {                                      /* element ht[]; */
117   int i;
118   printf("index    value0);
119   for (i=0; i<TABLE_SIZE; i++)
120     printf("[%3d] =    %s0,i,ht[i].key);
121 }
```

Program A.1: A Sample C Program

In Figure A.2 you see the list of error messages initially produced by a compiler on a SUN Sparcstation. Lines 13-18 all contain function prototypes, that is definitions of the function name and its arguments. K&R C does not support such definitions, although it does want the name to be declared. To remove these error messages one must delete the parameter specifications, as shown to the right within the comments. Line 20 violates K&R C by having a void listed as a parameter. This is easily corrected by removing it, as shown to the right. Once these changes have been made, one can re-compile the program with the result being a new set of warnings as shown in Figure A.3

```
"hash1.c", line 13: syntax error at or near type word "char"
"hash1.c", line 14: syntax error at or near type word "char"
"hash1.c", line 15: syntax error at or near symbol [
"hash1.c", line 15: element declared as parameter to non-function
"hash1.c", line 16: redeclaration of formal parameter, element
"hash1.c", line 16: syntax error at or near symbol [
"hash1.c", line 16: element declared as parameter to non-function
"hash1.c", line 16: element declared as parameter to non-function
"hash1.c", line 17: redeclaration of formal parameter, element
"hash1.c", line 17: syntax error at or near symbol [
"hash1.c", line 17: element declared as parameter to non-function
"hash1.c", line 17: element declared as parameter to non-function
"hash1.c", line 18: syntax error at or near symbol [
"hash1.c", line 18: element declared as parameter to non-function
"hash1.c", line 20: syntax error at or near type word "void"
"hash1.c", line 68: redeclaration of linear_insert
"hash1.c", line 74: item undefined
"hash1.c", line 77: ht undefined
"hash1.c", line 87: syntax error at or near variable name "item"
"hash1.c", line 87: redeclaration of formal parameter, element
"hash1.c", line 94: item undefined
"hash1.c", line 97: ht undefined
"hash1.c", line 109: syntax error at or near variable name "ht"
```

"hash1.c", line 113: ht undefined
"hash1.c", line 116: syntax error at or near variable name "ht"
"hash1.c", line 116: fatal error: too many errors

Figure A.2: Error messages produced by K&R C compiler

"hash1.c", line 27: warning: & before array or function: ignored
"hash1.c", line 33: warning: & before array or function: ignored
"hash1.c", line 36: warning: & before array or function: ignored
"hash1.c", line 44: warning: & before array or function: ignored
"hash1.c", line 48: syntax error at or near type word "char"
"hash1.c", line 54: key undefined
"hash1.c", line 60: syntax error at or near type word "char"
"hash1.c", line 64: key undefined
"hash1.c", line 67: syntax error at or near variable name "item"
"hash1.c", line 67: redeclaration of formal parameter, element
"hash1.c", line 74: item undefined
"hash1.c", line 77: ht undefined
"hash1.c", line 87: syntax error at or near variable name "item"
"hash1.c", line 87: redeclaration of formal parameter, element
"hash1.c", line 94: item undefined
"hash1.c", line 97: ht undefined
"hash1.c", line 109: syntax error at or near variable name "ht"
"hash1.c", line 113: ht undefined
"hash1.c", line 116: syntax error at or near variable name "ht"
"hash1.c", line 121: ht undefined

Figure A.3: Second set of error messages

Looking at Figure A.3 one sees several occurrences of the message:

"hash1.c", line 48: syntax error at or near type word "char"

This refers to the fact that K&R C does not permit argument specification as to type. Generally, a variable name is provided, but its type follows on another line. These changes are done on six pairs of lines, numbered: 48,49 60,61 67,68 87,88 109,110, and 116, 117. The only remaining error messages are those on lines: 27, 33, 36 and 44, namely

"hash1.c", line 27: warning: & before array or function: ignored

This is not a serious error as one can see it is ignored. Nevertheless, to remove it, one need only remove the & sign immediately preceding the variable key.

INDEX

Abstract data type
    array, 49-53
    bag, 17
    definition, 15
    graph, 257-272
    heap, 218-219
    natural number, 16-17
    polynomial, 59-65
    queue, 105-111
    set, 17
    sparse matrix, 66-78
    stack, 101-105
    string, 80-92
    symbol table, 395-396
Ackermann's function, 13, 245
Aho, A., 254, 568
Activity networks, 303-316
Adelson-Velskii, G., 482, 567
Aghili, H., 569
Algorithm
    analysis, 18-38, 453-454
    definition, 4
    performance measurement, 38-47
    recursive, 10-14
    specification, 4-14
Amortized complexity, 453-454
ANSI C, 570-578
Arithmetic expressions, 116-125
Arrays
    abstract data type, 49-53
    column major, 79
    one dimensional, 51-53
    representation, 78-80
    row major, 79
Asymptotic notation, 30-37
Atkinson, M., 469
AVL-trees, 480-496

B-trees, 528-542
B*-trees, 540
B´-trees, 541
Baase, S., 317, 393
Balance factor, 483
Bayer, R., 568

Bell, J., 428
Bent, S., 568
Bentley, J., 47
Biconnected components, 278-282
Big O, 31-32
Binary search, 6-11, 33-34, 321-322
Binary search trees
    AVL, 480-496
    definition, 226
    delete, 230-231
    height, 231
    insert, 228-230
    optimal, 470-480
    searching, 227-228
Binary trees
    abstract data type, 191-193
    balanced, 480-496
    AVL, 480-496
    complete, 192
    deap, 439-446
    extended, 446
    full, 195
    heap, 217-225
    height balanced, 480-496
    min-max heap, 430-438
    number of, 247-254
    optimal binary search tree, 470-480
    representation, 196-198
    search trees, 225-232, 480-496
    selection trees, 232-235
    skewed, 192
    threaded, 211-217
    traversal, 200-206
Binary tries, 449-450
Binomial heaps, 453-461
Binomial trees, 458
Bloom filters, 567-568
Breadth first search, 273-275
Breadth first spanning tree, 277
Brent, R., 428
Brooks, F., 47
Buffering, 378-385

Carlsson, S., 469
Chain, 157, 163
Circular lists, 157-161, 163
Coffman, E., 568
Complexity
    amortized, 453-454
    asymptotic, 30-37
    average, 30
    best, 30
    practical, 37-38
    space, 19-21
    time, 21-30
    worst, 30
Connected components, 262-276
Count sort, 393
Crane, C., 469, 567
Critical paths, 311
Cycle basis, 278

Data type, 15
Day, A., 428
Deap, 439-446
Deo, N., 317
Depth first search, 272-273
Depth first spanning tree, 272-273
Deque, 111
Differential files, 563-567
Digital search trees, 548-557
Dijkstra, E., 47
Dodd, M., 409, 428
Du, D., 428
Dwyer, B., 254

Enbody, R., 428
Equivalence relations, 166-171
Equivalence classes, 167, 247
Euler, L., 258, 316
Eulerian walk, 258
Eve, J., 568
Extended binary tree, 446
External node, 446
External path length, 472

Factorial function, 13
Fagin, R., 428
Fibonacci heaps, 461-469
Fibonacci numbers, 13, 465, 468
Flajolet, P., 428
Ford, L., 317
Forest
  binary tree representation, 236-237
  traversals, 237-238
Fredman, M., 469
Fulkerson, D., 317
Fuller, S., 568

Gabow, H., 469
Galil, Z., 469
Genealogical charts, 186-187
Gonzalez, T., 412
Gonnet, G., 393
Graham, R., 317
Graphs
  abstract data type, 257-272
  activity networks, 303-316
  adjacency matrix, 263-265
  adjacency lists, 265-267
  adjacency multilists, 267-269
  articulation points, 278-282
  biconnected components, 278-282
  bipartite, 284
  breadth first search, 273-275
  bridge, 284
  complete, 260
  connected components, 262, 276
  critical paths, 310
  definitions, 259-263
  degree, 262
  depth first search, 272-273
  digraph, 262
  directed, 259
  Eulerian walk, 258
  incidence matrix, 318
  inverse adjacency lists, 265
  multigraph, 260
  orthogonal lists, 268
  path, 260

  representations, 263-270
  shortest paths, 292-303
  spanning trees, 276-278, 284-292
  subgraph, 260
  transitive closure, 300-301
  undirected, 259
Gries, D., 47
Guibas, L., 568
Guttag, J., 47, 412

Harbison, S., 92, 131
Hash functions
  digit analysis, 401
  division, 399
  folding, 400
  mid-square, 399
  uniform, 399
Hash tables
  bucket, 395
  chained, 406-409, 410
  hash functions, 398-401
  identifier density, 397
  linear open addressing, 401-406, 409
  linear probing, 401-406, 409
  loading density, 397
  quadratic probing, 405, 410
  random probing, 405, 410
Hashing
  dynamic, 413-427
  extendible, 416
  hash functions, 398-401
  overflow handling, 401-409
  static, 395-413
Heap
  abstract data type, 218-219
  binomial, 453-461
  deletion, 223-224
  Fibonacci, 461-469
  insertion, 221-223
  max, 218
  min, 218
  min-max, 430-438
  skewed, 452
  sort, 347-350

Height balanced trees, 480-496
Hell, P., 317
Hill, T., 569
Hoare, C., 393
Holub, A., 131
Hopcroft, J., 568
Horner's rule, 13
Horowitz, E., 47
Hu, T., 317
Huang, B., 393
Huffman trees, 390-391

Infix notation, 118
Inorder, 201, 203
Insertion sort, 326-329
Internal path length, 472

Jaesche, R., 92

K&R C, 570-578
Karlton, P., 568
Kernighan, B., 47, 92, 131, 570
Knight's tour, 97-100
Knuth, D., 89, 92, 254, 393, 410, 428
    567, 568
Koehler, E., 568
Koenigsberg bridge problem, 257-258
Kruskal's algorithm, 285-289

Landis, E., 482, 567
Landweber, L., 132
Langston, M., 393
Larson, P., 428
Lawler, E., 317
Leeuwen, J., 254
Leftist trees, 446-453
Levisse, R., 47
Lewis, T., 428
Lindstrom, G., 254
Linear list, 59
Linear open addressing, 401-406, 409
Linear probing, 401-406, 409
List sort, 357-360

Lists
    available space list, 157
    chain, 157, 163
    circular, 157-161, 163
    doubly linked, 179-181
    erase, 156-159
    head node, 159
    linear, 59
    ordered, 59
    singly linked, 139-147
    verification, 322-324
Litwin, W., 428
Lloyd, J., 429
Lohman, G., 568
Lomet, D., 429
Lorin, H., 393
Loser tree, 234
Lum, V., 409, 428

Magic square, 34-36
Matrix
    addition, 23, 24, 33
    band, 94-95
    erase, 176-177
    linked representation, 171-177
    multiplication, 28, 73-77
    read, 174-176
    saddle point, 92
    sequential representation, 66-78
    sparse, 66-78, 171-177
    transpose, 29, 69-73
    triangular, 93
    tridiagonal, 93
Maze, 112-116
Mauer, W., 428
McCreight, E., 568
Melhorn, K., 567
Mendelson, H., 429
Merge sort, 335-347
Merging
    2-way, 335-340
    k-way, 376-378
    O(1) space, 336-340
Min-max heap, 430-438

Morris, R., 89, 92, 411, 428
Morrison, D., 568

Natural numbers, 16-17
Network
    AOE, 309-316
    AOV, 303-309
    weighted graph, 270
Nievergelt, J., 428, 567

Omega notation, 32
Optimal merge patterns, 389-391
Ordered list, 59
Overflow handling
    chaining, 406-409, 410
    linear open addressing, 401-406, 409
    linear probing, 401-406, 409
    quadratic probing, 405, 410
    random probing, 406, 410
    rehashing, 406, 410
    theoretical evaluation, 409-410

Partial order, 304
Patricia, 550-556
Pattern matching, 84-91
Performance analysis, 18-38
Performance measurement, 38-47
Permutations, 11-12
Pigeon hole principle, 13
Pippinger, N., 428
Plauger, P., 47
Pointers, 135-147
Polynomials
    abstract data type, 59-65
    addition, 63-65, 152-156, 158-161
    linked, 150-162
    sequential, 59-65
Postfix notation, 118-125
Postorder, 202
Power set, 14
Pratt, V., 89, 92
Precedence relation, 303
Prefix notation, 127

Preorder, 201
Prim's algorithm, 289-290
Priority queue
    deap, 439-446
    double ended, 430
    Fibonacci heap, 461-469
    heap, 218-224
    leftist tree, 446-453
    min-max heap, 430-438
Program step, 22
Propositional calculus, 208

Queues
    abstract data type, 105-111
    linked, 147-150
    many, 128-131
    priority, 219-221
    sequential, 107-111
Quadratic probing, 405-410
Quick sort, 329-332

Radix sort, 350-357
Radke, C., 428
Ramamohanrao, K., 429
Recursion, 10-14
Relations
    equivalence, 167
    irreflexive, 304
    precedence, 304
    reflexive, 167
    symmetric, 167
    transitive, 304
Rich, R., 393
Runs
    generation, 385-391
    optimal merging, 389-391

Sack, J., 469
Sahni, S., 47, 393
Santoro, N., 469
Sarnak, N., 568
Satisfiability, 206-210
Scholl, M., 429

Scroggs, R., 568
Search methods
    binary search, 6-11, 33-34, 320-321
    binary search tree, 226-232
    interpolation search, 322
    sequential search, 43-44, 320-321
Sedgewick, R., 47, 393, 568
Selection sort, 5-6, 41
Selection tree, 232-235
Set representation, 238-247
Sethi, R., 254
Severence, D., 428, 568, 569
Shortest path problems
    all pairs, 295-300
    single source, 292-295
Sleator, D., 568
Solitaire, 132-134
Sollin's algorithm, 290-291
Sommerville, I., 47
Sorting
    count sort, 393
    disks, 372-392
    exchange, 393
    external, 372-392
    heap sort, 347-350
    insertion sort, 326-329
    internal, 326-372
    list sort, 357-360
    merge sort, 335-347
    lower bound, 333-334
    quick sort, 329-332
    radix sort, 350-357
    selection sort, 5-6, 41
    shaker, 394
    stable, 326
    table sort, 360-365
    topological sort, 304-308
Spanning trees
    breadth first, 277
    depth first, 277
    minimum cost, 284-292
Spencer, T., 469
Splay trees, 542-548
Srinivasan, A., 569

Stacks
    abstract data type, 101-105
    linked, 147-150
    many, 128-131
    sequential, 103-105
Strings
    abstract data type, 80-92
    C functions, 82
    insertion, 83-84
    pattern matching, 84-91
Strong, H., 428
Structures, 53-58
Stubbs, D., 47
Symbol tables, 395-396
System life cycle, 1-4

Table sort, 360-365
Tarjan, R., 246, 254, 316, 469, 568
Test data, 44-46
Theta notation, 32
Topological order, 304
Topological sort, 304-308
Towers of Hanoi, 14
Traister, R., 182
Transitive closure, 300-301
Trees
    AVL, 480-496
    B-tree, 528-542
    B*-tree, 540
    B′-tree, 541
    binary, 191-199
    binomial, 458
    definition, 187
    diameter, 318
    digital, 548-557
    Huffman, 390-391
    leftist, 446-453
    m-way search tree, 528-530
    of losers, 234
    radius, 318
    red-black, 518-528
    representation, 189-191
    selection tree, 232-235
    spanning tree, 277, 284-292

splay trees, 542-548
terminology, 186-189
trie, 414, 549-550, 557-563
2-3, 496-509
2-3-4, 509-518
union-find, 238-247
Tries
  binary, 414, 549-550
  compressed, 550
  general, 557-563
  Patricia, 550-556

Ullman, J., 254, 568
Union-find trees
  collapsing rule, 244
  weighting rule, 242
Unions, 56-57

Webre, N., 47

Yuen, P., 409, 428